Virtual Community Participation and Motivation:

Cross–Disciplinary Theories

Honglei Li
Northumbria University, UK

Managing Director:	Lindsay Johnston
Senior Editorial Director:	Heather A. Probst
Book Production Manager:	Sean Woznicki
Development Manager:	Joel Gamon
Development Editor:	Mike Killian
Acquisitions Editor:	Erika Gallagher
Typesetter:	Nicole Sparano
Cover Design:	Nick Newcomer, Lisandro Gonzalez

Published in the United States of America by
Information Science Reference (an imprint of IGI Global)
701 E. Chocolate Avenue
Hershey PA 17033
Tel: 717-533-8845
Fax: 717-533-8661
E-mail: cust@igi-global.com
Web site: http://www.igi-global.com

Library of Congress Cataloging-in-Publication Data

Virtual community participation and motivation: cross-disciplinary theories / Honglei Li, editor.
     p. cm.
 Includes bibliographical references and index.
  ISBN 978-1-4666-0312-7 (hbk.) -- ISBN 978-1-4666-0313-4 (ebook) -- ISBN 978-1-4666-0314-1 (print & perpetual access) 1. Electronic villages (Computer networks) 2. Internet--Social aspects. 3. Computer networks--Social aspects. I. Li, Honglei, 1976-
  TK5105.83.V575 2012
  004.67--dc23
                                    2012008376

British Cataloguing in Publication Data
A Cataloguing in Publication record for this book is available from the British Library.

All work contributed to this book is new, previously-unpublished material. The views expressed in this book are those of the authors, but not necessarily of the publisher.

Editorial Advisory Board

Table of Contents

Section 2
Theories behind Virtual Community Participation

Detailed Table of Contents

Section 1
Virtual Community and Virtual Community Participation

Chapter 1

This chapter explores the theoretical and conceptual assumptions underlying the notion of virtual community. It discussed Internet as both technology and culture and how it shapes communities. The author concludes that studies of virtual communities must be contextualized according to historical and existing patterns of social life and offers a discussion on new challenges and questions facing mass communications research in this increasingly interdisciplinary area.

Chapter 2

The chapter starts with a short introduction to the complex phenomenon of Virtual Communities as part of media convergence process. The aim of the chapter is the analysis of Text-Based Communities through methodologies of ethnography and socio-semiotics, with specific focus, and analysis, of some virtual groups related to TV-Drama and linked to Fashion genre. The last part of the chapter is about the analysis of these virtual groups.

Chapter 3

This chapter demonstrates usage of a web-based participative learning environment, which has enabled graduate students in e-commerce classes on the Executive Master in Business Administration Programme taught by the Brazilian School of Public and Business Administration at Getulio Vargas Foundation, based in Rio de Janeiro, Brazil, to share and disseminate their knowledge among themselves. An illustrative single case study is applied in order to achieve this purpose.

Chapter 4

In this chapter, the authors discuss the benefits of community members generating content description by analyzing the current literature on the matter. Then, they present two studies they have held where they assess the metadata generated by users of an IPTV system and by members of two different virtual communities.

Chapter 5

Many studies look at participation from a static point of view and disregard different levels of participation. This chapter bring new angle of virtual community participation by looking at participation as an evolving process instead of as a one-time event, by giving voice to all participants of the community, and by studying the context within which communities emerge. A practice-based approach is suggested as a useful theoretical tool to deepen current understanding of online community participation.

Chapter 6

This chapter proposes the narrative network analysis methodology for application in the examination of online communities. The narrative network analysis provides a basis for systematic examination of online communities that has been missing from the literature. The chapter describes three online communities and their characteristics to demonstrate the possibilities of the methodology. From these descriptions, a proposed model of the communities is presented, and then an abbreviated narrative network analysis is developed.

This chapter outlines an infrastructural approach to understanding virtual communities (VCs) and applies it to a novel set of VCs. This chapter first outlines how the infrastructure approach is synthesised from current approaches to understanding VCs. Second, it uses the infrastructural approach to analyse three related meatspace communities' progress toward collaborating through specific data-sharing VCs. Third, it highlights merits and shortcomings of the infrastructural approach to understanding participation in virtual communities. Finally, it offers potential avenues of further VC research using the infrastructural approach.

Chapter 8
Sergey Rybas, Capital University, USA

Problematizing the historical, philosophical, and social foundations of online communities, this project lays out a theoretical framework of subjective performance in virtual spaces and uses it to examine interactions in one long-distance college class. The findings of this cyberethnographic study suggests that even though the collective perceptions of community remain relatively stable, yet idealized and evasive, the actual individual manifestations of online community are limited to the subjective performances of the members and are inseparable from their complex identities and literacies. Therefore, considering the subjective performances of online community is vital for understanding its goals, practices, principles, and limitations and critical for the assessment of its success.

Section 2
Theories behind Virtual Community Participation

Chapter 9
Weiyu Zhang, National University of Singapore, Singapore

The purpose of this work is to develop a theoretical framework to examine virtual community participation using the concept of subaltern public spheres. The theory of subaltern public spheres directs attention to the internal dynamics and external interaction of virtual communities. The theoretical framework is applied to analyze a case of Chinese online public spheres to illustrate the framework's utility.

Chapter 10
Jonathan Bishop, Centre for Research into Online Communities and E-Learning Systems, UK

With increased participation in social networking and services come new problems and issues, such as trolling, where unconstructive messages are posted to incite a reaction, and lurking, where persons refuse to participate. Methods of dealing with these abuses included defriending which can include blocking strangers. The Gamified Flow of Persuasion' model is proposed, building on work in ecological cognition and the participation continuum, the chapter shows how all of these models can collectively be used with gamification principles to increase participation in online communities through effective management of lurking, trolling, and defriending.

Chapter 11
Peter D. Gibbings, University of Southern Queensland, Australia
Lyn M. Brodie, University of Southern Queensland, Australia

In this chapter the authors demonstrate the importance of student focal awareness through investigating a case study Problem-Based Learning (PBL) course that utilises virtual learning communities to facilitate students' attainment of course objectives. This focal awareness has been shown to be influenced by reflective practices and also effective participation in virtual learning communities. It is therefore concluded that students' focal awareness and their effective participation are critical to their own learning in virtual communities.

The purpose of this conceptual chapter is to present and argue for a cross-disciplinary and systemic approach to the examination of motivations for sharing digital media objects via social mediating technologies. The theoretical foundation of this approach is built on two social theories from rhetorical analysis (Burke's pentad) and gift research (gift systems), respectively. A synthesis of these two theories provides an approach capable of producing more coherent and contextually grounded insights regarding online sharing motivations. This chapter argues for a consideration of situated and contextual motivations for contributing by highlighting the conceptual questions what, to whom, how, where, and finally, why.

The chapter investigates an actionable model of virtual participation for learning communities, in the context of holistic student development in college education. The framework of analysis is based on scenario-planning, accommodating the dynamics of strategic design, decision making, and prototyping of various organizational scenarios of learning in communities. This conceptualization is extensible in cyberspace in today's World Wide Web, especially promising for today's universities, under the mission of ensuring quality student learning.

This chapter develops a conceptual model to elaborate the dynamic interactions between Social Network Services (SNS) features, social capital factors, and motivational antecedents on continuous participation in knowledge sharing activities among Online Social Network (OSN) community members. A number of SNS features, social capital factors, and motivational antecedents are set forth in this chapter, and the mechanism that links these factors is reviewed. It is proposed that, with embedded social mechanism, SNS features can strengthen motivations to continued participation through social capital facilitators.

This study investigates the factors which motivate individuals to continue using a virtual community for information adoption. The proposed model integrates the IS continuance model with the information adoption model and is validated through an online survey of 240 users of a Bulletin Board System established by a local university in China. The results reveal that continuance intention within a virtual community is primarily determined by user satisfaction with prior usage, as well as by perceived information usefulness. The results also suggest that a long-term sustainable virtual community should be provided with high-quality and credible information.

Chapter 16

The aim of this chapter is to explore the application of data mining for analyzing participatory behavior of the students enrolled in an online two-year Master degree programme in project management. The main data sources were the operational database with the students' records and the log files and statistics provided by the e-learning platform. 129 enrolled students and more than 195 distinct characteristics/ variables per student were used. The association rules, clustering, and classification were applied in order to describe the participatory behavior of the students, as well as to identify the factors explaining the students' behavior, and the relationship between academic performance and behavior in the virtual learning environment. The results are very encouraging and suggest several future developments.

Chapter 17

This chapter contributes to the discussion of user generated content as labor by examining the process of building and maintaining an audience in the form of a friends list while simultaneously being an audience member in others' friends lists. This labor is examined in this chapter through looking at the motivations individuals cite for using Facebook and how those users describe their feelings about their friends list qua audience or how users describe themselves as members of an audience.

Chapter 18

This paper explores how people on the internet Mailing List, Cybermind, dealt with death on two occasions: firstly, just after the group's founding, and secondly, when the group had been established for eight years, and was in crisis. On both occasions the group was rocked by the deaths, and struggled to make a meaningful and ongoing List culture out of parts of offline culture, while transforming that culture within the constraints and ambiguities of List Life.

This study investigates participants' involvement, motives and behaviour and attempts to construct and validate a conceptual model of factors influencing members of virtual community of practice in immersive virtual world while they share their knowledge. In order to achieve these goals, quantitative and qualitative research were carried out with participants of a group in Second Life.

Foreword

The importance of virtual communities cannot be denied. In areas such as e-learning, e-health, and even e-commerce, virtual communities have become crucial in communication between people. As a result of this, virtual communities have gained attention by not only practitioners, but also researchers. This book gives an overview of state-of-the-art international research on virtual communities.

VIRTUAL COMMUNITY PARTICIPATION

The focus of this book is on the key aspect of virtual communities: participation. Without actively participating community members, there would be no virtual communities at all. This book takes a scientific approach to this proposition by defining participation and contribution to virtual communities in its first section. Theoretical and conceptual assumptions underlying the notion of virtual community are presented as well as different approaches in terms of analysis (e.g., ethnography, socio-semiotics, narrative network analysis, survey, and observational data) and case studies.

INTERDISCIPLINARY APPROACH

Even a brief look at the Table of Contents is enough to see that authors from several fields have contributed to this book. This is not limited to fields such as information systems and computer science, but also sociology, psychology, and philosophy. This is in line with the increasingly interdisciplinary approach needed to gain more insight into virtual communities. The chapters in this book are an important step towards integration of these fields with respect to their ideas on virtual community participation.

THEORIES BEHIND PARTICIPATION

Another commendable aspect of this book is that the second section of it is fully devoted to theories behind participation. Both theory development and validation are needed to gain more insight into the practice-based issue of virtual community participation. The importance of a theory-driven solution regarding this issue needs to be stressed in view of the omnipresence of virtual communities.

In sum, this book is highly relevant for both researchers and practitioners interested in virtual communities as it focuses on the key aspect: participation. The interdisciplinary approach employed within this book contributes to theory development and validation. This is exactly what is needed to push virtual communities forward.

Rik Crutzen
Maastricht University/CAPHRI, The Netherlands

Rik Crutzen *is a Psychologist and E-Communication Specialist by background and obtained his Ph.D. within the field of Health Promotion. Dr. Crutzen is based at the Department of Health Promotion, which is part of the CAPHRI – the School for Public Health and Primary Care, Maastricht University, The Netherlands. The overarching theme of his work is how technological innovations can be used to greatest effect in the field of health promotion to increase the public health impact of these innovations. An up to date overview of his publications can be found at www.crutzen.net.*

Preface

As an emergent field still in development, virtual community studies have been withstanding the growth of Internet itself. It has attracted a bundle of scholars from diversified fields, as shown in this book, to devote their time and energy to investigate all kinds of fascinating virtual community phenomenon. Starting around the early 1990's, various articles discussing virtual communities, debating its validity, and exploring human's behaviour difference in an seeming new world, have never ceased. Although the academic definitions on virtual communities are controversial and have never been concluded, the virtual community itself is growing to satisfy all kinds of human needs at individual, organizational, or societal level. Researches on virtual communities thus move away from virtual community definitions to virtual community design, management, and business functions.

Among all topics on virtual communities, virtual community participation, virtual involvement, or virtual community behavior, describing members' various activities including posting messages, browsing messages, post diaries, blogs, etc., in virtual communities is of essential importance for a virtual community to sustain and grow. The virtual community participation is also the prerequisite for knowledge accumulation of a community of practice. For this reason, virtual community participation has gained large attention from researchers from diversified disciplines from psychology, communication, sociology, education, information systems, business, marketing, engineering, and many other fields around the world. The motivations behind virtual community participation have accordingly been explored from communicational, psychological, social psychological, educational, informational, economical, information systems, marketing, engineering, and many other perspectives. This cross-disciplinary discussion of virtual communities provides an interesting and exciting angle to look at the virtual community itself considering the fact that virtual communities have been used for multiple functions in these disciplines. Theories explored in this book are in the very early stage in providing a sketch of the current virtual community participation research.

WHO SHOULD READ THIS BOOK?

The motivations and theories behind virtual community participation serve as not only a starting point to explore other potentials of virtual communities but also a guideline to direct practitioners to design, manage, and operate their virtual communities. The theories either generated or developed out of multiple disciplines lay the ground for further exploration of virtual community growth. The book targets readers who are interested in virtual community research and development. Researchers who would like to have an in-depth understanding of the development of the virtual community and members' participation, postgraduate students who would like to devote their efforts in pushing the field forward, and those practitioners, especially virtual community organizers, who want to explore members' participation beyond the superficial level of the behavior itself, would expect to enrich their knowledge on both virtual communities and virtual community participation by reading this book.

INTRODUCTION TO THE BOOK CHAPTERS

The book is divided into two sections based on the characteristics of the chapters. The first section gives readers an overview of the virtual communities and virtual community participation from different theoretical angels. The second section investigates various reasons and motivations behind virtual community participation framed up by cross-disciplinary theories.

Chapter 1 starts the book with the discussion of the evolution of virtual communities which could be traced back to the originality of communities, the development of Internet technologies, and the interactions between communities and the Internet. The most important function internet provides is communication! Building on the communicational perspective, this chapter played an important role by introducing readers to the perception of internet as both technology and culture, based on which virtual communities are evolving. It then further explored the evolution of the concept of community and how it has been changed in the modern civilization process from the sociological perspective. The psychological view of virtual communities on identities, imagined communities, online/offline intermix raised very interesting issues for the reader to ponder. Lastly, the author provides opportunities and challenges brought by virtual communities, i.e., Internet and community interactions at the macro level and Internet individual interactions at the micro level.

Chapter 2 extends chapter one by further discussing the concept of community and virtual community, and proposes an ethnography framework for analysis of a specific virtual community, Gossip Girl. The chapter has used the media coverage process to support the virtual community evolution process through an example. The characteristics of this chapter lies in the author's unique angle of viewing virtual community through the communicational perspective by tracking the origin of virtual communities back into the text-based community. By comparing the virtual community with the traditional media, such as TV through the media coverage theory, the author provides a very innovative perspective connecting the new media with the old media.

Chapter 3 illustrates a virtual educational learning community in Brazil and discusses several issues arising from virtual community environment. The author describes how a virtual community is forced, based on learning needs, in an executive MBA class. The virtual community shaped during the learning process could be categorized into the community of interest and is helpful in the collaborative learning process. The paper raises several interesting issues regarding virtual community participation based on number of messages analysed. Firstly, the author observes those members' participation level increases with the degree of distance. Secondly, the participation level increases greatly with the moderator's intervention. The empirical evidences in this chapter serve as a very good starting point for the opening of the theoretical exploration of virtual community participation.

Chapter 4 leads readers to ponder on news applications and products accompanying virtual communities by illustrating how virtual communities could generate metadata through demonstrating two research projects. User-generated contents are important to the future development of virtual communities and its importance grows along the growth of virtual communities. This chapter highlights how a small area of virtual community member participation could lead to changes in the traditional method of metadata generation process. This chapter will serve as a starting point for readers to explore more of such changes.

Chapter 5 redefines the virtual community participation in a more meaningful and rich context. In past literature, virtual community participation is generally categorized as either lurking or active participation, or no distinguishing between these two, and measured by time spent on virtual communities or frequency of visiting virtual communities, following the information systems traditional method of measuring information technology adoption approach. This chapter attempts to raise the issue that virtual community participation is different from general information technology adoption behavior and should be refined in a more meaningful way. The chapter brings forth the idea that virtual community stated that virtual community participation should be viewed in a more dynamic angle and be treated as an evolving process.

Chapter 6 introduces an ethnographical method of narrative network analysis to systemically analyse virtual community contents. This method has been used in the management field and is applied to analyse the discursive contents generated in virtual communities. Three virtual communities are analysed to demonstrate the method. The method enlightens authors to further explore new methods to systemically analyse virtual community participation behavior.

Chapter 7 introduces infrastructural approach to understanding virtual communities and demonstrates how to analyse virtual communities with this new approach. The author provides many implications for future researchers to analyse virtual communities using this approach.

Chapter 8 poses the following question: how are virtual communities embodied? The author discusses a theoretical framework of subjective performance and argues argues that members' subjectivity is is the key factor in the formation, functioning, and interpretation of virtual community.

Chapter 9 proposes a theoretical framework of subaltern public spheres and analyses how this framework could be applied to the Chinese internet environment, leading to diversified online communities. Specifically, the virtual community participation behavior of Chinese web-surfers could be traced back to their culture origins, and these cultures could confine and even diversify their behaviour. This chapter demonstrates how virtual community participation can be explained in an interesting and unique, yet academically systematically method.

Chapter 10 brings forth the issue of virtual community participation from a new angle. While previous studies tried to explain theoretical motivations for participation by focusing on the active participation, this paper explores the neglected de-friending behaviour in virtual communities and illustrated it by 'The Gamified Flow of Persuasion' model. The paper studies the lurking, defriending, and trolling behaviour, based on which the participation level could be increased. There are several interesting conclusions from this paper, particularly the effective management of lurking, trolling, and defriending behaviour could increase participation.

Chapter 11 further explores the strategy of increasing participation by studying a virtual learning community. The chapter reports that students' awareness of their own learning needs and attitudes are very important to their participation level, based on which the concept of focal awareness is developed and discussed. The focal awareness of the virtual community member is important to increase virtual community participation.

Chapter 12 introduces a systematic method to investigate online sharing motivation by incorporating rhetorical analysis and gift research. Based on these two theories, the chapter argues that virtual community participation is not only self-contained by members but also should consider the situational and cultural factors. The chapter highlights an important concept in virtual community participation- the social situation and the social context of virtual communities, from where future research could explore further and deeper in this area.

Chapter 13 describes a virtual community participation model for the student holistic development. The modern educational process calls for more community support for students and virtual educational community could serve as this purpose. The chapter illustrates the virtual community participation model by a campus project in the University of Macau educational system. The chapter provides a starting point for readers to ponder the links between virtual life and real life.

Chapter 14 seeks to explain the continuous virtual community participation through the social capital perspective. Although virtual community participation has been investigated by many studies, few have explored the continuous virtual community participation behaviour. This paper fills the gap by looking at the continuous involvement in the virtual community through the multiple dimensions of social capital theory.

Chapter 15 is another paper devoting to investigate the continuous virtual community participation behaviour through the information adoption perspective. The information adoption model was used to discuss the motivations for continuous virtual community participation. The paper is similar to chapter 14 by empirically testing the model using data collected from virtual community members. The results show that members' satisfaction and perceived usefulness are important factors in influencing members continued use of virtual communities.

Chapter 16 reports and analyses the data mining results of a virtual learning environment. The paper analyses the log records and participatory data from a master student programme's virtual learning environment. Several interesting findings show that participation is meaningful in predicting students' performance. The most interesting conclusion is that students with higher involvement have better performance and vice versa. The conclusion based on real data analysis leads us to ponder whether every part of our social life is meaningful or produces value in certain way.

Chapter 17 continues the discussion of value creation of virtual community participation activities. The paper investigates the Facebook activities with the immaterial labour theory and their analysis indicated that the respondents conscious of their time on Facebook as labour. The discussion here further opens new areas for us ponder on the values of virtual community participation. Will time and energy spent virtually produce values?

Chapter 18 raises an unnoticed issue in previous virtual community study—the death. While researchers are still trying to figure out the motivations for members' involvement in virtual communities, this paper demonstrates how death is dealt with in virtual communities through ethnography studies. The author himself has been in a Listserv for several years and observed the behaviour of members there. The paper has a unique perspective on culture development and shaping process interwoven with death.

Chapter 19 finishes the book with an exploration of the motivations for virtual world participation, a typical type of virtual community participations. Virtual world might be the future popular virtual communities. One of the interesting findings from this chapter lies in the social interaction patterns identified in virtual world despite the studied virtual world is intended for the purpose of business and entertainment.

This book is the first edited book to aim at giving readers a comprehensive view of virtual community participation. It pieced together theoretical reasons and motivations for virtual community participation from different disciplines with different research methods. When all these theories are compiled together to explain virtual community participation, they generate a dynamic picture of virtual community participation. Firstly, virtual community is still in development and the virtual community participation evolves with the development of the virtual community technology. For example, the virtual world participation in Second Life might be dramatically different from Listserv participation. Secondly, virtual community participation is better explained by social psychological, communicational, and psychological theories, supporting by various theories. Thirdly, the virtual community participation is closely associated with culture, social interactions, and interpersonal relationships. This opened the way for further exploration of virtual community participation theories.

Honglei Li
Northumbria University, UK

Acknowledgment

This book was first inspired by my previous colleague, Dr. Yogesh Dwivedi from School of Business & Economics in Swansea University, who has many experiences in editing books. I was inspired to edit a book on virtual communities while working with him and would like to give my first thanks to him.

There are many others without whom this book could not happen. They are all authors who contributed to this book, the editorial board members who have agreed to assistant me to distribute the information about this book, and the reviewers who have reviewed each chapter. To list name of those reviewers, they are Mamata Bhandar from National University of Singapore, Thierry Nabeth from Insead The Business School for the World, Kathryn Ruth Stam from Syracuse University, Rik Crutzen from Maastricht University/CAPHRI, Trudy Barber from University of Portsmouth, Mei Wu from University of Macau, Sunghee Shin from Queens College CUNY, Stephan Humer from University of the Arts Berlin, Kam Hou Vat from University of Macau, Jonathan Bishop from The Centre for Research into Online Communities and E-Learning Systems, Rivera Gonzalez from Sheffield University, Kevin Y. Wang from Butler University, Antonella Mascio from Università di Bologna, Francesca Comunello from Sapienza Università di Roma, Michael Baron from Baron Consulting, Jacquelyn Erdman from US Green Building Council, Jocelyn Williams from Unitec New Zealand, Kim Ballard from University of Minnesota, and Jonathan Marshall from University of Technology Sydney. Rik Crutzen has to be thanked again for encouraging me during the editing process and writing the Foreword of the book.

Besides all people, I would like to give special thanks to several professional Listservs where I met most of the authors and reviewers of this book. I will be attached to Air Listsrv (http://listserv.aoir.org/listinfo.cgi/air-l-aoir.org) after this book. The AISworld Listserv (http://www.aisnet.org/AIS_Lists/publiclists.aspx) also made a big contribution to the development of this book. I have been nurtured by these two communities during the editorial process. The other Listserv worth mentioning is IRMA (http://www.irma-international.org/irma-l/).

Finally, I would like to thank all the managing editors from IGI who have given me enough patience while editing this book. Special thanks go to Joel Gamon, the final managing editor who has given me enough patience and time.

Honglei Li
Northumbria University, UK

Section 1
Virtual Community and Virtual Community Participation

Chapter 1
Mixing Metaphors:
Sociological and Psychological
Perspectives on Virtual Communities

Kevin Y. Wang
Butler University, USA

ABSTRACT

This chapter explores the theoretical and conceptual assumptions underlying the notion of virtual community. Drawing from relevant literature, the author first examines the fundamental properties of the Internet as both technological and cultural artifact and argues that the Internet can embody different technological, functional, and symbolic meanings that will have direct implications for how communities are formed and experienced. Building on that framework, the second part of the chapter focuses on the sociological and psychological bases of community and explores how such conceptions change with the emergence of the Internet. The author concludes that studies of virtual communities must be contextualized according to historical and existing patterns of social life and offers a discussion on new challenges and questions facing mass communications research in this increasingly interdisciplinary area.

INTRODUCTION

With the rapid diffusion of the Internet, new media technologies are transforming the ways we organize daily lives, conduct businesses, and participate in political activities. As a result, many traditional social and political constructs are increasingly being meshed with technological innovations to create new terms, such as cyber-culture, hyper-text, and electronic-democracy. For social sciences research, this form of "convergence" may represent the best of times and the worst of times, as the pervasiveness of the Web has created a rich and fascinating interdisciplinary field of Internet studies, and yet the ever-changing technological environment challenges scholars to re-define what may have already been complex or contestable ideas. One of these problematic concepts is the notion of "virtual communities."

DOI: 10.4018/978-1-4666-0312-7.ch001

In the popular domain, virtual community is a term that can be used loosely to describe a variety of social groups interacting on the Internet, ranging from massively multiplayer online game (MMOG), online discussion forums, blogs, to a wide variety of social media sites or social networking sites. Despite its growing popularity in theory and in practice, there is no consensus regarding the appropriate definition or types of virtual communities (Porter, 2004). This difficulty is partly due to the ambiguous meaning of "community," but it is also due to the different ontological and epistemological approaches used by scholars to examine the subject matter. Such challenge, however, should not deter researchers from pursuing a better and richer understanding of virtual communities. As Howard Rheingold (1993) once wrote, "perhaps cyberspace is one of the informal places where people can rebuild the aspects of community that were lost when the malt shop became a mall. Or perhaps cyberspace is precisely the *wrong* place to look for the rebirth of community, offering not a tool for conviviality but a life-denying simulacrum of real passion and true commitment to one another. In either case, we need to find out soon" (p. 26).

Heeding Rheingold's call for further exploration, the purpose of this essay is to tease out some of the theoretical and conceptual assumptions underlying the notion of virtual community by mixing two important metaphors about community – that is, community as seen through the *sociological* and the *psychological* lens. The idea of a mixed metaphor involves using unrelated sources to make a senseless comparison. However, when scholars mix metaphors, it allows us to cross different disciplinary boundaries to examine the same issue under different lights. This essay hopes to do so by addressing the following research question from multiple theoretical perspectives: *How have conceptions of community shifted with the emergence of the Internet?* Drawing from relevant literature, I first examine the fundamental

properties of the Internet as both technological and cultural artifact and argue that the Internet can embody different technological, functional, and symbolic meanings that will have direct implications for how communities are formed and experienced. Building on that framework, the second part of the essay focuses on the sociological and psychological bases of community and explores how such conceptions might change with the emergence of the Internet. Finally, I conclude with a discussion on new challenges and questions facing mass communication scholars in the area of virtual communities.

THEORIZING THE INTERNET

Internet as Technology

The Internet itself was originally developed as a mechanism for national defense and can simply be treated in the literal sense as the hardware infrastructure that connects individual computers. However, after its rapid emergence and infiltration into public lives in the early 1990s, the Internet can be now be defined as "the electronic network of networks that links people and information through computers and other digital devices allowing person-to-person communication and information retrieval" (DiMaggio, Hargittai, Neuman, & Robinson, 2001). This view of the Internet as a "communication technology" is akin to what James Carey (1988) called the *transmission* view of communication, which emphasizes the idea of "imparting, sending, transmitting, or giving information to others" (p. 15). In other words, the Internet is no different from conventional mass media, such as print, radio, and television, in terms of its communicative purpose, but the ways in which such function is fulfilled (e.g., through a decentralized network) has sparked debates over whether the Internet may constitute a form of "new" media technology.

For example, some scholars (e.g., Barber, Mattson, & Peterson, 1997) have argued that individuals or marginalized groups can take advantage of the Internet's non-hierarchical modes of communication to bypass traditional intermediaries in politics and media to engage in social movements or political activities. However, others have pointed out that computer networking more often brings a reshuffling of the many functions of intermediaries to create different forms of hierarchy (Brown, Duguid, & Haviland, 1994) and can be used as a mechanism for control and surveillance in authoritarian countries, such as China (Kalathil & Boas, 2003). The extent to which these opposing propositions are accurate remains to be seen, as empirical research to date has generated varying support for both[1] (e.g., Margolis & Resnick, 2000; Xenos & Foot, 2005). Nevertheless, it is worth noting that such debate is inherently connected to two broader theoretical frameworks concerning the role of technology in human society, and similar discussions have occurred in the past as media technologies evolved. In order to fully understand the social implication of the Internet, it is necessary to explore the philosophical assumptions underlying these two contrasting views.

The first is the view of *technological determinism*. According to the determinists, technological innovations, such as cars and railroad, or communications technologies, such as print and television, are the fundamental sources of change in human society. New technology transforms human behavior and organization at every level: from day-to-day personal interactions to family lives and from social organizations to the formation of culture (cf. Howard & Jones, 2004; Wellman & Haythornthwaite, 2002). This strand of thought can be traced back to the Marxist belief that the base (e.g., economic and technological system) determines everything in the superstructure (e.g., social, political and intellectual), and technological determinism was embraced by many observers of technology and culture, such as Jacques Ellul

(1964) and Langdon Winner (1977). Technological determinism also has profoundly influenced many contemporary mass communications theorists (Chandler, 1995). For example, Marshall McLuhan's (1967) declaration of "the medium is the message" is reflective of such deterministic thinking. Other futuristic scholars, such as Alvin Toffler (1980), saw the coming of the "third wave society" and argued that electronic media will revolutionize the production of knowledge and accelerate social change. More recently, Manuel Castells' work on the information age points to digital information technology's potential to "provide the material basis for the pervasive expansion of the networking form of organization" in every realm of social structure (1996, p. 468).

In contrast to the deterministic view, the *social constructivism* approach emphasizes the role of human agency and social context in the development and impact of technology. Within this framework, technologies "do not suddenly leap into existence as the result of a momentous act by a heroic inventor" and do not determine human behavior or social organization. Rather, new technological artifacts are "gradually constructed or deconstructed in the social interactions of relevant social groups" (Bijker, 1993, p. 119). The idea of "interpretive flexibility" is central in the social construction of technology, that is, as Raymond Williams (1975) explained, "the process by which various relevant social groups attribute meaning and utility to such artifacts; and by which artifacts may find applications very different from those envisioned by the original inventors or developers" (p. 160). This process of social negotiation and contestation is invariably connected with the Gramscian notion of "ideology" and "hegemony" that are the set of social practices, cultural norms, and organizational forms that dominate the conception and the application of technology throughout its course of development. The social constructivist view of technology serves as the analytical foundation for critical cultural theorists who contend for a "democratization" of technology through a participatory process that includes the voices of ordinary citizens and relevant groups (Feenberg, 1999) in the decision-making process to reflect the broader public interests in the development of technology.

Internet as Culture

On the other hand, while the Internet can be treated as a network of networks, the sum total of all the computer networks out there and more, it has also become a fixture of our households today and can no longer be understood in purely a mechanical and technological sense. In other words, it can be said that the Internet's social meanings originated and were later amplified when people were connected at the societal, national, and global level through "something" that is available *via* the Internet. These "somethings" are not the hardware infrastructure itself, but the many Web sites, discussion forums, online games, and blogs that represent a "place" that people can "log on" and "log off" as part of their daily lives. In this sense, the Internet represents a conceptual place, often referred to as *cyberspace*, where cultures are formed and reformed (Hine, 2000). This view of the Internet as "culture" is closely aligned with the *ritual* view of communication proposed by Carey (1988), in which rituals and cultural symbols are created and maintained through a process of communication. The question for communications scholars is, then, whether the kind of "cyberculture" that transcends physical boundaries of time and space bears any meaning to the real world.

Early studies of computer-mediated-communication (CMC) found that, as a result of individual interaction with others in cyberspace, a form of virtual co-presence is established and becomes the basis for the formation of interpersonal relationships (Porter, 1996). Echoing such emphasis on the formation of authentic human experiences and relationships online, Turkle (1995) noted that "[individuals] participate with people from all over the world…people with whom [they] may have fairly intimate relationships but whom [they] may never physically meet" (p. 10). In thinking about the Internet as a symbolic space where new and existing values, identities, and desires converge to create real social implications offline, cyberspace can also be construed as a "third place" from a sociocultural perspective. Oldenburg (1999), in his seminal text *The Great Good Place*, argued that the disappearance of informal gathering places away from workplace and home in America has created a negative effect for both individuals and the communities. As a result, "the essential group experience is being replaced by the exaggerated self-consciousness of individuals…American lifestyles, for all the material acquisition and the seeking after comforts and pleasures, are plagued by boredom, loneliness, alienation" (p. 13).

By providing an alternative space for social interaction beyond the workplace and home, the Internet, through the rapid emergence of various online meeting places, may represent a rich ethnographic field where important issues concerning values, identities, and behaviors can be explored. Treating the Internet as a cultural phenomenon that does not exist in a vacuum, scholars are able to *contextualize* their research findings in relation to the broader historical, political, economic, and social milieu. For example, the formation of virtual communities can be seen as social networks (e.g., Wellman, 1997) encompassing personal, organization, and social realms. The use of the Internet in social activism and political movements can be studied through discourse analyses of the texts, images, and video streams surrounding these events in the online environment (e.g., Atton, 2006). Along the same line, as more and more women are connected to the Internet, women's studies researchers have used textual analysis and feminist theory to examine issues of gender and identity within cyberspace (e.g., Consalvo, 1997). Taken together, these areas of research make up what Silver (2000) observed the emerging interdisciplinary field of "critical cyberculture studies," which seeks to explore the "social, cultural, and economic interactions which take place online," and "analyzes a range of social, cultural, political, and economic considerations which encourage, make possible, and/or thwart individual and group access to such interactions" (p. 25).

Functional, Technological, and Symbolic Dimensions of the Internet

The two perspectives of the Internet discussed here, Internet as *technology* and as *culture*, are based on different analytical frameworks and will involve different methods and measures to address different kind of research questions. It is important to note that these two conceptualizations of the Internet should not be treated as dichotomous contrasts. Rather, they highlight the complex interactions and relationships that can be produced by these digital communication technologies, which may consequently shape the social meanings and implications of such technology. For example, voicing the need to strike a balance between the online versus offline world in studies of cyberspace, Hine (2000) cautioned, "a focus on [online] community formation and identity play has exacerbated the tendency to see Internet spaces as self-contained culture... [and] observing online phenomenon in isolation discounts social processes offline which contribute to an understanding of use of the Internet as a meaningful thing to do" (p. 27). Taken together, the technological and cultural views of the Internet intersect with one another and can be manifested in three broad dimensions.

First, when people talk about the Internet, they are most likely referring to its different *functional* characteristics. For example, the Internet can serve as a channel for interpersonal communication through tools like email, or as a mass communication source through popular Web sites. It can also serve as a destination for commerce, political activities, or education. In other words, these functional domains that are central to our day-to-day lives have found their ways to cyberspace as technology matures, and they make up different Web spheres (e.g., commercial, political, educational) that are composed of different specific and proprietary entities (e.g., a Web site, a blog). Our existing cultural values, identities, and beliefs may often shape how we use the Internet in unexpected ways (Contractor & Seibold, 1993). In turn, our patterns of usage may guide the future development of Internet technology – a process that reflects the idea of interpretive flexibility advocated by the social constructivist view of technology.

Second, by its very nature, the Internet is inherently *technological*, consisted of elements of information and communication infrastructures, such as telephone lines, broadband cables, computers, routers, servers, satellites, and so on. Its uses, however, vary from location to location, depending on how the Internet is set up and configured in the first place. For example, a typical online discussion forum may ensure a sense of anonymity and give the user privacy when communicating with others around the world. However, such user experience may change when a new technological platform is added (e.g., wireless mobile device) to the equation or when this process occurs in different locations. For instance, a user of Google in the United States will have a completely different experience than a user of Google in China because the Chinese version[2] (www.google.cn) contains filters that censor material deemed objectionable to authorities there (Mills, 2006). In other words, the structure and characteristics of the computer network (e.g., platform, point of access, bandwidth) will determine the characteristics and the quality of the communication (Bakardjieva & Feenberg, 2002).

Finally, as human interactions have become the common norm in cyberspace, scholars have argued, the online social world has also become something that is socially constructed, or *symbolic*. For instance, people who participate in online social networking sites may create personal images of one another (Walther & Borgoon, 1992), invent new forms of expression (Baym, 1995), or establish ethical and normative boundaries of behavior (e.g., netiquette) through a process of negotiation and interpretation (Dutton, 1996). Such symbolic dimension of the Internet may play a role in determining how people interact with other individuals or groups in cyberspace and, as a result, have an impact on people's online behavior. The formation and function of the virtual community, for example, may largely depend on a participant's perception and understanding of, and connection with the group, and is only given meaning by participants through their symbolic sense of community.

VIRTUAL COMMUNITIES: A SOCIOLOGICAL PERSPECTIVE

From Pastoral Village to Metropolis

As discussed previously, the technical, functional, and symbolic characteristics of the Internet may have changed the ways that communities are formed and experienced through a decentralized global communication network that transcends time and space. While this notion of "virtual community" is closely associated with the emergence of information communication technologies (ICTs), the idea that communities can be seen as series of social ties that vary in density, size and nature is not a novel concept. The rise of cities and urban centers as a result of industrialization have long concerned sociologists, many of whom (e.g., Wirth, 1938; Woodsworth, 1911) feared that traditional social relations that permeated folk communities may be transformed and even threatened by the growth of contemporary metropolis. The development of traditional mass media (e.g., print, radio, and television) had contributed to the process of urbanization by serving as a means of communication for both social and commercial activities. To understand what the Internet may mean for human communities in today's social

and technological context, it is necessary to first explore the changing conception of "community" before the arrival of computers.

While the existence of a community is typically defined by the types of social ties formed by its members (e.g., family or work) and by the physical boundaries that it occupies (e.g., neighborhoods or towns), the idea of community can be traced to ancient social and political thought, ranging from the five fundamental relationships in Confucianism to Plato's ideal republic. During the Enlightenment period, philosophers such as Locke (1988/1689) and Rousseau (1998/1762) wrote extensively about the ways in which individuals enter the covenant of community (or society) and its implication as antecedents for freedom and democratic governance. These abstract conceptions not only signify the sociological nature of community, that is, members are socially bounded together by common interests and traditions, but they also assert that community life, particularly a cohesive and connected one, is essential to the healthy functioning of human civilization. Studies of community in sociology and anthropology in the 19th century have reflected such normative concern.

For example, sociologist Ferdinand Tonnies (1957/1887) described two kinds of social life: Gemeinschaft (community) that is simple, intimate and familial, and Gesellschaft (society) that is sustained by instrumental goals of self interests and competitiveness. As the Industrial Revolution began to transform cities across Europe, Tonnies feared that the effect of rapid urbanization would lead to the loss of Gemeinschaft (Bruhn, 2004), echoing the earlier concerns of Marx and Engles (1844) that changing economic structures may result in different social interaction patterns.

As urbanization and industrialization began to take place in the U.S. in the early 20th century, sociologist Louis Wirth also observed that the division of labor and the new economic structure had attenuated communal ties. Relationships in the city were, in Wirth's words, "impersonal, transitory and segmental" (Wirth, 1938, p.12). As a result, urbanites are only bounded by weak and narrow "secondary" affiliations and the densely knit and interdependent kind of community life has been "lost."

The "lost" narrative dominated much of the early sociological studies of communities (cf. Gusfield, 1975; Nisbet, 1969; Wellman, 1979), as sociologists were concerned with the impact of the Industrial Revolution and the consequences of urbanization on community life. However, as hierarchical and class-based power structures of industrial society began to give way to information and network-based economic activities with improved transportation and communication technologies, the study of community also took on a different perspective to account for the processes of socio-economic transformation and the impact that such developments might have on the individuals.

The Rise of Information Society

The idea of the "information society" can be traced to the Cold War era when rapid technological developments were of central concern to political leaders as well as members of the scientific communities. For example, Bell (1973) posited that innovations such as nuclear energy and the digital computer will become the central thrust of a new socio-economic order. The information society, according to Bell, was represented by "a shift from manufacturing to services, the domination of science and technology-based industries, and the advent of new social stratification through the rise of new technical elite" (Day & Schuler, 2004).

Reviewing decades of scholarly research on the social, economic, and political implications of the information society, Webster (1995) attempted to tease out five distinct analytical paradigms, the first of which is *technological*. As technology progresses, innovations in information processing, storage and transmission reduce cost and increase the availability of information across all

segments of society. The information society is, in this sense, a result of the impact of drastically new technological innovations. Nevertheless, these information technologies interact in critical ways with economic, social, and political structures to produce benefits as well as problems (Steinfield & Salvaggio, 1989). To that end, the *economic* interpretation of the information society places an emphasis on "economics of information," where the production and distribution of "knowledge" (Machlup, 1962) becomes another form of goods and services to be bought and sold (Steinfield & Salvaggio, 1989) and a new kind of labor force may arise. The *occupational* perspective, therefore, stresses the possibility of occupational changes; that is, an information society is achieved when information work is predominant in occupations, and this is often combined with economic measures.

Building upon the abovementioned technological and economic interpretations, the last two perspectives focus on the sociocultural implication of the information society. The *spatial* conception emphasizes the information networks, which connect locations and consequently have substantial effects on the organization of time and space (Webster, 1995). The emergence of a network society and the significance of the flow of information are therefore of great concerns to scholars (Castells, 1989). Finally, the *cultural* conception focuses on the pattern of everyday lives, which now includes a sharp increase in the information in social circulation. Webster (1995) acknowledged this expansion of the informational content of modern life: "we exist in a media-saturated environment, which means that life is about symbolization, about exchanging and receiving" (Webster, 1995, p. 22).

Taken together, these paradigms offer insights into and perspectives on, the information society and what it might mean for the social, economic, and political structures of contemporary societies. Nonetheless, the important question remains: To what extent do these social changes undermine, transform, or facilitate community life? For example, is it the case that the rise of mass media would create isolated individual or misrepresentation of the world that would lead to a further erosion of community life and civic engagement, as many media scholars have suggested (e.g., Gerbner et al, 1986; Postman, 1985; Putnum, 1995)? Or is it possible that communication technologies, most recently with the arrival of the Internet and mobile phones, have provided another means to strengthen the social ties and community fabrics that were once thought to be lost? The following section will further explore the issue of community in the context of digital media and information communication technologies.

Cyberspace and the Networked Society

As we can see from the discussion above, one of the ways that the information society is fundamentally differently from the industrial society is that traditional economic and social activities have been transformed and re-organized into networks of hubs and nodes across physical time and space. Not only do multi-national corporations enjoy the benefits of global presence and the further specialization of skilled labors, individuals can also interact with one another and experience the world much differently than before via the Internet and other digital communication technologies. As Van Dijk (1999) argued, the social environment that we experience today is one "in which social and media networks are shaping its prime mode of organization and most important structures" (p. 248). A similar observation is also made by Benkler (2006), who argued that the emerging networked information economy, characterized by the collaborative production and distribution of information in a decentralized and non-market fashion, is ultimately beneficial to human welfare, development and freedom.

While the economic impact of this networked environment is evident, for example, in the proliferation of peer-production software and

creative commons in recent years Lessig, 2001, 2004), the extent to which such network culture may re-shape community life remains an issue of contention among scholars. For example, in his treatise on the information society, Castells (1996) pointed out that the "dominant functions are organized in networks pertaining to a space of flows that link them up around the world, while fragmenting subordinate functions, and people, in the multiple space of places, made of locales increasingly segregated and disconnected from each other" (p. 476). Such concern for the lost of community is reminiscent of the early sociologists' alarming call against the rapid urbanization at the turn of the century and is supported by empirical evidence that increasing computer and Internet usage is associated with greater loneliness, depression, and the decline of family and community ties (Kraut, 1998).

Nevertheless, as social media became popular, researchers studying the virtual community have indicated that in many instances, individuals, organizations, and communities are utilizing these technologies as ways to stay in touch with one another, and thus, strengthening their social ties in ways that were not possible before. For example, scholars have concluded that the interpersonal interactions that occur in cyberspace are authentic, and online social groups can be treated just the same as *real* communities (e.g., Baym, 1997; Jones, 1997). While it is too early to suggest conclusively that the Internet and other digital communication technologies could "save" community, longitudinal data seem to indicate that the erosion hypothesis may not be true. As Benkler (2006) pointed out, we are seeing two long term effects of the Internet on social ties. First is the "thickening of pre-existing relations with friends, family, and neighbors, particularly with those who were not easily reachable in the pre-Internet-mediated environment" (p. 357). In addition, the decentralized nature of the network enables the loosening of existing social hierarchy and the mobility of social relations, creating what

Benkler characterized as the "looser and more fluid, but still meaningful social networks" (p. 357).

This shift from the concept of the geographically bounded community and stable social relationships to a more flexible one that crosses through different boundaries has resulted in what sociologist Barry Wellman called "networked individuals." Rather than replacing face-to-face interpersonal relationships, the Internet is being integrated into the day-to-day context and existing patterns of social life (Koku, Nazer, & Wellman, 2001). According to Wellman (2003), "communities and societies have been changing towards networked societies where boundaries are more permeable, interactions are with diverse others, linkages switch between multiple networks, and hierarchies are flatter and more recursive." With networked individuals serving as the basis of networked society through their portable communication devices and ubiquitous connectivity, the basic premise of social ties has changed from "linking people-in-places to linking people at any place" (Wellman, 2003).

Indeed, with individuals interacting with one another or creating congregations of like-minded people in cyberspace, this is the new face of community in the age of digital communication technologies. As a result, it is the person, rather than issues associated with the change in physical environment (e.g., urbanization, migration), becomes the new focus of the community research in the information age from a sociological standpoint. For example, what motivates individuals to join virtual communities? In what frequency and capacity do individuals interact with multiple social groups? And to maintain what kind of social relations? These are some of the emerging questions that community scholars will soon have to answer. It is for this reason that the study of community must move beyond the realm of sociology and incorporate perspectives from psychology in order to obtain a more compete picture of what

has, and what has not, changed as a result of the networked environment at the individual level.

VIRTUAL COMMUNITIES: A PSYCHOLOGICAL PERSPECTIVE

Values, Rituals, and Symbols: The Imagined Community

In *The Community: A Critical Response*, Gusfield (1975) identified two dimensions of community as *territorial* and *relational*. While communities may obviously be defined by their physical boundaries, such as cities and neighborhoods, proximity to or occupation of certain territory does not necessarily constitute a community. From a psychological perspective, community exists in human emotion or perception and, consequently, influences the nature and the quality of relationships among members. Even when the sociologists worried that the process of urbanization and industrialization would result in the loss of community life, the primary concern was not about the disintegration of folk towns or pastoral villages, but about the weakening social ties and the disappearance of social capital. In that sense, the relational dimension that exists mostly in the human psyche should be considered as the key ingredient of community. As Dewey (1927) observed, "to learn to be human is to develop through the give-and-take of communication an effective sense of being an individually distinctive member of a community; one who understands and appreciates its beliefs, desires and methods, and who contributes to a further conversion of organic powers into human resources and values" (p. 154).

In other words, we can only realize and appreciate our sense of humanity by communicating with others through language and participating in shared experiences.

As Barney (2004) pointed out, the idea of *communication* and *shared interests* are the two defining elements that figure consistently throughout scholarly research and should be considered as the foundation of a community. The types of shared interests that community members embrace can be broadly understood in cultural terms: values, symbols, languages, traditions, and rituals that make each community unique. The function of the communication is not only to facilitate the sharing of experiences, but, echoing Carey's ritualistic view, to maintain shared meaning across time and space.

This characterization is similar to Benedict Anderson's (1991) notion of an *imagined community*, in that face-to-face interaction and physical boundaries are not the prerequisites for the sense of affinity and togetherness. Rather, as Anderson argued, "in the minds of each member lives the image of their communion" (p. 6); community is given meaning by its participants, and not necessarily bound by the structure or location of the community. For example, research has shown that many ethnic diaspora groups have relied on communications technologies to stay in contact with their homelands and to sustain a sense of belonging (Karim, 2003). The symbolic conceptualization of community is especially relevant in modern societies, as traditional communities, such as nuclear families and tightly knit villages, are increasingly being displaced by social organizations (Drucker, 1994) – organizations that are by nature voluntary and perhaps, virtual.

Psychological Sense of Community

If we accept the notion that a community can be defined by its *relational* meaning, the community question can be centered-on the individual perception, understanding and sense of connection towards a group. This "sense of community" was originally proposed by Sarason (1974), who defined it as "the perception of similarity to others, an acknowledged interdependence with others, a willingness to maintain this interdependence by giving to or doing for others what one expects from them, and the feeling that one is part of a

larger dependable and stable structure" (p. 157). In its early conception, social psychologists used sense of community as a construct to describe the basis of group cohesiveness, identity formation and communicative behavior at the community or neighborhood levels of social organization. For example, Ahlbrant and Cunningham (1979) found that those who were most satisfied with their neighborhoods enjoyed a stronger bond and interpersonal relationships, thereby increasing their commitment to the wellbeing of their communities. In the same vein, Bachrach and Zautra (1985), in their study of coping responses to a proposed hazardous waste facility, revealed that a stronger sense of community may lead to a greater sense of purpose and perceived control in dealing with an external threat. The factors that contribute to this sense of community as reflected in neighborhood attachment, satisfaction, and cohesiveness may include social bonding and behavior rooted-ness (Riger & Lavrakas, 1981), frequency and extent of residential roots and degree of social interaction with others in the nationhood (Riger, LeBailly, & Gordon, 1981).

The results from these studies of urban neighborhoods demonstrate that the experience of a sense of community does exist and that it can function as behavioral controls and predictors in day-to-day lives. However, as McMillan and Chavis (1986) suggested, it is not clear whether the elements used in these measures of sense of community contribute equally to an individual's experience or if some components are more important than others. Recognizing this problem, they proposed a framework to study sense of community that includes four fundamental elements: 1) *Membership*: the sense of belonging and emotional safety resulting from being part of a group community; 2) *Influence*: community cohesiveness and attractiveness depends on the community's influence on its members and the members' feelings of control and influence on the community; 3) *Integration and fulfillment of needs*: common needs, goals, beliefs, and values as the cohesive force that fulfills individual desires and binds the community together; and 4) *Shared emotional connection*: the bonds developed over time through positive interaction and shared history with other community members. The Sense of Community Index (SCI) that grew out of McMillan and Chavis's strand of research has been demonstrated as a robust instrument in measuring community cohesiveness across different geographical and economic sectors and is one of the cornerstones in community psychology research (cf. Chipuer & Pretty, 1999; Obst & White, 2004).

The Online/Offline Intermix

As Kurt Lewin (1946) noted more than half a century ago, behavior is a function of the person and his or her environment. In that sense, an individual's existing values, beliefs, or personalities may interact with today's network environment to result in different perceptions and meanings about community. In terms of personality, for example, prior research has indicated that, when using the Internet, extroverted individuals are more likely to seek out online interactions with others, become more involved in online communities; extroverts and thereby derive more emotional benefits from participating in these online social groups than introverted individuals (Kraut, Kiesler, Boneva, Cummings, Helgeson, & Crawford, 2002). This conclusion coincides with other studies that suggest people's personality difference can be used to predict how they might behave in a group or community setting *offline* (Lounsbury, Loveland, & Gibson, 2003). In other words, it appears that people's social and interpersonal behavioral patterns could remain relatively stable beyond face-to-face interaction and into the computer-mediated world. Yet, despite these findings, some scholars have argued that the unique characteristics associated with the Internet may prompt people to behave differently and therefore create different experiences for themselves and for people whom they interact with. For instance, Schwier and Balbar (2002) observed that although asynchronous platforms, such as bulletin boards or discussion forums, offer similar levels of convenience and enrichment as Internet chat sessions, real-time Internet chat gives users a sense of urgency and immediacy that ultimately creates a more dynamic environment and the added experience of togetherness.

Another area where the network environment and the personal values may converge is in the realm of "identity." While social identity and group identification can be attributed to one's fixed demographic attributes, such as race or gender (e.g., Yzerbyt, Rocher, & Schadron, 1997), the more fluid, subjective interpretation of values and beliefs (e.g., Hamilton, Sherman, & Lickel, 1998) may become more salient in the decentralized and mobile network environment. This is especially true in the case of virtual communities, when participation and membership is not given (as in the case of race or gender), but is entirely voluntary. For example, scholars have observed that individuals, particularly teenagers, are using online social groups as a means to develop their own sense of self, and in many instances, are "trying-out" new and different identities in cyberspace (e.g., Talamo & Ligorio, 2001; Turkle, 1995). The potential implication of such flexible processes may seem positive at face value as it opens up the individuals to more diverse experience. However, it should also be noted that conflicts may occur when competing interests arise from multiple group affiliations (e.g., between two online groups, or between one's online identification and his/her offline identification) because the networked environment enables people to take on more social identities, some of which will be inevitably incompatible. The different ways in which individuals may be able to navigate in, and juxtapose their connections between the online and offline world will be an important area for future studies.

CONCLUSION: OPPORTUNITIES AND CHALLENGES IN VIRTUAL COMMUNITY RESEARCH

In this chapter, I sought to explore the following research question: *How have conceptions of community shifted with the emergence of the Internet?* Looking at the technological and cultural properties of the Internet, I argued that its different technological, functional, and symbolic meanings will have direct implications for how communities are formed and experienced. Applying this framework to the changing conception of community through both sociological and psychological lens, we see that these aspects do converge and, in many ways, are intrinsically connected with the broader social, economic and political changes of our societies. Therefore, it is imperative for scholars in mass communication and other social science disciplines to recognize that the Internet does not exist in a void. Cyberspace may indeed transcend physical boundaries of time and space and allow people from diverse social or cultural backgrounds to converge. Nevertheless, its effect on individual and community must be contextualized, according to existing patterns of social life.

In the same vein, it is worth noting that we should be cautious about the deterministic undertone, whether positive or negative, that is often associated with new technological innovations. As we have seen, from the early European and American sociologists' apprehension over the consequences of urbanization and industrialization on community life, to mass media researchers' concern about the effect of television on social capital, to the recent debate on the utopian and dystopian impact of the Internet, the truth about the implication of these technological developments almost always lies somewhere between either extremes. Individuals and communities are inherently grounded by the environments they reside in, as it is important that scholars should never lose sight of the basic human needs, the larger cultural tradition, and most definitely, the historical and social context.

From the evidence presented in this chapter, it can be reasoned that two broad areas of opportunities and challenges exists for research on virtual community today. The first area is concerned with the interaction between the real world *communities* and the Internet. Scholars like Putnam (1995) have observed the erosion of social capital: fundamental features of social organization, such as networks, norms, and social trust that facilitate cooperation for mutual benefit and the functioning of a democratic society, has been in a steady decline. However, is it possible that, as Schudson (1996) argued, civic life does not die; it may just be manifest in different forms and different settings than we are used to, such as cyberspace? Therefore, the extent to which the Internet may empower members of a community, and serve as a catalyst to transform the well-being of community life either online or offline to result in higher levels of social capital is an important question worthy of further exploration. Such issue as the digital divide and computer literacy will play important roles, and relevant policy measures to facilitate digital literacy should be considered.

At a more micro level, the second area for research deals with the interaction between *individuals* and the Internet. The particular and even unique aspects of the Internet, whether functionally, technologically, or symbolically speaking, may interact with the personal characteristics of the individual to influence cognitive and behavior outcomes. In the realm of virtual community, it is reasonable to postulate that a person's dispositional attributes, prior values, beliefs, or even fantasies may propel certain individuals to join certain online group. This represents an opportunity for scholars to explore not only the formation of virtual communities, but the psychological and motivational bases of such behavior. Do people participate in these online groups to strengthen and maintain their existing values? Or do people participate because they want to "try out" new identities that may not be attainable in real life? These are some of the research questions that future scholars may wish to answer.

While the opportunities presented in these areas of research may be tremendous, the difficulty lies in the choices of methods and measurement. Whereas quantitative and experimental approaches may lend us insights into the psychological and cognitive processes in the computer-mediated communication situation, the motivation and the experiences that people may derive from these behaviors are perhaps better assessed using qualitative methods. At the macro level, the change in community life (or the structure of community) is gradual and may thus require longer periods of tracking and observation.

The challenge for future research is to generate innovative methods that combine the advantages of different methodologies to address these issues. To that end, Wellman's (2003) concern of "networked individualism" may prove to be a useful theoretical framework. By conceptualizing communities, physical or virtual, as series of networks shaped by the larger socio-economic environment, which can also be seen as larger networks (e.g., the network society) of national and global scale, we can contextualize individual differences in the broader social, historical, and cultural environment. Finally, with the multifacetedness of the Internet, studies that cross different disciplinary boundaries may help us better understand the complex web of relationships, cultures, and identities that are formed and reformed in cyberspace.

REFERENCES

Agre, P. (2002). Real-time politics: The Internet and the political process. *The Information Society*, *18*(5), 311–331. doi:10.1080/01972240290075174

Ahlbrant, R., & Cunningham, J. (1979). *A new public policy for neighborhood preservation*. New York, NY: Praeger.

Anderson, B. (1991). *Imagined communities: Reflections on the origin and spread of nationalism*. New York, NY: Verso.

Atton, C. (2006). Far-right media on the Internet: Culture, discourse and power. *New Media & Society*, *8*(4), 573–587. doi:10.1177/1461444806065653

Bachrach, K.M, & Zautra, A. (1985). Coping with a community stressor: The threat of a hazardous waste facility. *Journal of Health and Social Behavior*, *26*(2), 127–141. doi:10.2307/2136602

Bakardjieva, M., & Feenberg, A. (2002). Community technology and democratic rationalization. *The Information Society*, *18*(3), 181–192. doi:10.1080/01972240290074940

Barber, B. R., Mattson, K., & Peterson, J. (1997). *The state of the electronically enhanced democracy*. Rutgers, NJ: Walt Whitman Center.

Barney, D. (2004). Communication versus obligation: The moral status of virtual community. In Tabachnick, D., & Koivukoski, T. (Eds.), *Globalization, technology, and philosophy* (pp. 21–41). New York, NY: SUNY Press.

Baym, N. (1995). The emergence of community in computer-mediated communication. In Jones, S. (Ed.), *Cybersociety: Computer-mediated communication and community* (pp. 138–163). Thousand Oaks, CA: Sage Publications.

Baym, N. (1997). Interpreting soap operas and creating community: Inside an electronic fan culture. In Keisler, S. (Ed.), *Culture of the Internet* (pp. 103–120). Mahweh, NJ: Lawrence Erlbaum Associates.

Bell, D. (1973). *The coming of post-industrial society: A venture in social forecasting*. New York, NY: Basic Books.

Benkler, Y. (2006). *The wealth of networks*. New Haven, CT: Yale University Press.

Bijker, W. (1993). Do not despair: There is life after constructivism. *Science, Technology & Human Values, 18*(1), 113–138. doi:10.1177/016224399301800107

Bronfenbrenner, U. (1979). *The ecology of human development: Experiments by nature and design*. Cambridge, MA: Harvard University Press.

Brown, J., Duguid, P., & Haviland, S. (1994). Toward informed participation: Six scenarios in search of democracy in the information age. *Aspen Institute Quarterly, 6*(4), 49–73.

Bruhn, J. (2004). *The sociology of community connections*. New York, NY: Kluwer Academics.

Carey, J. (1988). *Communication as culture*. New York, NY: Routledge.

Castells, M. (1989). *The information city: Information technology, economic restructuring and the urban-regional process*. Oxford, UK: Blackwell.

Castells, M. (1996). *The rise of the network society*. Oxford, UK: Blackwell.

Chandler, D. (1995). *Technological or media determinism*. Retrieved March 10, 2008, from: http://www.aber.ac.uk/media/Documents/tecdet/tecdet.html

Chipuer, H., & Pretty, G. (1999). A review of the sense of community index: Current uses, factor structure, reliability and further development. *Journal of Community Psychology, 27*(6), 643–658. doi:10.1002/(SICI)1520-6629(199911)27:6<643::AID-JCOP2>3.0.CO;2-B

Consalvo, M. (1997). Cash cows hit the web: Gender and communications technology. *The Journal of Communication Inquiry, 21*(1), 98–115. doi:10.1177/019685999702100105

Contractor, N., & Eisenberg, E. (1990). Communication networks and new media in organizations. In Fulk, J., & Steinfield, C. W. (Eds.), *Organizations and communication technology* (pp. 143–172). Newbury Park, CA: Sage Publications.

Day, P., & Schuler, D. (2004). *Community practice in the network society: Local action/global interaction*. London, UK: Routledge.

Dewey, J. (1927). *The public and its problems*. Athens, OH: Swallow Press.

DiMaggio, P., Hargittai, E., Neuman, W., & Robinson, J. (2001). Social implications of the Internet. *Annual Review of Sociology, 27*, 307–336. doi:10.1146/annurev.soc.27.1.307

Drucker, P. (1994). The age of social transformation. *Atlantic Monthly*, (November): 53–80.

Dutton, W. (1996). Network rules of order: Regulating speech in public electronic fora. *Media Culture & Society, 18*(2), 269–290. doi:10.1177/016344396018002006

Ellul, J. (1964). *The technological society*. New York, NY: Alfred A. Knopf.

Feenberg, A. (1999). *Questioning technology*. London, UK: Routledge.

Gerbner, G., Gross, L., Morgan, M., & Signorielli, N. (1986). Living with television: The dynamics of the cultivation process. In Bryant, J., & Zillman, D. (Eds.), *Perspectives on media effects* (pp. 17–40). Hilldale, NJ: Lawrence Erlbaum Associates.

Gusfield, J. (1975). *Community: A critical response*. New York, NY: Harper & Row.

Hine, C. (2000). *Virtual ethnography*. Thousand Oaks, CA: Sage Publications.

Howard, P., & Jones, S. (2004). *Society online: The Internet in context*. Thousand Oaks, CA: Sage Publications.

Jones, S. (1997). *Virtual culture: Identity and communication in cybersociety.* London, UK: Sage Publications.

Kalathil, S., & Boas, T. (2003). *Open networks, closed regimes: The impact of the Internet on authoritarian rule.* Washington, DC: Carnegie Endowment for International Peace.

Karim, K. (2003). *The media of diaspora.* London, UK: Routledge.

Koku, E., Nazer, N., & Wellman, B. (2001). Netting scholars: Online and offline. *The American Behavioral Scientist, 44,* 1752–1772. doi:10.1177/00027640121958023

Kraut, R., Kiesler, S., Boneva, B., Cummings, J., Helgeson, V., & Crawford, A. (2002). Internet paradox revisited. *The Journal of Social Issues, 58*(1), 49–74. doi:10.1111/1540-4560.00248

Kraut, R., Patterson, M., Lundmark, V., Kiesler, S., Mukophadhyay, T., & Scherlis, W. (1998). Internet paradox: A social technology that reduces social involvement and psychological well-being? *The American Psychologist, 53*(9), 1017–1031. doi:10.1037/0003-066X.53.9.1017

Lessig, L. (2001). *The future of ideas: The fate of the commons in a connected world.* New York, NY: Random House.

Lessig, L. (2004). *Free culture: How big media uses technology and the law to lock down culture and control creativity.* New York, NY: Penguin Press.

Locke, J. (1988). *Two treatises of government.* New York, NY: Cambridge University Press. (Original work published 1689)

Lounsbury, J., Loveland, J., & Gibson, L. (2003). An investigation of psychological sense of community in relation to big five personality traits. *Journal of Community Psychology, 31*(5), 531–541. doi:10.1002/jcop.10065

Machlup, F. (1962). *The production and distribution of knowledge in the United States.* Princeton, NJ: Princeton University Press.

Margolis, M., & Resnick, D. (2000). *Politics as usual: The cyberspace "revolution.".* Thousand Oaks, CA: Sage Publications.

Marx, K., & Engles, F. (1848). Manifesto of the communist party. In Tucker, R. C. (Ed.), *The Marx-Engel reader* (pp. 331–362). New York, NY: Norton.

McLuhan, M. (1967). *Understanding media: The extensions of man.* New York, NY: McGraw Hill.

McMillan, D. W., & Chavis, D. M. (1986). Sense of community: A definition and theory. *Journal of Community Psychology, 14,* 6–23. doi:10.1002/1520-6629(198601)14:1<6::AID-JCOP2290140103>3.0.CO;2-I

Nisbet, R. (1969). *The quest for community.* New York, NY: Oxford University Press.

Obst, P., & White, K. (2004). Revisiting the sense of community index: A confirmatory factor analysis. *Journal of Community Psychology, 32*(6), 691–705. doi:10.1002/jcop.20027

Oldenburg, R. (1999). *The great good place.* New York, NY: Paragon House.

Porter, E. (2004). A typology of virtual communities: A multi-disciplinary foundation for future research. *Journal of Computer Mediated Communication, 10*(1). Retrieved April 10, 2007, from http://jcmc.indiana.edu/vol10/issue1/porter.html

Postelnicu, M., Martin, J., & Landreville, K. (2004). The role of campaign web sites in promoting candidates and attracting campaign resources. In Williams, A., & Tedesco, J. (Eds.), *The Internet election: Perspectives on the web in campaigning in 2004.* Lanham, MD: Rowman & Littlefield.

Postman, N. (1985). *Amusing ourselves to death: Public discourse in the age of show business*. New York, NY: Penguin.

Putnam, R. (1995). Bowling alone: America's declining social capital. *Journal of Democracy*, *6*(1), 65–78. doi:10.1353/jod.1995.0002

Rheingold, H. (1993). *The virtual community: Homesteading on the electronic frontier*. Cambridge, MA: MIT Press.

Riger, S., & Lavrakas, P. (1981). Community ties: Patterns of attachment and social interaction in urban neighborhoods. *American Journal of Community Psychology*, *9*, 55–66. doi:10.1007/BF00896360

Riger, S., LeBailly, R., & Gordon, M. (1981). Community ties and urbanites fear of crime: An ecological investigation. *American Journal of Community Psychology*, *9*, 653–665. doi:10.1007/BF00896247

Rousseau, J. J. (1998). *The social contract*. Hertfordshire, UK: Wordsworth Editions. (Original work published 1762)

Sarason, S. (1974). *The psychological sense of community: Prospects for a community psychology*. San Francisco, CA: Jossey Bass.

Schudson, M. (1996, March-April). What if civic life didn't die? *The American Prospect*, *25*, 17–20.

Schumpeter, J. (1947). *Capitalism, socialism, and democracy*. New York, NY: Harper.

Schwier, R., & Balbar, S. (2002). The interplay of content and community in synchronous and asynchronous communication: Virtual communication in a graduate Seminar. *Canadian Journal of Learning and Technology*, *28*(2), 21–30.

Silver, D. (2000). Looking backwards, looking forward: Cyberculture studies 1990-2000. In Gauntlett, D. (Ed.), *Web.Studies: Rewiring media studies for the digital age*. New York, NY: Oxford University Press.

Steinfield, C., & Salvaggio, J. L. (1989). Toward a definition of the information society. In Salvaggio, J. L. (Ed.), *The information society: Economic, social and structural issues* (pp. 1–14). Hillsdale, NJ: Lawrence Erlbaum Associates.

Talamo, A., & Ligorio, B. (2001). Strategic identities in cyberspace. *Cyberpsychology & Behavior*, *4*(1), 109–122. doi:10.1089/10949310151088479

Toffler, A. (1980). *The third wave*. New York, NY: Bantam.

Tönnies, F. (1957). *Community and society (Gemeinschaft und Gesellschaft)* (Loomis, C. P. (Trans. Ed.)). East Lansing, MI: Michigan State University Press. (Original work published 1887)

Turkle, S. (1997). *Life on the screen: Identity in the age of the Internet*. New York, NY: Simon & Schuster.

Van Dijk, J. (1999). *The network society: Social aspects of new media*. Thousand Oaks, CA: Sage Publications.

Walther, J., & Borgoon, J. (1992). Relational communication in computer-mediated interaction. *Human Communication Research*, *19*(1), 50–88. doi:10.1111/j.1468-2958.1992.tb00295.x

Webster, F. (1995). *Theories of the information society*. London, UK: Routledge.

Wellman, B. (1979). The community question: The intimate networks of East Yorkers. *American Journal of Sociology*, *84*(5), 1201–1231. doi:10.1086/226906

Wellman, B. (1997). An electronic group is virtually a social network. In Kiesler, S. (Ed.), *Culture of the Internet* (pp. 179–205). Mahwah, NJ: Lawrence Erlbaum Associates.

Wellman, B., & Haythornthwaite, C. (2002). *The Internet in everyday life*. Malden, MA: Blackwell Publishing. doi:10.1002/9780470774298

Wellman, B., Quan-Haase, A., Boase, J., Chen, W., Hampton, K., de-Diaz, I., & Miyata, K. (2003). The social affordances of the Internet for networked individualism. *Journal of Computer-Mediated Communication*, 8(3). Retrieved March 15, 2007, from http://jcmc.indiana.edu/vol8/issue3/wellman.html

Williams, R. (1975). *Television: Technology and cultural form*. New York, NY: Schocken. doi:10.4324/9780203450277

Winner, L. (1977). *Autonomous technology: Technics-out-of-control as a theme in political thought*. Cambridge, MA: MIT Press.

Wirth, L. (1938). Urbanism as a way of life. *American Journal of Sociology*, 44, 1–24. doi:10.1086/217913

Woodsworth, J. S. (1911). *My neighbor*. Toronto, Canada: University of Toronto Press.

Xenos, M., & Foot, K. (2005). Politics as usual, or politics unusual: Position-taking and dialogue on campaign web sites in the 2002 U.S. elections. *The Journal of Communication*, *55*(1), 169–185. doi:10.1111/j.1460-2466.2005.tb02665.x

ENDNOTES

[1] For a more thorough review, see Agre, P. (2002). Real-time politics: The Internet and the Political Process. *The Information Society,* 18(5), 311-331.

[2] Google began redirecting all google.cn traffic to its Hong Kong site starting March 22, 2010, thereby bypassing Chinese regulations and allowing uncensored search results.

Chapter 2
Asynchronous Text–Based Community:
Proposals for the Analysis

Antonella Mascio
University of Bologna, Italy

ABSTRACT

The chapter starts with a short introduction to the complex phenomenon of Virtual Communities as part of media convergence process. The aim of the chapter is the analysis of Text-Based Communities through methodologies of ethnography and socio-semiotics, with specific focus, and analysis, of some virtual groups related to TV-Drama and linked to Fashion genre. The last part of the chapter is about the analysis of these virtual groups.

INTRODUCTION

The Web actually hosts different kind of *communities*, subdivided into several typologies according to type of communications (synchronic or asynchronic), and by the way they present themselves on the screen (that is, in text-only or graphic versions). Through socio-semiotics and online-ethnography it is possible to describe – in a way - how Virtual Communities work. Those two methodologies are used in distinct steps of the analysis: in the former the virtual community is analyzed through the observation (whether participatory or not, it depends from case to case); in the latter the observed community can be delimited on specific boundaries and studied as a "text." Through the analysis of a – limited – body of online socialization settings dedicated to the connection between tv series (Gossip Girl) and *fashion discourse,* the chapter will focus on typical features in *fandom*, to highlight topics, value-laden features and dynamics which are offered to media fans of fashion products: *fandom*, therefore, as a practice for the setting-up of "elective" communities, as a space where identity-building elements are engendered, as a possibility of creating specific idiolects.

DOI: 10.4018/978-1-4666-0312-7.ch002

1. "VIRTUAL COMMUNITIES"

"Virtual communities" are social aggregations finding their place in specific Internet locations. They were established even before the birth of the Web (the BBS[1] for example) as a spontaneous and anarchical phenomenon. Since the second half of the 1990's the *communities* have become one of the most studied, analysed and explored elements of the Internet. A vast and heterogeneous literature has in fact developed around the concept of *virtual community*.

Virtual communities are quite varied: group members may *meet* by electronic means in some Internet spaces, or can exchange messages without ever experiencing actual moments of real-time *conversation*. The expression "virtual community" works therefore as a sort of umbrella term (Eco, 1979): its value does not lie in its expressing an unambiguous concept, but in its referring to a vast universe of meanings and values, where mailing lists, forums, e-groups may be found, as well as MUD, MOO and the 3D world of the web, environments describing and representing different inter-subjective relations. The configuration of the "virtual community" has further developed in recent years, thus coinciding with some forms of social network: Facebook, Linked In, Twitter and others also enable the establishment of forms of community, although according to new parameters and configurations. To some extent they may be seen as a clear evolution of communities, as the former share with the latter similar elements such as a shared culture and are characterised by a constantly changing outlook, so that making a correct and definite definition of what they are turns out to be quite difficult. Certainly the web 2.0 is contributing to change the idea of on-line community, thus stretching the boundaries of previous classifications[2].

On-line social aggregations are mostly characterised by the specificity of their environments where, despite the absence of a physical space, the *sense of place* is perceived quite strongly and is very present. A place to meet is there, it exists, although with different qualities than concrete environments, and the members of these aggregations perceive and experience it as a space they have in common. Or, at least, as the possibility of sharing a space they have in common. As Meyrowitz wrote, the idea is there that electronic media have substantially changed the meaning of physical presence, which is no longer necessary in some circumstances to experience social events. According the the author, "Electronic media have altered the significance of time and space for social interaction" (1986, p. viii).

The *communities* may be studied as laboratories where dynamics relating to the exchange of meanings, the construction of meaning, and the establishing of a culture may take shape and find their place.

As is often the case – and we will attempt to demonstrate it in the present article - virtual communities may also be linked to medial *source* texts: as for example the communities of fans meeting in the web to discuss their favourite *TV show*.[3] Audiences may also extend the pleasure deriving from the experience of watching by looking for further information regarding the series or by trying to enter into a Web community where the show is the focus of exchanges. And text boundaries would be blurred as a consequence.

This is why in studying these items, via the adoption of a socio-semiotic perspective[4], the notion of *textual network* becomes effective in describing the "network" which is generated around other texts, starting from *discursive formations*[5]. This is a process which is parallel to the process of *convergence*, referring to both the productive work expressed by participating communities, and the use of technologies enabling their existence[6].

In this article a textualist perspective has been adopted: both TV serials and on line discussions are analised as texts. Discursive productions developing around the series are observed through the approach of online ethnography. The wider framework being used is the framework of medial convergence: the series are analysed as a starting point of an intersection of discourses at times moving outside the boundaries of the "fictional" to enter those of the "real."

The analysis of *media-source* virtual communities must therefore take into account the medial text they refer to, and the work by its users or *consumers*; more or less passionate fans using them to express their ideas, starting precisely from those texts. In many instances they try to share in these spaces their pleasure in, and their interpretation of, the stories, so as to create a specific community of "taste."

The use of medial products may then be analysed as "a sort of cultural do-it-yourself, by which readers fragment the texts and reassemble the pieces according to their plans, saving large or small pieces of the objects encountered during the attribution of meaning to their social experience" (Jenkins, 1992, It. tr. 2007 p. 146). This is a full fledged activity of *braconnage* (poaching - de Certeau, 1990) merging into a new textual, community-based, shared, fluid experience based on the experience of recognising oneself together with others in the sharing of interests and passions.

Usually the social aggregations participating in the setting up of these networks represent not only a form of socialisation, but also a venue for the exchange of value-laden forms (news, spoilers, the latest gossip, new developments....). They can therefore be considered *indicators* of the setting up of knowledge bases through the complex system of symbolic elements they establish and the inter-textual reference system they create.

2. TEXT-BASED VIRTUAL COMMUNITIES

The first definition of virtual community found in literature was proposed by Rheingold in 1994, and it has remained a valid starting point for many:

Virtual communities are social aggregations that emerge from the Net when enough people carry on those public discussion long enough, which sufficient human feeling, to form webs of personal relationships in cyberspace (Rheingold, 1994, p. 5).

Today in the Web there are several forms of *communities* which are grouped on the basis of the type of communication they activate (synchronous and asynchronous) and the type of interface (text-only or graphic version):

After this general introduction, I will explore only the "text-based" communities operating asynchronously, as they represent the primary form of virtual community, although somewhat showing affinities with the most recent forms of web 2.0[7] sociality, in particular in the "quality of presence" and mostly in the user's "experience," which may also coincide. This is why the web 2.0 groups may be included in the first box of Figure 1. Each box of the table shows differing virtual communities in terms of layout, timing of operation, and type of sensory involvement offered to users: studies carried out on these items agree in stating that the maximum sensory involvement is reached in the cases pertaining to box 4.[8]

Asynchronous "text-based" communities use only the verbal-visual language to express themselves and at times to describe the spaces inhabited by them. In term of fruition time the "asynchronous" mode describes all the situations where the exchange between users does not take place in real time: this is the case for example of e-groups. This means that the "presence" in the same electronic space does not correspond to the contemporaneity of its use by users[9], unlike "synchronous" communication (for example, chat) where time and space are shared within the same virtual place.

At the beginning asynchronous text-based virtual communities had spaces where text-only posts[10] could be found. Progressively the interface has improved greatly and is now certainly much *friendlier.* This is a kind of communication

Figure 1. Virtual communities

Interface	TEXT BASED	3D GRAPHICS
Asincrono (staticità)	Mailing list, forum, e-groups, bacheche elettroniche, …	---
Sincrono (dinamicità)	Moo e MUD	3D Worlds - Chat

which in many instances tends to simulate the typical conversational exchange via the use of fake simulacra.

Today, users are also allowed to use more languages at the same time to express themselves (verbal-visual messages with attached music, visual or even audio-video files).

3. TEXT-BASED COMMUNITIES IN ASYNCHRONOUS MODE: PROPOSED ANALYSIS

In the study of virtual communities, recent literature has shown a general trend towards the use of ethnographic approaches. These are experiences of primary analyses referring to researchers particularly involved in the activity of the communities[11].

The first feature to emerge has been the fact that virtual communities usually give rise to at least two narrations, varyingly overlapping and woven together: the story based on *what people talk about* (the real information: therefore, the information level we find in the messages) and the story based on the *people who talk about it* (referring instead to the level of construction of roles and regimes inside the community, namely the level of inter-subjective conversation).

As ethnography deals with the description of a given social world according to a *non-obvious* perspective, understanding *what* users *do* in virtual communities is particularly useful. Thus a sort of

description of the organisation of a social group is configured, as well as the activities they carry out, the interpretation practices and cultural and symbolic elements which characterise them (Augé, 1994, Clifford & Marcus (ed.) 1986, Duranti, 1997, Dal Lago & De Biasi, 2002, Geertz 1973). An approach which therefore contributes to the definition of important answers with respect to the macro-questions researchers ask when encountering innovative forms of sociality.

From this perspective, asynchronous virtual communities may be considered interesting study example as they provide researchers with precious material for their analysis[12], although new problems may arise referring first of all to the outlining of the field of investigation: what should the boundaries be in view of the fact that a community-based environment constantly develops relations outside the perimeter being inhabited?[13] And for how long should an on-line community be observed, given the fact that the life of groups of this kind may be quite short, although very intense? And more: which participants are to be considered members of the community, as some of them leave behind very few signs of their presence?

For these and other reasons, the perspective to adopt may be focussed on the idea of "field" linked to the concepts of flow and connectivity. Following the approach adopted by many important Web ethnographers, like Christine Hine (2000), in fact, ethnography applied to the virtual world must take into due consideration this kind of specificity. For Howard (2002) as well, the concept of field must be adjusted to the specificities of the web: "First, the meaning of 'field sites' is adapted, and instead of choosing territorial field sites, the researcher has to choose a *perceived community* and select the important nodes in the social network as field sites." (Howard, 2002, p. 561, my italics). The fact of labelling communities as *perceived* highlights two different perspectives: the researcher looking from the outside and capable, after a close observation, of classifying some groups as community-based social forms, but also the internal outlook of the group, the fact of feeling (perceiving) themselves as part of the community or not, in view of the participation in a specific, although electronic, space, and the sharing of the passion for the topics being discussed there.

Hine writes ten principles about virtual ethnography which considers "the foundations for the experiments in ethnography" (2000, p. 63). In particular the focus should be on the fact that Hine insists on the differences in virtual ethnography: "The challenge of virtual ethnography is to explore the making of boundaries and the making of connections, especially between the 'virtual' and the 'real'. (…) Virtual ethnography is interstitial, in that it fits into the other activities of both ethnographer and subjects. Immersion in the setting is only intermittently achieved. Virtual ethnography is necessary partial." (Hine, 2000, p. 64 – 65).

Ethnography is therefore necessary for the definition of the specificities of the social group to be analysed and the practices being established by it. Virtual communities show in fact common traits; however each is characterised by specific elements and separate activities.

When we come to the core of the matter in the study of self-defined sociality, the virtual community should also be observed from the perspective of its specificity as a *text*[14], in according a socio-semiotic perspective.

The typical text of a *text-based* community appears therefore as a composite text: it is the result of different *utterances,* composed of a series of elements (written text, images, clips..) which bear traces and produce effects pertaining to the setting of the communication exchange. The textual structure comprises simulacrum-like[15] elements deriving from individual speech turns expressed in multiple spatial and time settings, which however seem to belong to a single instance. What is generated here is the simulated snapshot of a single moment which has never really occurred, starting from the use of an a-temporal present becoming evident in the different messages: each passage refers in fact to a different time-space. We quote an excerpt with three posts as in Figure 2.

In essence in a text-based community, the relationship between users is managed through their *simulacrum.* The interactive communication does not take place between two real subjects actually present together in a shared space, but rather in a sort of inter-space of symbolic nature, displayed on a screen. The sender prepares therefore a text for a recipient located *outside* the screen. The two subjects do not relate directly: the medium they use (either the computer or the mobile or something else) enables them to meet in a space which is different from the one they experience in their reality and at the same time. (Manetti, 1998)

The comparison of detected data through ethnographic tools with elements highlighted by the socio-semiotic analysis may be very useful for the interpretation of the community being studied as the two methodologies assist in outlining the social structure and its contents; hence, the meaning of its existence.

3.1. A Possible Chart…

The virtual community should therefore be observed for a medium-long period, in order to study the organisation of roles, dynamics, and practices which are being established (ethnographic per-

Figure 2. Example from the forum dedicated to the third season of Gossip Girl, found in the Italian website http://gossipgirl.forumcommunity.net dedicated to the whole series. The box on top shows the topic of discussion, followed by the sequence of messages listed in the order of "arrival."

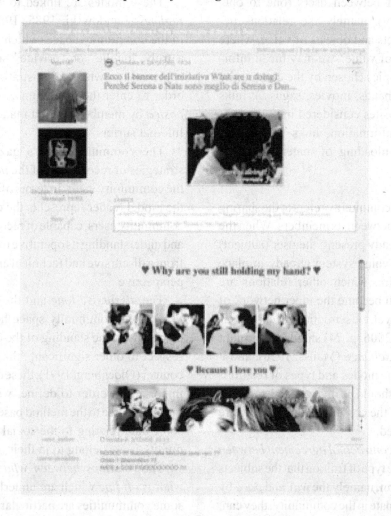

spective). This period is defined in the text-based communities by the selection of a time unit (usually ranging between one month and one year) and the diverse participations which characterise it. The text-based communities would enable to record not only the quantity of each user's participation, but also the diverse levels of discussions, subdivided into separate *topics*.

Starting from the discursive paths being originated, it becomes possible to study the inner *tension* and the level of intimacy between the members, as well as the different perspectives linked to the interest for topics emerging in the community. Also the *ways* in which users participate and the *frequency* of their "taking the floor" become significant in the perspective of studying the roles which are taking shape.

Community space and discourses circulating in it therefore become a complex context where two different types of contracts are established, which the user is invited to participate in:

• The contract between user and environment-community, namely between the subject and an already-established system of values and practices;

- The contract between users (one to one, one to many), namely the relations between subjects and objects of value, where by "objects of value" we may mean information on topics chosen by the community (TV series, bands, movies, sagas...), links to other websites considered important for additional information, links to websites for the downloading of materials, news, gossip....

The concept of community refers to the sharing of a value system between its members. When the community is already present, the user (subject) chooses to join a value system already in place (community) within which other relations are determined, which become the inner network of relations. At this level, the semiotic concept of *contract* (Fontanille, 2006, p. 74) should be brought closer to that of *exchange* (Mauss, 1950), and it is here that both the modes and types of relations between subjects should be investigated, together with the nature of the contextual universe where they are constituted.

In essence the *contractual agreement between subjects* evokes the type of fruition that the subjects themselves perform, namely the *way* and *pace* by which they participate in the community: they can, for example, remain in a space "at the threshold" and observe what is going one without participating (the *lurkers*[16]). They can, instead, participate actively, taking a predominant function and being identified by the others as community *opinion leaders*. Finally, they can choose an intermediate place between these two extremes and live the community space and social relations being developed inside it without playing an excessive protagonist's role nor being too absent. For each of the above modes of observation-participation, the community is experienced differently from a

functional perspective, and therefore it takes on different values.

These modes are linked to diverse *visibility regimes* (Landowski, 1985, 1989) taking place in the community space, which may seem to be a truly "public" or "private" space. The latter is the case in which a registration is required in order to enter the community, so that messages *posted* by members are not made available to all Internet surfers.

The community user's gaze activates the strategies of recognition of the *model reader*[17] of the community itself. In terms of textual strategy, the model reader represents the class of possible community users, capable of recognising its genre and understanding its operative mechanisms, both from a discursive and technical and technological perspective.

The *discursive tone* and the *language being used* in the community space help to generally comprehend the standing of the community with respect to other significant "third places" of encounter (Oldenburg, 1991): these elements become important in order to define, without having to make recourse to the method based on interviews, some data relating to the social group the community users belong to in their off-line lives.

The *relations between what is on line and what is off line* which are underlined at times by some communities are particularly relevant areas of investigation, especially when leading towards the concrete implementation, in the real world, of practices, actions, situations previously organised in the Internet. In these settings strategies, tactics, manoeuvres are activated which may be either solidarity-based or hostile, according to the attitude of individual members or different subgroups.

4. AN EXAMPLE: GOSSIP GIRL AND ITALIAN COMMUNITIES

Let us now take into consideration some virtual communities linked to the TV series Gossip Girl, based on the set of books with the same title written by Cecily von Ziegesar, narrating the stories of a group of young residents of Manhattan's Upper East Side. Gossip Girl is the nickname of a mysterious blogger whose identity is unknown, who publishes in her blog all the news referring to the lives of the protagonists. The narration develops following several lines: from love to friendships stories; from personal achievements to family events, from teenagers' carefree lives to their first responsibilities as young adults.

In Italy Gossip Girl started to be broadcast in 2008 and became an instant success in no time, with an audience of aficionados and real fans who publish in the Internet articles and photographs, run forums, make episodes visible and accessible, disseminate contents on the series and contribute to its growing success. In the on-line spaces dedicated to it (from blogs to forums, dedicated web sites, pages in social networks, chats, etc.) users discuss plots, the characters' development, their respective relations and lifestyles.

This paper will make an attempt to stress the relevance of "fashion" as a topic within the discourses of the observed virtual communities. Fashion in fact is a constant in the narrative, acting as a sort of identity card and a symbol of belonging to a specific social class. Fashion is mentioned in the lines spoken in particular by some characters, and it is visible in the clothes they wear, which are a sign defining the character of each of them; but it is even more evident when it is made explicit according to its grammar: the presence of a character representing a successful fashion designer (Eleonor Waldorf), her collections, runways, fashion shows and – at the same time – the presence of an aspiring young designer (Jenny Humphrey), the only character capable of radically changing her style (and therefore her personality) from one series to the next, place fashion in the list of the most covered topics.

4.1. The Fans of Gossip Girl

In the Web pages, Italian fans have colonised wide spaces to discuss their series: from forums inside dedicated websites, to collective blogs, Facebook groups. In general these environments respond to two macro functions linked to the virtual community: meeting "other" fans of the series and the search for information and news on the series and its characters-actors. There are innumerable pages in the Web dedicated to Gossip Girl[18], and only a few envisage spaces for discussion. What is clear is that the passionate audience enjoy more choices: they can read in-depth articles or participate in a community. In the latter case the surfers may decide to enter in a discussion group about Gossip Girl, where, besides having access to news, they can also meet other fans. The meaning assigned to the community experience is thus articulated on the basis of three main regimes[19]:

- For some surfer the experience of the virtual community coincides with *the pleasure of "being there,"* namely participating in a community experience with other fans of the series;
- For others, besides being there, *the pleasure of "showing themselves"* - therefore the desire to be seen and not only to be present in a given place, may become concrete; this means that within the group of Gossip Girl's fans there is the possibility of finding a place of prominence with respect to other participants;
- For others still, the main meaning may consist in the *sharing of information* which takes place inside the community, which goes beyond the possibility of socialising with other people, as it refers rather to the

acquisition of new knowledge on the series and its protagonists (love stories, breakups, places where they have showed up, new job offers....)

The pleasure of being there is what usually appears immediately in the communities. Three of the most popular Italian forums, Gossip Girl Italia, Gossip Girl First Italian Forum and Xoxo Gossip Girl Italian Forum[20] - which have been considered for the analysis here - clearly define *what they are* and *what they discuss about* to surfers that may encounter their pages.

The para-textual indices clearly point at the macro-themes shared by the community: the TV show Gossip Girl, developed along several discussion topics. The three forums are therefore dedicated to the series and are open to messages dedicated to the narration, as well as to individual characters, actors and their lives beyond Gossip Girl, and the opportunities of "using" the show "creatively." We know that in general the *user-reader* plays always a creative role: his/her activity of fruition/use is part of the process of text *realisation*, and it is observed as a full-fledged second-level production mode (de Certeau, 1990). A way of "picking from" the text through individual reading pathways: cultural consumers "fabricate" while looking at the screen. Therefore, the rigour of the order imposed by rules belonging to the universe of textual production blends at times with the fluidity of operations linked to forms of expenditure (Bataille, 1967) and based on *pleasure*, giving rise to a territory of new production, of hybridisation between *game* and *aesthetics*.

Who are therefore the users of forums of this kind? What happens inside these forums? Do members of this kind of communities coincide with a part of the audience of a show, or do they represent new medial roles? How many do coincide, with respect to the dissemination of news about the show?

4.2. Analysis of Forums

In the presence of community forms linked to "source" texts, defining the perimeter of the field upstream from the research becomes quite difficult. The forums that will be analysed here have been chosen first of all with respect to the traffic they were reporting in the time period taken into consideration, which is by itself a definition of a real sociality within them.

Starting from the title, the address and the images at the opening of the web page which in all sites show the protagonists of the series, the forum sites display in great evidence their macro-topic of reference, inviting the user-type they refer to, to enter. The presentation frame – the paratext - responds to the primary communication goal: it clearly shows a world which has been set up for people who are acquainted with the show and in most cases appreciate it.

The other very clear datum, also linked to the paratext, refers to the type of site we encounter: again, in all cases, these are forums, in reality multi-forums, as each of the three sites presents many autonomous topics of discussion, all referring to Gossip Girl. These are therefore community-based discussion spaces: thus the identikit of the model reader is further refined, a reader interested in reading and browsing material about that text and willing to discuss it with others.

A further remark should be added concerning the choice of the field of analysis: many exchanges taken into consideration had long "trails" before and after the chosen time span (March –April 2010). Some of them, in fact, had started in late 2009 and continued till September 2010, and were left open for new messages. In fact, only in some instances, when the forum is "off," community members cannot add new posts. This is why for some discussions covered by the observation exercise we have expanded the boundaries established beforehand.

One of the first spaces that the three above-mentioned forums offer users is the "welcome" section (actually quite typical of many forums) where participants introduce themselves with *posts* where they talk briefly of themselves, but mostly declare their *pleasure* in having found a place like the website, surfed by people sharing their very own passion for the series. Having "landed" in a discussion space engenders for many, according to their own statements, a sort of "relief effect": you are never alone in nurturing your passion, many share it with you, thus making it more real and meaningful[21].

Inside the individual sites, there are sections more specifically dedicated to the Gossip Girl text. You get therefore to the heart of individual discussions, each of which is branching out in its turn and subdivided into several sub-topics. Prior knowledge of the TV series becomes necessary in order to participate in the discussions, as the context where events develop is taken for granted: for example, the importance of New York City and its neighbourhoods; the protagonists' family relations; their backgrounds, and so on. Starting from an already acquired competence – and obviously taken for granted - users give rise to discussions, showing their individual skills and forecasting capabilities, as well as their participation in community life. One may find, therefore, together with the pleasure of belonging to a group, the pleasure linked to self-assertion, to the display of one's knowledge, of the scoops one's had taken hold of, referring either to the series or the actors playing in it. In the sections that are present in the web sites, there is in fact the one dedicated to the "news" and, also shared by different topics, there are many messages presenting the word "spoiler" in the title to introduce their content.

Users who participate the most are also those usually leading the discussions and in some instances acting as forum moderators and administrators as well. The observation of discussions over the period of two months seems to stress that their names appear frequently in the discussion pages: they often advance topics, points of view, in-depths or opinions on some narrative details of the show. From the perspective of an analysis concerning the type of sociality that takes place in these settings, we may say that this kind of users should also be considered *opinion leaders* in their communities: they win the trust of other members thanks to the timeliness and accuracy of the news they provide, and for the way they run their relations with the others. They are also very active in the multifunctional running of the forums: they can also be considered a full-fledged medium capable of providing information and materials on the series. In some instances, they work as "page indicators," groupings of web addresses, in order to find already broadcast episodes or entire seasons, so that fans may watch them again or for the first time. Forums work in this case as "basins" as they collect not only narrative nuclei created by the sequences of posts, but also the relational strategies referring to participating users, as well as the materials of the series or indications on the many places in the Internet where to find them, thus turning into essential connecting points. Fans behave therefore as a full-fledged participatory community offering a "collective intelligence" (Lévy, 1994) capable of producing contents and analyses on the series and providing "instruction for the Internet" to search for further in-depths.

The three macro-forums represent therefore effective examples of the way participatory culture works, and flow into the converging culture, namely in the flow of content across the multiple media platforms, in particolar from "the migratory behavior of media audiences who would go almost anywhere in search of the kind of entertainment experiences they want." (Jenkins, 2006b, p. 285).

The relations between users initiate and in some cases are further consolidated starting from the exchanges about Gossip Girl, which plays the role of "discursive anchor." At the same time the series operates also as a detonator, in view of the fact that its loyal audience produce contents which in some cases move away from specific topics covered there, to become autonomous texts. Therefore, on the one hand discursive productions focus on the source text, which remains the main reason of their existence; while on the other hand they mark a sort of evolution of the same text giving life to new narrations, new themes, new characters[22].

4.3. The Forums of Gossip Girl and Fashion

One of the established aims of the analysis referred to the presence – or absence – of the topic of "fashion" in discussions. The initial hypothesis was in fact that fashion, given its participation in the text, was perhaps discursivized in the forums under different modes.

As already mentioned above, fashion started to be woven into the plot from the pilot episode, although seemingly with a secondary role. The main focus is in fact on the stories involving the young protagonists. Each of them however stands out both for features linked to their role and the character they play, and for their dressing style.

The study of the forums has outlined that the attention for the topic of "fashion" emerges also in the analysed discussions: the item did not escape the fans' attention, thus giving rise to a full-fledged, very popular, discursive nucleus. In one of the three forums there is even a section called "Fashion, technology & New York" where the majority of discussions focus on fashion. Here some topics as an example: "Fashion for Blair," "Shopping Milan," "Style: Serena ot Blair?," "Style on Gossip Girl," "A clothing line inspired by Gossip Girl."

In many instances discussions on fashion operate as interstice between the forums themselves and the other Internet pages, where there are videos and in-depth news, which may be accessed to, thanks to the many links provided by the posts.

What is evident here is a sort of "ambiguity in communication" being developed on the double level of the discursive regime and the user's reality.

The ambiguity generates a persistent confusion between discursive topics relating to the universe of Gossip Girl and discursive topics relating to the *real life*, so much so that fashion may perhaps result in one of the major topics bringing continuity between the two worlds.

The observation of the forums enables therefore to stretch the perimeter of the analysis, which initially is circumscribed by the web sites where the forums are located, in order to consider the textual network comprising them, starting from the links they refer to, but also considering the discursive context they recall (functional vs real) (Cf. Meyrowitz, 1985, boyd, 2009).

This "journey outside the text" enables to activate a study process which is structured according to new paths: the fans indicate in fact new spaces linked to the topic of fashion, supporting the reference to Gossip Girl with their knowledge and skills linked to the fashion system. At times the messages report visual puzzles composed of fragments of images from the series together with fragments of pages from glossy fashion magazines, in order to show that the designers' clothes worn in a given "X" or "Y" episode have been identified and recognised as such (see Figure 3).

Of course the discourse on fashion does not stop to the analysis of individual garments, but expands further. In particular the majority of female users[23] look for advice, or offer advice, to make a "dream" come true: succeeding in replicating Gossip Girl's style in their "real life"[24]. From this point of view the analysed forums highlight a new and important function: they are placed at an intermediate level between the space of the fiction and the space of reality, thus providing a sort of "testing ground," where users can talk and get involved freely, showing themselves with words but also with photographs. The sharing and the opinion of a group with whom a good trustful relation has been established, and based on a shared passion, create such a climate of confidence that participants come to open up, to "reveal" themselves.

Figure 3. From the forum: Xoxo Gossip Girl Italian Forum (http://xoxogossipgirlitalian.forumfree.it/)

In some instances the photographs of the female protagonists are placed side by side the users' images, thus demonstrating the accomplished *gemmation* of style from fiction to reality. And the "fashion book of the show" appears in several posts, together with many images making the styles of individual characters even more explicit. All this makes us reread not only the forum setting linked to the series, which is clearly not only a space where to discuss the plots of the protagonists' lives, or the couple relationships that are initiated or broken up as the story progresses. The community environment is partially inhabited by truly fashion victims using it to reposition Gossip Girl within new in-depths: the text becomes then a "catalogue" of new styles as well, a sort of mix between innovative elements and cross-references to vintage, which are so appreciated by young fans. In the posts one can easily find many links to the many tutorials present in Youtube, "teaching" how to dress like a given protagonist or her rival. The clothing style very often coincides also with the appreciation for the character: the renewal of Jenny's look, for example, has produced as a consequence an increase in her character's recognition in the forums being analysed, and a special attention towards her look, both as Jenny Humphrey, and Taylor Momsen (see Figure 4).

The level of discussion on the fashion topic can therefore be used to observe the relation between fiction and reality: as a whole, the clothing and accessories found in the series and discussed in the communities become in many cases the place for a mediation between the virtuality of the fiction – and the discourses generated by it – and the reality of the off-line, thus assigning to Gossip Girl an "authorship" and authoritativeness in matters of new styles. The model reader tends then to change: as they do no longer coincide with the expected audience for a teen drama, we see then the participation of fashion experts or fans of the fashion world.

The elements coming from the filed of clothing or fashion open communication links between the text and its audiences: some in fact find a place in the everyday life of their fans. In this sense they operate as objects laden with symbolic value: audiences – and fans in particular – disassemble

Figure 4. From the forum: Xoxo Gossip Girl Italian Forum (http://xoxogossipgirlitalian.forumfree.it/)

the text in order to transfer some of its traits in their everyday lives, bearing on themselves the expression of the connection they experience both with Gossip Girl, and the fashion world it represents[25].

Naturally the favourable opinion on the style, the clothing, or the fashion styles in Gossip Girl does not generate solely in the on-line communities of its fans. The attention to dressing is part of the winning strategy of the text and is part of its production[26]. Gossip Girl's style has in fact been praised also by institutional media, and articles have been published in the most important Italian newspapers, like Corriere della Sera[27] or Repubblica[28], as well as in the US with the New York Times[29] and many fashion publications, such as Vogue Teen and Vogue America or Marie Claire, which have dedicated covers and articles to the female protagonists. The fact that the texts belong to the fashion discourse has been established and recognised as such by the fashion world itself: not only magazines, but also famous designers like Anna Sui who in 2008 created a collection

inspired by Gossip Girl's styles for the US retail chain Target[30].

The fans' response is however the element providing us with a clearer understanding of the scope of their appreciation: for many of them, their opinion spills out of the circuit of discussion to expand into their real lives. The Internet communities represent therefore an evaluation mode of the expected – and unexpected – effects produced by the source text, because they discuss it in a direct and passionate fashion and therefore represent an evident and quasi-immediate indicator of its effectiveness.

CONCLUSION

On-line discussion environments, increasingly varied and numerous, are really interesting for the observation of the social dynamics they contain. In particular, as we saw in relation to media texts, virtual communities can be studied to understand which are the elements that emerge from media stories, how audiences perceive and make them in their private life, "exporting" from the fictional material something to put in their real life.

The example of Gossip Girl has been interesting in this sense: through ethnographic observation and through the identification of the model reader, it has been possible to highlight several uses of the considered forums, in particular:

- The success of the virtual discussions (why the fans are there, what they will recognize, what and whom they hope to find);
- The success of the television series (in the cases examined focusing specifically on the topic of fashion. The study has revealed some important issues in this regard);
- The "coincidence" of interests (the passion for Gossip Girl that drives fans to search for specific on-line discussion; a passion for fashion, leading the same fans to discuss the two topics in parallel).

This is a *remediation* process (Bolter & Grusin, 1999) which deals not only with the network of connections between old and new media, but also with the intersection between "institutional" production logics on the one hand, and users' DIY practices on the other hand. What emerges thanks to the forum observation is therefore an understanding of dynamics that have found their place there, ranging from forms of personalisation of the series (interpretation of what is perceived "according to one's own view"), to the interpretation of individual characters (who is the best, who plays better, who should be imitated..), down to the creation of full-fledged information contents for the group (a sort of "daily news" on Gossip Girl). The construction of messages becomes increasingly sophisticated, so much so that community members call for the support of more expert participants. The connection between words, images and videos produces complex texts; in particular for the fashion topic, the result works very well, exactly because fashion needs visual language much more than other topics.

In general the studies about virtual communities, particularly those specifically related to media texts, on the one hand confirm the thesis of Jenkins on cultural convergence (2006a, 2006b). On the other hand these discussion groups stimulate the researcher to focus on single examples, to identify the many connections that each virtual community is able to determine, like a web that welcomes to discussions related to different issues and cultural areas.

Participants in these communities are often very witty model readers, with a good encyclopaedic competence[31], able to revise the contents in a complete and original way.

REFERENCES

Augé, M. (1994). *Pour une anthropologie des mondes contemporains*. Paris, France: Flammarion.

Bataille, G. (1967). *La part maudite: Precede de La notion de depense*. Paris, France: Minuit.

Baudrillard, J. (1981). *Simulacres et simulations*. Paris, France: Galilee. boyd, d., & Ellison, N. B. (2007). Social network sites: Definition, history, and scholarship. *Journal of Computer-Mediated Communication, 13*(1). Retrieved from http://jcmc.indiana.edu/vol13/issue1/boyd.ellison.html

Baym, N. K. (2000). *Tune in, log on*. Thousand Oaks, CA: Sage.

Boccia Artieri, G. (2009). SuperNetwork: Quando le vite sono connesse. In Mazzoli, L. (Ed.), *Network effect. Quando la rete diventa pop*. Torino, Italy: Codice Edizioni.

Bolter, J. D., & Grusin, R. (1999). *Remediation: Understanding new media*. Cambridge, MA: MIT Press.

boyd, d. (2008). *Teen socialization practices in networked publics*. http://www.danah.org/papers/talks/MacArthur2008.html

Clifford, J., & Marcus, G. E. (Eds.). (1986). *Writing culture: The poetics and politics of ethnography*. Berkeley, CA: University of California Press.

Coppock, P. J., & Violi, P. (1999). Conversazioni telematiche. In Garatolo, R., & Pallotti, G. (Eds.), *La conversazione: Un'introduzione allo studio dell'interazione verbale*. Milano, Italy: Raffaello Cortina.

Dal Lago, A., & De Biasi, R. (Eds.). (2002). *Un certo sguardo. Introduzione all'etnografia sociale*. Roma-Bari, Italy: Laterza.

de Certeau, M. (1990). *L'invention du quotidien. I Arts de faire*. Paris, France: Gallimard.

Duranti, A. (1997). *Linguistic anthropology*. Cambridge, UK: Cambridge University Press.

Eco, U. (1976). *A theory of semiotics*. Bloomington, IN: Indiana University Press.

Eco, U. (1979). *The role of the reader*. Bloomington, IN: Indiana University Press.

Eco, U. (1984). *Semiotics and the philosophy of language*. Bloomington, IN: Indiana University Press.

Eco, U. (1994). *The limits of interpretation*. Bloomington, IN: Indiana University Press.

Ferraro, G. (2001). *Il linguaggio del mito*. Roma, Italy: Meltemi.

Fontanille, J. (2006). *The semiotics of discourse*. New York, NY: P. Lang.

Fuch, C. (2006). The self-organization of virtual communities. *Journal of New Communications Research*, *1*(1), 29–68. Retrieved from http://fuchs.icts.sbg.ac.at/VC.pdf

Geertz, C. (1973). *The interpretation of cultures*. New York, NY: Basic Books.

Genette, G. (1987). *Seuils*. Paris, France: Seuil.

Greimas, A. J., & Courtés, J. (1979). *Sémiotique: Dictionnaire raisonné de la théorie du langage*. Paris, France: Hachette.

Hine, C. (2000). *Virtual ethnography*. London, UK: Sage.

Howard, P. N. (2002). Network ethnography and the hypermedia organization: New media, new organization, new methods. *New Media & Society*, *4*(4), 550–574. doi:10.1177/146144402321466813

Jenkins, H. (2002). *Textual poachers: Television, fans and participatory culture*. London, UK: Routledge.

Jenkins, H. (2006a). *Fans, gamers, and bloggers: Exploring participatory culture*. New York, NY: New York University Press.

Jenkins, H. (2006b). *Convergence culture*. New York, NY: New York University Press.

Jones, S. (Ed.). (1995). *Cybersociety*. Thousand Oaks, CA: Sage.

Jones, S. (Ed.). (1998). *Cybersociety 2.0*. Thousand Oaks, CA: Sage.

Landowski, E. (1985). Eux, nous et moi: régimes de visibilité. *Mots*, *10*, 9–16. doi:10.3406/mots.1985.1182

Landowski, E. (1989). *La société réfléchie*. Paris, France: Seuil.

Lévy, P. (1994). *L'intelligence collective. Pour une anthropologie du cyberspace*. Paris, France: La Découverte.

Manetti, G. (1998). *La teoria dell'enunciazione*. Siena, Italy: Protagon.

Marrone, G. (1999). *C'era una volta il telefonino. Un'indagine socio semiotica*. Roma, Italy: Meltemi.

Mascio, A. (2004). Virtual communities and the socio-semiotical approach. *Internet-Journal of INST, i.e. TRANS Internet-Zeitschrift fuer Kulturwissenschaften 15/2004, 1.2. Signs, Texts, Cultures. Conviviality from a Semiotic Point of View / Zeichen, Texte, Kulturen. Konvivialität aus semiotischer Perspektive*. Retrieved from http://www.inst.at/trans/15Nr/01_2/01_2inhalt_part1_15.htm

Mascio, A. (2008). *Virtuali comunità*. Milano, Italy: Guerini & Associati.

Mauss, M. (1950). *Sociologie et anthropologie*. Paris, France: Universitaires de France.

Meyrowitz, J. (1985). *No sense of place: The impact of electronic media on social behavior*. New York, NY: Oxford University Press.

Nonnecke, B., & Preece, J. (2000). Lurker demographics: Counting the silent. *Proceedings of CHI 2000*. The Hague, The Netherlands: ACM

Oldenburg, R. (1991). *The great good place: Cafés, coffee shops, bookstores, bars, hair salons, and other hangouts at the heart of a community.* New York, NY: Marlowe and Company.

Pozzato, M. P. (2001). *Semiotica del testo.* Roma, Italy: Carocci.

Preece, J. (2000). *Online communities: Designing usability, supporting sociability.* Chichester, UK: John Wiley & Sons.

Rheingold, H. (1994). *The virtual community.* London, UK: Minerva.

Roversi, A. (2001). *Chat line.* Bologna, Italy: Il Mulino.

Roversi, A. (2006). *L'odio in Rete.* Bologna, Italy: Il Mulino.

Schroeder, R. (Ed.). (2002). *The social life of avatars.* London, UK: Springer.

Stone, A. R. (1995). *The war of desire and technology, at the close of the mechanical age.* Cambridge, MA: M.I.T. Press.

Turkle, S. (1996). *Life on the screen: Identity in the age of the Internet.* London, UK: Weidenfeld & Nicolson.

Wallace, P. (1999). *The psychology of Internet.* Cambridge, UK: Cambridge University Press.

Wellman, B., & Haythornthwaite, C. (2002). *The Internet in everyday life.* Oxford, UK: Blackwell. doi:10.1002/9780470774298

ENDNOTES

[1] BBS (bulletin board system) is a usually an amateurs' data base, which can be accessed directly through a link to the modem installed on the provider's (called *sysop*) telephone number, and offers services of electronic mailing and download of software and shareware.

[2] For an exploration of the topic see: Boyd, d. m., & Ellison, N. B. (2007); Fuch, C. (2006).

[3] In particular the article will analyse three Italian virtual communities linked to the US TV series Gossip Girl.

[4] Socio-semiotics deals with the universality of culture and cultural specificities «in the attempt to systematically capture and analyse them […] Socio-semiotics […] should deserve the vast domain of social connotations» (Greimas and Courtés, 1979, under "socio-semiotics"). Like general semiotics, socio-semiotics as well may be considered as having – so to speak – a scientific vocation. Of the major scholars of the discipline, let us mention here Landowski (1989), Marrone (1999), Ferraro (2001) and Pozzato (2001). There is no univocal definition of socio-semiotics and we do not have here enough room to recall the respective views of the authors. We have chosen to focus on Gianfranco Marrone who defines socio-semiotics as a perspective integrating social observation with linguistic analysis (1999). For socio-semiotics, in fact, we mean "any linguistic utterance which is configured as an action, even before being an utterance of message; therefore an event taking place in a social context and acting on it, starting from actions preceding it, and giving rise to further actions. Likewise, every action taking place in the world entails social consequences, if and only if it is first and foremost an utterance, namely a production of meaning. In short, if saying is doing, doing is meaning" (1999, p. 23).

[5] *Textual net* is a concept emerging from the latest socio-semiotic literature (cf. Ferraro, 2001). By this concept, some classic - although non orthodox in semiotics - notions are recovered, like the concept of *discursive formations* (in Foucault's meaning) which

are produced around some texts. The reasons why some texts, under some conditions, bring forth the "emerging" of meaning, should therefore be explored.

6   *Convergence culture* is a process that interests media companies, media texts and media audiences. All of these have an active role in the convergence. As Jenkins writes, "media convergence impacts the way we consume media. A teenager doing homework may juggle four or five windows, scan the Web, listen to and download MP3 files, chat with friends, word-process a paper, and respond to e-mail, shifting rapidly among tasks. And fans of a popular television series may sample dialogue, summarize episodes, debate subtexts, create original fan fiction, record their own soundtracks, make their own movies – and distribute all of this world-wide via the Internet" (Jenkins, 2006b, p. 16). Cf. Jenkins, 2002, 2006a, 2006b.

7   When web 2.0 is mentioned, a reference is made to several communication modes which may be present in the same page at the same time. If reference is made to the layout, for example, in the case of a page of a Facebook group, one must take into account the presence of a modality which is somewhat similar to that of the forum and – at the same time – the possibility of being involved in real-time chatting. Of course let us not forget that forum and Facebook group are configured differently, not only for the communication opportunities they offer but also for their formation modes: the forum is an "open" space where anyone can access through registration. The Facebook group envisages instead the presence of a personal access to the system and the access request made to the group: thus group members may be monitored, so that the group may seem to be formally "close" (the exact number of participants is known; their Facebook identi-

ties may be observed; the group founder may be identified, ..). Cf. Boccia Artieri, 2009.

8   For an exploration of the topic, see Mascio, 2005, 2008.

9   Let us think, for example, at the space in a forum, where users can show their presence via e-mail messages sent at different times in the same day, or even in different days.

10   *To post* is commonly used in the Net to indicate the sending of a message to a given electronic place, the *poster* is the sender of the message; the "post" is the message.

11   Let us recall here, among others, the works by Baym, 2000, Jones (1995, 1998), Schroeder (2001), Stone (1995), Turkle (1996), Wallace, 1999 Wellman, 2000. In the Italian scenario, the studies by Antonio Roversi, (2001 and 2006) are particularly relevant.

12   The ethical question should always be considered: the possibility of performing analyses only for "open" communities and possibly the request to be allowed to observe in communities open only to registered members.

13   Let us think about the many links participants include in their messages, referring to other web sites and pages.

14   "Moreover what one usually calls 'message' is rather a text: a network of different messages depending on different codes, sometimes correlating different expressive substance with the same content (for example, a verbal message is always accompanied by paralinguist, kinesic or proxemic devices), sometimes making different contests depend on the same expressive substance (by virtue of intertwined subcodes)" (Eco, 1976, p. 141); "A text is not simply a communicational apparatus. It is a device which questions the previous signifying systems, often renews them, and sometimes destroyed them. (…) a textual machine made to liquidate grammars and dictionaries – is exemplary in this sense, but even rhetorical figures are

produced and become alive only the textual level. The textual machine empties the terms which the literal dictionary deemed univocal and well defined, and fills them with new content figures." (Eco, 1984, p. 25).

15 And therefore we encounter a *trace* and not a full-fledged presence of whoever has produced the act (cf. Baudrillard, 1981).

16 *Lurker* is term describing someone not participating, but just observing what is taking place and remaining silent. (Cf. Preece, 2000). In the Internet community the *lurker* is is seen as someone who "wants to get something without having to give something back (Preece, 2001: 64), therefore quite negatively, as discussion and interaction are perceived as vital and essential activities based on active participation.

17 In semiotics the "reader," or better still the "model reader" is meant to be "a set of textually-established felicitous conditions, which must be satisfied in order for the text to be fully actualized in its content potential" (Eco, 1979, p. 62).

18 With Google search engine, in Italian-only pages, if you enter "gossip girl" 866,000 results are displayed (date 1 july 2010).

19 Landowski, 1985, 1989.

20 They are found in the pages of: http://gossipgirl-italia.forumfree.it/ and http://gossipgirl.forumcommunity.net/ and http://xoxogossipgirlitalian.forumfree.it/ respectively. These are the forums used to analyse these pages, which were monitored in the April-May 2010 period.

21 "hallo, how nice to have found you, I did not know there was a forum dedicated to Gossip Girl!! xoxo" "Welcome!! all the fans are welcome!!" "hallo to all! I have just discovered this fantastic forum... I miss gossip girl a lot... I can't wait for the next series!! kiss kiss" are just some of the posts found in the two forums. A relevant difference between the two refers to the answers given to the presentation messages: while in Gossip Girl First Italian Community the majority of users respond with warm welcoming messages (the forum participants are almost all young women), in Gossip Girl Italia these types of messages do not receive any answer. The different relational style adopted by the two communities is clearly shown from the start.

22 For example in Gossip Girl First Italian Forum a whole section is dedicated to fans' creations (Fan Art - Fan Clubs/Appreciation Threads – Fan Fiction, to "rewrite" Gossip Girl's story) whose participation, to use Jenkins's words (2006), *amplifies the experience of the narrative*.

23 It should be remarked that the majority of users in these two forums are young women. This could open an analysis on the "model reader" of the TV series, which has probably appealed more to young girls' taste than young boys'.

24 "I could die now!!! I adore Blair and her style. Her way of dressing is very similar to mine, so I never miss an episode! I try to find an inspiration in what she wears and to interpret it. She is simply fantastic!" - "I worship her!! A unique style!!!! In any case I am letting my hair grow so that I can wear head-bands!!!!Xd!!! And I adore her coats, in 1 episode she wears a yellow one (photo) and C. an orange one!!they stand out so much !XD w chair" (in Gossip Girl First Italian Forum, topic: Fashion, Technology & New York!).

25 A striking example is Blair's hair-band, the focus of many discussions and displayed by the fans of the series through verbal statements or photographs attached to their messages.

26 Gossip Girl's fashion designer, Eric Daman, who had also worked with Patricia Field in *Sex and the City,* has recently published a book on the style of the series: "You Know You Want It: Style-Inspiration-Confidence,"

Clarkson N. Potter Publishers, New York, 2009.

27   Online at the address: http://www.corriere.it/cronache/08_luglio_10/gossip_girl_influenza_vendite_moda_7cff1968-4e75-11dd-a6e8-00144f02aabc.shtml

28   Online at the address: http://ricerca.repubblica.it/repubblica/archivio/repubblica/2008/09/10/in-tv-arriva-la-peggio-gioventu-che.html

29   Online at the address: http://www.nytimes.com/2008/07/08/fashion/08gossip.html

30   Online at the address: http://www.collegefashion.net/fashion-news/anna-sui-for-target-lookbook/

31   In *The limits of interpretation* (1994) Eco writes "Encyclopaedic competences can be represented in many ways" (238); "the spectator is brought to elaborate (…) on the nature of such a device and to acknowledge the fact that one has been invited to play upon one's encyclopaedic competence (…) an intertextual encyclopaedia. We have texts that are quoted from other texts, and the knowledge of preceding ones – taken for granted – is supposed to be necessary to the enjoyment of new ones. (…) Spectators (…) must, in short, have not only a knowledge of the text but also a knowledge of the world, of circumstances external to the texts."(89).

Chapter 3
A Web–Based E–Commerce Learning Community in Brazil

Luiz Antonio Joia
Brazilian School of Public and Business Administration, Getulio Vargas Foundation, Brazil

ABSTRACT

This chapter demonstrates usage of a Web-based participative learning environment, which has enabled graduate students in e-commerce classes on the Executive Master in Business Administration Programme taught by the Brazilian School of Public and Business Administration at Getulio Vargas Foundation, based in Rio de Janeiro, Brazil, to share and disseminate their knowledge among themselves. An illustrative single case study is applied in order to achieve this purpose. The structure of this virtual environment on the web is analysed. Findings about the participation level of the students in this group, the impact of regional influences – since classes are given throughout Brazil – and the role of the moderator in the leverage of this environment are also presented in this research, which attempts to establish how Internet technology can be effective in the development of virtual learning communities.

INTRODUCTION

The contemporary world economy has experienced a prolonged period of instability, with changes arising from different sources and paradigm shifts occurring systematically. This has given rise to a pressing need for establishing new mental models to deal with a turbulent environment marked by continuous technological innovations, which have affected the business and personal environments equally. Among these innovations, Internet technology and its applications have proved a veritable revolution and landmark. These changes – as a sole constant – have defied businesses and their executives to forecast future trends and develop their intellectual capital, so as to take advantage of the technological revolution which sweeps us all along in its wake.

DOI: 10.4018/978-1-4666-0312-7.ch003

Besides, we now live in a virtual knowledge economy, based on intangibility, intelligence and innovation (Roos *et al.*, 1997; Stewart, 1997; Sveiby, 1997). The elimination of distance made possible by real-time digital links connecting all the players involved in productive processes, has rapidly transformed political, economical, social and job-related relationships (Cairncross, 1997; Jarvenpaa & Tanriverdi, 2003).

For this reason, professionals working in the business arena have increasingly realized the need for ongoing training throughout life, as knowledge cannot be considered a mere commodity. They are returning to the lecture halls in a quest for analytical frameworks that can be used in their daily work. They are also looking for more "professional laterality" (Joia, 1999), in order to be of greater value to their companies, to leverage their employment prospects and/or to redirect their professional careers.

In this context, Executive MBAs are increasingly being offered in Brazil to make it possible for professionals unable to study on a full-time basis to get a master's degree in the management field, as it will be explained in the next section.

Thus, the general purpose of this chapter is essentially to examine how a participative tool based on the web, linking different e-commerce classes throughout Brazil, belonging to the Executive MBA of the Brazilian School of Public and Business Administration at Getulio Vargas Foundation, might be used to change the traditional teaching and learning *praxis*, so as to foster the creation of an alternative pedagogical framework. This would be one which, rather than replace the current instructivist and behaviouristic model completely (Sherry, 1996 and Boghossian, 2006), is able to complement it in such a way as to make it more constructivist (Piaget, 1974) and socially participative (Vygotsky, 1978). Therefore, this article strives to establish a balance between the real (brick and mortar) and virtual (click and buy) worlds, attaining a CAM (click and mortar) world (Lee & Whang, 2001 and Saeed *et al.*, 2003), which is considered the cornerstone in the strategic use of the Internet (Gulati & Garino, 2000; Porter, 2001).

Based on that, the main questions this research intends to tackle are:

- Does a web-based virtual environment enhance collaborative work? How?
- How does the physical location of the students influence their participation in a web-based environment?
- Why is a moderator needed in a web-based virtual environment and how can her/his importance be measured?

In order to answer these research questions, this chapter is structured as it follows. After this introduction, the context where the research problem is embedded is set forth, by analyzing the main characteristics of the Executive MBA programme under analysis, and the profile of the students that have taken part in this research is unveiled. Then, the concept of learning community is deployed so as to support this investigation as well as its findings and conclusions. It follows the presentation of the research method adopted in this work in order to have the research questions already presented answered. Then, after presenting the structure of the web-based learning community under scrutiny, it is analysed the interventions made by both the students (members of this aforementioned community) and the community's moderator, in order to consolidate the data collected. After analyzing the data collected for tendency curve estimation of time series, via statistical analysis based on linear and exponential regressions (Bianchi *et al.*, 1999 and Cameron, 2005), and data triangulation (Yin, 1994), concluding remarks are set forth in order to have the research questions answered, and recommendations for future research are presented.

CONTEXT

The Executive MBA Programme (EMBA) in Brazil intends to fulfill the objectives and targets of the Brazilian Ministry of Education, in which concerns to management development capacity building initiatives in the country.

The main characteristics of this EMBA Programme is the very concern with the actual application of the acquired knowledge by the students into their daily professional activities. In other words, the programme has as its main target to blend academic rigor with professional relevance, so as to allow the graduate students to play executive functions within their companies, to teach in a part-time basis in the Brazilian business schools, as well as to act as consultants in the business administration knowledge field.

The majority of the students that take part in this programme have been in the market for several years playing roles in the executive or operational level, with ages varying from 25 to 45 years old. Thus, the programme is attended in a part-time basis, in the evenings and weekends, as the students remains working in their organizations.

The programme started in 1999 in Rio de Janeiro and as Brazil is the fifth largest country in size in the world, it became paramount to offer classes throughout the nation. As such, as the programme is based in Rio de Janeiro, it was necessary to develop a feasible workflow to deploy this graduate course in cities far from Rio de Janeiro, such as Manaus in Amazonia and Curitiba in Southern Brazil.

Graduate students on the Executive MBA programme must enrol, study and be approved in ten mandatory courses and at least in two elective subjects. Besides that, the students are supposed to develop a thesis, to be assessed and approved by an academic committee compounded by three academics indicated by the programme's academic coordinator. All the course must last no more than 2.5 years.

Regarding the class under scrutiny in this research (e-commerce), it can be said that this has been an elective course on the Executive MBA programme lasting one term (45 class hours). The MBA coordination committee introduced this subject in May 2008.

As already said above, the course has also been offered in other cities. In this case, there are three meetings (usually starting on Thursday and ending on Saturday) spread over approximately two months. The teacher travels to different cities to give the classes on a lecture basis and monitors the students via distance learning on the Internet.

Based on that, a sample was chosen to investigate the role of a participative web-based learning community. As such, the sample of this research comprises a total of 43 pupils who attended the e-commerce elective class, from May 2008 to April 2009, namely 24.5% of all the Executive MBA graduate students. From this group of 43 students, 26 students were based in the city of Rio de Janeiro, 11 students were based in the city of Manaus (State of Amazonas, in the Amazon region) and 6 students were based in the city of Curitiba (State of Paraná in Southern Brazil), as shown in Figure 1.

These classes can be classified according to the parameters presented in Table 1, where:

- Class N. means the number of the class;
- City means the location where the students attended the class;
- Start means the start date of the course;
- End means the end date of the course;
- N. of Students means the total of students that attended the course.

In addition, Figure 2 presents the start and end dates of each class of the sample.

Ever since the planning phase of the pedagogical approach to be used in the class, there were concerns about using Internet technology to create a long-term virtual learning environment

Figure 1. Geographical distribution of graduate students in the e-commerce class

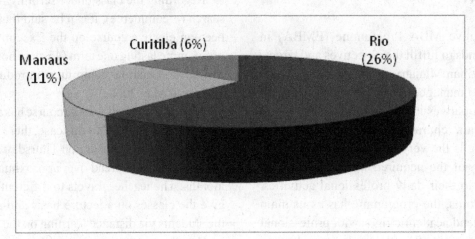

Figure 2. Time-schedule of the classes

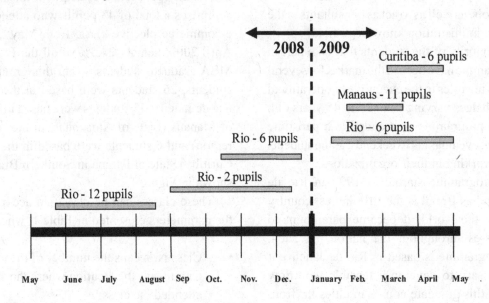

Table 1. E-commerce classes under analysis

Class N.	City	Start	End	N. of Students
1	Rio	5/23/2008	8/15/2008	12
2	Rio	8/31/2008	12/14/2008	2
3	Rio	10/10/2008	12/19/2008	6
4	Rio	1/17/2009	5/9/2001	6
5	Manaus	2/1/2009	3/17/2009	11
6	Curitiba	3/9/2009	4/28/2009	6

(Armstrong & Hagel III, 1996 and Dyson & Campello, 2004). In order to accomplish this end, a web-based participative environment was developed, which is called EBAP_ECOM, in order to handle and store the knowledge created during the course and thereafter. Hence, the 'education – anytime – anywhere' concept (Joia, 2000a) might be applied to students of the course.

The methodology used in the E-Commerce class is based both on an analytical approach – where the main theoretical concepts are addressed by using textbooks (Turban *et al.*, 2004) – and in case studies and analysis of papers. These two pedagogical mainstreams have been combined to form the methodological backbone of the course.

Furthermore, student evaluation is based on:

- Class participation – 20% of the final grade
- Preparation of an individual paper– 40% of the final grade
- Individual Assessment (test) – 40% of the final grade

The teacher's evaluation of student participation during the course is based on understanding of the subject content, through discussions and case presentations, as well as development of summaries of papers delivered during classes. Furthermore, interaction in the EBAP_ECOM virtual community is given considerable emphasis. The quality of participation rather than the frequency in attendance is given greater weight in evaluating student involvement on the course and in assessing class participation (20% of the final grade, as described above).

LEARNING COMMUNITIES

In this paper, the learning community concept lays on the concept of "Ba". "Ba" – which is Japanese for "place" – was a concept defined by Nonaka & Konno (1998), in accordance with the ideas first developed by Shimizu (1995), i.e., a shared virtual

space in order to create relationships. This space might be a physical one (e.g., business office), a virtual one (e.g., e-mail), a mental one (e.g., shared experiences and ideas) or even the combination of these former spaces (Shimizu, 1995). "Ba" provides a platform for the leverage of both individual and collective knowledge (Nonaka & Konno, 1998).

As such, learning community in this work is considered a place for interactions among professionals within an enterprise and among companies belonging to metabusinesses - as described by Keen (1991) -, in order to share and acquire knowledge. Freeman (1991) and Helble & Chong (2004) state the importance of both internal and external company networks as enablers of collaboration and innovation among the nodes of strategic ecosystems as defined by Moore (1996).

According to Soo *et al.* (2000), there is no academic consensus about the definition of community, since this is a very broad concept. Hence, taking advantage of the empirical results already developed in this realm, the framework developed by Soo *et al.* (2000) – based on two possible community structures – is followed:

1. **Communities based on Formal Collaboration**: Structures involving relationships ruled by formal agreements and structured protocols. As examples, we can cite: joint ventures between companies, strategic alliances, research collaboration and licensing. This structure is heavily used to formalise enterprise relationships, usually addressing the research and development of new products, deployment of new services in the market and so forth.

2. **Communities based on Informal Interaction**: Structures not limited to formal agreements and structured protocols. They are developed through unstructured meetings, *ad-hocs,* presenting characteristics of social networks among individuals. Web-based virtual communities, as analysed in

this article, have typical characteristics of this kind of structure.

Although considering learning communities as a structured mode of informal interaction, as explained above, Armstrong & Hagel III (1996) developed a very important taxonomy for a participative working environment on the web. According to the authors, these communities can be classified as:

A. **Communities of Transaction**: Developed to facilitate the buying and selling process of products and services and to give information about these transactions. The community's mediator is not necessarily a seller. It is only necessary to bring together a critical mass of buyers and sellers, so that commercial transactions can take place. These communities are also called marketspaces, linking not only professionals, but also companies (see, for instance, Ozuem *et al.,* 2008).

B. **Communities of Interest**: Developed to connect persons with common interests in one or more subjects. These are communities where interpersonal communication is far greater than in transaction communities. Sometimes transactions can take place within these communities but personal issues are rarely both addressed and discussed in this kind of community. So, it is not a social community per se (see, for instance, Cortes *et al.,* 2002).

C. **Communities of Fantasy**: Developed to enable the participants to create, in a collective way, their own fantasies, environments, characters and/or stories (see, for instance, Brent, 2004).

D. **Communities of Relationship**: Developed to enable the participants to exchange personal experiences usually of great impact in their personal lives, leading to strong personal ties (see, for instance, Hsu *et al.,* 2007).

Naturally, the taxonomy presented is very useful and important purely for academic purposes, as many existing communities can be classified into more than one specific community type. Communities rarely have the features of only one type, as they are normally a combination of some of the types presented above, which is presented in the Figure 3, where the mutual influence of the communities already presented is set forth, in order to foster the systemic characteristic of a community.

RESEARCH METHODOLOGY

The research methodology used in this article is of the single case variety. Case studies are particularly suitable for answering "how" and "why" questions and are also appropriate for generating and building theory in an area where little data or theory exists (Yin, 1994). It also enables the researcher to use "controlled opportunism" to permit a flexible response to new discoveries made while collecting new data (Eisenhardt, 1994). A single type 2 case study method (Yin, 1994) was used in this research, as multiple units of analysis were taken into account and measured. Yin's tactics (construct validity, internal validity, external validity and reliability) were carefully considered in this research.

In particular, construct validity was dealt with during the study through the use of multiple sources of evidence, the establishment of a chain of evidence and getting the members of the group to review the draft case study report. Internal and external validity of the findings was also taken into account, mainly by applying time-series analysis and replication logic respectively. Finally, the reliability of the results was established by using a case study protocol and developing a case study database.

An explanatory approach was applied in the case study. Explanatory case studies are useful to assess how intervention is working and why. This

Figure 3. Taxonomy of virtual communities

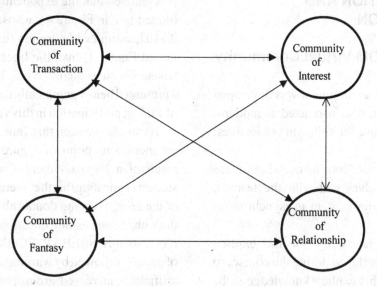

approach verifies whether there are problems and if modifications are needed in the intervention, and attempts to explain the causal effects found. Different sites are needed in order to develop a comparative analysis (see Table 1 and Figures 1 and 2). This was performed analysing the e-commerce classes in the cities of Rio de Janeiro, Manaus and Curitiba (Morra & Friedlander, 1999).

Hence, as already set forth in the introduction of this chapter, the main questions this research intends to tackle are:

- Did the web-based community under scrutiny in this work enhance collaborative work? How?
- How did the physical location of the students influence their participation in the virtual community under analysis?
- Why was a moderator needed in this web-based community and how can her/his importance be measured?

Finally, as an ancillary question, the study aims to determine the most adequate form of typology for the EBAP_ECOM community, as defined by Armstrong & Hagel III (1996) and presented earlier in this research.

Thus, in order to answer these research questions and develop the case study, it was collected data related to the dynamics of the learning environment, namely number of participants, number of messages per participant per region per month and the moderator's interventions – assessed by the number of messages sent and received by him throughout the period of analysis of the virtual environment. These data was then analysed via time series tendency curve estimation techniques (Bianchi *et al.*, 1999 and Cameron, 2005), whereby linear and exponential regressions were applied.

Furthermore, it was developed interviews with the participants as well as with the moderator, and it was analysed the content of some messages exchanged by the participants in the collaborative environment under investigation.

DATA COLLECTION AND CONSOLIDATION

The EBAP_ECOM Virtual Community

The EBAP_ECOM environment was developed by the class teacher, who also acted as moderator, in order to achieve the following objectives:

- To allow the students to exchange ideas among themselves and with the teacher, anytime and anywhere, in an asynchronous way;
- To create a repository for the explicit knowledge developed during the course, so as to enable this explicit knowledge to be transformed into tacit knowledge (internalisation), according to the knowledge spiral model of Nonaka & Takeuchi (1997);
- To enable synchronous events, such as chat room sessions among the students;
- To create a data centre for the whole course by storing the material used in the classes, the primary and secondary papers, as well as the most important bookmarks, in a secure environment;
- To allow the students to become more familiar with Internet tools and their potential.

The Evolution of the EBAP_ ECOM Virtual Community

Created in May 2008, the EBAP_ECOM virtual learning environment grew exponentially in relation to messages exchanged among its participants since its creation. This research studies the development of this community from its inception on the web to April 2009.

It was used the Least Square Method (Chumney & Simpson, 2006), in order to find out the best trend estimation for the time series of messages exchanged in the EBAP_ECOM virtual learning environment (solid line in Figure 4). Thus, it

was realized that the exponential regression line (dotted line in Figure 4), whose R^2 value equals 0.7103, estimated better the time series (dashed line in Figure 4) than the linear regression line, whose R^2 value equals 0.6477. Table 2 and Figure 4 presented below graphically depict the evolution of student participation in this virtual community.

It can also be seen that June 2008 was clearly an anomalous point in Figure 4. This was the result of a large number of messages sent by students indicating that they were already members of the group, voicing doubts about how to access the website and asking questions about the directory structure of EBAP_ECOM. The uploading of papers, followed by warnings to the group, also artificially increased group participation in that specific month. Hence, on-the-job construction of the website was the main cause for the surge in June 2008. On the other hand, the peak of messages in March 2009 can be ascribed to the high participation in the virtual community of students from Manaus and Curitiba, as it will be better explained in the next section of this work.

In Figure 5, the participation level of students who had already attended the e-commerce class but remained in the group was also compared to the participation level of students who were attending the course and, consequently, had a tacit obligation to participate effectively in the community, due to the participation grade (20% of the final concept).

As might be expected, the participation level of the students assisting the e-commerce course is far greater than the participation level of the other members. Analysing the participation of former students, it can be seen that, in general, although members of the group, only those working on a thesis on this theme participate actively, while the others remain in the group as lurkers (Ridings *et al.,* 2006). Figure 5 below depicts these observations through the consolidation of the number of messages exchanged per month per student throughout the time period under analysis

Figure 4. Time series and tendency curves of the total number of messages exchanged

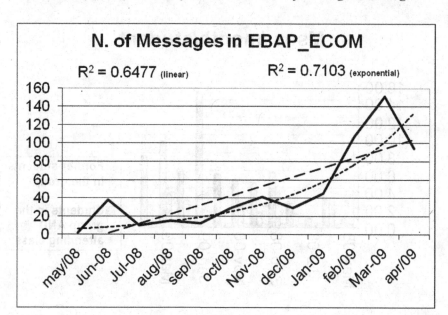

Table 2. Time series of messages exchanged in the virtual community

Month	N. of Msgs.	Students Reg. in the Group	Monthly Av. of Students Studying	Msgs./St. Reg. In the Group	Msgs/Monthly Av. of Students Studying
may/08	2	12	3	0.17	0.67
Jun-08	38	12	12	3.17	3.17
Jul-08	10	12	12	0.83	0.83
aug/08	15	12	6	1.25	2.50
sep/08	12	14	2	0.85	6.00
oct/08	29	20	6	1.45	4.83
Nov-08	41	20	8	2.05	5.13
dec/08	29	20	5	1.45	5.80
Jan-09	45	26	3	1.73	15.00
feb/09	107	37	17	2.89	6.29
Mar-09	151	43	16	3.51	9.44
apr/09	94	43	12	2.19	7.83

Geographical Distribution of Student Participation on the EBAP_ECOM Course

After the influx of the 11 students from the class in Manaus (Amazonia), on February 1st 2009, the participation level in the community (both in quantity and quality) experienced a quantum leap. This class started on February 1st 2009, as stated, and ended on March 17th 2009. In February, for instance, the rate of messages per member attained 2.89 msgs./member, which represents an increase of 67% against the January figure (1.73 msgs/member). The ratio is even more impressive when one considers that there are only 28 days

Figure 5. Number of messages exchanged per month per student

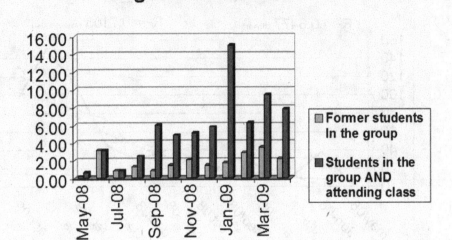

in February minus Carnival holidays (4 days in Brazil).

By the same token, the rate in March was 3.51 msgs/member – 21% higher than the previous month. Students from the class in the city of Curitiba (Southern Brazil) registered in the community during this month. Figure 6 below shows these figures.

Geographical Distribution of Student Participation on the EBAP_ECOM Course

After the influx of the 11 students from the class in Manaus (Amazonia), on February 1st 2009, the participation level in the community (both in quantity and quality) experienced a quantum leap. This class started on February 1st 2009, as stated, and ended on March 17th 2009. In February, for instance, the rate of messages per member attained 2.89 msgs./member, which represents an increase of 67% against the January figure (1.73 msgs/member). The ratio is even more impressive when one considers that there are only 28 days

in February minus Carnival holidays (4 days in Brazil).

By the same token, the rate in March was 3.51 msgs/member – 21% higher than the previous month. Students from the class in the city of Curitiba (Southern Brazil) registered in the community during this month. Figure 6 shows these figures.

As can be seen, both R^2 values for linear (dashed line) and exponential (dotted line) estimations shown in Figure 6 – 0.308 and 0.403 respectively – are not very high, according to Cohen's criterion (Cohen, 1992). Hence, the values cannot be explained statistically by either of these correlations. The very fact that June 2008 and April 2009 are salient points serves to illustrate this issue. In relation to the former month, the explanation has already been given above. In relation to the latter month (April 2009), the termination of the Manaus and Curitiba classes may explain this low point, as only one class was working in Rio de Janeiro. Anyhow, it is important to note that the further the class is from the main school site and the less the resources available for the students are, the more they take part in the community in comparison with the students from the main site (Rio de Janeiro).

A deeper analysis of these observations is presented below, by scanning the number of student participations in the community according to their geographical location.

Of the 107 messages sent by the group in February 2009, 38 were sent by students based in Manaus (nearly 3.5 messages/student), totalling 36% of the total of messages sent.

In March 2009, more than 45 messages were sent by the Manaus class (nearly 4.1 messages/ student and 30% of the total of messages sent), totalling 83 messages. Therefore, 38% of the total messages sent to EBAP_ECOM in February and March 2009 originated from the student group in Manaus.

In March 2009, the Curitiba group was responsible for 18 messages (nearly 3 messages/student and 12% of the total of messages sent that month).

Adding those values presented above, the group of students based away from the main site of the school (Manaus and Curitiba), totalling 17 students within a universe of 43 students taking part on EBAP_ECOM, was responsible for nearly 42%

of all the messages sent in March 2009. Taking into account that the moderator was responsible for 38 messages in March 2009 (25% of the message total), it can be deduced that students from Rio de Janeiro sent only 50 messages in that month (33% of the total).

Therefore, as might be expected, one may conclude that distance increases the engagement of the students in the community. Figure 7 shows these results.

The Moderator's Role

The moderator of the group is, in fact, the teacher of the e-commerce class. He had already used this feature in other classes, being therefore fully acquainted with this tool. This was not the case with the students, as most of them had never even experienced taking part in a simple discussion session. Some other discussion sessions were set up by MBA teams addressing administrative and generic issues.

In Rio de Janeiro, the classes had discussion sessions to debate academic issues (or purely for fun), as did the Manaus and Curitiba MBA classes.

Figure 6. Time series and tendency curves of the number of messages exchanged per member

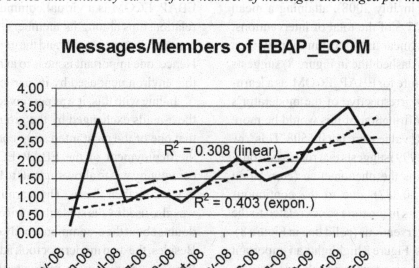

Figure 7. Number of messages sent per member per geography

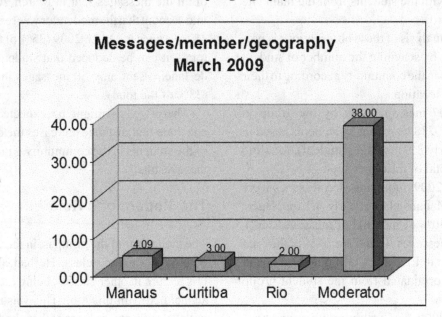

But, it became clear that e-mail was the single tool used in all of these communities.

Table 3 and Figure 8 show the role of the moderator in the EBAP_ECOM environment throughout the course of time, leading us to some conclusions.

As can be seen, the moderator's participation is high (attaining an astounding 80% of the message total sent in July 2008), attaining a mean average of 39.25% of the total of interventions. However, the linear trend estimation with a negative slope (dashed line in Figure 8) suggests a sustainable future for EBAP_ECOM, as a learning community, irrespective of the moderator's active role. Confirmation of this would be more positive if the R^2 value were not 0.1508. This low value (Cohen, 1999) suggests that regression only partially explains the phenomenon (correlation coefficient of −0.387), due to the continuous troughs and peaks in the time series related to the moderator's interventions (solid line in Figure 8).

Nonetheless, Figure 8 highlights an important fact detected during e-commerce classes, namely the need for the moderator to increase his participation intensively every now and again, in order to increase the participation of the members of the group. Hence, the success of the community depends very much on the moderator's engagement and commitment, so as to avoid a stalemate in the learning community.

Collaborative Work on EBAP_ECOM

EBAP_ECOM is a virtual community based on relationships among its members, namely the e-commerce classes pupils and the group moderator. Hence, one important issue is to analyse how was this environment used by its participants.

In line with this, it was perceived by analysing the e-mails exchanged by the group participants that one of the most interesting consequences of the deployment of the EBAP_ECOM learning community was to allow students to help each other in work on their theses. The learning community was also used by the students to arise questions and doubts about the e-commerce body of knowledge. Besides, the own moderator took advantage of the learning community to motivate the students to increase their participation in the class.

Table 3. Moderator's Participation

Month	No. Msgs. Moderator	% Participation	Total of Msgs./month
may/08	1	0.50	2
Jun-08	12	0.32	38
Jul-08	8	0.80	10
aug/08	4	0.27	15
sep/08	7	0.58	12
oct/08	6	0.21	29
Nov-08	20	0.49	41
dec/08	18	0.62	29
Jan-09	21	0.47	45
feb/09	33	0.31	107
Mar-09	38	0.25	151
apr/09	20	0.21	94
TOTAL	188	0.39	479
AVERAGE		39.25%	

As is well known, one of the greatest problems Internet users have on the web is tracking down what they want to find that is truly relevant (Saffo, 1989). The technology of Intelligent Agents will surely help Internet users to overcome this hurdle (Brandt, 2000), but until now, it is far from easy to get the right information on the web. Thus, the EBAP_ECOM environment helped the students to easily and fast find out what they were looking for, via interaction with their peers in the digital community. As such, although most e-mails sent should be transmitted privately, the moderator encouraged members to send their messages requesting assistance via EBAP_ECOM, as:

- It was impossible to know for certain whether either a question sent or material uploaded would be useful to other members of the group or not;
- The use of the learning community by members to share experiences and ask for help stimulated others to do the same.

CONCLUDING REMARKS

From the data collected and consolidated, the research questions posed at the beginning of this chapter can be answered in the following manner:

- Did the web-based virtual environment enhance collaborative work? How?

Clearly, collaborative work within the learning community existed and was developed, mainly, through e-mail threads and mutual help, on sub-

Figure 8. Moderator's intervention in percentage of the total messages

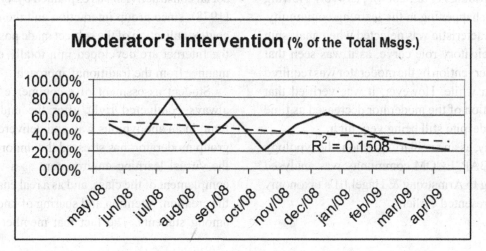

jects addressing the theses and dissertations of group members. Thus, papers, sites, bookmarks, among other items were shared and stored in the group repository by community members.

- How did the physical location of the students influence their participation in the group?

The further the members were from the educational base the greater their engagement and intervention in the group. The Manaus group (Amazonia) participated more than the Curitiba group. However this last group participated more actively than the Rio de Janeiro group. As the classes outside Rio de Janeiro were given in a shorter space of time, it was important for the students to develop strong ties with the teacher and the other members of the group. Hence, EBAP_ECOM was the ideal enabler for this.

- Why was a moderator needed and how can his importance be measured?

The moderator's role was highly relevant, as it was the incentive for the participation of the whole group. Students took part in the group proactively while attending the class. Afterwards, the students who were supervised by the moderator still continued to participate, whereas the others remained as lurkers (Ridings *et al.*, 2006), passively viewing what was happening in the learning community. This characteristic was detected when analysing the participatory role curve, as it was seen that heavy intervention by the moderator was required once in a while. However, it was verified that participation of the moderator decreased as time goes by, despite still being very high.

Finally, as an ancillary question, the typology of the EBAP_ECOM community was analysed according to Armstrong & Hagel III's taxonomy (1996) presented earlier.

A web-learning community about a specific subject has strong characteristic traces of an interest community. However, some characteristics of other typologies can be found. Commercial transactions typical of a transaction community might arise (e.g., exchange of books), trade-off of relationships typical of a relationship community might also arise (e.g., general questions, difficulties related to the elaboration of a thesis), and/or games and competitions might be developed by students, giving the community certain features of a fantasy community. In the case under analysis, strong characteristics of an interest community were detected, as well as some characteristics of a relationship community. Characteristics of transaction and fantasy Communities were not detected.

Although very recent, the use of a web-based collaborative tool as a pedagogical support in the e-commerce graduate class represented a quantum leap in the teaching and learning process. From a strictly instructivist standpoint, where students are seen as empty vessels to be filled by the teacher (Sherry, 1996 and Moule, 2007), one can progress to a piagetian constructivist approach, where knowledge is developed by the students themselves during and after the class, in line with the piagetian "assimilation" and "accommodation" model (Piaget, 1974). In addition to this, a discursive environment permits the development of social constructivism, as explained by Vygostsky (1978), since group interaction and the regional contextualisation of the subject made possible by the Internet are developed in a totally different manner from the traditional approach.

Student assessment of e-commerce classes, always conducted right after the end of the term, in an anonymous way and delivered to the group moderator, has stressed the importance of the virtual learning environment as a veritable complement of the class, and as a real enabler for the creation, retention and sharing of knowledge among students. The fact that members of the first classes – already terminated – still participated in the group is yet another indicator that the EBAP_ECOM community can be considered a technology of transformation, i.e., capable of transforming data and information into knowledge (Haeckel & Nolan, 1993; Joia, 2000b, Boisot & Canals, 2004).

A future step of this research to be envisaged involves analysis of the behaviour of a community in which no e-commerce class is being offered to students, so as to better understand both how the members take part in the group and whether the community is sustainable by itself. Furthermore, the reason why some students take part more actively than others and which issues motivate them to participate will be studied. A survey among members about the constructivist approach of this environment on the web is also forecast, so as to better study the metacognition effect developed by EBAP_ECOM (Reeves & Reeves, 1997; Joia & Costa, 2008; Lima & Joia, 2009).

Certainly, further results will emerge as the group increases with the intake on new e-commerce classes. Therefore, the persistence and transfer of knowledge among the students will be better understood (Argote *et al.*, 1990 and McEvily & Chakravarthy, 2002), permitting the use of this feature in an even more efficient way.

REFERENCES

Argote, L., Beckman, S., & Epple, D. (1990). The persistence and transfer of learning in industrial settings. *Management Science, 36*(2), 140–154. doi:10.1287/mnsc.36.2.140

Armstrong, A., & Hagel, J. III. (1996). The real value of on-line communities. *Harvard Business Review*, (May-June): 131–141.

Bianchi, M., Boyle, M., & Hollingsworth, D. (1999). A comparison of methods for trend estimation. *Applied Economics Letters, 6*(2), 103–109. doi:10.1080/135048599353726

Boghossian, P. (2006). Behaviorism, constructivism, and Socratic pedagogy. *Educational Philosophy and Theory, 38*(12), 713-722. Retrieved on June 18th, 2010 from http://www3.interscience.wiley.com/journal/118600926/abstract?CRETRY=1&SRETRY=0, DOI: 10.1111/j.1469-5812.2006.00226.x

Boisot, M., & Canals, A. (2004). Data, information and knowledge: Have we got it right? *Journal of Evolutionary Economics, 14*(1), 43–67. doi:10.1007/s00191-003-0181-9

Brandt, A. (2000). Agentes inteligentes: O próximo passo da Internet. *Inteligência Empresarial, 3*.

Brent, J. (2004). The desire for community: Illusion, confusion and paradox. *Community Development Journal, 39*(3), 213–223. doi:10.1093/cdj/bsh017

Cairncross, F. (1997). *The death of distance*. Harvard Business School Press.

Chumney, E. C., & Simpson, K. N. (2006). *Methods and designs for outcome research*. American Society for Health Systems Pharmacists.

Cohen, J. (1992). A power primer. *Psychological Bulletin, 112*(1), 155–159. doi:10.1037/0033-2909.112.1.155

Cortes, C., Pregibon, D., & Volinsky, C. (2002). Communities of interest. *Intelligent Data Analysis, 6*(3), 211–219.

Dyson, M. C., & Campello, S. B. (2004). Evaluating virtual learning environments: What are we measuring? *Electronic Journal of e-Learning, 2*(2). Retrieved June 15th, 2010, from http://www.ejel.org/volume-1-issue-1/issue1-art2.htm

Einsenhardt, K. M. (1989). Building theories from case study research. *Academy of Management Review, 14*(4), 532–550.

Freeman, C. (1991). Networks of innovators: A synthesis of research issues. *Research Policy, 20,* 499–514. doi:10.1016/0048-7333(91)90072-X

Gulati, R., & Garino, J. (2000). Get the right mix of bricks and clicks. *Harvard Business Review,* (July-August): 107–114.

Haeckel, S., & Nolan, R. (1993). Managing by wire. *Harvard Business Review,* (September-October): 122–132.

Helble, Y., & Chong, L. C. (2004). The importance of internal and external R&D network linkages for R&D organisations: Evidence from Singapore. *R&D Management, 34*(5), 605 – 612. Retrieved June 15th, 2010, from http://www3.interscience.wiley.com/journal/118761805/abstract

Hsu, M., Ju, T. L., Yen, C., & Chang, C. (2004). Knowledge sharing behavior in virtual communities: The relationship between trust, self-efficacy, and outcome expectations. *International Journal of Human-Computer Studies, 65*(2), 153–169. doi:10.1016/j.ijhcs.2006.09.003

Jarvenpaa, S. L., & Tanriverdi, H. (2003). Leading virtual knowledge networks. *Organizational Dynamics, 31*(4), 403–412. doi:10.1016/S0090-2616(02)00127-4

Joia, L. A. (1999). A new model for workers' retraining in Brazil. *Journal of Workplace Learning, 11*(4), 140–145. doi:10.1108/13665629910276070

Joia, L. A. (2000a). W3E - A web-based instruction system for leveraging corporate intelligence. *Journal of Workplace Learning, 12*(1), 5–11. doi:10.1108/13665620010309747

Joia, L. A. (2000b). Tecnologia da informação para gestão do conhecimento em organização virtual. *Produção, 9*(2).

Joia, L. A., & Costa, M. F. C. (2008). Some key success factors in web-based corporate training in Brazil: A multiple case study. *International Journal of Web-Based Learning and Teaching Technologies, 3*(4), 1–28. doi:10.4018/jwbltt.2009092201

Keen, P. (1991). *Shaping the future.* Harvard Business School Press.

Lee, H. L., & Whang, S. (2001). Winning the last mile of e-commerce. *Sloan Management Review, 42*(4), 54–62.

Lima, N. C., & Joia, L. A. (2009). Empirical evidence of key success factors in web-based corporate training. *Proceedings of the 15th Americas Conference on Information Systems.* Association for Information Systems - AIS.

McEvily, S. K., & Chakravarthy, B. (2002). The persistence of knowledge-based advantage: An empirical test for product performance and technological knowledge. *Strategic Management Journal, 23*(4), 285–305. doi:10.1002/smj.223

Moore, J. (1996). *The death of competition.* HarperCollins Publishers.

Morra, L., & Friedlander, A. C. (1999). *Case study evaluations.* OED (Operations Evaluation Department) Working Paper Series, No. 2, May, World Bank.

Moule, P. (2007). Challenging the five-stage model for e-learning: A new approach. *ALT-J, 15*(1), 37–50. doi:10.1080/09687760601129588

Nonaka, I., & Konno, N. (1998). The concept of 'Ba': Building a foundation for knowledge creation. *California Management Review, 40*(3), 40–54.

Nonaka, I., & Takeuchi, H. (1997). *Criação de conhecimento na empresa: Como as empresas Japonesas geram a a dinâmica da inovação* (pp. 65–71). Editora Campus.

Ozuem, W., Howell, K. E., & Lancaster, G. (2008). Communicating in the new interactive market-space. *European Journal of Marketing, 42*(9-10), 1059–1083. doi:10.1108/03090560810891145

Piaget, J. (1974). *Biology and knowledge.* Chicago, IL: University of Chicago Press.

Porter, M. (2001). Strategy and the Internet. *Harvard Business Review,* (3): 62–78.

Reeves, T. C., & Reeves, P. M. (1997). Effective dimensions of effective learning on the World Wide Web. In Kahn, B. H. (Ed.), *Web-based instruction* (pp. 59–66). Educational Technology Publications.

Ridings, C., Gefen, D., & Arinze, B. (2006). Psychological barriers: Lurker and poster motivation and behavior in online communities. *Communications of the Association for Information Systems, 18*(16). Retrieved from http://aisel.aisnet.org/cais/vol18/iss1/16

Roos, J., Roos, G., Dragonetti, N., & Edvinsson, L. (1997). *Intellectual capital.* MacMillan Press Ltd.

Saeed, K. A., Grover, V., & Hwang, Y. (2003). Creating synergy with a clicks and mortar approach. *Communications of the ACM, 46*(12), 206–212. doi:10.1145/953460.953501

Saffo, P. (1989). Information surfing. Retrieved on June 24th, 2010, from http://www.saffo.org/infosurfing.html

Sherry, L. (1996). Issues in distance learning. *International Journal of Distance Education, 1*(4), 337–365.

Shimizu, H. (1995). *Ba*-principle: New logic for the real-time emergence of information. *Holonics, 5*(1), 67–79.

Soo, C. W., Midgley, D. F., & Devinney, T. (2000). *The process of knowledge creation in organizations.* INSEAD Working Paper, 2000/71/MKT.

Stewart, T. A (1997). *Intellectual capital.* Double-day/Currency.

Sveiby, K. E. (1997). *The new organisational wealth.* Berret-Koehler Publishers, Inc.

Turban, E., Lee, J., King, D., & Chung, H. M. (2004). *E-commerce – A managerial perspective* (3rd ed.). Prentice-Hall, Inc.

Vygostsky, L.S. (1978). *Mind in society: The development of higher psychological processes.* Cambridge, MA: Harvard University Press.

Yin, R. (1994). *Case study research: Design and methods* (2nd ed.). Thousand Oaks, CA: Sage Publications.

KEY TERMS AND DEFINITIONS

Ba: A shared virtual space in order to create relationships.

Communities based on Formal Collaboration: Structures involving relationships ruled by formal agreements and structured protocols.

Communities based on Informal Interaction: Structures not limited to formal agreements and structured protocols.

Communities of Fantasy: Developed to enable the participants to create, in a collective way, their own fantasies, environments, characters and/or stories

Communities of Interest: Developed to connect persons with common interests in one or more subjects.

Communities of Relationship: Developed to enable the participants to exchange personal experiences usually of great impact in their personal lives, leading to strong personal ties

Communities of Transaction: Developed to facilitate the buying and selling process of products and services and to give information about these transactions.

Learning Community: A place for interactions among professionals within an enterprise and among companies, in order to share and acquire knowledge.

Chapter 4
Virtual Communities as Contributors for Digital Objects Metadata Generation

Joana Sócrates Dantas
Escola Politécnica da Universidade de São Paulo, Brazil

Regina Melo Silveira
Escola Politécnica da Universidade de São Paulo, Brazil

ABSTRACT

Description of online digital content is currently extremely necessary to facilitate a diverse amount of resource sharing over the internet. Many times, content is shared and reused within a virtual community. Virtual communities tend to have their own specific needs of resources, and tend to use a specific vocabulary to describe content. Members of virtual communities also tend to have specific motivations for participating and sharing information and knowledge with other members. In this chapter, the authors discuss the benefits of community members generating content description by analyzing the current literature on the matter. Then, the authors present two studies they have held where they assess the metadata generated by users of an IPTV system and by members of two different virtual communities.

1. INTRODUCTION

One of the most important revolutions the internet underwent in recent years was the emergence of Web 2.0. The term Web 2.0 was coined by Dale Dougherty and popularized by O'Reilly Media in 2004 and, in the words of O'Reilly himself, one of the insights on what was becoming the Web 2.0 back then was the network serving as a platform, where applications would learn and get better with people's use and contribution (O'Reilly & Battelle, 2009). Web 2.0 is both a usage and a technology paradigm that has consolidated the Web in a more collaborative and interactive manner. Being more dynamic it allows users to both access a web site and contribute to it. It can be understood as a collection of technologies, business strategies and social trends, which were ignited by social applications such as MySpace[1], Flickr[2], and YouTube[3] (Murugesan, 2007).

DOI: 10.4018/978-1-4666-0312-7.ch004

Web 2.0 has had a large impact on the way people use the Internet. This phenomenon can be appreciated in the vast and diverse multimedia content produced, exchanged and suggested by users online. Web sites supporting online collections of digital multimedia contents are very common nowadays, where people may exchange resources, opinions and information on content like music, video, books, periodicals and so on. Web 2.0 interactivity tools permit users to describe content for others or their own personal re-use.

Some examples of multimedia content services where users may participate at different levels are IPTV, online photo albums, bookshops, online radio and so on. Internet protocol television (IPTV) is the name given to a service that provides digital television over Internet Protocol (IP) for residential and business users (Xiao et al., 2007) with the aid of a set-top box connected to a TV set. as Another type of service is video over the Internet, that can be viewed on various devices such as TVs, PCs and mobile phones. For this reason IPTV and Internet TV present a convergence of communication, computing and content (Jain, 2005). Some online radio services such as Last FM rely greatly on users' contribution and interaction, where other users are cited based on common tastes. Similarly with Amazon, users may criticize and evaluate books and other products.

Web 2.0 has also promoted the development of virtual communities, which are, currently, large producers and consumers of digital multimedia content on the Web. In virtual communities members not only debate and exchange ideas, but also share information in the form of videos, articles, music etc, and suggest content for each other.

The vast availability of content on the web and the sharing and exchanging of this content within communities created the scenario where the Semantic Web became necessary. In Semantic Web, information is given well-defined meaning, better enabling computers and people to work in cooperation (Lee et al., 2001). The Semantic Web gives the traditional web far greater utility as us-

ers, within an area of interest, can use common terms to represent information. With semantic web tools, terms may be linked to each other and be understood automatically by different communities' web software (Feigenbaum et al., 2007).

Recently there has been intense research on user generated metadata alongside the social aspect involved in this activity. With all these new technologies and advances on the Internet, the need for metadata and the new active roles of users make us curious about how virtual communities relate to digital content online. Are virtual community members more active in generating content description? Do they generate higher quality description of content?

In the next section we will briefly elucidate on what a virtual community is and what motivates those involved in actively participating in a virtual community. In section 3 we will discuss the definition of metadata, different types of metadata promoted by the Web 2.0 technology and the quality of metadata generated by these new means. Section 4 will introduce the subject of virtual communities as metadata generators, while sections 5 and 6 will present the two studies we developed on the matter, their results and analysis. In section 7 we draw some conclusions on the subject and, finally, in section 7 some outlines for future work will be presented.

2. VIRTUAL COMMUNITIES

Howard Rheingold is one of the first enthusiasts and researchers of online communities. In 1985, when the internet was not yet broadly open and public, he became part of the WELL, a computer conferencing system, where people from all over the world would gather to have online conversations and discussions. In 1993, Rheingold wrote the book *Virtual Communities, Homesteading on the Electronic Frontier,* (re-edited and re-published by MIT Press in 2000), and was credited with inventing the term "Virtual Community". In the book he defines Virtual Communities as "social aggregations that emerge from the Net" where a group of people continuously participate in a public discussion with enough human feeling to form webs of personal relationships in cyberspace (Rheingold, 2000).

Virtual Communities seem to naturally arise as a consequence of people gathering to discuss subjects as diverse as hobbies, medical afflictions, personal experience, professional experience and house problems (Ridings et al., 2002). The frequent communication, the exchange of personal opinions and common interests promotes a development of connection between members, leading to a notion of association and belonging (Sproull & Faraj, 1997). This linkage between members leads to the sense of community and the development of norms and expectations for behaviors (Sproull & Kiesler, 1991).

In the ten years since he wrote *Virtual Community*, Rheingold observed a phenomenon about online behavior around the world and concluded: "Whenever computer-mediated communications technology becomes available to people anywhere, they inevitably build virtual communities with it, just as microorganisms inevitably create colonies."

Why do people gather to build virtual communities? What are the motivations for being actively participant in a virtual community? The reasons why are subject to extensive research resulting in theories that are entangled with the definitions of virtual community themselves.

2.1 Motivations for Virtual Community

One of the main reasons for success (and survival) of a virtual community lies in its members' motivation to actively participate in it (Ardichvili, A. 2008). With passive members a community would simply perish. Some motivations are related to the uses and applications of a virtual community, others lie on inherent social characteristics of the human kind.

Some significant influence over the decision to participate in a virtual community can be classified as social ties, trust, considerations of reciprocity and identification with the community and its goals (Chiu et al. 2006). Trust relates to how an individual expects members in a virtual community to follow an intrinsic set of rules, norms and principles (Chiu et al. 2006). And reciprocity refers to knowledge exchanges that are mutual and perceived by the parties as fair (Chiu et al. 2006).

Ardichvili, (2008), has conducted an extensive review and analysis of the current literature on the matter and developed a framework for motivational factors, enablers and barriers for knowledge sharing online. Although his research was institutionally focused, it is possible to extract some important points that are generic to the subject. Some of the social and emotional aspects mentioned by the framework are: Emotional benefits (sense of usefulness and by being able to contribute); intellectual benefits (developing expertise and expanding perspective), establishing ties with others, building the sense of community, protecting against external threats.

Rheingold believes that the technology that underlies the computer mediated communication enables and stimulates new activities between people. People recognize there is something valuable they can gain by gathering together. "Looking for a group's collective goods is a way of looking for the elements that bind isolated individuals into a community" (Rheingold, 2000). The three types of goods are: social network capital, knowledge capital and communion.

Knowledge capital includes the exchange and recommendation of content and information between members of a community, it was observed by Rheingold (2000) in the WELL as "an online brain trust representing a highly varied accumulation of expertise". Currier et al. (2004) analyses virtual communities according to their relationship to digital content, and describes two types of communities: one is based on sharing and re-using objects, the other is oriented towards producing texts, e-prints, papers, etc. However both communities have in common the aim of promoting digital content's sustainability, minimizing material production, and facilitating the content's access and discoverability (Currier et al., 2004).

A good example of knowledge capital is Wikipedia[iv], a worldwide virtual community of contributed and interactive knowledge, where people freely produce, correct and access information. The broad utilization and reliability of Wikipedia relies on the constant active participation of its members, with continuous collaboration and assessment.

In different models, besides Wikipedia's, the internet today is densely populated with the creation and exchange of digital resources, like IPTV services, online radio, social applications and so on. This broad production of content and the vast exchange of it must be facilitated by its description, that's when metadata comes to the fore.

3. WHAT IS METADATA?

Metadata can be seen as information about a thing, or data about data, more specifically; metadata is a record that comprises structured information about a resource. Metadata is a record on a resource that facilitates content management, discovery and retrieval (Al-Khalifa & Davis, 2006). The definition by Day, however, illustrates the importance of metadata to a system: "Metadata is normally understood to mean structured data about resources that can be used to help support a wide range of operations. These might include, for example, resource description and discovery, the management of information and their long term preservation." (Day, 2001).

Metadata can be of various formats and types in digital contents. They are accessible online and describe digital resources and multimedia resources. Some examples of the most common metadata are: *title*, *date of production*, *date of publishing*, *author*, *subject* and *abstract*. Of

course metadata has some variations according to the type of item it refers to. As an example a scientific article would have an abstract while a movie file would have a synopsis; a book would have an author, whereas a movie file would have a director and so on. A review on a film would also be considered metadata, proving metadata can also be subjective and express ideas and opinions on a given content.

Traditional metadata used to rely on well established vocabulary, thesauri or ontology. This orderly cataloguing approach guaranteed validation, consistency and quality control of terminology to be registered into an information system (Hammond, T. 2005). However, "terms in such a controlled vocabulary do not evolve with popular language and many of them are irrelevant or anachronistic." (Hunter et al., 2008).

Of course traditional metadata is adequate for standard types of content such as books on a shelf. However, the development of digital content production and publication methods has changed the characteristics of media resource collections. Currently we are witnessing increased abundance and diversity of resources, resulting in a heterogeneous pool of content subjects, characteristics and qualities (Duval, 2002). Moreover the successful implementation of Web 2.0 has influenced information access and therefore data description and management (Nack et al., 2005).

Considering the diversity and amount of digital content and user's queries on the Web, it is not surprising that metadata has, nowadays, an extremely important role in content's classification and retrieval. The same diversity of multimedia content that makes metadata so important also makes it hard to manage. "The variety of sources of data implies that associated metadata will not always be of the same granularity or even of the same type and in many cases will not even be available." (Currier et al., 2004).

Authoritative metadata creation can be very expensive since it requires time and effort of expert cataloguers (Hunter et al., 2008). In fact it is one of the most expensive initial tasks on a digital project such as the establishment of a digital repository or collection (Wilson, 2007). The difficulties and cost involved on metadata generation, together with the increasing demand for them led to what Wilson (2007) calls "Metadata Bottleneck". In order to alleviate this bottleneck alternative metadata generation methodologies were deployed.

3.1 Digital Objects Metadata Generation Alternatives

Traditionally metadata was produced only once and remained connected to the resource it described for its lifetime. Recently metadata can be seen as flexible, supporting subjective opinions and directly dependent upon the resource's context and intention of use (Nilsson et al., 2002). In a general analysis it is possible to distinguish two main concepts on metadata generation: a top down approach where metadata records are generated once and remain static, and a bottom up approach where information is collected over time generating relevant dynamic metadata (Dahl & Vossen, 2008).

Nowadays there are different possibilities for metadata generation, each of which has its own benefits and disadvantages. Some of the methods of metadata generation are described as follows:

- Metadata creation by an expert or authority.
- Automatic metadata generation by information extraction from digital objects and/or the context in which they are used.
- Hybrid systems where automatic and human metadata generation are combined.
- Collaborative metadata generation where users' or author's metadata maybe assessed by an expert cataloguer who performs authority control tasks in order to standardize the main fields in the metadata base (Greenberg et al., 2002).

- Social metadata generation: metadata created by a system's users generally in the form of tags and are not edited or conformed by metadata professionals.

3.2 Social Tagging

One of the many possible ways of describing content is by marking it with descriptive terms, also called keywords or tags, which may be used later for navigation, filtering and search. The novelty in this type of metadata is the collaborative tagging which consists of the practice of allowing users to attach tags to digital web content.

Digital libraries would enforce assigned keywords to their collections, which would be performed by an authority such as a librarian (Golder & Huberman, 2006). Tags, however, are free-form labels that are assigned by the users and are not drawn from a controlled vocabulary. Therefore tags can be seen as a "bottom-up" and personal approach whereas traditional classification structure follows a "top-down" and organizational approach (Hammond et al., 2005). Tagging mechanisms are simple and user-friendly, and by tagging items users create labels for online content (Rainie, 2007). In addition, each tag may also work as a link to other online resources containing the same tags (Marlow et al., 2006).

Social tagging occurs when a community of users applies free-form tags to digital objects. This phenomenon is social because the resources can be viewed and shared between users of a system (Zollers, 2007). Collaborative tagging is also known as *Folksonomy*, a blend of the words 'taxonomy' and 'folk' coined by Thomas Vander Wal and mainly used to describe the organic system of tag organization used in Web applications such as Delicious[1] and Flickr (Mathes, 2004).

One very important characteristic of social tagging is that the terms used to describe a resource are not predefined by a fixed, complex thesauri used in library authority files (Hunter et al., 2008). This lack of taxonomic frame permits social tags to rely on a social structure and relate to concepts and vocabulary pertinent to a user community (Marlow et.al., 2006). They also tend to be closely related to a given topic and more easily adaptable, becoming more relevant to users (Hunter et al., 2008).

Social tags offer a mechanism for distribution of time and expense of metadata generation across communities (Hunter, 2008). They are also extremely useful "when there is nobody in the 'librarian' role or there is simply too much content for a single authority to classify; both of these traits are true of the web, where collaborative tagging has grown popular" (Golder & Huberman, 2006).

3.3 Motivations for Tagging

The current studies found in the literature present diverse reasons why users tag content online. Some of these reasons relate to the design and ease of use of web page's tools, the usability of the site itself and the type of content; other reasons are the need for organization and social influences. For the purpose of our research we will focus on the social aspects of tagging motivation, which can be naturally related to virtual communities.

Zollers (2007) performed an exploratory study, on two websites tag clouds: Amazon.com[v] and LastFM[6]. She observed the most popular tags, and later investigated specific tags. The tags she closely examined presented characteristics resembling signs of social behavior. From the data analyzed, in LastFM web page 67% of the tags on tracks were opinion tags, while in Amazon, 33% in the book collection and 40% in the music collection were opinion tags.

The conditions and tools for free-for-all tagging vary by systems, however the tags are always visible to the public and therefore users might perceive an audience for their tags, implying that tagging is no longer a primarily organization activity for one's self, but has rather evolved to an audience context, where the act of tagging itself becomes a social and collaborative activity. The social motivators that are emerging in the tagging activity can be classified as: opinion expression, performance and activism (Zollers, 2007).

Marlow et al. (2006) analyzed the tags from Flickr, a popular web based photo sharing and tagging system. They observed that "…users are motivated both by personal needs and sociable interests" (Marlow et al. 2006). They categorize the motivations to tagging into two high level practices: *organizational* and *social*. The social aspect relates to the communicative nature of tagging, and how this activity may be used as a mean for users to express themselves and their opinions on the resource (Marlow et al. 2006). Some incentives that influence the tagging behavior are: contribution and sharing; attract attention; play and competition; self presentation; opinion expression (Marlow et al. 2006).

In 2006 some people in protest against the Millennium act started tagging DRM products with a "*defectivebydesign*" tag. The numbers involved in the activism was so high that the tag became one of the most common tags in the Amazon tag cloud (Zollers, 2007). This is a good example of activism motivation for social tagging.

3.4 Barriers for Tagging

Besides lack of motivation there are also barriers that might prevent users from broadly tagging digital content online. Some of these barriers are privacy concerns, avoiding extra tasks and a web sites' interface usability (Van Velsen & Melenhorst, 2009). It also appears that the fact that information submitted online is traceable and cannot be revoked averts some users from submitting information, who fear it could be traced back to their person (Van Velsen & Melenhorst, 2009).

Participants in the same research also identified themselves as information consumers and explicitly stated they only wanted to profit from the work done by others and would not be generating information on content themselves, unless the content was of high personal relevance (Van Velsen & Melenhorst, 2009).

3.5 Analysis on User Generated Metadata Quality

Users might be inclined sometimes to generate descriptions of content; however the metadata generated is not necessarily reliable or accurate. A certain quality of metadata is important to facilitate content retrieval and adequate assessment of that material to one's needs (Currier et al., 2004). Poor quality metadata may restrain content retrieval within a repository.

Greenberg et al. (2001) conducted a study that investigated the ability of content authors to produce acceptable metadata for resources on the National Institute of Environmental Health Sciences (NIEHS) in the United States. The study collected metadata generated by authors and analyzed its acceptability for its function in the database system. The study detected that all of the metadata records produced were considered to be of an acceptable level of quality, being intelligible, and data content values were properly placed in the correct metadata field (Greenberg et al., 2001).

However, an analysis of learning objects and e-prints repositories in three community-based archiving projects in the United Kingdom detected problems of inconsistency, spelling and incompleteness in the author-generated metadata (Currier et al., 2004; Barton et al., 2003).

Golder & Huberman (2006) and Mathes (2004) studied results from the collaborative tagging systems on the Del.icio.us[5] and Flickr websites. The observations presented issues around *ambiguity*, *lack of synonym* and *discrepancies in granularity*. In *ambiguity* the same words or expressions are used for different meaning. An example of an ambiguous word is *apple*; it may refer to the fruit or the computer company. In *synonyms* the same meaning is represented by different words or expressions. Synonyms like *lorry* and *truck*, or

the lack of consistency in the vocabulary chosen, for instance: *nyc* and *new york city*, or *Macintosh*, *Mac* and *Apple* can produce an undesired query result. Another issue observed was different levels of granularity in the tags: documents tagged *java* may be too specific for some users, but documents tagged *programming* may be too general for others, the same description of content may serve differently for different users.

Or-Bach (2005) presents an experiment developed among students of the Computer Science and Information Systems department at Emek Yezreel College in Israel. In the experiment, students were metadata generators for online learning resources in their educational program discipline. Some set of metadata were developed in groups of students. The experiment's resulting metadata tended to contain opinions, and included comparisons between resources, usage context, and anticipated content's re-use and not only its archive. Debates between the students regarding better ways to relate and compare content were observed. The overall quality of the metadata originated was considered high especially in its subjectivity and the value added (Or-Bach, 2005).

4. VIRTUAL COMMUNITIES AS METADATA CREATORS

From the aspects known about virtual communities it is reasonable to believe virtual community members could be more inclined to generate metadata for content that would be used by their community, this motivation may also result in metadata with an agreeable level of quality. It is also expected that the vocabulary selected for describing content would be pertinent to the area of interest of the community members and therefore would be more easily searched and understood by this community's members. Some research on virtual communities' behaviors in generating metadata is presented in the next section.

4.1 Researches on the Literature

A survey of readers in a public library in Ohio provided a tagging exercise that demonstrated the ability of fiction readers to generate a collection of tags adequately describing the content of a novel, but more significantly, readers would make recommendations and better describe the mood of a novel (Weaver, 2007). A virtual community of readers with similar tastes supplies enough information to make readers more satisfied when choosing a book than they would be without the extra subjective description.

Bermudez & Piasecki (2006) have observed the characteristics of Hydrology research's common vocabulary and the need for an ontology-based metadata technology focused on the community needs. In the area of Hydrology, standard descriptions for specific hydrologic data are not explicitly available. As a consequence, communities prefer to create their own specification by reusing elements of other specifications, or writing a completely new specification by themselves. One example of vocabulary with specific meanings is the difference of world realities bringing different understanding of the same word: in a search engine like Google the word "stage" means the measure for water surface elevation in the Hydrology field, but it has a different connotation and means a place for the performing arts field.

Noy et al. (2010) present a bio-medical community, active in updating and broadening an ontology for metadata in their area of activity. A portal called BioPortal relies on the contributions from bio-medical professionals to add suggestions of vocabulary, to help the development of ontology metadata and to review of and map the available ontology for specific sub-areas.

In Or-Bach (2005) (refer to section 3.5 - Analysis on user generated metadata quality), one of the main objectives of the experiment was to use the fact that computer language students would know best what other computer language students would search for on a learning object and therefore would describe that content in a more useful way than someone in a different position. The study also demonstrated that students suggested usages for the content and recommended related learning resources in the metadata field.

The researches mentioned above analyzed the metadata within a community, but did not compare the metadata generated by different communities. In the Study Number Two, presented in section 6, we analyze and compare the differences and similarities between the metadata generated by two different virtual communities and a control group. In Study Number One we have assessed the user generated metadata quality for a digital video repository in an IPTV system.

5. STUDY NUMBER ONE – USER GENERATED METADATA IN IPTV SYSTEM

In this study we have assessed the video metadata base of description generated by the users of an IPTV system. The video repository contained mainly academic related videos that were organized within communities according to their area of research.

5.1 Research Background

The University of São Paulo (USP), the largest university in Brazil, launched its experimental IPTV service in 2007, improving the dissemination of academic and scientific information in the university's community and in Brazilian society. So far USP IPTV stores and presents around 4,000 digital videos produced by different groups and departments in the university. At USP IPTV there are programs generated by live streaming transmission from real time events such as conferences, art exhibitions and sport competitions, as well as video on demand transmission from the current university video archive.

The users of the system have the option to subscribe to groups and communities according to the department they belong to or research group they are part of. The videos produced and uploaded by a community's member are classified and loaded as part of that community, so that each community has their own video content.

In the IPTV system the metadata is generated in two different ways: automatically by machine generation or created by users. In order to have a better knowledge of the repository's metadata quality we conducted an analysis of the system's database, where a sample of 100 entries was extracted from the collection of user generated metadata.

5.2 Research Objectives

The study aimed to evaluate the overall quality of the metadata generated by users of the system. To assess the characteristics and quality of metadata records contributed to the database, the following objectives were sought:

- Gauge the completeness of each record;
- Determine the types of errors (typographical/grammatical or semantic), if any, in each record;
- Identify the appearance and type of "value-added" or additional metadata in each record.

5.3 Research Methods and Records Evaluated

We have extracted 100 entries from the total of 4,099 videos uploaded at the system. The period of entries was limited to between 27 of August 2009 and 27 of November 2009. We analyzed the users' entries for Abstract and Keyword fields on the web form. The video content information is organized according to the content's identification, a primary key called EntityIdentifier. The EntityIdentifier is generated by an algorithm that calculates the content's diverse metadata as Title, Author and Timestamp. To reach the resulting 100 entries each entry was selected with an interval of 30 other entries.

5.4 Procedure

There is a large variety of data quality assessment methodologies; for the purpose of this study we have selected four data characteristics: *accuracy, completeness, value-added, understandability.*

- **Accuracy:** Two kinds of accuracy can be identified: a syntactic accuracy and a semantic accuracy. The syntactic accuracy relies on the fact that a given value in a table respects the corresponding definition domain. The semantic accuracy is related to whether the meaning of a given value is the same as the value in real life. For example, considering an author named "John", if the value author name on a given database is "Jhn", this value is both semantically and accurately incorrect, and if the value is "James" this value is semantically incorrect, but it is syntactically correct (Batini et al., 2009).
- **Completeness:** "The extent to which data is of sufficient breadth, depth, and scope for the task at hand" (Kahn et al, 2002)
- **Value-added:** Refers to the extent to which data is beneficial and provides advantage of use (Pipino et al., 2002).
- **Understandability:** Refers to the extent to which data is easily comprehended (Kahn et al., 2002; Pipino et al. 2002)

From the sample of 100 entries it was possible to analyze the *value-added* and *understandability* of the fields from the CreationType table. This table contained the following fields: *Title, Author, Type, Keywords* and *Abstract*, all of them inputted by the users via a web form.

Since a query on the metadata base is performed equally throughout all the description fields for a piece of content we considered that a term on one field that is the same as the one in another field for the same video content would not provide any value added. For understandability we assumed that acronyms that have syntactic accuracy problems (spelling errors) would also have no understandability.

5.5 Results

In a general observation our research has indicated the repository's metadata to be extremely heterogeneous, probably due to the users' background and profile diversity. The database is filled with some high quality metadata but at the same time it suffers from incomplete information, misspelling and unfilled fields (Dantas et al., 2010).

The analysis of the entries sample presented the following results: Regarding *Completeness*, keywords and abstract fields had almost 10% of missing fields. It is possible to note that a high percentage of Abstract fields had only one word as input, and many times that word would be the same word inputted in the Title and Keywords fields. Nevertheless, some entries presented a considerable completeness and semantic accuracy resulting in high quality metadata. On those entries, the keyword field is complete with many words related to the video, and the abstract field is comprehensive and informative. Some of the results from the research are presented in Tables 1, 2, 3, and 4.

5.6 Analysis and Consideration

From the observation of the metadata inputted by users we noted some high quality information on content, however the overall impression is that users do not feel inclined to input keyword and abstract information, probably due to the fact that those are the most time consuming fields to be filled in (Dantas et al., 2010).

Table 1. Incompleteness and lack of added value at CreationType table

	Number of Fields	Percentage
Total Entries	4,099	100%
Keywords = "-"	345	8.4%
Abstract = "-"	328	8.0%
ABSTRACT Not Informed	520	12.7%
Total Missing Fields	1,193	29.1%

Table 2. Quality levels on abstract and keyword fields at CreationType table

Total Number Of Analyzed Fields	200	100%
Empty Or Null Fields	13	6.5%
Fields With Low Metadata Quality	87	43.5%
Fields With Average Metadata Quality	41	20.5%
Fields With High Metadata Quality	59	29.5%

Table 3. Acceptable metadata quality at CreationType table

	Number of Fields	Percentage
Coherent & Informative Abstract	47	47%
Coherent & Informative Keywords	8	8%
Coherent & Informative Abstract & Keywords	9	9%
Acceptable Abstract	18	18%
Acceptable Keyword	17	17%
Acceptable Abstract & Keyword	6	6%

Table 4. Problems of value-added, accuracy, and understandability at CreationType table

	Number of Fields	Percentage
Title = File Name	5	5%
Author = Typing Error	5	5%
Keyword = Author	21	21%
Keyword = Title	41	41%
Abstract = Title	20	20%
Keyword & Abstract = Title	17	17%
Keyword = Acronym	5	5%

Even though the system's metadata present some quality issues most users manage to reach the desired content via their community's page. This phenomenon shows that classifying the video content by virtual communities became an extra tool for content retrieval and title browse.

6. STUDY NUMBER TWO: SIMULATION OF COMMUNITY MEMBER METADATA GENERATION

6.1 Research Background

With this experiment we intended to analyze whether members of a given virtual community would develop similar metadata if compared to a control group. In order to access this information we developed a simulation where participants would input metadata for a video resource in a web form.

6.2 Research Objectives

The study aimed to evaluate the differences and similarities of metadata generated by members of different communities and the overall quality of the metadata. To assess the characteristics and quality of metadata records contributed to the database, the following objectives were sought:

- Identify the similarities or discrepancies in the vocabulary chosen to describe the content between groups;
- Determine typographical errors (grammatical or semantic), if any, in each record;
- Identify the appearance of consistency issues throughout the records.

6.3 Research Methods

We have designed a simple web page containing a video and metadata inputting form. The web form contained four data input fields: two of them concerned the user's personal information: name and field of work or research. The two other fields concerned information about the video: keywords and abstract. The video selected was a video/animation presenting an introduction to Information Systems.

We sent emails to 3 different groups of people and asked them if they would be willing to participate in research on metadata by providing description of a video via a web form. We did not provide further information on the research, just mentioned it was metadata research. We offered to send the research's results as a motivational grant for the e-learning virtual community and for the Information Systems group. The replies would reach us via email, and with the responses we created a database that was later analyzed. The tested groups were divided as follows:

1. **Control Group:** Regular Internet users from diverse professions, all with undergraduate diplomas;

2. **E-Learning Virtual Community:** Researchers that exchange information, messages and take part in discussion forums on e-learning via the community's web page, they also exchange tutoring resources, blogs etc.

3. **IS Group:** Research group on Information Systems whose members meet monthly, to introduce their current research and production and debate via emails and forums.

6.4 Records Evaluated

1. **Control Group:** From 58 people that were contacted, 18 participated

2. **E-Learning Virtual Community:** From 37 people that were contacted, 12 we received record from

3. **SI Group:** From 88 people that were contacted, 20 participated

All the records received were evaluated.

6.5 Procedure

For this study we have selected two data quality characteristics: *syntax accuracy* and *consistency*. *Consistency*: relates to coherence of data as it is represented in different tables in the same database. One example of consistency is an attribute or a value that is always represented by the same exact words, and not by different synonyms throughout different tables on the same database (Pipino et al. 2002).

To evaluate the records, we developed the following data:

- Ratio of misspelled words (syntax accuracy problem) by total terms entered.

- Number of different words with the same meaning (consistency issue) by total terms entered.

- Numbers of recurring words for each group.

6.6 Results and Analysis

The reason why most people in each group were not willing to participate in the research was not assessed since this was not the aim of the study, however it is possible to infer the following hypotheses:

- Some virtual communities did not have extremely active members, so some members do not read all the messages received from the community, and therefore did not read the email about the metadata research.

- Some people did read the email but did not feel inclined to generate metadata because that is a time consuming task (Dantas et al., 2010), and they see themselves as information consumers and not generators (Van Velsen & Melenhorst,, 2009).

- People may not have perceived exchange of knowledge involved in the activity by taking part in the research (Chiu et al., 2006).

- Some people did not perceive a personal relevance on the content or on the purpose of the research (Van Velsen & Melenhorst, 2009).

From the records assessed we could observe that the overall quality of metadata generated was rather high. Misspelling was only detected in the IS group where it appeared in less than 1.50% of the words inputted; while consistency was present in all groups but in fewer than 1% of the total words (Table 5).

We did note a similar selection of words within each group (Figure 1). An interesting point is a slight recurrent selection of some words and

Table 5. Occurrences of quality problems vocabulary for digital content tested

Quality Problem	Occurrences in Information Systems Research Group	Occurrences in E-Learning Community	Number of Occurrences in Control Group
Misspelling	1.42%	0.00%	0.00%
Synonym	0.47%	0.29%	0.58%

expressions in the control group being more present than in the virtual community groups. One possible interpretation for that phenomenon is the fact that when someone must describe content on a subject they are not acquainted with, they tend to use the vocabulary used in the content, rather than words from their personal knowledge. One example is the word *Digital* that was used by many participants from the control group but not even once by members of the two virtual communities.

Even though the responders were not asked to make any remarks on the content's quality, some members of the e-learning community suggested improvements on the content and members of the e-learning community and the IS group commented on the content's downsides. As an ex-

ample three members from the e-learning community pointed out spelling errors in the content, four members from the IS group mentioned the content did not present the subject in satisfactory depth. This subjective approach on the responses could be extremely helpful in a scenario where the volume of available content is vast and personalized information could improve the content's re-use.

It is important to point out a downside in the study that most definitely interfered with the results achieved: the fact that the study was a simulation where participants knew they were taking part in a research project. An actual situation where members of a community were providing information for the re-use of content by other members could result in a higher number of responses,

Figure 1. Occurrences of words in keyword fields for digital content tested

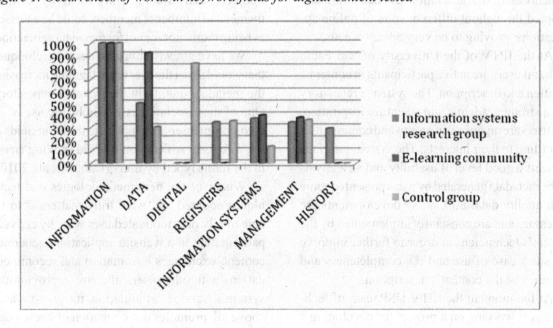

though it would not result in differences on the vocabularies used.

7. CONCLUSION AND FUTURE WORKS

Web 2.0 has enhanced the uses and characteristics of the Internet. Social interactive applications are, nowadays, extremely popular among diverse types of Internet users. The constant development of websites' interfaces guarantees the ease of use of the interactive tools available, resulting in increased communication between users and an abundant exchange of information and resources. Virtual communities formed by internet users with similar interests and goals become great producers of digital resources and also involved in a productive re-use of content available online.

In this new Internet communication scenario metadata generation and quality has become essential. The large dissemination of the Semantic web's tools enabled new practices for metadata generation and more efficient and dynamic engines for content retrieval. The collaboration of users, authors and community members in the process of content description generation has become broadly adopted throughout different sorts of online applications, proving to be very advantageous.

At the IPTV of the University of São Paulo in Brazil users are active participants in content's creation and description. The system's repository has a strong academic and scientific inspiration, and users are organized in groups and communities according to their interests. The system interface presents a good level of usability and an analysis of the metadata generated by users presented some high quality data. Still, many developments are necessary and are constantly implemented by the system's technicians in order to further improve the site's ease of use and the completeness and accuracy of the content's description.

At the moment the IPTV USP team of technicians is working on a project for developing a new Internet TV that would be used for learning purposes, called TV Escola (*School TV*). Its video content will be described by users, but its main novelty is the possibility to tag just a fraction of a video instead of the whole item. This tool will be of great assistance to teachers who are selecting parts of videos as resources for a discipline. Students and other teachers will be able to search and retrieve content related to that fraction without having to watch the complete video. This project, when launched, will be relying on virtual communities members to describe content in a more specific and targeted way, thus promoting a more adequate re-use of content to one's need. After the service becomes totally functional we intend to analyze the overall user's satisfaction with it, the difficulties the teachers have encountered when generating the metadata and the matches of content results for users queries.

Further and more detailed analysis on the metadata base of the IPTV USP repository is also required. An assessment of the metadata generated organized by the communities would make possible a future study on the characteristics of the different groups that promote them as generators of higher or lower quality of content description. Subjects such as community's activity, content themes and number of members could be assessed as being motivators or not for metadata generation.

We have already envisioned some techniques that would assist the user when tagging, increasing the metadata quality in the system's repository. One of these techniques would be the use of an auto-complete engine applied to the input fields in the web form which would avoid spelling errors in the terms typed by users (Dantas et al., 2010).

Whatever the new methodologies and techniques adopted are, what truly matters is to be able to rely on a motivated user who, by actively participating in a website application, generates content, exchanges information and recommendations with other users, thereby improving the system's service, stimulating its growth and, above all, promotes dissemination of knowledge and culture, justifying the restless evolution of communication technology.

REFERENCES

Al-Khalifa, H., & Davis, H. (2006). The evolution of metadata from standards to semantics in E-learning applications. *Proceedings of the Seventeenth Conference on Hypertext and Hypermedia*, (pp. 69-72).

Ardichvili, A. (2008). Learning and knowledge sharing in virtual communities of practice: Motivators, barriers, and enablers. *Advances in Developing Human Resources*, *10*(4), 541. doi:10.1177/1523422308319536

Barton, J., Currier, S., & Hey, J. (2003). Building quality assurance into metadata creation: an analysis based on the learning objects and e-prints communities of practice. *Proceedings of the 2003 International Conference on Dublin Core and Metadata Applications: Supporting Communities of Discourse and Practice—Metadata Research & Applications,* Dublin Core Metadata Initiative, (p. 5).

Batini, C., Cappiello, C., Francalanci, C., & Maurino, A. (2009). Methodologies for data quality assessment and improvement. *ACM Computing Surveys, 41*(3), 1–52. doi:10.1145/1541880.1541883

Bermudez, L., & Piasecki, M. (2006). Metadata community profiles for the Semantic Web. *GeoInformatica, 10*(2), 159–176. doi:10.1007/s10707-006-7577-2

Chiu, C., Hsu, M., & Wang, E. (2006). Understanding knowledge sharing in virtual communities: An integration of social capital and social cognitive theories. *Decision Support Systems, 42*(3), 1872–1888. doi:10.1016/j.dss.2006.04.001

Currier, S., Barton, J., O'Beirne, R., & Ryan, B. (2004). Quality assurance for digital learning object repositories: Issues for the metadata creation process. *ALT-J, 12*(1), 5–20. doi:10.1080/0968776042000211494

Dahl, D., & Vossen, G. (2008). Learning object metadata generation in the Web 2. 0 era. *International Journal of Information and Communication Technology Education, 4*(3), 1–10. doi:10.4018/jicte.2008070101

Dantas, J., Silveira, R. M., & Ruggiero, W. V. (2010). *Metadata in digital video repositories: An analysis on author-generated metadata.* International Conference on Information Society (i-Society 2010), June 28-30, 2010, London, UK.

Day, M. (2001). Metadata in a nutshell. *Information Europe, 6*(2), 11.

Duval, E., Hodgins, W., Sutton, S., & Weibel, S. (2002). Metadata principles and practicalities. *D-Lib Magazine, 8*(4), 1082–9873. doi:10.1045/april2002-weibel

Feigenbaum, L., Herman, I., Hongsermeier, T., Neumann, E., & Stephens, S. (2007). The semantic web in action. *Scientific American Magazine, 297*(6), 90–97. doi:10.1038/scientificamerican1207-90

Golder, S., & Huberman, B. (2006). Usage patterns of collaborative tagging systems'. *Journal of Information Science, 32*(2), 198–208. doi:10.1177/0165551506062337

Greenberg, J., Pattuelli, M., Parsia, B., & Robertson, W. (2001). Author-generated Dublin Core metadata for web resources: A baseline study in an organization. *Journal of Digital Information, 2*(2), 38–46.

Greenberg, J., & Robertson, W. (2002). Semantic Web construction: An inquiry of authors' views on collaborative metadata generation' *Proceedings of the 2002 International Conference on Dublin Core and Metadata Applications: Metadata for E-Communities: Supporting Diversity and Convergence*, Dublin Core Metadata Initiative, (pp. 45-52).

Hammond, T., Hannay, T., Lund, B., & Scott, J. (2005). Social bookmarking tools (I). *D-Lib Magazine, 11*(4), 1082–9873. doi:10.1045/april2005-hammond

Hunter, J., Khan, I., & Gerber, A. (2008). Harvana: Harvesting community tags to enrich collection metadata. *Proceedings of the 8th ACM/IEEE-CS Joint Conference on Digital Libraries*, (pp. 147-156).

Jain, R. (2005). I want my IPTV. *IEEE MultiMedia, 12*(3), 96. doi:10.1109/MMUL.2005.47

Kahn, B., Strong, D., & Wang, R. (2002). Information quality benchmarks: Product and service performance. *Communications of the ACM, 45*(4), 192. doi:10.1145/505999.506007

Lee, T., Hendler, J., & Lassila, O. (2001). The Semantic Web. *Scientific American, 284*(5), 34–43. doi:10.1038/scientificamerican0501-34

Marlow, C., Naaman, M., Boyd, D., & Davis, M. (2006). HT06, tagging paper, taxonomy, Flickr, academic article, to read. *Proceedings of the Seventeenth Conference on Hypertext and Hypermedia*, ACM, (pp. 31-40).

Mathes, A. (2004). *Folksonomies-Cooperative classification and communication through shared metadata*. Technical Report, Graduate School of Library and Information Science, University of Illinois Urbana-Champaign.

Murugesan, S. (2007). Understanding Web 2.0. *IT Professional, 9*(4), 34–41. doi:10.1109/MITP.2007.78

Nack, F., van Ossenbruggen, J., & Hardman, L. (2005). That obscure object of desire: Multimedia metadata on the Web, part 2. *IEEE MultiMedia, 12*(1), 54–63. doi:10.1109/MMUL.2005.12

Nilsson, M., Palmér, M., & Naeve, A. (2002). Semantic Web meta-data for e-learning–some architectural guidelines. *Proceedings of the 11th World Wide Web Conference*, (pp. 7-11).

Noy, N., Griffith, N., & Musen, M. (2010). Collecting community-based mappings in an ontology repository. *The Semantic Web-ISWC, 2008*, 371–386.

O'Reilly, T., & Battelle, J. (2009). *Web squared: Web 2.0 five years on*. Retrieved December 20, 2009.

Or-Bach, R. (2005). Educational benefits of metadata creation by students. *ACM SIGCSE Bulletin, 37*(4), 93–97. doi:10.1145/1113847.1113885

Pipino, L., Lee, Y., & Wang, R. (2002). Data quality assessment. *Communications of the ACM, 45*(4), 211–218. doi:10.1145/505248.506010

Rainie, L. (2007). *28% of online Americans have used the internet to tag content*. Pew Internet & American Life Project.

Rheingold, H. (2000). *The virtual community: Homesteading on the electronic frontier*. The MIT Press.

Ridings, C., Gefen, D., & Arinze, B. (2002). Some antecedents and effects of trust in virtual communities. *The Journal of Strategic Information Systems, 11*(3-4), 271–295. doi:10.1016/S0963-8687(02)00021-5

Sproull, L., & Faraj, S. (1997). Atheism, sex, and databases: The net as a social technology. In Kiesler, S. (Ed.), *Culture of the Internet* (pp. 35–51).

Sproull, L., & Kiesler, S. (1992). *Connections: New ways of working in the networked organization*. The MIT Press.

Van Velsen, L., & Melenhorst, M. (2009). Incorporating user motivations to design for video tagging. *Interacting with Computers, 21*(3), 221–232. doi:10.1016/j.intcom.2009.05.002

Weaver, M. (2007). Contextual metadata: faceted schemas in virtual library communities. *Library Hi Tech, 25*(4), 579–594. doi:10.1108/07378830710840527

Wilson, A. (2007). Toward releasing the metadata bottleneck: A baseline evaluation of contributor-supplied metadata. *Library Resources & Technical Services, 51*(1), 16–28.

Xiao, Y., Du, X., Zhang, J., Hu, F., & Guizani, S. (2007). Internet protocol television (IPTV): The killer application for the next-generation Internet. *IEEE Communications Magazine, 45*(11), 126–134. doi:10.1109/MCOM.2007.4378332

Zollers, A. (2007). *Emerging motivations for tagging: Expression, performance, and activism*. WWW 2007.

ENDNOTES

1. www.myspace.com
2. http://www.flicr.com
3. www.youtube.com
4. www.wikipedia.org
5. http://del.icio.us/
6. www.amazon.com
7. www.lastfm.com

Chapter 5

Redefining Participation in Online Community:
Some Neglected Topics

Gibrán Rivera Gonzalez
University of Sheffield, UK

Andrew Cox
University of Sheffield, UK

ABSTRACT

To be sustainable, online communities must have the ability to attract and retain members, who in turn must be willing to participate by giving their time, knowledge, and effort to provide benefits to others and themselves. Yet, many studies look at participation from a static point of view and disregard different levels of participation. There is a need to redefine the concept of participation. Furthermore, many studies explaining participation in virtual communities have focused their attention on the internal characteristics of these communities neglecting the importance of the external environment such as the competition that exists between online communities and alternative media; the multiple memberships people simultaneously have in different communities/practices; the organizational and social context in which online communities exist; and the social practices online communities support. By looking at participation as an evolving process instead of as a one-time event; by giving voice to all participants of the community; and by studying the context within which communities emerge, understanding of participation can be improved. To illustrate how these topics reshape a research agenda, the authors offer examples from a current study they are undertaking shaped by these concerns. By presenting the example the authors show how awareness of the "neglected topics" identified - as sensitizing ideas - expands research method and deepens understanding of participation in online communities. A practice-based approach is suggested as a useful theoretical tool to deepen current understanding of online community participation.

DOI: 10.4018/978-1-4666-0312-7.ch005

INTRODUCTION

Although there is no consensus regarding the concept of online communities (Komito, 1998; Lee et al., 2002; Ellis et al., 2004; Porter, 2004; Hansen, 2007), nobody questions that these social arrangements have been demonstrated to be a powerful opportunity to promote interaction and collaboration between individuals and organizations. Within the non-organizational context, for example, previous studies have explored how people interact in online communities in different ways such as providing emotional and informational support to others with similar diseases (Turner et al., 2001; Cummings et al., 2002); how people participate as volunteers to support survivors of natural disasters (Torrey et al., 2007); how open source software of high quality is developed (Lakhani and von Hippel, 2003; Lee and Cole, 2003); how people exchange stock-related information (Campbell, 2001; Gu et al., 2007); how people discuss TV programmes of which they are fans (Baym, 2000); how software programmers share knowledge (Wasko and Faraj, 2000), to name just a few. In the corporate context, organizations have found new opportunities in online communities and have been increasingly making significant investments to support them (Bateman, 2008). To name a few, multinational organizations such as Toyota (Dyer and Nobeoka, 2000), Siemens (Tiwana and Bush, 2005), Ford, Xerox (Mahar, 2007), Chevron. Raytheon, (Ellis, 2001), IBM (Gongla and Rizzuto, 2001; Mahar, 2007) (Ellis, 2001), Hewlett Packard (Devenport, 1996), Caterpillar (Ardichvili et al., 2002; Ardichvili et al., 2003), United Nations (Stoddart, 2007) have made of online communities a fundamental organizational tool through which they can get a wide range of benefits. Organizations have used online communities to facilitate their knowledge management strategies (Dyer and Nobeoka, 2000; Ardichvili et al., 2003; Tiwana and Bush, 2005; Bogenrieder and Baalen, 2007; Stoddart,

2007); to strengthen their innovation processes via firm-hosted user communities (Jeppesen and Frederiksen, 2006); to build brand loyalty (Porter and Donthu, 2008)

Because members' active participation in online communities is a key resource for them to succeed, much of the previous literature has focused its attention on understanding the benefits, motivations and barriers that lead (or prevent) online community members actively participating. Some of these studies for instance, have explained the different benefits that people obtain when they participate in online communities such as tangible returns, intangible returns and community-related benefits (Wasko and Faraj, 2000), extrinsic and intrinsic benefits (Kankanhalli et al., 2005), visibility, information, social and altruistic benefits (Butler et al., 2007). Others have focused on the motivations that enhance participation in online communities such as individual motivation n (Dholakia et al., 2004; Wasko and Faraj, 2005), social capital-related motivations (Dholakia et al., 2004; Wasko and Faraj, 2005; Chiu et al., 2006), individual and community-related outcome expectations (Chiu et al., 2006; Hsu et al., 2007); relational capital-motivation (Tiwana and Bush, 2005). Studies focusing on the costs and barriers to participate in online communities are also extensive in the literature (Ardichvili et al., 2003; Kankanhalli et al., 2005), just to name a few. Although still remains in the literature to develop a clear understanding of the motivational forces that affect people's decisions to participate in online communities (Ridings et al., 2002; Ardichvili et al., 2003; Ardichvili, 2008), some have suggested that an increasing consensus is being achieved (Faraj et al., 2011).

Without disregarding the relevance of active participation but at the same time acknowledging that some topics have been neglected in online community literature and thus have hindered our understanding of why people contribute to their communities, this chapter attempts to elaborate on the concept of participation 1) by looking at different types of participation (suggesting that participation can be seen from different perspectives that can be useful to deepen our understanding of the concept), 2) by looking at participation as a dynamic process instead of as a one-time event and 3) by widening the focus to look at factors beyond the internal mechanisms of the community as a bounded entity that shape participation (e.g. social environment or working practices).

As it will be shown in this chapter, some of these issues have been receiving recent attention, but still need further development. For example, a study within the e-learning context notes that online learner participation is not only about writing or reading behaviors, but it also embraces other more complex practices such as doing, communicating, thinking, feeling and belonging (Hrastinski, 2008), as well as maintaining relations with others, and demanding the use of physical and physiological tools (e.g. technologies and language) in order for participation to take place (Hrastinski, 2009). These studies go beyond the minimalistic conception of participation (e.g. posting behavior) that is found in a great number of previous online community studies. However, they still further development of these issues is required.

The approach is illustrated by giving examples of previous literature and explaining how these concerns influenced our own study of "CODECO", an online community established to support collaboration among dispersed University Human Resource staff as part of a project. While we suggest that broadening the concept of online community participation would provide a deeper understanding of this phenomenon, we also acknowledge the implications of this engagement. As Hrastinski (2008) suggests, in acknowledging participation as a complex phenomenon, it becomes more difficult not only to measure participation, but also to define the concept and explore it.

PARTICIPATION AS THE MAIN CHALLENGE OF ONLINE COMMUNITIES

Members' participation has been acknowledged as both the key resource and the biggest challenge for online communities to survive (Butler, 2001; Ardichvili et al., 2003; Wasko and Faraj, 2005; Chiu et al., 2006; Ardichvili, 2008). Regardless of their purpose, type, or the environment in which they reside, online communities' survival largely depends on their ability to attract and retain members who are willing to continuously participate. It is also the activity taking place in that attracts people to join. A common perspective taken in different studies to explain participation has been that implying a reductive cost-benefit model in online community literature. Butler (2001) for instance, has noted that online communities are sustained by members' willingness to contribute their time, knowledge, energy and emotional encouragement. Only when the perceived benefits of participating in an online community have greater value than the costs, will members engage in the community (Tiwana and Bush, 2005, Butler et al., 2007, Wang 2007). While these studies have deepened our understanding of participation, at the same time, adopting this cost-benefit perspective has also undermined other relevant issues that need further evaluation.

Kollock and Smith (1996) have noted that online communities are subjected to a public good dilemma meaning that an individual using a public good (e.g. knowledge contribution) does not undermine the ability of others to use the same resource. While active participation in online communities demands participants' time, energy, effort, and knowledge, accessing the contributions provided by active users tend to be costless. Because participation in online communities is often open and voluntary there is no assurance for contributors that those they are helping will ever contribute anything in return (Rheingold, 1993;

Wasko et al., 2004). Instead individuals have the privilege of benefiting from others' contributions; while at the same time they can avoid the costs associated with active participation. Free riding is one of the concepts associated with this idea. It is this public good dilemma which online communities face which makes participation a continuous challenge for communities. To remain attractive for participants, a certain level of activity is needed to take place via contributions of their members and thus when participation is dismissed so their attractiveness and the survival are too. Equally excessive activity can become a cost for participants as some studies have shown (Butler, 2001; Gu et al., 2007).

As the life of a community largely depends on its members' contributions, an immense body of literature has been aimed at understanding what motivates people to contribute with their effort, time and knowledge (Butler, 2001). In general, when evaluating this body of literature it can be noted that such studies can be classified into five main categories: 1) individual-related motivations such as personal benefits, needs, attitudes, etc., 2) community-related factors focusing on aspects such as shared norms, shared purposes, shared identity, trust and social capital, 3) structural characteristics of these communities such as membership, community size, roles, 4) technology-related issues, and 5) context-related factors including those aspects such as competition between online communities, cultural differences and the environment and organizational issues affecting member's online community participation.

While this literature has contributed to deepen our understanding of participation in online communities by suggesting that people have different motivations to participate and that this participation is shaped by different forces that go beyond the boundaries of these communities, in this chapter we argue that previous studies have neglected other relevant topics needed to better understand participation. With this aim in mind, first, we suggest seeing participation from two

different perspectives, one from the viewpoint of what motivates people to participate, and another based on the grounds of the behaviors different community members play in their communities, this in turn, allow us moving away from a narrow conception that tend to only consider contributing behaviors; second, we note that in order to understand online community participation we must not see it as a static one-time event with no previous history and a future orientation but rather to look at it as being shaped by past, present and future events, behaviors, interactions and intentions, and therefore conceptualizing participation as a dynamic process; and third, we argue that online communities must not be seen as isolated entities located in a vacuum, but rather as been embedded in specific environments and therefore suggesting that aspects such as competition, alternative media, social context, working practices being supported, and multi-memberships of participants need further consideration. In turn, in showing our awareness of "neglected topics" identified, there is a need to expand our research methods. Only by broadening the concept of participation and expanding our research methods to explore it will we have the ability to deepen our understanding of the success or failure of online communities.

REDEFINING THE CONCEPT OF PARTICIPATION

In the following sections, we discuss three issues related to participation, while at the same time we highlight some neglected topics that have hindered our understanding of online community in its complex nature. These perspectives are illustrated with an example of an online community, introduced to support knowledge sharing during the implementation of a Human Resource Project. The case study explores the methodological implications of an expanded understanding of participation. The remaining of this chapter is presented as follows. First, we discuss two different perspectives of participation; second, we discuss the issue of participation as evolving process; third, we look at the effects of external environment on participation; and finally we provide some conclusion for the chapter.

Motivation-Based Participation

Participation in online communities can be seen from the perspective of what motivates community members to contribute with their time, effort and knowledge to their peers.

Although many studies have found and discussed different motivations for why people contribute in online communities, no explicit differentiation has been made on how these distinct motivations lead to different sorts of participation; two main categories emerge from this.

On the one hand, participation can be seen as driven by individual motivations of members. In such cases, people's activity is often driven by self-interest, and unless tangible or intangible returns are in place, people will not be willing to participate (Wasko and Faraj, 2000). A great body of literature has identified how community members are more likely to participate when they receive extrinsic rewards such as personal information benefits (Wasko and Faraj, 2000; Ardichvili et al., 2003) or economic incentives such as monetary benefits, bonuses, or career advancement (Wasko and Faraj, 2000; Lerner and Tirole, 2002; Kankanhalli et al., 2005; Bjorkeng et al., 2009). On the other hand, a second reason motivating member' contributions to an online community can be when their members are motivated by community-related factors. Previous studies have suggested that when knowledge is seen as a public good owned and maintained by the community members, participation in online communities will not be motivated by self-interest but by community interests (e.g. altruism, reciprocity, sense of community, identify and norms, and moral obligation (Wasko and Faraj, 2000; Ardichvili et al., 2003; Bruce et al., 2005; Wasko

and Faraj, 2005; Ardichvili et al., 2006; Chiu et al., 2006; Zhou, 2011).

Previous research has noted that members who value different benefits from their communities are likely to contribute to the development of an online community in different ways (Butler et al., 2007).

In making visible the distinctiveness of motivations of people to participate in online communities the concept of participation could be better understood. The implications of this differentiation of participation based on what motivates people to participate are enormous for the survival of communities. While people motivated by self-interest could have a tendency to reduce their costs of participation as much as possible and therefore reduce their participation when the costs are perceived to be higher than the benefits they receive, those people driven not by self-interest but by community interest and moral obligation would be more willing to participate regardless of their costs of participation as far as they see the community being sustained.

Behavioural-Based Participation

Previous work in online community participation has been characterized by considering low-level conceptions of online community participation (Hrastinski, 2008). The most common differentiation of participation –but certainly in many studies ignored - is that made on the basis of type of participation (e.g. active and passive participation). Although active participation is the most basic type of investment in an online community (Butler et al., 2007), other kinds of participation need to be recognized; "solely equating participation with content contribution neglects members' roles as audience members" (Bateman, 2008:14). Focusing only on active contributors to the community, limits our understanding of participation since active participants that provide content to the community, only represent a small part of the entire population of the community. Furthermore, this small group of participants does not represent adequately the characteristics of members who participate in online communities.

Existing literature has typically examined why people actively participate in online communities by adding new content, by posting and solving questions, uploading videos, creating new discussions (e.g. Wang, 2007; Wasko and Faraj, 2005; Chiu et al., 2006). However, people who contribute content to the community represent only a small proportion of all participants (Nonnecke and Preece, 2001; Bateman, 2008; Zhang and Watts, 2008). Studies by Horowitz (2006), Nonnecke and Preece (2000) Katz (1998) and Mason (1999) have shown that only around 10% of the user population of online groups typically participate actively, suggesting that our current understanding of participation is reduced in that what has been studied has tended to ignore the majority of members participating in a community. Thus, highlighting the different sorts of behaviors online community members engage in could open new possibilities to increase our understanding of participation and look at it as a multifaceted concept in which content contribution behavior is acknowledged, but at the same time seeing as only one type of behavior giving life to an online community. Based on previous studies, in this chapter we highlight three main categories that show how online community member participation varies depending on the activities people engage in as members of their communities.

The most basic sort of engagement in an online community is content contribution behaviour, in the form of creating content to the community and thus making it available to other members. In online communities this sort of participation means posting messages, responding to other members' messages, uploading videos, photos, movies, etc. Many studies have recognized the attraction and retention power of content contributions for the survival of online communities (Bateman et al., 2006), and a generalized acknowledgement of its importance is present in most of the online com-

munity literature. Most of previous literature cited above in this chapter has focused its attention in this sort of behaviours.

Second, while the creation of content is essential for the community success, this sort of participation only represents one side of the communication equation (Bateman et al., 2006). Nonnecke and Preece (1999) were one of the first to observe that most of the online community literature has been developed based on observations of those who post, and that knowledge of lurkers would be valuable to better understand participation in online communities. Previous work initially defined lurkers as free-riders and were characterised by their lack of public participation and their self-centered use of resources without giving back to the communities (Kollock and Smith, 1996). Since then, however, many other studies have been conducted to understand lurking behaviour. This literature has criticised previous studies arguing that audience behaviours have been neglected, and the perception of lurkers itself has evolved. More recently, a general conception of lurkers has been developed acknowledging their fundamental role in online communities. Saying that participation in the form of content contribution only represents one side of the communication equation means that communities also need members who spend their time reading or looking at the contribution of others (Bateman et al., 2006). In order to remain viable members providing content contributions are not sufficient to maintain online communities, and thus members to read what other have post are also needed (Butler et al., 2007). Acknowledging the importance of lurking behaviours has been the focus of many studies and further literature has focused on understanding this phenomenon: measuring lurking levels in communities (Nonnecke and Preece, 2001), understanding why lurkers lurk (Nonnecke and Preece, 2001; Nonnecke and Preece, 2003; Preece et al., 2004), finding out the strategies lurkers use to deal with the content of their communities (Nonnecke and Preece, 2003), identifying strategies to provide social and technological support for lurkers (Nonnecke et al., 2004a), discussing similarities and differences among those who post and those considered as lurkers (Nonnecke et al., 2004b). Overall, these studies have led to a conception of lurkers as being fundamental for the survival of communities rather than seeing as 'second-class members' with a selfish free-riders attitude (Preece et al., 2004). Moreover, lurkers are also helpful to maintain the vitality of their communities. In a similar way in which learners of a practice, as peripheral participants (Lave and Wenger, 1991), may move toward full participation after some time, lurkers in an online community may engage into a more active participation.

Third, it has also been suggested in previous literature that in order to maintain the vitality of an online community different activities are needed, apart from those of actively contributing with content and engaging as audience members consuming the content others provide. Among the activities required to sustain online communities are those of control and encouragement, infrastructure administration and external promotion (Butler et al., 2007). Bateman et al. (2006) also suggested that important for the viability of online communities are community citizenship behaviours defining them as those activities through which members develop and propagate informal rules and guidelines for appropriate behaviours. Once acknowledging these sorts of behaviours, in many occasions enacted by community leaders (Butler et al., 2007) or core members (Johnson, 2010), our understanding of participation can be improved.

In our study of CODECO, given the importance of different levels of participation, we interviewed participants who had made a content contribution, participants with a more peripheral participation, and focal members acting as promoters of the community to better explore participation in CODECO. By giving voice to all the community whatever their apparent level of involvement,

we were able to further understand participation but at the same time this situation also made us face new challenges. The fact that we had a list with all participants of CODECO facilitated the access to them. Unfortunately we could not get permission to access the community log in which 'not-posting behavior' could have been observed. This would have given us an even clearer picture of different levels of participation. Nevertheless, by foregrounding the importance of non-users, low participants, and community promoters the agenda arising from the literature review refocused our attention from the interactions within the bounded group.

Member's Participation as an Evolving Process

Studies that give a snapshot of the life of an online group are abundant in online community literature. Yet unlike longitudinal studies (Tiwana and Bush, 2005; Wang, 2007; Faraj et al., 2011; Wang et al., 2011), studies that view participation as a static one time event are not able to explain how participation changes over time (Faraj et al., 2011). Since a community's sustainability depends not only on how communities attract new members, but also on how they retain current members, a focus on participation as a dynamic process is required, one that considers previous history participation, current behaviors and future needs of participants. To tackle this issue some studies have been conducted in which participation is seen as a dynamic process rather than as a one-time event (Tiwana and Bush, 2005; Wang, 2007; Wang et al., 2011).

Wang's (2007) study of seven Usenet newsgroups focuses on how current participation and prior participation affect the decision to stay in a community. He found that a higher current level of participation reduces the intention of participants to leave the community, suggesting that the expected benefits from participation increase the likelihood of staying in the community. Furthermore he also found that an individual with much prior participation in the community will be less likely to abandon the community. His findings, he says, "call for a shift from the current focus on single, isolated contributions in an online community to long term, ongoing exchange relationships between the participants and the online communities" (Wang, 2007:124). In a similar attempt, Tiwana and Bush (2005) studied an expertise-sharing network and found that individual users' intention to continue participating in the network is influenced by 1) their own reputation among peer users built on investments of time and effort in the form of active participation and by 2) the individuals users' relational capital manifested in close and trusting relationships with other participants of the community. As a consequence they develop goodwill, trust, sense of identity, and a reputation among their peer users which, in turn, enhances the value that they derive from participating in the community (Tiwana and Bush, 2005).

While these studies provide new insights to understand participation as an evolving process, their focus is on the idea that people will continue participating in the online community because they have invested a lot of time, knowledge and effort (e.g. to develop new relationships). Instead what we argue is that participation must be seen as continuously enacted and shaped by previous investments of their members, but also by the existence of norms, routines, experiences and interactions patterns developed in the past.

In our particular case of CODECO, for instance, we looked at participation as an evolving process but not only focusing on how previous investments made by their members influenced their intentions to remain in their communities. Looking at participation as an evolving process also allowed us to see how the continuous enactment of previous patterns of interactions (and the usage of specific media to support these encoun-

ters) shaped participation at CODECO. Similarly, conceiving participation not as a static event but continuously evolving, gave us the opportunity to see, for instance, how previous experiences with the community (having experiences leading to failure in looking for specific information), influenced future behaviors towards CODECO. As such, when we become interested in studying how the past influences current behavior different research methods are required. A preference for longitudinal studies over cross-sectional studies becomes preferable; and direct observation or ethnography could be more helpful to see the potential existing norms of routines embracing the use of particular online communities.

The Effects of the External Environment on Online Communities

Having argued for the need for a more inclusive definition of participation, in this section we move on to present how studying the external environment in which online communities are located may improve our understanding of online community participation. Many studies have focused on the internal features of online communities in order to give an explanation of why communities fail or succeed but still we have a limited understanding on how the presence of other similar communities compete for members to survive (Butler, 2001; Gu et al., 2007; Wang, 2007; Wang et al., 2011)how competing media affect the adoption and participation in a new technology -such as an online community- (Nardi and Whittaker, 2002; Woerner et al., 2004; Watson-Manheim and Bélanger, 2007); how multi-memberships of participants may increase or decrease participation in certain communities (Bogenrieder and Baalen, 2007); and how the offline contexts in which participants live, and the working practices online communities support affect their behaviour in online communities (Baym, 2000; Cox, 2008).

Competition among Online Communities and Alternative Media and Multi-Memberships of Participants

Although many studies have neglected to consider the effects of competition between communities and its effects on their success or failure, we found some studies that have investigated how similar communities compete for members to survive (Gu et al., 2007; Wang, 2007; Wang et al., 2011), how the existence of alternative media within a context affects participation in online communities (Nardi and Whittaker, 2002; Woerner et al., 2004; Watson-Manheim and Bélanger, 2007) and what the effects are of online community members' multi-memberships (Bogenrieder and Baalen, 2007; Jeppesen and Laursen, 2009; Dahlander and Frederiksen, 2011).

Competition among online communities and its consequences on online community participation has been acknowledged in some recent studies. Wang (2007), for instance, studied 241 newsgroups focusing on the ecological context and the pressures that this context has on communities. In his study, it is suggested that communities' capability to attract and retain members is largely influenced by the presence of other communities with similar content or shared members. Thus, in order to retain members, he argued, online communities should select different features to reduce the effect of competition. As he states: "only by recognizing the impact of potential competing forces, and by understanding how to cope with competition via managing internal dynamics" can online communities remain viable (Wang, 2007:88). In a further study by Wang and his colleagues they propose a similar thesis showing that communities that share members with other groups reduced their future growth rates and thus suggesting that overlapping memberships put competitive pressures on online groups (Wang et al., 2011). Another study by Gu et al., (2007) focused on how virtual communities grow and compete with each other. The authors

noticed that in order to understand the dynamics of how online communities grow and compete with each other there is a need to understand how participants value their communities. They argued that peoples' decision to stay or move from a certain community depend on the difference between the value received by participants and the costs which they incur. Participants' value-perceptions of their communities increase with high-quality postings but at the same time, the costs of participating in the community increases with community size. As a result of these trade-offs between community size and information quality, they suggest, online communities should adopt different strategies to differentiate themselves from other communities to attract and retain members.

In a comparable way in which similar online communities compete for members to survive, when a collaborative technology is introduced to support specific practices its usage and adoption is often threatened by competing media that already existing within the organization. Although the use of multiple media in organizations is a common practice rather than the use of one medium isolated from others (see Nardi and Whittaker, 2002; Woerner et al., 2004; Watson-Manheim and Bélanger, 2007), we still have very little understanding of how this combination of media usage occurs and how the existence of competing media may shape participation in an online community. Just as similar online communities compete for members to survive when CODECO was introduced to support the project implementation its usage and adoption was in competition with participants' pre-existing communities, be they formalized, named communities or existing implicitly within pre-existing patterns of media use. In many interviews it became apparent that employees used email, instant messaging, phone communication, face-to-face meetings and video-conferences to support the enactment of different practices, and that the usage of this media was highly routinised sometimes giving users of CODECO a perception of lack of control over their decision to choose the media to communicate. By looking at how online communities compete for members' participation –in this specific case how the existence of different media affects participation in CODECO-, we moved away from studying an online community as if it existed as a bounded entity, in a vacuum, isolated from other media, to a different level in which external aspects in the environment of CODECO became salient.

Competition between online communities (or between online communities and other alternative media) only represents one of the external forces of the environment that affects their sustainability. Another critical factor closely related to competition, are the tensions (and benefits) created by the multi-memberships of individuals in different communities (Wenger, 1998). For instance, Bogenrieder and van Baalen (2007) approached this issue recognizing that multiple memberships can be problematic for participation in a online community. According to them, people participate in different communities simultaneously in order to satisfy different individual interests but they may face tension and conflict due to the different practices and identities developed in different groups. Before members decide to participate in a community, the authors noticed, members bear in mind the possible consequences this might have on their future work and career (Bogenrieder and Baalen, 2007). They concluded that considering a community as an isolated entity may lead to wrong explanations based on the individual (i.e. motivation) or communal level (i.e. trust, psychological safety), that ignore the interrelationships presented within the communities and their context in which they are embedded. Other studies, however, have found that members who participate across several online communities (e.g. conducting boundary-spanning) are more prone to like sharing knowledge in their online communities (Jeppesen and Laursen, 2009). Similarly, Dahlander and Frederiksen (2011) found that participants being a 'cosmopolitan' who span multiple communities are in a better position to contribute with innovative ideas to their communities than those being 'too core' in a community.

When studying participation at CODECO, we found that when CODECO was introduced as a collaborative technology to support the project implementation its usage was threatened by competing media already existing within the organisation. Moreover of all existing media, face-to-face interactions, email, phone, the organisational intranet and instant messaging were reported to be the most common media used, and were found to be highly embedded in routinised within employees' day-to-day activities. Furthermore, these media were repeatedly used by participants to maintain their relationships developed in the past with members of other working communities. By acknowledging the influence of existing media and other factors affecting participation (e.g. multi-memberships) a need of broader questions is present; questions that go beyond the scope of a particular community and instead aim at understanding the overall context to which a particular community is embedded.

Social Context and Working Practices in which Online Communities Reside

Examining participation through studying only the activity of the online community would lead to overly simplistic understandings (Baym, 2000). The offline contexts and the practices taking place in that context are also important to explain participation in online communities (Wenger, 1998; Cox, 2007; Cox, 2008). Baym (2000) studied an online community devoted to soap operas arguing that one of the most important influences on online communities is the offline context in which participants live (Baym, 2000). She suggested that the medium used to communicate is not the only force that influences interaction in online communities, but also the topic, the purposes, the participants, the individuals and the offline contexts.

Cox (2007, 2008) studied a community of web production professionals in UK higher education and he found that participants in this community have overlapping but different membership and agendas, as a result of these, different factors of their environment such as the practitioners' local roles, positions and responsibilities, their orientation towards marketing or IT, the type of university which they belong to, the availability of resources they have and their identity to their profession, participants have different levels of participation on the online community.

Baym 2000 drew on an understanding of practice theory. More recently, other studies adopting a Practice-based approach have been providing interesting insights that seem to offer a new perspective to understand participation in online communities and use of technologies in general (Schultze and Boland, 2000; Schultze and Orlikowski, 2004; Vaast and Walsham, 2005; Orlikowski, 2007; Vaast, 2007; Feldman and Orlikowski, 2011). In general terms these studies used practice-based theories to explain participation (or adoption) of online communities under the assumption that practices in which online communities are established have a powerful influencing character on how these communities are used. These studies paid special attention, for example to how participation in online communities is a situated, collective, and historically shaped activity moulded by the different elements of the organization of the practices taking place.

In the particular case of CODECO, apart from looking at how different media compete for members' participation and how participants are involved in multiple and sometimes conflicting practices, we looked at other aspects of the real world context in which CODECO was introduced. These are further discuss in the last section of this chaper.

CONCLUSION

By extending the concept of participation and therefore looking at it as an evolving process and as a more inclusive concept which considers both active contributors, audience members and community citizenship behaviors; and by exploring different forces in the environment such the existence of alternative media to communicate and how these media create competition for members' participation; the multiple social practices online communities support; the participants' backgrounds and their attitude towards the use of IT's; and the existing social relationships and the social networks people bring to the online community, we show how our understanding of online community participation can be deepened. In turn, in this last section we discuss a bit further the case of CODECO and argue that adopting a Practice-based approach (Baym, 2000; Orlikowski, 2002; Reckwitz, 2002; Schatzki, 2005; Vaast and Walsham, 2005; Schatzki, 2006; Gherardi, 2009; Corradi et al., 2010; Feldman and Orlikowski, 2011) can be a potential approach with enough power to explain relevant issues neglected in previous studies. Four considerations are briefly tackled showing how practice theories provide useful insights to better understand participation. While this study was conducted within the corporate context we believe these concerns should also bear in mind when studying online communities in different contexts.

First, practice theories highlight the interconnectedness between practices and their elements. To understand participation at CODECO, we did not look at CODECO as an isolated element from the HR practices in which the community is embedded, but rather as being interrelated with other components of such practices (people having multiple memberships, existence of other technologies, etc.). In the same way in which these elements are interrelated, so are HR practices with

Table 1. Neglected topics and methodological implications

Neglected topic in previous literature	Examples	How practice theories deal with these issues	Methodological implications
Participation	• Reductive model of cost-benefit participation • Participation focusing on contributing behaviors only • Reductionist view of participation seeing as a static one-time event • Participation overlooking multi-memberships of potential participants	• Participation in a practice embraces doing and sayings, ways of feeling, thinking, communicating, etc. Motivation is only an aspect to consider. Previous history of membership, preferences, sensations, are also relevant. • Practices are enacted by a group of different practitioners, some of them having peripheral positions while others being considered as core to the practices (having the power, for example to introduce and promote the use of a new tool, i.e. CODECO) • Participation is seen as a evolving process, continuously produced and reproduced, and being shaped by existing structures (e.g.norms) • Practitioners of a set of practices belong to different communities, and their positions, relations, types of memberships, etc., will affect their membership (and behaviors such as willingness to use an online community) in a focal community	• There is a need to move from understanding individuals' motivations to understand participation as a social and collective process. • Giving voice to all relevant practitioners of a practice is a requirement to understand how practices are organized and how they are produced and reproduced. • Longitudinal studies are desirable to understand past events and previous enactment of practices, and to see how participation evolves over time. • Understanding the relations, connections and shared understandings supporting specific practices demand new methods that go beyond observing and measuring contributing behaviors.
Social environment and practices in which online communities reside	• Online communities are seen as isolated entities • Competition among communities tend to be ignored • Existence of alternative media is disregarded • Practices in which online communities reside are taken for granted	• Practices, and therefore their elements (e.g. people, technologies) coexist within a context (e.g. social site) and interact with other practices; in turn this context and other practices have powers of determination towards what occurs (exists) within their boundaries. • Practices are composed by a set of different entities which are interrelated to each other and acquire their meanings only when they are looked through the relations they sustain with other elements of practices • Every social practice has a specific flavour/ taste. This feature of practices guides and informs the right ways of doing things (i.e. to community using the online community or otherwise)	• A need for broader questions is required. These questions must explore beyond the boundaries of a specific community, and aim at understanding more than their members' behaviors in a particular community. • Practices, people, technologies are interrelated to each other and thus attention also must be given to how other elements of a practice shape participation in a specific community.

other practices. Thus in order to understand the use of CODECO we also acknowledged a need to understand not only the interconnections it holds with other elements of HR practices, but also the interdependences among other practices and HR practices.

Second, practices are the place where CODECO was introduced and they are repeatedly enacted so as that continuous repetition some elements are routinised. We looked at practices in which CODECO was introduced as consisting of a bundle of actions repeatedly performed so as that a routine ingredient is presented. As HR practices were repeatedly enacted by their practitioners, a series of habits, shared understandings, relationships, not reflective actions, were developed. This latent feature of routinization not only can affect the way HR practices are performed, but also, and of more relevance to this chapter, the way how and through what media (including CODECO) HR practices are supported.

Third, when people enact specific practices they tend to develop a set of shared knowing(s) through which they carry out their work competently. These shared knowing(s) (in addition to the specific skills and knowledge required to perform HR practices such as hiring, training, payroll, etc.) were performed in a collective and routinised way, and were reflected in HR practitioners' daily actions. Whether or not these shared knowing(s) were supported by CODECO was critical for its adoption.

And fourth, HR practices, like all practices of social life, have a specific flavour that characterizes them. This flavour was reflected in the actions that practitioners carry out routinely. If new elements (i.e. activities, actions, artefacts -e.g. CODECO), are to be institutionalized or adopted, they most probably be so if they 'fit' the flavour of the practices in which they are introduced. Thus, the ability of CODECO to 'fit' the flavour of HR practices was also crucial for its adoption. The following table shows how in adopting a practice-based approach previous neglected issues are brought to the fore of our analysis. Some methodological implications are also highlighted.

In adopting a practice-based approach, new avenues to explore online community participation emerge, while at the same time this approach also demands more complex methods for data collection. This approach should point researchers away from just observing communication activity inside online communities, as if they were neatly self contained entities, and point to the need to reach a wider range of participants (e.g. low and potential participants) and ask much broader questions about the context within which the community exists. The concept of online community is dynamic and complex, and thus the attempts to explain and understand them cannot be simplistic. Practice theories seem to offer theoretical tools that can be helpful to study participation and its complex dynamics.

REFERENCES

Ardichvili, A. (2008). Learning and knowledge sharing in virtual communities of practice: Motivators, barriers, and enablers. *Advances in Developing Human Resources*, *10*(4), 541–554. doi:10.1177/1523422308319536

Ardichvili, A., Maurer, M., Li, W., Wentling, T., & Stuedemann, R. (2006). Cultural influences on knowledge sharing through online communities of practice. *Journal of Knowledge Management*, *10*(1), 94–107. doi:10.1108/13673270610650139

Ardichvili, A., Page, V., & Wentling, T. (2002). Virtual knowledge-sharing communities of practice at Caterpillar: Success factors and barriers. *Performance Improvement Quarterly*, *15*(3), 94–113. doi:10.1111/j.1937-8327.2002.tb00258.x

Ardichvili, A., Page, V., & Wentling, T. (2003). Motivation and barriers to participation in virtual knowledge-sharing communities of practice. *Journal of Knowledge Management*, *7*(1), 64–77. doi:10.1108/13673270310463626

Bateman, P. J. (2008). *Online community referrals and commitment: How two aspects of community life impact member participation*. PhD Dissertation, University of Pittsburgh.

Bateman, P. J., Gray, P. H., & Butler, B. S. (2006). Community commitment: How affect, obligation, and necessity drive online behaviours. *Twenty-Seventh International Conference on Information Systems*, 2006, Milwaukee (pp. 983-1000). Milwaukee.

Baym, N. K. (2000). *Tune in, log on: Soaps, fandom, and online community*. Thousand Oaks, CA: Sage Publications.

Bjorkeng, K., Clegg, S., & Pitsis, T. (2009). Becoming (a) practice. *Management Learning*, *40*(2), 145–159. doi:10.1177/1350507608101226

Bogenrieder, I., & Baalen, P. (2007). Contested practice: Multiple inclusion in double-knit organizations. *Journal of Organizational Change Management, 20*(4), 579–595. doi:10.1108/09534810710760090

Bruce, B. C., Parliament, F., Kimmo, E. M., Studies, I., Reijo, E. M., & Sanna, E. M. (2005). Information literacy as a sociotechnical practice 1 Kimmo Tuominen, 2 Reijo Savolainen, 3 and Sanna Talja 4. *Most, 75*(3), 329–345.

Butler, B., Sproull, L., Kiesler, S., & Kraut, R. (2007). Community effort in online groups: Who does the work and why? In Weisband, S. P. (Ed.), *Leadership at a distance: Research in technologically-supported work*.

Butler, B. S. (2001). Membership size, communication activity, and sustainability: A resource-based model of online social structures. *Information Systems Research, 12*(4), 346–362. doi:10.1287/isre.12.4.346.9703

Campbell, J. A. (2001). Internet finance forums: Investor empowerment through CMC or market manipulation on a global scale? *Proceedings of AMCIS, 2001*, 2161–2163.

Chiu, C., Hsu, M., & Wang, E. (2006). Understanding knowledge sharing in virtual communities: An integration of social capital and social cognitive theories. *Decision Support Systems, 42*(3), 1872–1888. doi:10.1016/j.dss.2006.04.001

Corradi, G., Gherardi, S., & Verzelloni, L. (2010). Through the practice lens: Where is the bandwagon of practice-based studies heading? *Management Learning, 41*(3), 265–283. doi:10.1177/1350507609356938

Cox, A. M. (2007). Beyond information–factors in participation in networks of practice. *The Journal of Documentation, 63*(5), 765–787. doi:10.1108/00220410710827790

Cox, A. M. (2008). An exploration of concepts of community through a case study of UK university web production. *Journal of Information Science, 34*(3), 327–345. doi:10.1177/0165551507084354

Cummings, J. N., Sproull, L., & Kiesler, S. B. (2002). Beyond hearing: Where real world and online support meet. *Group Dynamics, 6*(1), 78–88. doi:10.1037/1089-2699.6.1.78

Dahlander, L., & Frederiksen, L. (2011). The core and cosmopolitans: A relational view of innovation in user communities. *Organization Science, 2011*, 1–20.

Dholakia, U. M., Bagozzi, R. P., & Pearo, L. K. (2004). A social influence model of consumer participation in network-and small-group-based virtual communities. *International Journal of Research in Marketing, 21*(3), 241–263. doi:10.1016/j.ijresmar.2003.12.004

Dyer, J. H., & Nobeoka, K. (2000). Creating and managing a high-performance knowledge-sharing network: The Toyota case. *Strategic Management Journal, 21*(3), 345–367. doi:10.1002/(SICI)1097-0266(200003)21:3<345::AID-SMJ96>3.0.CO;2-N

Ellis, D., Oldridge, R., & Vasconcelos, A. (2004). Community and virtual community. *Annual Review of Information Science & Technology, 38*(1), 145–186. doi:10.1002/aris.1440380104

Faraj, S., Jarvenpaa, S. L., & Majchrzak, A. (2011). Knowledge collaboration in online communities. *Organization Science, 22*(5), 1224–1239. doi:10.1287/orsc.1100.0614

Feldman, M. S., & Orlikowski, W. J. (2011). Theorizing practice and practicing theory. *Organization Science, 22*(5), 1240–1253. doi:10.1287/orsc.1100.0612

Gherardi, S. (2009). Practice? It's a matter of taste! *Management Learning, 40*(5), 535–550. doi:10.1177/1350507609340812

Gongla, P., & Rizzuto, C. R. (2001). Evolving communities of practice: IBM Global. *IBM Systems Journal, 40*(4), 842–862. doi:10.1147/sj.404.0842

Gu, B., Konana, P., Rajagopalan, B., & Chen, H. W. M. (2007). Competition among virtual communities and user valuation: The case of investing-related communities. *Information Systems Research, 18*(1), 68. doi:10.1287/isre.1070.0114

Hansen, D. L. (2007). *Knowledge sharing, maintenance, and use in online support communities*. PhD Dissertation, University of Michigan.

Hrastinski, S. (2008). What is online learner participation? A literature review. *Computers & Education, 51*(4), 1755–1765. doi:10.1016/j.compedu.2008.05.005

Hrastinski, S. (2009). A theory of online learning as online participation. *Computers & Education, 52*(1), 78–82. doi:10.1016/j.compedu.2008.06.009

Hsu, M. H., Ju, T. L., Yen, C. H., & Chang, C. M. (2007). Knowledge sharing behavior in virtual communities: The relationship between trust, self-efficacy, and outcome expectations. *International Journal of Human-Computer Studies, 65*(2), 153–169. doi:10.1016/j.ijhcs.2006.09.003

Jeppesen, L. B., & Frederiksen, L. (2006). Why do users contribute to firm-hosted user communities? The case of computer-controlled music instruments. *Organization Science, 17*(1), 45–63. doi:10.1287/orsc.1050.0156

Jeppesen, L. B., & Laursen, K. (2009). The role of lead users in knowledge sharing. *Research Policy, 38*(10), 1582–1589. doi:10.1016/j.respol.2009.09.002

Johnson, S. L. (2010). Should I stay or should I go? Continued participation intentions in online communities. *Proceedings of Academy of Management Annual Conference*, 2010, (pp. 1-6).

Kankanhalli, A., Tan, B. C. Y., & Wei, K. K. (2005). Contributing knowledge to electronic knowledge repositories: An empirical investigation. *Management Information Systems Quarterly, 29*(1), 113–143.

Komito, L. (1998). The Net as a foraging society: Flexible communities. *The Information Society, 14*(2), 97–106. doi:10.1080/019722498128908

Lakhani, K. R., & von Hippel, E. (2003). How open source software works: Free user-to-user assistance. *Research Policy, 32*(6), 923–943. doi:10.1016/S0048-7333(02)00095-1

Lave, J., & Wenger, E. (1991). *Situated learning: Legitimate peripheral participation*. Cambridge, UK: Cambridge University Press.

Lee, F. S. L., Vogel, D., & Limayem, M. (2002). Virtual community informatics: What we know and what we need to know. *35th Hawaii International Conference on System Sciences* (pp. 2863–2872).

Lee, G. K., & Cole, R. (2003). From a firm-based to a community-based model of knowledge creation: The case of the Linux kernel development. *Organization Science, 14*(6), 633–649. doi:10.1287/orsc.14.6.633.24866

Lerner, J., & Tirole, J. (2002). Some simple economics of open source. *The Journal of Industrial Economics, 50*(2), 197–234. doi:10.1111/1467-6451.00174

Mahar, G. (2007). *Factors affecting participation in online communities of practice*. PhD Dissertation, Nardi, B. A., & Whittaker, S. (2002). The place of face-to-face communication in distributed work. In P. Hinds & Kiesler, S. (Eds.), *Distributed work: New research on working across distance using technology*, (pp. 83-110). Cambridge, MA: MIT Press.

Nonnecke, B., Andrews, D., Preece, J., & Voutour, R. (2004a). *Online lurkers tell why* (pp. 2688–2694).

Nonnecke, B., & Preece, J. (1999). *Shedding light on lurkers in online communities* (pp. 123-128). Nonnecke, B., & Preece, J. (2000). *Lurker demographics: Counting the silent.* ACM SIGCHI CHI 2000 Conference on Human Factors in Computing Systems, The Hague.

Nonnecke, B., & Preece, J. (2001). *Why lurkers lurk.* Americas Confenrence on Information Systems 2001 Boston.

Nonnecke, B., & Preece, J. (2003). Silent participants: Getting to know lurkers better. *From Usenet to CoWebs: Interacting with Social Information Spaces,* (pp. 110-132).

Nonnecke, B., Preece, J., & Andrews, D. (2004b). What lurkers and posters think of each other. *Proceedings of the 37th Hawaii International Conference on System Sciences - 2004,* (pp. 1-9).

Orlikowski, W. J. (2002). Knowing in practice: Enacting a collective capability in distributed organizing. *Organization, 13*(3), 249–273. doi:10.1287/orsc.13.3.249.2776

Orlikowski, W. J. (2007). Sociomaterial practices: Exploring technology at work. *Organization Studies, 28*(9), 1435–1448. doi:10.1177/0170840607081138

Porter, C. E. (2004). A typology of virtual communities: A multi-disciplinary foundation for future research. *Journal of Computer-Mediated Communication, 10*(1), 00–00.

Porter, C. E., & Donthu, N. (2008). Cultivating trust and harvesting value in virtual communities. *Management Science, 54*(1), 113–128. doi:10.1287/mnsc.1070.0765

Preece, J., Nonnecke, B., & Andrews, D. (2004). The top five reasons for lurking: Improving community experiences for everyone. *Computers in Human Behavior, 20*(2), 201–223. doi:10.1016/j.chb.2003.10.015

Reckwitz, a. (2002). Toward a theory of social practices: A development in culturalist theorizing. *European Journal of Social Theory, 5*(2), 243-263.

Rheingold, H. (1993). *The virtual community: Homesteading on the electronic frontier.* Addison-Wesley Pub. Co.

Ridings, C. M., Gefen, D., & Arinze, B. (2002). Some antecedents and effects of trust in virtual communities. *The Journal of Strategic Information Systems, 11*(3-4), 271–295. doi:10.1016/S0963-8687(02)00021-5

Schatzki, T. R. (2005). Peripheral vision: The sites of organizations. *Organization Studies, 26*(3), 465–484. doi:10.1177/0170840605050876

Schatzki, T. R. (2006). On organizations as they happen. *Organization Studies, 27*(12), 1863–1873. doi:10.1177/0170840606071942

Schultze, U., & Boland, R. J. (2000). Knowledge management technology and the reproduction of knowledge work practices. *The Journal of Strategic Information Systems, 9,* 193–212. doi:10.1016/S0963-8687(00)00043-3

Schultze, U., & Orlikowski, W. J. (2004). A practice perspective on technology-mediated network relations: The use of internet-based self-serve technologies. *Information Systems Research, 15*(1), 87–106. doi:10.1287/isre.1030.0016

Stoddart, L. (2007). Organizational culture and knowledge sharing at the United Nations: Using an intranet to create a sense of community. *Knowledge and Process Management, 14*(3), 182–189. doi:10.1002/kpm.283

Tiwana, A., & Bush, A. A. (2005). Continuance in expertise-sharing networks: A social perspective. *IEEE Transactions on Engineering Management, 52*(1), 85–101. doi:10.1109/TEM.2004.839956

Torrey, C., Burke, M., Lee, M., Dey, A., Fussell, S., & Kiesler, S. (2007). *Connected giving: Ordinary people coordinating disaster relief on the Internet. HICSS 07* (*Vol. 40*, p. 2956). IEEE.

Turner, J. W., Grube, J. A., & Meyers, J. (2001). Developing an optimal match within online communities: An exploration of CMC support communities and traditional support. *The Journal of Communication, 51*(2), 231–251. doi:10.1111/j.1460-2466.2001.tb02879.x

Vaast, E. (2007). What goes online comes offline: Knowledge management system use in a soft bureaucracy. *Organization Studies, 28*(3), 283–306. doi:10.1177/0170840607075997

Vaast, E., & Walsham, G. (2005). Representations and actions: The transformation of work practices with IT use. *Information and Organization, 15*(1), 65–89. doi:10.1016/j.infoandorg.2004.10.001

Wang, X. (2007). *An ecological perspective on online communities*. Ph.D. Dissertation, University of Pittsburgh.

Wang, X., Butler, B., & Ren, Y. (2011). *The impact of membership overlap on growth: An ecological competition view of online groups* (pp. 1-36).

Wasko, M., & Faraj, S. (2000). It is what one does: why people participate and help others in electronic communities of practice. *The Journal of Strategic Information Systems, 9*(2-3), 155–173. doi:10.1016/S0963-8687(00)00045-7

Wasko, M., & Faraj, S. (2005). Why should I share? Examining social capital and knowledge contribution in electronic networks of practice. *Management Information Systems Quarterly, 29*(1), 35–57.

Wasko, M. M., Faraj, S., & Teigland, R. (2004). Collective action and knowledge contribution in electronic networks of practice. *Journal of the Association for Information Systems, 5*(11-12), 493–513.

Watson-Manheim, M. B., & Bélanger, F. (2007). Communication media repertoires: Dealing with the multiplicity of media choices. *Management Information Systems Quarterly, 31*(2), 267–293.

Wenger, E. (1998). *Communities of practice: Learning, meaning, and identity*. Cambridge, UK: Cambridge University Press.

Woerner, S. L., Orlikowski, W. J., & Yates, J. (2004). The media toolbox: Combining media in organizational communication. *Proceedings of the Academy of Management,* Orlando FL.

Zhang, W., & Watts, S. (2008). Online communities as communities of practice: A case study. *Journal of Knowledge Management, 12*(4), 55–71. doi:10.1108/13673270810884255

Zhou, T. (2011). Understanding online community user participation: A social influence perspective. *Internet Research, 21*(1), 67–81. doi:10.1108/10662241111104884

KEY TERMS AND DEFINITIONS

Competition between Online Communities: When communities with similar interests share members and "compete" for their participation.

External Environment of Online Communities: Environment surrounding an online community such as the existence of other communities (including both, online and offline communities); the organizational context in which communities are established; the existence of alternative media used to communicate.

Multi-Memberships of Participants: Different memberships developed by participants as a consequence of their participation in multiple communities/practices.

Participation in Online Communities: Contributions of time, knowledge and other resources made by the participants for an online community to give "live" to it. This definition includes different types/levels of participation.

Types of Participation: Different people may participate in different ways in their online communities. Participants could be motivated by self-interests or community-interests. Also, members of a community can participate by having contribution behaviours, audience behaviors, and community-citizenship behaviours.

Chapter 6
Toward an Understanding of Online Community Participation through Narrative Network Analysis

Michael R. Weeks
The University of Tampa, USA

ABSTRACT

This chapter proposes the narrative network analysis methodology for application in the examination of online communities. The narrative network analysis provides a basis for systematic examination of online communities that has been missing from the literature. The chapter describes three online communities and their characteristics to demonstrate the possibilities of the methodology. From these descriptions a proposed model of the communities is presented, and then an abbreviated narrative network analysis is developed. The network analysis demonstrates how an ethnographically informed model may be tested in a systematic manner with the narrative network analysis techniques. The chapter then concludes with a number of questions for future research in this area that have been proposed by other authors. These unanswered questions are likely candidates for future research using this promising methodology.

INTRODUCTION

Online communities are not a particularly new phenomenon in our rapidly changing technological landscape. Studies of the effectiveness of predecessors to the current communities precede the widespread acceptance of the world-wide web by over 20 years (Timm, 1976). Nevertheless, the ubiquitous adoption of graphical user interfaces in the early 1990s and the acceptance of the internet and world-wide web for mainstream communications in the mid-1990s created online communities of unprecedented significance (Horrigan, Rainie, & Fox, 2001).

DOI: 10.4018/978-1-4666-0312-7.ch006

Today's online communities are often comprised of thousands of members with multi-dimensional online identities, rich communication media, and complex social norms. These communities developed over time through the dynamic interaction of the members and evolved along distinct paths that influenced the subsequent interactions of the community, despite the constant ebb and flow of the membership (Rheingold, 1993). Just as traditional organizations seek to adapt to the community in which they operate, contemporary organizations will need to adapt to the dynamics of these new online communities through outreach, participation, and development. Despite these needs, online communities are difficult to study and the field is still emerging. Initial work was largely based on anecdotal evidence (e.g. Wellman & Gulia, 1999) and some authors have noted the slow development of empirical research (Kim, Choi, Qualls, & Han, 2008). More recent works in the field have adopted a variety of methodologies to explore the dynamics of online communities. These include surveys (Byoungho, Park, & Kim, 2010; Hung, Yiyan Li, & Tse, 2011; Yen, Hsu, & Chun-Yao, 2011), interpretive qualitative analyses (Jayanti & Singh, 2010), mixed methods (Benlian & Hess, 2011), and netnography (Kozinets, 2002, 2006)

The aim of this paper is to present a relatively new research methodology, narrative network analysis, which may help researchers better online communities more fully. Although the concept of narrative networks was developed several years ago by Pentland and Feldman (2007) and has wide applicability, the method has been not been utilized extensively. In fact, only one published article applying the techniques outlined by Pentland and Feldman can be found currently (Yeow & Faraj, 2011). Ultimately, the goal of this paper is to present an example of the application of the methodology to the study of online communities and thus extend research in this area that allows modern organizations to leverage the social and economic potential of these dynamic virtual networks.

THE EMERGENCE OF ONLINE COMMUNITIES

Online communities have developed over the past decade as an emergent internet phenomenon, largely created by the user community through incremental development processes (Baym, 1998; Rheingold, 1993). These groups are not randomly assigned the nomenclature of community without cause. As mentioned earlier, these online forums operate as virtual communities with many of the same characteristics of a traditional community such as moral voice, rights, responsibilities, and a public interest (Etzioni, 1993). Technological, sociological and economic forces have contributed to the emergence of online communities in the last decade.

The technological forces that contributed to this online phenomenon revolve around the development of the internet and World Wide Web and the adoption of graphical user interfaces. Early online communities adopted the simple text-based user interfaces of the time due to the limited bandwidth and processing capabilities of existing information communications technologies (ICTs) (Timm, 1976). The introduction of the Netscape Navigator internet browser in the mid-1990s and the penetration of broadband communication channels into the market in the late 1990s allowed more complex communities to develop. The communities became very specialized and the social identities of the members were quite well developed (Koh, Kim, Butler, & Bock, 2007).

These multifaceted communities emerged partly because ICT developments enabled a richness of communication not available in early e-mail groups and bulletin boards. Scholars were well-acquainted with the concept of media richness during this period, but did not quite anticipate the consequences of these emergent technologies. Daft and colleagues proposed a static classification scheme of media richness which consisted of face-to-face communication at the top, followed by telephone communication, personal documents, impersonal documents, and numeric documents (Daft & Lengel, 1986; Daft, Lengel, & Trevino, 1987). They concluded that communication channels with more direct human interaction provided increased richness for the sender and receiver of a message, thereby decreasing both uncertainty and equivocality in communication.

Early work on media richness theory preceded many of the current communication technologies and most subsequent research inserted electronic communications into the existing framework as equivalent to either personal or impersonal documents (Timmerman & Harrison, 2005). Nevertheless, some work proposed that richness could be improved by using multiple types of communications channels (Shepherd & Martz, 2001). The mainstream work in the area did not seem to anticipate that users would find ways to improve richness in existing media. For example, users quickly adopted emoticons (e.g.:), the well-known "smiley" face) to improve the richness of ICT environments. The dynamic creativity of the user environment coupled with improved bandwidth, which enabled pictures, video, and sound to be embedded in the media, dramatically improved the richness of the online communities.

Beyond technological development, a second set of sociological factors has also contributed to the emergence of contemporary online communities. Increased mobility of the workforce, longer work hours for many professionals, and globalization have resulted in a search for a sense of community beyond traditional geographic boundaries (Horrigan, et al., 2001; Putnam, 1995). Moreover, other sociological forces seem to be fostering this trend toward online communities. While two prominent sociologists, Etzioni and Maffesoli, predict differing results from trends in modern society, the search for community is a consistent theme for overcoming the travails of the modern world in their work. Etzioni is concerned that excessive individualism in modern society will have a detrimental effect on modern social institutions and values (Etzioni, 1993).

Conversely, Maffesoli predicts that a mass market society will result in a decline in individualism and therefore, modern tribes will be required to restore a sense of community (Maffesoli, 1996). Despite their differences, both authors argue that a sense of community is a prerequisite for a successful global society and emergent online communities seem to be fulfilling part of that need for many displaced and disenfranchised members of society, as well as those seeking a wider social network.

A final factor contributing to the growth of online communities is economic. Online communities are now big business for many sites and their owners. The sites discussed in this paper are communities focusing on photography and this research observed four business models for these organizations. The first types of sites are supported by advertising such as DigitalPhotographyReview.com (DP Review). The second model is a paid subscription model which requires users to pay a fee to participate in the forums. Next is a voluntary subscription model which asks users to contribute, but doesn't restrict access to those that do not subscribe. Finally, some sites also operate on a hybrid model with some parts of the site free, while other parts of the site require payment of a fee. None of the sites examined for this research are publicly traded, so definitive financial data is difficult to unearth. Nevertheless, some sense of the scale of the economic potential of these sites can be seen in the fact that DP Review has over 7 million unique visitors each month and was recently purchased by Amazon.com for an undisclosed sum (Anonymous, 2007; McCarthy, 2007)

THE CONCEPT OF NARRATIVE NETWORKS

The idea of narrative networks was developed by Pentland and Feldman as a framework to represent "patterns of technology in use." (Pentland & Feldman, 2007) Their work is based on prior work in structuration theory, actor-network theory, and organizational routines (Feldman & Pentland, 2003; Giddens, 1984; Latour, 2005; Law & Hassard, 1999; Pentland & Feldman, 2005). The narrative network is composed of three primary elements: the actants and their actions; the narrative fragments; and the narrative itself. A narrative network analysis then arranges these elements in a visual representation which provides a basis for analysis of the underlying themes and trends.

Given the linkages to actor-network theory in the framework, the concept of actant deserves more discussion. In addition to humans, actants in a narrative network can be any item or artifact that contributes to the social construction of the network (Faraj, Kwon, & Watts, 2004; Johnson, 1988). For example, discussion forum software, computer hardware, or networking equipment might all be actants at a given node of a narrative network.

Pentland and Feldman (2007) choose a simple example to illustrate the narrative analysis technique in their groundbreaking work. Their analysis uses the purchase of an airline ticket to develop the narrative network framework. This narrative network has a limited (but still substantial) number of actants and potential actions; yet, the task of buying an airline ticket is sufficiently constrained so that the resulting narrative network is manageable for exposition. Nevertheless, the resulting network provides a rich basis for analysis and illuminates a number of sociological and organizational issues that are present even in commonplace electronic transactions.

While the initial demonstration of the narrative network is necessarily constrained, this research begins to expand the network under study to more fully explore the explanatory potential of the device. For example, what if the actors in the network were expanded to include an audience? How would that factor affect the narrative? What if the audience could participate in the narrative? The observers could heckle or cheer the primary narrators and interject their own agenda into the narrative and take the plot in a completely new direction. How might the structure of the online forum affect the participation of the members? All of these developments are possible within a typical online community and must be considered in a narrative analysis of the entity.

THE NARRATIVE NETWORK METHODOLOGY IN USE

In order to construct a narrative network, Pentland and Feldman (2007) outline a number of steps that must be undertaken. The first is that we must choose a focal point and define its boundary. Second, one must choose a point of view for the analysis. Next, the narratives must be collected and the fragments coded. Finally, once the fragments are coded the researcher must relate the various nodes by sequence. Left unstated by Pentland and Feldman is the understanding that the researcher must then create a subsequent narrative to interpret the resulting narrative network. This work expands the concept of a narrative network to a community with multiple actants (both seen and unseen) as well as an environment with more nuanced social norms than a typical electronic commerce transaction.

Traditional narrative approaches have consisted of largely four types according to Czarniawska: "organizational research that is written in a story-like fashion; organizational research that collects organizational stories; organizational research that conceptualizes organizational life as story making and organization theory as story reading (interpretive approaches); and a disciplinary reflection that takes the form of a literary critique." (Czarniawska, 1998) The narrative network is a variation on the technique which conceptualizes organizational life as story making and organization theory as story reading. In some ways the network narrative variation changes the very nature of our understanding of organization. Rather than being in geographic proximity, the actors are in a virtual or symbolic proximity (Maffesoli, 1996). This changes ones focus from the traditional organization to more of a network focus, or a Czarniawska refers to the form, an "action net." (Czarniawska, 2004) By taking this approach, the study is released from geographic and temporal constraints.

At this point it is important to make a distinction in the terminology in use. The narrative fragments are the individual data that are used to construct the narrative network. The narrative network is a device or product which is produced *ex post* in relation to the events of the community. Finally, a concluding narrative is constructed from the narrative network which provides illumination of the phenomena under study. Each portion of the process builds on its predecessor to develop the final narrative for consumption and ultimate interpretation.

DISCUSSION FORUMS AND ONLINE COMMUNITIES

Online communities frequently operate in the world of discussion forums although some new types of communities have emerged recently such as Second Life (http://secondlife.com/). Typically members join a discussion forum through a registration process and then interact with the other members of the community through written discussion. The guidelines for the site outline the purpose for the community as well as acceptable topics for discussion. For example, some of the first communities were formed around specific heath issues. Sites dedicated to a particular disease or medical condition allowed users to swap information and seek comfort from others with the same predicament (Preece, 2000). Many sites have a forum within the community for off-topic discussions as well. Both on and off topic discussions provide narrative fragments that can be examined through the narrative network framework.

Photography Communities

Despite the proliferation of discussion forums, not all forums provide an optimum soil for the growth of a true community. Software design and membership policies result in very different user experiences for these sites. The number of members that participate in a forum also has a bearing on the richness of the community. Finally, the level of commitment of the users to the community also has an impact on the success of the operation.

This paper uses communities organized for photography as the research field. This selection is made primarily due to my familiarity with the communities and long-time participation in these forums. I have participated in all of the forums discussed here for a minimum of four years. Given the large amount of information contained in the archives of the forums, a multi-year experience with the forum provides a significant advantage when analyzing the interactions present on a daily basis. Although I have chosen photography communities for this research, my additional experience with other forums leads me to the conclusion that many forums share a number of common characteristics and the photography communities provide a reasonable representation of the discussion forum genre. This may partially be due to the limited number of software platforms available to run large communities as well as the cross-pollination by users (like me) that participate in a number of communities on a variety of topics.

To give a sense of the range of communities available even within the photography subject area I will describe three typical communities: Digital Photography Review, Nikonians, and I Love Photography (ILP). DPReview is a community based on the evaluation of equipment. Nikonians is a brand community (Prykop & Heitman, 2006) and ILP is a community dedicated to a particular type of photography (child portraiture).

Digital Photography Review (DPR)

Digital Photography Review (DPReview.com) is a site that evaluates photography equipment from all manufacturers. The site publishes its reviews online and is a widely read resource for many consumers. The site was founded by Phil Askey in December 1998 and is read by over 7 million unique visitors each month. The site also hosts forums that generate over 300,000 posts per month. In less than 10 years, the DPR forums have generated over 21 million messages from over 550,000 unique visitors (source: dpreview. com). Although DPR does not publish statistics about the users by gender, observation of the forums shows that the members of DPR forums are male by a large majority. The site was acquired by Amazon.com in 2007 for an undisclosed sum (Anonymous, 2007).

I Love Photography (ILP)

ILP (ILovePhotography.com) describes itself as a "site dedicated to the child portrait photographer." The site was started in 2003 by Eddie Bonfigli, a professional photographer and has over 23,000 members. The members have posted over 3 million messages on the board during the 5-year history of the site. Of those that identify their gender, the site's membership is approximately 90% female (source: ilovephotography.com). Many of the site's members are mothers that began photography businesses after they had children and developed an interest in photographing their offspring. This phenomenon has become so widespread that it was described in an article in the *New York Times* (Fairfield, 2007) and one of the ILP members was profiled in the story.

Nikonians

Nikonians (Nikonians.org) is a site that is dedicated to all things Nikon, the second leading manufacturer of film and digital cameras globally (Wakao,

2007). The site was started in 2000 by J. Ramon Palacios and Bo Stahlbrandt, two dedicated Nikon photographers. The site had over 40,000 unique visitors per day by early 2008. According to a press release available on the site, the typical site member is "a prosumer (i.e. an advanced amateur that buys professional level equipment): He uses a DSLR camera, is 45 years old, of high education level, earns $67,000 per year and spends more than $3,800 per year for his passion. 54 percent of the members say that Nikonians directly influenced their shopping decisions." (source: nikonians.org)

A PROPOSED MODEL OF AN ONLINE COMMUNITY

To begin to understand the online communities that specialize in photography I present a model of the communities with three elements: the community, the actor, and the audience (Figure 1) which are described in the following paragraphs. The model is proposed as a device for theory development and each element of the community will likely consist of multiple components. Moreover, the overlap displayed in the diagram between the elements represents the interdependencies extant in any complex community. This model is proposed as a starting point for examination to give structure to the analysis. In this way, the qualitative approach here is more in line with the hybrid approaches Miles and Huberman than a completely grounded approach demonstrated by Glaser and Strauss (Glaser & Strauss, 1967; Miles & Huberman, 1994).

In the narrative network framework, the model is a representation of the actants in the network. This model is based on extensive personal experience with the communities and gives a basis for structuring the narrative network analysis that is presented later in the paper. Participating in the communities for several years provides an ethnographic basis for the proposed model which is influenced by all of ethnography's

Figure 1. A model of the actants in an online community

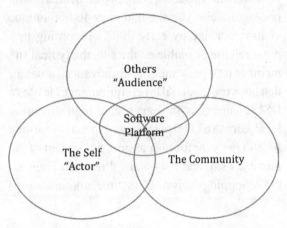

attendant advantages and problems (Stewart, 1998). The aim here is to develop an iterative process that refines the model of community as the narrative network analysis proceeds beyond the traditional ethnographic framework. In many ways, the research approach advocated here is one of meta-ethnography. Meta-ethnography enables: "critical examination of multiple accounts of an event, situation, and so forth; a way of talking about our work and comparing it to the works of others; and a synthesis of ethnographic studies." (Noblit & Hare, 1988)

The Community

The elements of the online discussion forum community are multi-dimensional and include technology, established rules and procedures, and the past narratives of the forum. On the technology front, the presentation of the community is partially dictated by the software selected to run the board. The software platform may dictate the richness of communication available to the members. For example, does the software allow private communication between members, personalized photo avatars, or emoticons (the ubiquitous smiley face is an example of an emoticon ☺)?

Beyond the software used for a community are a number of factors that influence behaviors within a community. The founders of a community often have a vision for the purpose of a given forum which defines the initial conditions for the emerging community. For example, Nikonians describes itself as the "friendly, reliable and informative; sharing, learning and inspiring community for Nikon users." (sic) The founders were unhappy with the lack of oversight as well as the often rude behavior at other photography sites. The founders had a vision for a more positive and inspiring community and created Nikonians.

Communities also establish terms of use which are published on the site to provide guidance for appropriate behaviors in the forums. Just as traditional communities have laws and regulation, on-line communities have terms of use. Failure to abide consistently by the terms of use will typically result in banishment from the community. Communities may also "anchor" significant threads at the top of the forums. These threads provide a sense of history for the new users. Moreover, the community often has a "frequently asked questions" (FAQ) section for its users.

Beyond the formal rules of the community, the users also develop behavioral norms that vary by community. They may also develop new words and abbreviations which are used during the conversations. For example, ILP is a community that is heavily populated by mothers with photography businesses. These users often refer to their family members with the abbreviations dh (dear husband), dd (dear daughter), and ds (dear son).

Discussion forums are typically formatted with various areas based on topic. The organization of the topics obviously has a significant role in the development of the community—often creating an "us versus them" dynamic within the community. For example, the DPR forums are largely organized by camera brand. This often creates conflict within the boards as members identify strongly with their camera brands. In fact, Nikonians was established partially in response to this brand dynamic. The founders wanted to avoid conflict created by users of other brands by constraining the conversation to one brand.

The Self

The on-line self is a multi-dimensional concept which is distinct from traditional constructs of the term (Jones, 1997). For example, some researchers discuss the effects of anonymity in computer-mediated communications (Watt, Lea, & Spears, 2002). Modern discussion forums make on-line anonymity almost a moot point. While it is true that user identities may be distinct from name and location, this does not mean that users are completely anonymous. In some ways, they are more transparent on-line than in a traditional relationship. Names are user selected and often tell a story in themselves (some examples from Nikonians: AndrewfromCanada, Crabby Guy, and amateurphotog). Beyond the name, the three forums under discussion for this research all allow users to post extensive user profiles which add richness to online identities. A final point for consideration is that all of a given user's postings on a forum are accessible from the profiles. This complete history is available at all times to all users—a much more complete picture of a user than is revealed in many personal relationships.

Others: The Audience

The remaining section of this model involves the audience. Traditional conversations have a limited audience of those present at the time of the conversation. Online discussions have an almost unlimited audience. The audience is not limited by geography or, notably, by time. The lack of a geographic limit means that the forums often have multi-cultural settings and heritages. The forums under examination here provide ample demonstration of this idea. The founder of DPR is British

and the site is headquartered in London. Nikonians was founded by two partners: a Swede living in Germany and a Mexican living in the US. ILP was founded in the U.S. and is based in Florida.

The nature of the forums also means that the communication is frequently asynchronous. Conversations take place over a period of days and can be resurrected at any time. Participants in the conversations can go to other web sites to check facts and continue the conversation after verification of any number of issues. The asynchronous element of the forum dynamic dramatically increases the potential audience. Moreover, the audience is likely to be much larger than those participating in the conversation. Many may observe the conversation and not choose to participate unless they see an unmet need in the conversation.

The Software Platform

A final actant in this model narrative network is the software platform that enables the conversation. Different forums use software that has various features to facilitate information flow. For example, some platforms allow users to post pictures of themselves and provide links or biographic information. In addition, the forums often provide a history of the user's previous postings and the date that the user joined the forum. This information provides a richer experience for the users and allows deeper relationships to emerge in the community. One can see from the central position of the software platform in Figure 1 that this actant affects all other participants in the narrative network.

THE NARRATIVE NETWORK IN USE

In this section, the narrative network is used to evaluate a discussion thread from two of the forums presented earlier and then draw a narrative network comparing the communities. The threads

Figure 2. An abbreviated narrative network analysis of discussion threads

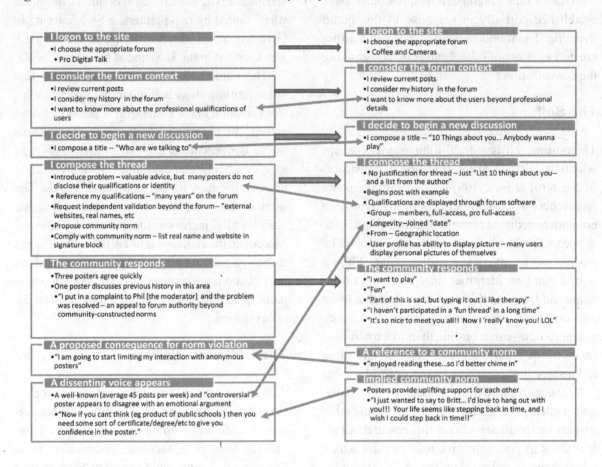

were selected by evaluating a week's worth of postings on each of the boards. The first thread is from the "Pro Digital Talk" area of DPR. The next is from the "Coffee and Cameras" area of ILP. These areas of the forums allow a broad range of conversation beyond the more strict limitations of subject matter imposed in some other areas of the forum. Selection of a single thread from among thousands is appropriate here given that this work is to provide an example of the research methodology, rather than to draw definitive portraits of the communities under study.

Threads selected from the individual forums had three primary characteristics. First, the thread needed more than 25 responses, to ensure the possibility of a rich conversation. Second, the thread

must have had no activity for at least 48 hours to give ample opportunity for the community to respond to the points under discussion. Finally, the threads were evaluated for a degree of reflexivity within the community. Threads were given priority that discussed the nature of the community and its participants.

The DPR Thread was titled by the original poster "Who are we talking to" and raised the question of professional qualifications of users posting comments in a forum titled "Pro Digital Talk." The ILP thread is titled "10 things about you" and asks users to post "10 random things about you." The brief narrative network analysis presented in Figure 2 provides an interesting view into the dynamics of the different communities.

DISCUSSION

Even from the abbreviated analysis presented in Figure 2, one can see some patterns of the boards emerge. For example, naming of the particular boards provides an expectation of certain norms among the participants. Moreover, forum identity is a complex concept which is context dependent and influenced by the software selection of the administrators. Finally, as in traditional instances of community, the analysis also indicates that norms are likely to be socially constructed over a lengthy period.

As tempting as it may be to discuss further the patterns of technology in use that emerge from Figure 2, much more analysis would be required to make truly informed pronouncements on the matter. However, one could see that adjustments and amendments to the model from Figure 1 would be expected from further analysis. Nevertheless, the issue here is the use of narrative network analysis as a technique to further understanding of online communities. Figure 2 is well-suited for this limited purpose. The network analysis shows a methodology that enables a rich analysis of complex narratives involving, not only discrete individuals, but also, technology, communities, and larger social contexts. Until now, researchers have used a hodgepodge of techniques to illuminate the complexities of online communities (e.g. (O'Brien, 1999)). The narrative network analysis gives a systematic way to examine the narratives while allowing patterns to emerge from the text.

Despite the promise of narrative network analysis, some significant difficulties arise when examining online communities in this manner. First, the sheer volume of the narratives will overwhelm any researcher. This begs the question of how to select narratives for analysis. One can use a random sample technique or, as in this case, use an ethnographically informed process which identifies threads with the most promise. More

than likely, some combination of the techniques will be used for most research. For example, ethnographically informed selection may be used for hypothesis development, while random samples may be used for hypothesis testing. Some researchers may hesitate to use an initial selection process so susceptible to personal bias; however, the hundreds of thousands of posts on many forums may defy more rigorous selection processes due to the volume of material created by thousands of users.

CONCLUSION

Narrative network analysis provides an exciting frontier for examination of online communities. The initial application of the technique by Pentland and Feldman (2007) was limited to a single electronic commerce transaction. This paper expands the use of the concept to complex communities with many participants, extensive technology variables, and rich social contexts. Previous studies of online communities have often used anecdotal data to draw conclusions about these complex beasts which have grown in importance with the development of the internet (Smith & Kollock, 1999). Wellman and Gulia (1999) propose seven questions concerning online communities in their work:

1. Are online relationships narrowly supported or broadly supportive?
2. In what ways are the weak ties on the Net useful?
3. Is there reciprocity online and attachment to virtual communities?
4. Are strong, intimate ties possible online?
5. How does virtual community affect "real-life" community?
6. Does the Net increase community diversity?
7. Are virtual communities real communities?

Wellman and Gulia conclude their paper with the following observation:

We have concluded this paper more like pundits and tellers of tales than like researchers. As others before us, we have argued often by assertion and anecdote. This is because the paucity of research into virtual communities has raised more questions than answers... It is time to replace anecdote with evidence. The subject is important: practically, scholarly, and politically. The answers have not yet been found. Indeed the, the questions are just starting to be formulated. (Wellman & Gulia, 1999)

I couldn't agree more, and I believe that this paper demonstrates that narrative network analysis is a tool that can help researchers overcome these difficult obstacles.

REFERENCES

Anonymous. (2007). Amazon.com acquires DPReview.com. *Business Wire Press Release.* Retrieved March 21, 2008, from http://www.dpreview.com/news/0705/07051402amazonacquiresdpreview.asp

Baym, N. K. (1998). The emergence of on-line community. In Jones, S. G. (Ed.), *Cybersociety 2.0: Revisiting computer-mediated communication and community* (pp. 35–68). Thousand Oaks, CA: Sage Publications.

Benlian, A., & Hess, T. (2011). The signaling role of IT features in influencing trust and participation in online communities. *International Journal of Electronic Commerce, 15*(4), 7–56. doi:10.2753/JEC1086-4415150401

Byoungho, J., Park, J. Y., & Kim, H.-S. (2010). What makes online community members commit? A social exchange perspective. *Behaviour & Information Technology, 29*(6), 587–599. doi:10.1080/0144929X.2010.497563

Czarniawska, B. (1998). *A narrative approach to organization studies* (*Vol. 43*). Thousand Oaks, CA: Sage Publications.

Czarniawska, B. (2004). On time, space, and action nets. *Organization, 11*(4), 773–791. doi:10.1177/1350508404047251

Daft, R. L., & Lengel, R. H. (1986). Organizational information requirements, media richness, and structural design. *Management Science, 32*(5), 554–571. doi:10.1287/mnsc.32.5.554

Daft, R. L., Lengel, R. H., & Trevino, L. K. (1987). Message equivocality, media selection, and manager performance: Implications for information systems. *Management Information Systems Quarterly, 11*(3), 355–366. doi:10.2307/248682

Etzioni, A. (1993). *The spirit of community: The reinvention of American society.* New York, NY: Touchstone.

Fairfield, H. (2007, April 15). Baby on board, and a photography business, too. *The New York Times.* Retrieved July 1, 2010, from http://www.nytimes.com/2007/04/15/business/yourmoney/15cameras.html?_r=1&oref=slogin

Faraj, S., Kwon, D., & Watts, S. (2004). Contested artifact: Technology sensemaking, actor networks, and the shaping of the Web. *Information Technology & People, 17*(2), 186–209. doi:10.1108/09593840410542501

Feldman, M. S., & Pentland, B. T. (2003). Reconceptualizing organizational routines as a source of flexibility and change. *Administrative Science Quarterly, 48*(1), 94–118. doi:10.2307/3556620

Giddens, A. (1984). *The constitution of society.* Cambridge, MA: Polity.

Glaser, B. G., & Strauss, A. L. (1967). *The discovery of grounded theory: Strategies for qualitative research.* New York, NY: Aldine de Gruyter.

Horrigan, J. B., Rainie, L., & Fox, S. (2001). *Online communities: Networks that nurture long-distance relationships and local ties*. Retrieved October 11, 2007, from http://www.pewinternet.org/pdfs/PIP_Communities_Report.pdf

Hung, K., Yiyan Li, S., & Tse, D. K. (2011). Interpersonal trust and platform credibility in a chinese multibrand online community. *Journal of Advertising, 40*(3), 99–112. doi:10.2753/JOA0091-3367400308

Jayanti, R. K., & Singh, J. (2010). Pragmatic learning theory: An inquiry-action framework for distripbuted consumer learning in online communities. *The Journal of Consumer Research, 36*(6), 1058–1081. doi:10.1086/648689

Johnson, J. (1988). Mixing humans and non-humans: The sociology of a door closer. *Social Problems, 35*(3), 298–310. doi:10.1525/sp.1988.35.3.03a00070

Jones, S. G. (1997). The Internet and its social landscape. In Jones, S. G. (Ed.), *Virtual culture: Identity and communication in cybersociety* (pp. 7–35). London, UK: Sage Publications.

Kim, J. W., Choi, J., Qualls, W., & Han, K. (2008). It takes a marketplace community to raise brand commitment: The role of online communities. *Journal of Marketing Management, 24*(3-4), 409–431. doi:10.1362/026725708X306167

Koh, J., Kim, Y.-G., Butler, B., & Bock, G.-W. (2007). Encouraging participation in virtual communities. *Communications of the ACM, 50*(2), 69–73. doi:10.1145/1216016.1216023

Kozinets, R. V. (2002). The field behind the screen: Using netnography for marketing research in online communities. *JMR, Journal of Marketing Research, 39*(1), 61–72. doi:10.1509/jmkr.39.1.61.18935

Kozinets, R. V. (2006). Click to connect: Netnography and tribal advertising. *Journal of Advertising Research, 46*(3), 279–288. doi:10.2501/S0021849906060338

Latour, B. (2005). *Reassembling the social: An introduction to actor-network theory*. Oxford, UK: Oxford University Press.

Law, J., & Hassard, J. (1999). *Actor network theory and after*. Oxford, UK: Blackwell.

Maffesoli, M. (1996). *The time of the tribes: The decline of individualism in mass society* (Smith, D., Trans.). London, UK: Sage Publications.

McCarthy, C. (2007). Amazon snaps up digital photography review. *CNet News*. Retrieved March 21, 2008, from http://www.news.com/2102-1038_3-6183488.html

Miles, M. B., & Huberman, A. M. (1994). *Qualitative data analysis: An expanded sourcebook* (2nd ed.). Thousand Oaks, CA: Sage.

Noblit, G. W., & Hare, R. D. (1988). *Meta-ethnography: Synthesizing qualitative studies* (*Vol. 11*). Newbury Park, CA: Sage Publications.

O'Brien, J. (1999). Writing in the body: Gender (re)production in online interaction. In Smith, M. A., & Kollock, P. (Eds.), *Communities in cyberspace* (pp. 76–104). London, UK: Routledge.

Pentland, B. T., & Feldman, M. S. (2005). Organizational routines as a unit of analysis. *Industrial and Corporate Change, 14*(5), 793–815. doi:10.1093/icc/dth070

Pentland, B. T., & Feldman, M. S. (2007). Narrative networks: Patterns of technology and organization. *Organization Science, 18*(5), 781–795. doi:10.1287/orsc.1070.0283

Preece, J. (2000). *Online communities: Designing usability, supporting sociability*. Chichester, UK: John Wiley & Sons.

Prykop, C., & Heitman, M. (2006). Designing mobile brand communities: Concept and empirical illustration. *Journal of Organizational Computing and Electronic Commerce, 16*(3/4), 301–323.

Putnam, R. D. (1995). Bowling alone: America's declining social capital. *Journal of Democracy, 6*(1), 65–78. doi:10.1353/jod.1995.0002

Rheingold, H. (1993). *The virtual community: Homesteading on the electronic frontier* (Revised ed.). Cambridge, MA: MIT Press.

Shepherd, M. M., Martz, J., & Benjamin, W. M. (2001). Media richness theory and the distance education environment. *Journal of Computer Information Systems, 47*(1), 114–122.

Smith, M. A., & Kollock, P. (1999). *Communities in cyberspace*. London, UK: Routledge. doi:10.5117/9789056290818

Stewart, A. (1998). *The ethnographer's method*. Thousand Oaks, CA: Sage Publications.

Timm, P. (1976). The bulletin board: Economy and effectiveness in organizational communication. *Journal of Business Communication, 13*(2), 37–44. doi:10.1177/002194367601300205

Timmerman, P., & Harrison, W. (2005). The discretionary use of electronic media. *Journal of Business Communication, 42*(4), 379–389. doi:10.1177/0021943605279059

Wakao, A. (2007). *Nikon eyes double-digit growth in compact digicams*. Retrieved March 24, 2008, from http://www.reuters.com/articlePrint?articleId=USTKU00283620070220

Watt, S. E., Lea, M., & Spears, R. (2002). How social is internet communication? A reappraisal of bandwidth and anonymity effects. In Woolgar, S. (Ed.), *Virtual society? Technology cyberbole, reality* (pp. 61–77). Oxford, UK: Oxford University Press.

Wellman, B., & Gulia, M. (1999). Virtual communities as communities: Net surfers don't ride alone. In Smith, M. A., & Kollock, P. (Eds.), *Communities in cyberspace* (pp. 167–194). London, UK: Routledge.

Yen, H. R., Hsu, S. H.-Y., & Chun-Yao, H. (2011). Good soldiers on the Web: Understanding the drivers of participation in online communities of consumption. *International Journal of Electronic Commerce, 15*(4), 89–120. doi:10.2753/JEC1086-4415150403

Yeow, A., & Faraj, S. (2011). Using narrative networks to study enterprise systems and organizational change. *International Journal of Accounting Information Systems, 12*(2), 116–125. doi:10.1016/j.accinf.2010.12.005

Chapter 7
Toward an Infrastructural Approach to Understanding Participation in Virtual Communities

Ben Li
University of Oulu, Finland

ABSTRACT

This chapter outlines an infrastructural approach to understanding virtual communities (VCs) and applies it to a novel set of VCs. The infrastructural approach explicitly links logics embodied in technical, social, and information systems to opportunities and motives for participation. This chapter first outlines how the infrastructure approach is synthesised from current approaches to understanding VCs. Second, it uses the infrastructural approach to analyse three related meatspace communities' progress toward collaborating through specific data-sharing VCs. Third, it highlights merits and shortcomings of the infrastructural approach to understanding participation in virtual communities. Finally, it offers potential avenues of further VC research using the infrastructural approach.

INTRODUCTION

One reason virtual communities (VCs) are broadly interesting is because they may incorporate and reflect dynamics of meatspace communities. In addition, their ICT-mediated nature may enable new large-scale socially and economically important behaviours and relationships. Efforts to replicate and apply findings from meatspace communities to VCs have experienced mixed success, but the "virtual" aspect of VCs has received less attention.

Simultaneously, the increasingly interdependent, intermediated, and invisible qualities of pieces that compose technical, social, and information components of individual VCs, and suites of related VCs increase the difficulty of conducting and generalizing piecemeal analysis (Kraut et al., 2010). Therefore, a new position must be adopted that respects and understands the particular qualities of each VC, but which also leverages and informs studies and ongoing practices in relation to other VCs.

DOI: 10.4018/978-1-4666-0312-7.ch007

The proposed infrastructural VC approach (IVCA) recognises that the qualities that make a virtual community "virtual" are the sets of generally assumed technologies and knowledges that enable individuals to share information online. Every online action engages ICTs to transmit and receive information. To consider "virtual communities" of interacting humans therefore requires us to consider the information infrastructures that underpin their distinctly "virtual" existence. While trace ethnography of the virtual yields insights about the 'what' questions about broadly distributed online phenomena (e.g., Geiger and Ribes, 2011), questions of 'how' and 'why' must be considered from the underpinning information infrastructures.

The virtual characteristic may impart dynamics difficult to reconcile with each other, let alone with knowledge about meatspace communities. Specifically, VC participants have fundamentally new or different possibilities, such as:

- The ability to search and discover communities and information through vast online search engines in addition to personal or local networks;
- Nearly instant storage and retrieval of remote information through high-speed data networks;
- Rapid responses from many interchangeable sources of information and assistance;
- Concurrency and parallelization of individual and group participation;
- Tools to rapidly entrench, retrench, and replicate/fork a community at low material cost; and
- The ability to take concurrent risks by participating in concurrent communities.

This chapter presents and investigates the IVCA by applying it to three related scientific communities in long-term ecological research (LTER) as they attempt to add VC components to share metadata. The LTER metadata VCs (LMVCs)

share some typical characteristics and dynamics of other VCs, yet are distinct in motivations, barriers to entry, and expectations of value. If the IVCA is worthwhile, it should reveal major conclusions about the LMVCs agreeing with conventional VC approaches (CVCAs) it incorporates, while also providing new kinds of questions and insights about unmet challenges of instantiating LMVCs. The IVCA also yields some testable predictions about kinds of infrastructural changes that may bring LMVCs closer to their goals.

The objective of this chapter is to address the basic scientific research question: How can we understand participation through data sharing in LTER VCs? Moving toward an answer requires understanding what a current state means to dynamic LMVCs, and the logics that govern their extensions into virtual realms.

This chapter proceeds as follows. First it outlines the infrastructural VC approach. Second, it traces how the IVCA arises from CVCAs to understanding VCs. Third, it uses the IVCA to analyse three LTER communities' work toward incorporating VCs. Fourth, it highlights the merits and shortcomings of the IVCA to understanding participation motives in virtual communities. Finally, it concludes that the IVCA provides many benefits of the CVCAs it incorporates, while leveraging their inconsistencies to explain some potential misunderstandings of VCs.

BACKGROUND

The Infrastructural VC Approach in Brief

Briefly stated, the IVCA assumes that concurrent logics both enable and restrict possible interactions in a community. It echoes ideas linking requisite variety to responses to environmental threats developed by Ashby (1958). IVCA is an infrastructural approach because it considers long-term assumed patterns of interactions (e.g.,

Bowker et al., 2010), but through their present and future effects rather than through their detailed particularities. By "logics" is meant the regular patterns of information flow that arise independently and compositionally from the various personal, social, technological, biological, and informational requirements and realities that intersect in a VC. Geels (2004) employs cognitive, regulative, normative, and formal rules to study socio-technical change as factors of stability, path-dependence and lock-in in innovation adoption. Lécuyer *et al.* (2010) have applied the idea of intersecting logics to understand pre-silicon local and virtual communities. "Logics" is used here in the same spirit.

As examples of logics, the rotation of the Earth, along with humans' circadian biology implies a pattern of reduced human interactions from each geographic location from 2:00-5:00 a.m. Of consequence, we expect VCs to have different qualities during the middle of the night than during the day. When a VC platform such as a wiki or content management system introduces a new social media sharing option as default, such as requiring all contributors to log in, a new technical logic becomes simultaneously available to be incorporated into many seemingly unrelated VCs and thereby potentially affect their social logics and behaviours.

Since the IVCA concerns dynamic human communities, the IVCA must also consider VCs' capacities to devise and adopt new logics, as well as to ignore/abolish existing logics. Thus its sensitivity to long-term features of VC logics, enables it to frame observations from traces as routines, accidents, or infrastructure changes. This approach is compatible with general systems theory (von Bertalanffy, 1968), and indeed echoes important broad ideas from it.

Incentives and motives are thought to underpin each individual's participation in VCs as they do in non-virtual communities (Tedjamulia et al., 2005). But unlike meatspace communities that can offer material and intangible resources for participation, ICT-mediated VCs are adapted to primarily deliver explicit information. The IVCA connects the personal logics of a VC's participants to the VC's sustainability via information flows. When overlapping logics interact to yield a system in which each participant can, on average, gain value from repeatedly interacting with it by contributing or gleaning information, the VC is sustained regardless of the motives or rewards of any individual participant. This concept is compatible with biological and ecological perspectives of change in communities as emergent phenomena (Reice, 1994).

"Virtual community" is deliberately not rigidly defined in the IVCA. Infrastructures facilitate activities at ranges of scales or intensities in general, rather than specific activities in particular. Therefore, IVCA can view through the same lens: a VC of five previously unconnected individuals elaborating on a technical invention for six days on a mailing list, a year-old virtual community of dozens of Mozilla contributors tasked with developing a particular aspect of Firefox's user interface, or the entire Mozilla Foundation. In each instance, users contribute and glean information under immediate logics—e.g., using the Bugzilla search tool—that may themselves be interpreted and operated through other logics—e.g., the distinctions between the Firefox web browser and its interface as different products. Empirically, all result in information interactions that are operationally sustained until participants receive no further gain from additional interactions. Each VC could thus be distinguished by its unique and dynamic combination of logics. For similar reasons, this chapter uses "member", "participant", "contributor" in their colloquial senses as the context demands.

As will be argued below, a fractal self-similar composition of virtual communities explains why a diverse range of interdependent VCs must exist for all to be sustained, why most VCs must exist at apparently small and "unsuccessful" scales (not necessarily "stages") of complexity, and how to consider information flows to gain better indicators of VCs' characteristics important for analysis.

In summary, the IVCA holds at its core that:

1. Logics arise from accumulated individual, social, technical, biological, and informational realities of a VC;
2. Logics enable and constrain present and future interactions by specifying default and possible behaviours;
3. Logics are maintained in effect when they generate value; and
4. Explicit and hidden logics of a virtual community collectively compose its "infrastructure".

Therefore, to apply the IVCA is to identify the individual logics of the VC and how they interact to form a sustainable infrastructure for information flows.

The Infrastructural VC Approach Arises from and Supports Conventional VC Approaches

The IVCA is implied by several current approaches to understanding VCs. This section elaborates the key points of the IVCA by contrasting with CVCAs.

To over-generalize, CVCAs frame VCs: through different tiers of VC participants (e.g., Rafaeli and Ariel, 2008); through individuals exercising various intrinsic and/or extrinsic motives (e.g., Preece and Shneiderman, 2009); through inhibitions due to fear of loss of social status or control; through predominantly economic expectations beneficial or harmful outcomes; or through individual studies of individual communities that are difficult to later compare.

Tiers of participants span the first-time new visitor to some trusted leader, and reflect enrolment from the perspectives of both the VC and participant. Additional categories include amateur/professional, number of posts/replies/ratings, duration of participation, etc. along or across the first range. These categories are not unique to the virtual setting, and meatspace communities and practices that have been virtualized may be used to understand the non-virtual originals. VC participants with different combinations of attributes have nuanced motives (Messinger et al, 2009) as in meatspace.

Personal and collective rewards are available for participation, including indicators of status, exclusivity, and desirability. VC participants are thought to choose their degree of participation by considering potential costs and potential benefits. Hesitation arises from uncertainty about expectations connecting participation to result, or from assuming that that inferior participation will lead to undesirable results.

From patterns of previous interactions at a particular VC or in meatspace, participants can develop expectations about how to obtain particular social, business, and/or personal returns. Meatspace constructs of social capital (e.g., Matchwick, 2007), profits (e.g., Iriberri and Leroy, 2008), feelings of accomplishment (Hinds and Lee, 2008) may also explain why VC participants expect others to behave in particular ways.

Authors often lament that the many different kinds of dynamics within and among VCs, and the observed variations in individual behaviours, make it difficult to reliably design (e.g., Lin, 2008) sustainable VCs or even to consistently apply CVCAs (e.g., Porter, 2004; de Moora and Weigandb, 2007). Abundant preserved evidence of inactive VCs is interpreted as an unacceptably high rate of failure of VCs (e.g., Preece and Shneiderman, 2009), usually without reference to the (quite possibly immeasurable) rate of failure of meatspace attempts at new community formation, operation, and decommissioning.

The few distinct characteristics of *virtual* communities, summarised in the introduction, receive inadequate attention. This is not surprising since theories borrowed from meatspace do not say much about the "virtual" parts of dynamic VC phenomena. Iriberri and Leroy (2008) recognized this distinction as a problem and opportunity: "in essence social networking sites are online communities that take advantage of the new and improved social computing technology for interaction and multimedia information exchange."

Although there are abundant frameworks and examples comparing snapshots of different VCs, it is rare to find work that cuts across several related VCs through a common period in time over short or long terms. This, too, is understandable due to operational challenges of scaling up ethnographic approaches to go beyond simply reassembling digital traces in a thinly descriptive account of VCs. Thus, the IVCA proposes to examine how the described features systematically arise in the first place.

These gaps are addressable by applying the IVCA to discover VCs' logics, as the following cases demonstrate.

THREE VIRTUAL COMMUNITIES' CHALLENGES SHARING DATA

Three long-term ecological research (LTER) communities were studied through semi-structured interviews, participant observation, and records analysis. The three aspiring virtual communities are influenced by people and practices instantiated in their corresponding physical communities decades ago with long histories of international collaboration. The broad goal of LTER is to gather, share, and mobilize ecological data over the long term (Aronova et al., 2010) through scientific collaboration and publication, public policy contributions, etc. The primary goal of the new *LTER metadata VC* aspect of these communities is to expose, and hopefully give to others, ecological data collected over decades (Gil et al., 2009) so that it may be (re)used for bigger science concerning research sites and systems beyond individual experiments. The primary challenge is to explicate descriptions of collected data (and

their dependent tacit knowledges) so that the datasets may be indexed and shared with other researchers (Greenberg et al., 2009) but these challenges need not be met through metadata alone (Zimmerman, 2007).

The several meatspace LTER communities have long histories of overlapping configurations, memberships, and politics in various formal and informal organizations and networks. Those who study and participate in such networks employ various, often disagreeing, units of analysis and reference depending on context (Ribes and Polk, 2012). This section does not intend to provide detailed chronologies of these communities—for which Furman and Peltola (2012), Gil et al., (2009), and Lin et al. (2008) are excellent references—but to focus on the *received* infrastructures and logics in the VCs.

Finland's LTSER

Size/Scope: The Finnish Long-Term Socio-Ecological Research (FinLTSER) network was established in the 2000s (formally in 2006) to support participating in data-intensive research in broader regional and global contexts. Although the network has tried to meet regularly, it is not funded as an entity or process. Participants include the field research stations of the country's major universities, national forestry and meteorological researchers, and assorted others in the community.

Sophistication: FinLTSER participants span a broad range of technical and scientific sophistication. At one end are individuals on short-term contracts digitizing data from logbooks, paper records, and boxes of decades-old uncharacterised samples. At the other end, organizations build and maintain digital metadata libraries for themselves and others. As a member of the International Long Term Ecological Research 'network of networks', FinLTSER adopted the Ecological Metadata Language (EML) as its standard for describing and sharing data (Knowledge Network for Biocomplexity, n.d.), but no technical EML infrastructure yet services the entire meatspace community. According to participants, data collaboration occurs almost exclusively through personal contact by email and other common Internet tools, and personal visits, not through the LMVC.

Virtual Dimensions and Motives: The FinLTSER network has largely not taken up unique "virtual" opportunities offered by VC infrastructure. The network possibly lacks critical mass in data, people, or resources to benefit from maintaining yet another set of logics intended to handle common datasets and interactions, with few datasets ready for widespread sharing. FinLTSER champions seek to participate more regularly in international research collaborations engaging more Finnish data and researchers. Some individual staff members are mildly motivated by their job descriptions to prepare data for eventual inclusion in LMVCs, but data digitization and sharing remain rare events. Network members report lots of data passing through their sites, but insufficient detail is collected in paper or online guestbooks/reservations to abstract and provide additional value.

Challenges: Lack of qualified individuals to perform data work, or to manage potential contributors having limited qualifications, have hampered FinLTSER's efforts to develop its internal LMVC. Despite being a small community in number of participants, for the virtual and meatspace community infrastructures, organizing potential collaborations remains a challenge. Retrofitting old data and collecting new long-term data remain relatively costly. A decade of inadequate coordination among national and international funders has acted as a barrier to building a sustainable technical infrastructure, and thus to new scientific logics of collaboration through the LMVC.

US LTER

Size/Scope: The US Long-Term Ecological Research Network is over three decades old and spans approximately two dozen sites (US LTER, n.d.) with a National Science Foundation mandate to share research data within and outside the network. The network has employed several generations of technical infrastructure to collect, store, and share data. Its virtual community predates most others on the Internet as collaborators made generous use of e-mail, gopher, teleconferencing, etc. between regular personal meetings. It continues to embrace newer technologies like Skype and Web 2.0 data collaboratories.

Sophistication: Sub-groups of the meatspace community work on the information sharing problem, having developed (among others): EML (KNB, n.d.), a cyber-infrastructure for EML (DataONE, n.d.), and EML tools (NCEAS, n.d.) for end-users to engage in the LMVC. Some information managers report insufficient time, knowledge, technical, or managerial support to meet changing data requirements. Others have specialized on the challenge. Their narratives expose different logics employed to observe and participate, but sufficient operational overlaps enable the community to endure.

Virtual Dimensions and Motives: An LMVC built on the common explicit EML logic provides one way to leverage diverse data and participants who bring many internal implicit and explicit logics.

Challenges: US LTER participants hold many often divergent views of the network, and of its social and scientific challenges. Many are common to large organizations, including human capital recruitment and retention, matching resources to needs, and knowledge management.

Taiwan Forestry Research Institute

Size/Scope: The Fire Ecology and Ecological Informatics division of the Taiwan Forestry Research Institute (TFRI) has become the technological and scientific gatekeeper for ecological data sharing standards within the Taiwan government and research community. (A small team centered on a technical manager and a technically minded director is responsible for the care and feeding of many metadata systems within Taiwan.) It has also become a regional leader by offering education and technical support to scientists in other nations to bootstrap ecological metadata systems.

Sophistication: TFRI's data management group is an informal group lacking official mandate, but engages several dozen team members. It develops/integrates/localizes foreign software and platforms for use in an Asian context. It is influenced by both US and European models of data management. It has also internalized and contributed to related VC technologies such as Drupal, wikis, etc. in order to manage its supporting knowledge, for example, about cloud computing platforms.

Virtual dimensions and motives: TFRIs external data collaborations rely heavily on infrastructures for VCs, including teleconferencing, content management systems, virtualized computing clusters and services, etc. Internally, many workflows have been digitized and interlinked so that leaders and team members from different divisions of the institute may discover, access, and contribute to knowledge held or developed at other divisions. TFRI also makes much of this infrastructure public so that they can use the data for whatever purpose, and contribute local knowledge or suggestions, for example, for species identification and distribution. Public members routinely access and revise TFRI's metadata about its domestic and international collections. TFRI also helped to instantiate the concept of data papers (Chavan and Penev, 2011).

Challenges: Labour in Taiwan is relatively inexpensive. TFRI also has volunteers to accumulate, manage, and share its information surplus. However, funding for information management remains soft (several TFRI divisions pool resources outside their budgets to operate the shared data management group), and there are political, cultural, and other challenges with respect to interoperating with Mainland China.

In short, LTER communities are simultaneously like and unlike other VCs, and their sub-community dynamics are not well explained by CVCAs. The following section interprets LTER communities through conventional and infrastructural VC approaches.

VC MOTIVATIONS UNDER THE INFRASTRUCTURAL VC APPROACH

Despite these many differences, the similarities suggest applying CVCAs to see what insights they may yield. Several aspects of LTER VCs reviewed in this section.

Motives

CVCAs state a VC participant can earn respect by demonstrating how their knowledge helps others. Extrinsic rewards from contributing to a VC are thought to be immediate and reinforcing of future contributions, through status displays such as the number of "upvotes" (or "likes" or "+1"s, etc.), re-shares, posts, or collected bounties. Longer-term rewards may come from accruing social capital and hence the ability to request information or actions from other members. Intrinsic rewards accrue to individuals immediately through personal feelings of accomplishment, discovery, satisfaction, etc.; and in the long term through visibility, sense of belonging, increases in responsibility and influence through promotion, etc. Open participation by novices is possible and encouraged through tiered classes of rewards and achievements, from "email verified", "first reply", "100 posts" up through "X-year veteran". Participation in special events may be rewarded with special indicators of status. VCs that form a new community are generally permissive of anonymous contributors, but may desire identification (with a consistent meatspace or virtual persona) for some purposes of responsibility. VCs that are supplemental to existing organizations and communities tend away from anonymity. Durable VCs provide opportunities to further specialize via interest groups or sub-communities. These all speak to reward systems adopted in bulk from meatspace community settings that connect personal participation to the group through well understood motivations.

LMVCs do not share important typical VC features. A contributor of public meta-data cannot direct that gift to anyone or any demand in particular. The knowledge externalization challenges that render data difficult to describe and document render it equally difficult for any contributor to offer to describe or clean up any other contributor's potential contributions. Extrinsic rewards from contributing data come rarely as one part of annual (or less frequent) reviews. Of consequence, it is difficult to evaluate, recognise and reward contributions based on quality or potential value to the LMVC. Intrinsic rewards are limited to personal satisfaction with detailed work accomplished (like a perfectly clean dataset) since contributing data to the LMVC is not a requirement to obtaining data from the LMVC. Anonymity is not substantially possible or desirable since the LMVC platform is designed to attach responsibility to data. And because the total number of LTER data managers is relatively small, the existing LTER community must seek to generalize a single data-sharing LMVC out of many specialized and fragmented interests based on data formats and research operationalization.

Gaining access to free but only vaguely related datasets confers little obvious individual or local meatspace community benefit. Research institutions, publishers, and funders do not consistently reward risk-taking to conduct broad multi-disciplinary synthetic work, despite demanding such work in their mission statements and strategies. Few CVCAs could be easily repurposed to overcome this coordination challenge, and no overarching "VC theory" as such provides guidance about developing a suitable approach.

The IVCA can decompose the activities and logics into the information flows they represent.

Specifically, from the perspective of a pure virtual community, all social and other information is conveyed through the same technical infrastructure, which is only capable of conveying and processing information, not motives or rewards or social capital or more abstract human concepts. (This is a convenient lie for now.) Then, to understand how such abstract concepts manifest through a VC is to understand its logics concerning the information flows that individually or collectively represent those abstract concepts.

Distinguishing Virtual Communities

Let us assume that VC participants seek advantages. Since a pure VC only conveys information, information must be the advantage, or embody the advantage. Since a pure VC only accepts information as the embodiment of participation, the method of seeking advantage from a pure VC must be to supply or receive information.

To develop a justified true belief that two VCs are different, we must have a basis to choose a small subset of all the possible characteristics of VCs to compare their similarities and differences. Pure VCs can only differ in the technical logics they express (everything else is brought in from meatspace communities) so therefore their logics about information flows must be a source (not cause) of differences among them. The IVCA would identify that the logics of conventional VCs and the logics of LMVCs are based on different assumptions and/or priorities with respect to decisions about how to transact in information.

In a pure virtual setting, socialization can only occur by making and responding to information requests, so status can only be gauged by the quality of information contributed in the view of the community and of any individual benefactors. Rating, directly or by referral, quality of contributions is not new to the virtual setting. What is new is the ability to quickly identify or become a non-interchangeable information source through verbatim external memories of information exchanges. The top three posters on a leaderboard (counted by volume, duration, number of replies, upvotes, or other mechanism) in a VC forum about species X in biome Y are likely to be or know highly relevant information sources about that topic. Their entire contributions to a particular VC are usually one click away from being evaluable by any information seeker. (How such a memory is used and the meaning of recall is a different topic).

But pure VCs do not exist. Community members also live outside each of their VCs, such communities cannot be isolated, and rewards of self-confidence or accomplishment in one must influence behavior in the other. The IVCA recognises different kinds of interfaces between intrinsic and extrinsic motives and rewards. For example, it recognises non-cash tangible rewards for VC participation as tight coupling between specific virtual and meatspace logics for the respective communities. Similarly, short- and long- term rewards may be viewed as parts of the same or different logics, having contradictions that may or may not appear sustained depending on how communities are delineated.

It is beneficial to understand how to structure motives, participation and rewards in VCs. These topics are addressed in detail below.

Risks and Rewards

A significant VC literature is built around expectations: those of individual community members, those of subsets of the community, those of the community as a whole, and (less frequently) those held about the community by others. Expectations as implicative logics can be made explicit by following information contributions and how they are elicited/processed in VCs. Incomplete understanding or misunderstanding of the logics in force can yield incorrect expectations, and inhibit risk-taking or potentially beneficial participation. This is not unique to VCs.

Unmet expectations can be ignored just as easily with a clear public record in VCs as offline. However, in VCs, potential participants can replay past interactions to gain heuristics about appropriate behavior before taking risks. (Having more instances of patterns to emulate can also cause an information-sorting problem). Digital infrastructure records instances of successes and mistakes forever, unlike in meatspace. Thus, the frame of reference for understanding the logics about novelty and risk-taking requires further consideration.

In LMVCs, it would be difficult to connect any (in)action of participation in LMVCs to particular positive or negative outcomes. CVCAs simply assume more activity is better: "As more members participate actively in the online community, more of these benefits are accrued for each member and for the community. As more members contribute to the community, the community sustains itself and achieves success." (Iriberri and Leroy, 2008).

Funders measure US LTER achievement in part by the number of datasets contributed via its LMVC. Peer evaluation of work is not rapid, since assessing contributed information for mobilization into a research work requires months or years of planning. Some LMVC members find automated tools to check contributed (meta-)data difficult to use. It is therefore not surprising that some under-resourced VC participants supply datasets at minimal accepted quality to avoid an adverse evaluation.

The IVCA understands this as a related but different problem. Since many small data points (informations) are needed to do a big data synthesis, very few syntheses ever arise, and hence syntheses are difficult to use as a measure or driver of the desired social practice.

Barriers to Participation

Users are assumed to face low barriers to participating in VCs since technical tools are readily accessible, for example, through a web browser or smart phone. Deploying infrastructure for new VCs is thought to also be simple using online service providers that host content management systems at low monthly rates, or using commodity personal computers (Ardichvili et al., 2003). Accessible installation instructions accommodate common configurations of VCs tools. CVCAs interpret the high rate of apparent failure of deployed VC platforms (indicated by few users, replies, interactions, etc.) as an outcome of poor community management, inadequate technical knowledge on the part of users, the failure of new social capital to manifest, etc., and prescribe better documentation and technical support for community managers. Yet the ease of publically experimenting with technical VC infrastructure will perpetually yield higher observable numbers and proportions of "failed" VCs.

CVCAs recognize a bootstrapping problem of lack of critical mass, poor community management, and inadequate motivating rewards. Unfortunately the implied resolutions have few accessible pathways. Seeding knowledge is structurally the same problem as the inadequate rewards and insufficient users, all of which compete for the same limited resources as a virtual community manager.

In contrast, high barriers to entry mean that there are few LTER VCs to categorize. While all the required software is open source, deploying it is difficult. One must download source code packages, configure a local Linux or Windows server, compile the software, install it, and configure an online application server, federate it with others, seed it with data, etc., mostly without access to the diverse experienced world-wide user-base enjoyed by, say WordPress VC managers. Instructions for LMVC software are outdated, of limited help to anyone not already expert at configuring application servers, and offered usually only in English.

Potential LTER VC members face an additional high barrier to entry in the form of accumulating several years of research data. Thus, LTER VCs cannot grow as rapidly as conventional VCs. TFRI

had been working to share data for a shorter period, but has a dedicated team of domain and technical experts larger than most US LTER site information management teams, and comparatively less legacy data to bring in. FinLTSER has perhaps a half-dozen individuals sporadically working on its LTER VC, and its decades-old datasets need not be immediately published.

Thus, the CVCA view that management or interventions of VCs may be both beneficially required or harmful is reconciled under IVCA by treating management (functions) and interventions as various degrees of short- or long- term, local- or broad- scope changes to logics. Benefit or harm then would simultaneously occur depending on which VC members and information functions are helped or hindered by the logic change.

Uncontrolled data inhibits LTER sites' local work. Too strictly controlled data prevents easily contributing sufficient but not well-documented data. TFRI flexibly adopted the hybrid GBIF standard, which is as controlled as users choose it to be. TFRI members also continually survey nearby technologies for advantageous logics as a team in a similar manner as the US LTER does as a network.

The IVCA suggests a logic modification to motivate good data sharing practices. Indeed, TFRI's work (and investments outside the immediate obvious LMVC technical system) has inspired such a modification to the ecological research system in Japan to recognise "data papers" (a scholarly publication which purpose is to publish sufficiently described raw data rather than novel analysis) with similar weight as conventional research papers via the *Ecological Research* journal and related data repository (Ecological Research, 2011). (This necessitated a previous logic change in which data papers became possible as a new variety of scholarly publication.) Of consequence, the interlocking problems of personal and professional motivation, money and time, and critical mass can resolve in unison, while community management becomes a minimal task of those who use the VC infrastructures as routine rather than as exception.

Competition for Recognition

Being subject to network effects, VCs' robustness depends on the particular kinds of enrolment, knowledge and links they attract. The US LTER VC shows that a strong network, a built-in tradition of mentorship, and a strong tradition of sharing knowledge outside the LMVC, are insufficient conditions to bootstrap wide participation in the LMVC. The exclusivity problem (framed as a combination of belongingness and risk mitigation in the current VC literature) is not overcome by the fact that new members of the VC (young people) are comparative masters of online VC tools as compared to senior members (established researchers) whose negative judgments could be most harmful.

Only two LMVCs compete with the EML-based system: an ontology approach based on Darwin Core (TDWG, 2009), and the GBIF hybrid of metadata and ontology (GBIF, n.d.). Darwin Core has gained some attention in continental Europe, but is technologically and conceptually incompatible with EML. Participants claim TFRI, using the GBIF standard, has become a technical success because they have de-emphasised their ecology mission to become more competitive at attracting funding to develop technical, social, and informational infrastructures to support their LMVC. By investing to become a net technical, social and informational resource, TFRI overcomes some challenges in the US, including access to technical skills, strict EML standard compliance, and designing new data collection methods to fit the received technical infrastructure. (Parts of the US LTER are also attempting new collection methods in addition to remediating existing data.) The leader of TFRI's information management group insists on assigning his staff to examine and try all kinds of potentially interesting technologies in combination in order to increase the size

of their potential toolset. By exploring, adopting, adapting and expanding on logics from US and European LTER approaches, and expanding on logics from nearby web services and collaboration fields, TFRI's internal experimentation saved the expense of forcing many existing sites of practice to fit a new experimental logic. FinLTSER would lack resources to conduct such experiments.

The same TFRI leader is evidently pleased with the outcome that "The first-ever peer-reviewed paper derived directly from a biodiversity metadata document has been published in the open-access ZooKeys journal." (GBIF, 2011) via the GBIF approach in late 2011.

Contributions and Contributors

Trivial and incremental contributions are easy to make in many VCs. Although their information contents may be small, their social content and context also provide value. But in LMVCs, the most basic information (data and meta-data) contributions can require hours or years of preparation. At more committed levels, the limited number of LMVC software tools, complexity of research policies, and de-localized responsibility for particular software packages, projects, and policies, can make it difficult to influence the community's logic. The IVCA suggests that a new logic that more strongly recognises incremental contributions—such as providing incomplete data or cleaning contributed data—would encourage and enable new community members to contribute. Indeed, the US LTER meatspace community has been pushing to recognise data custodianship as a form of scholarly contribution. Individual FinLTSER members have repurposed funding to support data cleaning at research sites. TFRI has given data custodianship responsibilities to research managers, a position of prestige.

However, recalling that "virtual" makes the difference, we must understand participant skills in terms of that infrastructure. In other VCs, up-votes and referrals are potentially good indicators of expertise that has been identified, but counts alone says little about how a VC is to sustainably acquire expert skills in both the virtual logic and in the logic of the substantive subject matter. A competent LMVC contributor is simultaneously adept at IT systems administration, data management, VC management, and ecology. Such domain and technical experts could participate to train younger members in VCs, but it is unclear what would motivate such well-reputed and rare experts obtain from recognitions offered by most VC tools. Personal motivations of experts, like passing on a craft, have no unique bearing on the virtual environment. Applying the IVCA to LMVCs provides some insight.

The availability of information management staff differs within and among each LTER network. But in all cases, by tacitly abstracting use and administration of information into a service (a defined set of logics), PIs who synthesize and make the most transformative uses of data need not participate in the LMVC at all. TFRI's strategy—to gather the many interested junior and senior people from several disciplines and then to cross-train them on many technologies in use by diverse LTER researchers across the world—internalizes knowledge discovery skills to operate, manage and grow the regional technical and social infrastructures. Those elaborate logics—that enable the US and Taiwan meatspace LTER communities to recruit potential allies—would lack members and information on which to operate in FinLTSER. In addition, the IVCA understands how all three LTER communities may be moving toward sustainable LMVCs, without needing to categorize any as being in a static or terminal state of success or failure.

The IVCA understands the roles of senior people as variously as a non-participant on a daily basis, or as the only participant when acting as a champion (net resource source) for their local community (net resource sink) depending on the logics required. Possible syntheses from shared data are rare and require much effort and vast numbers

data points and sets for each higher abstraction or stronger claim. Professional recognition logics offer rewards for such resource-consuming work. It is therefore unsurprising that those who stand to gain the most by occupying gatekeeper positions in the system can be the loudest champions, yet the least proficient users.

Scale of Participation, Motives, and Rewards

Scale brings us to operationalization. With many non-workplace VCs, one member's obtaining of data is not considered to diminish its value for future users (e.g., viewing a Wikipedia page does not make it more scarce). In contrast to the Knowledge Commons (Hess and Ostro, 2007) form of VC, LTERs' high-level science goal is not represented by just a knowledge production or knowledge transmission function. In contrast to the Commons-Based Peer Production form of VC (Benkler and Nissenbaum, 2006), "modules" of ecological data are highly non-substitutable, non-granular, and have high cost of integration, and converges on many similar but independent and unbounded goals (research outputs), rather than on producing or maintaining a bounded information source or code base.

Among LTERs, one user's synthesis of data for publication may pre-empt another's use of the same combination of data for publication due to "originality" requirements. Although some meatspace LTER *members* have agreed on internal logics on exclusivity over data and co-authorship, access to LMVCs and their data in general is not limited to those having formal LTER membership. (Information shared in LMVCs remains rival as with information shared in meatspace communities.) This reminds us that motives and rewards may not scale in obvious ways. But in both contexts, more available data may be viewed as more or less valuable depending on the costs of locating useful data, and information use may be helpful or harmful to the VC (depending, for example, on the performance characteristics of the underlying technical systems). We can reconcile these two interpretations by highlighting that the data itself is not valuable, but its combination and processing with other data in particular contexts (logics) conveys potential value.

The IVCA's modularity lets us understand how Japan apparently obtained the LMVC that TFRI sought, via specific adaptations of logics proposed by TFRI. Japan's LTER: professionally rewards data papers like traditional research papers; enjoys participation from several government agencies and institutions (JaLTER, n.d.); and employed an explicit program to learn tacit logics by embedding its scientists at LTER networks abroad. IVCA also highlights that such logics would not be operable in Finland for want of qualified personnel. One Finnish research station director recognizes data work, another station's data champion locally recognizes and rewards good data practices, but there is no system-wide logic.

IVCA also highlights long-term and long-distance logics (echoing Bayus, 2010) to explain the different states of the three LMVCs. TFRI's initial difficulties getting the US *Metacat* developers to accept their patches to enable compatibility with Chinese characters, and its investments to adapt other international (English-language) software infrastructure and documentation for local use, both helped TFRI to develop logics required for TFRI to help researchers in other countries build their LMVCs. IVCA helps situate the competing pressures (logics) on FinLTSER: the *virtual* community's high English, Finnish, scientific, and technical proficiency requirements are difficult to meet given the regional *meatspace* logics that yield few qualified individuals to fill envisioned roles.

Using similar reasoning, IVCA explains that a VC's finite static logics (from the virtual setting)—that support well defined parallel interactions of different kinds of participants and roles within and among LMVCs—must also be complimented by logics for resolving ambiguities among sets of logics. It would be costly for every member of a VC to

carry and apply such exceptional logic to all cases, so differentiation must occur. Such differentiation is consistent with, and explains, the conventional VC conclusion that users must always be able to find new value if they are expected to maintain participating in the VC. Yet the IVCA provides a way to study and potentially guide beneficial logic changes by identifying areas of the VC having high logic density, and those areas where many exceptions to logic occur. Such potential focal points of the most important current information flows for the VC must be where the virtual part of the community draws its ability to thrive. IVCA also addresses the optimality vs. interoperability (or specialization vs. generalization) tension by exposing both as different perceptions of a subset of VC logics, from different subsets of mounted *analytic logics*.

Summary

The IVCA profitably understands seemingly unusual LMVCs in the same terms as conventional VCs, and generally agrees with CVCAs' interpretations. IVCA explains some apparent conflicts among interpretations provided by CVCAs, such as the dynamics of recognition, community management, and bootstrapping. IVCA also begins to explain (through communities of VCs and motives): that not all VCs should be large scale; that non-large scale VCs may be valuable sub-communities of other communities, not "failed" VCs; why contributions to VCs must be understood through their information contents than through facts of interaction; and how to use such analyses to enhance long-term VC sustainability. Conventional case study and single-site or deep ethnographic approaches simply cannot mobilize comprehensive data over long time periods across and among many related VCs to easily reach such insights.

In addition, the IVCA demands that we pay attention to the context of every VC studied. Very few logic sets are simple enough to be broadly applicable to many communities, so there are only a small number of examples of VCs that operate across many sub-communities. Reddit's sub-reddits provide an obvious example of a VC technical infrastructure, as do WordPress, Linux, and MediaWiki whose software logics and changes are adopted but only sometimes adapted by hundreds of thousands of VCs worldwide.

Most easily discovered and contributed information is unexceptional, thus requiring little further review or action. Exceptional information or patterns of logic-breaking exceptions may indicate important changes in the environment, to which the VC's logic must efficiently respond with corresponding patterns. Big changes to fundamental logics require testing and evaluation among wide swaths of the VC, and therefore aggregation of many inputs.

SOLUTIONS AND RECOMMENDATIONS FROM THE INFRASTRUCTURAL VC APPROACH

The IVCA understands traces left in VCs as information transactions that support instantaneous and long-term reinforcement of the information infrastructure (logic) itself. Because researchers of VCs use the same kinds of measures as VC members, it may be fair to examine such traces' potential effects on the logics. On the other hand, traces may be deceptive for both VC members and researchers.

Design and Management of VCs

Given that the network measures suggested by the IVCA are highly context sensitive, they would seem to work against generalizing our understanding of individual VCs to VCs in general. The IVCA suggests developing ways to detect and understand concurrent logics and processes in existing meatspace and virtual communities relevant to a VC's stakeholders, and to gather

and augment intersecting logics that would enable a (prospective) managed VC. As discussed in the previous section, although designs to yield particular emergent phenomena are difficult to execute, incompatible or inhibiting logics may be modified or countered through additional logics under the influence of VCs. More importantly, since each particular sustainable VC's logics must continually respond to dynamic information gaps in their environments (broader logics), the design and management of a VC's logics must enable guided adaptability.

This also suggests that infrastructures of rules can be actively managed. Each VC's narratives and histories contain an unknowable number of factors, circumstances, and path dependencies (and not just among the VC members!) that yield the particular practices and logics evidenced at present. IVCA's ability to match practices with logics can help us differentiate active and inactive logics when studying VCs or considering revisions to its logics. Foundational logics and narratives that have been re-interpreted or de-interpreted through sufficient intervening logics so as to have no present operational expression are good candidates pointing to assumptions to be checked. By contrast, those logics whose infrequent but consistent application reinforces many other logics are good candidates pointing to critical compatibilities to be explicitly maintained.

Understanding VC Growth

CVCAs consider VCs in a linear or lifecycle model: "As the online community matures the need for a more explicit and formal organization with regulations, rewards for contributions, subgroups, and discussion of more or less specific topics is evident." (e.g., Iriberri and Leroy, 2008). It is not clear why this structure should be evident. The IVCA agrees with the CVCAs' reasoning that loyalty to shared employment, ethnic kin, professions, amateur interests, medical conditions, learning groups, etc. (Ren et al, 2007) are important to keeping a VC whole. But IVCA treats such factors as different instantiations of concurrent discoverable logics and participation. Discovering overlapping but complimentary logics may help to explain how and why VCs established for a particular online or offline purpose appear to spin-in or modularize additional sub-communities about general or specific interests also shared by some members of the main VC. CVCAs' adopted social capital framework does not convincingly explain the variety of scales among spawned sub-communities. This is evident in MMORPG virtual community discussion boards that discuss building personal computers, or Penny Arcade, Fark, Reddit who have spawned parallel and complimentary charitable operations.

Social capital alone does not capture the virtual dimensions of how motives for participating in the VC may become simultaneously diluted and reinforced by time spent on such related interests in different VCs. However, expansion and subsetting of high level VC logic, along with participants' individual logics, may explain how spawning sub-communities in nearby niches is rational and why different subsets yield vastly diverse sub-communities.

Designing VCs for Sustainability

CVCAs engage weak sustainability concepts (namely, incentives for repeatability, as discussed) but rarely attempt to explain how sustainability may be predicted or operationalized. The IVCA considers logic-bound information exchanges as a series of value-generating outcomes. Logics can be learned from formal specifications, or from observing practice. Actions and interactions are made explicit through the ICTs, but the VC members' reasoning may remain tacit. Yet most VC members must assume the same common reasoning for the explicit actions and interactions to be intelligible—an implied infrastructure. The ability to virtually elicit such common assumptions (or understandings)—not explicitly through

transmitted or transformed bits—raises questions about implicit information, or perhaps references to external or offline norms, routinely transmitted through explicit information.

Recalling the biological metaphors, there are few conditions that universally make "life" more or less successful, other than the ability to convert materials and energy into reproducing the organism's logic set. Biologically derived communities will be fundamentally limited by biological realities and logics. The fundamental logic of sustainable VCs must therefore convert information inputs into the ability to gather more inputs. This implies several other logics including those that recruit and retain community members' attentions at the individual level, those enabling technical and social information storage and retrieval logics around the VC level, and those high-level logics that devise new kinds of data to be collected outside the VC at a global level.

Summary

CVCAs indicate that a vibrant VC will emerge from LTER because individual community members are motivated, there are available infrastructures, and the tasks of sharing are well understood. Yet the assortment of theories and approaches has not noticeably helped community managers produce on demand a large abundance of VCs having long-term interactions. Several actions among LMVCs that are counter-intuitive from the CVCAs have helped the LMVCs, and seem plausible to apply to other VCs as well.

VC theory expects that any VC should be able to be made successful. Indeed, it suggests an obvious solution: to overpower all inhibitions and to create participation by extending large external rewards. (However, this expectation is wrong—large long-lived successful sustainable communities are the exception, rather than the norm.) This is not sustainable, but it does suggest a sustainable approach from the infrastructure perspective. Reliable sources of resources will tend to draw users.

VCs may seed useful resources to entice users as an attempt at infrastructure, but must not restrict users of those resources to any particular purpose, such that users can add their own value by completing the processing of the resources provided by the infrastructure. (They create their own personal infrastructures around it, from which they derive a reward, as knowledge workers do). If they also derive a reward by contributing information back to the VC, they may be enticed to do so, says current VC theory. Extending that, contributions back to the VC become potential uses (or a resource surplus) for other users. If users contribute resources (users may themselves be resources—see question-answer sites) that are overall complimentary to other users' needs, the effort is sustainable without knowing about the details of each contribution or use.

FUTURE RESEARCH DIRECTIONS

Several limitations are worth noting. The above LMVC descriptions, their challenges, their infrastructures, etc. are highly condensed. Important details from extensive ethnographic fieldwork have necessarily been omitted in order to not overwhelm presentation of the IVCA.

The above presentation of IVCA also ignores the reality that many activities in meatspace and virtual communities may be simply habitual or normal in the context of individuals' daily routines. Considering VCs from the logics exposed by IVCA brings these habits back into the foreground, but must be grounded in extensive human biological and other intersecting logics that are neither fully understood, nor easily summarized.

Although the IVCA suggests an approach to large-scale comparisons, it currently remains dependent on difficult to scale ethnographic methods for data collection. Note that this chapter also

made use of documentary references to understand logics at LMVCs. Content analysis of structures is a potential additional approach operationalize IVCA, and to conduct large-scale VC studies beyond individual sites. IVCA identifies similar opportunities and challenges as the biography of artifacts framework (Williams and Pollock, 2009), and accessibly operationalizes some of its ideas in VCs. Current VC theory does not prepare us to consider populations of VCs or their mutual dynamics with each other. The large number of detectable VCs invites a statistical approach, perhaps leveraging information flows as a synthesis of maligned but useful traces, with celebrated but resource-intensive contexts.

The IVCA probably also works for meatspace, in that VC participants are governed by as many different kinds of meatspace logics as VC logics. Of consequence, this approach may enable malicious individuals to design and deploy logics that structurally convert contributions from the whole to benefits only for a minority of the community. For environmental researchers in particular, the IVCA may also provide a structure to engage the multiplicity of demands they make of information systems (Normore and Tebo, 2011). Identifying when one set of logics and assumptions conflicts with another, the potentials for growth and change and innovation are great.

CONCLUSION

The original research of question of, *"How can we understand participation through data sharing in LTER VCs?"*, has been addressed through the IVCA which helps to discover and examine the logics that motivate and inhibit individuals' potential actions and expectations about sharing data. In addition to identifying some motives and inhibitors of participation within each LTER metadata VCs expected from CVCAs, it also highlights logics concerning dynamics among

LTER metadata VCs. IVCA's ease of exposing systematic comparisons yielded suggestions to enhance participation and contributions in LM-VCs agree with those suggested by CVCAs. This systematic approach enables us to discover how VC participants at several units of analysis collect and employ logics that work in their favour.

ACKNOWLEDGMENT

This work was funded by the Academy of Finland. It was made possible by informative discussions with the staff, students, and visitors at the University of Oulu's Oulanka Research Station, Helsinki University's Kilpisjärvi Biological Station, and the Taiwan Forestry Research Institute. The author thanks Helena Karasti, Nic Webber, and reviewers for their helpful comments.

REFERENCES

Ardichvili, A., Page, V., & Wentling, T. (2003). Motivation and barriers to participation in virtual knowledge-sharing communities of practice. *Journal of Knowledge Management*, 7(1), 64–77. doi:10.1108/13673270310463626

Aronova, E., Baker, K., & Oreskes, N. (2010). Big science and big data in biology: From the international geophysical year through the international biological program to the long term ecological research (LTER) network, 1957–present. *Historical Studies in the Natural Sciences*, 40(2), 183–224. doi:10.1525/hsns.2010.40.2.183

Ashby, W. R. (1958). Requisite variety and its implications for the control of complex systems. *Cybernetica*, 1(2), 83–99.

Bayus, B. L. (2010). Crowdsourcing and individual creativity over time: The detrimental effects of past success. Retrieved February 3, 2012, from http://ssrn.com/abstract=1667101

Benkler, Y., & Nissenbaum, H. (2006). Commons-based peer production and virtue. *Journal of Political Philosophy*, 4(14), 394–419. doi:10.1111/j.1467-9760.2006.00235.x

Bowker, G. C., Baker, K., Millerand, F., & Ribes, D. (2010). Toward information infrastructure studies: Ways of knowing in a networked environment. In Hunsinger, J., Klastrup, L., & Allen, M. (Eds.), *International handbook of internet research* (pp. 97–117). doi:10.1007/978-1-4020-9789-8_5

Chavan, V., & Penev, L. (2011). The data paper: A mechanism to incentivize data publishing in biodiversity science. *BMC Bioinformatics*, 12(Suppl 15), S2. doi:10.1186/1471-2105-12-S15-S2

DataOne. (n.d.) *About DataONE*. Retrieved February 2, 2012, from http://www.dataone.org/about

de Moora, A., & Weigandb, H. (2007). Formalizing the evolution of virtual communities. *Information Systems*, 32(2), 223–247. doi:10.1016/j.is.2005.09.002

Ecological Research. (2011). *Ecological research: Guidelines for data papers*. Retrieved February 26 from http://www.springer.com/cda/content/document/cda_downloaddocument/EcolRes11284_DataPaperGuidelines20110426.pdf?SGWID=0-0-45-1081937-0

Furman, E., & Peltola, T. (2012). Developing socio-ecological research in Finland: Challenges and progress towards a thriving LTSER network. In Singh, S. J., Haberl, H., Chertow, M., Mirtl, M., & Schmid, M. (Eds.), *Long term socio-ecological research: Studies in society: Nature interactions across spatial and temporal scales*. Springer.

GBIF. (2011). *First database-derived 'data paper' published in journal*. Retrieved February 2, 2012, from http://www.gbif.org/communications/news-and-events/showsingle/article/first-database-derived-data-paper-published-in-journal/

GBIF. (n.d.). *About GBIF*. Retrieved February 2, 2012, from http://www.gbif.org/index.php?id=269

Geels, F. W. (2004). From sectoral systems of innovation to socio-technical systems Insights about dynamics and change from sociology and institutional theory. *Research Policy, 33*(6-7), 897–920. doi:10.1016/j.respol.2004.01.015

Geiger, R. S., & Ribes, D. (2011). Trace ethnography: Following coordination through documentary practices. In *Proceedings of the 44th Annual Hawaii International Conference on Systems Sciences*.

Gil, I. S., Baker, K., Campbell, J., Denny, E. G., Vanderbilt, K., & Riordan, B. (2009). The long-term ecological research community metadata standardisation project: A progress report. *International Journal of Metadata. Semantics and Ontologies, 4*(3), 141–153. doi:10.1504/IJMSO.2009.027750

Greenberg, J., White, H. C., Carrier, S., & Scherle, R. (2009). A metadata best practice for a scientific data repository. *Journal of Library Metadata, 9*(3-4), 194–212. doi:10.1080/19386380903405090

Hess, C., & Ostrom, E. (2007). *Understanding knowledge as a commons - From theory to practice*. Cambridge, MA: MIT Press.

Hinds, D., & Lee, R. M. (2008). Social network structure as a critical success condition for virtual communities. In R. H. Sprague, Jr. (Ed.), *Proceedings of the 41st Hawaii International Conference on System Sciences – 2008,* (pp. 323-333).

Iriberri, A., & Leroy, G. (2009). A life cycle perspective on online community success. *ACM Computing Surveys, 41*(2), 11. doi:10.1145/1459352.1459356

Japan, L. T. E. R. (n.d.). *About JaLTER*. Retrieved February 25, 2012 from http://www.jalter.org/modules/about/

Knowledge Network for Biocomplexity. (n.d.). *Ecological metadata language (EML) specification*. Retrieved February 3, 2012, from http://knb.ecoinformatics.org/software/eml/eml-2.0.1/index.html

Kraut, R., Maher, M., Olson, J., Malone, T. W., Pirolli, P. L., & Thomas, J. C. (2010). Scientific foundations: A case for technology-mediated social-participation theory. *Computer Magazine, 43*(11), 22–28.

Lécuyer, C., Brock, D. C., & Last, J. (2010). *Makers of the microchip: A documentary history of fairchild semiconductor*. Cambridge, MA: The MIT Press.

Lin, C.-C., Porter, J. H., Hsiao, C.-W., Lu, S.-S., & Jeng, M.-R. (2008). Establishing an EML-based data management system for automating analysis of field sensor data. *Taiwan Journal for Science, 23*(3), 279–285.

Lin, C. F. (2008). The cyber-aspects of virtual communities: Free downloader ethics, cognition, and perceived service quality. *Cyberpsychology & Behavior, 11*(1), 69–73. doi:10.1089/cpb.2007.9932

Mathwick, C., Wiertz, C., & De Ruyter, K. (2007). Social capital production in a virtual P3 community. *The Journal of Consumer Research, 34*, 832–849. doi:10.1086/523291

Messinger, P. R., Stroulia, E., Lyons, K., Bone, M., Niu, R. H., Smirnov, K., & Perelgut, S. (2009). Virtual worlds - Past, present, and future: New directions in social computing. *Decision Support Systems, 47*(3), 204–228. doi:10.1016/j.dss.2009.02.014

National Center for Ecological Analysis and Synthesis (NCEAS). (n.d.). *Overview.* Retrieved February 26, 2012, from http://www.nceas.ucsb.edu/overview

Normore, L. F., & Tebo, M. E. (2011). *Assessing user requirements for a small scientific data repository.* ASIST 2011, October 9-13, 2011, New Orleans, LA, USA.

Porter, C. E. (2004). A typology of virtual communities: A multi-disciplinary foundation for future research. *Journal of Computer-Mediated Communication, 10*(1), Article 3.

Preece, J., & Shneiderman, B. (2009). The reader-to-leader framework: Motivating technology-mediated social participation. *Transactions on Human-Computer Interaction, 1*(1), 13–32.

Rafaeli, S., & Ariel, Y. (2008). Online motivational factors: Incentives for participation and contribution in Wikipedia. In Barak, A. (Ed.), *Psychological aspects of cyberspace: Theory, research, applications.* Cambridge, UK: Cambridge University Press.

Reice, S. R. (1994). Nonequilibrium determinants of biological community structure. *American Scientist, 82*(5), 424–435.

Ren, Y., Kraut, R., & Kiesler, S. (2007). Applying common identity and bond theory to design of online communities. *Organization Studies, 28*(3), 377–408. doi:10.1177/0170840607076007

Ribes, D., & Polk, J. B. (2012). Historical ontology and infrastructure. *Proceedings of the 2012 iConference,* Toronto, CA, (pp. 252-264).

Taxonomic Databases Working Group (TDWG). (2009). *Darwin Core.* Retrieved February 2, 2012, from http://rs.tdwg.org/dwc/

Tedjamulia, S., Olsen, D. R., Dean, D. L., & Albrecht, C. C. (2005). Motivating content contributions to online communities: Toward a more comprehensive theory. In J. F. Nunamaker, Jr. & R. O. Briggs (Eds.), *Proceedings of the 38th Hawaii International Conference on System Sciences – 2005, 03-06 Jan. 2005.*

US LTER. (n.d.). *About LTER.* Retrieved February 2, 2012, from http://www.lternet.edu/overview/

von Bertalanffy, L. (1968). *General system theory: Foundations, development, applications.* New York, NY: G. Braziller.

Williams, R., & Pollock, N. (2009). Beyond the ERP implementation study: A new approach to the study of packaged information systems: The biography of artifacts framework. In *Proceedings of the Thirtieth International Conference on Information Systems* 2009.

Zimmerman, A. (2007). Not by metadata alone: The use of diverse forms of knowledge to locate data for reuse. *International Journal on Digital Libraries, 7*(2), 5–16. doi:10.1007/s00799-007-0015-8

ADDITIONAL READING

Avgerou, C. (2003). New socio-technical perspectives of IS innovation in organizations. In Avgerou, C., & La Rovere, R. L. (Eds.), *Information systems and the economics of innovation* (pp. 141–161). Cheltenham, UK: Edward Elgar.

Borgman, C. L., Wallis, J. C., & Enyedy, N. (2006). Little science confronts the data deluge: Habitat ecology, embedded sensor networks, and digital libraries. *International Journal on Digital Libraries, 7*(1), 17–30. doi:10.1007/s00799-007-0022-9

Chan, C. M. L., Bhandar, M., Oh, L.-B., & Chan, H.-C. (2004). Recognition and participation in a virtual community. In *Proceedings of the 37th Hawaii International Conference on System Sciences - 2004, 5-8 Jan. 2004.*

Chen, C.-J., & Hung, S.-W. (2010). To give or to receive? Factors influencing members' knowledge sharing and community promotion in professional virtual communities. *Information & Management, 47*(4), 226–236. doi:10.1016/j.im.2010.03.001

Chiu, C.-M., Hsu, M.-H., & Wang, E. T.-G. (2006). Understanding knowledge sharing in virtual communities: An integration of social capital and social cognitive theories. *Decision Support Systems, 42*(3), 1872–1888. doi:10.1016/j.dss.2006.04.001

Daghfous, N., Petrof, J. V., & Pons, F. (1999). Values and adoption of innovations: A cross-cultural study. *Journal of Consumer Marketing, 16*(4), 314–331. doi:10.1108/07363769910277102

Ebner, W., Leimeister, J. M., & Krcmar, H. (2009). Community engineering for innovations: The ideas competition as a method to nurture a virtual community for innovations. R&. *Mana, 39*(4), 342–356.

Garrety, K., & Badham, R. (2000). The politics of sociotechnical intervention: An interactionist view. *Technology Analysis and Strategic Management, 12*(1), 103–118. doi:10.1080/095373200107265

Guldberg, K., & Mackness, J. (2009). Foundations of communities of practice: Enablers and barriers to participation. *Journal of Computer Assisted Learning, 25*(6), 528–538. doi:10.1111/j.1365-2729.2009.00327.x

Huber, M. J., Leimeister, J. M., & Krcmar, H. (2009). Towards a pattern based approach for designing virtual communities for innovations. In. *Proceedings der Tagung Mensch & Computer, 2009,* 42–47.

Hughes, T. P. (1989). The evolution of large technological systems. In Bijker, W., Hughes, T., & Pinch, T. (Eds.), *The social construction of technological systems* (pp. 51–82). Cambridge, MA: MIT.

Mathwick, C., Wiertz, C., & De Ruyter, K. (2008). Social capital production in a virtual P3 community. *The Journal of Consumer Research, 34*(6), 832–849. doi:10.1086/523291

Mumford, E. (2006). The story of socio-technical design: reflections on its successes, failures and potential. *Information Systems Journal, 16*(4), 317–342. doi:10.1111/j.1365-2575.2006.00221.x

Nov, O., Naaman, M., & Ye, C. (2009). Analysis of participation in an online photo-sharing community: A multidimensional perspective. *Journal of the American Society for Information Science and Technology, 61*(3), 555–566.

Sangwan, S., Guan, C., & Siguaw, J. A. (2009). Virtual social networks: Toward a research agenda. *International Journal of Virtual Communities and Social Networking, 1*(1), 2198–2210. doi:10.4018/jvcsn.2009010101

Trist, E. (1981). *The evolution of socio-technical systems: A conceptual framework and an action research program. Occasional paper No.2 June 1981.* Ontario Ministry of Labour, Ontario Quality of Working Life Centre.

Zhang, Z. (2010). Feeling the sense of community in social networking usage. *IEEE Transactions on Engineering Management, 57*(2), 225–239. doi:10.1109/TEM.2009.2023455

KEY TERMS AND DEFINITIONS

Conventional Virtual Community Approach (CVCA): Understands virtual communities predominantly through their internal dynamics and in terms of behaviours and theories replicated from understandings of offline communities.

Infrastructural Virtual Community Approach (IVCA): Understands virtual communities not only through their internal logics dynamics, but also through their members' and sub-communities' relationships with other communities as mediated by the unique properties of online technologies.

Infrastructure: Usually hidden and highly constant logics that indicate and influence individual and community dynamics in general, not just in specific instances or scales. Infrastructures are noticed when they fail, rather than when they operate correctly.

LTER Metadata VCs (LMVC): Virtual communities established to share data and meta-data in long-term ecological research (LTER).

Logics: The intersecting sets of local and non-local, tacit and explicit, personal and community conditions that both enable and restrict possible interactions in a community, as embodied in technical tools, social norms, personal characteristics, and terrestrial realities.

Metadata: Structured and searchable data that describes a particular dataset.

Virtual: The condition of being (largely) unconstrained by logics of physical or tangible interactions.

Chapter 8
Community Embodied:
Validating the Subjective Performance of an Online Class

Sergey Rybas
Capital University, USA

ABSTRACT

Problematizing the historical, philosophical, and social foundations of online communities, this project lays out a theoretical framework of subjective performance in virtual spaces and uses it to examine interactions in one long-distance college class. The findings of this cyberethnographic study suggests that even though the collective perceptions of community remain relatively stable, yet idealized and evasive, the actual individual manifestations of online community are limited to the subjective performances of the members and are inseparable from their complex identities and literacies. Therefore, considering the subjective performances of online community is vital for understanding its goals, practices, principles, and limitations and critical for the assessment of its success.

EXAMINING THE HYPE

The study of online collaboration has been a true companion of research projects on online teaching and learning. First envisioned by Licklider and Taylor in 1968 (Feenberg & Bakardjieva, 2004), online (or virtual) communities have now become "an accepted part of the lives of Internet users" (Bishop, 2007, p. 1881). Studies of communal interactions have emerged and thrived across

academic disciplines. Referring to the hype surrounding the exploration of online communities across the academic and professional worlds, Shumar and Renninger (2002) note that theorists, researchers, and practitioners of seemingly unrelated backgrounds and interests are equally enthused by the study of "the community enabled by the Internet" (p. 1). A number of studies, early and recent (e.g., Baym, 1998; Jones, 2002; Iriberri & Leroy, 2009; Nagel, Blignaut, & Cronje, 2009), have invested significant effort into exploring

DOI: 10.4018/978-1-4666-0312-7.ch008

questions ranging from whether online communities are to be built or if they "occur on their own, 'organically,'" to whether online communities are "imagined" or "real" (Jones, 2002, p. 368). Others have placed emphasis on the impossibility to analyze the virtual outside the "real" (e.g., Davis, Seider, & Gardner, 2008; Wellman & Gulia, 1999) and critiqued the treatment of online community as "a separate reality" and "an isolated social phenomenon," not taking into account how interaction on the Net fits other aspects of people's lives (Jones, 2002, p. 368). Finally, a spike of research activity has been observed in the areas of online community as a cultural, gender, and age specific phenomenon (e.g., Meyers, 2009; Peowski, 2010; Sum, Mathews, Pourghasem, & Hughes, 2009; Yi, 2008), as well as such uses and benefits of online (learning) community in areas of professional development (Duncan-Howell, 2010; Karagiorgi & Lymbouridou, 2009), graduate education (Glassmeyer, Dibbs, & Jensen, 2011), parenting (Farquharson, 2011; Winarnita, 2008), or political potential (Craig, 2010; In der Smitten, 2008).

The abundance of research of online communities, however, has not been able to address many of the basic questions on the concept, the mechanisms of construction and sustainment, as well as the ways of measuring the effectiveness of a learning community online. For instance, the questions of "presence" and "learning online" have largely remained limited to examining participant perception of satisfaction and learning (Akyol & Garrison, 2011). Few studies have "elucidated the relationships among online behaviors, online roles, and online learning communities" (Yeh, 2010, p. 140). Even less has been done to examine the multiplicity of performative functions, social expectations and user subjectivities embedded in the fabric of virtual interactions (Kehrwald, 2010; Liao & Hsieh, 2011; Saltmarsh-Sutherland-Smith, 2010). A dated statement by Wellman and Gulia (1999), therefore, has held true for over a decade:

The subject [on online community formation and functioning] is important: practically, scholarly, and politically. The answers have not yet been found. Indeed, the questions [emphasis added] are just starting to be formulated. (p. 188)

The embeddedness of online community in the experiences of everyday life and its reflection of and influence on the communication practices and patterns of identity formation make online community a colossal research enterprise that requires continuous investigation and theorizing. Grounded in the belief that online community is an active and productive discourse, which brings forth unique subjectivities of community members, this cyberethnographic study analyzes interactions in one online college class. Focusing on the performative nature of student subjectivities, embodying the online community itself yet reflecting the individual literacy of each community member, I argue that considering subjective performances of online community is vital for understanding its goals, practices and principles and limitations; and, is critical for the assessment of its success.

PROBLEMATIZING ONLINE COMMUNITY

An underlying foundation of much of research on online communities is the widely accepted idea of the communality of the cyberspace and its conduciveness to the formation of social binding that was quickly labeled as one of key futures of "online community." The social binding produced while interacting online remained a recurrent theme of much of research on online education throughout the 1990s. Rheingold (1994), a keen explorer of online communities, stresses *shared interests* of online communicators as the building blocks of community. Such shared interests, according to Rheingold, trigger social binding and lead to the formation of a communal space. Rheingold's belief in the automatism of the establishment of community online is as complete as it is striking. The process of community formation, according to Rheingold, is underwritten by the inherent desire of humans to socialize, while the internet technology is the right tool to accommodate that desire. In fact, online community is almost a by-product of the internet technology: "Whenever CMC technology becomes available to people anywhere, they inevitably build virtual communities with it, just as microorganisms inevitably create colonies" (p. 6). The idea of social bonding is echoed by Norris (2004) who attributes the blossoming of online community building to the active and open nature of the American Nation.

The social binding of online group interactions reinforced a well-established metaphor of community, whose value in social, educational, and professional settings is hard to overestimate. The adoption of the term "community," however, brings to the world of computer-mediated communication more confusion than convenience and clarity. Baym (1998) expresses a concern directly related to this project:

Despite – or perhaps because of – the term's intuitive appeal, these normative and ideological connotations have made its use controversial in the academic and popular work surrounding CMC. (p. 35)

Given the above mentioned controversy, it is fair to say that the ideas of *social binding* inherent in online communities and *communality* of cyberspace are in dire straits of establishing and upholding validity. The content of both ideas is heavily influenced, if not entirely controlled by the existing idea of community. The normative and ideological connotations Baym talks about reflect the imposed conventions of the existing discourse on community rather than letting online community speak in its own right as a unique discourse of the era of cyberlife.

This project posits that the existing assumptions about social binding and communality of online communities are affected by two complex themes that have defined practice and research of computer-mediated communication since its advent. The first theme is the egalitarian debate on online communication that was one of the prevalent arguments in the early scholarship on CMC. The essentializing of online communication bears a stamp on the theory and practice of online communities, while the positivist qualities assumed by any group interaction online result in an improbable expectation of any such interaction becoming an online community. The second theme is the overall drive toward community-building, which is informed by two conflicting concepts of community – *Gemeinschaft* (family- or village-like community) vs. *Gesellschaft* (community of large masses) – developed by German sociologist Ferdinand Tonnies. Human nostalgia for the now mythical and idealized communal closeness associated with Gemeinschaft, and the innate fear, antipathy, and rejection of Gesellschaft cannot but affect the meta idea of community, leading to essentializing its qualities, processes and uses, failing to embrace its fluidity and multiplicity.

The Egalitarian Debate

Among the celebrated and heavily debated topics in online education of the early 1990s, the alleged egalitarianism enabled by online communication has enjoyed a tremendous amount of spotlight. During that time, a recurrent theme in many publications was that of a more egalitarian nature of online interactions as compared to the face-to-face communication. Referring to several major journal publications and edited collections of the early 1990s, Blair and Monske (2003) point to the similarity of conclusions: "almost any networked activity will be a means to decenter the traditional classroom space and to disrupt the position of teacher as the figure of mastery … allowing students from all backgrounds to be heard" (p. 444).

However, as online education evolved over its first decade and made its way into campuses of most U.S. colleges, the egalitarian view of online discourse has been challenged by a number of research projects that, at best, criticize and, at worst, dismantle various constituents of its universally acclaimed goodness. For example, Jones (2002) questions the validity of the "democratic vs. undemocratic" debate:

Just because the spaces with which we are now concerned are electronic there is not a guarantee that they are democratic, egalitarian or accessible and it is not the case that we can forgo asking in particular about substance and dominance. (p. 20)

Romano (1993) calls the assumptions of egalitarianism engendered by technology "invidious." She explains: "if the technology is inflexible, infallible, and ever-enabling, then human beings absorb blame for [its] failure" (p. 25). Pointing at the social construction of technological spaces, Romano demands a more complex understanding of living and learning with technology, which renders the simplistic, egalitarian ideals of automation and neutrality irrelevant and untrue.

While the egalitarian promise of online education has been contested, problematized, revised, and/or rejected, the discussion of online community – its formation and functioning (which, undeniably, has developed parallel to the discussion of egalitarianism) – has remained influenced by the essentialist attitudes toward technology of the late 1980s-early 1990s. The inflexible belief that any limited-access online entity is susceptible to the formation of community or that any such entity can be interpreted, and/or classified using the language and categories of the face-to-face community points to the obvious intersection of the essentialist logic of the egalitarian view on online learning and the positivist logic of building communities online. That is, just like the egalitarian view, disregards the cultural, political, and economic situatedness of an online educational endeavor, a unified approach to an online community strips it of a situatedness in the contexts of online communication. Overall, while "commu-

nity building is frequently considered a desirable part of online learning, [and teachers] encourage students to build a community from which they later must depart or disengage" (Kazmer, 2005, p. 25), the scholarship on online communities pays very little attention to the type, structure, and specifics of *online communities*. It seems that the idea of a community that has long been associated with face-to-face interactions has been transferred to online interactions. The assumptions about such interactions, as well as the expectations from them, have made a similar inferential leap.

One does need to acknowledge, however, that a number of scholars have voiced similar concerns over essensializing online communities. Renninger and Shumar (2002), for example, have stressed that achieving the communal potential, which is inherent in online interactions, may not be "automatic, easy, or necessarily enduring." These authors have compared community building in online settings to freedom, which "is a fragile accomplishment that must be constantly worked at and watched over" (p. xxv). Wilbur (2000) has pointed to the many aspects of human identity that factor in the formation and interpretation of online community. He has emphasized that any study of online community will require a researcher to do "a difficult job of picking a path across a shifting terrain, where issues of presence, reality, illusion, morality, power, feeling, trust, love, and much more" (p. 54). The liberation of online community from the essentialist/positivist dogma of always accompanying online interactions is an important step toward a better understanding of human communication and a significant promise of more informed teaching and learning.

Conceptualizing Online Community

The second major theme that informs the meta discussion of communities, including those online, is the overall human drive toward communal interaction in a search for closeness, personal relationship, friendship, or support. Relying on

Ferdinand Tonnies, a forefather of contemporary sociological theory, Shumar and Renninger (2002) note that the notion of community has evolved from the pre-modern concept of *Gemeinschaft* (community as kinship or partnership), which stands for "coherent community in which culture and family are intact, and social life is whole because of this" (p. 3), to the modern concept of *Gesellschaft* (community as society, association, or company), which marks "a loss of traditional community values and structures and replaces them with impersonal relationships and fragmented cultural values" (p. 3). Gemeinschaft, Bell (2001) explains, is "a 'traditional' community where everyone knows everyone, everyone helps everyone, and the bonds between the people are tight and multiple" (p. 95). The bonds are naturally developed and easily preserved due to the small and typically closed-access character of a given group (e.g., a village or a family) and the considerable dependence of the group members on one another.

The evolutionary successor of Gemeinschaft is "the social arrangement" that Tonnies called Gesellschaft, which is brought to life owing to such processes as urbanization, industrialization, and, later, globalization and technologizing of the world. The new era people are "removed from Gemeinschaft-like situations and thrown together in the dense heterogeneity of the city" (Bell, 2001, p. 94). The relationships among the members of a Gesellschaft-like community are shallow and instrumental. Bell calls such relationships within such social arrangement "disembedding" and argues that it "impoverishes communities" (p. 94).

Studdert (2005) explains that while community (the Gemeinschaft type) "comes to represent … something lost [and] impossible" (p. 29), its altogether opposite positioning defines all social interactions.

In all, in Gesellschaft, kinship relations have been replaced by material capital while deliberate will and practicality have replaced essential will and organicity. The opposition of Gesellschaft and Gemeinschaft results, as Tonnies argues, in a consistent attempt by humans to regain or rebuild the lost ideal while relying on the material, the practices and the ideologies that do not correspond to it, if not finding themselves at odds with the pre-modern idea of community. Bell (2001) mentions "nostalgia" describing the influence of Gemeinschaft on both theory and practice of online communities. Elaborating on that idea, Shumar and Renninger (2002) say that "community" has remained in the hands of social scientists who "create a kind of fiction about the relation of time and historical movement that does not apply to many specific locales," as community is defined "as that we have lost to modernity" (p. 4).

Shumar and Renninger (2002) further argue that "the organization of community has become … individualized and less structured by larger social forces of class, work, geographic location and the like" (p. 5). They warn us that defining online communities in terms of or in contrast to Gemeinschaft and Gesellschaft "may keep us from recognizing forces that structure social relationships and … forms of social relationships that are being enacted in computer-mediated communication" (p. 5). Overall, the scholarship's dependence on the rigid dichotomy of Gemeinschaft and Gesellschaft in defining or otherwise handling online community inevitably leads to a disregard of the evolving discourse of online community, a failure to interpret its origin, meaning, and parameters, and a difficulty to utilize its potential for people communicating, co-existing, or collaborating online. The need for problematizing or re-visiting online community is, therefore, apparent while a rigorous effort driving such problematizing and re-visiting is long overdue. Haythornthwaite (2002) compares the exploration of online community to a black box that has yet to be looked into. This looking inside, she argues, should help "examine what types of interactions and associations make for a community" (p. 160). Stressing the need of "a turn toward [exploring] the nature of commitment in online social groups,"

Fernback calls to move "beyond community as a paradigm of online studies" (p. 66) and into a more critical and a more conscious examination of this phenomenon.

Community as Discourse

A theoretical foundation that challenges that inflexible understanding of online community is the concept of *discourse* in which conventional ways of meaning making are refuted. According to Foucault, "discourse," is a system in which certain knowledge is possible. Online communal interactions are a part of this system; they find themselves situated in a web of relationships with other discourse constituents – i.e., people, ideologies, and histories. In "What is an Author?," Foucault argues that discourse cannot only be analyzed by "its architectonic forms," such as codes and symbols embedded within the text. By the same token, the codes and symbols, online communal interactions being one of them, cannot be considered apart from the other discourse constituents with whom they are involved in an intricate interplay. Discourse, Foucault (1980) concludes, may only be analyzed with respect to its "placement" in a social context, which involves the dissemination and value of the discourse as well as the author's relationship to and society's adaptation of the discourse (p. 163). Acknowledging a limited agency of the speaker/observer, Foucault stresses that the knowledge produced in discourse is not a sole prerogative of either one of its members or constituents. Rather, it is a product of "relations between institutions, economic and social processes, behavioral patterns, systems of norms, techniques, types of classification, [and] modes of characterization" (Foucault, 1980, p. 143).

Applied to the current discussion, the Foucauldian idea of *discourse* is vital for the reconceptualization of online community, for which scholars, professionals, administrators and activists like Kazmer (2005), Haythornthwaite

(2002), Baym (1998), Bell (2001), Jones (2002), Huwe (2008), and Williams (2008) have called. A logical departing point for such reconceptualization is an examination of the unique power relations produced within the discourse of online community as well as the individual enactments and understandings of collaborating online. The culture of an online interaction serves as solid ground for the construction of subjectivities that, in their own turn, end up setting the parameters of online discourses. The promise of subjectivity inherent in online interactions calls for a closer examination of the mechanism by which the subjectivities of online learners shape and define the discourse of online community. The subject's ability to differentiate the self from the other (Lacanian subject), as well as see and act independently from the other, invokes the metaphor of vision as most appropriate for describing such mechanism. Vision as a feminist epistemology is given ample attention in the works of Anzaldua (1987), Harding (2004), Jaggar (2004), among others. Haraway (1991) believes that vision is a way to feminist objectivity, opposed to binary oppositions and honoring what Haraway calls *situated knowledge(s)*. Such situated knowledge(s), which she sees as legitimate ways of meaning making, are always "partial, locatable, critical knowledge(s) sustaining the possibility of webs of connections called solidarity in politics and shared conversations in epistemology" (p. 191). As with many other feminists, Haraway argues "for a doctrine and practice of objectivity that privileges contestation, deconstruction, passionate construction, webbed connections, and hope for transformation of systems of knowledge and ways of seeing" (p. 192).

Haraway also insists on "the embodied nature of all vision [and] reclaim[s] the sensory system that has been used to signify a leap out of the marked body and into a conquering gaze from nowhere" (p.188). This gaze, Haraway explains, "mystically inscribes all the marked bodies [and...] makes the unmarked category claim the power to see and not to be seen, to represent while escaping representation" (p.188). The subjective situated knowledge(s), along with feminist embodiment and feminist hopes for partiality and objectivity "turn on conversations and codes … in fields of possible bodies and meanings" (p. 201).

Interestingly, the idea of embodied vision, which, eventually, leads to the production of situated knowledge(s), does not imply that knowledge is produced solely by the subject, in opposition to or for a particular object. Merleau-Ponty, whose *Phenomenology of Perception* (1962) is an attempt to deconstruct Cartesian subject-object duality, described embodied knowledge as "knowledge in the hands, which is forthcoming only when bodily effort is made, and cannot be formulated in detachment from that effort" (p. 144). Harris (2003) explains embodied knowledge is "created in the unity between subjects and objects that is the direct result of having a body." The Lacanian subject is evident here: to perform as a subject, the discourse participant must also be an object. The "body" of the discourse participant is, thus, a unity of the subjective and the objective.

Further, Haraway's vision grounds itself in the web of "subjugated standpoints," the positionings of the subjects, which "promise more adequate, sustained, objective transforming accounts of the world" (p. 191). The hint here is that any study of subjectivities must embrace the idea of inconclusiveness and malleability of the discourse in which knowledge is produced. Any such study must also recognize the validity of embodied and situated knowledge(s) that are to define literacies, epistemologies, and pedagogies of the future.

Scope and Method

The empirical part of this project is an exercise in exploring newly-emerged "cultures" of the technologized world. The "culture" scrutinized is that of a single online class taught by me at a medium-sized university in the American Midwest. In an attempt to narrow "culture" to a more

manageable entity, the project limits itself to the theoretical concepts of subjugation of the online community member and his/her performance in the evolving community of one online class. That is, *online community*, or, precisely, the *discourse of online community and the sum of the constituents that produce this discourse* serves to define the "population" of the study, while the rules of the formation and functioning of such discourse, which Bourdieu (1988) would call *habitus*, replace the term "culture." The *subjectivity* of the online user is a crucial concept for the analysis of online community. Thus, taking a closer look at the subjectivities of online community members and exploring their *vision(s)*, the *subjugated standpoints*, and *situated knowledge(s)* help construct a representative picture of the "rules of the game" that embody online communities.

An important emphasis of this ethnographic project is on its departure from the traditional anthropological ethnography that has been known to simply document the uniqueness of a culture under investigation, as well as to defend and rationalize the revealed novelty, originality, or difference of such culture. A clearer idea about the assumptions, beliefs, and mechanisms of online community should help educators become better versed in the intricacies of its discourse and contribute to the formation and exchange of progressive, critical pedagogies of the information age. The project is positioned as a "critical ethnography" (Warren, 2006), an epistemological endeavor "giv[ing] life to people in context, mak[ing] embodied practices meaningful, and generat[ing] analysis for conditions that make the socially taken-for-granted visible as a process" (p. 318).

The Object(s) of Research: The Performances of Online Community

An analysis of user subjectivities and performances in/of online community is inseparable from a discussion of class interactions. To examine the participation dynamics in the class, the study summarized and assessed the weekly contributions of all seven students enrolled. Additional information on the student interactions was gathered from individual interviews, in which four students agreed to participate.

To measure the students' involvement in the online class discussions, the project employed the concept of democratic dialogue offered by Burbules (1993), who discusses three rules for an effective discussion in any educational setting:

1. The rule of participation, standing for any participant's ability to raise topics, pose questions, challenge other points of view, or engage in any other activities that define the dialogical interaction (p. 80);

2. The rule of commitment, implying a possibility for any participant to agree or disagree with other participants as well as the instructor (p. 81); and

3. The rule of reciprocity, implying reversible and reflexive behaviors for all participants of a dialogical interaction (p. 82).

The participation and involvement markers aid the data collection for RQ 1:

RQ 1: How was interaction performed online?

The power dynamics data collected as part of this project sets the direction for the examination of the subjectivity that is, arguably, internalized and performed by the participants of online interactions. RQ 1 provides insights into the actions, decisions, or beliefs on the part of the students that may account for their own understanding of selves as subjects. The unique agency enabled by the subjugation of the online user, as the earlier review demonstrates, allows for unique relations within an online group. The internalized subjugation bears consequences on the individual choices of online users, but also changes the features and dynamics of what constitutes an online community. Analyzing the qualitative and quantitative data

for RQ 1, the second question of the study (RQ 2) is advanced:

RQ 2: How was community performed online?

FINDINGS AND DISCUSSION

Performing Interaction Online (RQ1)

The metaphors of subjectivity, subjective performances, and situated knowledge(s) point at the need to examine the power relations in the online class. The data and the interview responses collected in reference to RQ 1 suggest that the roles assumed by the class participants, as well as the roles expected of the fellow class participants, reflected the individual literacy practices of the members of the class. As "literacy practices never occur dissociated from the broader social practices … [and] they are never context-neutral and value-free" (Braga & Burrsardo, 2004, p. 45), the roles, expected and performed in class, depended upon the skills of the participants and were affected by the format of any given interaction (e.g., small group discussion, dialogue based on personal knowledge and professional expertise, conversation with peers vs. instructor). The malleability of "role" stood in direct correspondence with the pliability of community that evolved in the duration of the online class.

First, only about half of all students' posts (51.5%) were dialogic in nature (i.e., containing a reaction to a previous post by a group member; expressing an opinion or judgment on an idea expressed by a class member; or asking for advice). An example of a dialogic post by a student could be this:

Thanks!!! Sometimes I am hypercritical of my writing and I fear it will become dull and over-edited if I'm not careful. Sometimes I think it would be interesting to be a technical writer, but I'm sure I'd add something I shouldn't just to see if the audience is paying attention. Not a great idea when it comes to job security, you know. (Seth)

Clearly, the student is building on the ideas of a previous post developing, thereby, an online conversation.

The principle difference between a dialogic and a monologic post is that the latter does not encourage further conversation and only responds to the very generic theme of the discussion forum set by the instructor. Here is an example of a message posted in a discussion forum dedicated to revision strategies of a major assignment:

Introduction (explanation of the purpose of the document and how it will detail the experience and knowledge acquired to justify course credit). Course Objectives (Listing of each objective followed by a statement of the understanding of the course objective with general information relating to the objective). Conclusion (A summary of the above information and request for course credit.) (Carl)

Carl's post looks and reads like his own report on the work done. Naturally, it does not generate any further discussion. While the student does "score" his participation points, his involvement in the discussion as an interaction of an entire class remains minimal. Another example of monologic posting could be a very common message like "Here's my draft" or "Attached is my revision," which are both very uninviting of further conversation or debate. The totals for both types of posts do not suggest a significant prevalence of either – 221 monologic vs. 235 dialogic.

The high number of monologic posts may be at odds with the ideas of involvement, support, responsiveness, or shared spirit of collegiality and brotherhood that saturates theory and practice of education in virtual classrooms. More importantly, however, the prevalence of online monologue contradicts some of the students' own statements. For example:

I think that we have to keep in mind that there could be more than 2 or 3 people involved in the on-line discussion, which means that we need to keep everyone involved as much as possible. I believe that my role will be to participate, read what others write, try to comprehend and consider what others write and then respond if applicable. (Ashley)

About half of Ashley's posts (just like those of her classmates) did not necessarily aim at involving people in the conversation. A statement from another student seems equally cliché:

My role will be to be aware of other student's postings and work and be willing to share feedback and information with the group. In order to gain the most from this course, it will be necessary for me to feel comfortable with "putting myself out there" and be willing to accept constructive criticism. (Seth)

Thus, while expecting and emphasizing interaction, both students, routinely, opted out of it, favoring the one-directional way of communicating their thoughts and ideas to the members of the online community.

Knowledge-Making in an Online Class (RQ 1)

Another discrepancy in the assumed and the performed roles in a virtual classroom was the low level of students' reliance on each other in knowledge-making. This was especially noticeable during the peer reviews, which students had to complete in small groups for each major assignment in the class. Even though the level of engagement was typically high and the students favored an opportunity to comment on the work of each other, at least three students (i.e., Ashley, Seth, and Kim) noted that it was the private feedback from the instructor that mattered the most.

The instructor also remained a paramount participation incentive for most (if not all) of the students, as well as an unchallenged authority in the construction of "truth" in online forums. Here are some instances:

Whenever in doubt, I tend to ask my instructor. I mean I tried to ask peers, too, but if it's an important question, I feel like asking the teacher. (Kim)

Kim's comment invokes the issue of trust and dependability that seemed to have weak representation in her online community. Ashley seconded Kim on the idea of credibility of knowledge produced in student-to-student interactions:

The instructor was much more credible to me than my fellow peers, after all, he is the instructor! I did, however, value many of the other students' comments, ideas, and suggestions.

Finally, Seth chose to ask his instructor and not the fellow students because he perceived meaning-making in a communal interaction more labor-and time-consuming:

I tried to interact with everybody. I mean I will interact with whomever on-line. As far as asking questions, asking the class instead of shooting an email to the instructor seemed like more work to me.

The idea of talking to the instructor as "less work" also prompts the following line of thinking: according to Seth, the instructor serves as a higher authority that can handily provide an answer to any question. In fact, the ever-present and available instructor, who, as the course statistics demonstrate, remained the most active participant in the class at all times, definitely contributed to Seth's limited understanding of the power arrangement in the online class.

Along with the earlier discussed patterns of question asking and private communication, these responses shed light on a striking trend – while the students were aware that the instructor was, above all, a participant in the class and "was lurking out there somewhere" (Kim), few, if any, students felt entitled to consider the instructor as a fellow community member, even though that was exactly the image I repeatedly tried to project in the class discussions and comments. The instructor's unintended domination of the public forum discussions, caused by the desire to fit in the role of "a good teacher" attending to the needs of all students, solidified the status quo in the class. In public forums, therefore, the role the class members assumed most of the time was that of *a student*, who is being examined and scrutinized not only by the teacher (every interviewee named the instructor as the primary examiner of all class content), but also by the fellow students (Seth and Kim implied that in their comments). The Foucauldian Panopticon worked its simple magic here. However, while the Panoptic eye controlled the online presence, the same Panoptic effect instilled an awareness of being observed in the students. This awareness, which the project considered as part of the subjugation process, led to the formation of an intricate public vs. private paradigm that informed all communication in this class, gave rise to a specific level of agency that guided the class participants through their choices in communal interactions.

The manifestation of this agency took various forms and shapes with some people asking more questions online (i.e., Kim), communicating with the instructor behind the scenes (all students, but especially Kim, Ashley, and Carl), minimizing participation while maintaining ample "invisible presence" online (e.g., David), or avoiding dialogic interaction (e.g., Allen, Ashley, and Seth). The variety of ways of interaction and participation triggered by the subjugation of the community members bore its unique mark on the formation of communal relations within the space of the online class. Like the evolving subjectivities of its members, the online community continued to evolve, connecting and empowering its members, yet also separating, limiting, and controlling them.

Performances of Online Community (RQ 2)

To explore community construction (RQ 2), the study assessed the students' understanding of "online community" and analyzed the patterns of community construction that revealed themselves in the work of the students. The multiple ways in which the students performed interaction in the online class, and the conflicting roles which they assumed for themselves and for others, suggested two consistent themes concerning the construction and functioning of an online community: a) online community is a by-product of an assignment-driven interaction located in time and fueled by *a need* to communicate rather than an opportunity to interact with others; and, b) online community is individually embodied by each of its members and is affected by their skill and need level.

To collect concrete insights into community construction and maintenance, one of the interview open-ended questions asked students about activities, roles, and practices that they believed were encouraged in the online class. All respondents mentioned the usual benefits of online learning (i.e., time, convenience, higher level of anonymity or impersonality, and ease of accessibility of class content). Strikingly, though, none of them emphasized building relationships, friendships, or establishing particular closeness within the group – the assumed qualities of a community. Countering these missing qualities were such characteristics as increased selectivity of participation, increased labor application and increased solitude. The sample responses read:

An online class encourages writing and weighing what you are going to write before actually posting it. It does not necessarily encourage building relationships, but maybe that is because I'm so far away. (Seth)

The writing and weighing of the content prior to posting it resonates with the earlier discussion of formality of online communication and the students' tendency to imitate academic discourse. The public display of posts coupled with the ever-present awareness of the class as a graded performance does not necessarily encourage or enable communality. Add to this the difference in the student level, age, interests and such communality appears an even less relevant concept.

Online class has forced me to think more. I worked a lot harder in this class. When you are out here on your own staring at a textbook and it doesn't make sense, you must engage your brain in a new way. (Kim)

Kim's desire to succeed in the class led to the application of additional effort to her studies, not relying on or requesting the help from her peers.

You are in a class full of people, but basically, you are always alone, all by yourself, faced with a need to say the right things to the right people, at the right time. You can't see people's reactions, facial expressions, so you have to be more aware of what your words are saying or APPEARING to say to someone reading them. (Ashley)

Ashley's feeling separated from the class was also at odds with the traditional assumption of the dynamics in an online community.

While some of the students' experiences directly contradicted common beliefs about egalitarity and inclusivity of online education, all three interviewees were enthusiastic in their admittance that community was a part of the class. Speaking of a connecting or communal element in the class, the three students gave similar responses, which stressed working to address "a common need" (i.e., developing an individual portfolio) (Seth), having "similar needs and abilities" (Ashley), and cultivating *"a sense of obligation that may be developed by working as a group" (Kim).*

The recurrence of the "need" theme in the responses of the students suggests that the core of the community was not in particular ways or patterns of interaction, but in developing *a need* to communicate. In other words, the community based itself *not* in *how* to communicate but *why* to communicate with others toward meeting a set objective. This finding is surprising as it contradicts prior research on knowledge-making communities (Hoadley & Pea, 2002), which emphasized interactivity over method or even content of online communication as vital for the learning in online communities. The emphasis on developing or realizing a need or a cluster of needs – as opposed to the mere addressing of it/ them by way of communal interaction – instilled further subjugation in the students: as they defined such needs for themselves (i.e., eliciting feedback or opinion, developing a vision or a plan for the completion of an assignment or class, etc.), they had to select or construct a means of addressing it. The means included, but were not limited to, an active interrogatory mode (public or private), practicing "invisible presence" online, or reliance on or avoidance of dialogue.

An online community structure that revolves around the agency of its members, rather than the tools that enable interaction, marks, in Holt's (2004) words, a move from passivity toward activity of the community member as a social actor (p. 53). Such social actor, Holt explains:

Is not only assumed to be more personally complex than is usual in monologic views, but is also viewed as capable of more diverse and broadly ranging activity. These expansions of potentiality, moreover, are situated in a reality allowing for myriad viewpoints that privilege subjectivity. (2004, p. 54)

Speaking in Foucauldian terms, the "self" of the social actor, located within the deep regimes of discourse and practice, breaks out of the web of classification, objectification and normalization instilled by the rigorous practice of communal interaction in the very general and traditional sense of the word. Online community, therefore, warrants a release of a new agency, paves way to the subjects' detachment of selves from the regimes of conventional truth, and allows for reconsideration and reconstruction of the very practices of everyday life, i.e., teaching and learning in an online environment.

A major implication of the need vs. format-based core of communal interaction for the distance education is this: those who do teaching and learning, as well as those who promote such forms of education, need to become cognizant of the communication practices available and fostered in computer-mediated classrooms. Any change in the structure of doing education implies modifying not only the methods of content delivery but, also, the forms and the processes of understanding that content, as well as ways of engaging the content and interacting with other people. An inflexible model of "communal" interaction, driven by a participation requirement and grounded in the belief that any closed-access entity is conducive to effective knowledge-making, bears a danger of ignoring the great liberating and empowering potential online technology extends to us - students, educators, administrators, or, simply, communicators.

COMMUNITY EMBODIED, COMMUNITY ... IMAGINED?

The performances of online communication suggest that the online community in the online class was largely an individually embodied experience for those involved in this educational endeavor. The idea of embodiment as a rhetorical tool is attributed to Haraway, who stresses "the politics embodied in knowledge – situated knowledge – in which the ideological implications for certain kinds of seemingly 'disinterested' knowledge are made articulate" (cited in Kates, 2002, p. 55). Embodied cognition research, according to Rambusch and Ziemke (2005):

Provides additional picture of the situated nature of situated-learning activity by putting emphasis on the close and mutual relationship between thinking and doing from a different point of view. Instead of reducing the body to an input-output device and explaining cognition in terms of mental symbol manipulation, researchers and scientists in embodied cognition now seek to emphasize the complex interplay between body and mind, between the agent and the world which it is part of and functions in. (p. 1803)

Embodied knowledge is also a vibrant topic in cognitive psychology. Cowart (2006) explains that embodied cognition is an outcome of "real-time, goal-directed interactions between organisms and their environment" and concludes that "the nature of these interactions influences the formation and further specifies the nature of the developing cognitive capacities." Pertaining to the online community that this project scrutinizes, embodiment was evident in the multiplicity of individual literacies (i.e., knowledge(s) situated in individual histories and experiences) of the community members. For example, a significant tendency in the weekly participation dynamics of the students was the apparent correlation between the level of participation and the personal matters that filled the "real" lives of the students. The level of Kim's involvement, for instance, was heavily affected by two factors: problems at work (her employer, a major newspaper in Northwest Ohio had just laid off half of its employees) and family issues (she was raising four daughters, working full-time, and taking nine credit hours of classes). The level of participation of Seth and David depended heavily on the specifics of their professional schedules (both had several business trips in the course of the class). The highest participation reading for

Seth (weeks 6, 9) was 7 posts, while the lowest (week 10) was 1. Finally, Felipe's participation dynamics reflected his struggle with English as a foreign language and the necessity to travel to his mother's funeral in the midst of the semester. All these personal circumstances, along with the existing skills, knowledge(s), and preferences pertaining to small group interaction and learning in environments where "students" and "teacher" corresponded to words, sentences, and messages were embodied in the frequency, content, and quality of communication.

Further, with six out of seven students in the class taking their first online class, participation was virtually a skill to develop. For example, Ashley stated: "I didn't know what to expect as far as *participating in classes* [online]," yet she stressed, it "was less complicated than I thought." A very conscientious students, Kim had a routine of an ideal student for any class:

I believe I took part in most discussions. Especially if those had questions that needed addressed. Even if I didn't feel that I could adequately help [to answer], I tried to at least respond to their question by posting a kind of "Hey, I was wondering about that too" message. I truly did try to acknowledge other people's posts.

Kim's pattern of interaction, however, was neither conventional for the communication in this group nor universally accepted. I dare presume that the large number of what Seth called "unsubstantial posts" from Kim and other participants – i.e., posts that did not contain ideas pertinent to the discussion theme – led to a disintegration of some students in particular conversations (i.e., Seth's own postings may have become more monologic as a result of that), or caused them to seek and practice alternate ways of participation in this class (i.e., private email exchange or "silent participation").

Subsequently, what Kim deemed "communal," corresponded to her individual body of knowledge on collaboration and communal interaction. Her frequent posts helped her employ and embody such knowledge. The physical and the imagined intersected here: being physically "present," "active," and "helpful," she all but contributed to the construction of what Anderson (1991) would call an imagined community, "limited and sovereign" (p. 7) in its individuality and exclusivity. How she positioned what she did or tried to do in the class was not always indicative of how the other students understood her actions as heterogeneous and multi-vocal, an image of community lived "in the minds of each participant" (p. 6). Represented in the physicality of online posts, online community resided not in an online class, but rather existed as an evasive, socially-enforced concept whose materialization was inseparable from the personal literacy histories of its members.

Speaking of the imagined communality of a nation and implying a similar nature for any community, Anderson (1991) notes that community is "always conceived as a deep, horizontal comradeship" (p. 7). Such concept, Anderson argues, while not representative of the actual connection between the common citizens of the nation, "makes it possible for so many millions of people ... to die for such limited imaginings" (p. 7). Even though the idea of community remains relatively stable, yet idealized and therefore evasive, the actual performance of community, as the findings in this study indicate, varies based on the individual illiteracies of the members. Moreover, the fact that community is embodied with the help of online technology, stresses the extent to which technology permeates communication. As Seliger and Engstroem (2007) suggest:

The matrix of technological materiality and our embodiment enter into ... practices, some of which are guided by preferences inherent in the artifact's design, some of which are guided by social expectations concerning its use, but all of which select, amplify, and reduce aspects of our experience as our perceptions of the world and our modes of relating to it change accordingly. (p. 576)

The technological materiality of an online class (i.e., the software, hardware, and the internet connection that make contact possible) provides a means for the projection of the subjective, situated knowledge(s) onto a larger screen of *performing an community*. Further research on online communities would benefit from a sustained practice of recognizing and validating subjective performances of individual participants and a systematic exploration of literacy practices – individual, generational, class, gender, etc. – that embody online communities.

CONCLUSION

The theoretical framework of subjugation of the online user drove this project to explore the students' performances in an online community of one online class. Positioning individual knowledge(s) of the participants of online educational interactions as building blocks of subjugation, the project maintained that the power and subject construction reside in the knowledge(s) with which the class participants interpreted the class rules and performed communication online. Originating and residing in the individual needs, knowledge(s), abilities – or, otherwise, literacies – of its participants, the online community appeared to be an embodied practice, while the meaning of communal interactions was individually constructed and negotiated through public and private communication enabled by the computer technology. I have argued that an awareness of the subjugated knowledge(s) of the course participants is a segway into more informed and effective uses of community online.

Ultimately, this project sought to encourage conversations on teaching and learning online as it called for an exploration of the forms and meanings of online interactions. The project's exploration of online power relations, agency, and subjectivity emphasized meaning construction as a social enterprise. According to Berlin (1987), the meaning "is never 'out there' in the material world or the social realm, or simply 'in here' in a private personal world" (p. 17). The meaning emerges "only as …the material, the social, and the personal interact," with language being "the agent of mediation" (p. 17). The intersection of the physical, the social, and the personal allows both creating and actively participating in a public forum relative to our own historical moment. While the subject is both the holder and maker of meaning, he or she is simultaneously a part of a larger enterprise – an episteme, which is a system of knowledge making good for a particular group, a particular time, and a particular place. It is imperative for us, as teachers, to locate online communal interaction in the individual space of the community members as well as in the broader fabric of education online. Students' and teachers' abilities to be critical about the multiplicity of online community, embodied by the members' physical lives, yet enabled by various technologies, must pave the way to effective pedagogies for the information age.

The growing enrollment in online classes, the blog revolution, and the world-wide march of the social network make the need of further exploration of online community massive and immediate. This project is part of an evolving conversation about online community that, as I argued throughout the project, resides in the subjective knowledge(s) and performances of the online learner and is fueled by the discursive power of online teaching and learning. A further discussion of subjective knowledge(s), performances, and the discourse of online community invites an online researcher on a journey of discovering the meaning of already existing embodied experiences and making sense of the practices of everyday life. A fuller idea of literacy as a complex phenomenon of human activity is imperative for a more accurate and informed judgment of the meaning, the function, and the performance of knowledge in the age of global technocultures.

REFERENCES

Akyol, Z., & Garrison, D. R. (2011). Understanding cognitive presence in an online and blended community of inquiry: Assessing outcomes and processes for deep approaches to learning. *British Journal of Educational Technology*, *42*(2), 233–250. doi:10.1111/j.1467-8535.2009.01029.x

Anderson, B. (1991). *Imagined communities*. London: Verso.

Anzaldua, G. (1987). *Borderlands/La Frontera*. San Francisco, CA: Spinsters/Aunt Lute.

Baym, N. K. (1998). The emergence of online community. In Jones, S. (Ed.), *Cybersociety 2.0 revisiting computer-mediated communication and community* (pp. 35–68). Newbury Park, CA: Sage Publications.

Bell, D. (2001). *An introduction to cybercultures*. London, UK: Routledge.

Berlin, J. (1987). *Rhetoric and reality: Writing instruction in American colleges, 1900-1985*. Carbondale, IL: Southern Illinois UP.

Bishop, J. (2007). Increasing participation in online communities: a framework for human-computer interaction. *Computers in Human Behavior*, *23*, 1881–1893. doi:10.1016/j.chb.2005.11.004

Blair, K. L., & Monske, E. A. (2003). Cui bono? Revisiting the promises and perils of online learning. *Computers and Composition*, *20*, 441–453. doi:10.1016/j.compcom.2003.08.016

Bourdieu, P. (1988). *Homo Academicus*. Stanford, CA: Stanford University Press.

Braga, D. B., & Busnardo, J. (2004). Digital literacy for autonomous learning: Designer problems and learner choices. In Snyder, I., & Beavis, C. (Eds.), *Doing literacy online* (pp. 45–68). Cresskill, NJ: Hampton Press.

Burbules, N. C. (1993). *Dialogue in teaching theory and practice*. New York, NY: Teachers College Press.

Cowart, M. (2006). Embodied cognition. *The internet encyclopedia of philosophy*. Retrieved January 24, 2012, from http://www.iep.utm.edu/e/embodcog.htm

Craig, J. (2010). Introduction: E-learning in politics. *European Political Science, 9*(1), 1–4. doi:10.1057/eps.2009.36

Davis, K., Seider, S., & Gardner, H. (2008). When false representations ring true (and when they don't). *Social Research, 75*, 1085–1108.

Duncan-Howell, J. (2010). Teachers making connections: Online communities as a source of professional learning. *British Journal of Educational Technology, 41*(2), 324–340. doi:10.1111/j.1467-8535.2009.00953.x

Farquharson, K. (2011). Doing 'race' on the internet: A study of online parenting communities. *Journal of Intercultural Studies (Melbourne, Vic.), 32*(5), 479–493. doi:10.1080/07256868.2011.593115

Feenberg, A., & Bakardijeva, M. (2004). Virtual community: No killer implication. *New Media & Society, 6*, 37–43. doi:10.1177/1461444804039904

Fernback, J. (2007). Beyond the diluted community concept: A symbolic interactionist perspective on online social relations. *New Media & Society, 9*, 49–69. doi:10.1177/1461444807072417

Foucault, M. (1980). *Power/knowledge: Selected interviews and other writings, 1972-1977* (Gordon, C. (Trans. Ed.)). New York, NY: Pantheon Books.

Glassmeyer, D. M., Dibbs, R. A., & Jensen, R. T. (2011). Determining utility of formative assessment through virtual community: Perspectives of online graduate students. *Quarterly Review of Distance Education, 12*(1), 23–35.

Haraway, D. J. (1991). *Simians, cyborgs, and women: The reinvention of nature*. New York, NY: Routledge.

Harding, S. (2004). Rethinking standpoint epistemology: What is "strong objectivity"? In Harding, S. (Ed.), *The feminist standpoint theory reader: Intellectual and political conversations* (pp. 127–140). New York, NY: Routledge.

Harris, A. (2003). *Notions of embodied knowledge*. Retrieved September 5, 2011 from http://www.thegreenfuse.org/harris/notions-of-ek.htm

Hawisher, G. E., & Selfe, C. L. (1992). The rhetoric of technology and the electronic writing class. *College Composition and Communication, 42*, 55–65. doi:10.2307/357539

Haythornthtwaite, C. (2002). Building social networks via computer networks. creating and sustaining learning communities. In Renninger, K. A., & Shumar, W. (Eds.), *Building virtual communities. Learning and change in cyberspace* (pp. 159–190). Cambridge, UK: Cambridge University Press. doi:10.1017/CBO9780511606373.011

Hoadley, C. M., & Pea, R. D. (2002). Finding the ties that bind: Tools in support of a knowledge-building community. In Renninger, K. A., & Shumar, W. (Eds.), *Building virtual communities: Learning and change in cyberspace* (pp. 321–354). New York, NY: Cambridge University Press. doi:10.1017/CBO9780511606373.017

Holt, R. (2004). *Dialogue on the internet: Language, civic identity, and computer-mediated communication*. Westport, CT: Praeger.

Huwe, T. (2008). Where the sidewalk ends and the community begins. *Computers in Libraries, 28*(4), 33–35.

In der Smitten, S. (2008). Political potential and capabilities of online communities. *German Policy Studies/Politikfeldanalyse, 4*(4), 32-62.

Iriberri, A., & Leroy, G. (2009). A life-cycle perspective on online community success. *ACM Computing Surveys, 41*, 11:1-11-29.

Jaggar, A. M. (2004). Feminist politics and epistemology. In Harding, S. (Ed.), *The feminist standpoint theory reader. Intellectual and political conversations* (pp. 55–66). New York, NY: Routledge.

Jones, S. G. (2002). Building, buying, or being there: Imagining online community. In Renninger, K. A., & Shumar, W. (Eds.), *Building virtual communities: Learning and change in cyberspace* (pp. 368–376). Cambridge, UK: Cambridge University Press. doi:10.1017/CBO9780511606373.019

Karagiorgi, Y., & Lymbouridou, C. (2009). The story of an online teacher community in Cyprus. *Professional Development in Education, 35*(1), 119–138. doi:10.1080/13674580802269059

Kates, S. (2002). *Elocution and African American culture: The pedagogy of Hallie Quinn Brown. Activist rhetorics and American higher education, 1885-1937* (pp. 53–74). Carbondale, IL: Southern Illinois University Press.

Kazmer, M. M. (2005). How technology affects students' departures from online learning communities. *ACM SIGGROUP Bulletin, 25*, 25–40.

Kehrwald, B. (2010). Being online: Social presence as subjectivity in online learning. *London Review of Education, 8*(1), 39–50. doi:10.1080/14748460903557688

Liao, P., & Hsieh, J. Y. (2011). What influences internet-based learning? *Social Behavior & Personality: An International Journal, 39*(7), 887–896. doi:10.2224/sbp.2011.39.7.887

Merleau-Ponty, M. (1962). *Phenomenology of perception*. London, UK: Routledge.

Meyers, E. M. (2009). Tip of the iceberg: Meaning, identity, and literacy in preteen virtual worlds. *Journal of Education for Library and Information Science, 50*(4), 226–236.

Nagel, L., Blignaut, A. S., & Cronje, J. C. (2009). Read-only participants: A case for student communication in online classes. *Interactive Learning Environments, 17*, 37–51. doi:10.1080/10494820701501028

Norris, P. (2004). The bridging and bonding role of online communities. In Howards, P. N., & Jones, S. (Eds.), *Society online the interned in context* (pp. 31–41). Thousand Oaks, CA: Sage Publications. doi:10.1177/108118002129172601

Peowski, L. (2010). Where are all the teens? Engaging and empowering them online. *Young Adult Library Services, 8*(2), 26–28.

Rambusch, J., & Ziemke, T. (2005). The role of embodiment in situated learning. *Proceedings of COGSCI 2005: XXVII Conference of the Cognitive Science Society*. Retrieved January 24, 2012, from http://www.cogsci.rpi.edu/CSJarchive/Proceedings/2005/docs/p1803.pdf

Renninger, A. K., & Schumar, W. (Eds.). (2002). *Building virtual communities*. Cambridge, UK: Cambridge University Press. doi:10.1017/CBO9780511606373

Rheingold, H. (1994). *The virtual community homesteading on the electronic frontier*. New York, NY: Harper Perennial.

Romano, S. (1993). The egalitarianism narrative: Whose story? Which yardstick? *Computers and Composition, 10*, 5–28.

Saltmarsh, S., & Sutherland-Smith, W. (2010). S(t)imulating learning: Pedagogy, subjectivity and teacher education in online environments. *London Review of Education, 8*(1), 15–24. doi:10.1080/14748460903557613

Seliger, E., & Engstrom, T. (2007). On naturally embodied cyborgs: Identities, metaphors, and models. *Janus Head*, *9*(2), 553–584.

Shumar, W., & Renninger, K. A. (2002). On conceptualizing community. In Renninger, K. A., & Shumar, W. (Eds.), *Building virtual communities: Learning and change in cyberspace* (pp. 1–20). Cambridge, UK: Cambridge University Press. doi:10.1017/CBO9780511606373.005

Studdert, D. (2005). *Conceptualizing community beyond the state and individual*. New York, NY: Palgrave/Macmillan.

Sum, S., Mathews, M., Pourghasem, M., & Hughes, I. (2009). Rapid communication: Internet use as a predictor of sense of community in older people. *Cyberpsychology & Behavior*, *12*(2), 235–239. doi:10.1089/cpb.2008.0150

Warren, J. T. (2006). Introduction: Performance ethnography: A TPQ symposium. *Text and Performance Quarterly*, *26*(4), 317–319. doi:10.1080/10462930600828667

Wellman, B., & Gulia, M. (1999). Virtual communities as communities. Net surfers don't ride alone. In Smith, M. A., & Kollock, P. (Eds.), *Communities in cyberspace*. London, UK: Routledge.

Wilbur, S. P. (2000). An archaeology of cyberspaces. Virtuality, community, identity. In Bell, D., & Kennedy, B. M. (Eds.), *The cybercultures reader* (pp. 45–55). London, UK: Routledge.

Williams, B. T. (2008). "Tomorrow will not be like today": Literacy and identity in a world of multiliteracies. *Journal of Adolescent & Adult Literacy*, *51*(8), 682–686. doi:10.1598/JAAL.51.8.7

Winarnita, M. S. (2008). Motherhood as cultural citizenship: Indonesian women in transnational families. *The Asia Pacific Journal of Anthropology*, *9*(4), 304–318. doi:10.1080/14442210802506412

Yeh, C. (2010). Analyzing online behaviors, roles, and learning communities via online discussions. *Journal of Educational Technology & Society*, *13*(1), 140–151.

Section 2
Theories behind Virtual Community Participation

Chapter 9
Virtual Communities as Subaltern Public Spheres:
A Theoretical Development and an Application to the Chinese Internet

Weiyu Zhang
National University of Singapore, Singapore

ABSTRACT

The purpose of this work is to develop a theoretical framework to examine virtual community participation using the concept of subaltern public spheres. The theory of subaltern public spheres directs attention to the internal dynamics and external interaction of virtual communities. Internal dynamics first refers to the inclusiveness of participation by looking at the access to virtual communities and the profiles of their participants. The nature of participation, as another aspect of internal dynamics, is estimated through examining the styles of the discourses and the types of participatory acts. The external interaction becomes another major focus of this theoretical framework and urges researchers to study how virtual communities interact with government apparatuses, commercial entities, the dominant public sphere, and other subaltern public spheres through discursive engagement and other means. The theoretical framework is applied to analyze a case of Chinese online public spheres to illustrate the framework's utility.

INTRODUCTION

Since the term *virtual community* was forged by Howard Rheingold (Rheingold, 1993), technologies have evolved rapidly (e.g., from Usenet to e-mail lists to Web 2.0) and computer-mediated communication (CMC) has become a common component of our everyday lives. The inquiry

into the virtual community has moved from the existence question (i.e., whether communities are able to exist virtually) to a range of research interests, including the psychological, social, political, and cultural dimensions of these mediated gatherings. This chapter centers on the political aspect of virtual communities and examines the democratic potential of the Internet through the lens of the public sphere. The initial efforts to

DOI: 10.4018/978-1-4666-0312-7.ch009

study virtual communities often focused on the social relations formed in these mediated spaces and the psychological well-being resulting from participation in such spaces. Many studies also concerned one particular virtual community and how it fostered the formation of a subculture identity or a marginalized group. This chapter, in contrast, emphasizes the political dimension of virtual communities, which is the mechanism of representing the community's interest to the larger society. The Habermasian public sphere as a theoretical framework has been applied to evaluate the democratic potential of the Internet (Dahlberg, 2001; Dahlgren, 2005; Papacharissi, 2002; Poster, 1995). However, the diverse and fragmented cyberspace seems to indicate a sphere that is far from universal and integrated. I proposed to take the criticism of the Habermasian public sphere seriously when examining online spaces (Zhang, 2006). This chapter presents the critique in detail and lays out a framework that follows the theory of subaltern public spheres. The usefulness of this theoretical approach is tested against an empirical case of the Chinese Internet.

BACKGROUND

The metaphor of community has caught the imagination of academics since the early age of Internet research in the 1980s. A famous debate in the CMC field was whether CMC is able to support communities as face-to-face (F2F) interactions do. The cues-filtered-out perspective claims that since CMC lacks nonverbal cues, it is less personal or socioemotional than F2F interaction, and therefore less capable of supporting communities (Rice & Love, 1987; Sproull & Kiesler 1986; DeSanctis & Gallupe 1987; Spears & Lea, 1992). On the other hand, researchers claim that CMC is able to foster the feeling of relational development over time (Walther, 1992), and communicators can successfully achieve collective goals if they

are work-oriented (Walther & Burgooon, 1990). The latter camp suggests that virtual communities are probable. Now it seems clear that the debate on the superiority/inferiority of CMC vs. F2F is a false comparison. CMC does not compete with F2F for the same kind of communities. Rather, CMC and F2F are integrated to build new types of communities that emerge out of the postmodern conditions of social lives.

The concept of community has gone through significant changes through history and across social contexts. According to Bell and Newby (1976), the idea of community first appeared in preindustrial societies. Communities in this period bore characteristics such as rural, homogenous, and densely knitted (Wellman, 1999). These communities had a local economic basis and a hierarchical power system (Bell & Newby, 1976). In agricultural societies, ownership of land was the crucial resource for the possession of power; thus, people were linked to the local form of territoriality. Power was exercised personally by the landowning elites via F2F interaction. Communities emphasized a common adherence to territory and solidarity of place, to both the elites and the subordinates.

The idea of community encountered its first critical challenge when societies were changed by the Industrial Revolution. When societies became unstable, dispersed, and heterogeneous, the rural community in the agricultural era broke down, and so did the local and personalized modes of control (Bell & Newby, 1976). This breakdown was not the end of community, however. Communities still existed in neighborhoods and operated as a method of social integration. Neighborhood communities retain three features of rural communities: locale, common ties, and social interaction (Bernard, 1973).

Researchers who are interested in modern communities suggest that we should understand communities as networks. Without presuming that a community is confined to a local area, social network analysis focuses on social relations and social structures (Wellman, 1999). This approach frees the conceptualization of community from a preoccupation with solidarity and neighborhood, and accommodates social changes. Social network researchers found that networked communities are specialized, sparsely knitted, and loosely bounded. However, these communities continue to be supportive and sociable, although social solidarity is not always necessary to them. The network approach to community suggests that the shared physical locality is not essential to communities. This reconceptualization of communities enables us to see virtual space such as the Internet as the locale of communities. Meanwhile, Anderson's imagined community (1991) provides another conceptual tool to study virtual communities. He defined the nation as an imagined community and explained that "it is imagined because the members of even the smallest nation will never know most of their fellow-members, meet them, or even hear of them, yet in the minds of each lives the image of their communion" (Anderson, 1991, pp. 6–7). Furthermore, "communities are to be distinguished not by the falsity/genuineness, but by the style in which they are imagined." In this sense, communities exist as long as they are perceived to exist.

It has taken a long transformation from rural communities to today's networked and imagined communities. The original purpose of community somehow became lost in the rhetoric of virtual communities. A community is aimed at building the social unit that connects individuals and society (Friedland, 2001). Watson (1997, p. 102) stated the purpose of community in one question: "how does a group struggle for greater representation in the larger society?" While social network research merely measures the individual relational network and limits the function of community to social support, the political connotation of community, implied in Watson's question, remains unexamined. The imagined nature of modern

communities also fails to address the concern of political representation through existing institutions such as congresses and mass media. It is in this situation that a concept of public becomes necessary to understand the political aspect of communities.

"The ideal of community refers to a model of association patterned on family and kinship-relations, on an affective language of love and loyalty, on assumptions of authenticity, homogeneity, and continuity, of inclusion and exclusion, identity and otherness" (Hansen, 1993, p. xxxvi). The notion of public, by contrast, refers to a specific social category that appears as a political actor (Splichal, 1999, p. 2). Community members become a public only if they engage in open contestations on issues that have consequences in their lives but are not under the members' full and direct control. The public sphere as the infrastructure that supports such contestations thus becomes a critical concept for understanding the political nature of communities, including virtual ones.

THE THEORY OF SUBALTERN PUBLIC SPHERES

Habermasian Public Sphere

In a central work, *The Structural Transformation of the Public Sphere*, Habermas "asks when and under what conditions the arguments of mixed companies could become authoritative bases for political action" (Calhoun, 1992, p. 1). More specifically, "what are the social conditions... for a rational-critical debate about public issues conducted by private persons willing to let arguments and not statuses determine decisions" (Calhoun, 1992, p. 1). The concept of public sphere indicates at least two social conditions. First, a liberal political culture that roots in motives and values. Second, an institutional system that supports rational-critical debates. The first condition could be considered as a set of norms of the public sphere. The second is also important because the success or failure of these institutions decides whether the public sphere is a utopian or an obtainable goal (Habermas, 1992, p. 453).

Habermas argued that, as the discursive aspect of civil society, the public sphere should be autonomous from both the state power and the market economy. Habermas also made a separation within civil society, which is family as the private realm and public sphere as the public realm (Peters, 1993). Habermas proposed a distinction between the lifeworld and the system to explain the fourfold structure. Family and the public sphere belong to the lifeworld, which is the everyday realm of conversations, experience, traditions, understandings, norms, and solidarity. The state and economy are ruled by abstract quantities such as power and money and thus considered the system. Since money and power are nondiscursive modes of coordination, "they offer no intrinsic openings to the identification of reason and will, and they suffer from tendencies toward domination and reification" (Calhoun, 1992, p. 6).

This fourfold structure implies that civil society is opposed to or at least competes with the state and economy in shaping public discourses. Habermas argued that the public sphere should be the birthplace of public opinion. All legislation and state administration should be consistent with the consensus generated from public deliberation. Habermas's opinion on the early-age relationship between the market economy and the public sphere is consistent with the understanding of civil society as the direct consequence of market economy. However, Habermas observed that, after years of transformation, the market economy is no longer a part of civil society. The market economy has become deeply involved with the state power, and the two systems are mingled together to control the whole society.

After discussing the structure that the public sphere exists in, it is time to specify the set of norms that the Habermasian public sphere advocates. The first dimension of the norms is related to inclusiveness or universal access, which means all citizens have the opportunity to enter and discuss in the public sphere despite their social status and personal interest. Citizens participate in the public sphere as private individuals and do not represent anyone other than themselves. The private participation reflects Habermas's distrust of representative democracy, which turns participants in democracy into viewers of democratic rituals. The second dimension regards the nature of discourses/speeches, which emphasizes rationality or reason. The concept of communicative rationality indicates several subsets of norms. First, the goal of the discussion is to reach mutual understanding instead of any dominant discourse. Second, the discussion is rational and critical, which means all the assertions are open to critique. Third, to ensure the goal of rationality, each participant must possess qualities such as reflexivity, ideal role-taking, and sincerity.

Even after all these norms are satisfied, the public sphere cannot be achieved without institutional support. From Habermas's historical analysis of various public spheres, we can see that the bourgeois public sphere is just one category of public sphere in history. At least four institutions of the public sphere have emerged: the representative public sphere, the literary public sphere, the bourgeois public sphere, and the mass media public sphere. These four forms of public spheres correspond to different historical conditions. As the earliest public sphere, the representative public sphere existed in the feudal society of the High Middle Ages. However, it was a pseudo-public sphere because there was no basis for division between the public sphere and the private domain at that time. "This publicity of representation was not constituted as a social realm, that is, as a public sphere; rather, it was something like a status attribute" (Habermas, 1989, p. 7). The prince and the estates of his realm represented their lordship not "for" but "before" the people. Here the people functioned as the backdrop before which the ruling estates displayed themselves and their status. The institutions of this public sphere were the great hall of court and the strict codes of noble conduct such as the famous Spanish ceremonial practices.

The public sphere in the world of letters, which is called the literary public sphere, built a bridge between the old courtly public sphere and the new bourgeois public sphere. This public sphere preserved certain continuity with the publicity involved in the representation enacted at the prince's court. In this sphere, one sees the combination of the urban aristocracy with writers, artists, and scientists. The bourgeois avant-garde learned the art of rational-critical public debate, and critical debate ignited by works of literature and art was extended to economic and political disputes. In this sense, the bourgeois public sphere evolved from the literary public sphere. The institutions of the literary public sphere were the salons that replaced the great hall at court.

When literary critiques turned into political debates, the bourgeois public sphere came into being. The new institutions were coffeehouses in Britain and salons in France. In both countries, these institutions were centers of criticism, literary at first and then political. In Germany, similar elements existed, beginning with the learning table societies and the old literary societies. If coffeehouses mainly provided meeting places, journals of opinions "linked the thousands of smaller circles" (Calhoun, 1992, p. 12). The social relationships among the participants were relatively loose because the bourgeois public sphere "disregarded status altogether" (Habermas, 1989, p. 36).

Finally, mass media replaced all the coffeehouses, salons, and societies to become the institutions of today's public sphere. However, mass media function poorly in this regard. They provide passive culture consumption and apolitical sociability rather than serious involvement in critical debates (Habermas, 1989, p. 166). The culture-consuming public takes part in noncommittal group activities such as watching movies in theatres instead of convivial discussion. The so-called debates in mass media are turned into a flourishing secondary business. The rational-critical discussions are lost in the mass media public sphere (Calhoun, 1992, pp. 21–22). If mass media once were able to reach the majority of society's members, the media segmentation made the media lose that ability (Katz, 1996). More and more media, such as MTV, are not for everybody but for a small, specific audience. Dispersed media spaces lead to the collapse of a shared public sphere.

Subaltern Public Spheres

The theory of subaltern public spheres criticizes the Habermasian public sphere on three different fronts: First, the historical exclusion of, namely women, proletariats, and racial minorities, in the bourgeois public sphere. The first critique of Habermas's public sphere is related to universal accessibility, which means all the social members could take part in one sphere in spite of their different social status. Habermas assumes that it is possible for a public sphere to bracket social inequalities. However, social inequalities themselves have determined who has permission to enter the sphere. At least the feminist counterpublic (Fraser, 1992) and the oppositional public of the working class (Negt & Kluge, 1993) did not have access. In addition, Habermas assumed that a single and comprehensive public sphere is always preferable to a nexus of subaltern public spheres. Fraser pointed out that a universal public sphere can work only for the advantage of dominant groups. Members of subordinated groups would have no arenas for deliberative discussions among themselves.

Habermas noticed that the bourgeois public sphere was class-limited. However, he did not deny the norms of the bourgeois public sphere because he believed that this open and rational discursive space can absorb "the others" without colonizing them. According to Habermas, the proletariat or the "plebian" public sphere was just a variant of the bourgeois public sphere. It was "a bourgeois public sphere whose social preconditions have been rendered null" (Habermas, 1992, p. 426). Although he admitted the exclusion of women has structural significance, he said that "this convincing consideration does not dismiss rights to unrestricted inclusion and equality, which are an integral part of the liberal public sphere's self-interpretation" (Habermas, 1992, p. 429). In his eyes, the success of the feminist movement reflects the potential of the bourgeois public sphere for self-transformation. However, the critiques from feminists and leftists go beyond inclusiveness and land on the norms themselves. In fact, both female and proletariat public spheres are substantially different from the bourgeois one. They disagree with the norms of the bourgeois public sphere, and thus, their institutions demonstrate totally different characteristics.

The second critique is about the rationality of the discourse. In a single public sphere bracketing social inequalities, it is impossible to reach real rationality. Deliberation is used only to obliterate the voice of the subordinates when the oppressed have no say in defining what constitutes rationality. Moreover, Habermas assumed that discourse in the public sphere should be restricted to deliberation about the common good, and that the appearance of private interests is always undesirable. What accounts for a matter of common good is decided through discursive contestation. However, the bracketing of inequalities puts the subordinate in an inferior position in this contestation. Discursive contestation is governed by protocols of style and decorum that are themselves correlations and markers of status inequality. Although bracketing of social inequality prevents formal exclusions, it also brings informal impediments to participatory parity. Subordinate groups sometimes cannot find the right voice or words to express their thoughts, and when they do, the groups find that they are not heard.

Fraser criticized the exclusion of women and questioned the sincerity of rationality in the bourgeois public sphere when rationality is based on fictitious universalism. However, she did not deny the belief of rationality and wanted to recover the real "rationality" within subaltern public spheres. She adhered to norms of procedural rationality as the best institutionalized procedures for excluding violence from the social arena (McLaughlin, 1993). For example, Fraser thought that the participants in the female public spheres are relatively equal and benefit from their critical discussions. These activities reinforce the common good of this specific group. In addition, she also pursued universal accessibility within the subaltern group and ignored the variety and internal conflicts among the group members. That is why Habermas (1992) did not think that the female public sphere overthrows the norms of the bourgeois public sphere. He thought the only difference between Fraser and him was the subjects of their theories. Habermas believed that the rationality of the bourgeois could help them to extend their class public sphere to finally absorb the other classes. Fraser questioned this possibility and claimed that full participation and rationality exist only in certain social groups who consider their own interests.

Felski (1989) criticized Habermas's public sphere from the perspectives of poststructuralism and feminism. In addition to asking the public sphere to account for gender differences, she continued Lyotard's (1984) question, whether a rational and uniform subject is the foundation for democracy. In her analysis of feminist literature, she found that autobiography and self-discovery narratives are very popular in the female public sphere because women can share their life experiences through these books. Not only rationality but also the affective experience can contribute to the construction of the female public sphere.

Negt and Kluge (1993) proposed an alternative definition of the public sphere without referring to discursive participation. They defined the public sphere as a horizon for the organization of social experience. While Habermas's notion of public life relies on the institutions of rational-critical discussions, Negt and Kluge emphasized questions of constituency, concrete needs, interests, conflicts, protest, and power (Hansen, 1993, p. xxx). The proletarian public sphere involves three elements: the experience of re/production under capitalism, the separation of the experiencing subjects from the networks of public expression and representation, and resistance and imaginative strategies as a response to the separation. In this sense, any practices that bring the proletarian experience into the visible horizon of social experience could be the embodiment of the public sphere. This definition overthrows Habermas's belief in rational debate and gives prominence to everyday experience. Negt and Kluge also found that rudimentary and ephemeral instances of the proletarian public sphere have already emerged. Habermas admitted that he was too pessimistic about the resistance from a pluralistic mass public (Habermas, 1992, p. 438).

The third front of contestation is the institutions of public sphere(s). Habermas lamented the failure of mass media to function as a public sphere because he fixed his eyes on broadcasting channels that are aimed at the entire population. This empirical focus is understandable because he favored a single public sphere that is accessible to all societal members. However, if we took the plural approach to public sphere(s), we would look at different institutional spaces in which the public expression of social experiences is made possible. Felski (1989) tried to locate the spaces that are open to feminist discourses in a variety of institutions such as health clinics, political action groups, bookstores, filmmaking collectives, welfare agencies, as well as corporations and Hollywood media firms. Negt and Kluge (1993) claimed that "life context" is where the proletarian

public sphere emerges from, and therefore, they looked at historical moments when the alternative organization of experiences becomes visible (e.g., English Chartism, Italian Maximalism, and certain moments in the October Revolution). Authors (Brouwer, 2001; Hauser, 2001; Squires, 2001) of the book *Counterpublics and the State* turned to prison writing, congressional hearings, the Black press, and so on to look for counterpublicity and its formation. The theory of subaltern public spheres directs our attention to the vivid and diverse lifeworld for the possibility of public exchange of everyday experiences. Virtual communities become one of the spaces where we can trace the development of subaltern public spheres.

A Dual-Function Framework Embedded in a Fourfold Structure

Our analysis of virtual communities benefits from the theory of subaltern public spheres in terms of the research foci. As Felski (1989) pointed out, the feminist public sphere as a type of subaltern public sphere serves a dual function:

Internally, it generates a gender-specific identity grounded in a consciousness of community and solidarity among women; externally, it seeks to convince society as a whole of the validity of feminist claims, challenging existing structures of authority through political activity and theoretical critique. (p. 168)

Consistent with this line of thought, our examination of virtual communities should look at the internal dynamics and the external interaction. I propose that our empirical examination of the internal dynamics should include, first, the inclusiveness of the subaltern public sphere, in other words, who are the members of the community and whose identity is being forged; second, the nature of participation, which encompasses the discourse(s), the way the discourse(s) are made, and any other participatory acts in addition to discursive engagement. Studies on virtual communities such as fans clubs (Baym, 2000), diasporas (Mallapragada, 2006), and extremist groups (Qiu, 2006) have done sufficient work on describing and signifying the internal dynamics but often lack a clear awareness of the external interaction these communities make (or do not make).

My second proposition regarding this theoretical framework is, thus, to bring the analysis of the external interaction into our routine examination of virtual communities. After defining what is internal to the virtual community in question, we need to specify what is external to it as well. Despite the critical take on the Habermasian public sphere, I argue that the theory of subaltern public sphere shares with Habermas its basic understanding of the fourfold structure, namely, state, economy, family, and civil society. Although feminist critiques questioned the division between family and civil society as disguising the oppression of women, there is still a difference between the two as empirical entities. By taking the fourfold structure as our basic understanding of the social conditions in which public spheres exist, our analysis of the external reach has clear targets now. Subaltern public spheres have to interact with the state apparatuses, the commercial entities, the dominant public sphere (often realized in the format of mass media), and other subaltern public spheres. The interaction can be found in discursive engagement in most times. However, interpersonal contacts, financial transfers, and even violent conflicts across the four arenas should be considered as the means of reaching as well.

As we can see now, the theoretical framework radically differs from the Habermasian approach in rejecting the two basic norms of his model of the liberal public sphere. The norm of universalism is rejected as both empirically impossible and conceptually undesirable. Instead, the fact that multiple publics coexist in our postmodern societies is fully admitted, and a model of multiculturalism guides our research. The norm of

rationality is also denied, and the vision of the public sphere is broadened to any practices that bring the social experiences of the oppressed into the visible horizon of the entire society. Although discursive engagement is still the main method of reaching wider publics, this framework does not pre-exclude other types of practices. However, the significance and influence of the different types of practices are evaluated instead of being assumed.

When the internal-external framework of subaltern public spheres is used, a variety of social groupings can be clearly organized and understood. Squires (2002) suggested that, since subaltern public spheres emerge out of various political and cultural contexts, not all could successfully achieve internal and external functions at the same time. Depending upon the resources the subaltern publics have and their strategies to engage wider publics, three types of subaltern public spheres can be distinguished. *Enclaved public spheres* enclave themselves, hiding counterhegemonic ideas and strategies in order to survive or avoid violence and disrespect from the state and the dominant public, while internally producing lively debate and planning. They have few material, political, legal, or media resources. These public spheres may have some contacts with the dominant public sphere but rarely with other public spheres. *Counterpublic spheres* usually emerge in response to a decrease in oppression or an increase in resources. Counterpublic discourses travel outside the safe and enclaved spaces to argue against the dominant conceptions of the group. Couterpublicity is facilitated by independent media resources and distribution channels. Some such spheres gain legal and political resources. *Satellite publics* seek separation from other publics for reasons other than oppressive relations but are involved in the wider public sphere discourse from time to time. These publics rely on the group media only to support internal discussions. Satellite publics can emerge from both dominant and marginalized groups.

A similar classification can be used when analyzing virtual communities. This classification not only helps us to draw a clear picture of the chaotic cyberspace but also enables us to have a comprehensive evaluation of the complicated role of the Internet in public life. The following analyses focus on a specific social, political, and cultural context of the People's Republic of China and utilize the framework to examine the various online spaces that are available for public contestations.

A CASE OF CHINESE ONLINE PUBLIC SPHERES

A research approach of case study is adopted in this chapter. The author has been an observer as well as a participant of the Chinese Internet for over ten years. A close participant observation of almost all aspects of the Chinese online public spheres was conducted with a longitudinal perspective. The empirical evidence is drawn from multiple sources including both quantitative (e.g., survey data) and qualitative (e.g., event analysis) ones. Key cases that are rich in providing insights regarding the theoretical framework are selected and reported.

If the public sphere has to be open to all publics, it is clear that the cyberspace in China does not hold to this standard. By the end of 2010, there were 457 million Internet users in China (China Internet Network Information Center [CNNIC], 2011). In contrast to the total population of 1.3 billion, the majority of the Chinese public (more than 70%) does not have access to this technology. The infrastructure of a Habermasian virtual public sphere is absent in China[1]. In addition, the heavy government control of online content (Qiu, 2000) limits the topics and issues that are allowed to be publicly debated. Understanding that the Chinese Internet is not completely open and free, I argue that subaltern public spheres flourish to provide limited yet viable spaces for public discussions.

Before describing the virtual spheres we can find in China, we have to answer the question of where the dominant public sphere is. Assessing from the reach and the influence of their content, traditional mass media still serve as the dominant channel through which the majority of Chinese get news and opinions. Although the government has toned down its repressive measures, it exerts passive yet powerful control over traditional mass media (Zhao, 2008). From a discursive perspective, the dominant public discourse conforms to the ideology of capitalist development led by an authoritarian government. It is against this backdrop that the Chinese Internet can be seen as an infrastructure supporting subaltern public spheres.

Subaltern public spheres on the Chinese Internet are most visible in various discussion forums. One of the unique features of the Chinese Internet is the popularity of discussion forums. When the Net (intra-net or LAN) was introduced to Chinese universities as an educational tool, the young students immediately turned it into a shared space to exchange feelings and thoughts regarding their everyday lives. During the late 1990s and the early 2000s, Bulletin Board Systems (BBSs) supported by the campus Net led the evolution of online public discussions. Commercial websites (e.g., xici.net) soon picked up this momentum and cultivated many discussion forums that attract millions of users. Discussion forums have become a default component of Chinese websites since then. Now we can find discussion forums on government portals, mass media sites, search engines, social networking sites, blogs, professional communities, video sites, and many more.

Although discussion forums as a collective category have been influential in the Chinese cyberspace, they function more like subaltern public spheres than a well-integrated discursive space. Users often visit only a few forums that they are interested in, and the number of forums that users really participate in is even smaller. Forums that users consistently visit and actively participate in often have clear boundaries and limited membership. A good example is the fan forum genre. Recently, successful TV shows such as *Supergirl* have created a group of very popular local celebrities. Their fans formed large-scale groups through forums. The fans express their affection, exchange information, and organize gatherings to extend their online relationship to offline. The fans are also involved in discussions such as drafting strategies to support their celebrity, and to help him or her to fight his or her competitors. Occasionally, the discussions go beyond the celebrity himself or herself and address broader issues such as cultural industry. In spite of the impressive number of members, these spheres mainly serve an internal function, which is to build and reinforce a fan's identity. Anyone who does not share this identity is excluded from the spheres. The connection between this kind of sphere and other subaltern public spheres is weak, and the external reach is made only when the internal integrity is threatened. Fan forums on the Chinese Internet thus stay close to the satellite public spheres, which keep their lively discussions inside the sphere and do not actively seek discursive engagement with other spheres unless under extreme conditions. One example is that, during the Shanghai Expo, a group of Chinese fans of a South Korean popular star caused turmoil due to their uncivil behavior when trying to get free tickets. Chinese netizens thought this was a "loss of face" that humiliated all Chinese and organized a virtual invasion of the home spaces belonging to these fans in June 2010. This incident was later on referred to as "the June 9th Conqueror." Fan groups had to react to the wider public(s) in this case.

Most users visit portal sites, mass media sites, and government portals to seek information and entertainment. For instance, 77% of Internet users read online news (CNNIC, 2011). I argue that these sites provide spaces that approach the model of counterpublic spheres. When discussions are initiated in these spheres, we tend to hear voices that are not just internal to one particular group.

Discourses flow between these sites and form a dynamic and interactive procedure of opinion exchange. In China, four portal sites have survived the fierce competition and become the leading online news portals. They are sina, sohu, netease, and tencent[2]. The first three sites were modeled after AOL or MSN to provide a combination of several basic services such as e-mail, searching, news, and forums. Tencent was founded as an instant messenger tool (i.e., QQ, similar to ICQ), but after conquering the market, tencent developed into a portal website. In addition to forums hosted on these sites, two things are unique: one is the comment function following all news items, and the other is the publication of news stories written by netizens themselves. Portal sites do not have a legal permit to collect their own news so the sites have to repost news from mass media or other websites. When news is reposted to these sites, a comment function is opened for users to discuss the news with each other. News, especially stories that involve government officials and their wrongdoings, often receive a great amount of attention and trigger vivid discussions. Emotional expressions such as outrageous replies are often seen side by side with rational reasoning. Commentators who hold contradictory views engage in flame wars against each other. Editors are responsible for deleting personal attack posts and those that are thought to have crossed the line set by the governmental rules and policies. Portal sites are also relatively open to citizen journalism, which refers to events and incidents reported by netizens. Driven by commercial interests, portal sites attempt to attract average Internet users through reposting such news. This mechanism enables portal websites to provide an alternative channel for different voices from the public(s).

Traditional mass media have a similar online presence. They host discussion forums, offer a commenting function, and report news. In addition to publishing news produced by their own staff, mass media sites also repost news from other mass media. However, mass media sites are strict with citizen journalists' work and re-post only those with the authors' real identities revealed (CNNIC, 2009). Users often rely on these sites to catch up with mainstream and high-profile events such as the Beijing Olympics. However, due to the restrictions imposed on mass media by the government, these sites are not often seen breaking citizen-initiated news. Nevertheless, we should not underestimate the influence of traditional mass media in amplifying the effect of online opinions. Although traditional mass media are reluctant to break news from nonofficial sources, these sites are quick to follow up if the news has been publicized by other official media (e.g., a commercial site). What is even more important is that the offline versions of these mass media are also involved in following up, and therefore, a handful of *online collective incidents* (in Chinese: *wangluo qunti shijian,* referring to incidents that trigger large-scale online responses) has successfully entered the dominant public sphere, triggering discussions among citizens who do not have access to the Internet.

Government portals, or e-government sites, played a significant role in recent online collective incidents. The commonly held idea is that government portals must be completely restricted, and we cannot see any meaningful discussions. However, studies (Jiang & Xu, 2009) have shown that government networks opened up spaces for public input in order to deflate social tension and remain the legitimacy of their governance. Government portals have become a popular space for citizens to report grievances and plead for support from the larger public. The reasons citizens do so should be understood in the context of the Chinese political system. China is a large country, and its political system relies on a strict hierarchy. Higher-tier officials have the power to appoint and fire lower-tier officials. Reciprocally, higher-tier officials are called to be responsible for lower-tier officials' wrongdoings. Chinese citizens are used to the mentality that, if they can catch the attention of higher-tier officials,

the citizens' grievances could be addressed and their problems solved. Posting a local event on a government portal that belongs to a higher-level administration is considered a convenient way to reach such a goal. In addition, breaking the news on a governmental portal softens the tone of challenging the government. It could be understood as an attempt to solve the problem within the official system. Thus, we have seen quite a few collective events first reported on government portals. A study (Yu, 2010) shows that among all the 2009 online collective incidents, 37.5% were first reported on government portals at the city level and another 1.7% on governmental portals at the province level. However, we have to be aware that only those incidents that are picked up and followed by portal sites and mass media sites eventually become influential.

I argue that the online spaces discussed above work together to function as counterpublic spheres. The discourses found there travel outside the spheres and reach the wider public. The events reported on government portals[3] reach portal sites and become known to the majority of the online public. If the events are further followed by mass media sites or even their offline versions, the events reach the dominant public, who are accessible only through traditional mass media. The theory of subaltern public spheres suggests that counterpublic spheres are able to influence the wider public because of an increase in their resources. The three types of spheres each have their own unique resources. Portal sites are commercial entities that enjoy the financial resources to mobilize the market. Mass media sites have their symbolic power to influence the opinion climate. Government portals are associated with political power and thus equipped with political capital that other spheres do not have direct access to. Whether these counterpublic spheres can persuade the majority of the public depends on their own efforts and the acceptance from the dominant public sphere. That is why we have seen the dynamics vary considerably across cases. The influence from the counterpublic spheres is far from being institutionalized, and the counterpublics always have to struggle to get their voices heard.

In between the counterpublic and satellite public spheres, numerous virtual spaces that engage in public discussions but lack the resources to push their discourses out of their own circle exist. We can see these spaces in BBS forums that focus on public issues (Zhang, 2006), blogs in which opinion leaders voice their concerns (Esarey & Xiao, 2008), and international virtual communities that pay attention to China (Yang, 2009). I call these spaces enclaved public spheres. Different from Squires's (2002) definition, these spaces are enclaved by others as well as enclaving themselves. International virtual communities include diasporic communities and bridge websites that are run by foreigners who are either based in China or interested in Chinese issues. One can find the most critical views from these spaces, but unsurprisingly, these sites are often blocked within mainland China. In this case, the Chinese government enclaves these spheres from accessing the public spheres in China, including the dominant and subaltern ones. Blogging in China has recently become a popular usage of the Internet. About 58% of Internet users either visit blogs or blog themselves (CNNIC, 2010). The most-visited blogs often belong to well-known individuals such as celebrities, professional experts, and famous scholars. Users visit these blogs due to interest in the individuals rather than engaging in a discussion with the bloggers. Most popular bloggers had to either close the comment function or never reply to the comments due to the large number of visitors. These blogs enclave themselves from two-way communications and cannot afford public discussions. Nevertheless, the blogs contribute to public discussions by providing sophisticated arguments and opinions that can be used in discursive contestations. However, opinion leaders cannot replace public engagement, and in this sense, blogs are at best enclaved public

spheres. BBS forums as a category involve a large variety in terms of the number of users, the diversity of users and opinions, and the degree of openness. I argue that, except for a few top forums (e.g., tianya.cn, xici.net, mop.com) that attract users who have the resources to influence the dominant public sphere, most are enclaved due to their limited membership. Different from the satellite public spheres, users of these forums intend to make them heard as widely as possible. However, the forums are simply not popular enough to reach a large audience. In other cases, the users are not influential enough to transform their discussions into a public debate. These enclaved public spheres hold the biggest potential to bring in social changes because of the spheres' openness to ideas. These spheres are also the most flexible in adapting to the sociopolitical environment by changing the degree to which they keep their discourses within themselves.

In short, the landscape of the Chinese Internet is highly diverse. Different components of this landscape are involved in dynamic and complicated interactions. Instead of looking for a universal public sphere, we should consider cyberspace in China as contentious virtual spheres that are open to many kinds of public discussions. Subaltern public spheres are found on the Chinese Net, and they serve different internal and external functions based on their membership, the resources they can mobilize, their relations to the government and the market economy, and the perceptions and reactions from the wider public(s). The internal and external functions also influence each other depending on the conditions. A virtual community that primarily serves an internal function (e.g., the online fans groups) may be forced to strengthen their external function when their internal activities caught attention from other publics. As another example, a community that once has extensive outreach (e.g., a popular online forum) may also have to close itself up in order to comply with the order from the state.

FUTURE RESEARCH DIRECTIONS

The case of Chinese online public spheres illustrates the utility of the framework that the theory of subaltern public spheres suggests. Future research should keep testing this framework against more empirical evidence. One way to expand the empirical test is to look at different contexts. These contexts may refer to different countries or even different regions when the idea of cross-national public spheres emerges out of regional alliances such as the European Union (EU) or the Association of Southeast Asian Nations (ASEAN). When the framework is tested against alternative evidence, I believe that new theoretical developments will come into being. Three types of subaltern public spheres have been identified in the Chinese cyberspace, but there must be more as the contexts change. Nevertheless, the emphasis on internal dynamics and external interaction serves as the first steps toward understanding how virtual communities become political entities through creating different subaltern public spheres.

CONCLUSION

The political significance of virtual communities should be understood in a structure of the state, economy, civil society, and family. Communities are seen as a social unit that is bigger than family but smaller than society. Communities are involved in politics when they try to clarify their interests and represent those interests to society through institutions such as policy-making procedures or media exposure. Information and communication technologies, especially the Internet, allow communities to be formed and provide limited yet viable discursive spaces for community members to engage in public discussions over concerns that are shared by the members. By taking a plural approach to virtual communities and the spheres they establish, this chapter shows that the theory of subaltern public spheres offers a more appropriate and comprehensive scheme that we can use to examine the Internet and its democratic potential.

I conclude that the Internet and the virtual communities it affords have shown and will continue showing to be highly relevant to politics. However, how much democratic progress they bring into the political procedure would have to be contingent on the political systems, cultures, and psychologies in the contexts. The case of Chinese online public spheres clearly demonstrates the diversity of virtual communities and their different strategies and practices in terms of representing their interests (or making their political claims) in front of state apparatuses, commercial entities, the dominant public, and other subaltern publics. However, due to the state-society structure in China (i.e., state overpowers society in most cases), virtual communities are still far from being an institutionalized representative mechanism that serves the democratic purpose as voting does. The same would be applicable to any other countries that clearly lack democratic components in their political systems (e.g., Vietnam). With regards to the well-developed liberal democracies (e.g., those in Europe and North America), the potential of the Internet to further their democratic progress would not be revolutionary. The reason is simply because the political system and culture there are already pro-democracy. What the Internet offers is only another tool, powerful indeed, to participate in an established democratic procedure that has already offered other means for participation (e.g., a free press). The democratic potential, I argue, is most promising in countries that have hybrid systems such as authoritarian democracies (e.g., Egypt), especially when they are facing fundamental unrests. These countries have the basic layout of a democratic setting (e.g., popular voting of parliament members and presidents) but have successfully suppressed these democratic mechanisms through other authoritarian means such as close control of mass media. The Internet fuels the oppositions that have been carried out by the political minorities for years and helps to change the balance between the ruling authorities and the opposing forces. It is at the moment of balance-breaking that the Internet releases its highest energy to democratize.

The theory of subaltern public spheres challenges the tendency to look at the Internet as one single entity without carefully examining the dynamics within the cyberspace. Instead of answering whether the Internet, as a whole, would facilitate democratization or not, we should study how different spheres within one particular cyberspace each function and how they interact with each other to influence the political procedure in one context. This theoretical framework, for instance, has led to empirical findings that complement previous studies on the Internet and politics in China. Previous research has exclusively focused on the struggle between the state and the so-called civil society, assuming that they are the only two players in the game. This chapter, by taking the approach of plural public spheres, introduces a four-player structure and provides an analysis that digs into the complexity of society (e.g., dominant pubic and multiple subaltern publics).

REFERENCES

Anderson, B. (1991). *Imagined communities: Reflections on the origin and spread of nationalism*. London, UK: Verso.

Baym, N. (2000). *Tune in, log on: Soaps, fandom, and online community*. Thousand Oaks, CA: Sage.

Bell, C., & Newby, H. (1976). Community, communion, class and community action: The social sources of the new urban politics. In D. T. Herbert & R. J. Johnston (Eds.), *Social areas in cities: Vol. II. Spatial perspectives on problems and policies* (pp. 189–207). Hoboken, NJ: Wiley.

Bernard, J. (1973). *The sociology of community*. Glenview, IL: Scott, Foresman.

Brouwer, D. C. (2001). ACT-ing up in congressional hearings. In Asen, R., & Brouwer, D. C. (Eds.), *Counterpublics and the state* (pp. 87–110). Albany, NY: State University of New York Press.

Calhoun, C. (1992). Introduction: Habermas and the public sphere. In Calhoun, C. (Ed.), *Habermas and the public sphere* (pp. 1–48). Cambridge, MA: MIT Press.

China Internet Network Information Center (CNNIC). (2009). *Research report on social events and the influence of online media*. Retrieved July 19, 2010, from http://research.cnnic.cn/img/h000/h11/attach200912231659420.pdf

China Internet Network Information Center (CNNIC). (2011). *Statistical survey report on Internet development in China*. Retrieved December 14, 2011, from http://www1.cnnic.cn/uploadfiles/pdf/2011/2/28/153752.pdf

Dahlberg, L. (2001). The Internet and democratic discourse: Exploring the prospects of online deliberative forums extending the public sphere. *Information Communication and Society*, *4*(4), 615–633. doi:10.1080/13691180110097030

Dahlgren, P. (2005). The Internet, public spheres, and political communication: Dispersion and deliberation. *Political Communication*, *22*, 147–162. doi:10.1080/10584600590933160

DeSanctis, G., & Gallupe, R. B. (1987). A foundation for the study of group decision support systems. *Management Science*, *33*, 589–609. doi:10.1287/mnsc.33.5.589

Esarey, A., & Xiao, Q. (2008). Below the radar: Political expression in the Chinese blogosphere. *Asian Survey*, *48*, 752–772. doi:10.1525/AS.2008.48.5.752

Felski, R. (1989). *Beyond feminist aesthetics: Feminist literature and social change.* Cambridge, MA: Harvard University Press.

Fraser, N. (1992). Rethinking the public sphere: A contribution to the critique of actually existing democracy. In Calhoun, C. (Ed.), *Habermas and the public sphere* (pp. 109–142). Cambridge, MA: MIT Press. doi:10.2307/466240

Friedland, L. A. (2001). Communication, community, and democracy: Toward a theory of the communicatively integrated community. *Communication Research, 28*(4), 358–391. doi:10.1177/009365001028004002

Habermas, J. (1989). *The structural transformation of the public sphere: An inquiry into a category of bourgeois society.* Cambridge, MA: MIT Press.

Habermas, J. (1992). Further reflections on the public sphere. In Calhoun, C. (Ed.), *Habermas and the public sphere* (pp. 421–461). Cambridge, MA: MIT Press.

Hansen, M. (1993). Foreword. In Negt, O., & Kluge, A. (Eds.), *Public sphere and experience: Toward an analysis of the bourgeois and proletarian public sphere* (pp. ix–xli). Minneapolis, MN: University of Minnesota Press.

Hauser, G. A. (2001). Prisoners of conscience and the counterpublic sphere of prison writing: The stones that start the avalanche. In Asen, R., & Brouwer, D. C. (Eds.), *Counterpublics and the state* (pp. 35–58). Albany, NY: State University of New York Press.

Jiang, M., & Xu, H. (2009). Exploring online structures on Chinese government portals: Citizen political participation and government legitimation. *Social Science Computer Review, 27*(20), 174–195. doi:10.1177/0894439308327313

Katz, E. (1996). And deliver us from segmentation. *The Annals of the American Academy of Political and Social Science, 546,* 22–33. doi:10.1177/0002716296546001003

Lyotard, J. F. (1984). *The postmodern condition: A report on knowledge.* Minneapolis, MN: University of Minnesota Press.

Mallapragada, M. (2006). Home, homeland, homepage: Belonging and the Indian-American web. *New Media & Society, 8*(2), 207–227. doi:10.1177/1461444806061943

McLaughlin, L. (1993). Feminism, the public sphere, media and democracy. *Media Culture & Society, 15,* 599–620. doi:10.1177/016344393015004005

Negt, O., & Kluge, A. (1993). *Public sphere and experience: Toward an analysis of the bourgeois and proletarian public sphere.* Minneapolis, MN: University of Minnesota Press.

Papacharissi, Z. (2002). The virtual sphere: The Internet as a public sphere. *New Media & Society, 4*(1), 9–27. doi:10.1177/14614440222226244

Peters, J. D. (1993). Distrust of representation: Habermas on the public sphere. *Media Culture & Society, 15,* 541–571. doi:10.1177/016344393015004003

Poster, M. (1995). *CyberDemocracy: Internet and the public sphere.* Retrieved July 20, 2010, from http://www.hnet.uci.edu/mposter/writings/democ.html

Qiu, J. L. (2000). Virtual censorship in China: Keeping the gate between the cyberspaces. *International Journal of Communications Laws and Policy, 4,* 1–25.

Qiu, J. L. (2006). The changing web of Chinese nationalism. *Global Media and Communication, 2*(1), 125–128. doi:10.1177/1742766506061846

Rheingold, H. (1993). *The virtual community: Homesteading on the electronic frontier*. Reading, MA: MIT Press.

Rice, R., & Love, G. (1987). Electronic emotion: Socioemotional content in a computer-mediated communication. *Communication Research, 14*(1), 85–108. doi:10.1177/009365087014001005

Spears, R., & Lea, M. (1992). Social influence and the influence of the 'social' in computer-mediated communication. In Lea, M. (Ed.), *Contexts of computer-mediated communication* (pp. 30–65). New York, NY: Harvester Wheatsheaf.

Splichal, S. (1999). *Public opinion*. Lanham, MD: Rowman & Littlefield.

Sproull, L., & Kiesler, S. (1986). Reducing social context cues: Electronic mail in organizational communication. *Management Science, 32*(11), 1492–1513. doi:10.1287/mnsc.32.11.1492

Squires, C. R. (2001). The black press and the state: Attracting unwanted(?) attention. In Asen, R., & Brouwer, D. C. (Eds.), *Counterpublics and the state* (pp. 111–136). Albany, NY: State University of New York Press.

Squires, C. R. (2002). Rethinking the black public sphere: An alternative vocabulary for multiple public spheres. *Communication Theory, 12*(4), 446–468. doi:10.1111/j.1468-2885.2002.tb00278.x

Walther, J. B. (1992). Interpersonal effects in computer-mediated interaction: A relational perspective. *Communication Research, 19*(1), 52–90. doi:10.1177/009365092019001003

Walther, J. B., & Burgoon, J. K. (1990). Relational communication in computer-mediated interaction. *Human Communication Research, 19*, 50–80. doi:10.1111/j.1468-2958.1992.tb00295.x

Watson, N. (1997). Why we argue about virtual community: A case study of the phish.net fan community. In Jones, S. G. (Ed.), *Virtual culture: Identity and communication in cybersociety* (pp. 102–132). Thousand Oaks, CA: Sage.

Wellman, B. (1999). The network community: An introduction. In Wellman, B. (Ed.), *Networks in the global village: Life in contemporary communities* (pp. 1–48). Boulder, CO: Westview Press.

Yang, G. (2009). *The power of the Internet in China: Citizen activism online*. New York, NY: Columbia University Press.

Yu, G. (2010). *Annual report on public opinion in China (2010)*. Beijing, China: People Daily Press.

Zhang, W. (2006). Constructing and disseminating subaltern public discourses in China. *Javnost-The Public, 13*(2), 41–64.

Zhao, Y. (2008). *Communication in China: Political economy, power, and conflict*. Lanham, MD: Rowman & Littlefield.

ENDNOTES

[1] The same criterion could be applied to other countries. If the Internet penetration rate does not reach a majority of the population, it is hard to say that a virtual public sphere exists. The infrastructure seems to be possible in countries that have almost a universal Internet access (e.g., Norway).

[2] See top sites in China, Alexa.com.

[3] The discourse that occurs on governmental portals is generally consistent with the dominant ideology. However, due to the complexity of political hierarchy, the actual practice of ideology control varies across

different spheres. Some meaningful discussions are seen in such official virtual spaces as Strengthen the Nation forum hosted by the leading party organ newspaper People Daily (Yang, 2009). In addition, governmental portals are often used as a channel to report/ release news or grievances, which become the trigger of large-scale online discussions. In these two senses, governmental portals have significant contribution to constructing counterpublic discourses.

Chapter 10
The Psychology of Trolling and Lurking:
The Role of Defriending and Gamification for Increasing Participation in Online Communities Using Seductive Narratives

Jonathan Bishop

Centre for Research into Online Communities and E-Learning Systems, UK

ABSTRACT

The rise of social networking services have furthered the proliferation of online communities, transferring the power of controlling access to content from often one person who operates a system (sysop), which they would normally rely on, to them personally. With increased participation in social networking and services come new problems and issues, such as trolling, where unconstructive messages are posted to incite a reaction, and lurking, where persons refuse to participate. Methods of dealing with these abuses included defriending, which can include blocking strangers. The Gamified Flow of Persuasion model is proposed, building on work in ecological cognition and the participation continuum, the chapter shows how all of these models can collectively be used with gamification principles to increase participation in online communities through effective management of lurking, trolling, and defriending.

INTRODUCTION

The study of online communities has led to such colourful expressions as trolling, flaming, spamming, and flooding being developed in order to describe behaviours that benefit some people while disrupting others (Lampe & Resnick, 2004). Since the proliferation of technologies like the '*circle-*

of-friends' (COF) for managing friends lists in online communities (Romm & Setzekom, 2008), the use of the Internet to build online communities, especially using social networking services has grown – but so has the amount of Internet abuse on these platforms. Facebook is currently one of the more popular COF-based websites (Davis, 2008). In addition to this, microblogging, such as Twitter, have 'status updates', which are as important a

DOI: 10.4018/978-1-4666-0312-7.ch010

part of social networks Facebook and Google+, as the circle of friends is. These technologies have made possible the instantaneous expression of and access to opinion into memes that others can access quickly, creating what is called, 'The public square' (Tapscott & Williams, 2010). The public square is the ability to publish and control editorial policy, and is currently available to all with access to and competency in using the Internet and online social networking services.

It is clear in today's age that there are a lot of demands on people's time, and they have to prioritise which social networking services, or other media or activity they use. This is often based on which is most gratifying and least discomforting. It has become apparent that introducing gaming elements into such environments, where they would not usually be – a concept called 'gamification' – can increase interest and retention in them. Such systems can promote positive activities by members and reduce the number of people not taking part, called 'lurkers' (Bishop, 2009c; Efimova, 2009). It can also promote activities like 'trolling' where content is created for the 'lulz' of it – that is for the fun of it. These can have upsides and downsides, but it is clear gamification can play a part in managing it.

The Problem of Lurking and Trolling Behaviour

Besides social software, gamification and consumerisation have been identified as the big themes for cloud applications (Kil, 2010). Gamification offers online community managers, also known as systems operators (sysops), the opportunity for a structured system that allows for equitable distribution of resources and fair treatment among members. Finding new ways to makes ones' website grow is a challenge for any sysop, so gamification may be the key. Often this is looked on in a technical way, where such platforms are encouraged to move from simple resource archives toward adding new ways of communicating

and functioning (Maxwell & Miller, 2008). It is known that if an online community has the right technology, the right policies, the right content, pays attention to the strata it seeks to attract, and knows its purpose and values then it can grow almost organically (Bishop, 2009c). A potential problem stalling the growth of an online community is lack of participation of members in posting content, as even with the right technology there is often still a large number of 'lurkers' who are not participating (Bishop, 2007b). Lurkers are defined as online community members who visit and use an online community but who do not post messages, who unlike posters, are not enhancing the community in any way in a give and take relationship and do not have any direct social interaction with the community (Beike & Wirth-Beaumont, 2005). Lurking is the normal behaviour of the most online community members and reflects the level of participation, either as no posting at all or as some minimal level of posting (Efimova, 2009). Lurkers may have once posted, but remain on the periphery due to a negative experience.

Indeed, it has been shown that lurkers are often less enthusiastic about the benefits of community membership (Howard, 2010). Lurkers may become socially isolated, where they isolate themselves from the peer group (i.e. social withdrawal), or are isolated by the peer group (i.e. social rejection) (Chen, Harper, Konstan, & Li, 2009). Trolling is known to amplify this type of social exclusion, as being a form of baiting, trolling often involved the Troller seeking out people who don't share a particular opinion and trying to irritate them into a response (Poor, 2005).

The Practice of Defriending in Online Communities

While the Circle of Friends allows the different techno-cultures that use online communities to add people as friends, it also gives them the power to remove or delete the person from their social network. This has been termed in the

United States of America as 'unfriending' or in the United Kingdom as 'defriending'. Defriending is done for a number of reasons, from the innocent to the malicious to the necessary. For instance, a user can innocently suspend their account or want to 'tidy-up' their Circle of Friends, so that only people they actually know or speak to are in it. There can be malicious and ruthless acts of 'cutting someone dead' or permanently 'sending them to Coventry' so that they are no longer in one's network or able to communicate with oneself (Thelwall, 2009). And users can do it, through a 'blocking' feature to cut out undesirable people who are flame trolling them so much that it impairs their ability to have a normal discourse. Being able to 'block' the people they don't want to associate with, this means that it is impossible for them to reconnect without 'unblocking'. Such practice on social networking sites can lead to users missing out on the context of discussions because they are not able to see hidden posts from the person they blocked or who blocked them, to them seeing ghost-like posts from people whose identities are hidden but whose comments are visible for the same reason. Any form of defriending, whether intended innocently or otherwise, can lead to the user that has been defriended feeling angry and violated, particularly if the rules for killing a community proposed by Powazek (2002) haven't been followed. This can turn the user into an E-Venger, whereby the user will seek to get vengeance against the person that defriended them through all means possible. If they're a famous person then this could mean posting less than flattering content on their Wikipedia page or writing negative comments about them in other online communities. If they're a close friend whose personal details they have to hand, then it could mean adding their address to mailing lists, or sending them abusive emails.

Gamification

As of the end of 2010, the Facebook game, Farmville, had more than 60 million users worldwide,

or 1 per cent of the world's population with an average of 70 minutes played weekly (Hurley, 2000). Concepts like "Gamification", which try to bring video game elements in non-gaming systems to improve user experience and user engagement (Yukawa, 2005) are therefore going to be an important part in current and future online communities in order to increase participation of constructive users and reduce that of unconstructive users. It seems however the gaming elements of online communities need not be 'designed' by the **sysops**, but developed independently by the users, in some cases unintentionally or unknowingly.

For instance, it has become a game on Twitter for celebrities to try and outdo one another by exploiting the 'trending' feature which was designed to tell users what was popular. Celebrities like the interviewing broadcaster, Piers Morgan, and reality TV personality Alan Sugar talked up in the press their programmes which went head to head, and Ms Morgan claimed victory because he and his guest, Peter Andre, on his Life Stories programme appeared higher in the most mentioned topics on Twitter. Also, consumers joined in this activity which could be called 'ethno-gamification' by agreeing to prefix 'RIP' to various celebrities names in order to get that term to appear in the trending column. In the same way 'hypermiling' has become a term to describe ethno-gamification where people try to compete with one another on how can use the least amount of fuel in their vehicles, so this could be called 'hypertrending' as people seek to try to get certain terms to trend higher than others. Examples of both of these are in Figure 1.

So it seems that gaming is essential to the way humans use computer systems, and is something that needs to be exploited in order to increase participation in online communities, which may not have the membership or status of established platforms like Facebook and Google+. Table 1, presents a restructuring of the extrinsic motivators and mechanical tasks in gamification identified by (Wilkinson, 2006) as interface cues, which are

Figure 1. Piers Morgan's Twitter page and 'RIP Adele' search results showing 'ethno-gamification' in the form of 'hypertrending'

'credibility markers' which act as mediating artefacts when attached to a user's cognitive artefacts (Bishop, 2005; Norman, 1991; Weiler, 2002). These are categorised according to whether they are 'authority cues,' signalling expertise, or 'bandwagon cues,' which serve as 'social proof' by allowing someone to reply on their peers. These are followed by and inclusion of the UK health

authority's guidance on communities and behaviour change (Esposito, 2010; Smith, 1996).

These stimuli and post types will need to be tailored to individuals dependent on their 'player type' and 'character type'. The dictionary, NetLingo identified four types of player type used by trollers; playtime, tactical, strategic, and domination trollers (Leung, 2010). Playtime Trollers are actors who play a simple, short game. Such trollers are relatively easy to spot because their attack or provocation is fairly blatant, and the persona is fairly two-dimensional. Tactical Trollers are those who take trolling more seriously, creating a credible persona to gain confidence of others, and provokes strife in a subtle and invidious way. Strategic Trollers take trolling very seriously, and work on developing an overall strategy, which can take months or years to realise. It can also involve a number of people acting together in order to invade a list. Domination Trollers conversely extend their strategy to the creation and running of apparently bona-fide mailing lists.

UNDERSTANDING ONLINE COMMUNITY PARTICIPATION

Increasing participation in online communities is a concern of most sysops. In order to do this it is important they understand how the behaviour of those who take part in their community affects others' willingness to join and remain on their website.

The Lurker Profile

Lurkers often do not initially post to an online community for a variety of reasons, but it is clear that whatever the specifics of why a lurker is not participating the overall reason is because of the dissonance of their cognitions that they have experienced when presented with a hook into a conversation. Cognitions include goals, plans, values, beliefs and interests (Bishop, 2007b), and may also include 'detachments'. These may include that they think they don't need or shouldn't post or don't like the group dynamics (Preece, Nonnecke, & Andrews, 2004). In addition some of the plans of lurkers causing dissonance has been identified (Preece et al., 2004), including needing to find out more about the group before participating and usability difficulties. The cognitions of 'goals' and 'plans' could be considered to be stored in 'procedural memory, and the 'values' and beliefs could be considered to be stored in 'declarative memory'. The remaining cognitions, 'interest' and 'detachment' may exist in something which the author calls, 'dunbar memory', after Robin Dunbar, who hypothesised that people are only able to hold in memory 150 people at a time. It may be that lurkers don't construct other members as individuals, and don't therefore create an 'interest' causing their detachment cognitions to be dominant. The profile of a reluctant lurker therefore is that of a socially detached actor, fearing consequences of their actions, feeling socially isolated or excluded, trapped in a state of low flow but high involvement. Lurkers, it has been argued are no more "tied" to an online community than viewers of broadcast television are "tied" to the stations they view (Beenen et al., 2004). However, it can be seen that some more determined lurkers are engaged in a state of flow with low involvement in doubting non-participation. Some have suggested lurkers lack commitment Building and sustaining community in asynchronous learning networks, but they are almost twice as likely to return to the site after an alert (Rashid et al., 2006). Indeed, lurkers belong to the community, and while they decide not to post in it, they are attracted to it for reasons similar to others (Heron, 2009). It has been argued that most lurkers are either shy, feel inadequate regarding a given topic, or are uncomfortable expressing their thoughts in written form (Jennings & Gersie, 1987), but others suggest lurking is not always an ability issue (Sherwin, 2006) .

Some researchers characterised lurkers as against hasty conversation rather than a problem for the community (Woodfill, 2009). Often lurkers are afraid of flame wars and potential scrutinising of their comments (Zhang, Ma, Pan, Li, & Xie, 2010). Marked and excessive fear of social interactions or performance in which the person is exposed to potential scrutiny is a core feature of social phobia (Simmons & Clayton, 2010), which has similar facets to lurking (Bishop, 2009d). Perhaps one of the most effective means to change the beliefs of lurkers so that they become novices is for regulars, leaders and elders to nurture novices in the community (Bishop, 2007b). It is known that therapist intervention can help overcome social phobia (Scholing & Emmelkamp, 1993). It could be that through 'private messaging' features that a leader could speak to a registered member who is yet to post. After all, a community is a network of actors where their commonality is their dependence on one another, so feeling a need to be present is essential.

Feelings of uncertainty over the use of posted messages is common to lurkers All social situations carry some uncertainty, which people with social phobia find challenging (Waiton, 2009). Lurking can potentially lead to social isolation, such as not naming anyone outside of their home as a discussion partner (Pino-Silva & Mayora, 2010). Lurkers are less likely to report receiving social support and useful information and often have lower satisfaction levels with group participation sessions (Page, 1999). Leaders can post more messages to encourage all members to post messages (Liu, 2007). Uncertainty caused by poor usability leads to non-participation by lurkers (Preece et al., 2004), and this can be tackled by having the right technology and policies (Bishop, 2009c). Developing trust involves overcoming, particularly in trading communities (Mook, 1987). Such trust was evident in The WELL (Whole Earth 'Lectronic Link), where members use their real names rather than pseudonyms (Rheingold, 2000). Requiring actors to use their real names

Table 1. Examples of interface cues and guidance for gamification use

Stimulus type (Post type)	Examples of interface cue	Guidance for use as mediating artefacts
Social (Snacking)	'group identity[1]', 'fun[2]', 'love[2]'	Users do perform snacking offer short bursts of content and consume a lot too. To take advantage of this, one should utilise local people's experiential knowledge to design or improve services, leading to more appropriate, effective, cost-effective and sustainable services. In other words allow the community to interact without fear of reprisals
Emotional (Mobiling)	'punishments[2]', 'rewards[2]'	Mobiling is where users use emotions to either become closer to others or make a distance from them. This can be taken advantage of to empower people, through for example, giving them the chance to increase participation, so as to also increase confidence, self-esteem and self-efficacy. This can be done through using leaders and elders to encourage newer members to take part.
Cognitive (Trolling)	'levels[1]', 'learning[2]', 'points[2]'	Trolling as a more generic pursuit seeks to provoke others, sometimes affect their kudos-points with others users. Such users should contribute to developing and sustaining social capital, in order that people see a material benefit of taking part.
Physical (Flooding)	'power[1]', 'mastery[2]'	Flooding is where users get heavily involved with others uses by intensive posting that aims to use the person for some form of gratification. Sysops should encourage health-enhancing attitudes and behaviour, such as encouraging members to abuse the influence they have.
Visual (Spamming)	'leader-boards[1]', 'badges[2]'	Spamming, often associated with unsolicited mail, is in general the practices of making available ones creative works or changing others to increase the success of meetings one's goals. Interventions to manage this should be based on a proper assessment of the target group, where they are located and the behaviour which is to be changed and that careful planning is the cornerstone of success. Designing visual incentives can be effective at reinforcing the message.
Relaxational (Lurking)	'meaning[2]', 'autonomy[1]'	Lurking is enacted by those on the periphery of a community. Their judgements for not taking part often relate to a lack of purpose or control. It is essential to build on the skills and knowledge that already exist in the community, for example, by encouraging networks of people who can support each other. Designing the community around allowing people to both see what others are up to, as well as allowing them to have a break from one another can build strong relationships. A 'd0 not bite the newbies' policy should be enforced.

could help a lurker overcome their uncertainties about others' true intentions.

The Troller Profile

A generic definition of trolling by '*Trollers*' could be 'A phenomenon online where an individual baits and provokes other group members, often with the result of drawing them into fruitless argument and diverting attention from the stated purposes of the group' (Moran, 2007). As can be seen from Table 2, it is possible to map the types of character in online communities identified by (Bishop,

2009b) against different trolling practices. Also included is a set of hypnotised narrator types which affect the approach a particular character can take to influence the undesirable behaviour of others without resorting to defriending, which is explored in the empirical investigation later.

This makes it possibly to clearly see the difference between those who take part in trolling to harm, who could be called 'flame trollers' from those who post constructively to help others, called 'kudos trollers'. A flame is a nasty or insulting message that is directed at those in online communities (Leung, 2010). Message in this context

Table 2. Troller character types and counter-trolling strengths as narrators

Troller Character Type	Hypothesised Narrator types	Description
Lurker	Stranger	Silent calls by accident, etc., clicking on adverts or 'like' buttons, using 'referrer spoofers', modifying opinion polls or user kudos scores.
Elder	Catalyst	An elder is an out-bound member of the community, often engaging in 'trolling for newbies', where they wind up the newer members often without question from other members.
Troll	Cynic	A Troll takes part in trolling to entertain others and bring some entertainment to an online community.
Big Man	Sceptic	A Big Man does trolling by posting something pleasing to others in order to support their world view.
Flirt	Follower	A Flirt takes part in trolling to help others be sociable, including through light 'teasing'
Snert	Antagonist	A Snert takes part in trolling to harm others for their own sick entertainment
MHBFY Jenny	Pacifist	A MHBFY Jenny takes part in trolling to help people see the lighter side of life and to help others come to terms with their concerns
E-Venger	Fascist	An E-Venger does trolling in order to trip someone up so that their 'true colours' are revealed.
Wizard	Enthusiast	A wizard does trolling through making up and sharing content that has humorous effect.
Iconoclast	Detractor	An Iconoclast takes part in trolling to help others discover 'the truth', often by telling them things completely factual, but which may drive them into a state of consternation. They may post links to content that contradicts the worldview of their target.
Ripper	Rejector	A Ripper takes part in self-deprecating trolling in order to build a false sense of empathy from others.
Chatroom Bob	Striver	A chatroom bob takes part in trolling to gain the trust of others members in order to exploit them.

could be seem to be any form of electronic communication, whether text based or based on rich media, providing in this case it is designed to harm or be disruptive. A 'kudos' on the hand can be seen to be a message that is posted in good faith, intended to be constructive.

The Effect of Gamification and Defriending on Online Community Participation

In 2007, as Facebook was emerging, (Bishop, 2007b) presented the ecological cognition framework (see Figure 2). The 'ECF' was able to show the different plans that actors make in online communities based on their different dispositional forces, which created 'neuro-responses' driving them to act, such as 'desires'. Four years earlier in 2003, research was pointing out that there were

unique characteristics among those people forming part of the *net generation* (i.e. those born between 1977 and 1997). These included having dispositional forces with preference for *surveillance* and *escape*, factors which were not part of the ECF.

These online social networking services have shown that the ties that used to bring people to form online communities are different than what they used to be prior to 2007. The personal homepage genre of online community (Bishop, 2009a) is now the most dominant model of online community enabled through these services. Through actors forming *profiles,* linked together with the circle of friends and microblogging content, they can control the visibility of objects such as actors (e.g. their friends) and artefacts (e.g. the content they want to see). They are in effect creating their own online community dedicated to the people they consider friends.

Figure 2. The ecological cognition framework

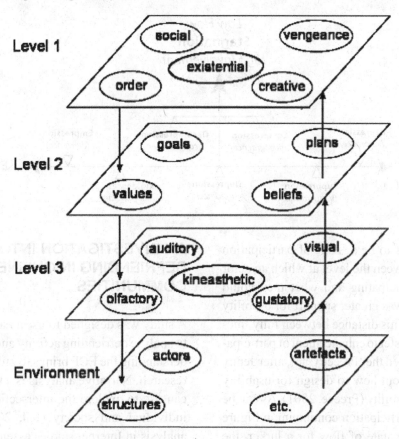

The Participation Continuum

One of the most important concepts in creating online communities that can harness gamification is the relationship between 'flow' and 'involvement'. When an actor is engaged in a state of flow their concentration is so intense that they forget about their fears and become fully immersed and completely involved in what they are doing (Csikszentmihalyi, 1990). Decision-making in such a state becomes more fluid and actors respond almost without thought for the consequences of their actions. In a high state of flow, Snerts will have low involvement cognitively and post flames with little restraint, often trolling for their own benefit, which then deters lurkers from becoming posters. A structure based on the ecological cognition framework for decision mak-

ing in human-centred computer systems has been proposed (Bishop, 2007a), which introduced the concepts of deference, intemperance, reticence, temperance and ignorance. This was extended through the participation continuum, to suggest that these cognitive states will lead to empression, regidepression, depression, suppression and repression respectively in the case of the original five judgements (Bishop, 2011b). A six cognitive state, proposed in that paper, reflects the dilemma that lurkers go through, which is compression when they experience incongruence due to congruence when trying to avoid cognitions which are not compatible with their ideal self. Decompression on the other hand is when they start to break this down. These concepts are presented in the model in Figure 3, called the participation continuum.

Figure 3. The participation continuum

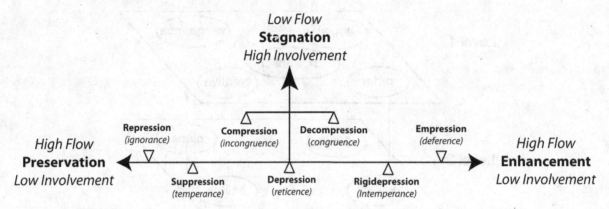

There appears to be a 'zone of participation dissonance', between the level at which an actor is currently participating and what they could achieve if there was greater support for usability and sociability. This distance between fully 'mediating' their transfer to enhancement of participation could be called the 'Preece Gap', after Jenny Preece, who set out how to design for usability and support sociability (Preece, 2001). As can be seen from the participation continuum in Figure 1, the higher the state of flow for a lurker, the more likely they are to be 'dismediating' from enhancement towards preservation by not to posting due to low involvement. Equally, the higher the state of flow for a poster the more likely they are to keep mediating towards enhancement and away from preservation within the community with little effort (i.e. involvement). The process in the middle resembles the visitor-novice barrier in the membership lifecycle (Kim, 2000). A lurker who has had bad experiences may be sucked into stagnation through rationalisation of non-participation, going from minimal posting (Efimova, 2009) to lurking (i.e. where they give up posting) and back out again after the intellectualisation process. This resembles a 'battering' cycle (Bishop, 2010), where the actor will be under a barrage of flaming abuse, then be told all is forgiven and they can come back as in (Bishop, 2009b).

AN INVESTIGATION INTO DEFRIENDING IN ONLINE COMMUNITIES

A study was designed to use a narrative analysis to analyse defriending activity and extend the understanding the ECF brings to online community research. Narrative analysis is a tool researchers can use to explore the intersection between the individual and society (Kil, 2010). Narrative analysis in Internet studies essentially uses both text and online "talk" to construct a holistic view of the online interactions, looking at cognition as well as affect (Yukawa, 2005). Narrative analysis is the most prevalent approach that has emphasized alternatives to categorising analysis, but much of narrative research, broadly defined, involves categorising as well as connecting analysis, and the distinction has not been clearly defined (Maxwell & Miller, 2008). Narratives were selected from Google's Blog Search by searching for the terms, "I deleted him as a friend", "he deleted me as a friend". "I deleted her as a friend" and "She deleted me as a friends". The ethnomethodological narrative analysis approach of (Bishop, 2011a) was then used to code the text in the blog posts to identify the different 'Methods', 'Memes', 'Amities', 'Rules' and 'Strategies' that impact on the decision to defriend someone or why someone was defriended.

Descriptives

The difficulties of a romantic relationship accounted for just over 2,700 (13.4%) of the cases where a female was defriended compared to less than 50 (0.47%) for men, suggesting that when a romantic relationship doesn't work out women are more likely to be defriended than men, or at least, people are more likely to disclose on a blog that they defriended a female because of relationship problems than they would males. Less than 20 males were defriended for a sex related issue compared to over 9,500 females. This may be because as Thelwall (2008) suggests, men use online social networking more for dating and women more for other forms of friendship. It became clear in the discourses there were often other people involved in the event leading to a person being defriended. In around 65 per cent of cases where males were defriended and 90 per cent where females were defriended there was another person involved. Over 3,000 females (16.4%) were defriended because someone was offended compared to only 4 males (0.08%) for the same reason (see Table 3).

Results

Analysing the data resulted in four key findings. Firstly, actors are provoked into responding to a state of disequilibrium, such as being defriended. Second, actors need to develop an awareness of the change in the environment before they are able to realise its impact on them. Thirdly, actors will first have a reaction to a state of disequilibrium before organising a response that causes them least dissonance. Fourthly and finally, actors will testify their experiences to others as a way of expressing their understanding in order to restore a state of equilibrium.

Finding 1: Actors are Provoked into Responding to a State of Disequilibrium

Understanding what drives actors to act is crucial to developing human-computer systems that adapt to and influence them. There has been extensive research into discovering what drives people, which has led to a number of theories, including psychoanalytic theory (Freud, 1933), hierarchical needs theory (Maslow, 1943), belief-desire-intention theory (Rao & Georgeff, 1998), which see desires as goals, and other desire-based

Table 3. Role of different factors in defriending narratives

Defriending discourse type	Males Defriended	Females Defriended
Effect of male on female friend	3,315	19,226
Effect of female on male friend	3,249	18,359
Employment mentioned	2,167	12,951
Sex	11	9,665
Break-ups and Dating	24	2,759
Offence	4	3,372
Little in common	3	1,835
Email related	25	1,386
Text message related	7	0
Application related	1	0
Total	*5,084*	*20,572*

theories, which see desires as instincts that have to be satisfied (Reiss, 2004). All of these theories suggest that actors are trying to satisfy some internal entity. This assumption ignores the role of the environment in shaping the behaviour of an actor and suggests that actors are selfish beings that only do things for shallow reasons.

There seemed from most of the narratives that there was something in the environment that provoked the actor to write about their defriending action. For instance, Era talking about a male she had known since the age of 12 who "made lots of sexual innuendos and jokes i.e. wolf whistles/comments about my make up, perfume etc." ended her narrative saying, "I told him goodbye and removed him as a friend on FB. I wished him all the best in his life. Then he replies and says he only likes me as a friend. He denied that he ever flirted with me and said I was crazy and that I over-analyse things," suggesting that recognition of her experience was important and writing in the blogosphere might be a way she saw to achieve it.

Finding 2: Actors Need to Develop an Awareness of the Change in the Environment before they Are Able to Realise its Impact on Them

It was apparent in the data that those writing their narratives needed to gain an awareness of how the stimulus that provoked them affects them, so that they can understand its impact more appropriately. In one of the weblog narratives, a blogger, Julie, said; "I deleted her as a friend on Facebook because after waiting six months for her to have time to tell me why she was upset with me I got sick of seeing her constant updates (chronic posting I call it)". This supports the view accepted among many psychologists that perception and action are linked and that what is in the environment has an impact on an actor's behaviour. Perceptual psychologists have introduced a new dimension to the understanding of perception and action, which is that artefacts suggest action through offering affordances, which are visual properties

of an artefact that determines or indicates how that artefact can be used and are independent of the perceiver (Gibson, 1986). This suggests that when an actor responds to a visual stimulus that they are doing so not as the result of an internal reflex, but because of what the artefact offers.

Finding 3: Actors Will First Have a Reaction to a State of Disequilibrium before Organising a Response that Causes them Least Dissonance

According to Festinger (1957) cognitive dissonance is what an actor experiences when their cognitions are not consonant with each other. For example if an actor had a plan to be social, but a belief that it would be inappropriate they would experience dissonance as a result of their plan not being consonant with their belief. Resolving this dissonance would achieve a state of consonance that would result in either temperance or intemperance. If this actor held a value that stated that they must never be social if it is inappropriate they could achieve consonance by abandoning the plan to be social which results in temperance. If the same actor had an interest in being social and a belief that it was more important to be social than not be social they might resolve to disregard their belief resulting in intemperance. If an actor experiences a desire without experiencing any dissonance they experience deference, as they will act out the desire immediately.

It became quite apparent early on in the analysis that those writing narratives would do to in such a way to cause least dissonance. For instance, one female blogger (Angie) when writing about a relationship breakdown with her friend, said, "I'm not sure if anything I write tonight will make any sense, but it's not as if anyone else reads these anyway so I guess it doesn't really matter how organized I keep it."

Finding 4: Actors Will Testify their Experiences to Others as a Way of Expressing their Understanding in Order to Restore a State of Equilibrium

It became apparent from looking at the weblog entries that bloggers got some sort of closure from writing the narratives. For instance, closing one of her blogs, Angie said, "As you can see, my brain is a ridiculously tangled ball of yarn at the moment and my thoughts are all over the place. Maybe some good old REM's sleep will massage the knots out. Until next time." Psychological closure, it is argued, is influenced by the internal world of cognition as well as the external world of (finished or unfinished) actions and (challenging or unchallenging) life events. Weblogs, according to some, serve similar roles to that of papers on someone's office desk, for example allowing them to deal with emerging insights and difficult to categorise ideas, while at the same time creating opportunities for accidental feedback and impressing those who drop by (Efimova, 2009).

REVIEW OF FINDINGS

The findings when mapped on to the ECF suggest several things. The first is that in online communities a stimulus is presented that provokes an actor into realising that an opportunity exists to post. For instance, a person may read something on an online news website which they disagree with so much that it provokes them into blogging about it. The next stage of the ECF, the impetus is governed by understanding and at is at this stage the actor beings to gain an awareness of how the stimulus affects them. The next stage is the realisation of its relevance to them and where they gain the intention to respond to it. In reference to the earlier example, it may be that the news article is disparaging about a particular cultural group they belong to, and it reignites old memories of discrimination that they want to respond to. The next narrative stage is where the reaction to this knowledge, where they may

form a plan to do something about giving them a sense of aspiration. The next stage of the ECF, Judgement, would be where the actor organises their responses to their reaction and weighs up the positives and negatives to acting on it. For example, their head may be flooded with emotions about how they responded to previous situations that were similar, which they may want to write down to contextualise the current situation. Once they have taken the bold step to write the post, they will then testify their opinions at the response stage and may cycle through their thoughts until they have given the response they are comfortable with. Table 4 presents the stages of the ECF and how these related to the findings of this study.

Towards the Gamification Flow of Persuasion Model

The constructivism proposed by Lev Vygotsky in *Mind in Society* (Vygotsky, 1930) says there is a gap between what someone can achieve by themself and what they can achieve with a more competent peer. Vygotsky called this the zone of proximal development, and suggesting that through mediating with artefacts, which the author interprets to include signs such as language or tools such as software, an actor can have help to achieve their potential, in this case in learning. The preeminent *Oxford Dictionary of Law,* which defines a mediator as someone who assists two parties in resolving a conflict but has no decision-making powers, and the process and mediation, supports this conceptualisation proposed by Vygotsky, the author accepts. Equally the term 'dismediation' is the process where an actor, either through reflection or the intervention of another actor returns to a former state of preserving their original status quo. The example given in some texts on cognitive dissonance is where a consumer orders a car from a dealer and then experiences doubt over whether they made the right decision. It has been argued that a courtesy call can help an actor feel more confidence in their decision and reduce the

Table 4. Description of stages of the ECF with reference to narrative stages

ECF Stage	Narrative Stage	Description
Stimuli	Provocation	There is a spark that makes someone want to post to an online community. This stimulus provokes an actor into seizing the opportunity to make a contribution.
Impetus	Awareness	Once someone has been given an incentive to post the next stage is to get an understanding of what they can do through gaining an awareness of what has happened.
Intent	Realisation	Once someone has an awareness of how an opportunity affects them the next stage is for them to realise how relevant it is to them to give them the intention to go further.
Neuroresponse	Reaction	Once someone has realised the relevance of a particular action to them they react to it without knowing the consequences giving them a feeling of aspiration.
Judgement	Organisation	Once someone has aspired to a particular course of action they may experience dissonance through organising the proposed action in line with their thoughts. They or their nervous system will then make the choice to take a particular action.
Response	Testimony	Once someone has made the judgement to take a particular action the next stage is to express that choice. In terms of narratives this is their testimony, which may encompass the various aspects of the previous stages.

Figure 4. The gamification flow of persuasion model

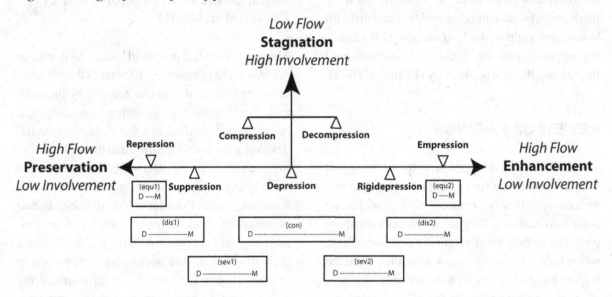

experience, which I call reticence, as an intervention to create mediation towards enhancement, which in this case is the benefit from a new car, which acts as the 'seduction mechanism'. The seduction mechanism in this context refers to an intervention that stimulates substantial change in an actor's goals, plans, values, beliefs, interests and detachments. An example, which can be found in the existing literature (Bishop, 2007c), is where someone who has been lurking is presented with a post that provokes them so much they feel compelled to reply. However, it is clear that not everyone reacts the same way to a seduction mechanism, as some may take longer to fully change their behaviour than others. A framework is therefore needed to explain these differences, and an extension to the participation continuum is presented in Figure 4.

DISCUSSION

Encouraging participation is one of the greatest challenges for any e-community provider. Attracting new members is often a concern of many small online communities, but in larger e-communities which are based on networks of practice, the concern is often retaining those members who make worthwhile contributions. These communities still have their 'classical lurkers' who have never participated, but they also appear to what could be called 'outbound lurkers', referred to as elders, who used to participate frequently, but now no longer do as much. One reason for this is that the actors have lost their ties through being 'defriended' by other actors in the network. Some of the reasons for this defriending behaviour has been explored in this chapter. They vary from issues in the workplace to difficulties in romantic relationships, whether romantic partners or strangers who take part in flame trolling. What is clear that defriending has an impact on those affected by them and are explained in the narratives they produce on weblogs. This suggests that while defriending can have an impact in one community, such as causing 'out-bound lurking', it can increase participation in another. Actors will always have a desire to share their experiences, and as has been shown through this chapter they follow a clear six-part cycle in expressing themselves, and their narratives take on 10 different personas based on their individual differences. It could therefore be concluded that one online communities loss is another's gain, as participation in these environments has now become so pervasive that if a person is forced not to participate in them and therefore become an 'outbound lurker,' or elder, they can always find another to meet their desires to express themselves.

This chapter has argued that essential to ensuring 'responsible trolling' is the use of gamification techniques. Gamification introduces elements from video gaming, such as points and leader-boards in order to incentivise positive behaviours and disincentivise negative ones. A model, called the 'gamified flow of persuasion' is presented, which builds on the earlier participation continuum. This explains how gamification based systems can be designed so as to help users transfer from one level of participation to another.

ACKNOWLEDGMENT

The author would like to thank those who provided feedback to earlier versions of this paper. In particular he would like to thank Jean Bishop for the thorough proof reading and for suggesting the names of the narrator types.

REFERENCES

Beenen, G., Ling, K., Wang, X., Chang, K., Frankowski, D., Resnick, P., & Kraut, R. E. (2004). Using social psychology to motivate contributions to online communities. *Proceedings of the 2004 ACM Conference on Computer Supported Cooperative Work,* (p. 221).

Beike, D., & Wirth-Beaumont, E. (2005). Psychological closure as a memory phenomenon. *Memory (Hove, England), 13*(6), 574–593. doi:10.1080/09658210444000241

Bishop, J. (2005). The role of mediating artifacts in the design of persuasive e-learning systems. *Proceedings of the First International Conferences on Internet Technologies and Applications,* University of Wales, NEWI, Wrexham, (pp. 548-558).

Bishop, J. (2007a). Ecological cognition: A new dynamic for human-computer interaction. In Wallace, B., Ross, A., Davies, J., & Anderson, T. (Eds.), *The mind, the body and the world: Psychology after cognitivism* (pp. 327–345). Exeter, UK: Imprint Academic.

Bishop, J. (2007b). Increasing participation in online communities: A framework for human–computer interaction. *Computers in Human Behavior, 23*(4), 1881–1893. doi:10.1016/j.chb.2005.11.004

Bishop, J. (2007c). Increasing participation in online communities: A framework for human–computer interaction. *Computers in Human Behavior, 23*(4), 1881–1893. doi:10.1016/j.chb.2005.11.004

Bishop, J. (2009a). Enhancing the understanding of genres of web-based communities: The role of the ecological cognition framework. *International Journal of Web Based Communities, 5*(1), 4–17. doi:10.1504/IJWBC.2009.021558

Bishop, J. (2009b). Increasing capital revenue in social networking communities: Building social and economic relationships through avatars and characters. In Dasgupta, S. (Ed.), *Social computing: Concepts, methodologies, tools, and applications* (pp. 1987–2004). Hershey, PA: IGI Global. doi:10.4018/978-1-60566-984-7.ch131

Bishop, J. (2009c). Increasing membership in online communities: The five principles of managing virtual club economies. *Proceedings of the 3rd International Conference on Internet Technologies and Applications - ITA09,* Glyndwr University, Wrexham.

Bishop, J. (2009d). Increasing the economic sustainability of online communities: An empirical investigation. In Hindsworth, M. F., & Lang, T. B. (Eds.), *Community participation: Empowerment, diversity and sustainability.* New York, NY: Nova Science Publishers.

Bishop, J. (2010). *Multiculturalism in intergenerational contexts: Implications for the design of virtual worlds.* Paper Presented to the Reconstructing Multiculturalism Conference, Cardiff, UK.

Bishop, J. (2011a). *The equatrics of intergenerational knowledge transformation in technocultures: Towards a model for enhancing information management in virtual worlds. Unpublished MScEcon.* Aberystwyth, UK: Aberystwyth University.

Bishop, J. (2011b). Transforming lurkers into posters: The role of the participation continuum. *Proceedings of the Fourth International Conference on Internet Technologies and Applications (ITA11),* Glyndwr University.

Chen, Y., Harper, F. M., Konstan, J., & Li, S. X. (2009). Group identity and social preferences. *The American Economic Review, 99*(1). doi:10.1257/aer.99.1.431

Csikszentmihalyi, M. (1990). *Flow: The psychology of optimal experience.* New York, NY: Harper & Row.

Davis, S. (2008). With a little help from my online friends: The health benefits of internet community participation. *The Journal of Education, Community and Values, 8*(3).

Efimova, L. (2009). Weblog as a personal thinking space. *Proceedings of the 20th ACM Conference on Hypertext and Hypermedia,* (pp. 289-298).

Esposito, J. J. (2010). Creating a consolidated online catalogue for the university press community. *Journal of Scholarly Publishing, 41*(4), 385–427. doi:10.3138/jsp.41.4.385

Festinger, L. (1957). *A theory of cognitive dissonance.* Evanston, IL: Row, Peterson.

Freud, S. (1933). *New introductory lectures on psycho-analysis.* New York, NY: W.W. Norton & Company, Inc.

Gibson, J. J. (1986). *The ecological approach to visual perception.* Lawrence Erlbaum Associates.

Heron, S. (2009). Online privacy and browser security. *Network Security,* (6): 4–7. doi:10.1016/S1353-4858(09)70061-3

Howard, T. W. (2010). *Design to thrive: Creating social networks and online communities that last.* Morgan Kaufmann.

Hurley, P. J. (2000). *A concise introduction to logic.* Belmont, CA: Wadsworth.

Jennings, S., & Gersie, A. (1987). *Drama therapy with disturbed adolescents* (pp. 162–182).

Kil, S. H. (2010). Telling stories: The use of personal narratives in the social sciences and history. *Journal of Ethnic and Migration Studies, 36*(3), 539–540. doi:10.1080/13691831003651754

Kim, A. J. (2000). *Community building on the web: Secret strategies for successful online communities.* Berkeley, CA: Peachpit Press.

Lampe, C., & Resnick, P. (2004). Slash (dot) and burn: Distributed moderation in a large online conversation space. *Proceedings of the SIGCHI Conference on Human Factors in Computing Systems,* (pp. 543-550).

Leung, C. H. (2010). Critical factors of implementing knowledge management in school environment: A qualitative study in Hong Kong. *Research Journal of Information Technology, 2*(2), 66–80. doi:10.3923/rjit.2010.66.80

Maslow, A. H. (1943). A theory of motivation. *Psychological Review, 50*(4), 370–396. doi:10.1037/h0054346

Maxwell, J. A., & Miller, B. A. (2008). Categorizing and connecting strategies in qualitative data analysis. In Leavy, P., & Hesse-Biber, S. (Eds.), *Handbook of emergent methods* (pp. 461–477).

Mook, D. G. (1987). *Motivation: The organization of action.* London, UK: W.W. Norton & Company Ltd.

Moran, J. (2007). Generating more heat than light? Debates on civil liberties in the UK. *Policing, 1*(1), 80. doi:10.1093/police/pam009

Norman, D. A. (1991). Cognitive artifacts. In Carroll, J. M. (Ed.), *Designing interaction: Psychology at the human-computer interface* (pp. 17–38). New York, NY: Cambridge University Press.

Page, S. E. (1999). Computational models from A to Z. *Complexity, 5*(1), 35–41. doi:10.1002/(SICI)1099-0526(199909/10)5:1<35::AID-CPLX5>3.0.CO;2-B

Pino-Silva, J., & Mayora, C. A. (2010). English teachers' moderating and participating in OCPs. *System, 38*(2). doi:10.1016/j.system.2010.01.002

Poor, N. (2005). Mechanisms of an online public sphere: The website slashdot. *Journal of Computer-Mediated Communication, 10*(2).

Powazek, D. M. (2002). *Design for community: The art of connecting real people in virtual places.* New Riders.

Preece, J. (2001). *Online communities: Designing usability, supporting sociability.* Chichester, UK: John Wiley & Sons.

Preece, J., Nonnecke, B., & Andrews, D. (2004). The top 5 reasons for lurking: Improving community experiences for everyone. *Computers in Human Behavior, 2*(1), 42.

Rao, A. S., & Georgeff, M. P. (1998). Decision procedures for BDI logics. *Journal of Logic and Computation, 8*(3), 293. doi:10.1093/logcom/8.3.293

Rashid, A. M., Ling, K., Tassone, R. D., Resnick, P., Kraut, R., & Riedl, J. (2006). Motivating participation by displaying the value of contribution. *Proceedings of the SIGCHI Conference on Human Factors in Computing Systems,* (p. 958).

Reiss, S. (2004). Multifaceted nature of intrinsic motivation: The theory of 16 basic desires. *Review of General Psychology, 8*(3), 179–193. doi:10.1037/1089-2680.8.3.179

Rheingold, H. (2000). *The virtual community: Homesteading on the electronic frontier* (2nd ed.). London, UK: MIT Press.

Romm, C. T., & Setzekom, K. (2008). *Social network communities and E-dating services: Concepts and implications.* London, UK: Information Science Reference. doi:10.4018/978-1-60566-104-9

Scholing, A., & Emmelkamp, P. M. G. (1993). Exposure with and without cognitive therapy for generalized social phobia: Effects of individual and group treatment. *Behaviour Research and Therapy, 31*(7), 667–681. doi:10.1016/0005-7967(93)90120-J

Sherwin, A. (2006, April 3). A family of Welsh sheep - The new stars of Al-Jazeera. *Times (London, England),* (n.d), 7.

Simmons, L. L., & Clayton, R. W. (2010). The impact of small business B2B virtual community commitment on brand loyalty. *International Journal of Business and Systems Research, 4*(4), 451–468. doi:10.1504/IJBSR.2010.033423

Smith, G. J. H. (1996). Building the lawyer-proof web site. Paper presented at the *Aslib Proceedings, 48,* (pp. 161-168).

Tapscott, D., & Williams, A. D. (2010). *Macrowikinomics: Rebooting business and the world.* Canada: Penguin Group.

Thelwall, M. (2008). Social networks, gender, and friending: An analysis of MySpace member profiles. *Journal of the American Society for Information Science and Technology, 59*(8), 1321–1330. doi:10.1002/asi.20835

Thelwall, M. (2009). Social network sites: Users and uses. In Zelkowitz, M. (Ed.), *Advances in computers: Social networking and the web* (p. 19). London, UK: Academic Press. doi:10.1016/S0065-2458(09)01002-X

Vygotsky, L. S. (1930). *Mind in society.* Cambridge, MA: Waiton, S. (2009). Policing after the crisis: Crime, safety and the vulnerable public. *Punishment and Society, 11*(3), 359.

Weiler, J. H. H. (2002). A constitution for Europe? Some hard choices. *Journal of Common Market Studies, 40*(4), 563–580. doi:10.1111/1468-5965.00388

Wilkinson, G. (2006). Commercial breaks: An overview of corporate opportunities for commercializing education in US and English schools. *London Review of Education, 4*(3), 253–269. doi:10.1080/14748460601043932

Woodfill, W. (2009, October 1). The transporters: Discover the world of emotions. *School Library Journal Reviews, 59.*

Yukawa, J. (2005). Story-lines: A case study of online learning using narrative analysis. *Proceedings of the 2005 Conference on Computer Support for Collaborative Learning: Learning 2005: The Next 10 Years!* (p. 736).

Zhang, P., Ma, X., Pan, Z., Li, X., & Xie, K. (2010). Multi-agent cooperative reinforcement learning in 3D virtual world. In *Advances in swarm intelligence* (pp. 731–739). London, UK: Springer. doi:10.1007/978-3-642-13495-1_90

Chapter 11
The Importance of Focal Awareness to Learning in Virtual Communities

Peter D. Gibbings
University of Southern Queensland, Australia

Lyn M. Brodie
University of Southern Queensland, Australia

ABSTRACT

Higher education today calls for transformative rather than transmissive education, and educators need to be particularly concerned with facilitating learners to fully focus on important elements, to make connections and properly process newly learned information. Educational approaches are beginning to place a greater emphasis on participation in community activities such as collaborative learning and team-work as opposed to individual inquiry. With the rise of the global community facilitated by the Internet and advances in communication technology, connected learners are forming virtual learning communities, which facilitate the individual and social aspect of learning through communication and team-based instruction models such as problem-based learning. To achieve this requires an education structure underpinned by pedagogical values that encourage student ownership of their learning and allows exploration of multiple perspectives by social interaction. One such educational structure may involve the use of virtual learning communities. The success of such a virtual learning community depends on developing key behaviours in students, which support them to focus on awareness of their own learning needs, attitudes and processes. This chapter argues therefore that students' focal awareness is critical to learning in virtual communities.

DOI: 10.4018/978-1-4666-0312-7.ch011

INTRODUCTION

Problem Statement

Whist learning communities have been well documented in general, there has often been some doubts raised about learning in online or virtual communities. Whilst people in close physical proximity may find it easy to learn from one another, it is reported to be much more difficult to establish learning communities in an online environment. Consequently, some discussions have appeared in the literature investigating possible impediments to the transfer of the traditional face-to-face learning communities to the development of virtual learning communities.

Although it may be more difficult, due to geographic, time and resource restraints, it is important that we gain more knowledge on how to develop and maintain effective learning communities in the virtual space. The key may be to look at the issue from the students' perspective, particularly as it relates to the theory of long term memory processes and focal awareness. In the context of this chapter, focal awareness refers to phenomena to which students' consciously direct their attention.

In this chapter we demonstrate the importance of student focal awareness through investigating a case study Problem-Based Learning (PBL) course that utilises virtual learning communities to facilitate students' attainment of course objectives.

Literature Review

The aim of online instruction is to promote student learning in accordance with well documented and well accepted education principles and theories. Learning fundamental theory often involves repeating a pattern of behaviour until it becomes automatic to the learner, but discussions surrounding higher order learning should also relate to the processes that occur in the mind of the learner. Cognitive psychology has demonstrated that learning is an internal process that involves memory, thinking and reflection (Ally 2004). This internal process involves creating linkages between existing and new information in the mind and this leads to greater retention of information (Mergel 1998). These linkages are made by the consolidation of information by the hippocampus in the brain to move it from short-term (focal or working) memory to long-term memory. It is appropriate to look at how these linkages are made in the cognitive architecture of the human brain with particular attention to focal awareness.

The limbic system is a complex set of brain structures that form the inner border of the brain's cortex on top of the brainstem. The limbic system is a fundamental processing centre in the brain that helps us process our sensory experiences (Ward 2006). It appears to be mainly responsible for motivation and emotions and therefore understandably one of its primal functions is the consolidation of memories and learning (Sousa 2001; Burton, Westen et al. 2009).

When data is processed from working memory to long-term memory, a specific hierarchy is followed (Sousa 2001). Data associated with survival is given priority, then experiences that evoke emotions are processed, and only after that do we process new information that might come from general learning activities. The consequence of this is that if students do not feel 'safe' (physically or emotionally), they will not properly process new information or focus on the learning activities. It is therefore critical to provide a 'safe' non-threatening environment in which students can learn. This applies particularly to the virtual learning environment where students often form, and participate in, learning communities. For example, Reuschle (2005, 2006) found that the online environment can support learning as a community activity provided the online learning environment offered a climate that was positive, supportive, safe, tolerant, respectful, nurturing, and participatory. In this context 'safe' means feeling comfortable enough to openly express ideas in the virtual environment without fear of ridicule or embarrassment – this is the 'easy to ask' environment mentioned by Postareff and Lindblom-Ylänne (2008, p. 116). When students feel safe participating in these online communities, they can focus on learning.

The aim of this chapter is to demonstrate the importance of students' focal awareness to their participation and learning in communities in virtual space. Our focus or awareness may be thought of as having a structure in terms of 'internal horizons' and 'external horizons' along the lines of Marton and Booth (1997). We are only aware and conscious of information that is being processed in our working memory. This represents what we are focussing on at a particular time or what is in the foreground of our focal awareness (Marton and Booth's internal horizon). There are other elements that we are less aware of that fade into the background of our focal awareness and these are at the outer limit of our perception (Marton and Booth's external horizon). Evidence suggests that the capacity of our working memory to focus on elements is very limited – if we are really trying to learn and properly process information this may be as low as two or three elements (Kirschner, Sweller et al. 2006). There are still many other elements in our memory that, at any particular time, we are not aware of and these are stored in our long-term memory (Kirschner et al. 2006). Educators need to be particularly concerned with facilitating learners to fully focus on important elements and to make connections and properly process newly learned information into their long-term memories.

Students' awareness and conception of their learning are central to the approaches they take and ultimately the quality of their learning (Marton & Booth 1997; Prosser & Trigwell 1999; Ramsden 2003). It is recognised that focal awareness does not necessarily lead to participation, and in turn participation (in this context participation in a learning community) does not necessarily lead to learning. However, one would need to participate in order to learn in a virtual community (although there are other ways of learning), and one should also need to be focally aware in order to participate in a properly constructed learning community. Students must effectively and actively participate in order to use their virtual communities for learning, since this cannot be a passive endeavour. The key then is to design virtual learning communities in such a way that they foster effective, focussed, participation.

In this chapter, when we discuss participation in a virtual learning community, we mean focus, engagement, thinking, active contribution, collaboration, and reflection of a nature that will foster the personal internal processes needed for learning. This definition is consistent with Rena and Pratt (2005) who believe the two key components for an online learning community are 'collaborative learning and reflective practice' (p1) and Palloff, and Pratt (2007) who believe the key to learning communities is the imparting of knowledge and co-creation of meaning. Such participation should encourage the creation of linkages between existing and new information in the mind and the consolidation of information by the hippocampus in the brain to move information from short-term short term memory to long-term memory.

Of course, recent literature exposes many barriers to effective learning in virtual communities. Palloff, and Pratt (2007) posed several questions: Are students engaged? Are they effectively participating? What if they are not? How important is team building and how do you do this effectively? How do you deal with conflict? How do you create a safe environment on discussion boards? Many of these barriers have been overcome by the authors and the strategies adopted will be discussed later in this chapter.

The latest thinking in professional education calls for transformative rather than transmissive approaches in professional education (Reushle 2005, p. 5). Reasons for this are evident and strongly promoted in contemporary adult education literature (Laurillard 2002; Reushle 2005,

2006). The transformative approach refers to learning that occurs when a student is empowered to reflectively transform their own individual meaning schemes (beliefs, attitudes, opinions) as a result of learning (Mezirow 1991). The process of students articulating their own ideas to others during peer discussions encourages them to develop their own thought processes and individual meaning schemes. This can lead to the discovery of misconceptions and disagreements with others, and the discourse also provides an opportunity for exposure to cognitive conflicts which, from a Piagetian perspective, is critical to intellectual growth (Anderson 2004). Even students who do not possess advanced knowledge benefit from communication with more knowledgeable peers (Vygotsky 1978; Misanchuk & Anderson 2001; Rovai 2002; Brook & Oliver 2003; Wallace 2003) in what Vygotsky (1978) might describe as their zone of proximal development. The nature of these discussions, and their role in facilitating student understanding, is central to the development of lasting knowledge in long-term memory that can be used by students in the future (Innes 2007). This sort of communication is often called 'discourse' in research literature since this term conveys a meaning of knowledge building through a community of inquiry as opposed to the more social connotation of 'conversation' (Anderson 2004).

Some educational approaches are beginning to change in recognition of the value of this community or social aspect of learning, for example a greater emphasis is beginning to be placed on collaborative learning and team work as opposed to individual inquiry. Education and knowledge advancement is often being considered a community activity rather than an individual achievement (Scardamalia & Bereiter 2006) and with the rise of the global community facilitated by the Internet and advances in communication technology, connected learners are finding it much easier to form virtual learning communities. These communities, although operating in virtual space, facilitate the individual and social aspect of learning through

communication and team-based instruction models such as PBL (Brodie & Gibbings 2007; Gibbings & Brodie 2008b) and are therefore ideal contexts to establish learning communities.

While PBL is not new to higher education, its application to distance education with students working in virtual teams has been sparsely discussed in the literature. There have been numerous references to PBL for distance students in various disciplines, however in nearly every case these students or student teams are required to meet face–to–face at least once during the course and often team members work entirely in a face–to–face mode. Alternatively, the literature describes courses that are not true interpretations of PBL, but simply use some form of technology to deliver course content.

Typically, the literature on 'distance PBL' refers to a course delivery process where students are either working away from the main campus on a satellite campus, or normal teamwork is supplemented by electronic communications with the lecturer, tutor or other team members (Brodie 2006). Wilczyski & Jennings (2003) note that "...*a general framework has not yet been presented to guide the formation and management of Internet–based design teams within engineering education*". Also, there is a distinct lack of published information on situated learning in virtual teams (Robey, Koo et al. 2000).

Most examples of situated learning involve communities of practice (CoP) that share space and time i.e. proximate (Robey et al. 2000; Gannon-Leary & Fontainha 2007). Virtual communities of practice have been most often referred to in the literature relating to business environments (Hildreth & Kimble 2000; Kimble, Barlow et al. 2000; Neus 2001). The research in this area has been driven by globalisation and organisations increasingly working in distributed environments. These trends are directly responsible for the increasing impetus for engineering graduates to be confident and skilled in working in virtual teams. This has been noted in the engineering education literature (Thoben & Schwesig 2002; Jamieson 2007) and recognised by accreditation agencies worldwide.

The literature, e.g Bos et al (2007) and Gannon-Leary (2007), distinguish between virtual CoPs and virtual learning communities. CoPs may 'share news and advice but are unlikely to undertake projects together'. This may generate informal learning and this involves the process of 'becoming a full participant in a socio-cultural practice'(Lave & Wenger 1991, p. 29). In this case the more experienced participants pass on to the less experienced skills and knowledge whereas learning community's main purpose is to increase the knowledge of participants. These communities have learning as their main goal.

CASE BACKGROUND

In 2000 the University of Southern Queensland (USQ), a regional Australian university specialising in distance education, introduced into the Faculty of Engineering and Surveying (FoES) a PBL course utilising virtual learning teams and communities to facilitate students' attainment of key graduate attributes such as teamwork, communication skill problem solving skills and life long learning skills required by professional accreditation bodies. The student cohort is very diverse, both in age, prior experience and education. The majority of students in the distance mode are in the 30 to 39 year age bracket whist for the on-campus mode only approximately 10% of students come directly to university from high school. This core course services students in all programs (two, three and four year degree and nine study majors).

Over the life of the course the academic team have made continuous improvements in all aspects following a rigorous evaluation schedule. In some cases the modifications have resulted from changes in technology i.e. discussion forums and team chat rooms due to new university

portal software and others from research into student learning outcomes. At present the initial assessment tasks, for teams and individuals, are focussed on forming a learning environment for the students to tackle the subsequent open-ended contextualised engineering problems/projects. These assessments focus on raising awareness of behaviours and processes that positively contribute to individual learning, the team outcomes, and hence the learning community. In this way, these initial tasks help to overcome some of the barriers to student participation in virtual learning communities identified earlier in this chapter.

The initial assessments in the first few weeks of the course focus on establishing individual and team learning goals and an agreed team process (rules of behaviour and engagement, communication and problem solving strategy and evaluations of peer contributions). It has been demonstrated that students' focus is changed as a result of learning activities and assessment strategies in this course (Gibbings & Brodie 2008a; Brodie 2009). In particular, students change from initially focussing on products and outputs to later focussing more on processes (both technical and individual learning processes). This change in focal awareness leads to desirable behaviour in teams and to participation as effective members of virtual learning communities. The authors do not suggest that focal awareness is the only consideration; simply that it is an important one with respect to participation and learning.

To enable participation in learning communities and facilitate a safe and supportive learning environment an effective communication and management system needs to be embedded in the course operation. For distance education and virtual learning communities this communication interface to enable the social and constructive dialogue to occur in a time and manner which suits all members of the community is a Learning Management System (LMS). The enforcement of rules surrounding the use of this LMS addresses a major barrier to participation identified in the introduction. So too does the development of a code of conduct by each of the PBL teams, and interested readers are referred to earlier publications for more details on how to establish and utilise a code of conduct to manage virtual PBL teams (Brodie & Porter 2008; Brodie 2009)

A LMS is commercial software for delivering, tracking and managing education. It enables the lecturer/facilitator to provide course material and supporting resources to students, and allows interactions and communication between lecturer/facilitator and students, and between students. It also provides other functionality including assignment submission and return, and student usage statistics.

In 2008, USQ moved from WebCT (now part of the Blackboard group) to the open source software Moodle as the LMS for the university. All courses at USQ have a presence on the LMS. This platform allows discussion boards, chat and whiteboard facilities, electronic submissions of all assessment items - individual and team, announcements and links to external URLs (e.g. team wikis). In building a learning community all these aspects may be used to enable a truly flexible and fully virtual community to flourish.

Assessment

Assessment in the course is a mixture of team tasks covering both team process and outcomes; peer and self assessment of individual effort and participation; and individual portfolios (Gibbings & Brodie 2008a). The assessment, to a large extent, focuses on *processes* and *progress* rather than just the final outcome. This caters for the range of student prior experience and forces teams to truly work as a team and not leave the work to the most talented and motivated members.

Portfolios, recording both product and reflective processes, are an effective alternative assessment instrument (Wolf, Bixby et al. 1991; Wade & Yarbrough 1996; Tillema 2001). This reflective learning has its roots in philosophy and was empha-

sised by the work of John Dewey (Orland-Barak 2005) and recording this reflective process in a portfolio has the potential to be conducive to make implicit knowledge (Schon 1987). Embedding this type of reflection, identified by Rena and Pratt (2005) as a key ingredient of an effective virtual learning community, into the course assessment, is important to ensure students both participate and reflect on that participation.

Although reflective portfolios are traditionally not used extensively in engineering or technical education, reflective portfolios can be used to encourage and support students to become independent learners. Students can anticipate their own learning needs and monitor their progress in their development (Heartel 1990; Wiggins 1993; Orland-Barak 2004). There is also an increasing emphasis on educating students to be 'reflective practitioners'. This is linked to life long learning and in engineering education and engineering practice it is increasingly used for professional development by Engineers Australia for accreditation procedures (Engineers Australia 2004).

STUDENT PARTICIPATION AND FOCAL AWARENESS IN VIRTUAL LEARNING COMMUNITIES

Methodology

Discussions in this chapter rely on data collected using research methods including student surveys, thematic analysis of student reflective portfolios, and phenomenography. Numerous investigations and analysis of student learning and behaviour that contributed to the formation of a virtual learning community has been undertaken since the foundation course was introduced. Results from a variety of methodologies have been investigated and validated through triangulation including surveys of students (Likert scale and short answer responses), a thematic analysis of student reflective portfolios and a phenomenographic study.

There were three main surveys used from the inception of the course to determine student perceptions on the course, their facilitator and their learning. These three surveys have continued to current offers and form the basis for a longitudinal study on student perceptions and learning. Responses were indicated on a five point Likert scale and by short answer. For this chapter survey data from three years has been analysed with total number of returns of 820 (n=820) at a response rate of 55.6% averaged over three years. Analysis was both quantitative and qualitative.

Student Portfolio entries fall into two main categories: product, and process, and both types of artefacts were scrutinized in a thematic analysis. Emergent patterns or themes were identified, coded and classified. This analysis validated the results of the surveys.

The final method of analysis was from the qualitative research method of Phenomenography. This is a well accepted and documented interpretative research method and the investigation concentrated on developing a representation of the qualitative variation in students' interpretations of their experience of learning in virtual space in the context of the PBL course. Unfortunately, due to its complex qualitative nature, it is not possible to fully document the phenomenographic method in this chapter, however the results are used here to aid in our understanding of students participation, conceptions, focal awareness, and learning in virtual communities. Readers are referred to to Gibbings, Bruce & Lidstone (2009) and Gibbings, Lidstone & Bruce (2008) for full details of the phenomenographic study.

Using these three methods of investigation with a mixture of qualitative and quantitative analysis provides a robust and rigorous examination of the interaction, student learning and self awareness of students working in a virtual environment forming a learning community to meet the diverse learning needs of its members.

Results and Analysis

For distance students, working in a student team in virtual space can be a novel experience. For most, the course offered by FoES provides their first opportunity to actively work with other students and to form learning communities in virtual space. Even though some students from different time zones and geographic locations meet 'asynchronously', the authors believe that virtual team meetings for distance students are as effective as physical meetings for on-campus students and foster the desirable attributes of teamwork, conflict resolution and negotiation of tasks.

The self perception surveys, validated by a thematic analysis of portfolios, indicate that students appreciate the social aspect of the learning, something which is novel to distance education students; they gained a raised awareness of the value of prior knowledge and experience (in long-term memory) of themselves and their colleagues and they appreciated the opportunity to determine their own learning goals, based on such prior knowledge and experience.

Results are shown in Figure 1.

During the analysis of results from the phenomenographical study (refer to Gibbings, Lidstone et al. 2008 for further details of this study; Gibbings, Bruce et al. 2009) attention was paid to the students' 'lived experience' of the course, what they thought was important, and therefore what they were focussing on (in short-term working memory). The phenomenographical study identified five conceptions which provide insights to the formation of learning communities in virtual space. Each represents a qualitatively distinct manner in which people voice the way they think about their learning experience. The conceptions are student-centred and during the data analysis, attention was paid to what they thought was important, and therefore what they were focussing on (their focal awareness with respect to short term working memory).

Figure 1. Student self perceptions of the social aspect of the course and effectively using student diversity in learning and problem solving in virtual space

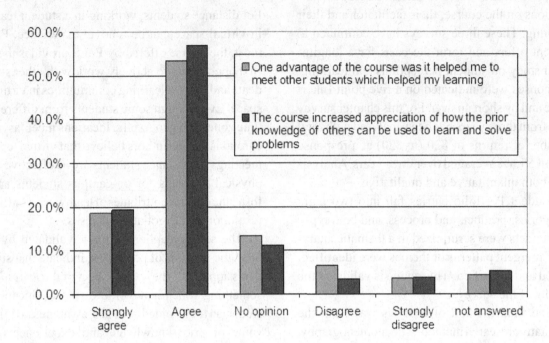

Five conceptions are:

1. A necessary evil for program progression
2. Developing skills to understand, evaluate, and solve technical Engineering
3. Surveying problems
4. Developing skills to work effectively in teams in virtual space
5. A unique approach to learning how to learn;
6. Enhancing personal growth

As part of the phenomenographical data gathering process, students were asked appropriate questions before and after the course. A comparison was then made between responses from before the course and those made after the course by dividing the data into two groups and totalling the numbers of responses falling into each conception. Doing this in each conception revealed variation in how students attend to learning in virtual space before

the course in comparison to after the course as indicated in Figure 2.

The trend is obvious and the inference is that the PBL course offered in virtual space was responsible for changing students' focal awareness in a positive way.

In this study it was discovered that the virtual space aspect to students' experience varied across the five conceptions:

- In conception one, there was an understanding that participating in team work in virtual space was necessary to solve the PBL scenarios in order to successfully submit assessment items, but this was restricted to the mechanics of team work participation and did not extend to how the team operates, nor issues associated with team dynamics.
- In conception two this awareness expands to realising the need for better communica-

Figure 2. Pre and post course response frequency (Gibbings et al. 2008; Gibbings et al. 2009)

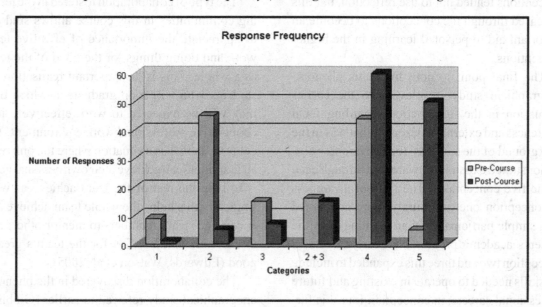

tion with the team in virtual space, since this was recognised as a skill that would be useful in future work. Although students were aware of the technical and other skills they had acquired, the ability to communicate effectively in virtual space was considered one of the major achievements from the course.

- In conception three the physical separation of the team caused students to consider learning to use the communication and other technology as an object of study itself and a means to aid better team work.
- In conception four, students understood that the learning in virtual space was quite a different experience from on-campus study, and as external students they also recognise that the PBL course was different from other external courses.
- In conception five, students had been issued a difficult challenge to study PBL in virtual space and when they successfully achieved this they experienced a great sense of accomplishment.

Three interesting aspects were discovered that demonstrate expanding awareness across the conceptions. One example relevant to this chapter is the manner in which students used their team with respect to communication, mentoring, critiquing, and evaluation. Students in the lower conceptions worked as individuals and only used the team to the extent they had to in order to pass assessments (participation only), whereas in higher conceptions the team became a critical part of learning with the use of communication, collaboration, mentoring and knowledge building all taking on increasing significance in the higher conceptions. Related to this, the second aspect was how students related to their team in the context of a virtual learning community and how they interacted with the team. Students in lower conceptions saw themselves as individuals and did not assimilate as being part of the team, whereas in higher conceptions they took an increased ownership of the team and genuinely saw themselves as part of a cooperative, collaborative team in virtual space. The third aspect revolved around how students used self reflection and feedback. Students in lower conceptions tended not to use reflection, but this increased through the conceptions to become an important aid to personal learning in the higher conceptions.

The final point to note from this phenomenographical study is relevant to the earlier discussion in the introduction regarding focal awareness and external horizons. What was in the background of the students' focal awareness also demonstrated expanding awareness through each of the five conceptions. The limit of awareness in conception one (seemingly more concerned with simple participation than learning) was the students' academic programs and early careers; in conception two and three this expanded to include the skills needed to operate in existing and future professional careers; in conception four this further expanded to life outside future careers with some indication that a social conscience may be emerging; and finally in conception five the limit of focal awareness was life in general and how the students as individuals, and their personal ethical values, could play a part in the broader context of developing a socially responsible society. Clearly then, the shift in focal awareness from before the course compared to after the course has been a beneficial one with respect to potential student learning.

Issues, Controversies, Problems

Team work skills and the ability to participate cooperatively in a virtual global environment began to take prominence in conception three, and in the course that was the subject of the study. The acquisition of these competencies relied heavily on students developing effective digital communication skills. These skills were largely transferable and include general team work skills, inter-personal dealings, relationship building, and conflict resolution skills all of which are necessary in workplace team environments regardless of whether the teams operate in the virtual environment or face-to-face.

The type of collaboration fostered in the learning communities in this course allows students to appreciate the importance of effective team work and doing things for the good of the team as a whole. This is an important realisation for students who will soon graduate at which time they will be expected to work effectively in a cooperative professional work environment. The course establishes a situation where the only way an individual can achieve their own personal goals is to help the rest of the team achieve as well. Logically this helps the whole team achieve and encourages team members to mentor others and to exert maximum effort for the team's greater good (Edwards, Watson et al. 2005).

The collaboration discovered in the phenomenographical study referred to earlier (Gibbings et al. 2008; Gibbings et al. 2009) expands from conception one where students really don't assimilate as part of the team at all, through later conceptions where they tend to make greater use of the team for skill development and learning, and finally on to deep collaboration and team knowledge building in conception five. The collaborative problem solving, undertaken in virtual learning communities, which was fostered by this course, engenders skills that are considered necessary for success in today's technologically advanced global markets. To achieve this requires a learning approach that is problem-centred and is underpinned by pedagogical values that encourage student ownership of their own learning and allows them to explore multiple perspectives by social interaction in the context of their learning (Edwards et al. 2005). This course has been shown to provide this type of learning environment, at least partly due of the formation of effective virtual learning communities.

Armed with this knowledge, pedagogical strategies may be devised to change the student's focal awareness and therefore effectively manage the student learning. While studying a well designed PBL course in virtual space, students may gain a deep appreciation of the need for lifelong learning and continuing professional development which will compel them to become confident, competent, and successful professional practitioners. Long after students have forgotten most of the knowledge they gained during their studies, they will be self sufficient and self motivated with respect to their own learning – and this may well be the most important attribute they acquire during their studies, as this will allow them to sustain their professional development and relevance throughout their future careers.

Solutions and Recommendations

Learning in a virtual environment and learning in teams needs careful scaffolding. The ability to work in a face-to-face group is not necessarily directly transferable to learning in an online virtual team. The main factor in developing a setting for online learning in a virtual team environment apart from the physical set up of appropriate communication channels and modes is developing trust. Walther's (1997) social information processing theory proposes that exchange of social information required to develop trust is not limited by computer–mediated communication. The only difference in this electronic communication from face–to–face communication is a slower rate of transfer. Thus communication is more a function of the context, setting, and timing than the characteristics of the media (Zack 1993; Markus 1994; Parks & Floyd 1996; Ngwenyama & Lee 1997). Pauleen and Yoong (2001) suggest that some electronic communication channels are more effective than others in building online relationships (including trust) and that the team *facilitator* plays a key role in strategic use of communication technologies. It is therefore recommended that facilitator training incorporates strategies to develop trust, deal with conflict and smooth communication difficulties.

Facilitators also play a key role in helping students understand 'life long and self directed learning'. Students can be well conditioned to passing the assessment items, but awareness of

their own learning comes from reflection. Where the assessment focuses on process and progress as well as identifiable outcomes, the focal awareness of students needs to be prompted by expert facilitator guidance.

FUTURE RESEARCH DIRECTIONS

Further investigation of students learning in a true virtual team environment will be of interest to many academics. The self efficacy, learning style, team role and individual personal characteristics of a student will all impact on their ability and motivation to participate, and learn, in a team environment. Doing this in a virtual environment is an additional complication and adds an aspect that warrants further study. The rise of the global community communicating through electronic media can link students in virtual learning environments which facilitate individual and social aspects of learning. This is a shift in direction from traditional classrooms where the teacher dictates the learning, the objectives and assessment. Developing the focal awareness of students on their own learning goals, and their attitudes and behaviors is required for a virtual learning community to fulfill the advantages such practices can deliver.

The current literature focuses on virtual teams which are formed in a 'contrived' business environment or have the ability to meet face–to–face to establish the basic fundamentals of a team e.g. a goal and trust between members. Little literature exists on teams formed without the use of 'sensory' communication devices like telephone, telephone conferencing and audio/visual conferences and formed for the purpose of *learning* as opposed to producing an outcome or artifact. Further investigation of the dynamics and formation of true virtual teams (with no face–to–face meetings or use of videoconferencing) formed for learning is recommended.

CONCLUSION AND FUTURE TRENDS

PBL, and more importantly PBL delivered utilising a virtual learning community, provides many required graduate attributes indicated by professional accreditation bodies. However, focussing on the individual and team outcomes, and indeed participation, does not necessarily deliver student *learning*. The success of a virtual learning community depends on developing key behaviours in students which support students to focus on awareness of their own learning needs, attitudes and processes. This focal awareness has been shown to be influenced by reflective practices and also effective participation in virtual learning communities. It is therefore concluded that students' focal awareness and their effective participation are critical to their own learning in virtual communities. By utilising a suitable pedagogical approach, underpinned by assessment tasks that focus on developing behaviours that support both individual and teams working in a collaborative and cooperative environment, students achieve deeper learning, and commit new information to long term memory, compared to approaches that place emphasis on the outcomes alone. The development of these learning skills set the foundation for future student learning.

So what can we expect for the future? The authors believe that in the future students will expect greater flexibility and mobility in how they engage in virtual learning communities. Portable devices are increasingly being used in learning environments for everything from e-reading to social networking and communication. In the future students will expect an approach that will help them to develop 'digital', 'flexible', 'portable' 'virtual' learning communities (how's that for a mouthful!) through the use of these portable devices. The challenge will be for educators to provide this flexibility and to do this in a manner

that does not detract from the lessons we have learned about the importance of participation and focal awareness to learning.

REFERENCES

Ally, M. (2004). Foundations of educational theory for online learning. In Anderson, T., & Elloumi, F. (Eds.), *Theory and practice of online learning* (pp. 3–31). Athabasca, Canada: Athabasca University.

Anderson, T. (2004). Teaching in an online learning context. In Anderson, T., & Elloumi, F. (Eds.), *Theory and practice of online learning* (pp. 273–294). Athabasca, Canada: Athabasca University.

Australia, E. (2004). *Accreditation management system. December 2004, Engineers Australia*. Melbourne: Aust.

Bos, N., Zimmerman, A., Olson, J., Yew, J., Yerkie, J., & Dahl, E. (2007). From shared databases to communities of practice: A taxonomy of collaboratories. *Journal of Computer-Mediated Communication Education, 12*(2).

Brodie, L. (2006). Problem based learning in the online environment – Successfully using student diversity and e-education. *Internet Research 7.0: Internet Convergences*, Hilton Hotel, Brisbane, Qld, Australia. Retrieved from http://conferences.aoir.org/viewabstract.php?id=586&cf=5

Brodie, L. (2009). E-problem based learning – Problem based learning using virtual teams. *European of Engineering Education, 34*(6), 497–509. doi:10.1080/03043790902943868

Brodie, L., & Porter, M. (2008). Engaging distance and on-campus students in problem based learning. *European Journal of Engineering Education, 33*(4), 433–443. doi:10.1080/03043790802253574

Brodie, L. M., & Gibbings, P. D. (2007). *Developing problem based learning communities in virtual space*. Connected International Conference on Design Education, University of New South Wales, Sydney, Australia.

Brook, C., & Oliver, R. (2003). Designing for online learning communities. *World Conference on Educational Multimedia, Hypermedia and Telecommunications 2003*, AACE, Honolulu, Hawaii, USA, (pp. 1494-1500). Retrieved January 13, 2007, from http://www.editlib.org/index.cfm/files/paper_14026.pdf?fuseaction=Reader.DownloadFullText&paper_id=14026

Burton, L., Westen, D., & Kowalski, R. (2009). *Psychology*, 2nd ed. John Wiley & Sons Australia Ltd.

Edwards, S. L., Watson, J. A., Nash, R. E., & Farrell, A. (2005). Supporting explorative learning by providing collaborative online problem solving (COPS) environments. *OLT 2005 Conference: Beyond Delivery*, QUT, Brisbane, (pp. 81-89). Retrieved February 8, 2008, from http://eprints.qut.edu.au/archive/00002146/02/2146.pdf

Gannon-Leary, P., & Fontainha, E. (2007). Communities of practice and virtual learning communities: Benefits, barriers and success factors. *eLearning Papers, 5,* 13. Retrieved January 3, 2010, from http://www.elearningeuropa.info/files/media/media13563.pdf

Gibbings, P., & Brodie, L. (2008a). Assessment strategy for an engineering problem solving course. *International Journal of Engineering Education, 24*(1), 153–161.

Gibbings, P. D., & Brodie, L. M. (2008b). Team-based learning communities in virtual space. *International Journal of Engineering Education, 24*(6), 1119–1129.

Gibbings, P. D., Bruce, C., & Lidstone, J. (2009). *Problem-based learning (PBL) in virtual space: Developing experiences for professional development*. VDM Verlag Dr Muller Aktiengesellschaft & Co KG.

Gibbings, P. D., Lidstone, J., & Bruce, C. (2008). *Using student experience of problem-based learning in virtual space to drive engineering educational pedagogy*. Paper presented to the 19th Annual Conference for the Australasian Association for Engineering Education - To Industry and Beyond, Yeppoon, Queensland, Australia, 7th - 10th December

Heartel, E. (1990). Performance tests, simulations and other methods. In Millman, J., & Darling Hammond, L. (Eds.), *The new handbook of teacher evaluation* (pp. 278–294). Newbury Park, CA: Sage.

Hildreth, P., & Kimble, C. (2000). Communities of practice in the distributed international environment. *Journal of Knowledge Management, 4*(1), 27–38. doi:10.1108/13673270010315920

Innes, R. B. (2007). Dialogic communication in collaborative problem solving groups. *International Journal for the Scholarship of Teaching and Learning, 1*(1), 1-19. Retrieved October 16, 2007, from http://www.georgiasouthern.edu/ijsotl/v1n1/innes/IJ_Innes.pdf

Jamieson, L. (2007). *Engineering education in the changing world*. Paper presented to the EPICS Conference, University of California, San Diego.

Kimble, C., Barlow, A., & Li, F. (2000). *Effective virtual teams through communities of practice*. Retrieved June 6, 2008, from http://ssrn.com/abstract=634645

Kirschner, P. A., Sweller, J., & Clark, R. E. (2006). Why minimal guidance during instruction does not work: An analysis of the failure of constructivist, discovery, problem-based, experiential, and inquiry-based teaching. *Educational Psychologist, 41*(2), 75–86. doi:10.1207/s15326985ep4102_1

Laurillard, D. (2002). *Rethinking teaching for the knowledge society*. Retrieved June 8, 2005, from http://www.educause.edu/ir/library/pdf/erm0201.pdf

Lave, J., & Wenger, E. (1991). *Situated learning. Legitimate peripheral participation*. Cambridge, UK: Cambridge University Press.

Markus, M. L. (1994). Electronic mail as the medium of managerial choice. *Organization Science, 5*(4), 502–527. doi:10.1287/orsc.5.4.502

Marton, F., & Booth, S. (1997). *Learning and awareness*. Lawrence Erlbaum Associates.

Mergel, B. (1998). *Instructional design and learning theory*. Retrieved November 28, 2005, from http://www.usask.ca/education/coursework/802papers/mergel/brenda.htm

Mezirow, J. (1991). *Transformative dimensions in adult learning*. San Francisco, CA: Jossey-Bass.

Misanchuk, M., & Anderson, T. (2001). Building community in an online learning environment: Communication, cooperation and collaboration, (pp. 1-14). Retrieved January 13, 2007, from http://www.mtsu.edu/~itconf/proceed01/19.html

Neus, A. (2001). Managing information quality in virtual communities of practice. In E. Pierce & R. Katz-Haas (Eds.), *6th International Conference on Information Quality at MIT*. Boston, MA: Sloan School of Management.

Ngwenyama, O. K., & Lee, A. S. (1997). Communication richness in electronic mail: Critical social theory and the contextuality of meaning. *Management Information Systems Quarterly, 21*(2), 145–167. doi:10.2307/249417

Orland-Barak, L. (2004). Portfolios as evidence of reflective practice: What remains untold. *Educational Research, 47*(1), 25–44. doi:10.1080/0013188042000337541

Palloff, R., & Pratt, K. (2005). Online learning communities revisited. *Proceedings of the 21st Annual Conference on Distance Teaching and Learning*. Retrieved from http://www.uwex.edu/disted/conference/Resource_library/proceedings/05_1801.pdf

Palloff, R., & Pratt, K. (2007). *Building online learning communities*. San Francisco, CA: John Wiley & Sons.

Parks, M. R., & Floyd, K. (1996). Making friends in cyberspace. *Journal of Computer-Mediated Communication, 1*(4). Retrieved from http://www.ascusc.org/jcmc/vol1/issue4/parks.html

Pauleen, D. J., & Yoong, P. (2001). Facilitating virtual team relationships via Internet and conventional communication channels. *Internet Research: Electronic Networking Applications and Policy, 11*(2), 190–202.

Postareff, L., & Lindblom-Ylänne, S. (2008). Variation in teachers' descriptions of teaching: Broadening the understanding of teaching in higher education. *Learning and Instruction, 18*(2), 109–120. doi:10.1016/j.learninstruc.2007.01.008

Prosser, M., & Trigwell, K. (1999). *Understanding learning and teaching: The experience in higher education*. Buckingham, UK: Open University Press.

Ramsden, P. (2003). *Learning to teach in higher education* (2nd ed.). London, UK: Routledge Falmer.

Reushle, S. E. (2005). *Inquiry into a transformative approach to professional development for online educators*. Doctoral thesis, University Southern Queensland, Toowoomba, Toowoomba.

Reushle, S. E. (2006). A framework for designing higher education e-learning environments. In T. C. Reeves & S. F. Yamashita (Eds.), *World Conference on E-Learning in Corporate, Government, Healthcare, & Higher Education*. Association for the Advancement of Computing in Education (AACE), Honolulu, Hawaii.

Robey, D., Koo, H., & Powers, C. (2000). Situated learning in cross-functional virtual teams. *IEE Transactions of Professional Communication, 43*(1), 51–66. doi:10.1109/47.826416

Rovai, A. (2002). Building sense of community at a distance. *International Review of Research in Open and Distance Learning, 3*(1), 1-16. Retrieved January 13, 2007, from http://www.irrodl.org/index.php/irrodl/article/view/79/153

Scardamalia, M., & Bereiter, C. (2006). Knowledge building: Theory, pedagogy, and technology. In Sawyer, R. K. (Ed.), *The Cambridge handbook of the learning sciences* (pp. 97–115). New York, NY: Cambridge University Press.

Schon, D. (1987). *Educating the reflective practitioner*. San Francisco, CA: Jossey-Bass.

Sousa, D. A. (2001). *How the brain learns: A classroom teacher's guide* (2nd ed.). Thousand Oaks, CA: Corwin Press, Inc., A Sage Publications Company.

Thoben, K., & Schwesig, M. (2002). *Meeting globally changing industry needs in engineering education*. ASEE/SEFI/TUB Colloquium, American Society for Engineering Education, Berlin, Germany. Retrieved from http://www.asee.org/conferences/international/papers/upload/Global-Education-in-Manufacturing.pdf

Tillema, H. H. (2001). Portfolios as developmental assessment tools. *International Journal of Training and Development, 5*(2), 126–135. doi:10.1111/1468-2419.00127

Vygotsky, L. S. (1978). *Mind in society*. Cambridge, MA: Harvard University Press.

Wade, R. C., & Yarbrough, D. B. (1996). Portfolios: A tool for reflective thinking in teacher education. *Teaching and Teacher Education, 12*, 63–79. doi:10.1016/0742-051X(95)00022-C

Wallace, R. M. (2003). Online learning in higher education: A review of research on interactions among teachers and students. *Education Communication and Information, 3*(2), 241. doi:10.1080/14636310303143

Walther, J. B. (1997). Group and interpersonal effects in international computer-mediated collaboration. *Human Communication Research, 23*(3), 342–369. doi:10.1111/j.1468-2958.1997.tb00400.x

Ward, J. (2006). *The student's guide to cognitive neuroscience*. Psychology Press - Taylor & Francis Group.

Wiggins, G. (1993). *Assessing student performance: Exploring the purposes and limits of testing*. San Francisco, CA: Jossey-Bass.

Wilczynski, V., & Jennings, J. (2003). Creating virtual teams for engineering design. *International Journal of Engineering Education, 19*(2), 316–327.

Wolf, D., Bixby, J., Glenn, J., & Gardner, H. (1991). To use their minds well. In G. Grant (Ed.), *Review of Research in Education, 17*, 31-74. Washington, DC: AERA.

Zack, M. H. (1993). Interactivity and communication mode choice in ongoing management groups. *Information Systems Research, 4*(3), 207–238. doi:10.1287/isre.4.3.207

Chapter 12
A Systemic Approach to Online Sharing Motivations:
A Cross-Disciplinary Synthesis of Rhetorical Analysis and Gift Research

Jörgen Skågeby
Stockholm University, Sweden

ABSTRACT

The purpose of this conceptual chapter is to present and argue for a cross-disciplinary and systemic approach to the examination of motivations for sharing digital media objects via social mediating technologies. The theoretical foundation of this approach is built on two social theories from rhetorical analysis (Burke's pentad) and gift research (gift systems), respectively. A synthesis of these two theories provides an approach capable of producing more coherent and contextually grounded insights regarding online sharing motivations. The reason these two theories were identified as useful is that they acknowledge and incorporate social and contextual factors. This is important to overcome the assumption that motivations to share are detached from the specifics of actors, situations, and sociotechnical means. As such, this cross-disciplinary combination challenges the limited, but common approach of trying to identify generic motivations for contributing to virtual communities. Instead, this chapter argues for a consideration of situated and contextual motivations for contributing by highlighting the conceptual questions what, to whom, how, where, and finally, why. In conclusion, the chapter fills a gap in the literature on online motivations mainly because current models focus on motivations as self-containing. Instead, this chapter suggests to consider sociotechnical means, types of relationships, values of media objects, identity, or culture in cohort.

DOI: 10.4018/978-1-4666-0312-7.ch012

INTRODUCTION

The question "why do people contribute to online communities?" has gained much attention from scholars interested in the incentive structures of Internet use. However, this generic question ignores the many contextual (social and technical) differences that the plethora of social network services of today enables. As such a systemic approach, that does not presuppose one specific incentive structure as more prevalent than others, seems viable in a context where media objects, social relations, technology, norms and markets co-exist. This paper proposes such a systemic approach.

Over the past decade we have seen an explosion in everyday, recreational social networking activities, applications, communities and services. Blogs, wikis, social networking, social bookmarking and media sharing are only some of the genres enveloped by the neologism social media. A central activity to all these genres of communication is, in a large sense, the sharing of various types of digital media objects (e.g. photos, movies, books, music files). By distributing artifacts, expertise, bandwidth and storage in connection to personal and social information these networks are bound together by the ties sharing creates. Thus, the emerging economy of sharing via social mediating technologies holds elements of both exchange and social bonding as well as self-centeredness and other-orientation. With the network effects of today it may well be that acts that are initially perceived as selfish may contribute to other-oriented benefits. As such, the notion of socially embedded (i.e. unspecified, other-oriented and focused on relationships) economies is gaining analytical traction, partly as a critique of pure transaction-centric markets (i.e. contractual, self-interest-maximizing and exchange-centered).

Few theorists adequately acknowledge social motives that transcend the gain imperative and instrumentalism, arising instead from social embeddedness in local communities, where individuals and groups are understood primarily as a part of social order. (Varman & Costa, 2008, p. 141)

As indicated by this quote much research on sharing motivations has been devoted to attempts at understanding sharing incentives in general, and somewhat counter-intuitively, by researching them as an isolated social phenomenon. The main drawback with such an approach is that it does not make the necessary connection between users, tools, relationships and environments. So, while many studies have been interested in understanding why people contribute to online communities in general, this chapter suggests that motivations are better understood through a systemic approach that can be applied to specific social mediating technologies. Consequently, the research question for this chapter is: how can we synthesize a model that approaches sharing motivations in a systemic way (i.e. that acknowledges social order and embeddedness)? Without foregoing the analysis, this paper will amalgamate a systemic conceptual framework by relating two partly overlapping, but mainly complementary theories on human motivation.

BACKGROUND

The technologies used to mediate human interaction are increasingly cheap, powerful, mobile and pervasive. As such, digital media objects are also becoming ubiquitous. Whether we use smartphones, netbooks, tablets or desktop computers to access the Internet, social networking sites, such as Facebook, are becoming hubs for sharing digital media objects. This paper focuses on social networking sites (SNS) because of their central position in everyday media use. SNS can be defined as:

web-based services that allow individuals to (1) construct a public or semi-public profile within a bounded system, (2) articulate a list of other users with whom they share a connection, and (3) view and traverse their list of connections and those made by others within the system. The nature and nomenclature of these connections may vary from site to site. (boyd & Ellison, 2007)

While profiles and connections are certainly the backbone of SNS, to an end-user the everyday use of social mediating technologies includes a mix of digital media objects, specific features of SNS and emergent ways of conduct. Superimposed on these three elements is then a network of weak to strong tie social relationships. The general practice can be understood as various media objects being shared to various people, depending on the type of relation and the available technical features. However, because of the great variety of social network sites currently available to end-users, we believe that a basic, but systemic, approach to sharing motivations, which are carried out via a variety of specific technologies, is vital. Such a framework would potentially support analysis and comparison of results.

SNS and the motivations to use them exist in a web of forces that pull them in different directions depending on the context. As mentioned there is a tension between social bonding and exchange. SNS are arguably rationalizing sociability. In many ways this is a contradiction in terms since sociability is dependent on qualitative measures and exchange on quantitative. Traditionally, any type of quantification of the strength of an interpersonal relationship (e.g. a monetary equivalent) would be seen as a deterioration of the relationship. In many SNS however, social relations and market mechanisms co-exist through various quantitative measurements, but also through a diffusion of individuals as 'personal brands' as well as corporations as 'personal friends'. There is also a tension between convergence and divergence. While there is a convergence in terms of features

in many SNS (e.g. some features are becoming the standard repertoire of SNS and some SNS defining these standards more than others) there is also a divergence both in terms of specialized services used for single purposes (e.g. outdoor sports gps tracking, social bookmarking, file syncing) and the technologies used to access them. More importantly there is also a divergence in terms of emergent practices. Different groups of users find new, "unintended", ways of utilizing features and consuming and producing material, which meet their specific needs. Finally, there is also an interesting tension between remediation and disruption. This tension has similarities to the convergence-divergence tension, but is also different. Remediation implies that SNS are taking on genre features from previous media forms – no media form is independent from previous ones (Bolter & Grusin, 2000). SNS are of course immediately related to such technologies as Usenet newsgroups, Internet relay chat (IRC) and ICQ. This suggests a fairly smooth transition where technologies 'evolve' over time, appropriating the most useful features. However, there are also certain conflicts that have emerged that are seemingly unique to SNS. These concern how participation through social media technologies can indeed create social dilemmas, conflicts of interest and personal insecurity. These disruptions, or 'inherent accidents' as Virilio would call them (Virilio, 2007), consist of such conflicts as work vs. non-work, public vs. private, pseudonymous vs. identified to name but a few (Skågeby, 2007, 2008, 2009b). The consequences for social practices is on the one hand a question about how people creatively use technologies in ways that were not intended by those who design and produce them (Margolin, 2009). On the other hand, there is also an element of how, previously non-mediated (i.e. face-to-face) social actions, are now mediated by technologies that "amplify certain, and reduce other possibilities in use" (Ihde, 2008, p. 15).

THEORETICAL FRAMEWORK

A recent survey of motivations in virtual communities (Kosonen, 2009) makes a typology of motivations consisting of individual motivations, personal characteristics, technical attributes and social capital. None of the 14 papers included in the survey by Kosonen considered all four categories and only two papers included three of the categories. To the author of this paper, this calls for an approach that considers motivations in a systemic way. To further the arguments, we shall now examine two systemic theories on motivation that stem from non-computer-mediated contexts. This section outlines the two theoretical frameworks used to create a systemic approach to sharing motivations. The two frameworks are Burke's pentad, stemming from rhetorical analysis, and gift systems, stemming from sociology and social anthropology.

Burke's Pentad

A common model for examining human motivations is what has been coined Burke's pentad (Burke, 1969) or the dramatistic pentad. This is a very comprehensive theory of symbolic action. The pentad (referring to the five elements included) stem from rhetorical and/or dramatistical analysis and contains act, scene, agent, agency and purpose. The general purpose of the pentad is to provide structure to human actions. It is an analytical tool in the sense that it provides analysts or managers with the basic terms for conducting analysis. Conceptualized as probing questions they can be formulated as:

- What was done? (act)
- When and where was it done? (scene)
- Who did it? (agent)
- How was it done? (agency)
- Why was it done (purpose)

Burke saw these fairly simple key terms as embracing the very essence of human motivation. At a later point Burke appended "attitude" as an addition to agency. Attitude refers to the manner in which an act is enacted. Although being very generic in nature, and used by other scholars prior to Burke, these key terms have been described as "universal heuristics of motives" (Rountree, 1998). In the context of this chapter they will serve as just that: a generic, but systemic, approach to motivations for sharing. An analysis using Burke's pentad will firstly focus on identifying what actually constitutes the different elements of a particular act. This may sound straightforward, but may require fundamental differentiation of layers of acts (e.g. non-present agents, primary/secondary issues, perceived versus claimed goals). Nevertheless, asking the questions above may provide significant insight into the structure of a particular act. This also points to the contextual nature of human actions (i.e. how a particular act needs to be considered in context to be fully understood). Clearly, the dramatistic pentad is an encompassing model (and has been criticized for being too broad). However, when applied to specific contexts, such as a specific SNS, the general elements of act, scene, agent, agency and purpose, are charged with more specific, and manageable, meaning.

Gift Systems

Gift-giving research has always been concerned with the social aspects of goods exchange (Adloff, 2006; Adloff & Mau, 2006; Sargeant & Woodliffe, 2007). Interestingly, many inquiries about the gift have deployed a conceptual model similar to Burke's pentad. A common generic research question in gift-giving research is thus to ask "who gives what to whom, when, how and why?" (Berking, 1999; Eckstein, 2001) An important addition compared to Burke, and which is particularly relevant when applied to social mediating technologies, is the probing question "to whom". Indeed, the prototypical bonds that are common in social networks (i.e. family, friends, acquaintances and strangers) seem highly relevant to the analysis of motivations for sharing.

Komter (2007) offers a comparable framework based in analyses of traditional ("offline") gifting. The framework consists of the object; the occasion; the ritual; the relationship; the spirit; and the principle. The object refers to the idea that any object can become a gift – a symbol of an existing or desired bond – by being charged with social bonding value. It is important to note that objects can be either material or virtual. Arguably, the digital object is positioned somewhere in between these terms, as it is normally not a material object, but still one that can be materialized in the shape of a representation (e.g. printed or burned to a CD). The occasion refers to the specific situation. Traditionally, gifts are often related to special occasions such as weddings, Christmas, Valentine's Day or exams. In the light of gifting theory, it is possible to say that SNS has revitalized gifting as an everyday practice. The ritual is concerned with the etiquettes and customs of gift-giving and gift-receiving. In a digital context the ritual is both connected to the means at hand for giving (i.e. the available sociotechnical features) and the emergent ways of conduct (i.e. netiquette or cultural norms). The relationship, as conceptualized by Komter, has not so much to do with interpersonal ties as with typical types of transactions. These transactions range from social sharing to market exchange. The spirit is concerned with the motivation behind of gifts, where common types are expressions of love or gratitude; relationship indicators; expressions of power, prestige or reputation; expectations of reciprocation; and pure self-interest. The principle encompasses the tension between selfishness and altruism. While this philosophical debate is clearly relevant to sharing issues, it is also one that is very hard to apply to actual situations or acts. As a result, several new conceptualizations of altruism have emerged (Andreoni, 1990; Hardin, 1982). These new views on altruism suggest that in its purest form, altruism rarely exists. However, this does not mean that people are not altruistic, they are just selective about how to distribute their altruism (Hardin, 1982). Another explanation suggests that altruistic acts bring a (selfish) feeling of warmth and of having done 'the right thing'. Andreoni refers to this as an impure altruism, where the inner feeling of 'warm glow' is significant (1990).

It is clear that much of Komter's framework is located at a socio-cultural level of gift systems. That is, all the key concepts, except possibly the object, are concerned with emergent values of specific communities or societies (e.g. norms, occasions, attitudes). We shall now move to create a synthesis of the two presented theoretical frames in order to create, what this chapter refers to as, a systemic approach towards sharing motivations in SNS.

Synthesis

The two theoretical frames just presented clearly have much in common. Separately, they do not cover all the central aspects of SNS, but in unison they form a coherent approach towards them. Table 1 illustrates how the concepts relate to each other.

Table 1. Key terms in motivation research

Level	Concept from theory	Focus when applied to SNS
What	Object, Act	Characteristics and perceived values of digital media objects
Who	Agent	Personal and social identity
To whom	Social bond	Relationship types and social dilemmas
How	Agency, Attitude and Relationship	Activities as mediated by social networking services and types of transactions
Where (& when)	Scene, Spirit, Ritual, Occasion and Principle	Present and emergent practices, social order and social representations
Why	Spirit, Purpose	Motivations as dependent on each of the key terms above

The levels of analysis presented above are not discrete entities or disconnected from each other and there is no definite linear causality from one to the next. Rather the levels co-exist within a larger system. However, from a research perspective, an extended analysis performed at one level will most likely see sociogenic patterns or details emerging driving the study towards the next level. The systemic approach is thus grounded in the interconnection of these elements to each other.

Because each of these elements is interconnected in the structure of action, in what Burke calls the "grammar of motives," our understanding of one term necessarily is tied to our understanding of all of the other terms (Rountree, 1998)

The synthesized theoretical frame developed in this chapter is conceptualized as a toolkit for analysis, debate and re)ection among researchers of SNS. We shall now move to discuss the relevance and application of these key terms to social mediating technologies. Each section also includes additional concepts that can be used to deepen the understanding of each key term.

WHAT? CHARACTERISTICS AND PERCEIVED VALUES OF DIGITAL MEDIA OBJECTS

Digital media objects can include music files, films, digitized books and text documents, but also combinations of objects such as personal profiles (that may include photos, texts, movies) or media collections (e.g. mp3 archives). By conceptualizing certain media objects as "digital" focus is put on the nature of goods and transmissions (i.e. being digital or binary). With the digital nature come a number of technical characteristics such as being perfectly replicable, easily storable and searchable. Furthermore, besides acknowledging these fairly technical qualities of digital media

objects, it becomes interesting to question what other values and qualities that emerge from the use of digital media objects. Use value and exchange value in relation to digital media objects has been discussed previously (Sterne, 2006). Use value refers to what practical use the object has to a person. Exchange value refers to what the object is worth in an economic exchange (e.g. market value in a trade or barter). Although Sterne partly dismisses exchange value in his analysis of digital music files (arguing that these digital media objects are rarely paid for) – it can stille be relevant to analyze exchange value in "micro-economic" and subscription-based services such as iTunes or Spotify. Further, that digital media objects are not always exchanged for money, but in fact traded for other digital media objects in differing kinds of peer-to-peer networks also highlights the analytical potential of the exchange value concept. It may also be that the sharing of media objects in SNS is not as prescribed or instantaneous as use or exchange values suggest. Rather, these contexts often present more interpersonal or collective reasons to share. Studies of sharing in non-computerized social contexts accentuate another category of value that users ascribe to objects, namely social bonding value (Godbout & Caillé, 1998). Social bonding value (often noted to be the most central aspect of gift-giving research) is focused on ties between people and how these are maintained via the exchange of goods and services. A question that, so far, has received rather little academic attention is how these values operate when the shared/gifted object is of digital nature, and when the milieu is a mediated semi-public social network (see Table 2).

By lifting the perspective from exchange and use values to include the social bonding values that people ascribe to digital media objects (compared to physical objects) we also shift focus towards new sets of contiguous activities, and ultimately practices and representations. Thus, media objects in a social context, are perhaps best

Table 2. Values and characteristics of digital media objects

Value	Characteristics
Use value	The practical utility to a person. What can/will it actually be used for?
Exchange value	The value of a media object in terms of what it can be exchanged for, in monetary or trading equivalents
Social bonding value	The value in relation to social ties and their management. It asks questions of how users socially authenticate and personalize media objects in order to convey social bonding intentions

Example 1.

Using the typology of values above to analyze the sharing of a photo in flickr would, in most cases, result in limited use and exchange values, but a significant social bonding value indicating an interesting tension in this particular media object

conceptualized as socio-digital objects (see Example 1).

WHO? PERSONAL AND SOCIAL IDENTITY

The importance of informal social networks as means of getting work done is increasingly being noted (Abrams, Cross, Lesser, & Levin, 2003; Nardi, Whittaker, & Schwartz, 2000; Papakyriazis & Boudoudrides, 2001). Further, personal and professional networks (and thereby identities) tend to mix and are progressively more becoming permeable thereby creating networks where social relationships are both work related and non-work related simultaneously (Haythornthwaite & Wellman, 1998). Sometimes this is working towards an advantage, but other times it becomes more problematic and potentially the cause of social dilemmas. Identity is of course a well-researched academic concept and there are two basic distinctions that can be made in relation to it: personal and social identity.

Example 2.

The increasing focus on the development of the 'personal brand' indicates an interesting merging of personal and social identities. Still, there is a need to differentiate between these identities as the contexts shift to avoid social tension. A close personal friend may find it offensive to have to interact solely with 'a personal brand'. Also, the public affiliation with certain group or organization (e.g. with strong political stance) on Facebook has been known to cause interpersonal ties to be terminated.

Personal identity typically refers to unique personal attributes – those assumed as not being shared with other people, or not seen as a mark of group belonging. Social identity, on the other hand, refers to an individual's perception of him- or herself as member of a group, particularly in terms of value and emotional attachment. (Alvesson, Ashcraft, & Thomas, 2008, p. 10)

In SNS it becomes clear that the transition between personal and social identity is not a clear-cut distinction, but rather a sliding scale. For example, in terms of social identity, a person can be part of both professional and recreational groups. No matter which identity that is predominant in a specific sharing act, it is likely to co-influence the underlying motivations. Is the sharing agent acting as a professional, as a fellow social media user or as a representative of an organization? The latter has become significantly more common in SNS such as Facebook and Twitter, where users can friend or follow representatives of organizations or even the organization itself themselves. Arguably, brands or organizations acting as personal network agents, is another sign that social and market economies converge in contemporary social media (see Example 2).

TO WHOM? RELATIONSHIP TYPES AND SOCIAL DILEMMAS

The question of "to whom" a sharing act is directed is fundamental to understanding motivation.

Table 3. Relationship levels

Level of relation	Group structures
Ego	Me, myself, and I
Micro	Small group of close peers, well-known friends
Meso	Small network of peers, recognized acquaintances
Macro	Large network of users, anonymous strangers

Example 3.

If the sharing of music can be seen as a relatively impersonal form of media, photo-sharing became an arena for more intimate and sensitive issues. In 2006, flickr supported four 'friend list' options to coordinate different types of relationships. These options were: public (photos visible to any and all); private (photos visible to oneself only); contacts (photos visible to personal list of contacts only); friends and family (photos visible to a select subset of the contact list). Perhaps needless to say this distinction was not enough for users who complained significantly when they discovered that for example their moms would access the same photos as their 'everyday peers'. Consequently, the lists included in flickr did not represent the variety or complexity of relationships out of flickr. Perhaps even more interesting, there were also users who were concerned that the added metadata that they themselves, or other users, attached to photos would compromise their social status. This could be for instance tags or comments that put the photo in a new light. That is to say that users were perhaps not concerned with a photo being public, but once 'social metadata', for example in the form of comments was attached, it was no longer clear that the photo should be public. So, when sharing digital media objects in a socially networked environment, the socially important metadata becomes part of the picture as well.

However, relationships are complex and the wide array of potential specific relationships requires a narrower typology to be used. The motivation to share something with a close friend is likely to differ significantly from sharing something in a public forum. Skågeby and Pargman (2005) separates between four structural levels of relationships: ego (myself), micro (close friends/family), meso (acquaintances) and macro (anonymous strangers) in order to understand potential conflicts of interest and social dilemmas (refer to Table 3).

The group structures used in the model is apparently based on tie strength (Granovetter, 1973). The model argues that an important focal point for analysis of sharing is situated in the relations between these levels. As such it is a useful tool for inferring potential conflicts between the different levels of relationships (see Example 3).

HOW? ACTIVITIES AS MEDIATED BY SOCIAL NETWORK SERVICES

The simplest way to investigate human interaction with digital media objects in SNS is to perform a feature or attribute analysis of a specific technology or SNS. The general features/activities that most SNS support are friend lists, sharing, tagging, consuming (reading, listening, viewing) and commenting. However, there are of course service-specific varieties of these general features, such as retweeting (Twitter), queues (Soulseek) and liking (Facebook) that need explication. This basic examination and description is of course

necessary to make research results understandable, but also to increase potential transferability. A careful description of the setting facilitates comparison to similar (or dissimilar) SNS. On a deeper level, there is a question of how features are utilized in cohort or in novel and innovative ways? In a context of social interaction via ICT:s, the digital also brings questions of persistence and ephemerality to light as goods and conversations can be copied, stored, re-shared or erased for social reasons.

An important theoretical contribution is that of attitude (i.e. in what manner an act is enacted). When referring to sharing in a converging context of social and economical markets, the manner in which a sharing act is performed is related to its type of transaction. This transaction is naturally concerned with both economic values and social values.

Fiske (1991) makes an interesting distinction that effectively combines social and economic considerations: community sharing; authority ranking; equality matching; and market pricing. Community sharing refers to the concurrent man-

Example 4.

Since online actions are so clearly mediated through specific features of tools (creating a truly social-technical milieu) we need to actively consider the specific model of sharing that underpins a specific feature of a specific SNS. In Facebook, multimedial sharing is taken to a new level – photo-sharing, locations, instant messaging, status updates, personal profiles, social gaming, friends of friends are examples of features of this 'mash-up' service. The key thing, when it comes to sharing with others is that the information provided to others can be directed through a configurable set of lists. As such, it is interesting to note that social media requires users to consider what we mean by friendship and what different types of friendships there are. To further this argument, an interesting question is, once we have configured our social relationships in Facebook, will we, when meeting people face-to-face, begin to consider them in terms of lists? If we subsequently connect on Facebook, we certainly have to. This indicates how important a specific feature can be in how we think about relationships.

agement of goods and social relations where all members of the group is treated equally. The social bond is comparable to all other members. Thus, no distinction needs to be made between recipients. Rather, all goods is shared to all members evenly. This type of transaction could also be based in social identification with others (Komter, 2007). Authority ranking is concerned with status and power positions. Goods and services are shared in order to show off and preferably to impress people higher in rank. Shared objects become symbols of supremacy. Equality matching entails a balanced reciprocity, where shared objects are weighted against consumed objects. Balance is important to maintain social order and each agency is compared to a corresponding agency. Market pricing consists primarily of exchange ratios of various kinds. They do not have to be monetary in nature, but they have to be socially meaningful. The exchange is however direct, contractual and unambiguous once settled.

Interestingly, many SNS show examples of all of these types of transactions concurrently. As such, determining common types of transactions in specific cases become important clues to understanding emergent social order (see Example 4).

WHERE? PRESENT AND EMERGENT PRACTICES, SOCIAL ORDER, AND REPRESENTATIONS

Common descriptions of culture define it as the attitudes and behavior that are characteristic of a particular social group or organization. Thus, defining the scene and setting is crucial for subsequent methodological choices. Particularly, how the studied phenomena permeates or does not permeate the online/offline border is of interest (online and offline methods can many times be used in conjunction (Garcia, Standlee, Bechkoff, & Cui, 2009; Silver, 2000)). Thus, the scene should be defined in both social and technical terms, illustrating for example system development processes, user base, historical background, characteristic social phenomena (if any), content of significance in FAQ:s, any official standards of conduct etc. The declaration of setting provides readers with the basic knowledge needed to contextualize the findings and insights presented later as well as judge how the studied phenomena relates to the chosen setting on a larger scale. A future reader can then make connections between the SNS genre, its features and the emergence of practices, social order and social representations.

Digital media sharing is now a common and persistent human activity. Like many other human activities it is also one that sees many paradoxes and tensions. Consequently, SNS are filled with parallel practices, which occasionally correlate and occasionally conflict. One defining reason for the emergence of concurrent practices is that online sharing has moved from being first and foremost goods-centric to being increasingly goods-and-person-centric. Of course, this highlights the motivations aimed at coordinating relationships between one self and the various groups of others to which one belongs. A related practical result of this change is that metadata used to be data mainly relating to media objects or technical resources. At present, media objects

Example 5.

> Soulseek is a music file-sharing service that emerged from the ruins of Napster. Up until 2004, Soulseek was an open "P2P system" (although, technically it relied on a central server) where users had access to all other online users material. However, in 2004, the introduction of 'the buddy list' came to divide the user community into two large groups. The buddy list was basically a list of selected friends, but the big cause of the stir was that users could choose to share their music with users on the buddy list exclusively. To the users who regarded open sharing as the ideal practice, this was an outrage. The creation of these small networks that could benefit from the overall pool of resources, but not give anything back went against their ethics of sharing. These users were what we may call instrumental in their use of Soulseek. They did not want to socialize or have chats about the weather each time someone wanted to download one of their files. In short, they wanted the biggest possible pool of resources. To the other group, whom we may call communicators, the buddy list was an improvement because it allowed them to make social connections as well as provide material directly to others whom they knew would enjoy it. Communicators also saw the buddy list as a way to ensure that others shared as much as them – somewhat counter-intuitively, only if you shared enough could you be on their buddy list. In all, the buddy list in Soulseek forced users to reflect on their intentions behind sharing, and its relation to the tension between the public and the private, at large.

are tagged with metadata about people and their (social) actions around the media objects.

The context in SNS often mixes educational, professional and recreational relationships, creating a stirring multiplexity – that is, a co-occurrence of different type relationships to the same people (e.g. personal friend and work mate). The mix of strangers, acquaintances and friends, the blending of contexts and multiplexity as well as the continuous development of new SNS functionality has to impact on sharing motivations. As such motivations are increasingly directed at coordinating the relationship between oneself and the various groups of the collective that one belongs to (see Example 5).

WHY? A SYSTEMIC APPROACH TO ONLINE SHARING MOTIVATIONS

Much research on online contribution has stressed the necessity to support self-centered end-user motivations and reward efforts in order to sus-

tain ongoing contribution. While partly supporting these arguments, this chapter also suggests that this is a limited view and instead points to a concurrent set of activities that include the acknowledgement of others' requests, coordination of social conflicts, emergent communal norms and even activities performed just for the fun of it. As such a systemic approach, that does not presuppose one specific incentive structure as more prevalent than others, seems viable in a context where media objects, social relations, technology, norms and markets co-exist. Asking, "why do people contribute to online communities?" ignores many contextual issues. The fact that social media and online communities exist in a cross-current of convergence and divergence calls for a systemic, but straightforward approach to motivational research. From the theories put forward in this chapter, motivations can only be clearly classified and understood when considered in relation to a specific service and its features as well as in relation to what is contributed, who is contributing it, how it can be contributed, and to whom it is contributed.

The Internet helps us test whether our theories are theories of social organization, or just social organization as we have known it to date. (Baym, 2005)

CONCLUSION, IMPLICATIONS, AND FUTURE RESEARCH

This chapter has proposed a systemic view of sharing motivations. This view is based in a wider reading of human motivations, including online identity; digital media object values; SNS features; mediated relationships; and sociotechnical emergent factors. In the words of Varman & Costa, it is:

[...] based on a broader interpretation of human motives: to be emotional, moral and at the same

Table 4. Conceptual framework

WHO	Personal identity	WHAT	General type (e.g. artifact, expertise, storage & bandwidth or social metadata)
	Social identity		Use value
			Exchange value
			Social bonding value
TO WHOM	Friends	HOW	Available technical features
	Family		Community sharing
	Acquaintances		Authority ranking
	Strangers		Equality matching
			Market pricing
WHERE	Setting	WHY	Regarded as a function of the other dimensions treated in cohort
	Present and emerging practices		
	Social order		

time purposeful. Here, community is offered as a celebration of human interdependence, the spirit of cooperation and sociality. This is a community that works not by the exclusion of other, but by having permeable boundaries that allow new bonds to be fostered. (p. 153)

The main contribution of this framework for managers is tools for a better understanding of how users share material. As sharing is at the very heart of collaborative hypermedia and social networks, managers will need know not only how to use social media tools, but also understand the fundamental underpinnings of social media and be able to apply that understanding strategically, for example to integrate it with corporate goals, marketing (research), and communication strategies. In a rapidly evolving, complex, globalized and multidisciplinary milieu, managers will need analytical tools that can be repeatedly applied to this social-technical flux. This paper has suggested a model that is generic enough, but still capable of delivering insights that pertain to a specific analytical target (see Table 4).

Future research naturally includes further testing of the framework as a way to structure empirical findings. However, preliminary studies have found it useful in the analysis of file-sharing (Skågeby, 2004), photo-sharing (Skågeby, 2008) and social metadata sharing (Skågeby, 2009a).

This paper has only begun to suggest dimensions that can be useful to further examine who; what; to whom; how; where and why. From that it is clear that the framework is flexible and allows for the creation of sub-categories that are adapted to specific SNS. As such, it shows developmental potential.

During its early conception, Internet was characterized by much volunteer effort and "community spirit": users shared advice, technical support, and good ideas. A plausible argument is even that in the early days of the Web, there was so little to receive that people who wanted, to share, drove much of its initial development. So, in a way, the Internet was always about giving and receiving, producing and consuming, uploading and downloading. Now, however, new services are building on each other through mashups and through the emerging social structures around them. SNS helps us to coordinate relationships and digital media objects, but social order, representations and practices develop in ways not determined by solitary technologies or their first-intended uses. Rather, the motivations for using social mediating technologies exist in force-complexes that affect them in different ways depending on the context. As seen from this chapter, these forces include tensions between social bonding and exchange; convergence and divergence; and remediation and disruption. The cross-disciplinary approach taken in this chapter paves way for more contextual inquiries that acknowledge the complexity of motivation and participation in virtual communities.

REFERENCES

Abrams, L. C., Cross, R., Lesser, E., & Levin, D. Z. (2003). Nurturing interpersonal trust in knowledge-sharing networks. *The Academy of Management Executive, 17*(4), 64–77. doi:10.5465/AME.2003.11851845

Adloff, F. (2006). Beyond interests and norms: Toward a theory of gift-giving and reciprocity in modern societies. *Constellations (Oxford, England), 13*(3), 407–427. doi:10.1111/j.1467-8675.2006.00399.x

Adloff, F., & Mau, S. (2006). Giving social ties, reciprocity in modern society. *European Journal of Sociology, 47*(1), 93–123. doi:10.1017/S000397560600004X

Alvesson, M., Ashcraft, K. L., & Thomas, R. (2008). Identity matters: Reflections on the construction of identity scholarship in organization studies. *Organization, 15*(1), 5–28. doi:10.1177/1350508407084426

Andreoni, J. (1990). Impure altruism and donations to public goods: A theory of warm-glow giving. *The Economic Journal, 100*(401), 464–477. doi:10.2307/2234133

Baym, N. K. (2005). Introduction: Internet research as it isn't, is, could be, and should be. *The Information Society, 21*(4), 229–232. doi:10.1080/01972240591007535

Berking, H. (1999). *Sociology of giving*. London, UK: SAGE.

Bolter, J. D., & Grusin, R. (2000). *Remediation: Understanding new media*. Cambridge, MA: MIT Press.

boyd, d. m., & Ellison, N. B. (2007). Social network sites: Definition, history, and scholarship. *Journal of Computer-Mediated Communication, 13*(1), article 11.

Burke, K. (1969). *A grammar of motives*. Berkeley, CA: University of California Press.

Eckstein, S. (2001). Community as gift-giving: Collectivistic roots of volunteerism. *American Sociological Review, 66*(6), 829–851. doi:10.2307/3088875

Fiske, A. P. (1991). *Structures of social life: The four elementary forms of human relations*. New York, NY: The Free Press.

Garcia, A. C., Standlee, A. I., Bechkoff, J., & Cui, Y. (2009). Ethnographic approaches to the internet and computer-mediated communication. *Journal of Contemporary Ethnography, 38*(1), 52–84. doi:10.1177/0891241607310839

Godbout, J., & Caillé, A. (1998). *The world of the gift* (Winkler, D., Trans.). Montreal, Canada: McGill-Queen's University Press.

Granovetter, M. (1973). The strength of weak ties. *American Journal of Sociology, 78*(6), 1360–1380. doi:10.1086/225469

Hardin, G. (1982). Discriminating altruisms. *Zygon, 17*(2), 163–186. doi:10.1111/j.1467-9744.1982.tb00477.x

Haythornthwaite, C., & Wellman, B. (1998). Work, friendship and media use for information exchange in a networked organization. *Journal of the American Society for Information Science, 49*(12), 1101–1114. doi:10.1002/(SICI)1097-4571(1998)49:12<1101::AID-ASI6>3.0.CO;2-Z

Ihde, D. (2008). *Ironic technics*. LaVergne, TN: Automatic Press/VIP.

Komter, A. (2007). Gifts and social relations: The mechanisms of reciprocity. *International Sociology*, *22*(1), 93–107. doi:10.1177/0268580907070127

Kosonen, M. (2009). Knowledge sharing in virtual communities - A review of the empirical research. *Journal of Web-based Communities*, *5*(2), 144–163. doi:10.1504/IJWBC.2009.023962

Margolin, V. (2009). Design history and design studies. In Clark, H., & Brody, D. (Eds.), *Design studies - A reader*. Oxford, UK: Berg.

McGee, K., & Skågeby, J. (2004). Gifting technologies. *First Monday*, *9*(12).

Nardi, B. A., Whittaker, S., & Schwartz, H. (2000). It's not what you know, it's who you know: Work in the information age. *First Monday*, *5*(5).

Papakyriazis, N. V., & Boudoudrides, M. A. (2001, May 17-18). *Electronic weak ties in network organizations*. Paper presented at the The 4th GOR Conference, Goettingen, Germany.

Rountree, J. C. (1998). Coming to terms with Kenneth Burke's Pentad. *American Communication Journal*, *1*(3).

Sargeant, A., & Woodliffe, L. (2007). Gift giving: an interdisciplinary review. *International Journal of Nonprofit and Voluntary Sector Marketing*, *12*(4), 275–307. doi:10.1002/nvsm.308

Silver, D. (2000). Looking backwards, looking forwards: Cyberculture studies 1990-2000. In Gauntlett, D. (Ed.), *Web studies: Rewiring media studies for the digital age*. London, UK: Arnold.

Skågeby, J. (2007). Analytical dimensions of online gift-giving: 'Other-oriented' contributions in virtual communities. *International Journal of Web-based Communities*, *3*(1), 55–68. doi:10.1504/IJWBC.2007.013774

Skågeby, J. (2008). Semi-public end-user content contributions: A case study of concerns and intentions in online photo-sharing. *International Journal of Human-Computer Studies*, *66*(4), 287–300. doi:10.1016/j.ijhcs.2007.10.010

Skågeby, J. (2009a). Exploring qualitative sharing practices of social metadata: Expanding the attention economy. *The Information Society*, *25*(1), 60–72. doi:10.1080/01972240802587588

Skågeby, J. (2009b). Online friction: Studying sociotechnical conflicts to elicit user experience. *International Journal of Sociotechnology and Knowledge Development - Special Issue on New Sociotechnical Insights in Interaction Design*, *1*(2), 62-74.

Skågeby, J., & Pargman, D. (2005). File-sharing relationships - Conflicts of interest in online gift-giving. *Proceedings of the Second International Conference on Communities and Technologies* (pp. 111-128). Milano, Italy: Springer.

Sterne, J. (2006). The mp3 as cultural artifact. *New Media & Society*, *8*(5), 825–842. doi:10.1177/1461444806067737

Varman, R., & Costa, J. A. (2008). Embedded markets, communities, and the invisible hands of social norms. *Journal of Macromarketing*, *28*(2), 141–156. doi:10.1177/0276146708314594

Virilio, P. (2007). *The original accident*. Malden, MA: Polity.

ADDITIONAL READING

Antoniadis, P., & Grand, B. L. (2007). Incentives for resource sharing in self-organized communities: From economics to social psychology. In the *Proceedings of ICDIM '07* (pp. 756-761). Lyon, France: IEEE.

Arakji, R., Benbunan-Fich, R., & Koufaris, M. (2009). Exploring contributions of public resources in social bookmarking systems. *Decision Support Systems*, *47*, 245–253. doi:10.1016/j.dss.2009.02.007

Arrow, K. (1972). Gifts and exchanges. *Philosophy & Public Affairs*, *1*(4), 343–362.

Bell, D. (1991). Modes of exchange: Gift and commodity. *Journal of Socio-Economics*, *20*(2), 155–167. doi:10.1016/S1053-5357(05)80003-4

Benbunan-Fich, R., & Koufaris, M. (2008). Motivations and contribution behaviour in social bookmarking systems: An empirical investigation. *Electronic Markets*, *18*(2), 150–160. doi:10.1080/10196780802044933

Bergquist, M., & Ljungberg, J. (2001). The power of gifts: Organizing social relationships in open source communities. *Information Systems Journal*, *11*(4), 305–320. doi:10.1046/j.1365-2575.2001.00111.x

Camerer, C. (1988). Gifts as economic signals and social symbols. *American Journal of Sociology*, *94*, 180–214. doi:10.1086/228946

Cheal, D. (1986). The social dimensions of gift behavior. *Journal of Social and Personal Relationships*, *3*, 423–439. doi:10.1177/0265407586034002

Constant, D., Kiesler, S., & Sproull, L. (1994). What's mine is ours, or is it? A study of attitudes about information sharing. *Information Systems Research*, *5*(4), 400–421. doi:10.1287/isre.5.4.400

Ebare, S. (2004). Digital music and subculture: Sharing files, sharing styles. *First Monday*, *9*(2).

Giesler, M., & Pohlmann, M. (2002). The anthropology of file sharing: Consuming Napster as a gift. In the *Proceedings of ACR Conference '02*, Atlanta, Georgia, USA.

Håkansson, M., Rost, M., & Holmquist, L. E. (2007). Gifts from friends and strangers: A study of mobile music sharing. In L. Bannon, I. Wagner, C. Gutwin, R. Harper & K. Schmidt (Eds.), *The Proceedings of ECSCW '07* (pp. 311-330), Limerick, Ireland: Springer.

Hemetsberger, A. (2001). Fostering cooperation on the Internet: Social exchange processes in innovative virtual consumer communities. In Broniarczyk, S. M., & Nakamoto, K. (Eds.), *The Proceedings of Advances in Consumer Research* (pp. 354–356). Austin, Texas.

Hew, K. F., & Hara, N. (2007). Empirical study of motivators and barriers of teacher online knowledge sharing. *Educational Technology Research and Development*, *55*, 273–295. doi:10.1007/s11423-007-9049-2

Janzik, L., & Herstatt, C. (2008, Sep 21-24). Innovation communities: Motivation and incentives for community members to contribute. In the *Proceedings of the 4th IEEE International Conference on Management of Innovation and Technology*, (pp. 350-355). IEEE.

Klamer, A. (2003). Gift economy. In Towse, R. (Ed.), *A handbook of cultural economics* (pp. 241–247). Cheltenham, UK: Edward Elgar Publishing.

Kollock, P. (1999). The economies of online cooperation: Gifts and public goods in cyberspace. In Smith, M. A., & Kollock, P. (Eds.), *Communities in cyberspace*. London, UK: Routledge.

LaRose, R., Lai, Y.-J., Lange, R., Love, B., & Wu, Y. (2005). Sharing or piracy? An exploration of downloading behavior. *Journal of Computer-Mediated Communication*, *11*(1). doi:10.1111/j.1083-6101.2006.tb00301.x

Levine, S. S. (2001). Kindness in cyberspace? The sharing of valuable goods on-line. In U. E. Gattiker (Ed.), *The Proceedings of 10th Annual EICAR Conference* (pp. 86-112), Munich, Germany.

Marett, K., & Joshi, K. D. (2009). The decision to share information and rumors: Examining the role of motivation in an online discussion forum. *Communications of AIS, 2009*(24), 47-68.

McGee, K., & Skågeby, J. (2004). Gifting technologies. *First Monday, 9*(12).

McLure Wasko, M., & Faraj, S. (2005). Why should I share? Examining social capital and knowledge contribution in electronic networks of practice. *Management Information Systems Quarterly, 29*(1), 35–57.

Moore, T. D., & Serva, M. (2007). Understanding member motivation for contributing to different types of virtual communities: A proposed framework. In the *Proceedings of 2007 ACM SIGMIS CPR Conference on Computer Personnel Research* (pp. 153-158), St. Louis, MO: ACM.

Offer, A. (1997). Between the gift and the market: the economy of regard. *The Economic History Review, 3*, 450–476. doi:10.1111/1468-0289.00064

Olivera, F. (2008). Contribution behaviors in distributed environments. *MIS Quarterly: Management Information Systems, 32*(1), 23–42.

Organ, D. W., Podsakoff, P. M., & Mackenzie, S. B. (2006). *Organizational citizenship behavior: Its nature, antecedents, and consequences*. Thousand Oaks, CA: Sage.

Otnes, C., & Scott, L. M. (1996). Something old, something new: Exploring the interaction between ritual and advertising. *Journal of Advertising, 25*(1), 33–50.

Pearson, E. (2006). Digital gifts: Participation and gift exchange in LiveJournal communities. *First Monday, 12*(5).

Peddibhotla, N. B., & Subramani, M. R. (2007). Contributing to public document repositories: A critical mass theory perspective. *Organization Studies, 28*(3). doi:10.1177/0170840607076002

Pfaffenberger, B. (2003). A standing wave in the web of our communications: Usenet and the socio-technical construction of cyberspace values. In Lueg, C., & Fisher, D. (Eds.), *From Usenet to CoWebs* (pp. 20–43). London, UK: Springer Verlag. doi:10.1007/978-1-4471-0057-7_2

Raban, D. R. (2008). The incentive structure in an online information market. *Journal of the American Society for Information Science and Technology, 59*(14), 2284–2295. doi:10.1002/asi.20942

Ranganathan, K., Ripeanu, M., Sarin, A., & Foster, I. (2004). To share or not to share: An analysis of incentives to contribute in collaborative file sharing environments. In the *Proceedings of CCGrid2004- 4th IEEE/ACM International Symposium on Cluster Computing and the Grid*, Chicago, USA.

Rehn, A. (2002). *Electronic potlatch*. Stockholm, Sweden: Royal Institute of Technology.

Ripeanu, M., Mowbray, M., Andrade, N., & Lima, A. (2006). Gifting technologies: A BitTorrent case study. *First Monday, 11*(11).

Skågeby, J. (2010). Gift-giving as a conceptual framework: Framing sociotechnical behavior in online networks. *Journal of Information Technology - Special issue on Social Networking through ICTs, 25*(2).

Sproull, L., Conley, C., & Moon, J. Y. (2005). Prosocial behavior on the net. In Amichai-Hamburger, Y. (Ed.), *The social net: Understanding human behavior in cyberspace*. Oxford, UK: Oxford University Press.

Voida, A., Grinter, R. E., Ducheneaut, N., Edwards, W. K., & Newman, M. W. (2005). Listening in: Practices surrounding iTunes music sharing. In the *Proceedings of CHI 2005*. Portland, OR: ACM.

Zeitlyn, D. (2003). Gift economies in the development of open source software. *Research Policy*, *32*(7), 1287–1291. doi:10.1016/S0048-7333(03)00053-2

KEY TERMS AND DEFINITIONS

Burke's Pentad: A model developed by Kenneth Burke used to examine and describe motivations in rhetorical analyses. The pentad includes the questions: what was done? (act); when and where was it done? (scene); who did it? (agent); how was it done? (agency); and why was it done (purpose).

Exchange Value: The value of an artifact in terms of what it can be exchanged for, in monetary or trading equivalents.

Gift System: A set of connected values or practices that come to form a complex economy which includes primarily social bonding values, but also use values and exchange values.

Motivation: Motivations can be described in term of incentive structures (i.e. as the general desire or willingness of someone to do something) or as individual motivations (i.e. as the reason or reasons one has for acting or behaving in a particular way).

Personal Identity: The unique personal attributes that separate an individual from other individuals.

Relationship Model: A theoretical model that separates between four structural levels of relationships: ego (myself), micro (close friends/family), meso (acquaintances) and macro (anonymous strangers) in order to understand potential conflicts of interest and social dilemmas.

Social Bonding Value: The value of an artifact in relation to social ties and their management.

Social Identity: An individual's perception of him- or herself as member of a group, particularly in terms of value and emotional attachment.

Use Value: The value of an artifact (e.g. media object) in terms of practical utility.

Chapter 13
Scenario-Planning for Learning in Communities:
A Virtual Participation Model to Support Holistic Student Development

Kam Hou Vat
University of Macau, Macau

ABSTRACT

The chapter investigates an actionable model of virtual participation for learning communities, in the context of holistic student development in college education. The framework of analysis is based on scenario-planning, accommodating the dynamics of strategic design, decision making, and prototyping of various organizational scenarios of learning in communities. This conceptualization is extensible in cyberspace in today's World Wide Web, especially promising for today's universities, under the mission of ensuring quality student learning. The premise in this exploration is situated in the design of living and learning programs in residential colleges that must integrate the genuine concerns of holistic development for both teachers and students. What is often argued in this mesh of organizational design is how exactly to connect members of the communities, albeit the very behavior of hoarding personal presence (or knowledge) is what makes people feel secured and successful. The virtual participation model responds to this need by emphasizing the presence of an appreciative form of community sharing that could be facilitated through some innovative electronic channels designed into the daily living and learning experiences. However, the task of identifying what to watch for in building an online community of learning (CoL) is not at all straightforward. The authors' investigation provides a basis to think of the generative potential of appreciative processes for interaction among different CoLs. The emergent challenge is to de-marginalize the concept of appreciative sharing among CoL members, expositing on the effective meaning behind the creation of such an environment through which purposeful individual or organizational learning could be enabled with the elaboration of suitable information technologies.

DOI: 10.4018/978-1-4666-0312-7.ch013

INTRODUCTION

The context of holistic student development (HSD) could be summarized in the Socratic dictum that "the unexamined life is not worth living." It is convinced an effective and ideal college education is one that centers on HSD, including the search for meaning and purpose in life. In launching any HSD programs today, many a university has included important concerns of who a student is and becomes, as well as what a student does during college (Barkley, 2010; Braskamp, Trautvetter, & Ward, 2006). Universities guide students to become what the college thinks and believes is a desired end. They educate and work with students on purpose. In particular, colleges develop students in ways that recognize and build on their purpose in life, intellectually and morally. They intentionally create environments that center on purpose, helping students reflect on such questions as – Who am I? What are my goals in life? How do I want to make a difference with my life? Addressing questions such as a life good to live, is an important part of holistic student development across many campuses today. Tellingly, endeavoring to develop our full potential as human beings is certainly not only about financial achievement and professional success, but also living a life that is fulfilling and meaningful. Indeed, the HSD approach presses students to acquire knowledge and to develop a life of purpose; it challenges students to obtain and improve competencies and to know themselves; it also encourages students to engage the world and to probe the relevance and power of personal commitments, perspectives, and even their shortcomings. The question is how best to facilitate such student development. This chapter is aimed to describe an emergent model of virtual participation to help foster student success in college education, addressing such questions as: What does college education desire students to become? What skills and patterns of behavior do students need to learn and develop? How do members of the campus community – faculty, staff, and administrators – contribute to the development of students by who they are as well as what they do? It is convinced that the answer lies in the cultivation of a virtual community of learning (CoL) comprising faculty dedicating themselves more fully to the totality of student life, colleges making an investment in students as whole beings, and students themselves becoming personally invested in their college experience. In particular, this chapter renders recommendations of how HSD could be enhanced if we could avail of the appropriate Internet technologies to support organizing online various student services, to be incrementally experienced throughout their college years of living and learning as members of the campus community.

Exploring Learning Communities for HSD

In an address at the Inaugural Conference on Learning Communities, Patrick Hill (1985) stated that learning communities (LCs) respond to and help alleviate a number of educational problems. He argues that LCs increase the intellectual interaction between faculty and students, as well as among students, and help students grasp not only the complexity of today's problems but also help them understand how various disciplines overlap to solve complex problems. Hill's comments remind us of colleges and universities effort to develop environments that foster student learning and development the holistic way. The implication, we have to confess, is that too often college learning is fragmented, and student lives outside the classroom are disconnected from the learning environment. Students take many individual, self-contained courses to meet basic requirements, but they do not often see how the courses may be related, especially if they are not connected with their majors. Indeed, Tussman (1969) describes the dilemma of students taking three, four, or five courses during a semester with "no attempt at horizontal integration." Each professor has a certain percentage of a student's time, but "no teacher is in a position to be responsible for ... the student's total educational situation (p.6)." Unquestionably, learning communities address important educational concerns, as Hill (1985) has voiced. Obviously, with the installation of various LCs within or outside the classroom setting (Stein & Hurd, 2000; Hurd & Stein, 2004; Vat, 2000), HSD could be enhanced through promoting intellectual communication between faculty members and students, making connections among courses, bridging students' academic and social worlds, as well as giving faculty members some new perspectives as reflective practitioners on collaborative student development. Eventually, as Tinto (1997) has pointed out, the perceived benefits that result from LCs should include enhanced student intellectual and social development; improved GPA, satisfaction and increased persistence to graduation. LCs that do include a residential element such as in the Residential Colleges (RCs), are supposed to benefit students the most because their connected courses enable them to feel attached to a peculiar community of learning (CoL).

Virtual Organizing Campus Communities for HSD

Accordingly, it is not surprising that many colleges and universities are looking to LCs to tackle their HSD concerns. Yet, Hurd and Stein (2004) remind us that there is no single way to organize LCs and no simple formula for creating successful LCs. Each campus should establish communities according to its unique culture. Each campus must develop its own vision of what a successful learning community is like. The nuts and bolts of organizing LCs require careful planning and work, whether the impetus for such an initiative comes from the college administrators, from faculty members, or from student affairs. The work entails much communication and negotiation among various campus entities. In particular,

it requires designing the specific LC model that works for the specific purpose, recruiting faculty members to develop the LC courses and teach in the LC, crafting the residence life component if it is meant to be a RC-based LC, recruiting students for the LC, and assessing the development of the LCs longitudinally. These steps serve as a hint of what goes into planning a LC, but whichever type of LC to be innovated, the conceptual issues of the LCs, must be closely examined and supported electronically to steer the course of LC planning, especially in the RC setting.

The Design Aspirations in LCs

The twentieth century has witnessed many an educational experiment based on Dewey's (1933) and Meiklejohn's (1932) ideas. Each such attempt has developed and refined our understanding about community and collaboration as part of the learning process. According to Gamson (2000), all such experimentations were based on three common premises: the best learning takes place in relatively small, cohesive communities; learning has to be relevant to students' commitment to a world larger than the university, considering both the academy and society as sites for making knowledge; and education is at its most productive using a combination of tradition and innovation (pp.114-115). The Evergreen State College in Olympia, Washington, and the University of California, Santa Cruz, on the central coast of California, both came into existence through state mandates to "develop an innovative structure that would not simply duplicate the existing academic resources of the state" (Yountz, 1984, p.95). Adams (2000) informs of their commitment to "innovative undergraduate education" that would be kept "intimate, personal, encouraging a sense of belonging" (p.131). The many small college buildings on the University of California, Santa Cruz, campus today are a remnant of the original intention to challenge disciplinary segregation by defining individual colleges through their own "coherent and independent undergraduate curricula, based upon distinctive thematic definitions of liberal education, and emphasizing interdisciplinary courses and innovative teaching techniques" (Adams, 2000, p.132). Evergreen also considers "Interdisciplinary Studies to be the centerpiece of curricular efforts," taking the opportunity in the first year to "design the strongest possible and most diverse set of Meiklejohn-like interdisciplinary program we could conceive" (Yountz, 1984, p.95). In *Learning Communities: Creating Connections among Students, Faculty, and Disciplines*, Gabelnick et al. see "recent work in such diverse areas as the social construction of knowledge, collaborative learning, writing and critical thinking, and cognitive and intellectual development, support and resonate with the learning community effort" as directly emerging from those earlier experiments (1990, p.17). Ruth Stein (2004) defines learning communities as the intentional arrangement of environments inside and outside the classroom to achieve learning outcomes by organizing more student interactions with faculty and between students around scholarship. LCs could have residential or non-residential and course or non-course components; however, the overarching goal is to construct seamless learning environments (Kuh, 1996) to enable the maximum potential of student learning and integration of material.

The Virtual Organizing Paradigm for LCs

Learning communities compel professionals to think about learning in different ways, and encourage the construction of environments that maximize learning outcomes. Such a mission very much requires resources, time to plan, and commitments from staff, faculty members, and students. Broadly put, LCs are one example of reform in learning that foster student participation to develop knowledge. In order to best facilitate such a reform, the idea of virtual organizing, at-

tributed to Venkatraman and Henderson (1998), can be considered as a method to galvanize an LC, dynamically assembling and disassembling nodes on a network of people or groups of people, to meet the demands of a particular learning context.

Robert Barr and John Tagg (1995) describe a paradigm shift in higher education from where students passively receive knowledge through instruction, to the *learning paradigm*, where students and instructors are active participants in the acquisition of knowledge. Meanwhile, LCs are said to exemplify and benefit from the rise of constructivist approach to education (Kim, 2005), where knowledge is construed "not as something that is transferred in an authoritarian structure from teacher to student, but rather as something that teachers and students work interdependently to develop" (Cross, 1998, p.5). In fact, while not a new approach in the context of online education, the emergence of virtual organizing in response to the concept of virtual organization, which appeared in the literature around the late twentieth century (Byrne, Brandt, & Port, 1993; Cheng, 1996; Davidow & Malone, 1992; Goldman, Nagel & Preiss, 1995; Hedberg, Dahlgren, Hansson, & Olve, 1997), has rendered a promising means to support a virtual participation model in the LCs.

Undeniably, LC's have been revived owing in part to some recent concerns about teaching and learning in college (Stein, 2004). In the 1998 final report, *Powerful Partnerships: a Shared Responsibility for Learning*, presented by the Joint Task Force on Student Learning (http://www.myacpa.org/pub/documents/taskforce.pdf), ten principles for higher education professionals from both academic and student affairs to improve student learning, have been proposed. Of particular relevance to LCs in the report include several essential contexts (pp. 3, 6-8): 1) learning is fundamentally about making and maintaining connections; 2) learning is done by individuals who are intrinsically tied to others as social beings; 3) learning is strongly affected by the educational climate in which it takes place; and 4) much learning takes place informally beyond the classroom walls. To facilitate such conditions for learning, virtual organizing renders two relevant assertions. Firstly, a virtual organization (say, an electronic form of LC) should not be considered as a distinct structure (such as a physical CoL) in an extreme and rigid form (Jagers, Jansen, & Steenbakkers, 1998), but virtuality is a strategic characteristic applicable to every organization (including a LC). Secondly, information and communications technology (ICTs) is a powerful enabler of the critical requirements for effective virtual organizing. Thereby, virtual organizing helps emphasize the ongoing process nature of the organization (LC), and it presents a framework of achieving virtuality in terms of three distinct yet interdependent vectors: a) virtual encounter for organization-wide interactions; b) virtual sourcing for asset configuration; and c) virtual expertise for knowledge leverage. The challenge for virtual organizing is to integrate the three hitherto separate vectors into an interoperable ICT platform that supports and shapes the new organizational initiative (LCs), paying attention to the internal consistency across the three vectors.

SCENARIO PLANNING OF LIVING-AND-LEARNING PROGRAMS

Indeed, through some intentional collaborative restructuring of the curriculum and some elaborate design of the spaces for learning, it is intended that well conceived HSD practices could be realized electronically, through virtual organizing, in various forms of RC-based learning communities. According to Michael Porter (1985), it is not uncommon to use scenarios in strategic planning to identify what types of practices are appropriate for specific organizations (campuses). Living-learning programs, also known as residential college programs, are characterized by scholarly

community, deep learning, strong sense of belonging, a careful integration of the intellectual and social dimensions of university life, and democratic education with a spirit of innovation and experimentation (Meiklejohn, 1932; Goodman, 1964; Newmann & Oliver, 1967; Boyer, 1987; Guarasci & Cornwell, 1997). These are elements organized to introduce and integrate academic and social learning in residence hall settings through faculty involvement with the goal of an enriched learning experience for all participants (Schoem, 2004). At their best, such programs represent the genuine model of learning and community (Ryan, 2001; Waltzer, 1992) that is so much desired but still so elusive at many of our colleges and universities; yet, the inadequacies observed on different campuses to fully tap into the rich intellectual potential of bringing our students and faculty members together do call for a renewal and strengthening of the bold vision represented by such programs.

The Nature of Collegiate Community

According to John Gardner (1990), "the community teaches. If it is healthy and coherent, the community imparts a coherent value system. If it is fragmented or sterile or degenerative, lessons are taught anyway – but not lessons that heal and strengthen. It is community and culture that hold the individual in a framework of values; when the framework disintegrates individual value systems disintegrate (p.113)". Colleges and universities exist for purposes beyond developing knowledge and skill in our students. They are the sanctuaries of our personal and civic values, incubators of intellect and integrity. A collegiate community must be more than a collection of buildings connected by wires and fiber cables; instead, it must be a set of relationships that recognize and celebrate a shared vision of purpose and values. In such a collegiate community, students must be recognized and respected as emerging scholars and are given voice to express ideas and opinions. In one of the most familiar and informing legacies of campus communities, Ernest L Boyer (1990) rendered some essential characterizations for campus LCs. Namely, they must be a purposeful community where students and faculty share learning goals; an open community where freedom of expression is nurtured and civility affirmed; a just community where diversity and the sacredness of each person is honored; a disciplined community, where individuals accept their obligations for the common good; a caring community where the nobility of service to others is upheld; and a celebrative community where the campus heritage and traditions are central to the values and culture of student development.

The Context of Virtual Organizing the Collegiate Community

The first of the three vectors in virtual organizing deals with the new challenges and opportunities for interacting with the members of an organization (a campus community). The second focuses on the organization's requirements to be virtually integrated in a network of interdependent (learning and knowledge) partners, so as to manage a dynamic portfolio of relationships to assemble and coordinate the necessary assets for delivering value for the organization. The third is concerned with the opportunities for leveraging diverse sources of expertise within and across organizational boundaries (different residential colleges, or even different university campuses) to become drivers of value creation and organizational effectiveness. All these three vectors are accomplishable by the provision of suitable information system (IS) support, under the auspices of modern ICTs, whose ongoing design represents the IS/ICT challenge of every organization (university campus) in this Internet age.

Virtual Encounter

The idea of providing remote (or online) interaction with the organization (campus community) is not new, but has indeed been refined with the advent of the Web technologies. Many campuses feel compelled to assess how their student services can be experienced virtually in the new medium of the Web 2.0 or Web 3.0 era (Li & Lee, 2010). The issue of customization is important. It requires a continuous information exchange with parties of interest, which in turn requires an organizational design that is fundamentally committed to operating in this direction. Pragmatically, organizations (campus communities) need to change from an inside-out perspective to an outside-in perspective. In the HSD context, this is often characterized by the emergence of different virtual communities of learning (CoLs), with the capacity to influence the organization's directions with a distinct focus in a wider campus community. Thereby, it is believed that as virtual organizing becomes more widespread (effective), organizations (universities) must recognize communities as an important part of the value system and respond appropriately in their operational strategies.

Virtual Sourcing

The idea is to focus on creating and deploying intellectual and intangible assets for the organization (campus community) in the form of a continuous reconfiguration of critical capabilities assembled through different relationships in the network of CoLs. The mission is to set up a resource network, in which the organization is part of a vibrant, dynamic network of complementary capabilities. The strategic leadership challenge is to orchestrate an organization's (CoL's) position in a dynamic, fast-changing resource network where the organization as a whole, and the individual CoLs can carefully analyze her relative dependence or inter-dependence on other players in the resource coalition and ensure her unique capabilities (or character in the making).

Virtual Expertise

The idea is to focus on the possibilities and mechanisms for leveraging expertise at different levels of the organization (university). In today's college campuses, many tasks are being redefined and decomposed so that they can be done at different locations and time periods. However, the obvious challenge in maximizing learning-unit expertise often rests not so much in designing the technological platform to support community (or in a smaller scale, group) work, but in designing the organizational structure and processes to facilitate such work. The message is clear: though knowledge, often alive in the human act of knowing, is more often an accumulation of experience that is more a living process than a static body of information. Thereby, it must be systematically nurtured and managed (or facilitated). In fact, many an organization (campus community) is increasingly leveraging the expertise not only from the domain of a local organization (individual residential college), but also from the extended network of broader campus community (other residential colleges, or CoLs around).

CASE INVESTIGATION OF RC PROGRAMS

Starting from the Fall-2010 semester, the University of Macau (UM) is launching its pilot residential college (RC) program called *Wonderful Life in Colleges* (http://www.umac.mo/rc/pilot_rcp.html), involving two newly established residential colleges, respectively named *East Asia College*, and *Pearl Jubilee College*. This program is an extensible project in a sense that many of the learning in the two RCs are emergent. UM is

learning to put together a unique RC experience for resident students; the pilot RC program at UM experimented at her Taipa (a part of Macau) campus (with two colleges from 2010 to 2013), is to accrue experience for follow-up continuous improvement to be realized in the official RC program (10 to 12 colleges) in her Hengqin (an island next to Macau's Taipa, inside mainland China) campus, twenty times the size of UM's Taipa campus, starting from the fall of 2013.

Assumptions about UM's RCs

1. The Residential College System (RCS) at UM is meant to be a four-year interdisciplinary liberal arts program integrating and realizing the vision and mission of an elite undergraduate education, with a unique relevance of General Education (GE), in the emergent context of a research university, emphasizing the quality of teaching and learning.

2. The relevance of GE in our RCS context remains the platform where students and teachers can together reflect on questions of common interest, and issues being mostly cross-disciplinary, are of concern to humanity and modern society. The goal is to nurture students to become educated persons in the modern, ever-changing world, with the intellectual and emotional ability and inclination to be able to appreciate and to become a positive force in any situation.

3. The Residential Colleges (RC's) could be characterized as a living-learning community because RC students live and learn in the same physical space. UM's RC community encourages and welcomes participation from different members of the UM family, including staff, students, faculty, friends, and alumni.

4. The RC's at UM should have a curriculum (activity-based learning, modeled after Harvard's experience) (Harvard, 2007,

p.19) of their own, which is largely interdisciplinary and engages students in creative exploration of the humanities, the social and the natural sciences, the engineering disciplines, the visual and performing arts, as well as some intensive foreign language study. The goal of the RC curriculum is to foster students' genuine appreciation and lifelong passion for learning, not merely individual quests for specialized knowledge, but preparation and encouragement that lead to effective and responsible engagement in the real world.

5. The RC's at UM should make a unique contribution to higher education, by combining typical residence hall facilities (dorm rooms, lounges, dinning halls, recreational rooms, and many others) with the academic and artistic resources required for a liberal arts education (classrooms, creative studios, faculty offices, performance and exhibition spaces, and different types of student support services). Each RC is meant to be a small college community fully integrated with the public University of Macau. It is guided by a philosophy of participatory education – basically everyone gets involved in our RC's.

Reading Club as Residential Education Program

The Reading Club is meant to be an activity-based learning embodiment of UM's pilot RC curriculum, presumably called *Think, Read, and Write* program. The requirements of this program are to conceive suitable learning activities for RC students to complete, so as to accomplish some specific RC curricular objectives. In the context of writing the learning outcomes for students joining the Reading Club, such outcomes are compliant with the SMART guideline (O'Neill & Conzemius, 2006): namely, to be strategic and/or specific, to be measurable, to be attainable, to be relevant and realistic, and to be tangible and/or time-bound.

1. **Strategic:** A Strategic Activity Has a Much Greater Chance of Being Accomplished
   ○ The mission of the Reading Club is not just to provide an opportunity for student residents to gather, to indulge in their reading hobby, and to participate in regular discussions about books they have read, but also to create a living and learning atmosphere for all student residents to experience UM's collegiate community, in close and constant association with one another, and with their tutors, advisors, coaches, and mentors, to experience pastoral care in a trust and safe environment so as to help students grow into an all-round character expected of a college student. So, it is the aim of the RC Reading Club to provide, through thoughtfully designed academic and social activities, an enjoyable opportunity and environment to share with one another, in order to facilitate character development and lifelong learning, to live up to the promise of holistic student development.

2. **Specific:** A Specific Activity Has a Much Greater Chance of Being Accomplished
   ○ **Who**: Reading groups are made up of individual RC students, who meet at regular intervals to discuss a specific topic such as a related book reading experience. Each group is assigned a facilitator played by volunteer teacher as coach and mentor to probe, to guide, and to steer the course of learning activities.
   ○ **What**: Reading group gatherings tend to be more personal and intimate since members have the chance to meet often, face-to-face and they usually could develop a strong social and intellectual dimension through mutual sharing. It is mentoring in ac-

tion, or rather in the terms of pastoral care, shepherding in action, especially when student writing is expected, such as from their own blogs.

○ **Where**: Popular places for reading groups to meet include RC meeting or recreational rooms, library discussion venues, café or even in restaurants over meals. In practice, students could also meet online through group e-spaces that should not be a big problem with current Web facilities.

○ **Why**: Each reading group tends not to grow too big (not more than 10 persons typically) so, as members they have more control over the choice of reading matter. Usually, the reading for each period (say, two weeks to a month) is voted from a list of suggested titles or the members may each take turns suggesting a book.

○ **When**: Typically, twice a month for face-to-face gathering, but unlimited online exchange is always plausible, with the setup of some group e-spaces. However, the small size per group also means the views and perspectives involved in the discussion can be limited. This could be compensated by timely bringing in two or more groups with the similar topic chosen during the same period, if RC's were to organize student residents in groups of 10 each for various reading club activities.

○ **How**: One possible mode of operations could be the single-title selection. This is the most common method, where one title is selected at a time and all members read the same book in the same time frame. They then meet to discuss the selected book and this method works particularly well for those who like intensive

discussion of books. Members are responsible for obtaining their own copy of each period's title, although they can either buy (new or second hand) or borrow from the library. It is nonetheless recommended that individual students keep a Web blog of what they experience during the reading so as to induce the reading and sharing with their fellow students.

3. **Measurable:** Establish Concrete Criteria for Measuring Progress toward the Attainment of a Specific Goal

○ **Kick-Off Activity:** Invite each entering RC student to sign in a form with a specific section called Reading Club Questionnaire (by default, every RC student resident is a member of the Reading Club, as an RC curriculum requirement, with the goal to develop student's *Think-Read-Write* ability through learning-by-doing).

▪ Provide a simple survey to conduct self-evaluation in proficiency of reading, thinking and writing: Good, Average, and Remedial.

▪ Provide some categories of reading materials to collect student reading favorites: Books, Magazine, Blogs, and many conceivable others.

▪ Ask how strongly student would like to see his or her abilities in reading, thinking, and writing improve, to get the most of his or her study at UM. Provide such choices as: strongly, average, not at all.

▪ Ask whether the student is aware that his or her achievement in college is closely related to the ability to think, to read, and to write.

4. **Attainable:** Goals Should Challenge Students to their Best, but they Need Also be Achievable

   ° **Starting Reading Club Blog:** Today, blogs are inexpensive: most of the popular blogging services offer free-of-charge hosting to bloggers. So, starting a blog will take very little time, though we should pay attention to some developmental questions before setting up student blogs in cyberspace: What is the purpose of the blog? Who will be privileged to post on the blog? Are comments allowed on one another's blogs? It is convinced that each RC should create the necessary blogging facilities to enable students in their Web blogs activities – writing their blogs, expressing themselves through blogging as their journaling activities after reading, preferably on a daily basis. There must be facilitators to lead the blogging activities by writing their own blogs to be the shepherds of students though.

5. **Relevant:** Goals Need to Pertain Directly to the Performance Challenge Being Managed. To be Realistic, Goals for Students to Achieve Must Represent an Objective toward which Students are Both Willing and Able to Work.

   ° **Reading Club Community-Minded Ideas:** While Reading Club is initiated with the intention of discussing books or other literatures, it is not uncommon that club activities may evolve into enjoyable social gathering and as members get to know one another, many would become keen on the idea of other activities. Group outings and themed nights based on a particular title, are popular alternatives, where members could organize food and music, for some good cause (charity perhaps) to match the book content, such as serving food and music that have significant meaning in the book or are the favorites of the characters or events in the book. RC Students may also surprise fellow students (those not living in the RC) with their momentum (or gift) of a book that their Reading Club has read and enjoyed, and invite non-RC students to join Reading Club activities, in preparation for their enrolling into the RC house the next school year.

   ° **The Key:** All such activities must be organized by the students in the reading groups themselves. So, facilitators among the reading groups must help lead the leadership training in each group to organize themselves and to plan and lead such activities. These are all learning-by-doing episodes, and are extremely important to develop students' abilities in creative problem solving, and other skills highly valued by the University. The underlying requirement is that programs like *Train-the-Trainer* for *Learn-To-Learn*, among students with such theme as *There-is-a-Leader-in-You*, become important.

6. **Timely:** Enough Time to Achieve the Goal-Not Much Time Can Definitely Affect Project Performance. Meanwhile, Goals Must be Tangible so that Students Could Experience them with their Senses

   A. RCs must provide opportunities for students to integrate the academic mission of UM with a community living environment. RC staff should assist students in creating a living and learning environment, conducive to students' understanding of cross-cultural differences, personal and community responsibility, as well as life (or career) planning.

B. RC staff should work hard to provide a supportive, involving and safe atmosphere within each residential college. A variety of activities and programs are scheduled during the year within each house to meet social and educational needs of students. Students are encouraged to discuss with RC staff their ideas about programs and their living environment.

C. The installation of RC Reading Club is meant to be an important means to meet the social and educational needs of resident students, especially to bring forth the perceived RC curriculum objectives. Students, after settling down in a specific RC, will be organized into different small groups, known as the Reading Groups. It is estimated that there could be up to about 15 to 20 groups in each RC, and such groups form the specific community of each RC.

D. Each of the RC reading groups must receive leadership training to manage themselves in terms of RC living and learning rules (or expectations) of the house, and be assigned a facilitator to advice and coach their living and learning activities. One of the important topics in leadership training is *Learn-to-Learn* (including upfront practice of *Think, Read, and Write*) among resident students.

E. Each of the reading groups under the Reading Club is to be equipped with an electronic group space, with individual electronic personal space for each group members, to encourage their blog writing, and to facilitate intra-group and subsequent inter-group communications. And the whole Reading Club should also be supported with an electronic portal space to facilitate any community-based announcement and activities. Through the personal e-spaces, students are expected to keep their individual learning portfolios in the form of their own blogs, sharable for others' reading. Such personal blogs are considered as a means to share student living and learning experiences, as an important part of their RC habits of learning. It is through students' blogs that their gains of common reading experience, could be made visible – it is an opportunity to learn to read, to think, to experience and to write – some concrete skills valuable throughout their four years of study and beyond.

F. There must be some electronic portfolios to keep track of individual students' development. Through active engagement, critical reflection and mentoring of others, the Reading Club activities can truly become the fiber of one's character. It is expected that students could retain at least 60% of what they do, 80% of what they do with guided reflection and 90% of what they teach or give to others. This model should form the basis for UM's RC-GE connection program to truly help students become active engaged citizens in their local and global communities. Throughout their four years, RC participants will reflect on their learning opportunities and service experiences through their electronic portfolios. Such reflections will be guided and responded to by peers, faculty and administrative staff (student affairs and academic affairs).

FUTURE TRENDS OF RC-BASED HOLISTIC STUDENT DEVELOPMENT

Today, an organization's ability to learn is often considered as a process of leveraging the collective individual learning of the organization. We identify with Peter Senge (1990) that the organizations which will truly excel in the future will be the organizations that discover how to tap people's commitment and capacity to learn, and to produce a higher-level organizational asset. For many organizations, that often means leading and fostering the kind of culture that mobilizes people to share what they know with their peers (co-workers or cohorts) without a fear of being questioned, critiqued, or put on the defense. In particular, this culture of sharing which should be in the driver's seat for conceiving and designing the paraphernalia of learning communities in the RC setting in support of holistic student development (HSD) could be developed from the idea of appreciative inquiry (Cooperrider & Whitney, 2005; Cooperrider, 1986; Vat, 2009b). Through such an inquiry, it is believed that an appreciative environment is needed in any design of living-learning experiences for the RC setting, in which developing an appreciative culture of knowledge sharing (collaborative learning) has the generative potential conducive to the fully functioning of HSD in any living-learning programs.

The Potential of Appreciative Coaching

The practice of appreciative coaching (AC) attributed to (Orem, Binkert, & Clancy, 2007) is developed from the context of appreciative inquiry whose philosophy is based on the assumption that inquiry into and dialogue about strengths, successes, hopes and dreams is itself a transformational process (Cooperrider & Whitney, 2005). AC describes an approach to coaching that shows individuals how to tap into or rediscover their own sense of wonder and excitement about their present life and future possibilities. It is an approach deemed very promising to enable students to grow psychologically, morally, intellectually and spiritually in the RC setting. AC is meant to guide individual students through different stages of appreciative development: discovery, dream, design and destiny – that inspire them to an empowering view of themselves and their future. The core process of AC begins with the selection of a topic, such as "enhancing student learning through implementing a LC in the RC setting." At the outset of the coaching relationship such as in the discovery stage, core questions serve to explore the student's strengths, past successes, work and personal values, and the one or two things he or she longs to have more of in life. From the answers to these questions come the tools for learning and change. Throughout the RC experience, as in the dream stage, student and coach/mentor come together to make sense of the answers to the core questions so that they may apply these answers to the chosen topic to create something with which both the student and the mentor can explore and experiment. Once the student client could bring his or her dream into clear view, it is time to design a plan for the dream. Design implies a plan or an impression or a mock-up of some future reality. There is no assumption that an initial design is the final design. Experimentation is the order of the day. The ultimate design should incorporate as many of the skills and strengths of the client as is possible or appropriate. Typically, student clients step into the destiny stage once they have begun to implement the concrete actions and practices they identified and designed in the design stage for realizing their desired future. The destiny stage is a time for student clients to acknowledge and celebrate the accomplishments they are making in either moving toward or actually realizing their dream. At the conclusion of this stage, students may choose to move to a second cycle of AC by expanding on other elements of their dream or creating a new dream. This is an excellent opportunity for coaches/mentors to help student clients reflect on the work they have done and appreciate the result they have achieved. This AC process of emphasizing the positive should turn out to be a pleasurable experience; hence, it is highly recommended as a practice of student HSD coaching or mentoring in the RC setting.

Appreciating the Flexibility of Virtual Participation

The idea of virtual participation, as introduced at the beginning of the chapter, is based on the blueprint of virtual organizing, attributed to Venkatraman and Henderson (1998), which could be considered as a means of galvanizing an LC, dynamically assembling and disassembling nodes on a network of people or groups of people, to meet the demands of a particular learning context. In practice, it is interesting to observe how the ideas of virtual participation can be applied to nurture the growth of the various CoLs in the campus environment. In the pilot RC setting at the University of Macau (UM), an attempt has been made to put in place a pilot RC wikis initiative for the convenience of supporting online participation from students, RC personnel as well as academic staff.

UM Pilot Wiki Initiative for RC Living-Learning Program

Under this pilot wiki program, each RC is provided with an electronic space (e-space) whose administration is supported by a coordinator designated by the RC. Under this RC e-space, accessible through the Internet, we could install an electronic space respectively for each volunteer academic member, for each student, for each course offered by the RC, as well as for each related project/ program of interest. Each such e-space could be managed (or administrated) by the respective person involved: an e-space for an academic staff member by his or her own self; an e-space for a student by him- or herself; a course e-space by

the course instructor; and a project e-space by the project leader. Access control could be set for such spaces by the administrator of the page, under basic regulations of the CLE (collaboration and learning environment) scheme. This wiki-based CLE could afford individuals the ability to edit their e-spaces to serve their respective educational purposes (teaching, learning, assessment, and research), or in the context of RC, activity-based learning, such as Reading Club. Through this CLE, our RCs aim to serve such purposes as (the list being not exhaustive):

1. To encourage student-centered learning: Even our students can build their web pages, embed images and video, and post documents on their e-spaces.
2. To encourage teacher-student collaboration: Both teacher and students could be invited into one another's e-spaces to participate in such activities as sharing, discussing, advising, coaching, and mentoring.
3. To assist teaching/learning support: At the discretion of individual staff, coordinate day-to-day teaching work and activity schedules. Timely share and comment on assessment findings. Possibly centralize links to outside resources and upload presentations.
4. To facilitate RC coordination: Manage projects, coordinate meeting agendas and document action-items and decisions. Share reports and presentations to a broader audience.

Virtual Encountering RC-Based CoLs

From a nurturing perspective, it is important to identify what CoLs are desirable in the RC setting, and how, if they already exist, but are not already online, to enable them to be online in order to provide more chances of virtual encounter of such communities, to the organizational members. For those communities already online, it is also important to design opportunities of interaction among different online communities, to activate their knowledge sharing. Since it is an important CoL practice not to reduce learning (knowledge) to a transferable object, what counts as learning (knowledge) is often produced through a process of communal involvement, which includes all the possible controversies, debate and accommodations. This collective character of knowledge construction is best supported online with individuals given suitable ICT support to participate and contribute their own ideas. An ICT subsystem, operated through virtual encounter, must help achieve many of the primary tasks of a CoL, such as encouraging student participation, establishing a common baseline of knowledge and scaffolding what should be well understood so that people in the community can exercise their creative energies on the learning issues of interest to the community's collective growth

Virtual Sourcing RC-Based CoLs

From the discussion built up above, it is not difficult to visualize the importance of identifying the specific expertise of each potential CoL in the organization (the RCs), and if not yet available, planning for its acquisition through a purposeful nurture of expertise in various CoLs related to different RC curricula of studies. This vector focuses on creating and deploying intellectual and intangible assets for the specific RC in the form of a continuous reconfiguration of critical capabilities scattered among the CoLs, assembled through different relationships in the network of CoLs distributed within and across the RCs. An ICT subsystem, operated through virtual sourcing, must help the RC understand precisely what knowledge will give it the unique edge. The RC then needs to acquire or develop this knowledge, keep it on the cutting edge, deploy it, leverage it in operations, and steward it across the networks of CoLs.

Virtual Expertizing RC-Based CoLs

It is important to understand that not everything we know can be codified as documents and tools for the use of the RCs. Sharing tacit knowledge requires interaction and informal learning processes such as storytelling, conversation, coaching, and apprenticeship. The tacit aspects of knowledge often consist of embodied expertise – a deep understanding of complex, interdependent elements that enable dynamic responses to context-specific problems. This type of knowledge is very difficult to replicate. In order to leverage such knowledge, an ICT subsystem, operated through virtual expertise, must help hooking people with related expertise into various networks of CoLs, in order to facilitate sharing such knowledge to the rest of the RC communities.

Remarks for Continuing Challenge

The major challenge to support virtual participation in a RC program lies in the installation of an appreciative knowledge environment (AKE) (Vat, 2010, 2009a) in which electronic support for AC (appreciative coaching) to enable collaborative knowledge work among students and between teachers and students is made available, especially in their respective work and study settings. Currently, the challenges of how to enhance the value of RC-specific knowledge work have rendered, at least, three main design reflections: 1) support the actual practices and daily tasks of the participants (teachers and students); 2) collect experiences and represent them in an accessible and equitable manner; and 3) provide a framework to guide the knowledge process.

Support the Actual Practices and Daily Tasks of the Participants

The AKE environment should support the actual practices and daily tasks of teachers by helping them guide students' learning process through the creation of a visible history of student work. For students, the AKE should support learning practices and tasks by making the thinking of their peers more visible and by illustrating the process of collaborative problem solving through both individual and group inquiry activities. Moreover, from a knowledge integration perspective, the design of living and learning programs involves developing a repertoire of models for explaining situations. What type of knowledge integration framework can best help students and teachers in their daily practice?

Collect Experiences and Represent them in an Accessible and Equitable Manner

The AKE environment should collect experiences and represent them in an accessible and equitable manner to promote the process of connecting ideas so that participants (students and teachers) can use them in subsequent tasks such as during follow-up clarification and illustration. Communities, if viewed as a network of relationships and resources, can be structured to elicit ideas, develop shared understanding, and promote the integration of a diverse set of perspectives. It is important to investigate the potential of structuring discussions in different ways based on the type of discussion and the associated pedagogical goals. Linking different types of pedagogical goals to design strategies is a challenging task because most of the students are yet to get accustomed to reflecting on the nature of their contributions.

Provide a Framework to Guide the Knowledge Process

The AKE environment should encourage participants to make sense of their learning by creating a culture where people ask each other for justification and clarification. It is essential to investigate how participants adjust their learning behavior as their peers prompt them to support their ideas with evidence. One strategy is to create some commonly agreed upon criteria and to examine

how these criteria are adopted and transformed by community members as they interact with one another. For communities to maintain coherence and develop a sense of what is desirable behavior, it is important that a strong community culture be established with a common set of values and criteria for making contributions. Student communities need a general framework to help define the mission and vision for their knowledge process.

CONCLUSION

Today, many educational institutions across the world have implemented electronic learning (e-learning) environments (Curran, 2004; Salmon, 2005; OECD, 2005; HEFCE, 2005, 2009; JISC, 2007, 2010), for the convenience of their teachers and students. This new way of facilitating teaching and learning, coupled with the RC setting has the potential to extend learning methodologies, to open up opportunities for flexible online learning as well as to challenge more traditional methods of course delivery (Vat, 2009a). At the same time, it adds a degree of complexity to educational development and curriculum design. It is experienced that the key to student success is to concentrate on not merely thinking of how to integrate different sorts of content resources, but also on developing educational processes that blend online with face-to-face interactions. In this regard, the idea to support RC-based program participation online is to empower students to learn through various Web-based materials and activities including text-reading, simulations, video demonstrations or dialogue, and such resources as chat rooms, message boards, wikis, podcasts, and RSS feeds that have been purposely built for RC living and learning experience. Indeed, the increasing adoption of collaborative learning and the growth in online support has reflected the current shift away from teaching as a means of transmitting information towards enabling learning as a student-generated activity. Collaborative learning online is a timely example of a blended learning experience for both teachers and students. In fact, the context of blended learning (Eklund, Kay, & Lynch, 2003) offers the possibility of changing our attitudes not only as to where and when learning takes place, but in terms of what resources and tools can support learning and the ways in which these might be used. In particular, blended learning fosters integration of different spaces, allowing students to learn from university, or from home or residence hall or on the move. It offers flexibility in the time when learners can participate in courses, reducing or removing restrictions arising from the balancing of school or home commitments with study. It opens up the range of media resources that can be used for learning. The blend of space, time and media offers new possibilities as to the sorts of activities students can carry out and the ways they can collaborate, using available electronic tools. Literally, the integration of physical and online spaces means that communities can form and interact in ways that were previously unimagined. It introduces the possibility of interacting in real time (synchronously) in conjunction with opportunities to collaborate over a period of time (asynchronously). This in turn allows exploration of different forms of dialogue and new types of learning. New media resources and tools open up possibilities for students to create their own resource banks, integrating self-generated intellectual assets with more formal materials sourced from libraries around the world. This brings into question some of the traditional values of education, such as who owns, creates and controls resources and knowledge. New types of learning activities thereby challenge our thinking as to how learning might be facilitated, creating new etiquettes of learning and teaching, and shifting the locus of control from the teacher to the learner. This is the essence of holistic student development that could be enhanced through virtual participation, especially in the RC context.

REFERENCES

Adams, W. (2000). Getting real: Santa Cruz and the crisis of liberal education. In DeZure, D. (Ed.), *Learning from change: Landmarks in teaching and learning in higher education from Change Magazine, 1969-1999* (pp. 131–134). Sterling, VA: Stylus.

Barkley, E. F. (2010). *Student engagement techniques: A handbook for college faculty*. San Francisco, CA: Jossey-Bass.

Barr, R. B., & Tagg, J. (1995). From teaching to learning: A new paradigm for undergraduate education. *Change, 27*(6), 154–166.

Boyer, E. L. Sr. (1987). *College: The undergraduate experience in America*. New York, NY: HarperCollins.

Boyer, E. L. Sr. (1990). *Campus life: In search of community – A special report for the Carnegie Foundation for the Advancement of Teaching*. Lawrenceville, NJ: Princeton University Press.

Braskamp, L. A., Trautvetter, L. C., & Ward, K. (2006). *Putting students first: How colleges develop students purposefully*. San Francisco, CA: Jossey-Bass.

Byrne, J. A., Brandt, R., & Port, O. (1993, February 8). The virtual corporation. *Business Week*, 36-41.

Cheng, W. (1996). The virtual enterprise: Beyond time, place and form. *Economic Bulletin*. Singapore International Chamber of Commerce, 5-7 February.

Cooperrider, D. (1986). *Appreciative inquiry: Toward a methodology for understanding and enhancing organizational innovation*. Unpublished Doctoral dissertation. Case Western Reserve University, Cleveland, Ohio.

Cooperrider, D. L., & Whitney, D. (2005). *Appreciative inquiry: A positive revolution in change*. San Francisco, CA: Berrett-Koehler.

Cross, K. P. (1998). Why learning communities? Why now? *About Campus*, *3*(3), 4–11.

Curran, C. (2004). *Strategies for e-learning in universities*. Research & Occasional Paper Series: CSHE.7.04. Center for Studies in Higher Education, University of California, Berkeley

Davidow, W. H., & Malone, M. S. (1992). *The virtual corporation – Structuring and revitalizing the corporation for the 21st century*. New York, NY: HarperCollins.

Dewey, J. (1933). *How we think*. Lexington, MA: Heath.

Eklund, J., Kay, M., & Lynch, H. (2003). *E-learning: Emerging issues and key trends*. Australian Flexible Learning Framework discussion paper. Retrieved from http://www.flexiblelearning.net.au

Gabelnick, F., MacGregor, J., Matthews, R. S., & Smith, B. L. (1990). *New directions for teaching and learning: No. 41. Learning communities: Creating connections among students, faculty, and disciplines*. San Francisco, CA: Jossey-Bass.

Gamson, Z. F. (2000). The origins of contemporary learning communities: Residential colleges, experimental colleges, and living and learning communities. In DeZure, D. (Ed.), *Learning from change: Landmarks in teaching and learning in higher education from Change Magazine, 1969-1999* (pp. 113–116). Sterling, VA: Stylus.

Gardner, J. (1990). *On leadership*. New York, NY: Free Press.

Goldman, S., Nagel, R., & Preiss, K. (1995). *Agile competitors and virtual organizations: Strategies for enriching the customer*. New York, NY: van Nostrand Reinhold.

Goodman, P. (1964). *Compulsory mis-education and the community of scholars*. New York, NY: Random House.

Guarasci, R., & Cornwell, G. (1997). *Democratic education in an age of difference*. San Francisco, CA: Jossey-Bass.

Harvard (2007). *Report of the Task Force on General Education*. Last retrieved on 2012FEB22 at: http://www.sp07.umd.edu/HarvardGeneral-EducationReport.pdf.

Hedberg, B., Dahlgren, G., Hansson, J., & Olve, N. (1997). *Virtual organizations and beyond: Discover imaginary systems*. New York, NY: John Wiley & Sons Ltd.

HEFCE. (2005). *HEFCE strategy for e-learning. Higher Education Funding Council for England (HEFCE), Joint Information Systems Committee (JISC), and Higher Education Academy*. HEA.

HEFCE. (2009). *Enhancing learning and teaching through the use of technology: A revised approach to HEFCE's strategy for e-learning. Higher Education Funding Council for England*. HEFCE.

Hill, P. J. (1985). *The rationale for learning communities*. Paper presented at the Inaugural Conference of the Washington Center for Improving the Quality of Undergraduate Education, Olympia, WA.

Hurd, S. N., & Stein, R. F. (Eds.). (2004). *Building and sustaining learning communities: The Syracuse University experience*. New York, NY: John Wiley & sons, Inc.

Jagers, H., Jansen, W., & Steenbakkers, W. (1998). Characteristics of virtual organizations. In P. Sieber & J. Griese (Eds.), *Organizational Virtualness, Proceedings of the VoNet-Workshop*, April 27-28. Bern, Switzerland: Simowa Verlag.

JISC. (2007). *Transforming institutions through e-Learning*. Retrieved December 19, 2011, from http://www.elearning.ac.uk/features/Transformation

JISC. (2010). *New study urges colleges to develop e-learning strategies for higher education.* Retrieved December 19, 2011, from http://www.jisc.ac.uk/news/stories/2010/12/vle.aspx

Kim, J. S. (2005). The effects of a constructivist teaching approach on student academic achievement, self-concept, and learning strategies. *Asia Pacific Education Review, 6*(1), 7-19. Retrieved January 24, 2012, from http://www.eric.ed.gov/ERICWebPortal/search/detailmini.jsp?_nfpb=true&_&ERICExtSearch_SearchValue_0=EJ728823&ERICExtSearch_SearchType_0=no&accno=EJ728823

Kuh, G. D. (1996). Guiding principles for creating seamless learning environments for undergraduates. *Journal of College Student Development, 37*(2), 135–148.

Li, H. L., & Lee, K. C. (2010). Behavior participation in virtual worlds: A Triandis model perspective. *Proceedings of the 2010 Pacific Conference in Information Systems (PACIS2010)*, Paper 94. Retrieved January 24, 2012, from http://aisel.aisnet.org/pacis2010/94/

Meiklejohn, A. (1932). *The experimental college.* New York, NY: HarperCollins.

Newmann, F., & Oliver, D. (1967). Education and community. *Harvard Educational Review, 37*(1), 61–106.

O'Neill, J., & Conzemius, A. (2006). *The power of SMART goals: Using goals to improve student learning.* Bloomington, IN: Solution Tree.

OECD. (2005). *E-Learning in tertiary education: Where do we stand?* OECD Publishing. Retrieved January 24, 2012, from http://www.oecd.org/dataoecd/55/25/35961132.pdf

Orem, S. L., Binkert, J., & Clancy, A. L. (2007). *Appreciative coaching: A positive process for change.* San Francisco, CA: Jossey-Bass.

Porter, M. (1985). *Competitive advantage.* New York, NY: The Free Press.

Ryan, M. (2001). *A collegiate way of living: Residential colleges and a Yale education.* New Haven, CT: John Edwards College, Yale University.

Salmon, G. (2005). Flying not flapping: A strategic framework for e-learning and pedagogical innovation in higher education institutions. *ALT-J. Research in Learning Technology, 13*(3), 201–218. doi:10.3402/rlt.v13i3.11218

Schoem, D. (2004). Sustaining living-learning programs. In Laufgraben, J. L., & Shapiro, N. S. (Eds.), *Sustaining and improving learning communities* (pp. 130–156). San Francisco, CA: Jossey-Bass.

Senge, P. M. (1990). *The fifth discipline: The art and practice of the learning organization.* London, UK: Currency Doubleday.

Stein, R. F. (2004). Learning communities: An overview. In Hurd, S. N., & Stein, F. S. (Eds.), *Building and sustaining learning communities: The Syracuse University experience* (pp. 1–18). Boston, MA: Anker.

Stein, R. F., & Hurd, S. N. (2000). *Using student teams in the classroom: A faculty guide.* Boston, MA: Anker.

Tinto, V. (1997, November/December). Classrooms as communities: Exploring the educational character of student persistence. *The Journal of Higher Education, 68*(6), 599–623. doi:10.2307/2959965

Tussman, J. (1969). *Experiment at Berkeley.* London, UK: Oxford University Press.

Vat, K. H. (2000). Training E-commerce support personnel for enterprises through action learning. In *Proceedings of the 2000 ACM SIGCPR Conference* (pp. 39-43). April 6-8, Chicago, Illinois, USA.

Vat, K. H. (2009a). Developing REALSpace: Discourse on a student-centered creative knowledge environment for virtual communities of learning. *International Journal of Virtual Communities and Social Networking*, *1*(1), 43–74. doi:10.4018/jvcsn.2009010105

Vat, K. H. (2009b). The generative potential of appreciative inquiry for CoP: The virtual enterprise's emergent knowledge model. In Akoumianakis, D. (Ed.), *Virtual community practices and social interactive media: Technology lifecycle and workflow analysis* (pp. 60–85). Hershey, PA: Information Science Reference. doi:10.4018/978-1-60566-340-1.ch004

Vat, K. H. (2010). Virtual organizing professional learning communities through a servant-leader model of appreciative coaching. In Inoue, Y. (Ed.), *Cases on online and blended learning technologies in higher education: Concepts and practices* (pp. 183–206). Hershey, PA: Information Science Reference.

Venkatraman, N., & Henderson, J. C. (1998). Real strategies for virtual organizing. *Sloan Management Review*, *40*(1), 33–48.

Waltzer, K. (1992, Fall). Mad about Madison. *MSU Alumni Magazine*.

Yountz, B. (1984). The Evergreen State College: An experiment maturing. In Jones, R. M., & Smith, B. L. (Eds.), *Against the current: Reform and experimentation in higher education* (pp. 93–118). Cambridge, MA: Schenkman.

KEY TERMS AND DEFINITIONS

Appreciative Coaching: A coaching method derived from the change management philosophy called appreciative inquiry developed in the 1980s in the US, whose philosophy is based on the assumption that inquiry into and dialogue about strengths, successes, hopes and dreams is itself a transformational process.

Holistic Student Development: A learner-centered student nurturing practice based on the essence of whole-person education, emphasizing the holistic development of a person including various aspects such as intellectual, physical, social, moral, and spiritual development of our students, especially in higher education.

Learning Communities: A learning community is a group of people who share common values and beliefs, are actively engaged in learning together from each other. Such communities have become the template for a cohort-based, interdisciplinary approach to higher education today.

Scenario Planning: Also referred to as scenario thinking or scenario analysis, is a strategic planning method some organizations use to make flexible long-term plans. It is often regarded as the act of testing various solutions to a problem situation through enacting it against possible futures.

SMART Scheme: A practical scenario planning method, emphasizing that any activity must be specific or strategic, implying a much greater chance of being accomplished (S); any activity must be measurable, implying that measuring progress toward the attainment of a specific goal must start with establishing concrete criteria (M); any activity planned must be attainable (A), implying that such goals should challenge the persons involved, to their best, to accomplish some achievable goals; any activity planned must be relevant or realistic (R) implying that such goals to be achieved, must represent an objective towards which students are both willing and able to work; any activity must be timely and tangible, implying that such goals could actually be experienced with our senses given enough time to effect the goals.

Virtual Organizing: An organization development blueprint to make use of Web and mobile technologies to organize online various knowledge assets, services, and activities for the convenience of learning and transfer among people in the form of learning communities.

Virtual Participation: An organizational development scheme to encourage online participation of learning activities, say, in the context of higher education institution (university) where students and teachers need to participate online to facilitate, encourage, and reflect on learning online.

Chapter 14
Continuous Knowledge Sharing in Online Social Network Communities:
Service Features, Social Capital Facilitators, and Impact on Motivations

Stella W. Tian
The University of Hong Kong, Hong Kong

Doug Vogel
City University of Hong Kong, Hong Kong

Felix B. Tan
Auckland University of Technology, New Zealand

ABSTRACT

Drawing upon Jasperson, Carter, and Zmud's feature-centric view of technology (Jasperson, Carter, & Zmud, 2005) and Nahapiet and Ghoshal's three dimensions of social capital factors (Nahapiet & Ghoshal, 1998), this chapter develops a conceptual model to elaborate the dynamic interactions between Social Network Services (SNS) features, social capital factors, and motivational antecedents on continuous participation in knowledge sharing activities among Online Social Network (OSN) community members. A number of SNS features, social capital factors, and motivational antecedents are set forth in this chapter. And the mechanism that links these factors is reviewed. It is proposed that, with embedded social mechanism, SNS features can strengthen motivations to continued participation through social capital facilitators.

DOI: 10.4018/978-1-4666-0312-7.ch014

1. INTRODUCTION

The rapid growth of Social Network Services (SNS) in the U.S. and around the globe has attracted millions of users who actively participate in all kinds of Online Social Networking (OSN) activities. For example, Facebook had 845 million monthly active users at the end of December 2011, and approximately 80% of these users were outside the U.S. and Canada (Facebook, 2011). These OSN users spontaneously form into large-scale groups (Waterson, 2006) who exchange information regularly via SNS platforms. These online groups become "online communities" when the interaction and togetherness between group members lasts long enough to form a set of habits and conventions (J. Lee & Lee, 2010).

One of the major habitual and conventional activities among OSN community members is knowledge sharing through social networking services. A study in 2009 found that four out of five photos were located by traversing the social network links on Flicker (Mislove, 2009). This means that social networks have become the major venue for locating content. Thus the value of OSN communities, to a great extent, depends on the levels of member involvement and engagement in knowledge sharing activities (M. H. Hsu, T. L. Ju, C. H. Yen, & C. M. Chang, 2007). As a result, continued participation in knowledge sharing through social networking services becomes critical for the thriving of online communities.

Continued participation in knowledge sharing through social networking services is not about initial adoption of SNS platforms, it is about people's continued involvement in a complex IT platform post-adopting a core set of technologies for social interactions and information exchange. Previous studies have differentiated the continuance intention to Information Systems (IS) usage from initial adoptions (Bhattacherjee, 2001; Chiu, Hsu, Sun, Lin, & Sun, 2005; Hong, Thong, & Tam, 2006; Jasperson, et al., 2005; S. S. Kim & Malhotra, 2005; Limayem & Cheung, 2008; Limayem, Hirt, & Cheung, 2007). Built on these, researchers have highlighted the role of social factors in facilitating continuance intentions to participate in knowledge sharing in online communities. For instance, in community of transaction or community of consumption, there are factors such as sociability (Kim et al., 2008), shared vision and trust (Wang & Chiang, 2009); in community of practice, there are three dimensions of social capital factors (Wasko and Faraj, 2005; Chiu, Hsu et al., 2006); in professional virtual communities for expertise sharing, there are factors such as norms of reciprocity and trust (Lin, Hung, & Chen, 2009), and social interaction ties (I. Y. L. Chen, 2007).

However, many studies have examined a complex information system as a whole, rather than looked into the feature level factors. Very few studies have explicitly investigated the relationship between certain features and user behaviors, for example, Xiao and Benbasat (2007) studied the relationship among recommendation agents use, characteristics and consumer decision making outcomes. In this chapter, we emphasized the importance of adopting a feature-centric view of technology (Jasperson, et al., 2005). Because users do not necessarily use the same information system although on the same SNS platform, in the sense that each of them chooses their own collection of social networking services and activities; online social networking becomes a routine for OSN members while the relationship between SNS features, social interactions, and motivation to participate in knowledge sharing activities is still unclear. In order to conceptualize social interactions, this chapter adopts a social capital perspective, since the social capital theory provides a multi-dimensional view of social interactions which will allow us to form a bigger picture.

The purpose of this chapter is therefore to develop a set of theoretical links in a conceptual model which synthesizes the dynamic interactions between SNS features, social capital factors, and motivations to participate in knowledge sharing activities among OSN members. Based on Jasperson, Carter and Zmud's feature-centric view of technology (Jasperson, et al., 2005) and Nahapiet and Ghoshal's classification of the structural, relational and cognitive dimensions of social capital factors (Nahapiet & Ghoshal, 1998), we hope the model will provide theoretical underpinnings to explain the links between technological, social capital and motivational factors in SNS platforms.

In the rest of the chapter, we first elaborate the theoretical background of feature-centric view of technology and the multi-dimensions of social capital factors. Then, we examine the characteristics of SNS websites and the embedded social mechanisms so as to generalize the links between SNS features and social capital factors. Next, we investigate the link between social capital factors and motivational factors to participate in knowledge sharing in OSN communities. After this, we present the conceptual model and discuss implications for future research and practice. Conclusion is drawn.

2. THEORETICAL BACKGROUND

2.1 Feature-Centric View

The feature-centric view of technology is rooted in the social construction of technology, in which features are interpreted (and possibly adapted) by individual users so as to constitute a technology-in-use (Jasperson, et al., 2005). In the post-adoptive context, a feature-centric view of technology is valuable because the set of IT application features recognized and used by an individual likely changes over time (Jasperson, et al., 2005). In this chapter, we follow Jasperson et al's definition of feature: a technology's features are the building blocks or components of the technology, some features reflect the core of the technology, collectively representing its identity, other features are not defining components and their use may be optional (Jasperson, et al., 2005).

There are a few crucial steps to conceptualize the features to be investigated, suggested by Jasperson et al (2005): 1) to appropriately define the scope of the *core* feature sets and *ancillary* feature sets, 2) to investigate features from *designers' view* (i.e., use a set of predefined features) or from *users' view* (i.e., use a social construction of the technology-in-use as defined collectively by a specific user community), and 3) to focus on *discrete, elemental* features or on meaningful *bundles* of these elemental features.

In this chapter, we investigate core features that are based on key elements of SNS websites which support social interactions. Then bundles of features are investigated from OSN community users' view. The features used in this chapter are not a comprehensive review of all features implemented in SNS platforms, but are features that are commonly known by users or specifically mentioned in literature.

2.2 Three Dimensions of Social Capital Factors

The role that *social capital* plays in facilitating knowledge sharing has been heavily illustrated in recent years (Adler & Kwon, 2002; C. J. Chen, 2004; C.-M. Chiu, M.-H. Hsu, & E. T. G. Wang, 2006; C. M. Chiu, M. H. Hsu, & E. T. G. Wang, 2006; M.-H. Hsu, T. L. Ju, C.-H. Yen, & C.-M. Chang, 2007; Koka & Prescott, 2002; Mu, Peng, & Love, 2008; Nahapiet & Ghoshal, 1998; Nielsen, 2005; Phang, Kankanhalli, & Sabherwal, 2009; Smedlund, 2008; Tian & Tan, 2009; Tseng & Kuo, 2010; M. M. Wasko & Faraj, 2005). From the *Social Capital Theory* perspective, there are three dimensions of social capital factors: the *structural, relational,* and *cognitive* dimensions (Nahapiet & Ghoshal, 1998).

The *structural* dimension of social capital refers to the overall pattern of connections between actors (Nahapiet & Ghoshal, 1998). The most salient manifestations of this dimension are: 1) network ties, such as strong and weak ties; and 2)

Table 1. Examples of SNS artifacts supporting OSN elements

Element	Example of technology artifacts
Individual users	Personal profile (boyd & Ellison, 2008; Ma & Agarwal, 2007; Mislove, 2009).
Groups	Access control (Mislove, 2009); group profiling (H.-s. Kim, et al., 2008).
Social connections	Social network navigation (Mislove, 2009); recommendation system (Yimam-Seid & Kobsa, 2003); awareness features (Huysman & Wulf, 2006).
Content	Content management such as storage, tag, index, rating, searching (Mislove, 2009); recommender system (Yimam-Seid & Kobsa, 2003); awareness features (Huysman & Wulf, 2006).
Communication	Information exchange tools such as IM, discussion groups, chat rooms, white boards (Molly McLure Wasko & Faraj, 2000); Collocated communication spaces with complex materials (Fischer, Scharff, & Ye, 2004).

network configuration or morphology describing the pattern of linkages in terms of such measures as density, connectivity, and hierarchy (Nahapiet & Ghoshal, 1998).

The *relational* dimension of social capital refers to the assets created and leveraged through relationships such as respect and friendship, which bond the actors together and influence their behavior (Nahapiet & Ghoshal, 1998). The most import facets of this dimension are: 1) trust and trustworthiness, 2) norms and sanctions, and 3) identity and identification (Nahapiet & Ghoshal, 1998).

The *cognitive* dimension of social capital refers to those resources that provide shared representative actions, interpretations, and systems of meaning among parties. The most representative facets include shared language and codes, and 2) shared narratives (Nahapiet & Ghoshal, 1998).

3. LINKING SNS FEATURES TO SOCIAL CAPITAL FACTORS

3.1 Characteristics of SNS Websites

SNS websites are web-based services that allow individuals to: 1) construct a public or semi-public profile within a bounded system, 2) articulate a list of other users with whom they share a connection, and 3) view and traverse their list of connections and those made by others within

the system (boyd & Ellison, 2008). What makes social network sites unique is not that they allow individuals to meet strangers, but rather that they enable users to articulate and make visible their social networks (boyd & Ellison, 2008). It has facilitated a new form of information exchange. For example, Mislove's study on Flicker has found that social network becomes the major venue for locating content as four out of five photos were located by traversing the social network links (Mislove, 2009).

The characteristics of online communities vary, based on the quality or depth of their social relationships that members form with other individuals within the digital environment, as well as on their mutual goals and shared interests (H.-s. Kim, Park, & Jin, 2008). Although OSN sites have implemented a wide variety of technical features, their backbone consists of visible profiles that display an articulated list of Friends who are also users of the system (boyd & Ellison, 2008). Therefore, technology artifacts in OSN sites deal with five indispensable elements: individual users, groups, social connections, content, and communication. Table 1 provides examples of artifacts related to each element.

3.1.1 Users

Full participation in online social networks requires users to register a (pseudo) identity with the network, though some sites do allow browsing public data without explicit sign-on. Users may volunteer information about themselves, all of which constitutes the user's profile (Mislove, 2009).

A *profile* generated by an individual user typically includes information such as age, location, background, experience interests, and habits. Most sites also encourage users to upload a profile photo. The visibility of a profile varies by site and according to user discretion (boyd & Ellison, 2008). For example, Facebook allows users who are part of the same "network" to view each other's profiles, unless a profile owner has decided to deny permission to those in their network (boyd & Ellison, 2008). In general, the profile supports users' self-representation, the social searching, and social browsing (Lampe, Ellison, & Steinfield, 2006) of individual users' information, which to a large extent, has enhanced individuals' ability to process information about people.

3.1.2 Groups

Groups can be established by any members in the OSN sites. A group can be founded in a topic-centered way, or a member-centered way. Either type of group can have a *group profile*. The rationale of a group profile is the same as that of the individual profile – to provide group information and a group image. Groups have *access control* to allow or forbid new members joining. Groups will have their own spaces for group profiles and group content repositories.

3.1.3 Social Connections

The public display of social connections (also known as "social networks" or "social links") is a crucial component of SNSs. The *social network navigation* is based on such visibility of social connections. After joining a social network site, users are prompted to identify others in the network with whom they have a relationship (Mislove, 2009). For the establishment of online relationships,

users have to send a request to each other to be accepted as a "Friendship". The characteristics of *social network navigation* are: 1) mutual, 2) public un-nuanced, and 3) de-contextualized (Donath & boyd, 2004), as explained below.

1. Mutual

Most OSN sites require bi-directional confirmation for Friendship. Mutual means: if User A shows User B as a connection, then User B has also agreed to show User A as a connection.

2. Public Un-Nuanced

On most OSN sites, the list of Friends is visible to anyone who is permitted to view the profile. Therefore, after the mutual confirmation, the social connections become public since they are permanently on display for others to see. However, some OSN sites do have a more strict policy of showing the social connections. For example, LinkedIn allows you to see only the connections made by your immediate links, and only if they allow it.

Also, the social connections are un-nuanced: there is no distinction made between a close friend with whom the user chats every day and a near stranger with whom the user has idly chatted online one night. However, the users can label their online friends as "Special Friends," "Relatives," "Fans," etc., to categorize them.

3. De-Contextualized

The social connections are de-contextualized because there is no way of showing only a portion of one's network to some people. Some sites do allow users to adjust the closeness by degree of the people who are to be allowed to see their connections - but still - within that degree everyone can see all connections. Thus, there is no approach to segregate one's social connections currently (Donath & boyd, 2004).

To leverage the massive volume of social connections established on OSN sties, the *recommendation system* and the *awareness features* are adopted. The *recommendation system* (Yimam-Seid & Kobsa, 2003) is commonly used to recommend "friends" to users based on the analysis of the overlap of two users' social connections. The *awareness features* capture selected activities of individual users and make them visible to their friends (Huysman & Wulf, 2006). These two artifacts have made the OSN sites much more "clever" and more socially intelligent. The Friends list contains links to each Friend's profile, enabling viewers to traverse the network graph by clicking through the Friends lists (Mislove, 2009).

3.1.4 Content

In OSN sites, the unique characteristic of the contents is that they are user generated. The *User Generated Content (UGC)* comes from regular people who voluntarily contribute data, information, or media that then appear before others in a useful or entertaining way, usually on the Web - for example, restaurant ratings, wikis, and videos (Krumm, Davies, & Narayanaswami, 2008). The UGC in OSN communities covers a wide range of content types, which can be media files, chat logs, documents, etc., that are created by users during the interaction.

As mentioned earlier, the way contents are located and viewed by users is shifting to a social paradigm in OSN sites. For example, four out of five photos were located by traversing the social network links on Flicker (Mislove, 2009). This means that social networks have become the major venue for locating content.

3.1.5 Communication

Without doubt, the communication in OSN sites is a practice of *Computer-Mediated Communication (CMC)*. The communication in OSN sites takes place in one-to-one, one-to-many, and many-to-

many patterns in a synchronous or asynchronous manner.

For one-to-one communication, most OSN sites provide a mechanism for users to leave messages on their Friends' profiles. This feature typically involves leaving "comments," although sites employ various labels for this feature (boyd & Ellison, 2008). In addition, OSN sties often have private messaging features, such as the Instant Messenger and Webmail services.

For one-to-many and many-to-many communication, discussion groups and chat rooms are widely accepted; sometimes, however, "comments" can also be adopted in a one-to-many communication channel, as many users can make comments on one user's posts.

In addition, a boundary-spanning communication has emerged which frequently takes place in collocated communication spaces with complex materials (Fischer, et al., 2004). This type of interaction is gathered around certain content that could have complex materials attached. As long as the content is initiated or shared by a user, everyone in that user's whole social network can participate in the communication discourse that links to the original source. Thus, it quickly bridges spatial and temporal boundaries of one user's social connections (Huysman & Wulf, 2006).

3.2 Embedded Social Mechanism in SNS Platforms

Many SNS applications straddle the virtual and real social worlds, as they entail online and offline interactions and various forms of visual and verbal connectivity in both synchronous and asynchronous modes (M. J. W. Lee & McLoughlin, 2009). The most frequently mentioned social mechanisms supported by the SNS applications are: 1) social presence within a virtual environment, 2) transactional control of communication, and 3) social connectivity.

3.2.1 Social Presence within a Virtual Environment

The term social presence is defined as "the degree to which a medium facilitates awareness of the other person and interpersonal relationships during the interaction" (Fulk, Schmitz, & Steinfield, 1990). The "Users" and "Groups" elements mentioned in the above section are the exact medium which facilitates awareness of the other person's social interaction.

The *Social Presence Theory (SPT)* postulates that the inability of mediums to transmit nonverbal cues has a negative effect on interpersonal communication (Short, Williams, & Christie, 1976). Based on the *SPT*, electronic and paper-based communication media have traditionally been viewed as low in social presence, whereas Face-to-Face (FtF) communication has been viewed as high in social presence (Fulk, et al., 1990). Therefore, it is suggested that the awareness of the online presence of fellow members could be reinforced through offline interaction which would influence online community activity. Offline interaction helps virtual community members understand, trust, and identify with one another, providing a stronger base for online community activity (Koh, Kim, Butler, & Bock, 2007). For example, by choosing collaboration software that promotes social presence, trust can be enhanced in distributed and culturally diverse teams (Lowry, Zhang, Zhou, & Fu, 2010).

How can we choose collaboration software to promote social presence in virtual environments? The *Media Richness Theory (MRT)* posits that rich communication channels can bridge different frames of reference and make issues less ambiguous *(Daft & Lengel, 1986)*; thus, the medium's capacity to support highly affective interpersonal interactions depends on its richness. The determinants of media richness include the medium's capacity for immediate feedback, the number of cues and senses involved, personalization, and language variety (Rice, 1992). With the rise

of richer Computer-Mediated Communication media, some research suggests that social presence can be manipulated in technology design (Hassanein & Head, 2006; Miranda & Saunders, 2003). For example, by increasing social presence through the use of collaborative software, it is possible to lessen the negative impact of increasing group size of task groups (Roberts, Lowry, & Sweeney, 2006).

3.2.2 Social Connectivity

OSN sites enable individuals to connect with one another by providing the "social connections" element. Although people connect with each other in the offline environment, Culnan and Markus (1987) point out that computer-mediated communication networks can create communities based on interest "rather than by geography, social position, and prior acquaintance" (p. 34). Thus, the online social ties create a significant impact on group connectivity (Haythornthwaite, 2005).

First, the social connectivity through OSN sites facilitates the latent tie connectivity on which weak and later strong ties may grow (Haythornthwaite, 2005). The concept of latent social network ties is developed by Haythornthwaite in the *Latent Tie Theory* (Haythornthwaite, 2002). Latent ties refer to social ties that are technically possible but not yet activated socially (Haythornthwaite, 2002). They are only activated, i.e., converted from latent to weak, by some sort of social interaction between members, e.g., by telephoning someone, attending a group-wide meeting, reading and contributing to a web board, emailing others, etc. (Haythornthwaite, 2005).

Second, the social connectivity through OSN sites facilitates the effectiveness of communication. Sohn et al. (2007) have found that a network-generalized exchange (e.g., blogging system in OSN sites) is a more effective structure than group-generalized exchange (e.g., electronic bulletin) for many-to-many communication particularly when a large number of individuals are involved.

Third, the social connectivity and behavior diffusion in OSN is initiated in a flourishing way. Mark Zukerberg, the 23 year old founder of Facebook, has claimed that: "… as our ties become stronger with one another online, we begin to utilize different types or combinations of media to strengthen ties. Thus, simple online text communication is no longer sufficient. We desire to see photographs, have voice conversations and see films, digital video and moving pictures in order to solidify our sense of identification with the other. So, as our needs begin to change, so do our online communities, and for this reason exclusively, social networking sites such as Facebook emerge and flourish" (Olaniran & Williams, 2009). Why can such influence be created by Facebook? Based on an experiment in artificially structured online communities, Centola (2010) suggest two possible explanations: 1) individual adoption is much more likely when participants receive social reinforcement from multiple neighbours in the social network, and 2) the behavior spreads farther and faster across clustered-lattice networks than across corresponding random networks. In real life, such social reinforcement from multiple neighbours takes longer and is less visible. However, in OSN sites, each individual user has his (or her) own clustered-lattice networks, while social reinforcement is made strong and visible via SNS applications.

3.2.3 Transactional Control of Communication

The concept of transactional control of communication is rooted in the learning literature. One stream of the literature is about the *Transactional Distance Theory* (Moore, 1972), which is originally used to investigate pedagogical relationships existing in a distance education environment (Jung, 2001). In this theory, the construct of "learner autonomy" is built which refers to the extent to

which learners make decisions regarding their own learning and construct their own knowledge based on their own experience (Moore & Kearsley, 1996). The theory posits that when the communication between instructors and learners increases, their transactional distance decreases (Moore & Kearsley, 1996). According to constructivists, how learners choose to learn is considered to be a direct consequence of the level of choice they are given in learning (Olaniran & Williams, 2009). Therefore, by incorporating features and functionalities that can provide extensive scaffolding to learning environments, the learners' autonomy can be promoted, and thus the learning ttransactions between the instructor and learners can be enhanced (Jung, 2001; Vovides, Sanchez-Alonso, Mitropoulou, & Nickmans, 2007).

What does the transactional control of communication mean to the social interaction in virtual communities? First, as individuals have to manage a large volume of interactions taken place randomly, the autonomy to communicate asynchronous and synchronous is necessary. It is reported that greater use of both asynchronous and synchronous communication via the use of social software tools is likely to enhance social interaction within an online learning community and thus facilitate a sense of community (McInnerney & Roberts 2004). Second, it is a big challenge for individuals in virtual communities to manage the following modes of interaction simultaneously: one-to-one, one-to-many, and many-to-many (Dron 2007). However, the social software provides easy-to-use ways to communicate, collaborate, and participate on an unprecedented scale (Farkas 2007).

3.3 SNS Features and Social Capital Factors

There is scant literature specifically focused on the SNS features that support multi-dimensions of social capital development. From a socio-technical perspective, understanding the interplay between

SNS features and social capital development provides IT designers with the social requirement analysis for electronic tools to support knowledge sharing (Huysman & Wulf 2006). This section attempts to link SNS features to the structural, relational and cognitive dimension of social capital factors.

3.3.1 Features Support Structural Social Capital Development

Structural social capital development relates to the formation and strengthening of network ties and configuration.

Technological determinists suggest that new media features for structural social interaction induce social change by enabling new forms of communication and cultivating distinctive skills and sensibilities (DiMaggio et al. 2001). For example, the social browsing and social search features make the maintaining of social ties cheap and easy, by means of "remove barriers to interaction" or "expanding interaction networks" (Resnick 2002); the social recommending feature based on user data analysis suggests opportunities for establishing social ties; the awareness feature on SNS automatically reminds individuals if their friends are in the same virtual place, thus creating a virtual co-presence among individuals who have already built up a social tie; the member-centered or topic centered-spaces allows individuals to become "boundary spanners," "roamers," or "outposts" who take care of various facets of social network configurations (Wenger, 1998).

3.3.2 Features Support Relational Social Capital Development

Although there are several sub-dimensions of relational social capital, their developments are not directly supported by SNS features. However, SNS may take part in the control or manipulating of the process.

First, certain SNS features are related to the control or communication of identity. Interactions where people are not informed about each other's identity can sometimes allow people to transcend their stereotypes or take productive risks (Turoff 2001). Similarly, the suppression of certain sensory information (smell, tone of voice, facial expressions) can, in some circumstances, allow people to transcend emotional reactions that would interfere with collaborating with each other (Resnick 2002). Access controls (e.g., a joint request to a group based on which group moderators approve new members and new messages) are another example of restricting information flows. This can help build social capital in two ways: 1) it can create a sense of boundaries, reducing the risks of participation and fostering a group identity among those who do have access, and 2) according people different access privileges can reify roles (Resnick 2002).

Second, reciprocity can be facilitated by dependency management, such as the notification feature. For example, calendar programs remind people of appointments, and notification services alert them when messages arrive or other events occur (Resnick 2002).

3.3.3 Features Support Cognitive Social Capital Development

Cognitive social capital development relates to the enhancement of shared language, codes, and narratives.

One of the SNS features is the "Explicit Feedback" (Resnick 2002) where individuals comment on the quality of each others' posts in an explicit way (e.g., "tagging," "share," and "like" buttons on Facebook). Such activities can promote the publicity and diffusion of the posts, and thus direct other members to view the same narratives.

3.3.4 Features Support Multi-Dimensional Social Capital Development

Some features support multi-dimensional social capital development. For example, the features that support history maintaining make the residuals of previous interactions visible. These features can be useful in several ways, including: 1) presenting a cognitive map to new members, 2) contributing to the development of roles and a sense of collective identity (people can reflect on past patterns of interactions), and 3) contributing to the development of to trust (the visibility of interaction logs and explicit feedback can create accountability) (Resnick 2002).

4. LINKING SOCIAL CAPITAL FACTORS TO MOTIVATIONS

Motivation is a psychological state, whereas actual behaviour is the outcome of that state (Mitchell & Daniels, 2003). In this section, motivational antecedents on participating knowledge sharing are divided into two aspects: self-related and socially-related.

4.1 Self-Related Motivational Antecedents

The self-related motivations derive from a core set of individual needs that the user wants to fulfill. The *Uses and Gratifications* approach is a well-established paradigm to explain these needs (U. M. Dholakia, R. P. Bagozzi, & L. K. Pearo, 2004). It was originally developed and employed by communications researchers as an approach to study the gratifications that attract and hold audiences to the kinds of media and the types of content that satisfy their social and psychological needs (Ruggiero, 2001). It is also used to explain the internet-specific gratifications that guides the assessment of user motivations for online media

usage and access (Stafford, Stafford, & Schkade, 2004). Applied to the use of online social network websites, these needs include: 1) the information need, 2) the instrumental need, 3) the self-discovery need, and 4) the entertainment need.

4.1.1 Information Need

The information needs are derived from getting and sharing information in the virtual community, such as the needs of information retrieval, information giving, and conversation capabilities (Flanagin & Metzger, 2001).

4.1.2 Instrumental Need

The instrumental need is derived from accomplishing specific tasks, such as solving a problem, generating an idea, influencing others regarding a pet issue or product, validating a decision already reached or buying a product through online social interactions (Utpal M. Dholakia, Richard P. Bagozzi, & Lisa Klein Pearo, 2004).

4.1.3 Self-Discovery Need

The self-discovery need derives from self-realization values that can be traced back to the work of the eudaemonists, existentialists, and other related work in studying the philosophy of personal identity (Waterman, 2004). It is a type of individual intrinsic motivation that the individual needs to form a personal identity.

4.1.4 Entertainment Need

The entertainment need, also included in the uses and gratifications framework, is derived from the value of having fun and relaxation through playing or otherwise interacting with others. Studies have shown that many participants do this for entertainment through exploring different fictional identities, as well as encountering and solving virtual challenges, etc. (McKenna & Bargh, 1999).

4.2 Socially-Related Motivational Antecedents

While the above four needs are self-referent, the socially-related motivations are based on a set of social needs derived from the value of viewing oneself in relation to other group members (Utpal M. Dholakia, et al., 2004).

4.2.1 The Need of Maintaining Connectivity and Social Status

The socially-related motivations can derive from social needs such as the need of maintaining interpersonal connectivity, and the need of enhancing social status. These needs can be explained from the *Social Integration* perspective (Berkman & Glass, 2000) and the *Social Exchange Theory* (Emerson, 1976).

The *Social Integration* perspective includes the view that individuals need social support, social influence, and social engagement so that their self beliefs can be reinforced for their well-being. Maintaining interpersonal connectivity can benefit individuals with social support, friendship, and intimacy. Empirical studies have found that engaging in virtual communities can help members stay connected, and provide greater benefits for users experiencing low self-esteem and low life satisfaction (Ellison, Steinfield, & Lampe, 2007).

The *Social Exchange Theory* claims that the anticipation of social rewards and punishments forms the incentive for individuals to exchange favours or act in a collective way (Gächter & Fehr, 1999). Thus, the value of enhancing social status is derived from contributing to the community so as to gain acceptance and reciprocity of other members, and as a result, enhance one's social status within the community (Baumeister, 1998).

4.2.2 The Need of Exerting Social Influences

The socially-related motivations can also derive from social influences, which Bagozzi and Dholakia (2002) summarize into: a) compliance (i.e., normative influence of others' expectations), b) internalization (i.e., congruence of one's goals with those of group members), and c) identification (i.e., conception of one's self in terms of the group's defining features). However, in virtual communities, Bagozzi and Dholakia (2002) point only to the significant effect of internalization and identification. The non-significant result for compliance is not surprising since participation in virtual communities is usually voluntary and anonymous, and members are able to leave without much effort (U. M. Dholakia, et al., 2004). The constructs frequently used to study social influences in virtual communities are social identity and social norms. The social identity captures the main aspects of an individual's identification with the group in the sense that the person comes to view himself or herself as a member of the community, as "belonging" to it (U. M. Dholakia, et al., 2004). The social norms can be in the form of the community norm or the group norm which is defined as "the understanding of, and a commitment by, the individual member to a set of goals, values, beliefs, and conventions shared with other group members" (U. M. Dholakia, et al., 2004).

4.3 Self and Socially Related Motivational Antecedents

4.3.1 The Need of Fulfilling Social Cognitions

The socially-related motivations can derive from individuals' cognitions in inter-personal relationships. According to the *Social Cognitive Theory*, a person's behavior is partially shaped and controlled by the influences of social network and the person's cognition, such as expectations and beliefs (Bandura, 1989). Two types of expectation and beliefs have been identified as the major cognitive forces guiding behavior: outcome expectations and self-efficacy. Information Systems (IS) researchers have demonstrated the importance of self-efficacy and outcome expectations for predicting and improving the performance of IT usage; for example, the computer self-efficacy in the computer training environment (Agarwal, Sambamurthy, & Stair, 2000) and outcome expectations in virtual community context (C.-M. Chiu, et al., 2006).

Although the focus of the *Social Cognitive Theory* is on the inter-personal configuration of linkages between people or units, the motivational constructs derived from this theory have overlaps with the other self-related and socially-related motivational antecedents mentioned above. This is because: 1) the individuals' expectations and beliefs are closely related to the individuals' intrinsic needs and personal characteristics; and 2) the assets embedded within the impersonal linkages, such as trust, group norms and group identification (C.-M. Chiu, et al., 2006), are also shaped by social influences. For example, based on the *Social Cognitive Theory*, Hsu et al. have found that multi-dimensional trusts for environmental influences, as well as self-efficacy and outcome expectations for personal influences, show significant effect on knowledge sharing in professional virtual communities (M.-H. Hsu, et al., 2007). Therefore, the *Social Cognitive Theory* has covered multi-dimensions of the antecedents of knowledge sharing in communities.

4.4 Why Social Capital Factors Facilitate Motivations

Table 2 lists some salient constructs related to social capital theory and their implications for why knowledge sharing is facilitated. These constructs are derived from conceptual work such as Adler and Kwon's (2002) and Huysman

and Wulf's (2006) assertions in conjunction with empirical findings in virtual communities by other IS researchers. Drawing upon the findings of why certain social capital factors facilitate knowledge sharing, the links can be established between social capital factors and motivational antecedents.

It can be seen that structural social capital factors facilitate knowledge sharing mainly by strengthening self-related motivational antecedents. For example, centrality affects the one's self-discovery need, and network ties affect one's instrumental need and information need.

Relational social capital factors facilitate knowledge sharing mainly by strengthening socially-related motivational antecedents. For example, trust, norms of reciprocity, reciprocity, and identification are incubators for obtaining connectivity and social status, while perceived identity verification gives rise to individual's social influences.

Cognitive social capital factors facilitate knowledge sharing by sustaining both self-related and socially-related needs. For example, shared codes and language can stimulate the information need because it promotes users' transactional control of communication, while individual expertise can encourage self-discovery need. Shared value and vision, on the other hand, will generate expectation and beliefs to fulfil users' social cognitions.

5. CONCEPTUAL MODEL

5.1 Conceptual Framework

Previous sections have established two links: 1) the link between SNS features and social capital factors, and 2) the link between social capital factors and motivational antecedents to participate in knowledge sharing activities in OSN communities. Based on the links, we present the conceptual framework in Figure 1.

Although some research has suggested that the influence of user interaction on continuance

Table 2. Social capital factors facilitating knowledge sharing in virtual communities

Social capital dimension	Construct	Why facilitate knowledge sharing	Source of empirical study
Structural dimension			
Network configuration	Centrality	High levels of network centrality enable individuals to contribute more helpful responses	(M. M. Wasko & Faraj 2005)
Network ties	Social interaction ties	A cost-effective way of assessing a wider range of knowledge sources	(Chiu et al. 2006)
	Social interactivity	Opportunity to interact and network with knowledgeable members	(Phang et al. 2009)
Relational dimension			
Trust	Trust	Trust creates intrinsic motivation to share	(Chiu et al. 2006)
Norms	Norms of reciprocity	Participants expect mutual reciprocity which can justify their effort in KS activities	(Chiu et al. 2006)
	Reciprocity	When there is a strong norm of reciprocity in the collective, individuals trust that their contribution efforts will be reciprocated, thereby rewarding and ensuring ongoing contribution	(M. M. Wasko & Faraj 2005)
Identification	Identification	Sense of belong and positive feeling toward community	(Chiu et al. 2006)
	Perceived identity verification	Similar identity helps to build relationships with each other	(Ma & Agarwal 2007)
Obligations and expectations	Commitment	Commitment to a collective conveys a sense of responsibility to help others	(M. M. Wasko & Faraj 2005)
Cognitive dimension			
Shared codes	Knowledge tracking fulfillment	System supported ability to track knowledge activities	(Phang et al. 2009)
Shared language	Shared language	Facilitating common understanding of collective ways of acting in virtual community	(Chiu et al. 2006)
Shared value, vision	Shared vision	Common goals, interests and visions that members of a virtual community share will help them see the meaning of knowledge	(Chiu et al. 2006)
Individual expertise	Self-related expertise	Higher levels of expertise enable individuals to provide more useful advice	(M. M. Wasko & Faraj 2005)
	Tenure in the field	Longer tenure in the shared practice are likely to enable individuals to better understand the practice and share relevant knowledge	(M. M. Wasko & Faraj 2005)

intention in online community can be mediated by the creation of various dimensions of social capital (Wang & Chiang, 2009), we would like to leave the discussion open. In the model, social capital development factors are treated as facilitators, as there are multi-dimensional factors, they have the potential to exert mediating or moderating effect, or both, which depends on the specific type of features, social capital factors, and motivational antecedents.

5.2 Implications for Research

There are several directions for future research based on the findings in this chapter. First, further theoretical model can be developed to explain the relationship between specific factors mentioned in this chapter, or to extend the theoretical scope to decision making constructs. In addition, whether social capital facilitators are moderators or mediators deserves further investigation.

Figure 1.Conceptual framework

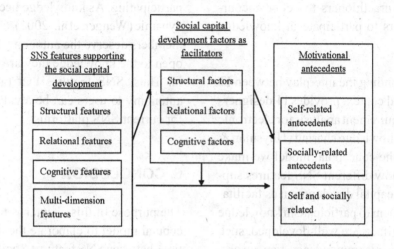

Second, more theoretical perspectives can be adopted to examine the influences of SNS features. In this chapter, we introduced social capital theory as the theoretical lens for exploratory studies. There are plenty of facilitators or barriers that can be obtained from other theories. How SNS features relates to these facilitators or barriers, and what are the mechanisms, are possible directions for future study.

Third, the advancement of technology such as mobile technology has created many new opportunities and challenges for adaptive SNS feature usage. For example SNS apps on smart phone, twitter, accepts a shorter length of content but has much more frequent updates of content; while foursquare, provides Location Based Services (LBS) plus SNS that can create more ways of online community engagement. From a feature-centric view of technology, how will the new bundles of technologies and adaptive SNS features change people's social networking behavior? How will the interaction between core features (e.g., LBS and SNS), and other ancillary features influence users' post-adoptive behavior? How will they influence people's motivation to participate in online social networking? These can be possible inquiries for the future.

Last, future research can target various types of online social network communities and take into account of the nature of communities, to study the relationship between the nature of online communities, SNS adoptions, and user' motivation to participate. For example, a community of practice for doctors and patients that provides a platform for healthcare knowledge exchange and a community of transaction or consumption frequently hosted by firms to promote commercial exchanges (H.-s. Kim, et al., 2008). How do the social mechanisms vary on different types of online communities? How will users' motivation be altered due to the interplay between community conventions and SNS features? These can be interesting issues for future research.

5.3 Implications for Practice

The implications from the exploratory findings are twofold:

1. For IT designers to pay attention to the social mechanisms to better support online communities as incubators for knowledge sharing,

2. For online social network community managerial practitioners to better encourage members to participate in knowledge sharing.

First, understanding the interplay between IT features and social context provides IT designers with the social requirement analysis for electronic tools to support knowledge sharing (Huysman & Wulf, 2006). In the conceptual model we make propositions on how different SNS features support users' social capital development as facilitators to motivate them to participate in knowledge sharing. Some artifacts are well-developed, such as social browsing, recommender system, awareness features; some might need further refinement on new forms of communication medium such as mobile platforms. In addition, how to design the combination of various SNS features, and deliver them to support knowledge sharing more efficiently, remains a challenge.

Second, for OSN community managerial practitioners, who expect to promote an effective knowledge sharing and creative learning environment, it is common to emphasize the convenience of IT infrastructure and the enhancement of material rewards. However, they should also pay attention to the interactive basis of the relationship among the OSN members (Guo, Shim, & Otondo, 2010). Apart from IT infrastructure and material rewards, facilitating the use of SNS features to cultivate social capital can also strengthen members' motivation to share knowledge. For example, creating and organizing communication spaces on relevant topics to the interest of the community of practice will facilitate cognitive social capital development (Wenger, McDermott, & Snyder, 2002).

Third, for both IT designers and community managers, it is important to notice that individuals have to cope with the increasing information overload problem in online spaces (Jones, Ravid, & Rafaeli, 2004). Motivating community members to share knowledge will bring benefit to them, but information overload can be a barrier to continuous participating. As knowledge becomes social and dynamic (Wenger, et al., 2002), online community members deserve the autonomy to be selectively open to the knowledge they are really interested in. Thus, SNS features that provide sufficient autonomy to users can be a value-added feature for current SNS platforms.

6. CONCLUSION

The purpose of this chapter is to develop a conceptual model to elaborate the dynamic interactions between SNS features, social capital factors, and motivational antecedents to participate in knowledge sharing activities among OSN members. Based on Jasperson, Carter and Zmud's feature-centric view of technology (Jasperson, et al., 2005) and Nahapiet and Ghoshal's three dimensions of social capital factors (Nahapiet & Ghoshal, 1998), we set forth a number of SNS features and explain their links to social capital factors. Then, we reviewed a number of theories to explain the mechanism that links social capital factors to motivational antecedents.

It is summarized in the conceptual framework that several core sets of SNS features can support different social capital factors, which will in turn facilitate motivational antecedents to participate knowledge sharing activities. It is concluded that, with embedded social mechanism, SNS features can strengthen motivations to continued participation in knowledge sharing activities through social capital facilitators. We hope that our ideas stimulate others to more intensive study of this flourishing behavior in SNS platforms.

REFERENCES

Adler, P. S., & Kwon, S.-W. (2002). Social capital: Prospects for a new concept. *Academy of Management Review, 27*(1), 17–40.

Agarwal, R., Sambamurthy, V., & Stair, R. M. (2000). Research report: The evolving relationship between general and specific computer self-efficacy--An empirical assessment. *Information Systems Research, 11*(4), 418. doi:10.1287/isre.11.4.418.11876

Bagozzi, R. P., & Dholakia, U. M. (2002). Intentional social action in virtual communities. *Journal of Interactive Marketing, 16*(2), 2–21. doi:10.1002/dir.10006

Bandura, A. (1989). Social cognitive theory. In Vasta, R. (Ed.), *Annals of child development* (pp. 1–60). Greenwich, CT: Jai Press LTD.

Baumeister, R. F. (1998). The self. In Gilbert, D. T., Fiske, S. R., & Lindzey, G. (Eds.), *The handbook of social psychology* (pp. 680–740). New York, NY: McGraw-Hill.

Berkman, L. F., & Glass, T. (2000). Social integration, social networks, social support, and health. In Berkman, L. F., & Kawachi, I. (Eds.), *Social epidemiology* (pp. 137–173). New York, NY: Oxford University Press.

Bhattacherjee, A. (2001). Understanding information systems continuance: An expectation-confirmation model. *Management Information Systems Quarterly, 25*(3), 351–370. doi:10.2307/3250921

boyd, D., & Ellison, N. (2008). Social network sites: Definition, history, and scholarship. *Journal of Computer-Mediated Communication, 13*(1), 210–230. doi:10.1111/j.1083-6101.2007.00393.x

Centola, D. (2010). The spread of behavior in an online social network experiment. *Science, 329*(5996), 1194. doi:10.1126/science.1185231

Chen, C. J. (2004). The effects of knowledge attribute, alliance characteristics, and absorptive capacity on knowledge transfer performance. *R & D Management, 34*(3), 311–321. doi:10.1111/j.1467-9310.2004.00341.x

Chen, I. Y. L. (2007). The factors influencing members' continuance intentions in professional virtual communities—A longitudinal study. *Journal of Information Science, 33*(4), 451–467. doi:10.1177/0165551506075323

Chiu, C. M., Hsu, M. H., Sun, S. Y., Lin, T. C., & Sun, P. C. (2005). Usability, quality, value and e-learning continuance decisions. *Computers & Education, 45*(4), 399–416. doi:10.1016/j.compedu.2004.06.001

Chiu, C.-M., Hsu, M.-H., & Wang, E. T. G. (2006). Understanding knowledge sharing in virtual communities: An integration of social capital and social cognitive theories. *Decision Support Systems, 42*(3), 1872–1888. doi:10.1016/j.dss.2006.04.001

Culnan, M. J., & Markus, M. L. (1987). Information technologies. In Jablin, F. M., Putnam, L. L., Roberts, K. H., & Porter, L. W. (Eds.), *Handbook of organizational communication: An interdisciplinary perspective* (pp. 420–443). Newbury Park, CA: Sage.

Daft, R. L., & Lengel, R. H. (1986). Organizational information requirements, media richness and structural design. *Management Science, 32*(5), 554–571. doi:10.1287/mnsc.32.5.554

Dholakia, U. M., Bagozzi, R. P., & Pearo, L. K. (2004). A social influence model of consumer participation in network- and small-group-based virtual communities. *International Journal of Research in Marketing, 21*(3), 241–263. doi:10.1016/j.ijresmar.2003.12.004

Donath, J., & Boyd, D. (2004). Public displays of connection. *BT Technology Journal, 22*(4), 71–82. doi:10.1023/B:BTTJ.0000047585.06264.cc

Ellison, N. B., Steinfield, C., & Lampe, C. (2007). The benefits of Facebook 'friends': Social capital and college students' use of online social network sites. *Journal of Computer-Mediated Communication, 12*(4), 1143–1168. doi:10.1111/j.1083-6101.2007.00367.x

Emerson, R. M. (1976). Social exchange theory. *Annual Review of Sociology, 2,* 335–362. doi:10.1146/annurev.so.02.080176.002003

Facebook. (2011). *Company information.* Retrieved from http://newsroom.fb.com/content/default.aspx?NewsAreaId=22

Fischer, G., Scharff, E., & Ye, Y. (2004). Fostering social creativity by increasing social capital. In Huysman, M., & Wulf, V. (Eds.), *Social capital and information technology* (pp. 355–399). Cambridge, MA: MIT Press.

Flanagin, A. J., & Metzger, M. J. (2001). Internet use in the contemporary media environment. *Human Communication Research, 27*(1), 153–181. doi:10.1093/hcr/27.1.153

Fulk, J., Schmitz, J., & Steinfield, C. (1990). A social influence model of technology use. In Fulk, J., & Steinfield, C. (Eds.), *Organizations and communication technology* (pp. 117–142). Newbury Park, CA: Sage.

Gächter, S., & Fehr, E. (1999). Collective action as a social exchange. *Journal of Economic Behavior & Organization, 39*(4), 341–369. doi:10.1016/S0167-2681(99)00045-1

Guo, C., Shim, J., & Otondo, R. (2010). Social network services in China: An integrated model of centrality, trust, and technology acceptance. *Journal of Global Information Technology Management, 13*(2), 76–99.

Hassanein, K., & Head, M. (2006). The impact of infusing social presence in the Web interface: An investigation across product types. *International Journal of Electronic Commerce, 10*(2), 31–55. doi:10.2753/JEC1086-4415100202

Haythornthwaite, C. (2002). Strong, weak, and latent ties and the impact of new media. *The Information Society, 18*(5), 385–401. doi:10.1080/01972240290108195

Haythornthwaite, C. (2005). Social networks and Internet connectivity effects. *Information Communication and Society, 8*(2), 125–147. doi:10.1080/13691180500146185

Hong, S. J., Thong, J. Y. L., & Tam, K. Y. (2006). Understanding continued information technology usage behavior: A comparison of three models in the context of mobile internet. *Decision Support Systems, 42*(3), 1819–1834. doi:10.1016/j.dss.2006.03.009

Hsu, M.-H., Ju, T. L., Yen, C.-H., & Chang, C.-M. (2007). Knowledge sharing behavior in virtual communities: The relationship between trust, self-efficacy, and outcome expectations. *International Journal of Human-Computer Studies, 65*(2), 153–169. doi:10.1016/j.ijhcs.2006.09.003

Huysman, M., & Wulf, V. (2006). IT to support knowledge sharing in communities, towards a social capital analysis. *Journal of Information Technology, 21*(1), 40–51. doi:10.1057/palgrave.jit.2000053

Jasperson, J. S., Carter, P. E., & Zmud, R. W. (2005). A comprehensive conceptualization of post-adoptive behaviors associated with information technology enabled work systems. *Management Information Systems Quarterly, 29*(3), 525–557.

Jones, Q., Ravid, G., & Rafaeli, S. (2004). Information overload and the message dynamics of online interaction spaces: A theoretical model and empirical exploration. *Information Systems Research, 15*(2), 194–210. doi:10.1287/isre.1040.0023

Jung, I. (2001). Building a theoretical framework of web-based instruction in the context of distance education. *British Journal of Educational Technology, 32*(5), 525–534. doi:10.1111/1467-8535.00222

Kim, H.-s., Park, J. Y., & Jin, B. (2008). Dimensions of online community attributes: Examination of online communities hosted by companies in Korea. *International Journal of Retail & Distribution Management, 36*(10), 812–830. doi:10.1108/09590550810901008

Kim, S. S., & Malhotra, N. K. (2005). A longitudinal model of continued IS use: An integrative view of four mechanisms underlying postadoption phenomena. *Management Science, 51*(5), 741–755. doi:10.1287/mnsc.1040.0326

Koh, J., Kim, Y. G., Butler, B., & Bock, G. W. (2007). Encouraging participation in virtual communities. *Communications of the ACM, 50*(2), 69–73. doi:10.1145/1216016.1216023

Koka, B. R., & Prescott, J. E. (2002). Strategic alliances as social capital: A multidimensional view. *Strategic Management Journal, 23*(9), 795–816. doi:10.1002/smj.252

Krumm, J., Davies, N., & Narayanaswami, C. (2008). User-generated content. *IEEE Pervasive Computing / IEEE Computer Society and IEEE Communications Society, 7*(4), 10–11. doi:10.1109/MPRV.2008.85

Lampe, C., Ellison, N., & Steinfield, C. (2006). *A Face (book) in the crowd: Social searching vs. social browsing.* Paper presented at the CSCW-2006, New York.

Lee, J., & Lee, H. (2010). The computer-mediated communication network: exploring the linkage between the online community and social capital. *New Media & Society, 12*(5), 711–727. doi:10.1177/1461444809343568

Lee, M. J. W., & McLoughlin, C. (2009). Social software as tools for pedagogical transformation: Enabling personalization, creative production, and participatory learning. In Lambropoulos, N., & Romero, M. (Eds.), *Educational social software for context-aware learning: Collaborative methods and human interaction* (pp. 1–22). Hershey, PA: Information Science Reference. doi:10.4018/978-1-60566-826-0.ch001

Limayem, M., & Cheung, C. M. K. (2008). Understanding information systems continuance: The case of Internet-based learning technologies. *Information & Management, 45*(4), 227–232. doi:10.1016/j.im.2008.02.005

Limayem, M., Hirt, S. G., & Cheung, C. M. K. (2007). How habit limits the predictive power of intention: The case of information systems continuance. *Management Information Systems Quarterly, 31*(4), 705–737.

Lin, M. J. J., Hung, S. W., & Chen, C. J. (2009). Fostering the determinants of knowledge sharing in professional virtual communities. *Computers in Human Behavior, 25*(4), 929–939. doi:10.1016/j.chb.2009.03.008

Lowry, P. B., Zhang, D., Zhou, L., & Fu, X. (2010). Effects of culture, social presence, and group composition on trust in technology-supported decision-making groups. *Information Systems Journal, 20*(3), 297–315. doi:10.1111/j.1365-2575.2009.00334.x

Ma, M., & Agarwal, R. (2007). Through a glass darkly: Information technology design, identity verification, and knowledge contribution in online communities. *Information Systems Research, 18*(1), 42–67. doi:10.1287/isre.1070.0113

McKenna, K. Y. A., & Bargh, J. A. (1999). Causes and consequences of social interaction on the internet: A conceptual framework. *Media Psychology*, *1*(3), 249–269. doi:10.1207/s1532785xmep0103_4

Miranda, S. M., & Saunders, C. S. (2003). The social construction of meaning: An alternative perspective on information sharing. *Information Systems Research*, *14*, 87–106. doi:10.1287/isre.14.1.87.14765

Mislove, A. (2009). *Online social networks: Measurement, analysis, and applications to distributed information systems*. Doctor of Philosophy PhD Thesis, Rice University, Houston, Texas.

Mitchell, T. R., & Daniels, D. (2003). Motivation. In Borman, W. C., Ilgen, D. R., & Klimoski, R. J. (Eds.), *Handbook of psychology, volume twelve: Industrial and organizational psychology* (*Vol. 12*, pp. 225–254). New York, NY: John Wiley.

Moore, M. G. (1972). Learner autonomy: The second dimension of independent learning. *Convergence*, *5*(2), 76–88.

Moore, M. G., & Kearsley, G. (1996). *Distance education: A systems view*. New York, NY: Wadsworth.

Mu, J., Peng, G., & Love, E. (2008). Interfirm networks, social capital, and knowledge flow. *Journal of Knowledge Management*, *12*(4), 86–100. doi:10.1108/13673270810884273

Nahapiet, J., & Ghoshal, S. (1998). Social capital, intellectual capital, and the organizational advantage. *Academy of Management Review*, *23*(2), 242–266.

Nielsen, B. B. (2005). The role of knowledge embeddedness in the creation of synergies in strategic alliances. *Journal of Business Research*, *58*(9), 1194–1204. doi:10.1016/j.jbusres.2004.05.001

Olaniran, B. A., & Williams, I. M. (2009). Web 2.0 and learning: A closer look at transactional control model in e-learning. In Lambropoulos, N., & Romero, M. (Eds.), *Educational social software for context-aware learning: Collaborative methods and human interaction* (pp. 23–37). Hershey, PA: Information Science Reference. doi:10.4018/978-1-60566-826-0.ch002

Phang, C. W., Kankanhalli, A., & Sabherwal, R. (2009). Usability and sociability in online communities: A comparative study of knowledge seeking and contribution. *Journal of the Association for Information Systems*, *10*(10), 721–747.

Rice, R. E. (1992). Task analyzability, use of new media, and effectiveness: A multi-site exploration of media richness. *Organization Science*, *3*(4), 475–500. doi:10.1287/orsc.3.4.475

Roberts, T. L., Lowry, P. B., & Sweeney, P. D. (2006). An evaluation of the impact of social presence through group size and the use of collaborative software on group member voice in face-to-face and computer-mediated task groups. *IEEE Transactions on Professional Communication*, *49*(1), 28–43. doi:10.1109/TPC.2006.870460

Ruggiero, T. E. (2001). Uses and gratifications theory in the 21st century. *Mass Communication & Society*, *3*(1), 3–37. doi:10.1207/S15327825MCS0301_02

Short, J., Williams, E., & Christie, B. (1976). *The social psychology of telecommunications*. Toronto, Canada: Wiley.

Smedlund, A. (2008). The knowledge system of a firm: Social capital for explicit, tacit and potential knowledge. *Journal of Knowledge Management*, *12*(1), 63–77. doi:10.1108/13673270810852395

Sohn, D., & Leckenby, J. D. (2007). A structural solution to communication dilemmas in a virtual community. *The Journal of Communication*, *57*(3), 435–449. doi:10.1111/j.1460-2466.2007.00351.x

Stafford, T. F., Stafford, M. R., & Schkade, L. L. (2004). Determining uses and gratifications for the Internet. *Decision Sciences, 35*(2), 259–288. doi:10.1111/j.00117315.2004.02524.x

Tian, W., & Tan, F. B. (2009). *Guanxi, social capital and knowledge exchange: A cross-dimensional view*. Paper presented at the the 6th International Conference on Knowledge Management, Hong Kong, China.

Tseng, F.-C., & Kuo, F.-Y. (2010). The way we share and learn: An exploratory study of the self-regulatory mechanisms in the professional online learning community. *Computers in Human Behavior, 26*(5), 1043–1053. doi:10.1016/j.chb.2010.03.005

Vovides, Y., Sanchez-Alonso, S., Mitropoulou, V., & Nickmans, G. (2007). The use of e-learning course management systems to support learning strategies and to improve self-regulated learning. *Educational Research Review, 2*(1), 64–74. doi:10.1016/j.edurev.2007.02.004

Wang, J. C., & Chiang, M. J. (2009). Social interaction and continuance intention in online auctions: A social capital perspective. *Decision Support Systems, 47*(4), 466–476. doi:10.1016/j.dss.2009.04.013

Wasko, M. M., & Faraj, S. (2000). "It is what one does": Why people participate and help others in electronic communities of practice. *The Journal of Strategic Information Systems, 9*(2-3), 155–173. doi:10.1016/S0963-8687(00)00045-7

Wasko, M. M., & Faraj, S. (2005). Why should I share? Examining social capital and knowledge contribution in electronic networks of practice. *MIS Quarterly: Management Information Systems, 29*(1), 35–57.

Waterman, A. S. (2004). Finding someone to be: Studies on the role of intrinsic motivation in identity formation. *Identity: An International Journal of Theory and Research, 4*(3), 209–228. doi:10.1207/s1532706xid0403_1

Waterson, P. (2006). Motivation in online communities. In Dasgupta, S. (Ed.), *Encyclopedia of virtual communties* (pp. 334–337). Hershey, PA: Idea Group. doi:10.4018/978-1-59140-563-4.ch062

Wenger, E. (1998). *Communities of practice*. New York, NY: Cambridge University Press.

Wenger, E., McDermott, R. A., & Snyder, W. (2002). *Cultivating communities of practice: A guide to managing knowledge*. Boston, MA: Harvard Business Press.

Xiao, B., & Benbasat, I. (2007). E-commerce product recommendation agents: Use, characteristics, and impact. *Management Information Systems Quarterly, 31*(1), 137–209.

Yimam-Seid, D., & Kobsa, A. (2003). Expert-finding systems for organizations: Problem and domain analysis and the DEMOIR approach. *Journal of Organizational Computing and Electronic Commerce, 13*(1), 1–24. doi:10.1207/S15327744JOCE1301_1

Chapter 15
The Continued Use of a Virtual Community:
An Information Adoption Perspective

Xiao-Ling Jin
Shanghai University, China

Matthew K.O. Lee
City University of Hong Kong, Hong Kong

Christy M.K. Cheung
Hong Kong Baptist University, Hong Kong

Zhongyun (Phil) Zhou
Tongji University, China

ABSTRACT

With the advent of the Internet, so too came several new means by which people share and acquire information. One such method is the use of virtual communities. Virtual communities are steadily becoming a valuable resource for today's organizations. However, a large number of virtual communities fail because their members withdraw from using them. Motivated by this concern, this study investigates the factors which motivate individuals to continue using a virtual community for information adoption. The proposed model integrates the IS continuance model with the information adoption model and is validated through an online survey of 240 users of a Bulletin Board System established by a local university in China. The results reveal that continuance intention within a virtual community is primarily determined by user satisfaction with prior usage, as well as by perceived information usefulness. The results also suggest that a long-term sustainable virtual community should be provided with high-quality and credible information. The findings of this study contribute to both theory building in virtual community continuance and practice in virtual community management.

DOI: 10.4018/978-1-4666-0312-7.ch015

1. INTRODUCTION

Due to the low cost, bidirectionality, and lack of temporal and physical constraints, virtual communities are becoming unprecedentedly popular for both organizations and individuals. Virtual communities, also known as online communities, are computer-mediated spaces where a group of people generate content and share such content among themselves (Hagel & Armstrong, 1997). In this definition, *computer-mediated space* and *member-generated content* are considered to be the two key elements of a virtual community. *Computer-mediated space* implies that the activity is taking place in cyberspace, helping virtual communities overcome time and space constraints (Rheingold, 1993; Wellman & Gulia, 1999; Preece, 2001). This creates new opportunities for users to discuss ideas, share knowledge and extend social networks. *Member-generated content* denotes that the words and ideas in a virtual community are all generated in discussions conducted by its members (Rheingold, 1993; Hagel & Armstrong, 1997; Preece 2001; Lee et al. 2003). These two elements emphasize the unique nature of purposeful social interaction in cyberspace and distinguish virtual communities from other online information services and offline communities.

A successful virtual community can and do provide valuable benefits for both business and organizations. On the one hand, a sustainable virtual customer community (e.g., eBay, Amazon) can decrease the cost of customer retention and customer service, increase product sales and overall consumer satisfaction, and make a brand stronger (Banks & Daus, 2002; Wenger et al., 2002). On the other hand, an employee community of practice (e.g., IBM employee community) can not only facilitate knowledge flow between geographically dispersed coworkers within organizations (Constant et al., 1996), but can also help employees gain access to external knowledge resources cross organizational boundaries (Wasko & Faraj, 2005). These benefits are generated from community size and volume of communication activity (Butler, 2001). Despite the benefits of participating in virtual communities, a lot of virtual communities fail to retain their members and foster members' long-term participation (Sangwan, 2005). Discerning how to establish a sustainable virtual community is still an appealing objective for both researchers and practitioners (Sangwan, 2005; Ma, 2005).

A significant amount of work has been done to investigate the factors which attract members to use virtual communities for information (or knowledge) sharing and adoption (e.g., Jarvenpaa & Staples, 2000; Wasko et al., 2004; Wasko & Faraj, 2005; Sussman & Siegal, 2003; Zhang & Watts, 2003). Although attracting new members is the first step toward realizing virtual community success, the long-term sustainability of a virtual community depends on the extent to which it maintains its existing members. Butler (2001) claimed that *"the efforts to attract new members are likely to be wasted if these social structures fail to maintain the membership necessary to provide valuable benefits over a longer term"* (p. 347). To fill this research gap, this study investigates the antecedents of user intention to continue using virtual communities. A virtual community is useless if it is not being used for information adoption, regardless of content generation. For this reason, this study investigates specifically the continuance intention to use virtual communities for the purpose of information adoption.

The remainder of the paper is structured as follows. The next section describes the IS continuance model and the information adoption model. Based on this theoretical background, the third section discusses the research model and hypotheses. The research design, data analysis and results, are then presented in the fourth and the fifth sections respectively. Finally, this paper concludes by reflecting on the key findings, theoretical and practical implications, and areas of further research.

2. THEORETICAL BACKGROUND

With the increasing popularity of virtual communities, research on them has become more and more important. In order to understand the sustainability of virtual communities in general, and user intention to continue using virtual communities for information adoption in particular, we provide a review on the literature of information system continuance and information adoption.

2.1 Information Systems Continuance

The long-term sustainability of an information system (IS) depends on its sustained use rather than initial adoption (Venkatesh & Davis, 2000; Bhattacherjee, 2001; Kim & Malhotra, 2005). Several longitudinal studies have been conducted to understand the IS post-adoption phenomena by investigating users' psychological states at different IS adoption stages (e.g., Karahanna et al., 1999; Venkatesh & Davis, 2000). They used the same model, i.e., the same variables, to explain both acceptance and continuance. Although continuance and acceptance are correlative, users have different psychological beliefs and motivations in different adoption stages based on their first-hand experience with initial usage (Bhattacherjee, 2001; Limayem et al., 2003; Jasperson et al., 2005). These studies are otherwise impossible to explain the "acceptance-discontinuance anomaly"—people withdraw after initial adoption (Bhattacherjee, 2001).

Bhattacherjee (2001) assumed that IS users' continuance decision is similar to consumers' repurchase decision. Like repurchase decision, IS continuance decision has three steps: (1) users first accept a new IS; (2) they evaluate the outcomes of initial usage; (3) they make a decision to continue or withdraw the usage of that IS based on their first-time experiences. Building upon this assumption, Bhattacherjee (2001) extended the expectation confirmation theory (Oliver, 1980)

to the new context of IS continuance and developed a theory of IS continuance. The objective of the IS continuance model is to understand the factors that motivate users to continue using an IS after initial adoption. It goes beyond prior IS adoption models to include users' post-adoption psychological motivations (e.g., satisfaction and confirmation) (see Figure 1). This IS continuance model was empirically validated by a field survey of online banking users. The results indicated that user satisfaction with prior IS use was the strongest predictor of continuance intention. Post-adoption expectation–perceived information usefulness had a significant but weaker effect on IS continuance intention. Satisfaction and perceived usefulness were in turn affected by expectation-performance discrepancy (i.e., disconfirmation).

2.2 Information Adoption Model

Sussman and Siegal (2003) proposed and empirically examined a theoretical model of information adoption to explain how people are influenced to adopt the information posted in computer-mediated communication (CMC) contexts. This model is adapted from the elaboration likelihood model (ELM) which is a dual-process model of informational influence (Petty & Cacioppo, 1986). ELM posits that a message can influence people's attitudes and behaviors through two routes: central route and peripheral route. The former refers to the nature of augments in the message while the later refers to issues or themes that are not directly related to the subject matter of the message (Petty & Cacioppo, 1986). When adapted to the CMC contexts, the information adoption model has two key propositions. First, the information adoption model considers augment quality (information quality) as the central route and source credibility as the peripheral route (Sussman & Siegal, 2003). Augment quality (information quality) is identified as the extent to which users think that information is relevant, timely, accurate, and complete (Lee et al., 2002). It reflects the features of the content

Figure 1. IS continuance model (Bhattacherjee, 2001)

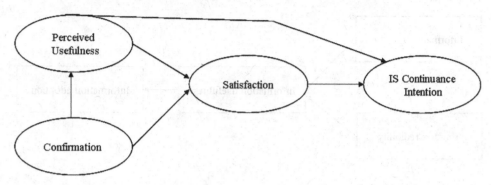

contained in a message. Source credibility captures the extent to which users think that they can trust a piece of information or that the information is contributed by an expert (Rieh, 2002). It offers the heuristic information evaluation and reflects the characteristics of the informational source. The importance of information quality and source credibility has also been highlighted and strongly validated in prior research on information seeking (e.g., Rieh, 2002; Zhang & Watts, 2003; Davy, 2006; Xu et al., 2006; Hong, 2006; Sundar et al., 2007). Second, information usefulness, the key construct in adoption theories, is more strongly related to information adoption than information quality and source credibility. Information usefulness, therefore, mediates the relationship between these two aspects of informational routes and information adoption. Figure 2 presents the information adoption model.

3. RESEARCH MODEL AND HYPOTHESES

This study attempts to explain the motivations of continued use of virtual communities by information users. Building upon Bhattacherjee's IS continuance model (2001) and the information adoption model (Sussman & Siegal, 2003), a research model is developed in the context of Internet bulletin board-based communities (see

Figure 3). Research hypotheses are discussed in this section.

3.1 Behavioral Intention of Continued Use of a Virtual Community for Information Adoption

Information adoption is a process in which people purposefully engage in using information. Information adoption behavior is one of the principle activities that users want to conduct in virtual communities. For example, people read the opinions and comments posted by others before they make a buying decision (Pitta & Fowler, 2005). Similarly, they solicit a virtual community for help by posting questions when they have some problems (Sussman & Siegal, 2003). According to the "China Internet Community User Development Report 2006" (iResearch, 2006), 70% of community users in China rated "Content" as the most important factor for an attractive virtual community. The specific cognitive beliefs of information adoption behavior in virtual communities are, therefore, essential to investigating virtual community continuance. Continuance intention to use a virtual community for information adoption is regarded as an individual's subjective likelihood of continuing to perform information adoption behavior in a virtual community. Prior research (e.g., Davis et al., 1989; Taylor & Todd, 1995) has found that intention is strongly related to behavior.

Figure 2. The information adoption model (Sussman & Siegal, 2003)

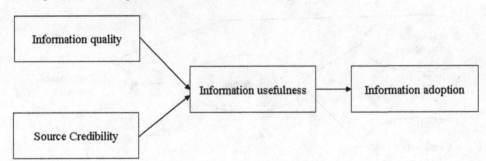

Figure 3. Research model of continuance intention to use a virtual community for information adoption

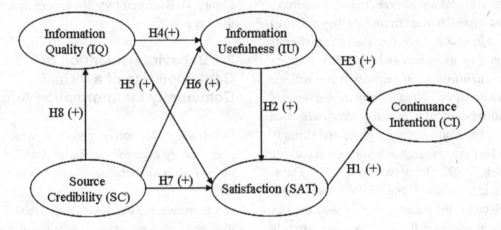

3.2 User Satisfaction

In the IS continuance model, user satisfaction with prior IS use is the primary predictor of continuance intention (Bhattacherjee, 2001). Several continuance studies provided empirical support for this proposition as well. Tiwana and Bush (2005) found that user satisfaction was the most salient determinant of continuance intention to use expertise-sharing networks. Hsu et al. (2004) also found that the more an individual user was satisfied with prior use, the higher probable that he would continue to use the World Wide Web. In the context of virtual communities, user satisfaction with a virtual community is regarded as an emotional affect toward the outcome of using a virtual community. It is found to be the surrogate of frequency and the duration of users' participation in virtual communities (Langerak et al., 2003). Consistent with these studies, we infer that users' level of satisfaction with prior use of a virtual community has a strong and positive impact on their intention to continue using the virtual community for information adoption. Therefore:

H1: User satisfaction with prior use of a virtual community has a positive impact on continuance intention to use the virtual community for the sake of information adoption.

3.3 Perceived Information Usefulness

The technology acceptance model posits that perceived usefulness and perceived ease of use are two significant beliefs influencing IS initial adoption intention (Davis et al., 1989; Adams et al., 1992). However, building upon past empirical research, Bhattacherjee (2001) argued that *"usefulness impacts attitude substantively and consistently during stages of IS use"* (p. 356), while *"ease of use has an inconsistent effect on attitude in the initial stages, which seems to further subside and become non-significant in later stages"* (p. 356). Accordingly, only ex post perceived usefulness is adopted as the post-adoption belief of IS continuance (Bhattacherjee, 2001). As for information adopters in the virtual community, perceived information usefulness captures the same meaning of perceived usefulness (Sussman & Siegal, 2003). Information usefulness refers to the degree to which the information is perceived to be valuable, informative and helpful (Sussman & Siegal, 2003). A great amount of empirical evidence indicates that perceived (information) usefulness is positively associated with user satisfaction (e.g., Bhattacherjee, 2001; Limayem et al., 2003) and IS continuance intention (e.g., Karahanna et al., 1999; Bhattacherjee, 2001; Limayem et al., 2003; Kim & Malhotra, 2005). In accordance with these observations, we posit that the more useful a user perceives the information posted in the virtual community, the more satisfied he will be with the virtual community and, simultaneously, the more likely that he will continue to use that virtual community for information adoption. Therefore:

H2: Perceived information usefulness has a positive impact on user satisfaction with the virtual community use.

H3: Perceived information usefulness has a positive impact on continuance intention to use the virtual community for the sake of information adoption.

3.4 Perceived Information Quality

Drawn from the IS success model (DeLone & McLean, 1992; DeLone & McLean, 2003), information quality has a significant effect on IS use and user satisfaction. Information quality captures the characteristics (e.g., timeliness, completeness and correctness) of the content contained in the information per se. Prior research showed that web information quality has a significant relationship with customer satisfaction (McKinney et al., 2002) and information usefulness (Sussman & Siegal, 2003). Out-dated, irrelevant, incomplete or inaccurate information will cause users to lose their confidence in the usefulness of the virtual community, become unsatisfied with their usage experiences, and thereby withdraw from using the virtual community. Consistent with these observations, information quality is expected to positively affect information usefulness and user satisfaction. Therefore:

H4: Perceived information quality has a positive impact on perceived information usefulness.

H5: Perceived information quality has a positive impact on user satisfaction with the virtual community use.

3.5 Perceived Source Credibility

Source credibility refers to the recipient's perceptions of the trustworthiness and expertise of the information provider (Dholakia & Sternthal, 1977; Grewal et al., 1994). Information provided by high credible sources is perceived to be useful and reliable, thereby facilitates knowledge transfer (Ko et al., 2005). By analogy, in the context of virtual communities, participants tend to consider the information useful and credible when they perceive the source is trustworthy and from experts (Sussman & Siegal, 2003), much like the way in which readers consider the news published in authorized newspapers to be valuable and convincing (Donath, 1999). Source credibility has been validated to have a significant impact on satisfaction as well. For instance, Albright and Levy (1995) conducted an experiment to investigate the effect of source credibility on recipients' reactions and found that the more credible of the source, the more favorable of the recipient's reactions. Therefore:

H6: Perceived source credibility has a positive impact on perceived information usefulness.

H7: Perceived source credibility has a positive impact on user satisfaction with the virtual community use.

Furthermore, source cue is the heuristic judgment of information quality (Rieh et al., 1998). For example, consumers often use source credibility to judge the quality of health information in the Internet (Bates et al., 2006). That means information from identified trustworthy experts will be perceived to be of high quality in the context of virtual communities. Therefore:

H8: Source credibility has a positive impact on perceived information quality.

4. RESEARCH DESIGN

Virtual communities can be established technically through various computer-mediated communication media such as Listservs, online chat rooms, bulletin board systems (BBSes), newsgroups, instant messaging and Weblogs (Lazar & Preece, 1998; Ridings et al., 2002). In this study, we focus on virtual communities that are built on Web-based BBSes, one of the most common Web-based communication media. A Web-based BBS provides an asynchronous, interactive, text-based virtual environment for chatting, learning, trading, playing games, meeting peers, and performing other social and functional activities (Pena-Shaff & Nicholls, 2004). It typically consists of multiple sub-forums of distinct topics managed by mod-

erators and administrators. In each sub-forum, messages are listed in chronological order grouped by topic threads (Pena-Shaff & Nicholls, 2004; James et al., 1995). Registered members of a BBS, distinguished by unique usernames, usually have additional privileges to start new topic threads, to edit their previous posts and to personalize their individual settings and profiles accessible to other users. Attached to each message is the member's information, including the username, a graphical representation, the membership level and the number of points earned. The latter two are determined by the quantity, and sometimes the quality as well, of the messages the member has posted.

This study aims at investigating users' intention to continue using Web-based BBSes for the sake of information adoption. Data collection was conducted in China for its large growing population of BBS users. Based on the statistics by China Internet Network Information Center, there were 26.5 million Internet users in 2001 and 9.0% of them used BBSes (CNNIC, 2001). The figures jumped to 123 million and 43.2% respectively five years later (CNNIC, 2006). These figures mean that Web-based BBSes have become extraordinarily popular in China, making it an ideal site for data collection.

4.1 Data Collection

We posted an invitation message with the hyperlink to a self-administered online English questionnaire in three of the most popular sub-forums of a Web-based BBS owned by a local university in mainland China. Everyone, either inside or outside the campus, can browse the BBS anonymously, but pre-registration is needed to obtain the privilege to post messages on the BBS.

Our choice of using an online survey rather than traditional paper-based survey was motivated by three considerations. First, online survey has little missing data (Boyer et al., 2002). Second, the data entry of online survey is more accurate

Table 1. Demographics of respondents

Demographics		Number	Percentage
Gender	Male	185	22.9%
	Female	55	77.1%
Age	<21	29	12.1%
	21-25	172	71.7%
	>25	39	16.2%
Education Level	High school certificate or less	11	4.6%
	Vocational/Technical school	2	0.8%
	Undergraduate degree	90	37.5%
	Postgraduate or higher degree	137	57.1%
Experience with virtual community (BBS)	More than 3 years	191	79.6%
	Less than 3 years	49	20.4%

and takes less time due to automated data entry (Boyer et al., 2002; Parasuraman & Zinkhan, 2002). Third, data collected by online survey has largely comparable reliability, validity and quality compared with those collected by print survey (Boyer et al., 2002).

To encourage participation in the online survey, incentives of USB memory drives were offered as lucky draw prizes among respondents. A preventive measure was taken to avoid repetitive completion of the questionnaire from the same respondents by rejecting two pieces of data with the same IP address. The response rate was 18.1% (240 reponses/1327 views) according to the method suggested by Tiwana and Bush (2005) for measuring online response rate. This response rate is Among these respondents, 77.1% were male and 22.9% were female (see Table 1). This ratio is similar to the ratio of male and female students in the university. A majority of the respondents were aged between 21 and 25 and had a bachelor degree or above. They were also frequent and experienced users of the BBS. Around 80% of them visited the BBS everyday and the average usage experience with the BBS was more than three years. Statistical tests show that there is no significant difference between the

respondents of the messages posted in the three respective sub-forums of the Web-based BBS.

4.2 Measurement Development

The constructs in the research model were all measured by using multiple-item scales adopted from previous studies with minor modifications to ensure contextual consistency. The scale items used seven-point semantic differential scales. Items that had low loadings on the corresponding construct were eliminated to enhance reliability. Table 2 shows the measures of all the constructs and their sources.

5. DATA ANALYSIS AND RESULTS

Data analysis was performed using Partial Least Squares (PLS), a structural equation modeling technique that has become widely accepted in recent years due to its accuracy and utility. PLS allows researchers to simultaneously analyze both how well the measures relate to each construct and how the independent variables influence the dependent variables. Moreover, PLS does not require a normal distribution of the data and is applicable to small samples (Chin, 1998), mak-

Table 2. Constructs and sources

Construct	List of Items	Sources
Continuance Intention (CI)	The degree to which I intend to continue using this BBS in the next few weeks for the sake of information adoption is CI1: very unlikely/ very likely. CI2: strongly unlikely/ strongly likely.	(Bagozzi & Dholakia, 2002)
BBS-User Satisfaction (SAT)	My overall experience of using this BBS is SAT1: very dissatisfied/ very satisfied. SAT2: very displeased/ very pleased. SAT3: very frustrated/ very contented. SAT4: absolutely terrible/ absolutely delighted.	(Bhattacherjee, 2001)
Information Usefulness (IU)	Based on my experience of using this BBS, the messages posted in this BBS are IU1: invaluable/ valuable. IU2: uninformative/ informative. IU3: harmful/ helpful.	(Sussman & Siegal, 2003)
Information Quality (IQ)	Based on my experience of using this BBS, the quality of information provided in this BBS is IQ1: useless/ useful. IQ2: irrelevant/ relevant. IQ3: inappropriate/ appropriate. IQ4: inapplicable/ applicable. IQ5: out-date/ current. IQ6: insufficiently timely/ sufficiently timely. IQ7: insufficiently out-of-date/ sufficiently out-of-date. IQ8: inaccurate/ accurate. IQ9: incorrect/ correct. IQ10: unreliable/ reliable. IQ11: incomplete/complete. IQ12: The information in this BBS sufficiently satisfies my needs. (disagree/ agree) IQ13: The information provided in this BBS includes all necessary values. (disagree/ agree) IQ14: The information provided in this BBS covers my need. (disagree/ agree) IQ15: The information provided in this BBS has sufficient breadth and depth. (disagree/ agree)	(Lee et al., 2002)
Source Credibility (SC)	Based on my experience of using this BBS, people who post messages in this BBS are SC1: not very knowledgeable/ very knowledgeable. SC2: not expert/ expert. SC3: not trustworthy/ trustworthy. SC4: not reliable/ reliable.	(Sussman & Siegal, 2003)
Note: The scale of each item is (-3, +3).		

ing it the most appropriate data analysis tool for this study.

5.1 Assessment of the Measurement Model

Convergent validity, which indicates the extent to which the items of a scale that are theoretically related to each other relate to each other in reality, was verified by examining the internal consistency reliability (ICR) and the average variance extracted (AVE). Acceptable values of ICR and AVE should be greater than 0.70 and 0.50 respectively (Fornell & Larcker, 1981). As Table 3 shows, all ICR and AVE values of the items meet the recommended threshold and almost the entire factor loadings are more than 0.70 except one item of Information Quality (i.e., IQ15).

Discriminant validity measures whether a given construct is different from other constructs. It was assessed by one criterion: the square root of AVE for each construct should exceed the cor-

Table 3. Psychometric properties of measures

	Item Loading	Means	Standard Error	t-statistics
Information Quality (IQ)			CR = 0.96, AVE = 0.62	
IQ1	0.81	1.38	0.03	31.60
IQ2	0.81	1.35	0.03	28.48
IQ3	0.85	1.31	0.02	37.63
IQ4	0.84	1.27	0.02	33.41
IQ5	0.80	1.37	0.04	21.92
IQ6	0.79	1.20	0.04	17.57
IQ7	0.83	1.14	0.03	26.56
IQ8	0.80	1.19	0.03	22.98
IQ9	0.83	1.25	0.03	30.13
IQ10	0.80	1.32	0.04	23.72
IQ11	0.78	0.97	0.04	22.57
IQ12	0.73	0.80	0.04	18.82
IQ13	0.70	0.60	0.04	16.32
IQ14	0.72	0.62	0.03	18.54
IQ15	0.65	0.57	0.04	15.52
Source Credibility (SC)			CR = 0.91, AVE = 0.72	
SC1	0.84	0.88	0.03	33.17
SC2	0.83	0.75	0.02	34.85
SC3	0.87	1.05	0.02	46.71
SC4	0.87	1.02	0.02	46.86
Information Usefulness (IU)			CR = 0.92, AVE = 0.80	
IU1	0.90	1.00	0.02	56.28
IU2	0.90	1.09	0.02	45.77
IU3	0.88	1.04	0.02	38.30
User Satisfaction (SAT)			CR= 0.92, AVE = 0.75	
SAT1	0.87	0.67	0.02	41.91
SAT2	0.88	0.90	0.02	38.96
SAT3	0.85	0.74	0.03	26.75
SAT4	0.86	0.77	0.03	27.68
Continuance Intention (CI)			CR = 0.97, AVE = 0.94	
CI1	0.97	1.70	0.01	156.00
CI2	0.97	1.67	0.01	176.32
Note: CR - Composite Reliability, AVE - Average Variance Extracted				

Table 4. Correlation matrix and psychometric properties of key constructs

	AVE	IQ	SC	IU	SAT	CI
IQ	0.62	**0.79**				
SC	0.72	0.76	**0.85**			
IU	0.80	0.72	0.72	**0.89**		
SAT	0.75	0.42	0.48	0.48	**0.87**	
CI	0.94	0.44	0.45	0.45	0.60	**0.97**

Notes: Bolded diagonal elements are the square root of AVE for each construct
Off-diagonal elements are the correlations between constructs.

relations between this construct and other constructs (Fornell & Larcker, 1981). It is shown in Table 4 that the square root of AVE for each construct exceeds the correlations between the constructs and all other constructs (i.e., the off-diagonal elements in the corresponding rows and columns), demonstrating adequate discriminant validity of all the constructs.

5.2 Assessment of the Structural Model

The examination of the structural model involves estimating the path coefficients, which represent the strengths of the relationships between the dependent and independent variables, and the R-square values, which stand for the amount of variance in dependent variables explained by their antecedents. Together, the R-square values and the path coefficients (including the loadings and the significance levels) demonstrate how well the data validated the research model. Figure 4 presents the results of the PLS structural model assessment with the overall explanatory power, the estimated path coefficients (all significant paths are indicated with an asterisk), and the associated t-values of the paths. Tests of significance of all paths were performed using the bootstrap resampling procedure.

As shown in Figure 4, 40% of the variance in continuance intention was explained by satisfac-

tion and information usefulness (β=0.50, p<0.001 and β=0.21, p<0.01 respectively), providing support to Hypotheses 1 and 3. Satisfaction, in turn, was predicted by information usefulness (β = 0.29, p<0.05) and source credibility (β = 0.26, p<0.05), providing support to Hypotheses 2 and 7 respectively. Surprisingly, information quality had no significant influence on satisfaction. As a whole, 27% of the variance in user satisfaction with virtual community usage was explained. Information usefulness was significantly explained by both information quality (β = 0.41, p<0.001) and source credibility (β = 0.42, p<0.001). These two factors explained nearly 60% of the variance in information usefulness. Finally, 58% of variance in information quality was explained by source credibility (β = 0.76, p<0.001), i.e., Hypothesis 8 was supported.

6. DISCUSSION

This study empirically examined a theoretical model to explain and predict continuance intention to use a virtual community for information adoption. In this section, we will first discuss the findings, and we will then address the implications for research and practice.

Figure 4. PLS results of the research model

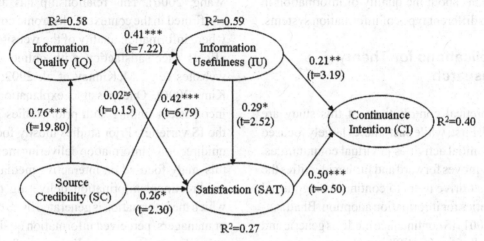

*p<0.05 **p<0.01 ***p<0.001 ns: nonsignificant

6.1 Key Findings

The results show that the measurement model was validated with adequate levels of convergent and discriminant validities. The results also provide sufficient support to the research model. A major finding of this research is that continuance intention to use virtual communities (e.g., Web-based BBSes) is primarily determined by satisfaction and secondarily determined by perceived information usefulness. This finding is consistent with prior studies of IS continuance (e.g., Bhattacherjee, 2001; Hsu et al., 2004; Tiwana & Bush, 2005; Kim & Malhotra, 2005). Since actual behaviour is strongly predicted by intention (Davis et al., 1989; Taylor & Todd, 1995), satisfaction and perceived information usefulness are anticipated as the important predictors of actual continuance behaviour in virtual communities. In addition, source credibility has a significant impact on information quality, meaning that users often use source credibility to judge the quality of the messages posted in virtual communities. Furthermore, information quality and source credibility have

indirect effects on information adopters' intention to continue using virtual communities mediated by information usefulness or satisfaction. This finding suggests that both the features of content and resource are critical to the sustainability of virtual communities.

Finally, contrary to the findings of prior IS studies (e.g., DeLone & McLean, 1992; McKinney et al., 2002; Park & Kim, 2006), the results show that there is no significant relationship between information quality and user satisfaction. This inconsistency may be due to the fact that the information system investigated in this research is fundamentally different from those in previous studies. Past research mostly focused on information delivering information systems which are unidirectional, e.g., company Web Site. The information in such kind of information systems is generated by IS operators or managers. This study, however, focused on interactive media which are bidirectional, e.g., Web-based BBSes. The content in this kind of information systems is generated by their users. Users may have different expectations about the quality of information in these two different types of information systems.

6.2 Implications for Theory and Research

The theoretical contributions of this study are threefold. First, while past studies largely focused on users' initial activities in virtual communities, this study moves forward and further identifies the factors that drive users to continue using virtual communities for information adoption. Bhattacherjee's (2001) IS continuance model is generic and does not distinguish different purposes of using IS. It needs to be integrated with other theories to understand continued use of virtual communities for special purposes, e.g., information adoption. This theoretical structure expands the boundary of Bhattacherjee's (2001) IS continuance model and thus serves as an example for future attempts to integrate theories for investigating IS continuance intention for various purposes.

Second, satisfaction is the primary predictor of users' continuance intention to use a virtual community for information adoption. Satisfaction is also claimed to be the key explanation of "acceptance-discontinuance anomaly" (withdrawal after initial adoption) (Bhattacherjee, 2001). This means that information adopters will discontinue using a virtual community mostly because they are dissatisfied with their first-hand experience, even though they may consider the information posted in the virtual community to be useful. This finding suggests that satisfaction should be paid great attention to in future research on the long-time success of virtual communities.

Third, information quality was found to have no significant impact on user satisfaction. This finding is inconsistent with that of the end-user computing satisfaction literature in which the relationship between information quality and user satisfaction is very well established (e.g., DeLone & McLean, 2003; Iivari, 2005; Wu &

Wang, 2006). This relationship has also been confirmed in the context of electronic commerce, where information quality of the website content affects user satisfaction with online shopping websites (e.g., McKinney et al. 2002; Park & Kim, 2006). One possible explanation of this inconsistent finding with prior studies is due to the IS varieties. Prior studies mostly focused on unidirectional information delivering media while this study focused on interactive media. For the unidirectional information delivering media in which the information is generated by IS operators or managers, perceived information quality plays a significant role in evaluating the performance of IS use. Accordingly, the higher information quality is perceived, the more satisfied users will be. For interactive media, the content is generated by users during the process of communication. The quality of such member-generated content is difficult to evaluate. Perceived information quality plays a small role in evaluating the performance of IS use. Another possible explanation of this inconsistent finding with prior studies lies in the characteristics of the system users. In the web-based virtual community, members mostly use the virtual community with a specific purpose, which is to look for useful information. They expect to get something that is directly useful for them to make decision. In addition, this type of web-based virtual community normally comprises of members of strangers. To some extent, users have lower expectation on the quality of information generated by other users. When they come to the decision to continue to adopt the information, the usefulness of the information, as well as the credibility of the source will play a more important role to determine both user satisfaction and continuance intention. Future studies should continue to explore this issue with the specific focus on the nature of the virtual communities used by the public against functional information systems used in organizations. Hence, the relationship between information quality and user satisfaction varies given the nature of information systems and the characteristics of system users.

6.3 Implications for Practice

A sustained virtual community can bring important values for organizations and transactions. The proposed virtual community continuance model describes a concrete set of factors that may help providers and managers of virtual communities to retain their members.

User satisfaction remains as the most important factor in determining user intention to continue using the virtual community for information adoption. It serves as an important measure for virtual community sustainability, and thus community managers should closely monitor changes in user satisfaction levels by conducting some user satisfaction surveys.

Practitioners of virtual communities should also address the issue of information usefulness which has a significant impact on both user satisfaction and user continuance intention. For example, community designers can provide a rating system for members to review and rate other people's posted messages regarding the messages' usefulness. This rating mechanism is similar to those used in popular Internet websites such as Amazon.com, where users are able to review and rate the usefulness of the comments in the customer review sections. This mechanism can also motivate users to contribute useful information and help information adopters find useful information.

A long-term sustainable virtual community should offer high-quality and credible information. Community managers should build in incentive mechanisms to motivate members to contribute high-quality content, such as raising their membership level or providing points to contributors of high value message with which they can exchange for accessibility to other valuable messages. For example, "Baidu Zhidao" (http://zhidao.baidu.com/), a famous knowledge-based virtual community in China, uses extrinsic rewards (e.g., gifts) to encourage users to contribute high quality content. In addition, community managers should also enhance the perception of the credibility of the message contributed by members by offering a recognition mechanism, in which the information providers can get recognition for the expertise reflected in their contribution to the virtual community. Finally, to enhance the credibility of a virtual community, virtual community administrators can irregularly invite reputable experts to post a series of messages in that virtual community.

6.4 Limitations and Suggestions for Future Research

This study has several empirical and theoretical limitations, which call for additional research. First, since the questionnaire was posted on a web-based BBS, most respondents had been using the BBS for years and intended to continue using it. The responses from the continuers may be biased in contrast to discontinuers. Hence, a longitudinal study of the new users should be conducted in future research. Second, we selected only one particular virtual community (a Web-based BBS established by a local university in China) as our research site. The research results are somehow affected by the nature of the BBS and the background of the respondents. Future research examining different kinds of virtual communities and comparing the results will help to enhance the generalization of our research model. Third, from the results of our study, only 40% of the variance of users' continuance intention to use the Internet BBS was explained by information usefulness and user satisfaction. There must be other predictors of virtual community continuance intention that were unexplored in this study. Some related social factors (e.g., social identity, group norm, etc.) may be useful in explaining intention to continue using virtual communities (Bagozzi

& Dholakia, 2002; Dholakia et al., 2004). Future research should take the social factors into account. Lastly, our study just examined the motivations for information adopters' continued usage of virtual communities. Future research studying the factors motivating information contributors to continue using virtual communities is anticipated to help us realize another aspect of virtual community continuance.

CONCLUSION

The goal of this study was to explore the antecedents of continued use of virtual communities. By integrating the IS continuance model with the information adoption model, the research model particularly explained users' intention to continue using virtual communities for information adoption. Data collected from an online survey among BBS users provide empirical support for the research model and the hypotheses. This study increases our understanding of the factors predicting users' continuance intention to select a virtual community as a channel of information adoption. Future research should continue to enrich this line of research by extending the investigation in other types of Internet-based media that support virtual communities in different cultures, and examining the diverse motivations for continued use of virtual communities by different kinds of users (including both information adopters and contributors).

ACKNOWLEDGMENT

The authors acknowledge with gratitude the generous support of the Hong Kong Baptist University for the project (HKBU 240609).

REFERENCES

Adams, D. A., Nelson, R. R., & Todd, P. A. (1992). Perceived usefulness, ease of use, and usage of information: A replication. *Management Information Systems Quarterly*, *16*, 227–247. doi:10.2307/249577

Albright, M. D., & Levy, P. E. (1995). The effects of source credibility and performance rating discrepancy on reactions to multiple raters. *Journal of Applied Social Psychology*, *25*, 577–600. doi:10.1111/j.1559-1816.1995.tb01600.x

Bagozzi, R. P., & Dholakia, U. M. (2002). Intentional social action in virtual communities. *Journal of Interactive Marketing*, *16*, 2–21. doi:10.1002/dir.10006

Banks, D., & Daus, K. (2002). *Customer community: Unleashing the power of your customer base*. San Francisco, CA: Jossey-Bass.

Bates, B. R., Romina, S., Ahmed, R., & Hopson, D. (2006). The effect of source credibility on consumers' perceptions of the quality of health information on the Internet. *Medical Informatics and the Internet in Medicine*, *31*, 45–52. doi:10.1080/14639230600552601

Bhattacherjee, A. (2001). Understanding information systems continuance: An expectation-confirmation model. *Management Information Systems Quarterly, 25*, 351–370. doi:10.2307/3250921

Boyer, K. K., Olson, J. R., Calantone, R. J., & Jackson, E. C. (2002). Print versus electronic surveys: A comparison of two data collection methodologies. *Journal of Operations Management, 20*, 357–373. doi:10.1016/S0272-6963(02)00004-9

Butler, B. (2001). Membership size, communication activity, and sustainability: A resource-based model of online social structures. *Information Systems Research, 12*, 346–362. doi:10.1287/isre.12.4.346.9703

Chin, W. W. (1998). The partial least squares approach to structural equation modeling. In Marcoulides, G. (Ed.), *Modern methods for business research* (pp. 295–336). Mahwah, NJ: Lawrence Erlbaum Associates.

China Internet Network Information Center (CNNIC). (2001). *The 8th Statistical Survey Report on the Internet Development in China.* July 2001. Retrieved from http://j2j.cn/download/2003/10/10/171539.pdf

China Internet Network Information Center (CNNIC). (2006). The 17th Statistical Survey Report on the Internet Development in China, January 2006. Retrieved from http://www.cnnic.org.cn/images/2006/download/2006011701.pdf

Constant, D., Sproull, L., & Kiesler, S. (1996). The kindness of strangers: The usefulness of electronic weak ties for technical advice. *Organization Science, 7*, 119–135. doi:10.1287/orsc.7.2.119

Davis, F. D., Bagozzi, R. P., & Warshaw, P. R. (1989). User acceptance of computer technology: A comparison of two theoretical models. *Management Science, 35*, 982–1003. doi:10.1287/mnsc.35.8.982

Davy, C. (2006). Recipients: The key to information transfer. *Knowledge Management Research & Practice, 4*, 17–25. doi:10.1057/palgrave.kmrp.8500081

DeLone, W. H., & McLean, E. R. (1992). Information systems success: The quest for the dependent variable. *Information Systems Research, 3*, 60–95. doi:10.1287/isre.3.1.60

DeLone, W. H., & McLean, E. R. (2003). The DeLone and McLean model of information systems success: A ten-year update. *Journal of Management Information Systems, 19*, 9–30.

Dholakia, R., & Sternthal, B. (1977). Highly credible sources: Persuasive facilitators or persuasive liabilities? *The Journal of Consumer Research, 3*, 223–232. doi:10.1086/208671

Dholakia, U. M., Bagozzi, R. P., & Pearo, L. K. (2004). A social influence model of consumer participation in network- and small-group-based virtual communities. *Journal of Research in Marketing, 21*, 241–263. doi:10.1016/j.ijresmar.2003.12.004

Donath, J. S. (1999). Identity and deception in the virtual community. In Smith, M. A., & Kollock, P. (Eds.), *Communities in cyberspace* (pp. 29–59). New York, NY: Routledge.

Fornell, C., & Larcker, D. F. (1981). Evaluating structural equation models with unobservable variables and measurement error. *JMR, Journal of Marketing Research, 18*, 39–50. doi:10.2307/3151312

Grewal, D., Goflieb, J., & Marmorstein, H. (1994). The moderating effects of message framing and source credibility on the price-perceived risk relationship. *The Journal of Consumer Research, 21*, 145–153. doi:10.1086/209388

Hagel, J., & Armstrong, A. G. (1997). *Net gain: Expanding markets through virtual communities.* Boston, MA: Harvard Business School Press.

Hong, T. (2006). The influence of structural and message features on Web Site credibility. *Journal of the American Society for Information Science and Technology, 57*, 114–127. doi:10.1002/asi.20258

Hsu, M. H., Chiu, C. M., & Ju, T. L. (2004). Determinants of continued use of the WWW: An integration of two theoretical models. *Industrial Management & Data Systems, 104*, 766–775. doi:10.1108/02635570410567757

Iivari, J. (2005). An empirical test of the DeLone-McLean model of information system success. *The Data Base for Advances in Information Systems, 36*, 8–27. doi:10.1145/1066149.1066152

iResearch. (2006). *China internet community user development report 2006*. Retrieved from http://www.iresearch.com.cn

James, M. C., Wotring, E., & Forrest, E. J. (1995). An exploratory study of the perceived benefits of electronic bulletin board use and their impact on other communication activities. *Journal of Broadcasting & Electronic Media, 39*, 30–50. doi:10.1080/08838159509364287

Jarvenpaa, S. L., & Staples, D. S. (2000). The use of collaborative electronic media for information sharing: An exploratory study of determinants. *The Journal of Strategic Information Systems, 9*, 129–154. doi:10.1016/S0963-8687(00)00042-1

Jasperson, J., Carter, P., & Zmud, R. (2005). A comprehensive conceptualization of post-adoptive behaviors associated with IT enabled work systems. *Management Information Systems Quarterly, 29*, 525–557.

Karahanna, E., Straub, D. W., & Chervany, N. L. (1999). Information technology adoption across time: A cross-sectional comparison of pre-adoption and post-adoption beliefs. *Management Information Systems Quarterly, 23*, 183–213. doi:10.2307/249751

Kim, S. S., & Malhotra, N. K. (2005). A longitudinal model of continued is use: an integrative view of four mechanisms underlying post-adoption phenomena. *Management Science, 51*, 741–755. doi:10.1287/mnsc.1040.0326

Ko, D. G., Kirsch, L. J., & King, W. R. (2005). Antecedents of knowledge transfer from consultants to clients in enterprise system implementations. *Management Information Systems Quarterly, 29*, 59–85.

Langerak, F., Verhoef, P. C., Verlegh, P. W. J., & de Valck, K. (2003). *The effect of members' satisfaction with a virtual community on member participation*. ERIM Report Series Research in Management, Reference No. ERS-2003-004-MKT, Erasmus Research Institute of Management, Erasmus University Rotterdam.

Lazar, J., & Preece, J. (1998). Classification schema for online communities. *Proceedings of the Americas Conference on Information Systems 1998* (pp. 84-86). Association for Information Systems.

Lee, F. S. L., Vogel, D., & Limayem, M. (2003). Virtual community informatics: A review and research agenda. *Journal of Information Technology Theory and Application, 5*, 47–61.

Lee, Y., Strong, D., Kahn, B., & Wang, R. (2002). AIMQ: A methodology for information quality assessment. *Information & Management, 40*, 133–146. doi:10.1016/S0378-7206(02)00043-5

Limayem, M., Cheung, C. M. K., & Chan, G. W. W. (2003). Explaining information systems adoption and post-adoption: Toward an integrative model. *Twenty-Fourth International Conference on Information Systems* (pp. 720-731).

Ma, M. (2005). *IT design for sustaining virtual communities: An identity-based approach*. Dissertation, Decision of Information Technologies Department, University of Maryland, Maryland.

McKinney, V., Yoon, K., & Zahedi, F. M. (2002). The measurement of web-customer satisfaction: An expectation and disconfirmation approach. *Information Systems Research, 13*, 296–315. doi:10.1287/isre.13.3.296.76

Oliver, R. L. (1980). A cognitive model for the antecedents and consequences of satisfaction. *JMR, Journal of Marketing Research, 17*, 460–469. doi:10.2307/3150499

Parasuraman, A., & Zinkhan, G. M. (2002). Marketing to and serving customers through the Internet: An overview and research agenda. *Journal of the Academy of Marketing Science, 30*, 286–295. doi:10.1177/009207002236906

Park, C.-H., & Kim, Y.-G. (2006). The effect of information satisfaction and relational benefit on consumers' online shopping site commitments. *Journal of Electronic Commerce in Organizations, 4*, 70–90. doi:10.4018/jeco.2006010105

Pena-Shaff, J. B., & Nicholls, C. (2004). Analyzing student interactions and meaning construction in computer bulletin board discussions. *Computers & Education, 42*, 243–265. doi:10.1016/j.compedu.2003.08.003

Petty, R. E., & Cacioppo, J. T. (1986). *Communication and persuasion: Central and peripheral routes to attitude change*. New York, NY: Springer-Verlag.

Pitta, D. A., & Fowler, D. (2005). Internet community forums: An untapped resource for consumer marketers. *Journal of Consumer Marketing, 22*, 265–274. doi:10.1108/07363760510611699

Preece, J. (2001). Sociability and usability in online communities: Determining and measuring success. *Behaviour & Information Technology, 20*, 347–356. doi:10.1080/01449290110084683

Rheingold, H. (1993). *The virtual community: Homsteading on the electronic frontier*. Reading, MA: Addison-Wesley.

Ridings, C. M., Gefen, D., & Arinze, B. (2002). Some antecedents and effects of trust in virtual communities. *The Journal of Strategic Information Systems, 11*, 271–295. doi:10.1016/S0963-8687(02)00021-5

Rieh, S. Y. (2002). Judgment of information quality and cognitive authority in the Web. *Journal of the American Society for Information Science and Technology, 53*, 145–161. doi:10.1002/asi.10017

Rieh, S. Y., & Belkin, N. J. (1998). Understanding judgment of information quality and cognitive authority in the WWW. *Proceedings of the 61st Annual Meeting of the American Society for Information Science* Vol. 35 (pp. 279-289). Retrieved from http://www.si.umich.edu/rieh/papers/asis98.pdf

Sangwan, S. (2005) Virtual community success: A uses and gratifications perspective. *Proceedings of the 38th Hawaii International Conference on System Sciences*. Los Alamitos, CA: IEEE Press.

Sundar, S. S., Knobloch-Westerwick, S., & Hastall, M. R. (2007). News cues: Information scent and cognitive heuristics. *Journal of the American Society for Information Technology, 58*, 366–378. doi:10.1002/asi.20511

Sussman, S. W., & Siegal, W. S. (2003). Informational influence in organizations: An integrated approach to knowledge adoption. *Information Systems Research, 14*, 47–65. doi:10.1287/isre.14.1.47.14767

Taylor, S., & Todd, P. A. (1995). Understanding information technology usage: A test of competing models. *Information Systems Research, 6*, 144–176. doi:10.1287/isre.6.2.144

Tiwana, A., & Bush, A. A. (2005). Continuance in expertise-sharing networks: A social perspective. *IEEE Transactions on Engineering Management, 52*, 85–101. doi:10.1109/TEM.2004.839956

Venkatesh, V., & Davis, F. D. (2000). A theoretical extension of the technology acceptance model: Four longitudinal field studies. *Management Science, 46*, 186–204. doi:10.1287/mnsc.46.2.186.11926

Wasko, M. M., & Faraj, S. (2005). Why should I share? Examining social capital and knowledge contribution in electronic networks of practice. *Management Information Systems Quarterly, 29*, 35–57.

Wasko, M. M., Faraj, S., & Teigland, R. (2004). Collective action and knowledge contribution in electronic networks of practice. *Journal of the Association for Information Systems, 5*, 493–513.

Wellman, B., & Gulia, M. (1999). *Net*-surfers don't ride alone: Virtual communities as communities. In Wellman, B. (Ed.), *Networks in the global village* (pp. 331–366). Boulder, CO: Westview Press.

Wenger, E., McDermott, R., & Snyder, W. M. (2002). *Cultivating communities of practice: A guild to managing knowledge*. Boston, MA: Harvard Business School Press.

Wu, J.-H., & Wang, Y.-M. (2006). Measuring KMS success: A respecification of the DeLone and McLean's model. *Information & Management, 43*, 728–739. doi:10.1016/j.im.2006.05.002

Xu, Y., Tan, C. Y., & Yang, L. (2006). Who will you ask? An empirical study of interpersonal task information seeking. *Journal of the American Society for Information Science and Technology, 57*, 1666–1677. doi:10.1002/asi.20339

Zhang, W., & Watts, S. (2003). Knowledge adoption in online communities of practice. *2003 Twenty-Fourth International Conference on Information Systems* (pp. 96-109).

KEY TERMS AND DEFINITIONS

Behavioral Intention of Continued Use of a Virtual Community: An individual's subjective likelihood of continuing to use a virtual community.

Information Adoption: A process in which people purposefully engage in using information.

Information Quality: The characteristics (e.g., timeliness, completeness and correctness) of the content contained in the information per se.

Information Usefulness: The degree to which the information is perceived to be valuable, informative and helpful.

Satisfaction: An emotional affect toward the outcome of using a virtual community.

Source Credibility: The recipient's perceptions of the trustworthiness and expertise of the information provider.

Virtual Communities: Computer-mediated spaces where a group of people generate content and share such content among themselves.

Chapter 16
Mining Student Participatory Behavior in Virtual Learning Communities

Constanta-Nicoleta Bodea
Academy of Economic Studies, Romania

Vasile Bodea
Academy of Economic Studies, Romania

Ion Gh. Roşca
Academy of Economic Studies, Romania

Radu Ioan Mogos
Academy of Economic Studies, Romania

Maria-Iuliana Dascalu
Politehnica University of Bucharest, Romania

ABSTRACT

The aim of this chapter is to explore the application of data mining for analyzing participatory behavior of the students enrolled in an online two-year Master degree programme in Project Management. The main data sources were the operational database with the students' records and the log files and statistics provided by the e-learning platform. 129 enrolled students and more than 195 distinct characteristics/ variables per student were used. Due to the large number of variables, an exploratory data analysis through data mining is decided, and a model-based discovery approach was designed and executed in Weka environment. The association rules, clustering, and classification were applied in order to describe the participatory behavior of the students, as well as to identify the factors explaining the students' behavior, and the relationship between academic performance and behavior in the virtual learning environment. The results are very encouraging and suggest several future developments.

DOI: 10.4018/978-1-4666-0312-7.ch016

INTRODUCTION

Educational Data Mining (EDM) is a discipline, concerned with "developing methods for exploring the unique types of data that come from educational settings, and using those methods to better understand students and the settings which they learn in" (International Working Group on Educational Data Mining, 2010). (Romero & Ventura, 2007) present the main findings of an educational data mining survey covering the period 1995-2005. (Baker & Yacef, 2009) made another survey covering the latest data mining approach in education domain. Both surveys show that the number of data mining applications in education is constantly increasing, and they cover a lot of educational processes such as: enrollment management, academic performance, web-based education, retention. Many case studies on data mining techniques in education are cited in the literature (Luan, 2002), (Ma & al, 2000), (Barros & Verdejo, 2000), (Ranjan & Malik, 2007). These case studies aim at predictions of student performance, mainly through cluster analysis to identify relevant types of students. Using data mining, it is possible to discover students' behavior pattern and the relationship between behavior pattern and student performance.

(Baker & Yacef, 2009) comment an important EDM methods category, named "discovery with models". Such methods are relying on models previously developed through any process which are used as components of data mining analysis. "Discovery with models has become an increasingly popular method in EDM research, supporting sophisticated analyses such as how different type of student behavior impact students' learning in different ways (Cocea et al, 2009) and how variations in intelligent tutor design impact students' behavior over time (Jeong & Biswas, 2008)".

Students' behavior in the virtual environment is a complex topic, too difficult to be address only based on an unstructured exploratory analysis, as it is done in data mining. A model-driven discovery process has the potential to reveal unusual behavioral profiles or unexpected relationships between different characteristics and the behavior pattern in a more structured way, reducing the complexity and making the process more manageable. In this chapter, the authors considered Unified Theory of Acceptance and Use of Technology (UTAUT) as the model to be used for structuring the EDM process.

The UTAUT model (Venkatesh et al, 2003) integrates different theoretical frameworks and variables that influence the behavioral intention of technology adoption and use. The four constructs that were considered as direct determinants of user acceptance and usage behavior are the following: performance expectancy, effort expectancy, social influence and facilitating conditions. The *performance expectancy* represents the degree to which an individual believes that using the technology will help him/her in performance gains. The *effort expectancy* is the level of simplicity associated with the use of the system. The *social influence* is defined as the extent in which an individual perceives that important others believe that he/she should use the system. And finally, the *facilitating conditions* reflect the degree to which an individual believes that an organizational and technical infrastructure exists to support the use of the system. The UTAUT model incorporates also moderator variables such as age, gender, prior experience and voluntariness of the technology use.

UTAUT was already used to discover the factors that influence medical teachers' acceptance of information and communication technology (ICT) integration in the classroom (Birch & Ervine, 2009), to investigate the determinants of mobile Internet acceptance and to find out the extent to which students used and accepted M-Learning as an education delivery method (Williams, 2009).

Table 1. AES education & training portfolio for 2009-2010

AES Education &Training Programs	Total Number	Online Programs
Bachelor's degree in Economics	13	0
Continuing education (Trainings)	75	16
Scientific Master's degree	29	0
Professional Master's degree	56	10
International Master's degree	9	0
Doctor's degree	10	0
Total	**192**	**26**

THE RESEARCH CONTEXT

The Academy of Economic Studies (AES) is a national university. The education and training programs are delivered based on a public budget, coming from the Education and Research Ministry, and also on its own resources. It also has freedom and autonomy according the law. AES is considered a remarkable representative of superior economic studies in Romania. The university has 10 faculties, over 49.000 students and course attendants; 35500 - graduation cycle, 9400 - master programs, 2500 - PhD enrolled, over 1600 in academic schools and post-graduation courses and 2000 didactical staff and technical and administrative personnel. In 2009-2010, AES has delivered more than 192 education & training programs, 26 delivered as online programs (see Table 1).

AES delivers 26 online programmes, ten of them being master degree programmes, with more than 5000 enrolled students. The *Computerized Project Management programme*, known as MIP, is one of the online master degree programme delivered by AES. In 2009-2010, 181 students were enrolled in MIP, 52 students in the first year and 129 in the second year.

The main characteristics of the students enrolled in the MIP programme, class 2010 as shown in Figure 1 are the following:

- **Age:** Most of the students were below 30 years old (18% of them were between 22-24, 36% were between 25-26, 25% were between 27-30 and just 21% were above 31 years old);
- **Practical Experience in Project Management:** 63% had no experience in project management, 33% were junior (between 1 and 4 years of experience, just 4% of them were seniors (over 4 years of working in project management);
- **Previous Graduated Programme:** According this characteristics, the student collectivity is highly heterogeneous. The students graduated bachelor degree programme in engineering, economics, business, science etc.
- **Experience in Others Online Trainings/ Courses:** Just 15% of them were engaged in previous online trainings or courses, and 86% of them did not experienced this kind of activities;
- **Their Field of Activity:** Most of the students come from IT (70%), others come from telecommunications, banking, research, education, commercial, logistics, financial consulting, constructions; the most common jobs among our students are: software developer, IT analyst, business analyst, consultant, engineer, researcher, team leader, project manager.

Figure 1. The main students' characteristics

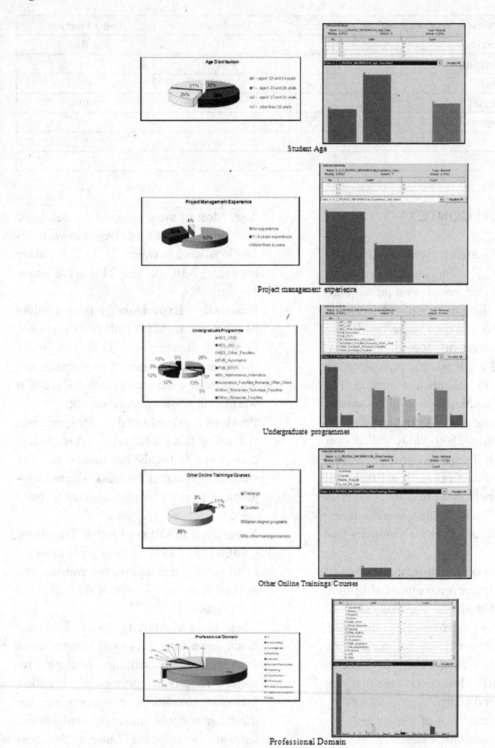

Student Age

Project management experience

Undergraduate programmes

Other Online Trainings/Courses

Professional Domain

Several e-learning platforms are used in the AES, but Moodle is preferred for the majority of online programmes. Moodle (http://moodle.org/) is a Course Management System (CMS), also known as a Learning Management System (LMS) or a Virtual Learning Environment (VLE). Figure 2 presents some of the MIP learning contexts, defined in Moodle. As we can see, the virtual learning environment has the following two distinct areas:

- **Teaching Area**: Organized for each modules in two sections; the course and the laboratory/seminar section.
- **Administrative Area**: Including the organizational forums, calendars, participant profiles, log files and visual reports on participants' activities.

The lessons are organized by week, in individual folders. Every week, the lesson is centered on one topic and reading materials are published by the teacher. Homework is assigned every week. Quizzes are scheduled at fixed dates. In order to do the homework and to prepare the quizzes and final exam, the students read the didactic materials and could ask questions to teacher and colleagues on the course and seminar forums. Teachers could answer and ask additional questions for clarifying the discussed issues. The students should upload the homework results in the didactic area, dedicated to this kind of materials. The virtual communication is organized on threads, naming a communication topic. The teachers and the students could initiate new threads. Initiating a thread means that the participant is making proposals to other participants and is taking initiative in the communication process. The final exam should be taken by every student in a campus room, as a classic examination.

In the administrative area, general materials, such as regulation, guidelines etc. are available. Events calendar is regularly updated, in order to indicate the active module, the quizzes and exam dates, the schedule of the face-to-face meetings. The students could read these materials, asking question to teacher or colleagues or answering questions. In the administrative area, the virtual communication is organized on threads, naming a communication topic. Both teachers and students could initiate new threads in the administrative area.

Types of Actions Defining the Participatory Behavior in the Virtual Learning Environment

The following types of actions, defining the student participatory behavior in the virtual environment were considered for the first year:

- Reading materials in the teaching area, the course X section, the first year, the first semester;
- Reading materials in the teaching area, the course Y section, the first year, the second semester;
- Reading materials in the teaching area, the seminar X section, the first year, the first semester;
- Reading materials in the teaching area, the seminar Y section, the first year, the second semester;
- Reading materials in the administrative area, the forum section, the first year, the first semester;
- Reading materials in the administrative area, the forum section, the first year, the second semester;
- Reading materials in the administrative area, the participant section, the first year, the first semester;
- Reading materials in the administrative area, the participant section, the first year, the second semester;
- Upload materials in the teaching area, the course X section, the first year, the first semester;

Figure 2. The Moodle platform used on the MIP program

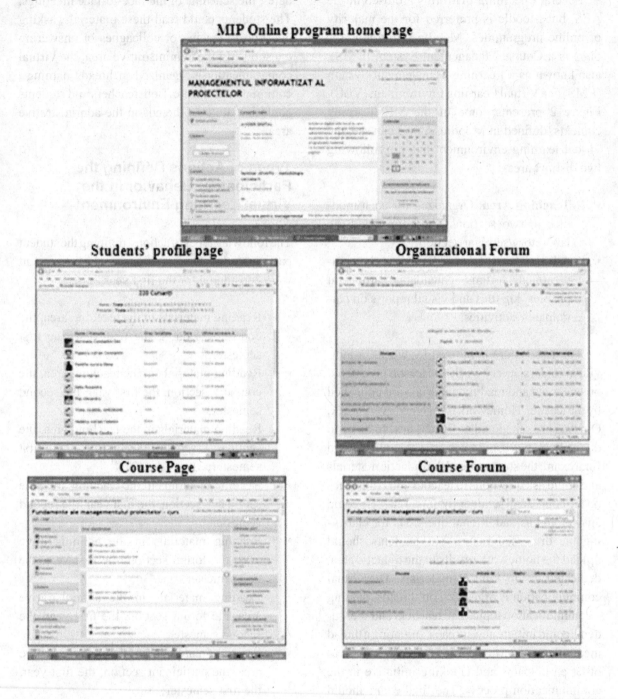

- Upload materials in the teaching area, the course Y section, the first year, the second semester;
- Upload materials in the teaching area, the seminar X section, the first year, the first semester;
- Upload materials in the teaching area, the seminar Y section, the first year, the second semester;
- Upload materials in the administrative area, the forum section, the first year, the first semester;
- Upload materials in the administrative area, the forum section, the first year, the second semester;
- Ask teacher in the teaching area, the course X section, the first year, the first semester;
- Ask teacher in the teaching area, the course Y section, the first year, the second semester;
- Ask teacher in the teaching area, the seminar X section, the first year, the first semester;
- Ask teacher in the teaching area, the seminar Y section, the first year, the second semester;
- Ask colleagues in the teaching area, the course X section, the first year, the first semester;
- Ask colleagues in the teaching area, the course Y section, the first year, the second semester;
- Ask colleagues in the teaching area, the seminar X section, the first year, the first semester;
- Ask colleagues in the teaching area, the seminar Y section, the first year, the second semester;
- Ask teacher in the administrative area, the forum section, the first year, the first semester;
- Ask teacher in the administrative area, the forum section, the first year, the second semester;
- Ask colleagues in the administrative area, the forum section, the first year, the first semester;
- Ask colleagues in the administrative area, the forum section, the first year, the second semester.
- Answer to teacher in the teaching area, the course Y section, the first year, the second semester;
- Answer to teacher in the teaching area, the seminar X section, the first year, the first semester;
- Answer to teacher in the teaching area, the seminar Y section, the first year, the second semester;
- Answer to colleagues in the teaching area, the course X section, the first year, the first semester;
- Answer to colleagues in the teaching area, the course Y section, the first year, the second semester;
- Answer to colleagues in the teaching area, the seminar X section, the first year, the first semester;
- Answer to colleagues in the teaching area, the seminar Y section, the first year, the second semester;
- Answer to teacher in the administrative area, the forum section, the first year, the first semester;
- Answer to teacher in the administrative area, the forum section, the first year, the second semester;
- Answer to colleagues in the administrative area, the forum section, the first year, the first semester;
- Answer to colleagues in the administrative area, the forum section, the first year, the second semester
- Propose to teacher in the teaching area, the course Y section, the first year, the second semester;

Figure 3. The participatory behavior of the students enrolled in the MIP programme, the class 2010

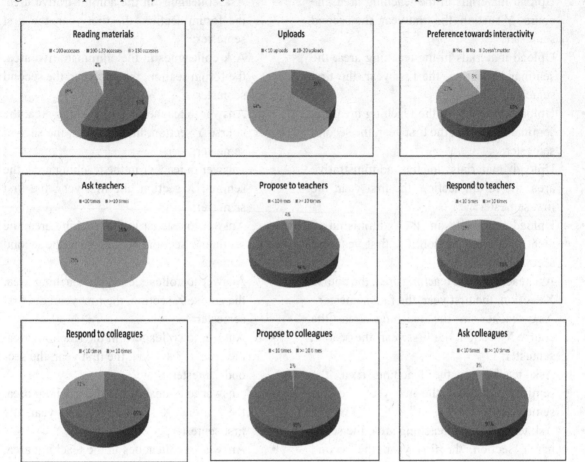

- Propose to teacher in the teaching area, the seminar X section, the first year, the first semester;
- Propose to teacher in the teaching area, the seminar Y section, the first year, the second semester;
- Propose to colleagues in the teaching area, the course X section, the first year, the first semester;
- Propose to colleagues in the teaching area, the course Y section, the first year, the second semester;
- Propose to colleagues in the teaching area, the seminar X section, the first year, the first semester;

- Propose to colleagues in the teaching area, the seminar Y section, the first year, the second semester;
- Propose to teacher in the administrative area, the forum section, the first year, the first semester;
- Propose to teacher in the administrative area, the forum section, the first year, the second semester;
- Propose to colleagues in the administrative area, the forum section, the first year, the first semester;
- Propose to colleagues in the administrative area, the forum section, the first year, the second semester

Figure 4. The correlation between the activities with colleagues and activities with teachers

Dependent Variable: ACTIVITIES_WITH_COLLEAGUES				
Sample: 1 129				
Included observations: 129				
Variable	Coefficient	Std. Error	t-Statistic	Prob.
ACTIVITIES_WITH_TEACHERS	0.723584	0.037289	19.40455	0.0000
C	-3.956399	0.951461	-4.158234	0.0000
R-squared	0.677789	Mean dependent var		12.60221
Adjusted R-squared	0.675989	S.D. dependent var		9.946345
S.E. of regression	5.661655	Akaike info criterion		6.316298
Sum squared resid	5737.727	Schwarz criterion		6.351640
Log likelihood	-569.6250	F-statistic		376.5366
Durbin-Watson stat	1.532010	Prob(F-statistic)		0.000000

The same types of actions are considered for the second year. The Figure 3 presents the main information about the participatory behavior of the students enrolled in the MIP programme, the class 2010, during the second year.

As one can see from the graphics, the favourite types of actions in the e-learning environment are:

- Reading materials: 57% from the students read the materials between 1 and 100 times, 39% do this type of actions between 100 and 130 times and the rest do it more than 130 times;
- Uploading materials: 36% make less than 10 uploads and the rest between 10 and 20 uploads, in the whole learning programme; of course the number of uploads increases as the students progress with theis studies;
- Ask and respond to teachers: 75% of the students ask the teachers more than 10 times, but just 19% of them respond to the teachers' request more than 10 times;
- Propose to teachers: just 4% of the stundents make more than 10 proposals during the entire master; the rest of them limit to less than 10 proposals;

- Ask and respond to colleagues' requests: just 3% of the students ask the colleagues more than 10 times, the rest ask them less than 10 times; 31% of them answer the colleagues more than 10 times, to the online students have a collaborative attitude;
- Propose to colleagues: just 1% make more than 10 proposals; most of them make no proposals

According to R square (Figure 4), the activities with colleagues depend very much on the ones with the teachers: meaning, they are explained in 67% by the ones with the teachers.

The main reasons for choosing an e-learning programme are the interest towards the domain (49%) and professionally improving (46%). A few of the respondents said that they considered the training to be useful (3%) and the programme to be more accessible than a traditional one (2%). These reasons dictate also the behavior in online environments. 65% of the students prefer interactive activities and just 27% of them said they didn't like interactivity. After analyzing the correlation between the teaching participation, the administrative access and resources uploading, on one hand and grades, as a performance measure,

Figure 5. The correlation between the teaching participation, the administrative participation, resources uploading, and grades

Dependent Variable: GRADES
Method: Least Squares
Sample: 1 129
Included observations: 129

Variable	Coefficient	Std. Error	t-Statistic	Prob.
TEACHING	0.001291	0.001316		
ADMIN_ACCESS	-0.0011	0.001147	0.980929	0.328
RESOURCES	0.001324	0.001375	-0.95817	0.3393
C	7.504581	0.102791	0.963371	0.3367
			73.00813	0
R-squared	0.009714			

on the other hand, we noticed that there is no connection for the first year of study (Figure 5). R square has a very low value (0.009), so the statistic model is not trusTable.

After analyzing the influence of the same independent variables (forums, platform access and resources access) on the grades obtained on the second year, we notice a stronger correlation.

RESEARCH QUESTIONS AND METHODOLOGY

The research objective is to identify the main participatory behavior patterns of the students in virtual learning environment. The research questions are:

- Are there specific participatory behavior patterns for students during the first and second year of the programme?
- Which are the similarities/differences between the student participatory behavior during the first and the second year of the programme?

- Which are the most relevant attributes explaining the participatory behavior of students (in the first and the second year) and what are the main relationships between these attributes?
- Are there relevant relationships between participatory behavior and behavioral intention, external factors and moderator variables?
- Are there relevant relationships between participatory behavior and the academic performance?

In virtual learning environment, the student participatory behavior is too difficult to be analyzed using the statistics approach (too many attributes related to the student behavior). Also, the multiple interdependencies between behavioral characteristics make the unstructured exploratory analysis, as it is done by data mining very difficult to be validated. Only a model-driven discovery process has the potential to reveal unusual behavioral profiles or unexpected relationships between different characteristics and the behavior pattern in a more structured way, reducing the complexity and making the process more manageable.

Figure 6. The model used in the exploratory data analysis

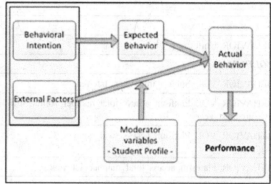

a) The UTAUT Model

b) The research model

In this chapter, the authors considered Unified Theory of Acceptance and Use of Technology (UTAUT) as the model to be used for structuring the EDM process. General UTAUT and the UTAUT adapted model for this research (named as the research model) are presented in Figure 6.

The participatory behavior (named in the research model as the actual behavior) is defined based on student activities in the virtual learning space. The following criteria for the activities differentiation are used:

- The platform area where the student is acting (administrative or teaching area);
- The type of activity performed by the student (reading materials, uploading materials, answering questions, asking questions or making proposals);
- The activity partner (teacher or colleague)

Tables 2 and 3(a) present the summary of the behavior characteristics defined as numeric and nominal attributes. The values of these indicators were calculated using the log files and the statistics offered by the e-learning platform (Figure 9).

The construct and the indicators of the behavior intention, external factors and student profile are defined based on a **survey** performed in February 2010. The survey was designed to collect

students' opinions about the MIP online programme, in general, and specifically, regarding the e-learning platform, the educational resources available online, the communication with trainers, the assessment, the practical approach of different disciplines.

The questionnaire was developed in order to collect a large amount of interesting information. The questionnaire is structured into five main parts:

- Questions regarding organization aspects and technical platform;
- Trainee's needs (motivation to participate into an online education programme);
- Trainee's commitment towards the project management educational programme;
- Syllabus and expectations from training providers;
- Trainers' involvement;

Both open and multiple-choice questions were addressed. The questionnaire was given to the students in the second year. The data included in filled questionnaires was processed and recorded in an excel database, for further analysis (Figure 8). Tables 3(b), 4, 5, 6 and 7 include the summary of the questionnaire items related to the behavioral intention, external factors and student profile.

Table 2. The constructs and indicators of the first year participatory behavior (actual behavior) defined as numeric attributes

UNIFORMITY	
BEHAVIOR_Uniformity_Class_1st_Year	The uniformity of the platform access in the first year
VOLUME	
BEHAVIOR_VOL_Subject_initiatives_1st_Year	The number of the subject initiatives
BEHAVIOR_VOL_Platform_access_total_number_Administrative_area_1st_year	The total access number in the administrative area in the first year
BEHAVIOR_VOL_Platform_access_total_number_Teaching_area_1st_year	The total access number in the teaching area in the first year
BEHAVIOR_Platform_access_total_number_1st_year	The total access number in the first year
ACTIVITY TYPE: READ	
BEHAVIOR_READ_Platform_Administrative_Action_Type_Reading_Materials_I	The total access number in administrative area in the first year for reading the administrative materials.
BEHAVIOR_READ_Platform_Teaching_Action_Type_Reading_Materials_TOTAL_I	The total access number in teaching area in the first year for reading the educational materials.
ACTIVITY TYPE: UPLOAD	
BEHAVIOR_UPLOAD_Platform_Administrative _Action_Type_Uploading_Materials_I	The total access number in administrative area in the first year for uploading administrative materials.
BEHAVIOR_UPLOAD_Platform_Teaching _Action_Type_Uploading_Materials_TOTAL_I	The total access number in teaching area in the first year for uploading projects.
ACTIVITY TYPE: ASK	
BEHAVIOR_ASK_Platform_Administrative _Action_Type_Ask_Teachers_I	The total access number in administrative area in the first year for asking teacher administrative questions.
BEHAVIOR_ASK_Platform_Administrative _Action_Type_Ask_Colleagues_I	The total access number in administrative area in the first year for asking colleagues administrative questions.
BEHAVIOR_ASK_Platform_Teaching_Action_Type_Ask_Teachers_TOTAL_I	The total access number in teaching area in the first year for asking teachers didactic-related questions.
BEHAVIOR_ASK_Platform_Teaching_Action_Type_Ask_Colleagues_TOTAL_I	The total access number in teaching area in the first year for asking colleagues didactic-related questions.
ACTIVITY TYPE: ANSWER	
BEHAVIOR_ANSWER_Platform_Administrative _Action_Type_Responde_Teachers_I	The total access number in administrative area in the first year for answering to the teachers' administrative questions.
BEHAVIOR_ANSWER_Platform_Administrative _Action_Type_Responde_Colleagues_I	The total access number in administrative area in the first year for answering to the colleagues' administrative questions.
BEHAVIOR_ANSWER_Platform_Teaching_Action_Type_Responde_Teachers_TOTAL_I	The total access number in teaching area in the first year for answering to the teachers' questions.
BEHAVIOR_ANSWER_Platform_Teaching_Action_Type_Responde_Colleagues_TOTAL_I	The total access number in teaching area in the first year for answering to the colleagues' questions.
ACTIVITY TYPE: PROPOSE	
BEHAVIOR_PROPOSE_Platform_Administrative _Action_Type_Proposal_Teachers_I	The total access number in administrative area in the first year for making a proposal to teachers.
BEHAVIOR_PROPOSE_Platform_Administrative _Action_Type_Proposal_Colleagues_I	The total access number in administrative area in the first year for making a proposal to colleagues.
BEHAVIOR_PROPOSE_Platform_Teaching_Action_Type_Proposal_Teachers_TOTAL_I	The total access number in teaching area in the first year for making a proposal to teachers.
BEHAVIOR_PROPOSE_Platform_Teaching_Action_Type_Proposal_Colleagues_TOTAL_I	The total access number in teaching area in the first year for making a proposal to colleagues.

Table 3(a). The constructs and indicators of the second year participatory behavior (actual behavior) defined as numeric attributes, defined as numeric attributes

UNIFORMITY	
BEHAVIOR_Uniformity_Class_2nd_Year	The uniformity of the platform access in the second year
VOLUME	
BEHAVIOR_VOL_Subject_initiatives_2nd_Year	The number of the subject initiatives
BEHAVIOR_VOL_Platform_access_total_number_Administrative_area_2nd_year	The total access number in the administrative area in the second year
BEHAVIOR_VOL_Platform_access_total_number_Teaching_area_2nd_year	The total access number in the teaching area in the second year
BEHAVIOR_Platform_access_total_number_2nd_year	The total access number in the second year
ACTIVITY TYPE: READ	
BEHAVIOR_READ_Platform_Administrative_Action_Type_Reading_Materials_II	The total access number in administrative area in the second year for reading the administrative materials.
BEHAVIOR_READ_Platform_Teaching_Action_Type_Reading_Materials_TOTAL_II	The total access number in teaching area in the second year for reading the educational materials.
ACTIVITY TYPE: UPLOAD	
BEHAVIOR_UPLOAD_Platform_Administrative_Action_Type_Uploading_Materials_II	The total access number in administrative area in the second year for uploading administrative materials.
BEHAVIOR_UPLOAD_Platform_Teaching_Action_Type_Uploading_Materials_TOTAL_II	The total access number in teaching area in the second year for uploading projects.
ACTIVITY TYPE: ASK	
BEHAVIOR_ASK_Platform_Administrative_Action_Type_Ask_Teachers_II	The total access number in administrative area in the second year for asking teacher administrative questions.
BEHAVIOR_ASK_Platform_Administrative_Action_Type_Ask_Colleagues_II	The total access number in administrative area in the second year for asking colleagues administrative questions.
BEHAVIOR_ASK_Platform_Teaching_Action_Type_Ask_Teachers_TOTAL_II	The total access number in teaching area in the second year for asking teachers didactic-related questions.
BEHAVIOR_ASK_Platform_Teaching_Action_Type_Ask_Colleagues_TOTAL_II	The total access number in teaching area in the second year for asking colleagues didactic-related questions.
ACTIVITY TYPE: ANSWER	
BEHAVIOR_ANSWER_Platform_Administrative_Action_Type_Responde_Teachers_II	The total access number in administrative area in the second year for answering to the teachers' administrative questions.
BEHAVIOR_ANSWER_Platform_Administrative_Action_Type_Responde_Colleagues_II	The total access number in administrative area in the second year for answering to the colleagues' administrative questions.
BEHAVIOR_ANSWER_Platform_Teaching_Action_Type_Responde_Teachers_TOTAL_II	The total access number in teaching area in the second year for answering to the teachers' questions.
BEHAVIOR_ANSWER_Platform_Teaching_Action_Type_Responde_Colleagues_TOTAL_II	The total access number in teaching area in the second year for answering to the colleagues' questions.
ACTIVITY TYPE: PROPOSE	
BEHAVIOR_PROPOSE_Platform_Administrative_Action_Type_Proposal_Teachers_II	The total access number in administrative area in the second year for making a proposal to teachers.
BEHAVIOR_PROPOSE_Platform_Administrative_Action_Type_Proposal_Colleagues_II	The total access number in administrative area in the second year for making a proposal to colleagues.
BEHAVIOR_PROPOSE_Platform_Teaching_Action_Type_Proposal_Teachers_TOTAL_II	The total access number in teaching area in the second year for making a proposal to teachers.
BEHAVIOR_PROPOSE_Platform_Teaching_Action_Type_Proposal_Colleagues_TOTAL_II	The total access number in teaching area in the second year for making a proposal to colleagues.

Table 3(b). Summary of the questionnaire items related to the behavioral intention, for the second year

SATISFACTION_SYLLABUS_Interactivity	The attribute shows if the student favorite subjects have a higher degree of interactivity.
SATISFACTION_SYLLABUS_EvaluationMethods	The attribute shows what kind of evaluation methods should be used.
SATISFACTION_PLATFORM_PreviousTraining	The attribute shows if it would be necessary to organize a technical training session prior to platform usage.
SATISFACTION_PLATFORM_Forums	The attribute shows how important are for the student the online discussions with colleagues.
SATISFACTION_PLATFORM_ForumsParticipation	The attribute shows how often student participates in online discussions.
SATISFACTION_PLATFORM_FaceMeetings	The attribute shows if the student considers useful the face-to-face meetings.
BEHAVIOR_COMMITMENT_ExtraRessourcesUse	The attribute shows if student uses extra resources.
BEHAVIOR_COMMITMENT_TeamWork	The attribute shows if student prefers the projects developed individually or developed in team.
BEHAVIOR_COMMITMENT_Evaluation	The attribute shows in student opinion if there is any connection between his involvement in online activities and evaluation results.
SATISFACTION_COMMITMENT_WorkSupport	The attribute shows if the colleagues at work support students in attending this master programme.
SATISFACTION_INSTRUCTORS_Impact	The attribute describes how important is the instructor's role
SATISFACTION_INSTRUCTORS_Role	The attribute describes the teacher role in the student's point of view.
BEHAVIOR_INSTRUCTORS_CommunicationMethod	The attribute describes the preferred method for communicating with the teacher.
SATISFACTION_INSTRUCTORS_CommunicationEffeciency	The attribute describes how student rate in terms of efficiency his communication with the teachers.
BEHAVIOR_INSTRUCTORS_CommunicationInvolvement	The attribute describes the involved degree of the student in communication with the teacher.
SATISFACTION_INSTRUCTORS_InteractivityTechniques	The attribute describes the techniques that a teacher should use to ensure a good interactivity
SATISFACTION_INSTRUCTORS_MaterialsQuality	The attribute describes the materials quality.

The performance measures were defined based on the following elements:

- The grades at all 14 disciplines scheduled in the first academic year and 6 disciplines included in the curricula for the second year.
- Number of failures at first academic year exams
- Number of failures at second year exams

The main performance measures are the following:

- Grade Point Average in the first academic year (GPA_I)
- Grade Point Average in the second academic year (GPA_II)
- Aggregated Performance in first academic year (EVALUATION_PERFORMANCE_CLASS_I)
- Aggregated Performance in the second academic year (EVALUATION_PERFORMANCE_CLASS_II)

EVALUATION_PERFORMANCE_CLASS_I is defined as follow:

Table 4. Summary of the questionnaire items related to the external factors, for the second year

SATISFACTION_NEEDS_InitialRequirements	The attribute describes if students consider that MIP met their requirements
SATISFACTION_SYLLABUS_Content	The attribute describes how important are the clear thematic content and course requirements.
SATISFACTION_SYLLABUS_RessourceSufficiency	The attribute describe the sufficiency of the resources provided in order to acquire the needed knowledge.
SATISFACTION_SYLLABUS_ProjectsRelevancy	The attribute describes if the students consider that the projects have a proper weight in the final grade
SATISFACTION_SYLLABUS_WorkImpact	The attribute describes how students see the programme impact over their work.
SATISFACTION_SYLLABUS_Homework	The attribute shows how important are the homework assignments.
SATISFACTION_SYLLABUS_EvaluationRelevancy	The attribute describes what students think about the results of evaluations, if they reflect their knowledge or not.
SATISFACTION_PLATFORM_Adequacy	The attribute shows if the students consider the platform as adequate or not.
SATISFACTION_PLATFORM_Flexibility	The attribute shows if the students consider the platform as flexible.
BEHAVIOR_COMMITMENT_CandidatesSelection	The attribute shows how students consider the program admission.
BEHAVIOR_COMMITMENT_PerformanceFactor	The attribute shows which is the most important element for student performance.
SATISFACTION_COMMITMENT_AppliedKnowledge	The attribute shows whether students apply the acquired knowledge at work.
SATISFACTION_INSTRUCTORS_IdealInstructor	The attribute shows how students see the ideal teacher.
MOTIVATION_NEEDS_Reason	The attribute shows why students chose to follow this online programme.
MOTIVATION_NEEDS_ReasonOnlineMIP	The attribute relive the students enrollment reasons
MOTIVATION_NEEDS_Benefits	The attribute describes what students think about the benefits of the online programme
MOTIVATION_NEEDS_PreviousOnlineProgrammes	The attribute shows whether the student has followed or not other online programmes.
SATISFACTION_SYLLABUS_CertifiedProgramme	The attribute describes how important is the programme certification.
SATISFACTION_SYLLABUS_CertifiedProviders	The attribute describes how important is certification of the organization.
SATISFACTION_SYLLABUS_MaterialsFormat	The attribute describes if student considers that the projects have a proper weight in the final grade or not.
SATISFACTION_SYLLABUS_ProjectRelevancyInGrade	The attribute describes how students consider the project relevancy for different disciplines.
SATISFACTION_SYLLABUS_Assessment	The attribute describes if student prefers the ongoing assessment or the summative one.
SATISFACTION_PLATFORM_Continuity	The attribute indicates if the student considers that the program should continue next year.
PROFILE_INFORMATION_OtherTrainings	The attribute indicates if the student has followed other project management trainings.
PROFILE_INFORMATION_ActivityField	The attribute describes the student activity domain.

Table 5. Summary of the questionnaire items related to the moderator factors (student profiles)

INFORMATION_Age_Class	The student age
PROFILE_INFORMATION_GraduatedFaculty	The student graduated faculty
INFORMATION_Experience_Class	The student work experience
PROFILE_INFORMATION_OrganisationPosition_Class	The attribute describes the student position in the organization
PROFILE_INFORMATION_Income	The attribute offers information about student income
INFORMATION_DailyActivity_Class	The attribute shows student daily activity in virtual environment (in hours)
PROFILE_INFORMATION_RelativesFamilyInPM	The attribute indicates if other members of the student family are working in Project Management domain

Table 6. Summary of the first year performance variables

PERFORMANCE_EVALUATION_Average_1st_year	The attribute shows the student average performance for the first year.
PERFORMANCE_Failed_Exams_1st_year	The attribute shows the number of failed exams in the first year.
PERFORMANCE_Class_1st_year	The attribute is the performance class for the first year having the following values: 0 – average grade between 6 and 7 1 – average grade between 7.01 and 8 and over 3 failed exams 2 – average grade between 7.01 and 8 and less than 2 failed exams 3 – average grade over 8.01 and less than 2 failed exams.

Table 7. Summary of the second year performance variables

PERFORMANCE_EVALUATION_Average_2nd_year	The attribute shows the student average performance for the second year
PERFORMANCE_Failed_Exams_2nd_year	The attribute shows the number of the failed exams in the second year
PERFORMANCE_Class_2nd_year	The attribute is the performance class for the first year having the following values: 0 – average grade between 6 and 7 1 – average grade between 7.01 and 8 and over 3 failed exams 2 – average grade between 7.01 and 8 and less than 2 failed exams 3 – average grade over 8.01 and less than 2 failed exams.

- EVALUATION_PERFORMANCE_CLASS_I = 0, if GPA_I is between 6 and 7
- EVALUATION_PERFORMANCE_CLASS_I = 1, if GPA_I is between 7.01 and 8 and over 3 failed exams
- EVALUATION_PERFORMANCE_CLASS_I = 2, if GPA_I is between 7.01 and 8 and less than 2 failed exams
- EVALUATION_PERFORMANCE_CLASS_I = 3, if GPA_I is over 8.01 and less than 2 failed exams

EVALUATION_PERFORMANCE_CLASS_II is similarly defined, using GPA and number of failures from the second academic year.

In order to answer to the research questions, the following data mining methods were used:

- Attribute importance
- Association rules
- Clustering
- Classification

Figure 7. Conceptual schema of the operational database

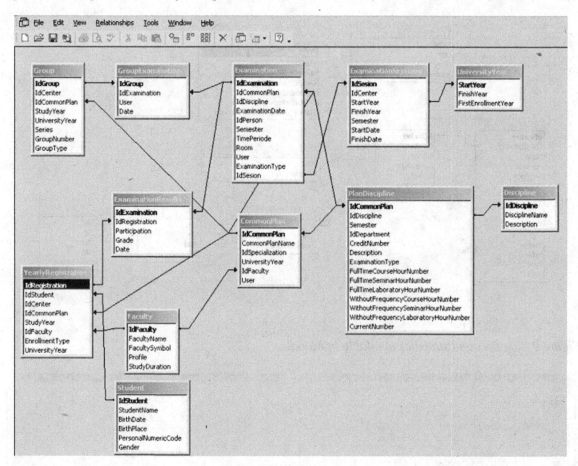

DATA SOURCES

The main data sources used on this research are:

- **The Operational Database**: Administered at the university level (Figure 7). This database is developed and updated by the IT Department, using the secretary network. The data reflect the academic curricula and the academic performance (the grades and the failed exams) for each student. The data are stored into the database through a software application.
- **The Questionnaire Database**: The data collected was stored in a database, having the conceptual schema shown in Figure 8.

- **The Moodle Platform's Log Files and Statistics**: Which offers analytical and graphical data regarding the student behavior, such as: the number of platform access, per day, month, semester, year, entire programme, the number of new subject initiated by a student, the time spent on the virtual space, the area of virtual space visited by the student. Figure 9 presents some of the facilities offered by Moodle. As we can see, some students have a uniform platform accessing pattern, others access platform only during the exam period, and others did not use the platform, using additional communication solutions (e-mail groups) in order to be informed.

Figure 8. Conceptual schema of the questionnaire database

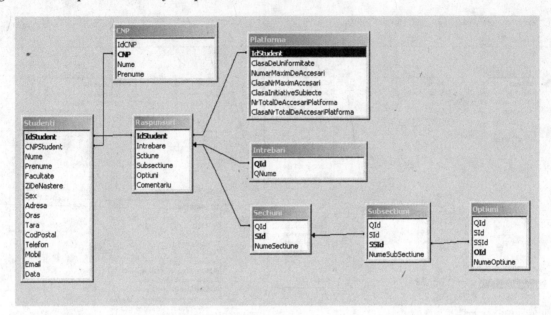

Figure 9. Log files and statistics available in Moodle

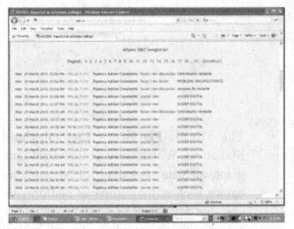 

In order to be used on the data mining processes, data a preprocessed. The main preprocessing task is to transform the numerical attributes into nominal ones, in order to be used by data mining algorithms. Table 8 presents the attributes included in Table 2, after they are transformed in nominal attributes.

DATA MINING PROCESSES

Participatory Behavior Patterns Analysis Using Clusters and Association Rules

Cluster analysis was used in order to identify the main patterns of the participatory behavior for the students enrolled in the MIP programme,

Figure 10. Data workflow for discovering Actual Behavior patterns for the first and second year

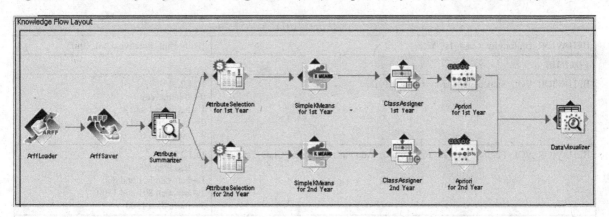

class 2010. The patterns are discovered separately for the first and second year of the programme, a longitudinal analysis being made. Based on the pattern differences, we tried to characterize and explain the dynamics of the participatory behavior for MIP students, defining associative rules between the most important attributes of the students' participatory behavior.

Data workflow, presenting the main applied processes and algorithms, is shown in Figure 10.

As we can see, the following processes should be performed in order to discover the participatory behavioral patterns:

- Input data, organized as "arff" file is loaded in Weka environment;
- Data is preprocessed. Weka environment offers many visualizing and preprocessing tools, such as Attribute Summarizer, filters, updating algorithms. Data is stored for later use;
- Attributes selection is done, for each academic year;
- Simple K-Means algorithm is applied for each academic year in order to find out the number of clusters and their characteristics, in terms of considered attributes
- The cluster label is assigned at each instance as a new attribute. This new attribute will be used as a class attribute.

- The results visualization is finally performed, in order to validate the results.

During the analysis process performance, the following algorithms were used:

A. **Simple K-Means Algorithm:** It can use either the Euclidean distance (as default) or the Manhattan distance. If the Manhattan distance is used, the cluster centroids are computed as the component-wise median rather than mean. The main algorithm options are: *displayStdDevs* (to display the standard deviations of numeric attributes or the counts of nominal attributes), *distanceFunction* (the distance function to be used for instances comparison. As a default is weka.core.EuclideanDistance), *dontReplaceMissingValues* (to replace globally the missing values with mean/mode), *maxIterations* (to set the maximum number of iterations), *numClusters* (to set the number of clusters), *preserveInstancesOrder* (to preserve order of instances), *seed* (the random seed number to be used). After several simulations, the number of clusters was chosen. This number is 3. Figure 11a. indicates the setup parameters window used for running Simple K-Means algorithm.

Table 8. Summary of the actual behavior characteristics for the first year, defined as nominal attributes

UNIFORMITY	
BEHAVIOR_Uniformity_Class_1st_Year	{Non_Unif, Relative_Unif, Unif}
VOLUME	
BEHAVIOR_VOL_Subject_initiatives_Class_1st_Year	{0,1,2,3} 0 – 0 initiatives 1 – between 1 and 3 2 – between 4 and 6 3 – more than 6
BEHAVIOR_VOL_Platform_access_total_number_Administrative_area_Class_1st_year	{0,1,2,3} 0 – less than 500 1 – between 501 and 800 2 – between 801 and 1500 3 – more than 1500
BEHAVIOR_VOL_Platform_access_total_number_Teaching_area_Class_1st_year	{0,1,2,3} 0 – less than 1000 1 – between 1001 and 3000 2 – between 3001 and 4000 3 – more than 4000
BEHAVIOR_Platform_access_total_number_Class_1st_year	{0,1,2,3} 0 – less than 1000 1 – between 1001 and 3000 2 – between 3001 and 5000 3 – more than 5000
ACTIVITY TYPE: READ	
BEHAVIOR_READ_Platform_Administrative_Action_Type_Reading_Materials_Class_I	{0,1,2} 0 – between 0 and 3 1 – between 4 and 8 2 – more than 8
BEHAVIOR_READ_Platform_Teaching_Action_Type_Reading_Materials_TOTAL_Class_I	{0,1,2} 0 – between 0 and 30 1 – between 31 and 32 2 – more than 32
ACTIVITY TYPE: UPLOAD	
BEHAVIOR_UPLOAD_Platform_Administrative_Action_Type_Uploading_Materials_Class_I	{0,1,2} 0 – 0 or one activity 1 – equal to 2 2 – more than 2
BEHAVIOR_UPLOAD_Platform_Teaching_Action_Type_Uploading_Materials_TOTAL_Class_I	{0,1} 0 – between 0 and 3 1 – more than 3
ACTIVITY TYPE: ASK	
BEHAVIOR_ASK_Platform_Administrative_Action_Type_Ask_Teachers_Class_I	{0,1,2) 0 – between 0 and 4 1 – between 5 and 8 2 – more than 8
BEHAVIOR_ASK_Platform_Administrative_Action_Type_Ask_Colleagues_Class_I	{0,1,2} 0 – no activity 1 – one activity 2 – more than 1

continued on following page

Table 8. Continued

UNIFORMITY	
BEHAVIOR_ASK_Platform_Teaching_Action_Type_Ask_Teachers_TOTAL_ Class_I	{0, 1, 2} 0 – between 0 and 3 1 – between 4 and 6 2- more than 6
BEHAVIOR_ASK_Platform_Teaching_Action_Type_Ask_Colleagues_TOTAL_ Class_I	{0, 1, 2} 0 –no activity 1 –one activity 2 – more than one
ACTIVITY TYPE: ANSWER	
BEHAVIOR_ANSWER_Platform_Administrative _Action_Type_Responde_Teachers_ Class_I	{0,1,2} 0 – 0 or 1 activity 1 –2 or 3 activities 2 – more than 3
BEHAVIOR_ANSWER_Platform_Administrative _Action_Type_Responde_Colleagues_ Class_I	{0,1,2} 0 – between 0 and 2 1 – between 3 and 5 2 – more than 5
BEHAVIOR_ANSWER_Platform_Teaching_Action_Type_Responde_Teachers_TOTAL_ Class_I	{0,1,2} 0 – 0 or 1 activity 1 – 2 activities 2 – more than 2
BEHAVIOR_ANSWER_Platform_Teaching_Action_Type_Responde_Colleagues_TOTAL_ Class_I	{0,1,2,3} 0 – no activity 1 – one activity 2 – 2 or 3 activities 3 – more than 3
ACTIVITY TYPE: PROPOSE	
BEHAVIOR_PROPOSE_Platform_Administrative _Action_Type_Proposal_Teachers_ Class_I	{0,1,2} 0 - 0 or 1activity 1 – 2 or 3 activities 2 – more than 3
BEHAVIOR_PROPOSE_Platform_Administrative _Action_Type_Proposal_ Colleagues_ Class_I	{0,1} 0 – 0 activity 1 – more than 0
BEHAVIOR_PROPOSE_Platform_Teaching_Action_Type_Proposal_Teachers _TOTAL_Class_I	{0,1} 0 –0 or 1 activity 1 – more than 1
BEHAVIOR_PROPOSE_Platform_Teaching_Action_Type_Proposal_ Colleagues _TOTAL_Class_I	{0,1} 0 –0 or 1 activity; 1 – more than 1

B. **InfoGainAttribute Evaluator:** It evaluates the worth of an attribute by measuring the information gain with respect to the class. The algorithm options are: *binarizeNumericAttributes* (to use 0/1 on discrete values of the numeric attributes), *missingMerge* (to distribute counts for missing values. The counts are distributed across other values according their frequency. Otherwise, a missing value is treated as a separate value). Figure 11b. indicates the setup parameters window used for running InfoGainAttribute Evaluator algorithm.

C. **Ranker ordering Method:** The method ranks attributes according their individual evaluations (Figure 11c). As attribute evalua-

Figure 11. The algorithms parameters used in the clustering analysis

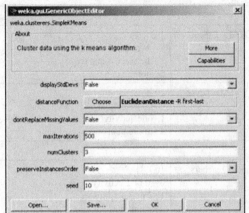

a) *Simple K-Means* parameters

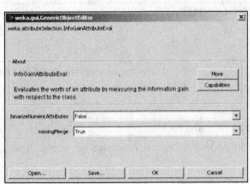

b) *InfoGainAttribute evaluator*

c) *Ranker ordering evaluator*

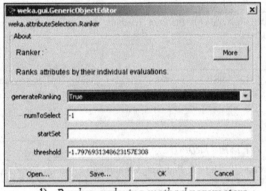

d) *Ranker ordering method* parameters

tors there are: *InfoGain*, *ReliefF*, *GainRatio*, *Entropy*, etc. The main options of the ranker ordering method (Figure 11d.) are: *generateRanking* (it is a constant. The method is capable only to generate attribute rankings), *numToSelect* (to specify the number of attributes to be retained. The default value is (-1), indicating that all attributes are to be retained. In order to reduce the attribute set, this option or a threshold could be used), *startSet* (to specify a set of attributes to be ignored. When the ranking is generated, the Ranker method will not evaluate this attribute list. This is specified as a comma separated list of attribute indexes, starting with 1), *and threshold* (to set the threshold at which the

attributes can be discarded. Using the default value no attributes will be discarded).

D. **Apriori Algorithm:** The algorithm (Agrawal & Srikant, 1994) iteratively reduces the minimum support until it finds the required number of rules with a given minimum confidence. The algorithm can discover class association rules, when it is adapted as explained in (Liu, Hsu & Ma, 1998). The main algorithm options are: *car* (if this option is enabled, then the class association rules are mined instead of general ones), *classIndex* (the index of the class attribute. If it has the value -1, the last attribute is taken as class attribute), *delta* (the factor of iteratively support decreasing. The support will be

Figure 12. The Apriori Algorithm parameters

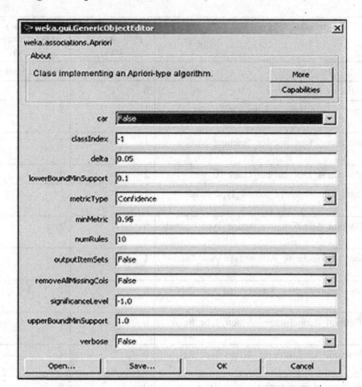

reduced until the min support is reached or required number of rules has been generated), *lowerBoundMinSupport* (the lower limit of the minimum support), *metricType* (the metrics used to rank the rules. Usually, the rule confidence, defined as the proportion of the examples covered by the premise that are also covered by the consequence, is used as a rule ranking metrics. The Class association rules can only be mined using the rule confidence), *minMetric* (the minimum metric score. There are considered only the rules with higher scores than this value), *numRules* (to number of rules to be mined), *outputItemSets* (if this option is enabled, then the itemsets are considered also as output), *removeAllMissingCols* (to remove columns with all missing values), *significanceLevel* (the significance level of the rule confidence to be used by the significance test), *upperBoundMinSupport* (the upper bound for the

minimum support, which is iteratively decreased), *verbose* (to activate the verbose mode). Figure 12 indicates the parameters setup window used for the Apriori Algorithm.

THE MAIN FINDINGS

Student Participatory Behavior Patterns during the First Academic Year

The *Simple K-Means* algorithm was applied to the first year attributes (see Algorithm 1) of all instances, and results were obtained (the cluster centroids are presented in Table 9).

Cluster 0. The students belonging to this cluster tend to visit platform the administrative are more than the teaching one, being less interested on communicating with colleagues and teachers on academic subjects. Their initiative in

Table 9. The cluster centroids for the first year participatory behavior

Attributes	Cluster 0 (57 instances, 44%)	Cluster 1 (48 instances, 37%)	Cluster 2 (24 instances, 19%)
BEHAVIOR_Uniformity_Class_1st_Year	Non_Unif	Relative_Unif	Relative_Unif
BEHAVIOR_Subject_initiatives_Class_1st_Year	0	0	0
BEHAVIOR_Platform_access_total_number_Administrative_area_Class_1st_year	1	2	2
BEHAVIOR_VOL_Platform_access_total_number_Teaching_area_Class_1st_year	1	2	2
BEHAVIOR_VOL_Platform_access_total_number_Class_1st_year	2	2	3
BEHAVIOR_READ_Platform_Administrative_Action_Type_Reading_Materials_Class_I	1	2	1
BEHAVIOR_UPLOAD_Platform_Administrative_Action_Type_Uploading_Materials_Class_I	0	2	2
BEHAVIOR_ASK_Platform_Administrative_Action_Type_Ask_Teachers_Class_I	1	2	2
BEHAVIOR_ASK_Platform_Administrative_Action_Type_Ask_Colleagues_Class_I	0	1	1
BEHAVIOR_ANSWER_Platform_Administrative_Action_Type_Responde_Teachers_Class_I	0	1	2
BEHAVIOR_ANSWER_Platform_Administrative_Action_Type_Responde_Colleagues_Class_I	0	1	1
BEHAVIOR_PROPOSE_Platform_Administrative_Action_Type_Proposal_Teachers_Class_I	0	0	2
BEHAVIOR_PROPOSE_Platform_Administrative_Action_Type_Proposal_Colleagues_Class_I	0	0	0
BEHAVIOR_READ_Platform_Teaching_Action_Type_Reading_Materials_TOTAL_Class_I	0	1	2
BEHAVIOR_UPLOAD_Platform_Teaching_Action_Type_Uploading_Materials_TOTAL_Class_I	1	0	0
BEHAVIOR_ASK_Platform_Teaching_Action_Type_Ask_Teachers_TOTAL_Class_I	0	1	2
BEHAVIOR_ASK_Platform_Teaching_Action_Type_Ask_Colleagues_TOTAL_Class_I	0	0	2
BEHAVIOR_ANSWER_Platform_Teaching_Action_Type_Responde_Teachers_TOTAL_Class_I	0	1	2
BEHAVIOR_ANSWER_Platform_Teaching_Action_Type_Responde_Colleagues_TOTAL_Class_I	1	2	3
BEHAVIOR_PROPOSE_Platform_Teaching_Action_Type_Proposal_Teachers_TOTAL_Class_I	0	1	1
BEHAVIOR_PROPOSE_Platform_Teaching_Action_Type_Proposal_Colleagues_TOTAL_Class_I	0	1	1

Algorithm 1. First year attributes

kMeans
=====
Number of iterations: 4
Within cluster sum of squared errors: 851.0
Missing values globally replaced with mean/mode
Clustered Instances
0 57 (44%)
1 48 (37%)
2 24 (19%)
0.8885 16 BEHAVIOR_ASK_Platform_Teaching_Action_Type_Ask_Teachers_TOTAL_Class_I
0.8331 19 BEHAVIOR_ANSWER_Platform_Teaching_Action_Type_Responde_Colleagues_TOTAL_Class_I
0.6495 18 BEHAVIOR_ANSWER_Platform_Teaching_Action_Type_Responde_Teachers_TOTAL_Class_I
0.6026 1 BEHAVIOR_Uniformity_Class_1st_Year

proposing new topics is also reduced. It can be conclude that the students are not very interested in acquiring knowledge, being focused on the administrative issues instead.

Cluster 1. The interest of the students for the administrative issues is high, but the teaching topics are not neglected. The students tend to interact with their colleagues in a large degree, making proposals for new topics. Reading the didactic materials provided by teacher is not a significant activity for these students, maybe because additional information / clarifications are obtained communicating with the other participants.

Cluster 2. Students belonging to this cluster are clearly focused on the academic activities, and have a low interest for the administrative issues. These students have the highest value for the attribute "answers to colleagues' questions" and we can expect these students to have a high academic performance.

Figure 13 presents these clusters, which are visualized using the attribute: *BEHAVIOR_ASK_Platform_Administrative_Action_Type_Ask_Teachers_Class_I*. Most of the students belonging to the first cluster (named as *cluster 0* in Table 9 and *cluster 1* in the Figure 13) asked questions to teachers once up to five times for clarification during the whole first year. The students from the other two clusters have a more intense activity in this regard.

According to these results we can conclude that despite specific characteristics, usually the students do not take initiative in the communication process, allowing the professor to decide the communication flow.

Student Participatory Behavior Patterns during the Second Academic Year

The *Simple K-Means* algorithm was applied to the second year attributes (see Algorithm 2) of all instances, and the following results were obtained (the cluster centroids are presented in Table 10):

Cluster 0. Like for the first year, the students belonging to this cluster shows a low interest for the teaching area, preferring just to get some information from the administrative one, and loading various materials. The e-learning platform is exploited in a small extent, the access volume being minimal (class 0). The platform accesses for downloading are at a minimum level. The teachers and classmates are not considered as an option when students solve problem and prepare

Figure 13. Clusters visualization using BEHAVIOR_ASK_Platform_Administrative_Action_Type_Ask_Teachers_Class_I

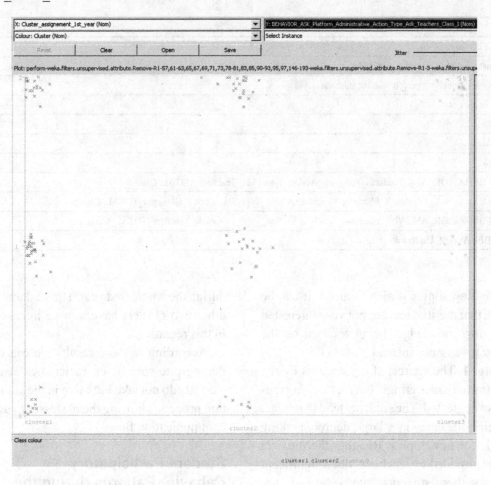

themselves for exams. A possible explanation is the lack of time, students mentioning it as the first reason for choosing an online programme.

Cluster 1. The students belonging to this cluster tend to access more often the teaching area comparing with the administrative one. It can be assumed that a minimum presence in the administrative area is always necessary but the attention pay to this area should not exceed the teaching focus. Reading materials is weak, as well as the communication with peers and teachers. It can be observed a high resemblance between the first two patterns in terms of attitude towards colleagues and teachers.

Cluster 2. The students belonging to this cluster appear to be most interested in the aca-

demic content and communication with teachers and peers. The uniformity of their presence in the online activities indicates a constant work performance. Contact with teachers is higher than the communication with the colleagues. The main activities with teachers are asking for clarification and reading the materials. Even when they are trying to deal with the administrative issues, they are more interested to communicate with teachers instead of peers. Regarding the initiative, we cannot find a good score.

According to these results, we can conclude that in the second year of the programme, the students do not take initiative in the communication process, allowing the professor to decide the

Table 10. The cluster centroids for the second year participatory behavior

Attributes	Cluster 0 (72 Instances, 55%)	Cluster 1 (24 Instances, 19%)	Cluster 2 (33 Instances, 26%)
BEHAVIOR_Uniformity_Class_2nd_Year	Non_Unif	Non_Unif	Relative_Unif
BEHAVIOR_Subject_initiatives_Class_2nd_Year	0	0	0
BEHAVIOR_Platform_access_total_number_Administrative_area_Class_2nd_year	0	1	3
BEHAVIOR_VOL_Platform_access_total_number_Teaching_area_Class_2nd_year	1	0	3
BEHAVIOR_VOL_Platform_access_total_number_Class_2nd_year	0	1	2
BEHAVIOR_READ_Platform_Administrative_Action_Type_Reading_Materials_Class_II	0	0	2
BEHAVIOR_UPLOAD_Platform_Administrative_Action_Type_Uploading_Materials_Class_II	2	0	1
BEHAVIOR_ASK_Platform_Administrative_Action_Type_Ask_Teachers_Class_II	0	1	2
BEHAVIOR_ASK_Platform_Administrative_Action_Type_Ask_Colleagues_Class_II	0	0	1
BEHAVIOR_ANSWER_Platform_Administrative_Action_Type_Responde_Teachers_Class_II	0	1	1
BEHAVIOR_ANSWER_Platform_Administrative_Action_Type_Responde_Colleagues_Class_II	0	0	1
BEHAVIOR_PROPOSE_Platform_Administrative_Action_Type_Proposal_Teachers_Class_II	0	1	2
BEHAVIOR_PROPOSE_Platform_Administrative_Action_Type_Proposal_Colleagues_Class_II	0	0	1
BEHAVIOR_READ_Platform_Teaching_Action_Type_Reading_Materials_TOTAL_Class_II	0	1	2
BEHAVIOR_UPLOAD_Platform_Teaching_Action_Type_Uploading_Materials_TOTAL_Class_II	1	1	2
BEHAVIOR_ASK_Platform_Teaching_Action_Type_Ask_Teachers_TOTAL_Class_II	0	1	2
BEHAVIOR_ASK_Platform_Teaching_Action_Type_Ask_Colleagues_TOTAL_Class_II	0	1	1
BEHAVIOR_ANSWER_Platform_Teaching_Action_Type_Responde_Teachers_TOTAL_Class_II	0	1	1
BEHAVIOR_ANSWER_Platform_Teaching_Action_Type_Responde_Colleagues_TOTAL_Class_II	0	1	1
BEHAVIOR_PROPOSE_Platform_Teaching_Action_Type_Proposal_Teachers_TOTAL_Class_II	0	1	1
BEHAVIOR_PROPOSE_Platform_Teaching_Action_Type_Proposal_Colleagues_TOTAL_Class_II	0	1	1

Algorithm 2. Second year attributes

kMeans
======
Number of iterations: 4
Within cluster sum of squared errors: 648.0
Missing values globally replaced with mean/mode
Clustered Instances
0 72 (55%)
1 24 (19%)
2 33 (26%)
0.8539 14 BEHAVIOR_READ_Platform_Teaching_Action_Type_Reading_Materials_TOTAL_Class_II
0.7292 8 BEHAVIOR_ASK_Platform_Administrative_Action_Type_Ask_Teachers_Class_II
0.6744 17 BEHAVIOR_ASK_Platform_Teaching_Action_Type_Ask_Colleagues_TOTAL_Class_II
0.6744 21 BEHAVIOR_PROPOSE_Platform_Teaching_Action_Type_Proposal_Colleagues_TOTAL_Class_II

communication flow. This is very similar with the student participatory behavior during the first year.

Figure 14 presents these three clusters, which are visualized using the attribute: *BEHAVIOR_READ_Platform_Teaching_action_Type_Reading_Materials_TOTAL_Class_II*. We can see a big difference between the clusters considering the selected attribute. The first cluster (named as *cluster 0* in Table 10 and *cluster 1* in the Figure 14) has 0 as this attribute value, and the other clusters have the value 1 and, respectively, 2. So, the students belonging to the last two clusters are most interested in reading the teaching materials published in the teaching area.

Similarities between the Student Participatory Behavior during the First and the Second Year of the Programme

- Three profiles of the student participatory behavior can be identify during each year: one of these profile has a weak participation on the virtual learning environment, and we can mention that the representativeness of this group increases from 44% in the first year to the 55% in the second year. Another profile has a moderate participation on the virtual learning environment and the representativeness of this profile decreases from 37% in the first year to 19% in the second year. The last profile is characterized by an active participation. The representativeness of this profile increases slightly from 19% in the first year to 26% in the second year.

- The active students tend to initiate sessions on topics proposed by the teachers.

The students characterized by an active participation are very present in the administrative area not only during the first year, but in the second year as well.

Differences between the Student Participatory Behavior during the First and the Second Year of the Programme

- The interest for teaching activities decreases dramatically from the first to the second year, especially at the students belonging to the first two clusters. One explanation might be that the students are more fo-

Figure 14. Clusters visualization using BEHAVIOR_READ_Platform_Teaching_action_Type_Reading_Materials_TOTAL_Class_II

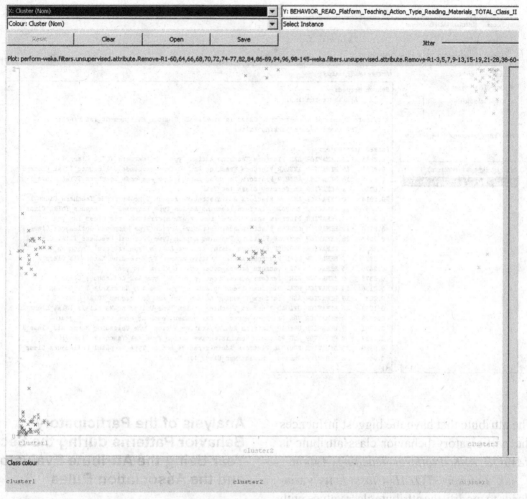

cused to work to complete their master thesis, instead to participate in the learning environment.

• Each year, the most important activities in the virtual environment are different. During the first year, the students are mostly involved to respond to peers and teachers and also to ask questions to teachers. During the second year, the most important activities are directed towards colleagues, and those related to the didactical materials.

Analysis of the Participatory Behavior Patterns during the First Year Using the Attribute Evaluator and the Association Rules

A. Relevant Behavior Attributes Selection

The attributes defining the participatory behavior of students during the first year are evaluated using *InfoGainAttribute Evaluator* and *Ranker ordering* method (Figure 15) in respect to the relevance for the participatory behavior class (see Attribute Evaluator 1).

Figure 15. Evaluation of the participatory behavior attributes for the first year using InfoGainAttribute Evaluator and Ranker ordering Method

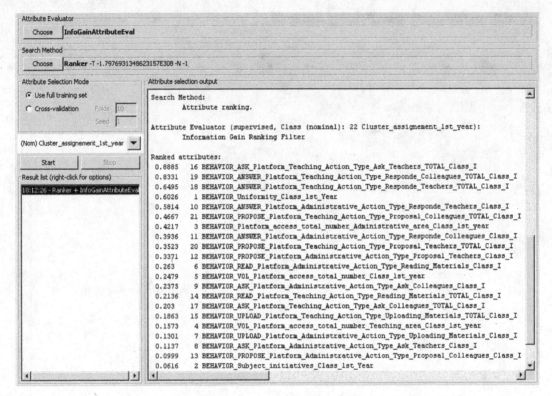

The attribute that have the biggest influences on the participatory behavior class attribute is *BEHAVIOR_ASK_Platform_Teaching_Action_Type_Ask_Teachers_TOTAL_Class_I*. Its variation leads to modify the attribute class values with highest probability. It can be said that communication with teachers is the most important factor for characterizing the participatory behavior profile.

B. Association Rules for the Most Relevant Behavior Attributes

In order to identify the relationship between the most relevant behavioral characteristics, the association rules are induced using the Apriori Algorithm, with the most six relevant attributes (see Results 1 and 2).

Analysis of the Participatory Behavior Patterns during the Second Year Using the Attribute Evaluator and the Association Rules

A. Relevant Behavior Attributes Selection

The attributes defining the participatory behavior of students during the first year are evaluated using *InfoGainAttribute Evaluator* and *Ranker ordering* method (Figure 16) in respect to the relevance for the participatory behavior class (see Result 3).

The attribute that have the biggest influences on the participatory behavior class attribute is *READ_Platform_Teaching_Action_Type_Reading_Materials_TOTAL_Class_II*. Its variation leads to modify the attribute class values with highest probability. Its variation leads to modify the attribute class values with highest probability.

Attribute Evaluator 1.

Search Method:
Attribute ranking.
Attribute Evaluator (supervised, Class (nominal): 22 **Cluster_assignement_1st_year**):
Information Gain Ranking Filter
Ranked attributes:
0.8885 16 BEHAVIOR_ASK_Platform_Teaching_Action_Type_Ask_Teachers_TOTAL_Class_I
0.8331 19 BEHAVIOR_ANSWER_Platform_Teaching_Action_Type_Responde_Colleagues_TOTAL_Class_I
0.6495 18 BEHAVIOR_ANSWER_Platform_Teaching_Action_Type_Responde_Teachers_TOTAL_Class_I
0.6026 1 BEHAVIOR_Uniformity_Class_1st_Year
0.5814 10 BEHAVIOR_ANSWER_Platform_Administrative_Action_Type_Responde_Teachers_Class_I
0.4667 21 BEHAVIOR_PROPOSE_Platform_Teaching_Action_Type_Proposal_Colleagues_TOTAL_Class_I
0.4217 3 BEHAVIOR_Platform_access_total_number_Administrative_area_Class_1st_year
0.3936 11 BEHAVIOR_ANSWER_Platform_Administrative_Action_Type_Responde_Colleagues_Class_I
0.3523 20 BEHAVIOR_PROPOSE_Platform_Teaching_Action_Type_Proposal_Teachers_TOTAL_Class_I
0.3371 12 BEHAVIOR_PROPOSE_Platform_Administrative_Action_Type_Proposal_Teachers_Class_I
0.263 6 BEHAVIOR_READ_Platform_Administrative_Action_Type_Reading_Materials_Class_I
0.2479 5 BEHAVIOR_VOL_Platform_access_total_number_Class_1st_year
0.2375 9 BEHAVIOR_ASK_Platform_Administrative_Action_Type_Ask_Colleagues_Class_I
0.2136 14 BEHAVIOR_READ_Platform_Teaching_Action_Type_Reading_Materials_TOTAL_Class_I
0.203 17 BEHAVIOR_ASK_Platform_Teaching_Action_Type_Ask_Colleagues_TOTAL_Class_I
0.1863 15 BEHAVIOR_UPLOAD_Platform_Teaching_Action_Type_Uploading_Materials_TOTAL_Class_I
0.1573 4 BEHAVIOR_VOL_Platform_access_total_number_Teaching_area_Class_1st_year
0.1301 7 BEHAVIOR_UPLOAD_Platform_Administrative_Action_Type_Uploading_Materials_Class_I
0.1137 8 BEHAVIOR_ASK_Platform_Administrative_Action_Type_Ask_Teachers_Class_I
0.0999 13 BEHAVIOR_PROPOSE_Platform_Administrative_Action_Type_Proposal_Colleagues_Class_I
0.0616 2 BEHAVIOR_Subject_initiatives_Class_1st_Year
Selected attributes: 16,19,18,1,10,21,3,11,20,12,6,5,9,14,17,15,4,7,8,13,2: 21

Result 1. Most relevant behavior attributes

Apriori
=======
Minimum support: 0.35 (45 instances)
Minimum metric <confidence>: 0.9
Number of cycles performed: 13
Best rules found:
1. BEHAVIOR_ASK_Platform_Teaching_Action_Type_Ask_Teachers_TOTAL_Class_I=0 BEHAVIOR_ANSWER_Platform_Teaching_Action_Type_Responde_Teachers_TOTAL_Class_I=0 45 ==> BEHAVIOR_PROPOSE_Platform_Teaching_Action_Type_Proposal_Colleagues_TOTAL_Class_I=0 45 conf:(1)
If students not to ask questions to their teachers and also they do not answer to their questions then it is very likely that they do not have communication initiatives with their colleagues (see Results 2).

Result 2. Other relevant association rules

2. Cluster_assignement_1st_year=cluster1 57 ==> BEHAVIOR_PROPOSE_Platform_Teaching_Action_Type_Proposal_Colleagues_ TOTAL_Class_I=0 57 conf:(1)
3. BEHAVIOR_Uniformity_Class_1st_Year=Non_Unif Cluster_assignement_1st_year=cluster1 54 ==> BEHAVIOR_PROPOSE_Platform_Teaching_Action_Type_Proposal_Colleagues_TOTAL_Class_I=0 54 conf:(1)
4. BEHAVIOR_Uniformity_Class_1st_Year=Non_Unif BEHAVIOR_ANSWER_Platform_Teaching_Action_Type_Responde_Teachers_TOTAL_Class_I=0 45 ==> BEHAVIOR_PROPOSE_Platform_Teaching_Action_Type_Proposal_Colleagues_TOTAL_Class_I=0 45 conf:(1)
5. BEHAVIOR_ANSWER_Platform_Teaching_Action_Type_Responde_Teachers_TOTAL_Class_I=0 58 ==> BEHAVIOR_PROPOSE_Platform_Teaching_Action_Type_Proposal_Colleagues_TOTAL_Class_I=0 58 conf:(1)
6. BEHAVIOR_ANSWER_Platform_Teaching_Action_Type_Responde_Teachers_TOTAL_Class_I=0 Cluster_assignement_1st_year=cluster1 45 ==> BEHAVIOR_PROPOSE_Platform_Teaching_Action_Type_Proposal_Colleagues_TOTAL_Class_I=0 45 conf:(1)
7. BEHAVIOR_ASK_Platform_Teaching_Action_Type_Ask_Teachers_TOTAL_Class_I=0 50 ==> BEHAVIOR_Uniformity_Class_1st_Year=Non_Unif 49 conf:(0.98)
8. BEHAVIOR_ASK_Platform_Teaching_Action_Type_Ask_Teachers_TOTAL_Class_I=0 BEHAVIOR_PROPOSE_Platform_Teaching_Action_Type_Proposal_Colleagues_TOTAL_Class_I=0 47 ==> BEHAVIOR_Uniformity_Class_1st_Year=Non_Unif 46 conf:(0.98)
9. BEHAVIOR_ASK_Platform_Teaching_Action_Type_Ask_Teachers_TOTAL_Class_I=0 BEHAVIOR_PROPOSE_Platform_Teaching_Action_Type_Proposal_Colleagues_TOTAL_Class_I=0 47 ==> BEHAVIOR_ANSWER_Platform_Teaching_Action_Type_Responde_Teachers_TOTAL_Class_I=0 45 conf:(0.96)
10. Cluster_assignement_1st_year=cluster1 57 ==> BEHAVIOR_Uniformity_Class_1st_Year=Non_Unif 54 conf:(0.95)

It can be said that, the importance gave by the students to published didactic materials has a great influences on the participatory behavior profile. Therefore, a variation in how students access didactic materials may lead to another participatory profile.

B.   Association Rules for the Most Relevant Behavior Attributes

In order to identify the relationship between the most relevant behavioral characteristics, the association rules are induced using the Apriori Algorithm, with the most six relevant attributes (see Reults 4 and 5).

ANALYSIS OF THE RELATIONSHIPS BETWEEN PARTICIPATORY BEHAVIOR AND BEHAVIORAL INTENTION, EXTERNAL FACTORS, AND MODERATOR VARIABLES

The designed workflow for analyzing the relationships between participatory behavior and behavioral intention, external factors and moderator variables is shown in Figure 17.

When *BEHAVIOR_ASK_Platform_Administrative_Action_Type_Ask_Colleagues_Class_II* attribute has value 0 (meaning that the students do not put any question to their colleagues) and when the *BEHAVIOR_ANSWER_Platform_Administrative_Action_Type_Responde_Colleagues_Class_II* attribute has value 0 (meaning that students do not give any answer to their colleagues) then the Actual Behavior are strongly related to the external factor *MOTIVATION_NEEDS_Benefits* having the value *Access_to_info_without_going_to_class*, meaning that the students cannot come to classes (see Result 6). This rule describes the reason for getting enrolled in the online program is associated with the participatory behavior during the second year. If students fail to ask and answer questions to their colleagues then their reason for applying to this online program is the lack of time. Confidence factor for this rule is one (maximum). A number of 91 students respect both the rule first and the second part (see Result 7).

When the attributes:

Figure 16. Evaluation of the participatory behavior attributes for the second year using InfoGainAttribute Evaluator and Ranker ordering Method

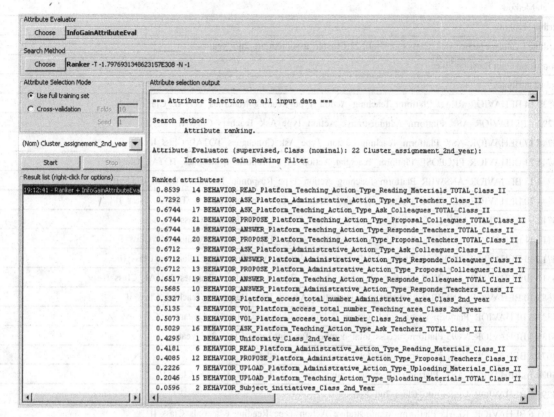

BEHAVIOR_ANSWER_Platform_Administrative_Action_Type_Responde_Colleagues_Class_II and BEHAVIOR_ASK_Platform_Administrative_Action_Type_Ask_Colleagues_Class_IIhave value 0, meaning that the student has not responded and do not put any questions to colleagues, then the participatory behavior is strongly related to the external factor explaining that reason for choosing an online program is *Lack_of_ time* and the platform offers satisfaction to the student. Therefore, the amount of available time is a very important element for the participatory behavior during the second year. A number of 85 students are aligned with this rule (see Result 8).

When *MOTIVATION_NEEDS_ReasonOnlineMIP* attribute has value *Lack_of_time*, *SATISFACTION_INSTRUCTORS_IdealInstructor*has value *Involved* (meaning that students ask to their

teacher to be very engaged in virtual environment). *PROFILE_INFORMATION_Income*attribute has value *>1500* (meaning that students have an income of more than 1500 RON) then the following attributes. *BEHAVIOR_PROPOSE_Platform_Administrative_Action_Type_Proposal_Colleagues_Class_II*, *BEHAVIOR_ASK_Platform_Administrative_Action_Type_Ask_Colleagues_Class_II* and *BEHAVIOR_ANSWER_Platform_Administrative_Action_Type_Responde_Colleagues_Class_II*have values 0 (meaning that the students do not make proposals, do not ask and not answer to questions). 85 of the students respect this rule (see Result 9).

The rules 165, 203, 204, and 205 confirm that the students with poor a communication with their colleagues ask for a greater involvement of the teachers on virtual environment. It is supposed

Result 3.

Search Method:
Attribute ranking.
Attribute Evaluator (supervised, Class (nominal): 22 **Cluster_assignement_2nd_year**):
Information Gain Ranking Filter
Ranked attributes:
0.8539 14 BEHAVIOR_READ_Platform_Teaching_Action_Type_Reading_Materials_TOTAL_Class_II
0.7292 8 BEHAVIOR_ASK_Platform_Administrative_Action_Type_Ask_Teachers_Class_II
0.6744 17 BEHAVIOR_ASK_Platform_Teaching_Action_Type_Ask_Colleagues_TOTAL_Class_II
0.6744 21 BEHAVIOR_PROPOSE_Platform_Teaching_Action_Type_Proposal_Colleagues_TOTAL_Class_II
0.6744 18 BEHAVIOR_ANSWER_Platform_Teaching_Action_Type_Responde_Teachers_TOTAL_Class_II
0.6744 20 BEHAVIOR_PROPOSE_Platform_Teaching_Action_Type_Proposal_Teachers_TOTAL_Class_II
0.6712 9 BEHAVIOR_ASK_Platform_Administrative_Action_Type_Ask_Colleagues_Class_II
0.6712 11 BEHAVIOR_ANSWER_Platform_Administrative_Action_Type_Responde_Colleagues_Class_II
0.6712 13 BEHAVIOR_PROPOSE_Platform_Administrative_Action_Type_Proposal_Colleagues_Class_II
0.6517 19 BEHAVIOR_ANSWER_Platform_Teaching_Action_Type_Responde_Colleagues_TOTAL_Class_II
0.5685 10 BEHAVIOR_ANSWER_Platform_Administrative_Action_Type_Responde_Teachers_Class_II
0.5327 3 BEHAVIOR_Platform_access_total_number_Administrative_area_Class_2nd_year
0.5135 4 BEHAVIOR_VOL_Platform_access_total_number_Teaching_area_Class_2nd_year
0.5073 5 BEHAVIOR_VOL_Platform_access_total_number_Class_2nd_year
0.5029 16 BEHAVIOR_ASK_Platform_Teaching_Action_Type_Ask_Teachers_TOTAL_Class_II
0.4295 1 BEHAVIOR_Uniformity_Class_2nd_Year
0.4181 6 BEHAVIOR_READ_Platform_Administrative_Action_Type_Reading_Materials_Class_II
0.4085 12 BEHAVIOR_PROPOSE_Platform_Administrative_Action_Type_Proposal_Teachers_Class_II
0.2226 7 BEHAVIOR_UPLOAD_Platform_Administrative_Action_Type_Uploading_Materials_Class_II
0.2046 15 BEHAVIOR_UPLOAD_Platform_Teaching_Action_Type_Uploading_Materials_TOTAL_Class_II
0.0596 2 BEHAVIOR_Subject_initiatives_Class_2nd_Year
Selected attributes: 14,8,17,21,18,20,9,11,13,19,10,3,4,5,16,1,6,12,7,15,2: 21

Result 4. Most relevant behavior attributes

Apriori
=======
Minimum support: 0.1 (13 instances)
Minimum metric <confidence>: 0.9
Number of cycles performed: 18
1. BEHAVIOR_ANSWER_Platform_Teaching_Action_Type_Responde_Teachers_TOTAL_Class_II=0 BEHAVIOR_PROPOSE_Platform_Teaching_Action_Type_Proposal_Teachers_TOTAL_Class_II=0 BEHAVIOR_PROPOSE_Platform_Teaching_Action_Type_Proposal_Colleagues_TOTAL_Class_II=0 81 ==> BEHAVIOR_ASK_Platform_Teaching_Action_Type_Ask_Colleagues_TOTAL_Class_II=0 81 conf:(1)
This rule describe the student who are not actives, therefore most often they do not answer teachers questions and do not make proposals to the teachers. Also, the communication with colleagues is not good. In this situation, it is likely that the student would not want to communicate with colleagues. Other relevant association rules are:

Result 5. Other relevant association rules

2. BEHAVIOR_ASK_Platform_Teaching_Action_Type_Ask_Colleagues_TOTAL_Class_II=0 BEHAVIOR_PROPOSE_Platform_Teaching_Action_Type_Proposal_Teachers_TOTAL_Class_II=0 BEHAVIOR_PROPOSE_Platform_Teaching_Action_Type_Proposal_Colleagues_TOTAL_Class_II=0 81 ==> BEHAVIOR_ANSWER_Platform_Teaching_Action_Type_Responde_Teachers_TOTAL_Class_II=0 81 conf:(1)
3. BEHAVIOR_ASK_Platform_Teaching_Action_Type_Ask_Colleagues_TOTAL_Class_II=0 BEHAVIOR_ANSWER_Platform_Teaching_Action_Type_Responde_Teachers_TOTAL_Class_II=0 BEHAVIOR_PROPOSE_Platform_Teaching_Action_Type_Proposal_Colleagues_TOTAL_Class_II=0 81 ==> BEHAVIOR_PROPOSE_Platform_Teaching_Action_Type_Proposal_Teachers_TOTAL_Class_II=0 81 conf:(1)
4. BEHAVIOR_ASK_Platform_Teaching_Action_Type_Ask_Colleagues_TOTAL_Class_II=0 BEHAVIOR_ANSWER_Platform_Teaching_Action_Type_Responde_Teachers_TOTAL_Class_II=0 BEHAVIOR_PROPOSE_Platform_Teaching_Action_Type_Proposal_Teachers_TOTAL_Class_II=0 81 ==> BEHAVIOR_PROPOSE_Platform_Teaching_Action_Type_Proposal_Colleagues_TOTAL_Class_II=0 81 conf:(1)
5. BEHAVIOR_PROPOSE_Platform_Teaching_Action_Type_Proposal_Teachers_TOTAL_Class_II=0 BEHAVIOR_PROPOSE_Platform_Teaching_Action_Type_Proposal_Colleagues_TOTAL_Class_II=0 81 ==> BEHAVIOR_ASK_Platform_Teaching_Action_Type_Ask_Colleagues_TOTAL_Class_II=0 BEHAVIOR_ANSWER_Platform_Teaching_Action_Type_Responde_Teachers_TOTAL_Class_II=0 81 conf:(1)
6. BEHAVIOR_ANSWER_Platform_Teaching_Action_Type_Responde_Teachers_TOTAL_Class_II=0 BEHAVIOR_PROPOSE_Platform_Teaching_Action_Type_Proposal_Colleagues_TOTAL_Class_II=0 81 ==> BEHAVIOR_ASK_Platform_Teaching_Action_Type_Ask_Colleagues_TOTAL_Class_II=0 BEHAVIOR_PROPOSE_Platform_Teaching_Action_Type_Proposal_Teachers_TOTAL_Class_II=0 81 conf:(1)
7. BEHAVIOR_ANSWER_Platform_Teaching_Action_Type_Responde_Teachers_TOTAL_Class_II=0 BEHAVIOR_PROPOSE_Platform_Teaching_Action_Type_Proposal_Teachers_TOTAL_Class_II=0 81 ==> BEHAVIOR_ASK_Platform_Teaching_Action_Type_Ask_Colleagues_TOTAL_Class_II=0 BEHAVIOR_PROPOSE_Platform_Teaching_Action_Type_Proposal_Colleagues_TOTAL_Class_II=0 81 conf:(1)
8. BEHAVIOR_ASK_Platform_Teaching_Action_Type_Ask_Colleagues_TOTAL_Class_II=0 BEHAVIOR_PROPOSE_Platform_Teaching_Action_Type_Proposal_Colleagues_TOTAL_Class_II=0 81 ==> BEHAVIOR_ANSWER_Platform_Teaching_Action_Type_Responde_Teachers_TOTAL_Class_II=0 BEHAVIOR_PROPOSE_Platform_Teaching_Action_Type_Proposal_Teachers_TOTAL_Class_II=0 81 conf:(1)
9. BEHAVIOR_ASK_Platform_Teaching_Action_Type_Ask_Colleagues_TOTAL_Class_II=0 BEHAVIOR_PROPOSE_Platform_Teaching_Action_Type_Proposal_Teachers_TOTAL_Class_II=0 81 ==> BEHAVIOR_ANSWER_Platform_Teaching_Action_Type_Responde_Teachers_TOTAL_Class_II=0 BEHAVIOR_PROPOSE_Platform_Teaching_Action_Type_Proposal_Colleagues_TOTAL_Class_II=0 81 conf:(1)
10. BEHAVIOR_ASK_Platform_Teaching_Action_Type_Ask_Colleagues_TOTAL_Class_II=0 BEHAVIOR_ANSWER_Platform_Teaching_Action_Type_Responde_Teachers_TOTAL_Class_II=0 81 ==> BEHAVIOR_PROPOSE_Platform_Teaching_Action_Type_Proposal_Teachers_TOTAL_Class_II=0 BEHAVIOR_PROPOSE_Platform_Teaching_Action_Type_Proposal_Colleagues_TOTAL_Class_II=0 81 conf:(1)

that the students consider that this involvement will compensate their own weak involvement on different activities.

ANALYSIS OF THE RELATIONSHIP BETWEEN PARTICIPATORY BEHAVIOR AND ACADEMIC PERFORMANCE

The workflow, as described in the Figure 18, includes the following processes:

- Input data, organized as "arff" file is loaded in Weka environment;
- Data is preprocessed. Weka environment offers many visualizing and preprocessing tools, such as Attribute Summarizer, filters, updating algorithms. Data is stored for later use;
- The most six relevant attributes for the participatory behavior pattern in the first and second year are selected using the InfoGainAttribute algorithm;

Figure 17. Workflow for the relationship analysis

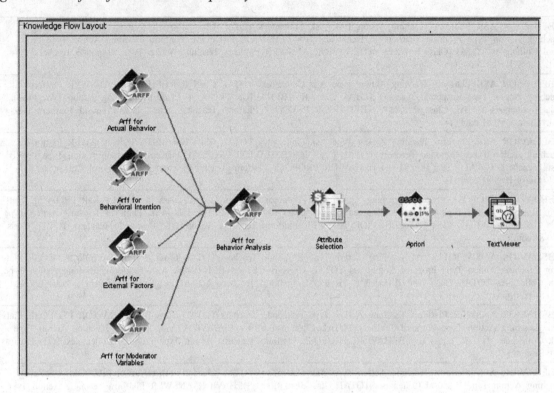

Result 6.

28. BEHAVIOR_ASK_Platform_Administrative_Action_Type_Ask_Colleagues_Class_II=0 BEHAVIOR_ANSWER_Platform_Administrative_Action_Type_Responde_Colleagues_Class_II=0 91 ==> 1_3_MOTIVATION_NEEDS_Benefits=Access_to_info_without_going_to_class 91 conf:(1)

Result 7.

136.MOTIVATION_NEEDS_ReasonOnlineMIP=Lack_of_time
SATISFACTION_PLATFORM_Continuity=YES
BEHAVIOR_ANSWER_Platform_Administrative_Action_Type_Responde_Colleagues_Class_II=0 85 ==> BEHAVIOR_ASK_Platform_Administrative_Action_Type_Ask_Colleagues_Class_II=0 85 conf:(1)

Result 8.

163.MOTIVATION_NEEDS_ReasonOnlineMIP=Lack_of_time
SATISFACTION_INSTRUCTORS_IdealInstructor=Involved
PROFILE_INFORMATION_Income=>1500
BEHAVIOR_PROPOSE_Platform_Administrative_Action_Type_Proposal_Colleagues_Class_II=0 85 ==> BEHAVIOR_ASK_Platform_Administrative_Action_Type_Ask_Colleagues_Class_II=0 BEHAVIOR_ANSWER_Platform_Administrative_Action_Type_Responde_Colleagues_Class_II=0 85 conf:(1)

Result 9. Other relevant rules

165.MOTIVATION_NEEDS_ReasonOnlineMIP=Lack_of_time
SATISFACTION_INSTRUCTORS_IdealInstructor=Involved
PROFILE_INFORMATION_Income=>1500
BEHAVIOR_ASK_Platform_Administrative_Action_Type_Ask_Colleagues_Class_II=0 85 ==> BEHAVIOR_ANSWER_Platform_Administrative_Action_Type_Responde_Colleagues_Class_II=0 BEHAVIOR_PROPOSE_Platform_Administrative_Action_Type_Proposal_Colleagues_Class_II=0 85 conf:(1)
203.MOTIVATION_NEEDS_ReasonOnlineMIP=Lack_of_time SATISFACTION_PLATFORM_Continuity=YES SATISFACTION_INSTRUCTORS_IdealInstructor=Involved BEHAVIOR_PROPOSE_Platform_Administrative_Action_Type_Proposal_Colleagues_Class_II=0 84 ==> BEHAVIOR_ASK_Platform_Administrative_Action_Type_Ask_Colleagues_Class_II=0 BEHAVIOR_ANSWER_Platform_Administrative_Action_Type_Responde_Colleagues_Class_II=0 84 conf:(1)
204. MOTIVATION_NEEDS_ReasonOnlineMIP=Lack_of_time SATISFACTION_PLATFORM_Continuity=YES SATISFACTION_INSTRUCTORS_IdealInstructor=Involved BEHAVIOR_ANSWER_Platform_Administrative_Action_Type_Responde_Colleagues_Class_II=0 84 ==> BEHAVIOR_ASK_Platform_Administrative_Action_Type_Ask_Colleagues_Class_II=0 BEHAVIOR_PROPOSE_Platform_Administrative_Action_Type_Proposal_Colleagues_Class_II=0 84 conf:(1)
205. MOTIVATION_NEEDS_ReasonOnlineMIP=Lack_of_time SATISFACTION_PLATFORM_Continuity=YES SATISFACTION_INSTRUCTORS_IdealInstructor=Involved BEHAVIOR_ASK_Platform_Administrative_Action_Type_Ask_Colleagues_Class_II=0 84 ==> BEHAVIOR_ANSWER_Platform_Administrative_Action_Type_Responde_Colleagues_Class_II=0 BEHAVIOR_PROPOSE_Platform_Administrative_Action_Type_Proposal_Colleagues_Class_II=0 84 conf:(1)

Figure 18. Workflow for analyzing the relationship between academic performance and participatory behavior

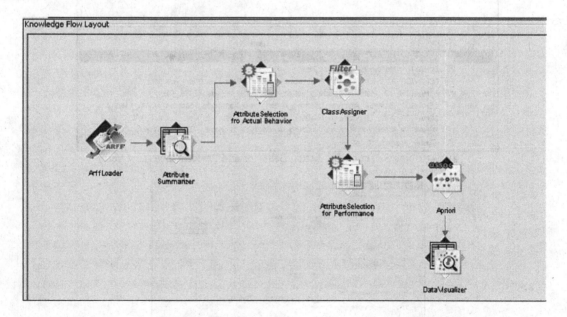

- The participatory behavior class label is added to dataset as a distinct attribute;
- The attributes *PERFORMANCE_Class_1st_year*, and *PERFORMANCE_Class_2nd_year* are added to dataset;
- The association rules are induced using the Apriori algorithm.
- The results visualization is finally performed, in order to validate the results.

Association Rules for Academic Performance and Participatory Behavior Class in the First Year

The Apriori algorithm is used to induce the association rules (see Result 10) expressing the relationships between the participatory behavior and the academic performance. In Figure 19 the preparatory actions are shown.

Rule 63: If the student average grade is between 7 and 8, she/he has two failed exams, the participatory behavior is not uniform, and the student does not intend to propose topics for discussion to colleagues then in the first year the student

should be included in the first cluster, as it was defined during the cluster analysis.

Rule 67: If the student average grade is over 8, the participatory behavior is not uniform, and the student does not intend to propose topics for discussion to colleagues then in the first year the student should be included in the cluster 1.

Considering these two association rules, we can conclude that the student could still get good results at school even her/his participation in the virtual environment is weak. When the student does not access the e-learning platform very often, her/his academic performance is medium.

Figure 19. Preparing the Apriori Algorithm application for the first year

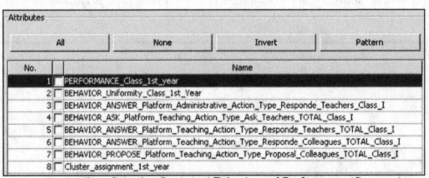

a) Attribute Selection for Actual Behavior and Performance (first year)

b) Apriori algorithm parameters

Association Rules for Academic Performance and Participatory Behavior Class in the Second Year

The Apriori algorithm is used to induce the association rules (see Result 11) expressing the relationships between the participatory behavior and the academic performance. In Figure 20 the preparatory actions are shown.

Based on obtained rules, we can say that when the student average grade is between 7 and 8, and she/he has less than two failed exams) then the student belongs to the behavior cluster 1, during the second year

This correlation is preserved from one year to another, so it is really very hard for a student to get a good academic performance when she/he is no up to date with the platform activities and she/

Result 10. Induced association rules

63. PERFORMANCE_Class_1st_year=2 BEHAVIOR_Uniformity_Class_1st_Year=Non_Unif BEHAVIOR_ANSWER_Platform_Teaching_Action_Type_Responde_Teachers_TOTAL_Class_I=0 BEHAVIOR_PROPOSE_Platform_Teaching_Action_Type_Proposal_Colleagues_TOTAL_Class_I=0 16 ==> Cluster_assignment_1st_year=cluster1_1st_year 16 conf:(1)
64. PERFORMANCE_Class_1st_year=2 BEHAVIOR_Uniformity_Class_1st_Year=Non_Unif BEHAVIOR_ANSWER_Platform_Teaching_Action_Type_Responde_Teachers_TOTAL_Class_I=0 16 ==> Cluster_assignment_1st_year=cluster1_1st_year 16 conf:(1)
65. PERFORMANCE_Class_1st_year=2 BEHAVIOR_ASK_Platform_Teaching_Action_Type_Ask_Teachers_TOTAL_Class_I=0 BEHAVIOR_ANSWER_Platform_Teaching_Action_Type_Responde_Teachers_TOTAL_Class_I=0 16 ==> Cluster_assignment_1st_year=cluster1_1st_year 16 conf:(1)
66. PERFORMANCE_Class_1st_year=2 BEHAVIOR_ASK_Platform_Teaching_Action_Type_Ask_Teachers_TOTAL_Class_I=0 BEHAVIOR_PROPOSE_Platform_Teaching_Action_Type_Proposal_Colleagues_TOTAL_Class_I=0 16 ==> Cluster_assignment_1st_year=cluster1_1st_year 16 conf:(1)
67. PERFORMANCE_Class_1st_year=3 BEHAVIOR_Uniformity_Class_1st_Year=Non_Unif BEHAVIOR_PROPOSE_Platform_Teaching_Action_Type_Proposal_Colleagues_TOTAL_Class_I=0 16 ==> Cluster_assignment_1st_year=cluster1_1st_year 16 conf:(1)
71. PERFORMANCE_Class_1st_year=2 BEHAVIOR_ASK_Platform_Teaching_Action_Type_Ask_Teachers_TOTAL_Class_I=0 BEHAVIOR_ANSWER_Platform_Teaching_Action_Type_Responde_Teachers_TOTAL_Class_I=0 BEHAVIOR_PROPOSE_Platform_Teaching_Action_Type_Proposal_Colleagues_TOTAL_Class_I=0 16 ==> Cluster_assignment_1st_year=cluster1_1st_year 16 conf:(1)

Result 11. Induced association rules

49. PERFORMANCE_Class_2nd_Year=2 BEHAVIOR_READ_Platform_Teaching_Action_Type_Reading_Materials_TOTAL_Class_II=0 23 ==> Cluster_assignment_2nd_year=cluster1_2nd_year 23 conf:(1)
50. PERFORMANCE_Class_2nd_Year=2 BEHAVIOR_READ_Platform_Teaching_Action_Type_Reading_Materials_TOTAL_Class_II=0 BEHAVIOR_ASK_Platform_Teaching_Action_Type_Ask_Colleagues_TOTAL_Class_II=0 23 ==> Cluster_assignment_2nd_year=cluster1_2nd_year 23 conf:(1)
51. PERFORMANCE_Class_2nd_Year=2 BEHAVIOR_READ_Platform_Teaching_Action_Type_Reading_Materials_TOTAL_Class_II=0 BEHAVIOR_ANSWER_Platform_Teaching_Action_Type_Responde_Teachers_TOTAL_Class_II=0 23 ==> Cluster_assignment_2nd_year=cluster1_2nd_year 23 conf:(1)
52. PERFORMANCE_Class_2nd_Year=2 BEHAVIOR_READ_Platform_Teaching_Action_Type_Reading_Materials_TOTAL_Class_II=0 BEHAVIOR_PROPOSE_Platform_Teaching_Action_Type_Proposal_Teachers_TOTAL_Class_II=0 23 ==> Cluster_assignment_2nd_year=cluster1_2nd_year 23 conf:(1)
53. PERFORMANCE_Class_2nd_Year=2 BEHAVIOR_READ_Platform_Teaching_Action_Type_Reading_Materials_TOTAL_Class_II=0 BEHAVIOR_PROPOSE_Platform_Teaching_Action_Type_Proposal_Colleagues_TOTAL_Class_II=0 23 ==> Cluster_assignment_2nd_year=cluster1_2nd_year 23 conf:(1)
58. PERFORMANCE_Class_2nd_Year=2 BEHAVIOR_READ_Platform_Teaching_Action_Type_Reading_Materials_TOTAL_Class_II=0 BEHAVIOR_ANSWER_Platform_Teaching_Action_Type_Responde_Teachers_TOTAL_Class_II=0 BEHAVIOR_PROPOSE_Platform_Teaching_Action_Type_Proposal_Colleagues_TOTAL_Class_II=0 23 ==> Cluster_assignment_2nd_year=cluster1_2nd_year 23 conf:(1)

Figure 20. Preparing the Apriori Algorithm application for the second year

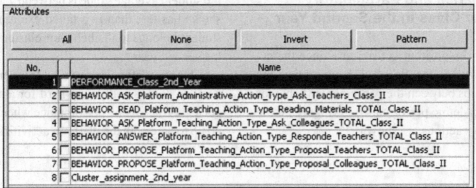

a)   Attribute Selection for Actual Behavior and Performance (the second year)

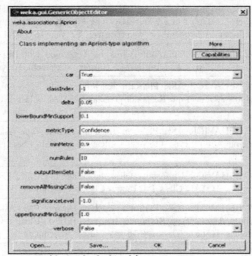

b) Apriori algorithm parameters

he is not communicating with other participants in the virtual environment.

FUTURE DEVELOPMENT

The data collection, transformation and analysis processes described in this chapter could be used to extract knowledge about further analysis. An improvement to the current data set would be if some attributes will be added. These attributes will be used to describe students' performance during their faculty years. Also, a new analysis direction could be based on some new attributes

that describe the teachers' point of view regarding students' activity, projects quality, the quality of their questions and answers. Analyses about teachers' expectations from their students will help to configure an initial check/test for the future students that will enroll to this online master programme.

CONCLUSION

Data mining processes reveal interesting patterns existing in data. Three student participatory behavior patterns in the first academic year were discovered. The students associated with the first pattern tend to visit platform the administrative are more than the teaching one, being less interested on communicating with colleagues and teachers on academic subjects. Their initiative in proposing new topics is also reduced. It can be conclude that the students are not very interested in acquiring knowledge, being focused on the administrative issues instead. The students associated with the second pattern have a high interest for the administrative issues, but the teaching topics are not neglected either. The students tend to interact with their colleagues in a large degree, making proposals for new topics. Reading the didactic materials provided by teacher is not a significant activity for these students, maybe because additional information / clarifications are obtained communicating with the other participants. Students presenting the last behavioral pattern are clearly focused on the academic activities, and have a low interest for the administrative issues. These students have the highest value for the attribute "answers to colleagues' questions" and we can expect these students to have a high academic performance.

Three student participatory behavior patterns in the second academic year were discovered. Like for the first year, the students showing this pattern have a low interest for the teaching area, preferring just to get some information from the administrative one, and loading various materials. The e-learning platform is exploited in a small extent, the access volume being minimal (class 0). The platform accesses for downloading are at a minimum level. The teachers and classmates are not considered as an option when students solve problem and prepare themselves for exams. A possible explanation is the lack of time, students mentioning it as the first reason for choosing an online programme. The students associated with the second pattern tend to access more often the teaching area comparing with the administrative one. It can be assumed that a minimum presence in the administrative area is always necessary but the attention pay to this area should not exceed

the teaching focus. Reading materials is weak, as well as the communication with peers and teachers. It can be observed a high resemblance between the first two patterns in terms of attitude towards colleagues and teachers. The students associated with the last pattern appear to be most interested in the academic content and communication with teachers and peers. The uniformity of their presence in the online activities indicates a constant work performance. Contact with teachers is higher than the communication with the colleagues. The main activities with teachers are asking for clarification and reading the materials. Even when they are trying to deal with the administrative issues, they are more interested to communicate with teachers instead of peers. Regarding the initiative, we cannot find a good score.

According to these results, we can conclude that in the second year of the programme, the students do not take initiative in the communication process, allowing the professor to decide the communication flow. This is very similar with the student participatory behavior during the first year.

The main similarities between the student participatory behavior in the first and the second year of the programme are:

- Three profiles of the student participatory behavior can be identify during each year: one of these profile has a weak participation on the virtual learning environment, and we can mention that the representativeness of this group increases from 44% in the first year to the 55% in the second year. Another profile has a moderate participation on the virtual learning environment and the representativeness of this profile decreases from 37% in the first year to 19% in the second year. The last profile is characterized by an active participation. The representativeness of this profile increases slightly from 19% in the first year to 26% in the second year.

- The active students tend to initiate sessions on topics proposed by the teachers.

The students characterized by an active participation are very present in the administrative area not only during the first year, but in the second year as well.

The main differences between the student participatory behavior in the first and the second year of the programme are:

- The interest for teaching activities decreases dramatically from the first to the second year, especially at the students belonging to the first two clusters. One explanation might be that the students are more focused to work to complete their master thesis, instead to participate in the learning environment.
- Each year, the most important activities in the virtual environment are different. During the first year, the students are mostly involved to respond to peers and teachers and also to ask questions to teachers. During the second year, the most important activities are directed towards colleagues, and those related to the didactical materials.

The attribute that have the biggest influences on the participatory behavior class attribute in the first year is *BEHAVIOR_ASK_Platform_Teaching_Action_Type_Ask_Teachers_TOTAL_Class_I*. Its variation leads to modify the attribute class values with highest probability. It can be said that communication with teachers is the most important factor for characterizing the participatory behavior profile. If students not to ask questions to their teachers and also they do not answer to their questions then it is very likely that they do not have communication initiatives with their colleagues.

The attribute that have the biggest influences on the participatory behavior class attribute in the second year is *READ_Platform_Teaching_Ac-*

tion_Type_Reading_Materials_TOTAL_Class_II. Its variation leads to modify the attribute class values with highest probability. Its variation leads to modify the attribute class values with highest probability. It can be said that, the importance gave by the students to published didactic materials has a great influences on the participatory behavior profile. Therefore, a variation in how students access didactic materials may lead to another participatory profile.

When *BEHAVIOR_ASK_Platform_Administrative_Action_Type_Ask_Colleagues_Class_II* attribute has value 0 (meaning that the students do not put any question to their colleagues) and when the *BEHAVIOR_ANSWER_Platform_Administrative_Action_Type_Responde_Colleagues_Class_II* attribute has value 0 (meaning that students do not give any answer to their colleagues) then the Actual Behavior are strongly related to the external factor *MOTIVATION_NEEDS_Benefits* having the value *Access_to_info_without_going_to_class*, meaning that the students cannot come to classes. This rule describes the reason for getting enrolled in the online program is associated with the participatory behavior during the second year. If students fail to ask and answer questions to their colleagues then their reason for applying to this online program is the lack of time. Confidence factor for this rule is one (maximum). A number of 91 students respect both the rule first and the second part.

When *BEHAVIOR_ANSWER_Platform_Administrative_Action_Type_Responde_Colleagues_Class_II* and *BEHAVIOR_ASK_Platform_Administrative_Action_Type_Ask_Colleagues_Class_II* have value 0, meaning that the student has not responded and do not put any questions to colleagues, then the participatory behavior is strongly related to the external factor explaining that reason for choosing an online program is *Lack_of_time* and the platform offers satisfaction to the student. Therefore, the amount of available time is a very important element for the participatory behavior during the second year. A number of 85 students are aligned with this rule.

When *MOTIVATION_NEEDS_ReasonOnlineMIP* attribute has value *Lack_of_time*, *SATISFACTION_INSTRUCTORS_IdealInstructor* has value *Involved* (meaning that students ask to their teacher to be very engaged in virtual environment). *PROFILE_INFORMATION_Income* attribute has value *>1500* (meaning that students have an income of more than 1500 RON) then the following attributes. *BEHAVIOR_PROPOSE_Platform_Administrative_Action_Type_Proposal_Colleagues_Class_II, BEHAVIOR_ASK_Platform_Administrative_Action_Type_Ask_Colleagues_Class_II* and *BEHAVIOR_ANSWER_Platform_Administrative_Action_Type_Responde_Colleagues_Class_II* have values 0 (meaning that the students do not make proposals, do not ask and not answer to questions). 85 of the students respect this rule.

Other induced association rules confirm that the students with poor a communication with their colleagues ask for a greater involvement of the teachers on virtual environment. It is supposed that the students consider that this involvement will compensate their own weak involvement on different activities.

If the student average grade is between 7 and 8, she/he has two failed exams, the participatory behavior is not uniform, and the student does not intend to propose topics for discussion to colleagues then in the first year the student should be included in the first cluster, as it was defined during the cluster analysis. If the student average grade is over 8, the participatory behavior is not uniform, and the student does not intend to propose topics for discussion to colleagues then in the first year the student should be included in the cluster 1. Considering these two association rules, we can conclude that the student could still get good results at school even her/his participation in the virtual environment is weak. When the student does not access the e-learning platform very often, her/his academic performance is medium.

Based on the association rules, we can say that when the student average grade is between 7 and 8, and she/he has less than two failed exams) then the student belongs to the behavior cluster 1, during the second year. This correlation is preserved from one year to another, so it is really very hard for a student to get a good academic performance when she/he is no up to date with the platform activities and she/he is not communicating with other participants in the virtual environment.

REFERENCES

Agrawal, R., & Srikant, R. (1994). Fast algorithms for mining association rules in large databases. In *20th International Conference on Very Large Data Bases*, (pp. 478-499).

Arbaugh, J. B. (2004). Learning to learn online: A study of perceptual changes between multiple online course experiences. *The Internet and Higher Education*, *7*, 169–182. doi:10.1016/j.iheduc.2004.06.001

Baker, R., & Yacef, K. (2009). The state of educational data mining in 2009: A review and future visions. *Journal of Educational Data Mining*, *1*, 3–17.

Barros, B., & Verdejo, M. F. (2000). Analyzing student interaction processes in order to improve collaboration: The degree approach. *International Journal of Artificial Intelligence in Education*, *11*, 221–241.

Bauer, L. (2010). *Measuring student behavior and learning in an online environment*. Distance Learning Symposium, Learning Enhancement Center, Metropolitan College of New York. Retrieved from http://vimeo.com/12856497

Birch, A., & Irvine, V. (2009). Preservice teachers' acceptance of ICT integration in the classroom: Applying the UTAUT model. *Educational Media International*, *46*(4), 295–315. doi:10.1080/09523980903387506

Bodea, V. (2003). Standards for data mining languages. *The Proceedings of the Sixth International Conference on Economic Informatics - Digital Economy*, (pp. 502-506). ISBN 973-8360-02-1

Bodea, V. (2007). Application and benefits *of knowledge management in universities – A case study on student performance enhancement. Informatics in Knowledge Society, The Proceedings of the Eight International Conference on Informatics in Economy*, May 17-18, (pp. 1033-1038).

Bodea, V. (2008). *Knowledge management systems*. Ph.D thesis, supervised by Prof. Ion Gh. Roşca, The Academy of Economic Studies, Bucharest.

Bodea, V., & Roşca, I. (2007). Analiza performanţelor studenţilor cu tehnici de data mining: Studiu de caz în Academia de Studii Economice din Bucureşti. In Bodea, C., & Andone, I. (Eds.), *Managementul cunoaşterii în universitatea modernă. Editura Academiei de Studii Economice din Bucureşti*.

Bouckaert, R., Frank, E., Hall, M., Kirkby, R., Reutemann, P., Seewald, A., & Scuse, D. (2010). *WEKA manual for version 3-6-2*. Hamilton, New Zealand: University of Waikato.

Brew, L. S. (2008). The role of student feedback in evaluating and revising a blended learning course. *The Internet and Higher Education, 11*, 98–105. doi:10.1016/j.iheduc.2008.06.002

Bulu, S. T., & Yildirim, Z. (2008). Communication behaviors and trust in collaborative online teams. *Journal of Educational Technology & Society, 11*(1), 132–147.

Chapman, C., Clinton, J., & Kerber, R (2005). *CRISP-DM 1.0, Step-by-step data mining guide.*

Charpentier, M., Lafrance, C., & Paquette, G. (2006). *International e-learning strategies: Key findings relevant to the Canadian context.* Retrieved from http://www.ccl-cca.ca/pdfs/CommissionedReports/JohnBissInternationalE-LearningEN.pdf

Cocea, M., Hershkovitz, A., & Baker, R. S. J. D. (2009). The impact of off-task and gaming behaviors on learning: immediate or aggregate? *Proceedings of the 14th International Conference on Artificial Intelligence in Education*, (pp. 507-514).

CRoss Industry Standard Process for Data Mining. (n.d.). Retrieved from http://www.crisp-dm.org/

Davenport, T. (2001). Successful knowledge management projects. *Sloan Management Review, 39*(2).

Delavari, N., Beikzadeh, M. R., & Amnuaisuk, S. K. (2005). Application of enhanced analysis model for data mining processes in higher educational system. *Proceedings of ITHET 6th Annual International Conference*, Juan Dolio, Dominican Republic.

Delavari, N., Beikzadeh, M. R., & Shirazi, M. R. A. (2004). A new model for using data mining in higher educational system. *Proceedings of 5th International Conference on Information Technology based Higher Education and Training: ITEHT '04*, Istanbul, Turkey.

European Commission. (2005). *Mobilizing the brainpower of Europe: Enabling universities to make their full contribution to the Lisbon Strategy.* Brussels, Communicate no. 152.

Eurostat. (2009). *The Bologna Process in higher education in Europe, key indicators on the social dimension and mobility, European Communities and IS, Hochschul-Informations-System G mbH, 2009.* Retrieved from http://epp.eurostat.ec.europa.eu/portal/page/portal/education/bologna_process

Guardado, M., & Shi, L. (2007). ESL students' experiences of online peer feedback. *Computers and Composition*, *24*, 443–461. doi:10.1016/j.compcom.2007.03.002

Haddawy, P., & Hien, N. (2006). *A decision support system for evaluating international student applications. Computer Science and Information management program.* Asian Institute of Technology.

International Working Group on Educational Data Mining. (2010). *Educational data mining.* Retrieved from http://www.educationaldatamining.org/

Jeong, H., & Biswas, G. (2008). Mining student behavior models in learning-by-teaching environments, *Proceedings of the 1st International Conference on Educational Data Mining*, (pp. 127-136).

Kelly, H. F., Ponton, M. K., & Rovai, A. P. (2007). A comparison of student evaluations of teaching between online and face-to-face courses. *The Internet and Higher Education*, *10*, 89–101. doi:10.1016/j.iheduc.2007.02.001

Kumar, T. (2001). An introduction to data mining in institutional research. Retrieved from www.ir.uni.edu/dbweb/pdf/present/dm_intro.pdf

Liu, B., Hsu, W., & Ma, Y. (1998). Integrating classification and association rule mining. In *Fourth International Conference on Knowledge Discovery and Data Mining*, (pp. 80-86).

Luan, J. (2001). *Data mining applications in higher education. New directions for institutional research* (1st ed.). San Francisco, CA: Jossey-Bass.

Luan, J. (2002). Data mining and its applications in higher education. In Serban, A., & Luan, J. (Eds.), *Knowledge management: Building a competitive advantage for higher education. New directions for institutional research, No. 113*. San Francisco, CA: Jossey Bass. doi:10.1002/ir.35

Luan, J., Zhai, M., Chen, J., Chow, T., Chang, L., & Zhao, C.-M. (2004). *Concepts, myths, and case studies of data mining in higher education.* AIR 44th Forum, Boston.

Ma, Y., Liu, B., Wong, C. K., Yu, P. S., & Lee, S. M. (2000). Targeting the right students using data mining. *Proceedings of the Sixth ACM SIGKDD International Conference on Knowledge Discovery and Data Mining*, Boston, (pp. 457-464).

McDonald, M., Dorn, B., & McDonald, G. (2004). A statistical analysis of student performance in online computer science courses. *Proceedings of the 35th SIGCSE Technical Symposium on Computer Science Education*, Norfolk, Virginia, (pp. 71-74).

McFarland, D., & Hamilton, D. (2006). Factors affecting student performance and satisfaction: Online versus traditional course delivery. *Journal of Computer Information Systems*, *46*(2), 25–32.

Monolescu, D., & Schifter, C. (2000). Online focus group: A tool to evaluate online students' course experience. *The Internet and Higher Education*, *2*, 171–176. doi:10.1016/S1096-7516(00)00018-X

Piccoli, G., Ahmad, R., & Ives, B. (2001). Web-based virtual learning environments: A research framework and a preliminary assessment of effectiveness in basic IT skills training. *Management Information Systems Quarterly*, *25*(4), 401–426. doi:10.2307/3250989

Priluck, R. (2004). Web-assisted courses for business education: An examination of two sections of principles of marketing. *Journal of Marketing Education*, *26*(2), 161–173. doi:10.1177/0273475304265635

Ranjan, J. (2008). Impact of Information Technology in academia. *International Journal of Educational Management*, *22*(5), 442–455. doi:10.1108/09513540810883177

Ranjan, J., & Malik, K. (2007). Effective educational process: A data mining approach. *Vine, 37*(4), 502–515. doi:10.1108/03055720710838551

Romero, C., & Ventura, S. (2007). Educational data mining: A survey from 1995 to 2005. *Expert Systems with Applications, 33*, 135–146. doi:10.1016/j.eswa.2006.04.005

Sargenti, P., Lightfoot, W., & Kehal, M. (2006). Diffusion of knowledge in and through higher education organizations. *Issues in Information Systems, 3*(2), 3–8.

Shyamala, K., & Rajagopalan, S. P. (2006). Data mining model for a better higher educational system. *Information Technology Journal, 5*(3), 560–564. doi:10.3923/itj.2006.560.564

Talavera, L., & Gaudioso, E. (2004). Mining student data to characterize similar behavior groups in unstructured collaboration spaces. *Workshop on Artificial Intelligence in Computer Supported Collaborative Learning at European Conference on Artificial Intelligence,* Valencia, Spain, (pp. 17-23).

Tallent-Runnels, M.-K. (2005). The relationship between problems with technology and graduate students' evaluations of online teaching. *The Internet and Higher Education, 8*, 167–174. doi:10.1016/j.iheduc.2005.03.005

Venkatesh, V., Morris, M. G., Davis, G. B., & Davis, F. D. (2003). User acceptance of information technology: Toward a unified view. *Management Information Systems Quarterly, 27*(3), 425–478.

Waiyamai, K. (2004). *Improving quality of graduate students by data mining.* Faculty of Engineering, Kasetsart University, Frontiers of ICT Research International Symposium.

Williams, P. W. (2009). *Assessing mobile learning effectiveness and acceptance.* US: ProQuest Information & Learning.

Witten, I., & Frank, E. (2005). *Data mining: Practical machine learning tools and techniques.* Elsevier.

Young, A., & Norgard, C. (2006). Assessing the quality of online courses from the students' perspective. *The Internet and Higher Education, 9*, 107–115. doi:10.1016/j.iheduc.2006.03.001

Zapalska, A., Shao, D., & Shao, L. (2003). *Student learning via WebCT course instruction in undergraduate-based business education. Teaching Online in Higher Education (Online).* Conference.

ADDITIONAL READING

Anjewierden, A., Kollöffel, B., & Hulshof, C. (2007). Towards educational data mining: Using data mining methods for automated chat analysis to understand and support inquiry learning processes. *Proceedings of International Workshop on Applying Data Mining in e-Learning 2007,* Crete, (pp. 27-36).

Bodea, C. (2007). An innovative system for learning services in project management. In *Proceedings of 2007 IEEE/INFORMS International Conference on Service Operations and Logistics. And Informatics.* Philadelphia, PA: IEEE.

Castells, M., & Pekka, H. (2002). *The information society and the welfare state. The Finnish model.* Oxford, UK: Oxford University Press. doi:10.1093/acprof:oso/9780199256990.001.0001

Demirel, M. (2009). Lifelong learning and schools in the twenty-first century. *Procedia Social and Behavioral Sciences, 1*, 1709–1716. doi:10.1016/j.sbspro.2009.01.303

Garcia, A. C. B., Kunz, J., Ekstrom, M., & Kiviniemi, A. (2003). *Building a project ontology with extreme collaboration and VD&C. CIFE Technical Report #152.* Stanford University.

Gareis, R. (2007). *Happy projects!* Romanian version ed. Bucharest, Romania: ASE Printing House.

Guardado, M., & Shi, L. (2007). ESL students' experiences of online peer feedback. *Computers and Composition*, *24*, 443–461. doi:10.1016/j.compcom.2007.03.002

Kalathur, S. (2006). An object-oriented framework for predicting student competency level in an incoming class. *Proceedings of SERP '06 Las Vegas*, 2006, (pp. 179-183).

Kanellopoulos, D., Kotsiantis, S., & Pintelas, P. (2006). Ontology-based learning applications: A development methodology. In *Proceedings of the 24th IASTED International Multi-Conference Software Engineering*. Innsbruck, Austria, 2006.

Lytras, M. D., Carroll, J. M., Damiani, E., & Tennyson, R. D. (2008). *Emerging technologies and information systems for the knowledge society*. In First World Summit on the Knowledge Society, WSKS. Athens, Greece, 2008.

Markkula, M. (2006). *Creating favourable conditions for knowledge society through knowledge management, eGorvernance and eLearning*. Budapest, Hungary, 2006. FIG Workshop on eGovernance, Knowledge Management and eLearning.

Teekaput, P., & Waiwanijchakij, P. (2006). *E-learning and knowledge management, symptoms of a reality*. In Third International Conference on eLearning for Knowledge-Based Society. Bangkok, Thailand, 2006.

Turner, R. J., & Simister, S. J. (2004). *Gower handbook of project management*. Romanian version ed. Bucharest, Romania: Codecs Printing House.

Young, A., & Norgard, C. (2006). Assessing the quality of online courses from the students' perspective. *The Internet and Higher Education*, *9*, 107–115. doi:10.1016/j.iheduc.2006.03.001

KEY TERMS AND DEFINITIONS

Association Rule: Is an implication expression of the form $X => Y$ where X and Y are disjoint conjunctions of attribute-value pairs. Strength of association rules can be measured in terms of support and confidence. Support determines how often a rule applies to a data set and confidence determines how frequently items appear in transactions that contain X. Association analysis has as objective to find hidden relationships in large sections of data sets.

Classification: Is the process consisting in learning function f, which assigns a predefined class label y to each set of attributes X. The function f is known as the model for classification. A classification model can serve as an explanatory tool to distinguish between instances of different classes. In this case, the classification is considered as a descriptive modeling. A classification model can also be used to predict the class label for the unknown instances. In this case, the classification is considered as a predictive modeling. Classification techniques are better suited for prediction or description of data sets for binary or nominal attributes.

Clustering: Is a technique by which similar instances are grouped together. All the instances grouped in the same cluster have a certain understanding, a certain utility, or both. Clusters capture the natural structure of data and so, the clustering process might be the starting point for other data handling processes such as summarization.

Data Mining: Is the process of extracting previously unknown, valid, and operational patterns/models from large collection of data. Essential for data mining is the discovery of patterns without previous hypotheses. Data mining is not aimed to verify, confirm or refute hypothesis, but instead to discover "unexpected" patterns, completely unknown at the time of the data mining process take place, which may even contradict the intuitive perception. For this reason, the results are truly valuables.

Educational Data Mining: Is an emerging discipline, concerned with developing methods for exploring the unique types of data that come from educational settings, and using those methods to better understand students, and the settings which they learn in.

E-Learning: Is a type of distance education in teaching-learning interaction is mediated by an environment set up by new information and communication technologies, in particular the Internet. Internet is both the material environment, as well as the communication channel between the actors involved.

Chapter 17
Social Net/work(ing) on Facebook:
An Analysis of Audiences, Producers, and Immaterial Laborers

Robert N. Spicer
Rutgers University, USA & DeSales University, USA

ABSTRACT

Reactions to new media vary from utopian pronouncements about their democratizing potential to fear about social deviance. The news media spend a great deal of time discussing new media, especially as they relate to young people. Again, sometimes these media are reported on as democratizing forces as when Time magazine declared "You" to be the person of the year (Grossman, 2006). Other times they are described as a source of social anxiety, for example, when NBC News (2011) reported on flash mobs as "swarms of mostly young people organized through social media, texting, tweeting, using Internet sites, and increasingly turning violent in cities across the country" (para. 4). However, social media are rarely discussed in terms of their capacities to tap into users' activities as forms of labor. This chapter contributes to the discussion of user generated content as labor (Cohen, 2008; Peterson, 2008; van Dijck, 2009) by examining the process of building and maintaining an audience in the form of a friends list while simultaneously being an audience member in others' friends lists. This labor is examined in this chapter through looking at the motivations individuals cite for using Facebook and how those users describe their feelings about their friends list qua audience or how users describe themselves as members of an audience.

INTRODUCTION

The site under analysis in this study, Facebook, falls under the category of a social network site as defined by danah boyd and Nicole Ellison (2007) as "web-based services that allow individuals to (1)

construct a semi-public profile within a bounded system, (2) articulate a list of other users with whom they share a connection, and (3) view and traverse their list of connections and those made by others within the system" (p. 211). One argument this chapter will make is that Facebook breaks down the distinction between social network sites and social networking sites.

DOI: 10.4018/978-1-4666-0312-7.ch017

It will also be argued that Facebook can be defined as a virtual community. Blanchard (2004) defines virtual communities as "groups of people who interact primarily through computer-mediated communication and who identify with and have developed feelings of belonging and attachment to each other" (p. 55). She argues for two kinds of virtual communities: place based and dispersed. The place based communities are those communities which include face-to-face (FtF) communication and a virtual component, such as a message board about the place in which the FtF communication takes place. A dispersed virtual community is one that does not have any FtF component. Functionally speaking, Facebook could be seen as serving both forms of virtual communities. On one hand, groups can be formed *because* they are made up of individuals who are geographically separated from one another and then find each other on Facebook. For example, one respondent to the survey for this study voiced a common theme saying Facebook is "a great tool to help keep in touch with friends that live far away." There were also respondents who discussed Facebook as a way to maintain relationships that do not have an FtF component but are strictly in a dispersed virtual community. One respondent said she uses Facebook because, "I like the social element as I live in a rural, isolated location." Another respondent noted that Facebook can serve as an aid for combating shyness, saying, "it's helped me stay friends with people … I'm very introverted, and tend to tunnel into my house … that usually meant friends would drift off to more social people." This echoes research that has examined uses of social media for those with varying degrees of social anxiety (Blumer, 2010; Orr et al., 2009). However, most respondents framed this dispersed community in professional terms, using Facebook as a way to network with others in their profession whom they have not met FtF.

This chapter will begin with a literature review discussing the definition and distinction between social network and social networking websites.

It will also look at research on immaterial labor in the use of those sites. The method section will explain the implementation of the survey for this study. This will be followed by a discussion of the data, broken into two sections. The first will discuss the quantitative data; the second involves an interpretive analysis of the open-ended questions from the survey. Finally, the chapter concludes by discussing the theoretical implications of Facebook users thinking of themselves as audience members rather than content producers.

LITERATURE REVIEW: IMMATERIAL LABOR, AUDIENCE STUDIES, AND SOCIAL NETWORKS

The overarching argument of this chapter is that the creation of content within social network(ing) websites is a form of free labor which, while it may be of value or create pleasure for the user generating it, is engaged in on behalf of whatever institution happens to own the website with which the user has an account. This research builds on work that makes this same argument about a variety of online, user generated content (Zwick 2008; Arvidsson, 2006; Banks and Humphrey, 2008) and employs Maurizio Lazzarato's (2006) theory of immaterial labor, which is defined as, "the labor that produces the informational and cultural content of the commodity" (p. 132). In this case the commodity is a social network(ing) website. The informational aspect of immaterial labor is, "where the skills involved in direct labor are increasingly skills involving cybernetics and computer control," the cultural aspect is "a series of activities that are not normally recognized as 'work' … defining and fixing cultural and artistic standards, fashions, tastes, consumer norms, and, more strategically, public opinion" (p. 132).

It is also important to define precisely what is meant by social network(ing) websites and how the concept of immaterial labor fits into the way this research conceptualizes them. Boyd and Ellison (2008) make a distinction between social network websites and social networking websites. This research conflates the two into social network(ing) websites. The distinction between the two is that social network websites allow for the maintenance of existing "real world" networks in the forum of the website. This is distinct from social networking websites that allow users to connect to strangers, to engage in the activity of networking (p. 210-211). This chapter conflates the two because of the way in which immaterial labor is inserted into the discussion and the question of how the respondents conceive of themselves as either members of an audience or as performers. The term networking carries with it the obvious connotations of the labor of making connections for the advancement of professional interests. Facebook, as this research demonstrates, tends to be more of a social network website in that it is used for the maintenance of existing networks, not the labor of networking, creating new networks that can be professionally advantageous. However, the theory of immaterial labor is employed here to argue that even the maintenance of personal networks is a form of labor and value creation. Thus the term used in this chapter, social network(ing), is employed for its implication that Facebook users are value creators engaged in labor even if that labor is mainly directed toward personal relationships rather than professional ones.

The conflation of social network and social networking also acknowledges findings in the data of this study that indicate that Facebook users use it for personal relationships with friends and family while also cultivating professional relationships with strangers who work in their field. Ellison, Steinfield and Lampe (2007) note, "Previous research suggests that Facebook users engage in 'searching' for people with whom they have an offline connection more than they 'browse' for complete strangers to meet" (p. 1144). Their research, along with Blanchard's, indicates that Facebook is predominantly used for relationships that have both online and offline elements. The data

collected here confirms that argument. However, it also shows that there are valuable online only relationships and that Facebook users are creating an environment where personal and professional relationships are mixing with one another. This builds on earlier audience studies research about attention and value creation for "old" media such as print, television and radio; traditional media which are advertiser supported. In their examination of "watching as working" Jhally and Livant (2006) argue that one way media as technology create economic value is through the speed at which they circulate information about commodities and how they thus increase the speed at which they are consumed (p. 26). Value is also created through media in how they tap into the audience's capacities, their capacities to act, to purchase and to pay attention to a message, their capacity to watch.

Jhally and Livant define watching as the "activity through which human beings relate to the external physical world and to each other" (p. 26). The problem for Jhally and Livant is that what is being created when media present content in order to attract attention is a somewhat "fuzzily described" process (p. 26). Watching is a broad, general capacity employed by the audience and harnessed by "old" media and "because watching is an unspecialized, general-purpose capacity, it is capable of being modified by its objects, by what we watch, how we watch, and under what conditions we watch" (p. 27). Social network(ing) websites present an example of the modification to which Jhally and Livant refer. While engaging the audience it also invites that audience to perform for those whom they are simultaneously watching. The audience/performer distinction begins to break down and that breakdown is what is being examined in this research. The question is, when this breakdown happens which role more prominently makes up the users' self-identities: audience or performer?

The creation of content in websites like Facebook can also be seen as a form of "online personal brand management" (Cote and Pybus, 2007, p. 95). Cote and Pybus argue for "capital as a logic which increasingly flows through more and more otherwise discrete social relations, and finds passage in different political and social techniques and practices" (p. 93). Examples of these social techniques and practices are found in the maintenance of the digital body, the on-line extension of self, the "entrepreneurial skills necessary for forging effective links" that help the digital body to be "valorized and to extend one's social network and hence cultural capital" (p. 94). Theses techniques are also demonstrated through the management of others' perceptions of the user through things like one's profile picture on Facebook (Mendelson and Papacharissi, 2011). Similar to Cote and Pybus, Scholz (2007) argues that social networking sites do "not even need to own the created content. The created sociality is the value" (para. 18). In other words, Facebook is not just a site "for forging effective links," but also one for forging "affective links," emotional ties between users, connections that become valu-able to advertisers.

In Joshua Meyrowitz's (1986) terms, Face-book walls turn metaphoric and literal walls into windows increasing "our access to each other's social performances" (p. 37). These social per-formances come described in varied language from the sterility of "uploading data" to the far more friendly "sharing." Along with "sharing" comes the notion of affective connections through media, where the user is not simply telling her audience something, there is reciprocity, and in this connection is part of an attempt to obtain or spend social capital within the network. The frame of capital turns the individual into a brand necessitating management that is described by Arvidsson (2006) as creating, on dating sites for example, "a problematic emphasis on the self and its experiences and complexities" (p. 682). This gets to the essence of Facebook as Chris Cox its director of products described it in an article for *New York* magazine in 2009.

A lot of times users—well, I don't want to say they undervalue sharing, but a lot of times they don't want to share initially...And then eventually, they say, 'Okay, I'll put a profile picture up here. I'll do it.' Immediately, their friends comment on it, and there are no tacky, weird strangers around, and suddenly they start to realize, 'Hey, wait, this is different. I am on the Internet, but I am in a safe place.' (Grigoriadis, 2009, para. 15)

Unfortunately, the act of defining privacy and "a safe place" can come with a bit of ambiguity. Users, at times, may not think about the act of sharing as inherently threatening to privacy or privacy as necessitating total secrecy.

Boyd (2008) uses the phrase "security through obscurity" (p. 15). The loss of security through the ending of obscurity, boyd argues, was caused by the creation of News Feed on Facebook. Users' actions were suddenly being announced for their entire friends list to see. This was problematic because of the compartmentalization of relationships that happens in "the real world" and some users may expect in the "digital world" of Facebook. There are two fundamentally different perceptions of the impact of News Feed that reflect, as Wellman (2002) argues, a more complicated social milieu. Wellman presents the example of people who shout into cell phones when in a public place. In this instance the individuals' "awareness and behavior are in private cyberspace even though their bodies are in public places" (p. 16). This "un-awareness" is reflected in the responses in this study that skew toward a discourse about being an audience rather than a performer. This is the main theme that will be explored in the results section of this chapter.

METHOD

The survey used for this study was simultane-ously an attempt to obtain user responses and to observe the functionality of a social network, how easily an item might flow through it. As much as this research was attempting to answer some questions about Facebook users there was also a secondary function in the research of attempting to play with research methods in social media. With this in mind, a survey was sent to 182 people in the researcher's Facebook friends list. Recipients were sent a message with a link to an online survey. They were asked to respond to the survey and forward the link to any "Facebook friends" they thought would be interested in taking it. The rationale behind this method of distribution was two-fold. First, it was done with the intention of attempting to find how effective it would be. This is an experimental research method that was intended to test the boundaries of research methods in social networks. There is functionality in Facebook that creates "pass-along" or circulation value, the ability to more easily circulate content. The research method is being used to test that "pass-along" value, how easily a survey could be circulated, testing the responsiveness of the network and quantifying the results as evidence of the power of the network's circulation capabilities. The results of this methodological approach will be discussed in the quantitative data section.

While there is a quantitative aspect to the data collected, the primary research method of this study is qualitative and interpretive. The survey circulated contained some demographic data with closed-ended questions about the number of people in each respondent's friends list and the amount of time they spend on Facebook. However, the purpose of the research was to gather qualitative responses to questions about participation in the Facebook community. Being qualitative and interpretive in its nature, the first research question this chapter attempts to answer is how respondents would describe their use of Facebook when given an open-ended question. Specifically, do they speak in terms of being members of an audience or in terms of engaging in a performance for an audience? When asked, "Why do you use Facebook," how will they respond? Will they discuss Facebook functions like sharing content

with others through things like posting pictures or self-expression via status updates? Or, will they describe their reasons for using Facebook through the terms of viewing others' activities? Simply put, when asked, "Why do you use Facebook," will the respondents talk about "watching" or "being watched?" The questions given in the survey for this study, with the exception of demographic questions, were open ended; respondents were given the freedom to give whatever information they felt was relevant to their experiences with Facebook. The goal of this project was to then weave these responses into a discussion of theory surrounding affective connections, immaterial labor and audiences in new media. The survey results were examined for common threads in responses to the questions.

RQ 1: Do Facebook users discuss their use of Facebook in audience-oriented or producer-oriented terms?

The second research question interrogates the respondents' self-perception as audience or performer by asking about their feelings about their friends list and the number of friends in it. The respondents were asked how many "friends" they have on Facebook. Respondents were then asked to "describe the value they place on that number" and "why they value it in that way." By asking the rationale behind the value they place on their friends list we can find another avenue of insight into the audience/performer split in their thinking about their Facebook use. Some respondents may speak in terms of valuing a large number of Facebook friends because they are looking for a lot of people with whom they will be able to share information. On the other hand, they may respond with ideas about having others to "watch" via Facebook.

RQ 2: How are users' perceptions of their friends list part of their audience-oriented or producer-oriented perceptions?

This research method was also chosen for its utility in collecting both quantitative and qualitative data. The goal of this research was to have quantifiable data about the ways in which users think about their Facebook experience. However, more than that, the goal of the research was to dig deeper into that thinking. This is an attempt to give respondents the ability to express their perceptions of their experience and to analyze those answers as texts. This is done with the goal of giving greater insight into that thinking, more than just categorizing their expressions as "audience-oriented" or "producer-oriented." To possibly answer why the respondents feel the way they do or to look at what constitutes an "audience-oriented" or "producer-oriented" response. The discussion of the responses has been broken up into the next two sections. The first section will discuss the quantitative data; the second will discuss the qualitative responses.

Quantitative Data: A Living Address Book

The most interesting part of the quantitative data for this research is the number of respondents. As explained in the method section this research was conducted in an attempt to experiment with research methods in social media. The survey for this study was distributed to 182 users in the researcher's Facebook friends list. In a little over a month after sending the link to the survey 272 responses were received. This in and of itself raises some interesting questions, for future research about the flow of information within the network. On the day the survey was distributed there were 34 responses. By second day there were 163, by the tenth day 261. This is when the rate of responses began to taper off with 272 responses reached on day 41.

Of the 272 responses, 164 people were willing to give their e-mail addresses if they were interested in receiving a copy of the results once they were compiled. Of those 164 e-mail addresses, 119

belonged to people who were not Facebook friends with the researcher. This indicates that the survey was forwarded by some of the respondents and that at least a little less than half, approximately 44%, of the total respondents were at least one degree of separation in the network from the researcher, possibly more.

The data that partially answers RQ 2 was that which asked about the respondents' experiences with Facebook and that would give some insight into their perceptions of their friends list. Specifically, the questions were asked to investigate whether the respondents saw their use of Facebook as reflecting the role of a sender/creator of messages (producer-oriented) or a receiver/viewer of messages (audience-oriented) or engaged in a mutual, interpersonal form of communication. First, respondents were asked how many people they had on their friends list. This data is contained in Table 1.

This data reflects a wide range in the number of friends in each respondent's list. However, the largest group fell in the range of 100-300 friends. This is similar to results in other research (Ellison et al., 2007; Orr et al., 2009). Respondents were then asked to describe, in an open-ended question, what kind of value they place on the number of friends they have on Facebook. This yielded some interesting results with some common themes popping up throughout many of the answers. The overwhelming majority of respondents gave an answer indicating that they see no inherent value in having a high number of friends on Facebook. The numbers for this response are contained in Table 2. One interesting aspect to this response was that many of the respondents used the words "quantity" and "quality" frequently noting that they saw Facebook as a medium that is useful for maintaining social ties with friends and family. They described looking for "authenticity" in their relationships on Facebook rather than looking for a large number of people to interact with in ways they saw as having little or no value. Respondents also noted an aversion to "friending" people just

Table 1. Numbers of users in respondents' friends lists

Amount	N	%
Less than 100	59	22%
100-300	122	45%
300-500	56	21%
500-700	17	6%
700-1000	5	1%
More than 1000	6	2%
No answer	7	3%

Table 2. What value do you place on your number of Facebook friends?

Response	N	%
See no inherent value	225	83%
See some value in a high number	32	12%
Did not answer	15	5%

to have a higher number, a practice in which they claimed to see others engaging.

What makes these responses interesting is the reason why the respondents gave the answers they did. Those who saw value in having a higher number of friends spoke both in terms of networking and professional development on one hand, and social, familial and personal connections on the other. One respondent who saw value in a higher number said Facebook was useful for "network[ing] for information or spread[ing] details about events I'm promoting for my work." Others spoke of maintaining quick and easy connections to friends and family with one respondent referring to Facebook as "a living address book." Another respondent said she valued the high number of contacts because it made it possible for her to connect to members of her father's side of her family and to build a family tree with them.

Of most interest in the responses from those who saw some value in having a high number of friends was the mixture of social and professional value. This is evidence for two arguments. First, it reinforces this chapter's argument that Facebook is a conflation of social network and social net-working websites, the notion of Facebook as social network(ing). Throughout many of the responses, both those who saw value in quantity and those who did not, there was a conflation of business and pleasure, professional and social relationships. In other words, Facebook is a site of what boyd (2008) calls social convergence, "when disparate social contexts are collapsed into one" (p. 18).

The second argument these results support is the argument for Facebook use as a form of immaterial labor. While Lazzarato defines immaterial labor as made up of the dual components of informational and cultural work, Michael Hardt argues that the most important aspect of it, an aspect that is important to this research, is the affective component. Over and over, throughout a significant portion of the responses to the survey for this study, respondents spoke in both interpersonal and professional terms. They described Facebook as part of their personal network and professional networking. When communicating with that personal network the respondents are engaged in the "affective labor of human contact and interaction," they are working with the binding element of immaterial labor (Hardt, 1999, p. 95).

Table 3. Why do you use Facebook?

Response	N	%
Interpersonal communication	221	81%
Audience-oriented	88	32%
Producer-oriented	41	15%
n/a	20	7%

Addressing RQ 1, one open-ended question asked respondents "Why do you use Facebook?" The responses to this question were then interpreted and placed into three categories. The first included answers that described an experience of mutual interpersonal communication with other users, using phrases such as "keep in touch." The second category comprised responses describing the Facebook experience as being "audience-oriented." These responses used words like "watching," "viewing" or "seeing" and focused on being an audience member for others. The third category contained answers that were "producer-oriented." These responses described experiences of producing content for others to view and used words such as "sharing." Some of the responses contained multiple reasons for using Facebook and thus were placed in multiple categories. For example, some responses contained both an audience-oriented and an interpersonal component. The breakdown of these categories is contained in Table 3.

This categorization also ties into RQ 2. It was expected that most respondents would describe their Facebook experience either in terms of interpersonal communication or in terms of being an audience for others' "performances" on Facebook. As Table 4 demonstrates, this expectation was clearly met. Because the questions were open-ended there was the possibility that a respondent's answer could be categorized in more than one of the three categories. Even though respondents could potentially give an answer that encompassed all three categories only a small number of the respondents spoke explicitly in

terms of being a producer of content and about sharing that content with others. This is an important point to take away from this data. When given the opportunity to describe their Facebook experience a strong majority of the respondents excluded "sharing" from the list of reasons that most readily came to mind.

Of the 272 responses to the question in Table 4, 183 were categorized as only falling under one of the three categories (interpersonal, audience or producer), 80 gave multifaceted responses that involved two of the categories and nine responses contained elements of all three. The 183 single-category responses reinforce the trend of respondents speaking of their Facebook experience in strictly interpersonal terms. Out of those 183, 136 wrote exclusively about interpersonal communication, 23 thought of themselves as audiences for others' posts and only five respondents wrote strictly in terms of being producers of content. Although the respondents may not be speaking the precise language of the theory of immaterial labor, this is what they are talking about here. A central issue this research points out is that Facebook users do not see the time they spend on the website as a form of labor or value creation for the owners of Facebook. Even when users are engaged in the interpersonal, affective labor of "keeping in touch" that so many of the respondents describe, they are still creating value. Whether responding to a private message, commenting on a status update or "liking" a photograph posted by a friend, they are always giving and attracting attention to the site; attention that is then sold to advertisers.

This section of the chapter discussed the quantifiable aspects of the data collected from the survey for this project. While there was some discussion of specific quotes from the respondents, this section was not an attempt at delving into those responses in depth, but rather to present illustrations of what was being discussed in the numbers. The next section will focus on probing further into the qualitative responses to the open-ended questions. It will discuss what can potentially be learned about the respondents' perceptions of their use of Facebook from their responses to the questions. It will also connect those responses to the theory of immaterial labor in social network(ing) websites discussed in the literature review.

QUALITATIVE DATA: "STALKER BOOK"

One unexpected and interesting result from this research was the number of respondents who indicated feeling that there was something strange to the "wacky ritual," to use one respondent's words, of collecting Facebook friends. Another respondent who said they saw some value in having a larger number of Facebook friends described it this way.

It's better to have more [Facebook friends] because people tend to see it as a status symbol and a symbol of your ability to socialize. But you also can't add people indiscriminately because it also lowers your status (in the real world) if you add a ton of people you don't even know. So there's a balance between those two competing goals. I don't particularly care about the number and don't make it a goal to maximize that number, but I know some people who do.

What is especially interesting in this response is that there is a sort of tension between the social capital that comes with a large number of friends and some perceived negative social consequences of having "too many" friends. This respondent reinforces and adds to Blanchard's (2004) arguments about the effects of dispersed virtual communities on FtF communities. Blanchard says that a network member may spend too much time on a dispersed virtual community because of its "greater socioemotional rewards" (p. 56). The respondent above notes similarly that the perception that one has *too many* Facebook friends

may reduce the user's social capital in their FtF networks. The use of the word "indiscriminately" indicates that the high number of friends is a sign that the user does not take care in thinking about with whom they associate and that others may perceive that lack of care in that large number. This response reinforces Blanchard (2004) and Ellison et al.'s (2007) findings that Facebook users' online networks are closely connected to and influenced by their FtF networks.

When asked about what value they placed on their number of Facebook friends quite a few respondents commented on this as an issue of social capital, but also problematized it in a way, often speaking in terms that drew a contrast between the "quantity" and "quality" of relationships on the social network. One respondent said he is "always deleting people [he does not] talk to. People who just request your online friendship in order to have a higher friend count." Here again there is a tone of judgment in his assessment, implying that the desire for a higher number of Facebook friends is not something worth pursuing. There is also an underlying implication about the "quantity/quality" issue, saying that some people "friend" others only to have a higher friend count, not to have any kind of meaningful connection.

This is echoed by another respondent who says, "I'm the sort of person who values having genuine friendships with smaller groups of people rather than casual friendships with tons of people who you end up not really knowing that well." This respondent expresses a desire for a smaller and more meaningful network of personal relationships. In one very brief response to the question, a respondent strikes a similar note saying simply, "I think it's kind of strange. I'm not sure i [sic] actually know 301 people." This again draws attention to the question of personal relationships and how many any individual can realistically manage in life.

Coming from the opposite direction, one respondent described seeking out Facebook connections with people he does not know that well.

He noted that tendency to friend someone and then never have any meaningful contact, "or you friend a girl you're totally crushing on, but then realize it's incredibly creepy/lame to hit on her via the interwebs [sic] and you then run and hide (sometimes literally)." This is a statement on the link between social capital in a virtual community and an FtF community and the expectations for pursuing romantic relationships. It is "creepy" or "lame" to pursue a girl in the virtual as opposed to in the FtF context.

These relationships in the virtual community become something that requires an immaterial labor of audience management. A few respondents spoke of needing to go through their friends list and remove some people. One respondent in particular said that the number of people in his list was "ridiculous. I don't have that many real life friends and I really ought to go through and delete people to which I don't have significant real life connections." Here there is a sense of list management as a chore for the user to complete. Another user expressed list management as a privacy issue, saying "I only want people I know reading/seeing my site." This privacy concern is contrasted with a publicity concern, a way of thinking about audience management as performative. What is happening here is what Cote and Pybus (2007) call an "online personal brand management" (p. 95). One respondent described her list management as being part of both her personal network and professional networking. She said, "Facebook has been great for catching up with old friends I haven't heard from in years. Although it hasn't paid off yet, I think it will also be valuable in terms of networking in my field." Another respondent who indicated he is a librarian said, "I think I have too many [friends]. The bulk of my extraneous friends are other librarians. It seems professionally helpful somehow, [or] else I'd delete most of them." Once again, with this statement the respondent notes the networking usefulness of Facebook to the point where he feels obligated to maintain connections that are potentially "professionally helpful."

Another way to frame the "audience-oriented" responses is through the issue of surveillance. Delving into the qualitative responses to the questions one finds users who freely admit to their own acts of surveillance of others but very rarely did a respondent discuss any concern about being the target of others' surveillance. One respondent said, "I like to be friends with everyone I've ever met so I can creep on their profile randomly." These responses give further evidence to support Kennedy's (2006) findings that Internet users fail to distinguish "between being anonymous and feeling anonymous" (p. 866). However, where Kennedy's research was about how the subject's feeling of anonymity was tied to online identity, the results in this study find a feeling of anonymity in the expression of feeling free to surveil others.

One respondent combines in one answer, thoughts about sharing with friends via Facebook, while also having surveillance opportunities. He said Facebook "is a good way to post stuff that no one else really cares about except for the rest of your nerdy friends. It makes a great blackmail tool as well … people certainly like to post drunk/slutty/drunkslutty pictures of themselves within the public domain." An interesting point about this response is that he frames his own sharing as "stuff that no one else really cares about." In other words, sharing for him is safe because not many people are going to be interested, only the people who matter (i.e. nerdy friends). This is contrasted by his claim that other users are guilty of carelessly posting "drunkslutty" images that reflect badly on them and can potentially be used as "blackmail." He follows his statement about blackmail by saying, "In all seriousness though, it is a quick and streamlined system to get in touch with people." Although there is a hint of humor in this response, the point stands, that he sees some people posting photographs that reflect badly on them, while he merely posts niche items only interesting to his circle of "nerdy" friends, creating no danger of infringement on his privacy.

Other respondents presented similar ideas, stating that what is important to them about Facebook is "the keeping up with other people's lives (i.e. "stalker" book)" and the ability to "find out more about new acquaintances." Another respondent also mixed the personal with the professional in her response saying Facebook allows her "to keep track of people … stay[ing] up to date and informed on important milestones." She also said she used Facebook "as a networking tool to gain information about possible job inquiries." Yet another respondent was even bolder in his admission that he uses Facebook for surveillance purposes saying it lets him "keep in touch with friends and it helps me to keep tabs on what my staff is up to in their personal lives." Again, almost every respondent spoke in terms of *being* the audience, not *having* an audience. One respondent wrote that Facebook "has become the one-stop website for catching up with a lot of my friends from all over the place. Photos and status updates are integrated well so I find it a nice way to see what my friends are up to." This respondent speaks strictly in the language of being the audience for others engaged in content creation, but does not include content creation as part of her own experience. Another respondent wrote, "I don't have to talk to my friends now to find out what's going on with them. This is supposed to be a 'social' site, but I rarely leave comments for others. I look at it more than I update it or type to others." Here again we see a construction of others as producers and the self as audience. Most respondents seem to be saying, "others are self-expressing and I am consuming their self expression." This particular person does not even participate in the content creation process via commenting on others' content. She describes her experience as simply one of consumption.

This is a potential problem, the fact that the overwhelming majority of these respondents do not view their friends list as an audience, or at least *did not articulate an explicit vision of them*

as such. Those who did articulate a sense of their friends list as an audience seemed to recognize that Facebook can be used to great effect as a self-promotional tool for event organizers and musicians, businesses and even ideologies. For example, one respondent said:

I use Facebook to network with people who share the same ideals and who want to articulate those ideals to others and convince them of their value. I use my profile as a means of displaying what I truly care about and share important information that I want others to read, see, or hear.

Another, when asked about how she values the number of friends she has on Facebook said, "I think the number of people on my list is very important. The more people on my list, the more exposure to my home based [sic] business." Here there is a sense of the immaterial labor practiced in Facebook as beneficial not only to Facebook, but also to the user who has a business to promote. Relationships are built and the users of Facebook and other social media, as Banks and Humphrey (2008) argue, "are often quite competent and canny participants in the making of these relationships" (p. 405). The problem, as this research indicates, is that users are more likely to see those relationships from the perspective of an audience member or interpersonally more than from the perspective of a content producer. Thus, they may be unlikely to fully realize the potential value a social network(ing) website like Facebook may hold for them.

CONCLUSION

Immaterial labor, especially when it is done for free, is an essential concept in research examining social network(ing) sites such as Facebook. However, in attempting to essentialize this concept one must ask, what are the consequences of studying the labor of virtual communities in general or

Facebook in specific? What are the consequences of theorizing this audience/producer split? The rise of the "prosumer" and immaterial labor in social network(ing) sites draws attention to the problem in neoliberalism identified by Foucault, that it ignores labor as a factor to be studied, and that labor itself must be reinserted into the study of economics. Sites like Facebook open up such an opportunity of reinsertion and bring out what Foucault (2008) says is the first problem to arise when attempting to reinsert labor, the necessity of analyzing "how the person who works uses the means available to him" (p. 223).

The responses to the survey for this study demonstrate that Facebook users are fully aware of the time and energy they invest in Facebook, but they are not "conscious" of their labor. In other words, they may not be explicitly thinking in these terms, but respondents repeatedly spoke the language of immaterial labor. Their descriptions answer that question of how the person who works uses Facebook, engaging in the informational, cultural and affective aspects of immaterial labor. They discussed the informational component describing the management of their friends list. This is a process of deciding with whom to share information and/or from whom to receive information. The maintenance of such a list is a necessary labor for more effectively participating in the Facebook community. As one respondent noted, one cannot "indiscriminately" add friends. The maintenance of a friends list is labor like the pruning of a tree for many of the respondents. It requires time, thought, energy and care, and respondents noted that it translates into FtF social capital. In other words, there is a labor of audience management and an "entrepreneurialism of the self," as Foucault called it. One need not simply theorize the management of the friends list as a sort of labor, the respondents to this survey frame it this way.

Immaterial labor is also reflected in an expressed awareness of the professional networking potential in Facebook. Social capital is both (inter) personal, relevant to social relationships and it is a professional social capital. One respondent said he uses Facebook to "maintain personal and work relationships." Another saw utility in Facebook allowing her to "collaborate with colleagues [and] network." A third said she started using Facebook "because as an academic librarian I wanted to keep up with current technological trends that affect youth and young adults." In all three responses there was a sense of the importance of being able to easily share information with others and a connection of that information sharing to their labor.

Respondents also discussed the cultural component of immaterial labor in how they associate with others interpersonally, using Facebook as a way to rekindle and maintain social ties. One respondent also acknowledged the use of Facebook in taste making and sharing popular culture artifacts saying he used it to, "maintain records of movies/cds watched/listened to." This is just a new way of maintaining a book or music collection as an outward expression of self. Much like Walter Benjamin (1968) unpacking his library, apps in Facebook act as the immaterial fetishization of immaterial objects. Or as another respondent put it, Facebook is "an archive of my own life." We cannot place mp3s on a shelf, but we can have a virtual shelf on Facebook and we do not need to invite people into our homes in order to show it off.

Finally, there is Hardt's affective component of immaterial labor that is expressed in the many responses about interpersonal/social contacts. There was the repeated use of the words like "touch" and "contact," the physical, embodied aspect of FtF communication effortlessly slides into the realm of social network(ing). One respondent said she uses Facebook for "keeping in touch with friends, [and to] monitor who my Mom is dating (no, really)." Another described Facebook as a way to "share my life (photos, news, etc.)," a phrase that begs to be used in marketing for any social media. What is problematic in all of this is the high number of respondents who are apparently not thinking about their uses of Facebook in producer-oriented terms at all, the fact that labor does not seem to be at all conscious of itself. The labor of Facebook goes beyond just content creation to include "tastes, preferences, and general cultural content construction therein" (Cote and Pybus, 2007, p. 89-90). The audience, who is creating the content they are consuming, is also doing the marketing. Andrejevic (2007) describes this as a process of "co-creating unique value," the work done by a "free focus group" (p. 25). Simply put, what social networks do is create "multiple lines of valorization (both social and capitalist)" (Cote and Pybus, 2007, p. 95). This self-valorization is achieved through the creation of an audience, or in terms of Facebook, a "friends list." Facebook is essentially an audience creation tool. As one respondent put it "I think a lot of people get a feeling of satisfaction and social acceptance when they log on and find that somebody wrote on their wall, commented on their status, tagged them in a photo."

This comment encompasses multiple lines of valorization; writing on a friend's wall is an engagement of communication, giving a sense of value that another was interested in communicating; a status comment that tells another user, "I noticed what you're doing and I care enough to respond without direct solicitation;" tagging you in a photo is an act of purposeful content creation that includes you, is about you, marking you as a worthy subject. Every act of content creation within Facebook is an act of calling the audience into being. These cohering relations are present in Facebook in how they work toward "allowing the impression of being a 'friend' as opposed to a consumer" (Pybus, 2007, para. 18). Its most powerful effect is in the user's feeling of self-identifying as an audience to others even as the user is working to create content to attract an audience and not realizing the acts of creation and/or watching are in and of themselves labor.

REFERENCES

Andrejevic, M. (2007). *iSpy: Surveillance and power in the interactive era*. Lawrence, KS: University Press of Kansas.

Arvidsson, A. (2006). Quality singles: Internet dating and the work of fantasy. *New Media & Society*, *8*(4), 671–690. doi:10.1177/1461444806065663

Banks, J., & Humphrey, S. (2008). The labour of user co-creators: Emergent social network markets? *Convergence*, *14*(4), 401–418. doi:10.1177/1354856508094660

Benjamin, W. (1968). Unpacking my library: A talk about book collecting. In Arendt, H. (Ed.), *Illuminations* (pp. 59–68). New York, NY: Schocken Books.

Blanchard, A. (2004). The effects of dispersed virtual communities on face-to-face social capital. In Huysman, M., & Wulf, V. (Eds.), *Social capital and information technology* (pp. 53–73). Cambridge, MA: The MIT Press.

Blumer, T. (2010). Face-to-face or Facebook: Are shy people more outgoing on social networking sites? In N. Carpentier, I. Trivundza, P. Pruulmann-Vengerfeldt, E. Sundin, T. Olsson, R. Kilborn … B. Cammaerts (Eds.), *Media and communication studies interventions and intersections* (pp. 201-212). Estonia: Tartu University Press.

boyd, d., & Ellison, N. (2007). Social network sites: Definition, history, and scholarship. *Journal of Computer-Mediated Communication, 13*(1), 210-230.

boyd, d. (2008). Facebook's privacy train wreck: Exposure, invasion, and social convergence. *Convergence, 14*(1), 13-20.

Cohen, N. (2008). The valorization of surveillance: Towards a political economy of Facebook. *Democratic Communiqué*, *22*(1), 5–22.

Cote, M., & Pybus, J. (2007). Learning to immaterial labour 2.0: MySpace and social networks. *Ephemera*, *7*(1), 88–106.

Ellison, N., Steinfield, C., & Lampe, C. (2007). The benefits of Facebook "friends:" Social capital and college students' use of online social network sites. *Journal of Computer-Mediated Communication*, *12*(4), 1143–1168. doi:10.1111/j.1083-6101.2007.00367.x

Foucault, M. (2008). *The birth of biopolitics: Lectures at the College de France*. New York, NY: Picador.

Grigoriadis, V. (2009, 13 April). Do you own Facebook? Or does Facebook own you? *New York Magazine*. Retrieved from http://nymag.com

Grossman, L. (2006, December). You – yes, you – are *Time's* person of the year. *Time*, *168*(26). Retrieved from http://time.com

Hardt, M. (1999). Affective labor. *Boundary 2*, *26*(2), 89–100.

Jhally, S., & Livant, B. (2006). Watching as working: The valorization of audience consciousness. In *S. Jhally (Author), The spectacle of accumulation: Essays in culture, media, & politics* (pp. 25–43). New York, NY: Peter Lang. doi:10.1111/j.1460-2466.1986.tb01442.x

Kennedy, H. (2006). Beyond anonymity, or future directions for identity research. *New Media & Society*, *8*(6), 859–876. doi:10.1177/1461444806069641

Lazzarato, M. (2006). Immaterial labor. In Virno, P., Buckley, S., & Hardt, M. (Eds.), *Radical thought in Italy* (pp. 133–150). Minneapolis, MN: University of Minnesota Press.

Mendelson, A., & Papacharissi, Z. (2011). Look at us: Collective narcissism in college student Facebook photo galleries. In Papachariss, Z. (Ed.), *A networked self: Identity, community, and culture on social network sites* (pp. 252–273). New York, NY: Routledge.

Meyrowitz, J. (1986). *No sense of place*. Oxford, UK: Oxford University Press.

NBC News. (2011, August 13). Flash mobs turning violent across the country. *NBC Nightly News with Brian Williams*.

Orr, E., Sisic, M., Ross, C., Simmering, M., Arseneault, J., & Orr, R. (2009). The influence of shyness on the use of Facebook in an undergraduate sample. *CyberPscyhology & Behavior*, *12*(3), 337–340. doi:10.1089/cpb.2008.0214

Peterson, M. (2008). Loser generated content: From participation to exploitation. *First Monday*, *13*(3). Retrieved from http://frodo.lib.uic.edu/ojsjournals/index.php/fm/article/view/2141/1948

Pybus, J. (2007). Affect and subjectivity: A case study of Neopets.com. *Politics and Culture*, *2*. Retrieved March 27, 2008, from http://aspen.conncoll.edu/politicsandculture/page.cfm?key=557

Scholz, T. (2007). What the MySpace generation should know about working for free. *Re-Public*. Retrieved from http://www.re-public.gr/en/?p=138

Silverstone, R. (1990). From audiences to consumers: The household and the consumption of communication and information technologies. In Hay, J., Grossberg, L., & Wartella, E. (Eds.), *The audience and its landscapes* (pp. 281–296). Boulder, CO: Westview. doi:10.1177/0267323191006002002

Van Dijk, J. (2009). Users like you? Theorizing agency in user-generated content. *Media Culture & Society*, *31*(1), 41–58. doi:10.1177/0163443708098245

Wellman, B. (2002). Little boxes, glocalization, and networked individualism. In Tanabe, M., van den Besselaar, P., & Ishida, T. (Eds.), *Digital cities II: Computational and sociological approaches* (pp. 10–25). Berlin, Germany: Springer. doi:10.1007/3-540-45636-8_2

Zwick, D., Bonsu, S., & Darmody, A. (2008). Putting consumers to work: Co-creation and new marketing governmentality. *Journal of Consumer Culture*, 8(2), 163–196. doi:10.1177/1469540508090089

Chapter 18
Culture, Disorder, and Death in an Online World

Jonathan Paul Marshall
University of Technology Sydney, Australia

ABSTRACT

Death strikes everywhere, even online. Death poses problems personally, existentially, and culturally, and is potentially destructive to person and group. Yet many social theories of death posit some kind of social integration as normal, downplaying the potential for disorder. This chapter explores how people on the internet mailing list, Cybermind, dealt with death on two occasions: firstly, just after the group's founding, and secondly, when the group had been established for eight years, and was in crisis. On both occasions the group was rocked by the deaths, and struggled to make a meaningful and ongoing mailing list culture out of parts of offline culture, while transforming that culture within the constraints and ambiguities of List Life. This was a disorderly exploratory process, which verged on disintegration. Social disorder cannot be seen as simply pathological or an error; it is a vital part of cultural processes and must be taken seriously in itself.

INTRODUCTION

Death online is rarely explored.[1] This contrasts radically with the huge amount written about other aspects of life online, and makes a surprising gap given death's importance for indicating the disorderly differences, similarities, and ambiguous boundaries between online and offline life. Death, ending and decay are vital parts of social life, and ignoring them implies that online life is somehow unreal, or remains untouched by fundamental existential and social problems. This is simply not true. I use ethnographic research to elucidate the death of Michael Current, a founder of the internet mailing list Cybermind, at the beginning of the List's life, and the death of popular member, Rose Mulvale, during a time of conflict. I analyse the way List members dealt with, or failed to deal with, death in their ventures towards cultural creation. I begin with a short description of the List, discuss ethnography, culture and death, and then give a comparative account of the deaths on Cybermind.

DOI: 10.4018/978-1-4666-0312-7.ch018

CYBERMIND

For a full history and ethnography of Cybermind see Marshall (2007). Cybermind is an internet Mailing List founded in 1994 by Alan Sondheim and Michael Current to discuss "the philosophical and psychological implications of subjectivity in cyberspace". It has been a voluminous List and is still active today, although much reduced. Onlist conversation has wandered over many fields other than the advertised ones. People have talked at length about their offline lives, and have used the List to organise offline meetings and even a conference in Perth, Western Australia. They have conducted love affairs, given personal counselling, had flame wars, been invaded by other Lists, and carried out co-operative work, including the group authored 'Cybermind Novel', a 'ficto-criticism' of internet theory and List life (Rosewood, 2008). It is impossible to observe Cybermind and argue for a simple division between online and offline life.

Despite many members evincing ideologies of role-play and multiplicity, as has been widely reported, or anticipated, in the literature (e.g. Turkle, 1995; Poster, 2001), long-term members largely present themselves, and take each other, as real 'authentic' people, although perhaps able to express more of themselves online than offline (cf. Kendall 2002, p.8-9). However, authenticity is always problematic as, despite claims of spontaneity, it has to be indicated by conventional 'ritual displays' and etiquette (Marshall, 2007 p.105ff.). Consequently, manifestations of authenticity are frequently misconstrued, and struggles over authenticity and meaning form part of the group's dynamics, not least when faced with death.

Surveys over the group's history show that visible members were generally 'intellectual middle class', usually with leftist politics, and precarious means of livelihood. Almost all members lived in the Western English Speaking World, and English was the only language used onlist. The majority of members seem to have been male, but the number of posts from women exceeded their proportion of membership. However, only a relatively small number of the total membership wrote frequently; the majority of the List posted rarely or never (Marshall 2007, p.281ff.).

While much of the frequently posting population was stable over the research period, the group experienced considerable membership change, making it hard to assess how changes in group behaviour relate to internal development, wider world events, or to change of population. Disordering and flux of group culture and membership, was ongoing. Flux and mess is as much part of living on Cybermind, if not more so, than is fixity, order and patterning.

ETHNOGRAPHY, CULTURE, AND DEATH

Ethnography

For detailed comments on online ethnography as a method, and its similarity to living online generally, see Marshall (2010; 2007, p.7-10). In general, ethnographic fieldwork depends upon living with people and engaging in extended observation as a participant. It aims to gain familiarity with ways and patterns of living, and modes of understanding, and to make a meaningful and relatively explicit model of social life. It is not primarily an interview or statistical method although it may employ both in its attempts to make sense of peoples' lives. Ethnography is destabilising, as there is only a messy difference between facts and analysis. What counts as facts, depends on meaning and interpretation. The same act can have different meanings or consequences, depending on actors and context. Clifford Geertz (1975) elaborates this issue by pointing to Gilbert Ryle's discussion of the difference between a twitch of the eye, a wink, a parody of a wink, a faked wink, a rehearsed wink and so on. All of these events appear similar and it is our understanding of the cultural context which enables us to differentiate (p.6-7). Some misunderstanding is inevitable, as in social life generally. With Cybermind, my fieldwork involved participating on the List daily, raising questions, and interacting with members offlist.

The research was conducted between 1995 and 2005. Cybermind was chosen accidentally as I originally joined the group for its official topics while searching for an online field site, but found List members so apparently open about their offline lives that it seemed fieldwork would be less disruptive here than elsewhere. I discussed carrying out research with the moderator Alan Sondheim, who advised me to participate on the List before proceeding further. After several months of participation he asked me to announce my intentions to the List. The announcement caused little stir, and there has never been any overt objection to my presence or questioning, perhaps because my onlist writings fitted in with the List's blend of confessional, analysis, and political work. Other members have also written about their experiences on Cybermind.[2]

All my ethnographic writings, including this paper, have been made available to List members before publication for comment and/or protest. This has proven a useful way of getting further information and correcting misunderstandings. However, even with feedback, ethnography is always incomplete and partial. No one can speak to everyone, or perceive everything. There were many long-term members of the List, people who passed through the List or who 'lurked' on the List, with whom I had no contact at all, merely observing the traces left by their email. This is not that different to offline fieldwork or social life in general. No one ever knows everything that is happening, and ignorance is socially distributed. Social perception is inherently disordered. Furthermore all description is abridged, and disciplinary demands force a level of fictional order and regularity upon the data. When the analyst says that people do, or believe, certain things, this glosses over those

who don't speak or do. Order, while providing comprehension, disorders the reality by deletion. Disordering is paradoxically fundamental to any social analysis. I have given as many actual words and examples as possible, but the account is still an abridgment of complexity. We do our best to make sense of life, and express this sense, as individuals in collaboration and competition, and, as I shall argue later, this generates the dynamics of our, always incomplete, 'culture'.

As ethnography is collaborative, acknowledgement is important. Changing names is standard in internet ethnography (cf Kendal 2002, p.241-2) as publication can accidentally produce problems for the group, or individuals (Reid 1996). However, it was impossible to hide Cybermind when I began writing, as it was easy to locate the group and the people referred to through search engines. More importantly removing names removes acknowledgement from people who influenced my understanding of the group and deletes honouring the creative 'community' of Cybermind. In this paper, I have named people less than I wished, to protect privacy, but the decision is not easy.

As an ethnographer, my own experience informs my discussion of the deaths described. I was distant from Michael's death, and knowledge of the reactions around his death was gained through archives, interviews and people's spontaneous musings on List. This produced a sense of indirect closeness. I wrote to the List in 1997 that: "Memory of the List for me starts with the presence of michael in discussion". Rose, on the other hand, was the first person to respond to my writing onlist; in many ways she was a mentor for me. She was important to me and her death was something I struggled with and engaged with. Like Behar (1991), in her account of death in a Spanish village, for whatever reason, I was not an uninvolved spectator however much that might be the ethnographic convention (pp.372, 377). I was part of building group culture.

Culture

Discussing death involves discussing culture. The many differences in academic ideas about 'culture' (the 'culture of culture') show us that culture is changing, argumentative, and both diverse and shared. Barth (1989) suggests that assumptions that culture is ordered and whole, encourage the analyst to discard what may seem like 'oddities', 'failures' or 'disorders' rendering academic descriptions of society monochromatic while deleting important parts of social-being (pp.121, 125). As Barth writes, people "participate in multiple, more or less discrepant universes of discourse; they construct different, partial and simultaneous worlds in which they move" (p.130). Culture is composed of a set of divergent 'models' that allow people to make sense of their lives and the lives of others.

In this view, culture is both contested, and constructed tentatively. People make, and seize, *essays* towards a successful encapsulation of mood, or towards a conceptualisation of what is happening to them and of what others are doing. In this sense, culture is imagistic or poetic, making an often complex mystery manifest (Barth 1990, p.45). It is both a set of tools for expression and interaction, and a model helping a person understand (or misunderstand) what other people do. Culture is therefore tied to rhetoric, structures of communication, and power, as people attempt to persuade others of the truth of their (incomplete) vision, images or understanding – just as we do in writing academically.

Online groups, so far, build culture from offline resources with the potential to anchor some common procedures or understanding, and perhaps transforming them in the process. Some offline death customs proved to be important and presented problems to the group on both occasions; in particular customs around kin ties, or links to the dead, lines of distribution of information, appropriate expression and intensity of expression.[3]

One major difference between Michael's and Rose's deaths was the involvement of Rose's kin, who used Rose's email in her final days to communicate with the List thus breaking the sharper boundaries between on- and offline present in Michael's day, and perhaps enabling a more coherent response. However, culture on Cybermind was diverse, argumentative and unstable. It could easily dissolve before an influx of new people. People who didn't like the culture, or the way they saw the culture heading, could easily leave; although people were often surprisingly persistent in attempting to change List culture to meet their expectations. With this constant flux, or threat of flux, the culture of Cybermind was often on the edge of disorder.

Ethnography and Death

Historically ethnography has been entangled with death as it has aimed to preserve supposedly dying (rather than changing) customs and social orders through description. Early ethnographers often attempted to protect the validity of disrupted societies by suggesting they would have continued indefinitely were it not for contact with conquering cultures. Even today, social theorists underplay both the disordering effects of death and the ongoing role of disorder and flux in culture generally.

It would be inconsistent, after drawing attention to cultural disorder, to claim all ethnographers approach death the same way, nevertheless it is frequently asserted that death rituals and behaviours are integrative; even while giving examples which suggest otherwise. Bonsu & DeBerry-Spence (2008) write that:

Death ritual occasions … facilitate family harmony and enhance the bereaved family's competitive edge in the pursuit of status in the community. The cohesion sought may extend beyond the family into the broader community (p.701).

They give stories of unity repaired or established for the first time, showing how funerals instigate new patterns of gift exchange, build patterns of care and strengthen beliefs (pp.704-5). Examples of disordering are given, but are not considered significant, such as a dispute about appropriate behaviour (pp.706, 709). While the intention of some in that dispute might have been to reinforce traditions and family, their actions could equally activate long-term bad feelings and disruption. Similarly:

At the bereaved family meetings... I observed the unscripted intimidation, superiority complexes, and outright show of disrespect that characterized discussions on death ritual choices... Insult trading was not uncommon (Bonsu 2007, p.206-7).

The omission of some family connections in obituaries and the emphasis of others (p.212) also suggests fracturing. Frequent ritual innovations occur which involve "a high degree of risk taking" (Bonsu & DeBerry-Spence 2008, p.713). Yet these disruptive, risky and potentially 'failed' events are made secondary to integration.

While Counts and Counts (2004) recognise possible disruption in New Britain, writing: "Bad deaths are the result of and the expression of social dysfunction and may lead to further destruction of peace and social order", they emphasise that people "usually manage to agree on the cause of and culpability for death and reach an acceptable closure before more deaths occur and social relationships and social order are destroyed" (p.896). 'Usually' can cover a lot of uncertainty and variation, and integration is the implied normality. O'Rourke (2007) suggests that interactions between identity, ritual and death can be "messy open ended, and inherently incomplete" (p.388), but writes that "the ritual no longer functions as part of a complex of beliefs and actions that make up shared culture, both supporting and drawing support from a sense of community" (p.399), implying that disorder is

a fall from once prevailing harmony. In contrast, while Giddens (1991) claims that death cannot "be brought within the internally referential systems of modernity" (p.162), this disjunction plays little part in his general sociology, despite the commonness of death.

Death may be customary and ritualised, but those rituals may not always work. Death can disrupt social life, as death *is* a significant threat to social stability, to the systems of meaning and hence to people's ontological security. In a small-scale society, the loss of one person, or the disruption of an apparently minor process can have major effects. Sometimes humans triumph over circumstances, chance and destruction, but at other times they fail. The focus of researchers on social continuity and survival perhaps becomes what Becker (1973) calls an 'immortality project', allaying their own anxiety about death and dysfunction. Similarly, if social life is subject to unpredictable contingency, then it may undermine ambitions of constructing a 'science' of society if science is thought of as imlying continuity, deterministic order and control.

DEATH ON CYBERMIND

We now explore how people on Cybermind faced, and made manifest, the mystery of death, expressing their feelings and understandings in others' company with the cultural resources available. Offline resources may not work well either. No one displayed satisfaction with contemporary Western mourning rituals. Discussions of funerals, particularly while Rose was "living with cancer", indicated that people found funerals unsatisfactory. Three different people wrote on separate occasions:

The rampant manipulation and price-gouging of the American funeral industry offends me more than I can express.[...]

It's in situations of this kind that one realizes one can still be oppressed by religious rituals and institutions one does not believe in or accept.[...]

What is said at funerals is sometimes ludicrous, farcical... The ritual is designed to ease loss, but for some reason it often fails miserably.[...]

The closest anyone came to defending funerals was to say:

funerals are for the living. We've learnt to need ceremonies and rituals to organise events in our minds and hearts, to start and finish this

Even this implies conventional rituals are arbitrary and untrusted. So, how do people construct satisfactory mourning online with such broken tools?

It is also frequently suggested that sequestration of the dead and dying is common in Western English Speaking cultures (Metcalf and Huntington 1991, pp.193-6; Baudrillard 1993, p.126; Mulkay 1993). However, these writers' disapproval indicates dissatisfaction. In a letter to Cybermind, Elizabeth encapsulates the hostility:

Surveys show that the most feared form of death – alone, in a hospital, in pain – is by far the most common in America. Which is insane.

Sequestration can be forced upon people online with even greater force than offline. Michael's death was effectively concealed, only being revealed to List members through a complex trajectory. People online can have low priority in the conventional process of being informed or valued by immediate survivors.

Almost two years later, Alan recalled the ambiguities and lack of information around Michael's death as follows:

When Michael died, I knew something was wrong only by virtue of the fact I hadn't heard from him for two days. I worried about him if I didn't hear on a day by day basis. On Friday I started to make inquiries (after hearing [from him] late Wed. night - on Saturday the obituary came over the wires. But the initial announcement was no announcement at all, no enunciation, and that silence became more and more perturbing...

The trajectory seems to have been that Linda posted notification of the death to soc.motss, a gay newsgroup. This was read by tommyc who rejoined FutureCulture "where I expect his friends will want to reminisce and mourn", but found nothing. So he forwarded Linda's post there writing "I have no independent knowledge of the contents and have no independent verification of this information". This email was forwarded to Cybermind by Mike the same day. Two hours later, Alan wrote to Cybermind, FutureCulture and other Lists, confirming the news:

I just received a message that Michael Current has died; I called his home in Des Moines and it is true. Michael and I corresponded daily and intensely, through email, Unix talk, and telephone. I never met him in person. I miss him more than I can tell you. We spoke the night he died. This is horrible.

The offlist closeness Alan establishes to Michael in this post gives him permission to have made contact with those at Michael's home, to break the boundaries of cyberspace and establish contact in the 'real world'. While Michael's kin and lover played no further part in Cybermind's mourning, establishing ties to the deceased became an important part of the culture of coping with distress.

In contrast, when Rose died after a long illness in 2002, emails from the List were read to her until quite late and her daughter, Kate, wrote to the list, even though Rose herself was sequestered away from the world. In this case online life, to an extent, broke the boundary of sequestration. Thus, 10 Oct 2002, Kate wrote:

she does not have the energy to read and compose e-mail directly, however if you do care to send a personal e-mail [her friend] Julie and I will ensure it gets delivered. I know such messages would be greatly be appreciated

And then:

I'm sitting in Mom's hospital room [...] Dr. Ruth cannot tell us how much longer Mom has, but from looking at her, it cannot be long. Mom has asked that no visitors, outside of family and Julie, be permitted.

Another List member, a personal friend (through the List) in contact with the family, wrote that day:

For the last week she has been confined to bed and having Cybermind and your messages printed out and read to her. She was playing the same friendly, wise, inspiring and generous role on some cancer lists. Early yesterday morning she was taken to hospital and is unlikly to return home.

About three hours after she died, the List was notified by her daughter.

Hi:
This is Kate writing from Rose's account. She died this afternoon at 3:15pm. B... was with her. Her brother H... and I were making preparations at the local funeral home at the time.
Mom left the following mail draft as well as a list of all the people she wanted it sent to (and who

are receiving this message now). She wrote this on April 27, 2002:
This is to inform you that Rose Mulvale has died. She didn't lose her "battle with cancer"; she won (after living well with it, she left – and took it with her...) Please pass this information on.

Boundaries were further broken by the family, when an email from Cybermind member Salwa was read at Rose's funeral service:

[Rose] you've been an example of a life well lived: you know what matters in life, what's worthwhile, what's really worth pursuing; you see beauty where most see ordinariness, magic where we see nothingness, hope where we complain of spleen; your posts have defamiliarized for me the "average," "the normal," "the mundane," making me view reality in a different, more enriching, light.

Between Michael and Rose's death there may have been a shift in public and professional attitudes towards death, and this, along with increasing familiarity with the internet, overflowed into the contact possible with the List. Gibson (2007) suggests that the "modern experience of 'sequestered death' has passed. Death images and events are now thoroughly mediated by visual and communication technologies used and accessed by a vast number of citizens across the globe." Certainly during that period there was a change in attitudes towards people using the internet, and an increase in public use of the internet to memorialise the dead and contact the dying (Roberts & Lourdes 1999-2000).

While Michael died of an unexpected heart attack, Rose's death had been prepared for. Rose had written to the List about her death, discussed how she wanted her body disposed of, announced she had set up a notice of her death to be posted out, and had sent various List members gifts and received gifts in return. She was part of the pattern of exchange until her death, and to an extent afterwards. Her family continued this, for a short time, crossing the boundaries between online and offline life, making her death something people, who knew her online, could be involved in.

However, boundaries remained in people's experience, as they sometimes struggled to explain their grief to those offline. Much later, a list member wrote to me:

I remember distinctly being very upset yet feeling that, in front of [my] family members, I had to pull myself together, because the very process of grieving over the loss of someone I had never "seen" could not be explained and was somewhat embarrassing, as in believing in ghosts or something! I remember my husband trying to commiserate, and expressing sympathy; yet, somewhere I could detect a pinch of irony... It was as if grieving over Rose had to take place in the very privacy of my heart and thoughts, because externalizing it would have been unseemly and hard to comprehend by people who have not had the same kind of online bond or experience.

Similar problems of explanation and expression, although less marked, occurred in my own offline life, with people often seeming somewhat puzzled unless they too had ongoing online lives.

A significant problem faced by some people in both deaths was the intensity of their grief. Hockey (1993) suggests that it is common to fear that emotion will disrupt funerals (p.129), or disturb those with a legitimate claim to grieve, so grief may be a standard cultural disrupter and hard to place. People felt they both knew Michael and didn't know him, or they knew him and he didn't know them, or that this knowing was somehow incomplete and a problem to be dealt with, within offline conventions about grief and distance. Many people expressed surprise at the strength of their feelings, feeling their grief was out of proportion. As Argyle (1996) reports: "What was going on with me? Why was I so upset? Why did I have to read all these messages. Why do I still think about

it now?" (p.136). Slightly over 6 months after Michael's death, Greg wrote about the visceral and disordering ambiguity he felt, as boundaries and conventions clashed:

I never knew Michael in RL, and I only barely knew him in cyberspace.[...] When I read the post informing the lists of Michael's death, I was alone in my apartment and I began to cry, but, almost immediately, I stifled my emotions, telling myself that 'Hey, this is someone you don't even really know.' I was trying very hard at that time to maintain the veil that this bizarre text-based medium allows us, perhaps because I was not willing to extend my circle of concern out across the network to people who existed, in my life, only as words and pixels, not as flesh and blood.

This disordering was a vital part of his experience. Surrounded by the usual disorder of messages on different subjects online, any reiteration of mood (be it 'flame', lust or grief) produces an unusual consistency of interpretative cues which magnifies people's responses (Marshall, 2007, pp.20, 269), disrupting the usual disorder.

This strength of feeling was also present at Rose's death, although less remarked upon. Just before Rose's death Salwa wrote expressing the disorders of division between kin and non-kin and degrees of closeness:

Yes, I speak, therefore I am; how about I feel therefore I am? Can one relay feelings through cyberspace without sounding embarrassingly mushy? Can/may I admit to just wanting to sit down and have a good cry? I feel guilty about taking the news about Rose so badly; after all, how can I possibly feel a fraction of what Kate and other family members are feeling?

She also explains that Rose "became a *necessary* individual in our lives, someone we looked up to, someone we turned to for answers and guidance". Closeness was established in terms of Rose's personal abilities and her functions as guide and peacemaker for many on Cybermind. Elizabeth (and later others) responded to this letter, stressing the 'rightness' of the feeling and commonality:

Grief is not something you can chop up into discrete chunks and measure with a spoon or a scale. Your sorrow at losing Rose does not deny or infringe upon theirs, although if you choose to share, you may all find yourselves feeling less miserable. [...]
Just think: if we all attended Rose's funeral in the flesh, we'd have to rent a *cathedral* to fit everyone in!

Distance proved less of an issue with this death; Rose's daughter responded:

I saw Salwa's note on CM this morning via Mom's inbox, and it broke my heart - please do not for one minute minimize your sadness and compare it to ours! I don't hurt more than you, I just hurt differently. I feel almost guilty, writing to you all and knowing that I have had her for my whole life, and you're only had her such a short time. You all are her family, too. I can't tell you what your support means to us, so I'm not going to try. Just thank you. [...] When [Rose] found CM, it was like a whole world unfolded right before her eyes, in this very dining room.

Permissions were given and the boundaries could become permeable, if only for a moment.

Without family participation, people justified their feelings in Michael's case by attempting to establish ties and familiarities; making a claim to the right to grieve while investigating the nature of those ties and feelings. Alan was the first to do so: "Michael and I corresponded daily and intensely, through email, Unix talk, and telephone. I never met him in person. I miss him more than I can tell you". Others wrote:

The cyber cliche is true: I've never met him somatically but felt closer to him than 90% of those I have[...]. We talked via email several times - already receding[...]. He was going to ask me to xerox another article for him.

I didn't _know_ Michael, but read his letters with interest and respect. I can imagine his death comes as quite a shock to you who did know him better, but also be assured it gives me pause as well[...]

I never had a brother, and was surprised to discover at some point that I felt as if Michael was my brother[...]. I didn't know what he looked like, how he walked, gesticulated, sat down.

Sometimes this issue was used to justify a delay in speaking as when Mike wrote:

I didn't know Michael Current except from his posts and one reply to a request-decent, knowledgeable, sympathetic, useable. So I have been lurking as others have publicly grieved.

Some people emphasised that they shared other lists with Michael. One member of both Cybermind and FutureCulture forwarded parts of Michael's last letter to him, which he had not read until after Michael's death. The letter established the receiver's relationship to Michael and acted as an image of Michael's good nature.

With Rose, people also needed to establish their contact with her to justify themselves, and to puzzle through the issue of grief for someone they both knew and felt they did not know. Some of these messages seem like ways of sharing her actions in their lives.

Over the years, we exchanged books and small presents. The last one she sent me was a little thing that Kerry had picked up in India many years ago. I was touched...[...]

We enjoyed so much the chance to meet her in Halifax last year.[...]

Rose brought the reality of the net home to me when she sent me a feather from a golden pheasant - prompting a kind of 'in-joke' about feathers and connections...

References to the conventional awkwardness of expression seemed more frequent around Rose's death than around Michael's:

I've tried several times to put something down about Rose. Each time I failed. My vocabulary 'taint strong enough to [do] justice to her.[...]

I never know what to say when it comes to times like this.
I never knew an e-mail could make me cry. Man, death sucks.[...]

by lack of words that express my emotions properly I'll just use the stockphrase; my condolences.

With Michael's death, the main offline conventions employed centred upon using praise of the dead to show loss: "Michael was, IS the most net-beautiful person I know", "Michael was indeed beautiful – on the net, and by acclamation, every-where else". Around the time of Rose's death conventional expressions flowed more easily; when the wife of one member died, and to Rose's family. When kin was involved it seemed easier to know what to do.

Another common response, especially with Michael, implies that standard conventionalities accepted in offline death, such as remarks on the peace of the body, were excluded by the rules of authenticity (cf. Elias, 1985, pp.23-7), by the absence of a body to evoke them, and by silence being a mark of non presence (Marshall, 2007, pp.105 ff.). Therefore some people responded with a slightly strained originality; "How does one send a dirge with ASCII", "Unfortunately,

his beauty has too perfectly become itself – by virtue(?) of its ephemerality", or "Michael has finessed the fleshmeet question with, as usual, a devastatingly simple gesture". Despite this striving for authenticity, other people expressed a need for ritual, or conventional actions.

Never before having lost an e-mail friend, I don't know the protocol for this – but does anyone know what the funeral arrangements for Michael are? And to whom could one send a card? [...]

I'm finding it difficult to respond To Michael Current's death....
This is too difficult to write about. I have no homologous context in which to inscribe or experience. Damn, as someone said already. Damn. I wish I could say more - thank you. Michael. Damn[...]

Mike wrote that he was:

bothered I guess, by the fact that there are no rituals of loss, mourning, passage. The personal statements of some is being followed with no evident break or closure by the noise of more or less inane net chatter.

There was no conventional quietness around the death. The lack of something to distinguish the 'territory' of public grief from normal behaviour and noise disturbed him. He suggested that:

some sort of ritual is called for what exactly its form would take I'm not sure: -closing 'his' lists to postings for a day -posting and re-posting a memorium for a period of time[...] He was a person who mattered to others and his passing should not be un 'marked' even in this markerless medium.

Some people suggested putting together a collection of Michael's writings, but others were more ambivalent, implying that grief is largely private and cannot be shared:

i wouldn't mind seeing posts of his that people wish to share, though i don't think they will Demonstrate why it is i or you or he or she or we grieve. grief, sort of like despair, comes from a place that can't be illuminated by example or demonstration, for me,

Alan also expressed his belief that group rituals would not be sufficient:

I think whatever rituals there are in regards to Michael are private, personal; perhaps one of the things we can learn from the Net is that there _is_ no closure. Stopping posts for a day silences others, for example. On the Net, all one has of the other is text, and these survive, and are a memorial. This is just my opinion of course.

The hesitation at the end is probably to show that his opinion is not meant to carry added weight from his position as moderator and as Michael's most visible friend, and is cast in terms of individualisation of death, grief and ritual; these are private matters. As Alan implies, conventional silence also has problems. Silence onlist is an absence, not a kind of being together. It fails to convey anything and prevents presence.

It is hard to know what kind of private rituals were developed, but some people shared them. One person refused to let his mail program automatically delete "the messages of sorrow", while another wrote:

For me the ritual has already begun in the cycling of messages repeated and repeated from list to list and I leaf through five, six, seven copies of the same awkward anguish, one copy for each place we haunted together, one current copy, and one copy bouncing off to [Michael's email address]

The difficulties of organising people on a Mailing List, of gaining authority to organise, and the semi-hidden nature of participation, made it almost impossible to arrange memorials, or get agreement to them. A fund was announced by an offline friend of Michael's, "to continue the studies Michael was interested and involved in". There are no references to this on the obvious websites mentioning Michael, or discussions of it on Cybermind. When asked offlist, Alan responded: "As far as I know, nothing came of it". Attempts to pay tribute to Rose online by collecting her writings failed, but some List members privately contributed to charities, or planted flowers or trees in her honour. I have discussed elsewhere (Marshall, 2007, pp.222-5) the ways that some people tried to make Michael's death an origin of community, to convey its power and the way it harmonised mood among many, but not all, List members. In that way the List itself becomes a monument. Similarly, when Rose died some took the opportunity to suggest that List members stop fighting amongst themselves (over the politics in the lead up to the Iraq war), in memory of her:

There's enough going on out there in the World like that, and most of you are smart enough to do things Differently I think/hope...there's good fights[...] and bad Fights (where other folks get hurt and insulted etc). [...]Rose was An inspiration to many of you to "fight the good fight"...in a loving And strong way. Can we have more of that stuff please?

These appeals did not work, and it is possible that the loss of a person who was respected as a peacemaker and often described as the "heart of the list", allowed the arguments to flare without check.[4] In both cases, some people continued on without reference to the dead, as is customary in the Western English speaking world (Kearl 1989, pp.85-6). Mourning could not be maintained, and a week after Michael's death, the main topic was a comic flame war. Sometime after Rose's death, a List member wrote to me that she had felt that a "certain solemn tone needed to be maintained and observed" and the return of some members to their normal practice of issuing one line jokes had surprised her.

Other people found List dialogues about death openly discordant, threatening to leave, or apologizing for leaving because they were too busy to deal with the volume of mourning postings. Newcomers could feel markedly outsiders: "pardon my lack of knowledge, who was (is) Micheal CUrrent? Is he dead? And what were some of his profound opinions that made him famous?" The grief disrupted group function for some members and they moved on. Communication can promote discord and mutual incompatibility, not just harmony. However, Rose herself, stated at that time, that she found the grief for Michael humanized the group; she stayed, instead of leaving as she had planned.

Another hard issue for people to deal with was the blurred boundaries between online presence and absence. There is no general numinous image to which the deceased can pass in transition, other than that class of people who are now nonexistent: those who no longer post or who leave. This category is general but vague, consisting of people who have never posted or existed for the List, people who posted for a short while and never became known, people who were known and left, and recognisable people who were thrown out. Being part of this category conveys only confusion. One person wrote:

to put it plainly, he made contact with me and touched me at the level that i wish to touch others. especially In Here; everything's so tenuous, it's absurd. but that ABSENCE can be an incredibly strong presence as well. before he left, he and i had been talking a lot (he had with many people here-in) about the vitality and cruciality of the flesh, of presence, of embodiment or the effects a lack there-of has on interaction, the mind, the heart. The Irony of The Situation is not lost to me to be sure, but i feel sick in my soul because of it. he wanted to BE HERE to SEE THIS, blossoming of CONTACT

Absence and presence are not absolutes, and the ambiguity adds to the pain being felt. The writer goes on to suggest that connections between narratives give the net its depth, and thus Michael's "absence tears apart the connections between the dialogues, as it would in any community". Months later, Karen, in the middle of a letter about people being in differing time zones and the presence and absence that creates, wrote;

Presence is attenuated, so _on_ isn't as powerfully present as it is in rl, and absence is often simply a matter of the happenstance of simultaneity, so I don't necessarily think anything of someone's silence or absence unless it goes on for a while or something reminds me of his or her absence.
But Michael's absence is complete. That's I think what shocked me the most[...]. And it really brought home to me the fragility of this kind of contact. I now read the holiday unsub messages with a certain urgency—"you'll be back? You're sure you'll be back?"

The absent could be dead. However, there is no group uniformity; Fido protested a little later that death was "distinctly different from signoff, no matter what anyone says". People also experienced a degree of interaction with the dead; Michael's emails arriving after they heard of his death, and presents from Rose arriving after her death, (as did spam spoofing her email address); boundaries were not quite clear. At the time Alan posted a disconnected but moving meditation on the body, the net and silences, which also speaks to this issue:

The body is fragile as the Net is fragile, motions, nodes, unavoidable toxins, and the body is irreal as the Net is irreal, but the body is all we have to offer. The body leaves speech and leaves speech behind, and finally speech is abandoned.
At the limits of the body, speech is abandoned, death sinks in, the Net is hidden speech. And at

the limits, cries and murmurs are heard. Broken, disconnected, this is all we have to offer.

Another 'memorial' to Michael, is 'Care of the Body' a piece written by Michael which Alan has forwarded to the List many times, especially on anniversaries of his death. Michael was nervous about mailing it to the List but sent it to Alan. In the absence of the body, this text about the body substitutes for the body. The text is elusive. Michael describes or imagines a person writing to him, who might actually be him. He wonders about the problem of us abandoning the body for the machine, and yet as the person writes he strokes both his penis and the surrounding books which become sensual as much as intellectual objects. He turns off the computer sleeps then briefly wakes:

feeling, for a moment, as he falls back into sleep - something like. . concerned. 'We must not abandon the body,' he murmurs...
In the corner, the computer listens for his breathing to steady, then switches itself on and dials, disks spinning with anticipation.

In some ways Michael's text can be seen as foreshadowing his death, warning of abandonment of the body; an incantation of what metaphorically becomes his passing into the wires, emphasising, in a different way, the ambiguities and disorders of boundaries around life online.

With Rose, it seemed more explicit that the dead can still be with us and part of social life, as a call to keep on expressing her ways of doing things:

[I] know that that in some way Rose will always be part of cybermind
Personally, for a host of reasons, I need Rose. I need her whole. I need her healthy. I know it's immature, silly, and embarrassing to speak this way, but this is precisely how I feel, I who, like Alan, can't resort to any metaphysical notions to ease the pain of parting.[...]

do not let her go. Let her live on in your memories and actions. Show what you have gleaned from her cyber-touch and continue in that vein. I know I hope to.[...]

your death will be pain, but i have saved your words and archived your wit and wisdom - when needed, the words can be called, and the ripples of your soul will be felt again and again and again.[...]

Rose is all over the place - in everyone she knows she has left part of herself, as a message one can read if one observes carefully. [...]
I think everyone we know leaves a message engraved in our souls, some of them are painful, some soothing ... Rose's message no doubt is an everlasting joy - like the coolest tattoo ever![...]

At the time of Rose's death, but not at Michael's, it was possible for many members to speak about their certainty of continuance after death. Even so, there was no unity as to what that continuance would be, and others stated that hopes of continuance were delusions. What was largely agreed was that Rose continued in their hearts and in the List's own presence.

CONCLUSION

Ethnography constructs culture as a model of human behaviour which grows out of interaction with people and interpretation of their actions. It is a joint work, which resembles the ongoing construction of culture in the societies studied, particularly when those cultures are relatively new, and have little tradition and few tools or artefacts to anchor them. This paper aims to capture the divergences and disorder within the apparent order, so that we can see how precarious, multifarious and contingent the construction of culture is, and how people can experience, express and conceive of disruptive events such as death. There is no finality, only flux, from which an emergent but momentary order or disorder can arise.

People on Cybermind constructed their own cultures dealing with death using cultural items from the offline world, within the limitations of Mailing List structures. These cultures were not uniform but depended on a tentative rhetorical deployment, and the embrace or rejection of the proposed motions. They attempted to express the mysteries, disorderings, challenges and interpretations of life, in making sense of death online to themselves and others.

As Kirkby (2007) suggests in consideration of Derrida's attitude to mourning, mourning can be an opportunity for a continuing engagement with the legacy of those dead who remain within us and yet beyond us, and whose presence becomes a call to responsibility, and possibly, we might add, of failure. With Michael's death, while the List could have collapsed with his loss, it continued and built something out of the death, or after the death. With Rose, although the call was more urgent, the conflicts of the time overrode any temporary unity, and the loss of her peacemaking skills added to the group's difficulties. Yet both of the deceased continued in remembrance, resisting closure just as much as a text, social life, or culture itself. People were transformed, reorganised and reconstituted in relation and response to their loss and to each other, but this was not through any wholeness. Sometimes it was simply through shifting away from the focus of death.

The messy and troubled constructions around death were disturbed by shifting and ambiguous boundaries, by insufficiencies and conflicts. It was never clear what others were doing, only what they said they were doing. Actions were surrounded by silence; there was no guaranteed meeting place of-flist to discuss actions before bringing them to the List, so cultural hesitations could not be tried out in relative privacy; everything had to be exposed before it was fully built. As well, members had to use tools from offline culture that were considered broken, that to some extent marginalised being

online, or were not that applicable. List members seemed particularly troubled by a perceived need to justify their feelings, by the need to establish contact with the deceased as rationale for that grief, and by the forms by which they could express that grief. These troubles tied in with offline cultural notions about the importance of kin, appropriate degrees of closeness, and difficulties with disruptive emotion. Ideals of authenticity, important to group identity and self-presentation, conflicted with and disrupted the possibilities of maintaining memorials for the dead, especially when no one could take responsibility for organising group rituals. Ambiguities over the role of the group, of authority, and over whether the group would participate, also made such rituals difficult.

The cultures made by the group were not integrated, not replications of previous responses, or offline culture, but essays, or attempts, which involved collaboration. The process was not orderly, nor finished, and it always risked the pain of rejection. Almost by necessity cultures in a new or infrequent situation are hesitant. These attempts provoked arguments and fractures, and were affected by contingency of messages. Often attempts failed: proposals were agreed upon but not carried out, some left when faced with grief, and others protested that they would leave. Those who stayed built some understandings, but there was no demand these understandings be mutual, any way to enforce mutuality, or any guarantee they would last. There was no completely shared position and previous feuds continued. Online cultures may be disorderly and fragmentary but they give some order to perceptions of life, and as such they constitute philosophies and an ever-modified way of living in an ambiguous environment. This failure of synthesis or integration is normal, and in this disorder lies potential for creative response.

Without recognising the disorder present in people's attempts to make models of action and behaviour for themselves and for each other, especially in a relatively new environment, we lose the sense of what social and cultural life is actually like, especially in a time of crisis. We smooth out the variations, without seeing them as essential for the dynamics of social life. We render life more secure than it is, and lose the sense of the risks inherent in either invention, or in attempting to remain the same when all has changed. We need to accept that social life is varied, not always integrated, involves mutually misunderstanding actors, and always has the potential to undermine its own order or produce disorder or even its own death.

REFERENCES

Argyle, K. (1996). Life after death. In Shields, R. (Ed.), *Cultures of the internet: Virtual spaces, real histories, living bodies*. London, UK: Sage.

Barth, F. (1989). The analysis of culture in complex societies. *Ethnos*, *34*, 120–142. doi:10.1080/001 41844.1989.9981389

Barth, F. (1990). *Cosmologies in the making*. Cambridge, UK: Cambridge UP.

Baudrillard, J. (1993). *Symbolic exchange and death*. London, UK: Sage.

Becker, E. (1973). *The denial of death*. New York, NY: Simon & Schuster.

Behar, R. (1991). Death and memory: From Santa Maria del Monte to Miami Beach. *Cultural Anthropology*, *6*(3), 346–384. doi:10.1525/can.1991.6.3.02a00050

Bonsu, S. K. (2007). The presentation of dead selves in everyday life: Obituaries and impression management. *Symbolic Interaction*, *30*(2), 199–219. doi:10.1525/si.2007.30.2.199

Bonsu, S. K., & DeBerry-Spence, B. (2008). Consuming the dead: Identity and community practices in death rituals. *Journal of Contemporary Ethnography*, *37*(6), 694–719. doi:10.1177/0891241607310631

Clark, D. (Ed.). (1993). *The sociology of death*. Oxford, UK: Blackwell.

Counts, D. A., & Counts, D. (2004). The good, the bad, and the unresolved death in Kaliai. *Social Science & Medicine*, *58*(5), 887–897. doi:10.1016/j.socscimed.2003.10.040

Elias, N. (1985). *The loneliness of the dying*. Oxford, UK: Blackwell.

Geertz, C. (1975). *The interpretation of cultures*. New York, NY: Basic Books.

Gibson, M. (2007). Death and mourning in technologically mediated culture. *Health Sociology Review*, *16*, 415–424. doi:10.5172/hesr.2007.16.5.415

Giddens, A. (1991). *Modernity and self identity: Self and society in the late modern age*. Stanford University Press.

Hockey, J. (1993). The acceptable face of human grieving? The clergy's role in managing emotional expression during funerals. In Clark, D. (Ed.), *The sociology of death: Theory, culture, practice* (pp. 129–148).

Kearl, M. C. (1989). *Endings*. New York, NY: Oxford University Press.

Kendall, L. (2002). *Hanging out in the virtual pub: Masculinities and relationships online*. Berkley, CA: University of California Press.

Kirkby, J. (2006). Remembrance of the future: Derrida on mourning. *Social Semiotics*, *16*(3), 461–472. doi:10.1080/10350330600824383

Marshall, J. P. (2007). *Living on cybermind: Categories, communication and control*. New York, NY: Peter Lang.

Marshall, J. P. (2010). Ambiguity, oscillation and disorder: Online ethnography and the making of culture. *Cosmopolitan Civil Societies Journal*, *2*(3), 1-22. Retrieved from http://epress.lib.uts.edu.au/ojs/index.php/mcs/article/view/1598

Metcalf, P., & Huntington, R. (1991). *Celebrations of death: The anthropology of mortuary ritual* (2nd ed.). Cambridge University Press.

Mulkay, M. (1993). Social death in Britain. In Clark, D. (Ed.), *The sociology of death: Theory, culture, practice*.

O'Rourke, D. (2007). Mourning becomes eclectic. *American Ethnologist, 34*(2), 387–402.

Poster, M. (2001). *What's the matter with the internet?* Minneapolis, MN: University of Minnesota Press.

Reid, L. (1996). Informed consent in the study of on-line communities: A reflection on the effects of computer-mediated social research. *The Information Society, 12*(2), 169–174. doi:10.1080/713856138

Roberts, P., & Lourdes, A. V. (1999-2000). Perpetual care in cyberspace: A portrait of memorials on the web. *Omega, 40*(4), 521–545.

Rosewood, B. (2008). *Cybermind novel*. Sydney, Australia: Alchemical Elephant. Retrieved from http://uts.academia.edu/jonmarshall/Books/130911/Cybermind_Novel

Saarinen, L. (2002). Imagined community and death. *Digital Creativity, 13*(1), 53–61. doi:10.1076/digc.13.1.53.3212

Turkle, S. (1995). *Life on screen: Identity in the age of the internet*. New York, NY: Simon and Schuster.

KEY TERMS AND DEFINITIONS

Culture: Culture is a central term in social theory; it can even become *the* central term as in 'Cultural Studies'. However, it is hard to define Culture. Culture like many other categories is 'ill formed', or disorderly, and escapes definition. It is something 'we know when we see' rather than can be precise about, and definitions of culture, even in the one discipline, are not always shared. In their 1952 book *Culture: A Critical Review of Concepts and Definitions* Kroeber and Kluckhohn pronounced that "culture is the central concept of anthropology" (p.36). They then went on to display "close to three hundred 'definitions' [of culture]" (p.149). There is no evidence to suggest that this flourishing of different definitions has diminished over the years. Importantly, this cultural diversity in the meaning of term 'culture' shows that cultural variation is not simply an epiphenomenon, but essential to culture itself. As a good enough guide, it could be asserted that culture consists of those models, meanings, beliefs, modes of communication and expression, that people use to make sense of the world and each others' actions. The term as used in anthropology includes 'high culture', the great exemplars of art or science, and the everyday culture of sport, conversation, household cooking and so on. 'Cultural difference' implies some degree of lack of mutual understanding, and can be pronounced even in the same social group.

Cybermind: A particular internet Mailing List, which acts as a social group. It is obviously different from offline social groups, but has some similarities and some advantages.

Disorder: Disorder is another ambiguous term. One person's disorder can be another person's order, or it can represent a challenge to a repressive order. A central cultural debate can be about the allocation and definition of order and disorder. As there are more ways that disorder can occur than order can, people can agree on what constitutes disorder, but may not agree on what constitutes correct order. In normal social theory perceived disorder is usually bypassed as a sign of external pathology or as evidence of failure, or as completely marginal to the analysts interests, rather than as the way things are. Disorder tends to be removed by the tools that we use to analyse things, so much everyday disorder remains unconsidered. 'Disorder Theory' asserts that disorder is interesting and not necessarily pathological. It aims to explicate necessary social disorder and asserts that modes of ordering tend to produce their own disorders, and so order and disorder are not separate but tied together in an order/disorder complex.

Ethnography: Ethnography is a mode of research; it is also the product of that research. In anthropology, ethnographic research usually means spending at least a year living with the people you are studying and engaging in as much of daily life with them as is possible. Ideally you should learn the language, study the customs and culture, and catch malaria. Then you write the understandings produced, and elucidated by the theories you have found most useful, up as a thesis or book – which is called an ethnography. All ethnographies produced since the 1960s are different from each other. Without a familiarity with many ethnographies, people tend to think the culture of their own society is the way humans are, or the way good humans should be.

Mailing List: A Mailing List is one of many ways that people can form groups using the Internet. Like all internet social formations the structures of communication have a great effect on what people find easy to do and what is difficult to do. On a Mailing List people send email to a central server which is then sent out to everyone who subscribes to that List. The moderator of the List, is usually the person who performs the maintenance that keeps the List working. They have certain privileges and can, for example, block mail from certain addresses. Mailing Lists were among the original modes of internet communication along with newsgroups. Nowadays, most scholars tend to think of them as terribly old

fashioned and thus less interesting than Facebook which also has the advantage of encouraging much simpler interactions. However, Mailing Lists are still common and in use and form the basis of much discussion.

ENDNOTES

[1] The relatively large amount of writing on the way people use memorial websites or form grief communities (see writings in the *Omega Journal*, especially Vol 49 no.1), does not generally discuss online life. Saarinen (2002) is a rare exception who looks at both group dynamics and relations between online and offline life. Argyle (1996), writing about one of the deaths discussed here seems to see death online as separated from offline 'reality', and analyses it in terms of Carnival, inversion of rules, and freedom from restraint, something which ignores the connection between on and offline life and does not match the effects on the group, or on her own search for meaning when faced with her reactions.

[2] An inventory of writings about the List can be found at: http://en.wikipedia.org/wiki/Cybermind

[3] Saarinen (2002) describes how in a death in a 'virtual community' devoted to the television character Xena warrior princess, despite the group's positive valuation of same sex relationships, the deceased's online lesbian lover was marginalised in comparison to her offline kin. The group's 'rhetorical vision', could not stand up to offline conventions (p.56-7).

[4] I briefly describe the destructive arguments over the Iraq war in Marshall (2007, pp.204-8).

Chapter 19
Virtual Communities of Practice in Immersive Virtual Worlds:
An Empirical Study on Participants' Involvement, Motives, and Behaviour

Grzegorz Majewski
University of the West of Scotland, UK

Abel Usoro
University of the West of Scotland, UK

ABSTRACT

Immersive virtual worlds such as Second Life have recently gained much attention from education and business because of their adaptability to address real world challenges such as: online presentations, meetings, collaboration, 3D data visualization, and online knowledge sharing. These features make immersive virtual worlds a convenient place for knowledge sharing activities that occur in Virtual Communities of Practice (VCoP). A great number of virtual communities exist in Second Life to serve various purposes ranging from business to entertainment. Knowledge sharing in this environment may thus serve diverse purposes. There is, however, little research into knowledge sharing in immersive virtual worlds. Therefore, the purpose of this research is to fill this gap in knowledge. This study investigates participants' involvement, motives, and behaviour and attempts to construct and validate a conceptual model of factors influencing members of VCoP in immersive virtual world while they share their knowledge. In order to achieve these goals, quantitative and qualitative research were carried out with participants of a group in Second Life.

DOI: 10.4018/978-1-4666-0312-7.ch019

1. INTRODUCTION

Modern organisations realize that their market value is to a high degree dependent on their employees and on the employees' knowledge in particular. It is noteworthy that to achieve full potentials, this knowledge needs to be shared between employees. Thus, knowledge management activities have gained much attention just like other business processes. One of the ways to capture and share knowledge is to use a collaborative virtual environment (CVE) which is a "software environment that emulates some of the features of the real world" (Tomek 2001, pp 458-459). The characteristics of the real world that are useful for knowledge sharing activities and are usually emulated include: the concept of space, the representation of an object, the representation of a human (in a form of avatar), and various tools that can be used to interact with other objects. To share knowledge in this environment, a participant does not need to type texts using the keyboard as she would do with other knowledge sharing media. Instead she uses her avatar to act out the knowledge that she wants to share. This approach is very useful especially when sharing tacit knowledge which cannot easily be reduced to text or even realised by the knowledge owner. A simple example is the instruction to change a car wheel. In the "flat" static ICT environment, such as a discussion board, the participant would have to use a text description of how to change the wheel with detailed description of each step. A CVE knowledge recipient would rather observe how it is performed in practice. Although it is in a virtual environment it is easy to copy the behaviour into the real world. Generally speaking, CVE essentially captures relevant parts of the work process, organizes it and provides data retrieval and data mining functions. It is a very efficient and productive way of managing participants' knowledge which includes the tacit form. Apart from that, it is also more attractive and richer than the static web based media. Therefore it is possible to benefit from increased motivation of employees to share their knowledge by combining work and entertainment-like functions. (Tomek 2001, p 459).

2. THEORETICAL BACKGROUND

Knowledge is embedded in people, and knowledge creation occurs in the process of social interaction. – Karl Erik Sveiby

As was described in the previous paragraph, knowledge sharing activities may be enhanced by the use of a CVE. Immersive virtual worlds such as Second Life (SL) may be perceived as a form of CVE. An immersive virtual environment is a 3D environment which also "help[s] [to] develop a common understanding in a collaborative mind set and engage people through appealing and memorable experiences" (Schmeil & Eppler 2008, p 667). Participants are encouraged to be creative and to develop stronger social ties compared to a static web discussion board or forum.

While utilizing an immersive virtual world in knowledge management and collaboration related activities it is necessary to consider the following characteristics of this environment (Tomek 2001, Ondrejka 2008, Schmeil & Eppler 2008):

- Physical topology can be emulated as a natural metaphor, a useful feature for a successful groupware.
- People, information and knowledge can be organized spatially.
- Awareness of co-workers, usage policies for tools and objects is enhanced.
- Content is produced by residents of the world; developers provide powerful tools designed to be used by everyone.
- Group and private chat functionality, as well as object sharing, provide inherent collaboration possibilities (additionally all communication can be logged instantly).

- Social and collaborative aspects exist – inherent collaboration between avatars.
- Constructivist aspect – playing or creating objects and so creating correlations and knowledge from current structures - is inherent in Second Life (SL) (Antonacci, 2005).
- Collaborative problem solving engaging several avatars is supported in Second Life.

Environments based on Virtual Reality mimic the physical reality and because of that the engagement of a participant is much easier and usually it is of a higher degree. The disadvantage associated with such environments is the steep learning curve (3D models may be difficult to use and may require more manipulation of the user's avatar as compared with "flat" environments). Sometimes the richness of the environment may distract the participant from the communication (Tomek 2001, p 461). This can happen in "flat" environments as well (e.g. bad design of a discussion board by overemphasis of graphical elements).

Virtual Communities of Practice as a Knowledge Management Tool

Large organizations, reflectively structured, are well positioned to be highly innovative and deal with discontinuities. If their internal communities have a reasonable degree of autonomy and independence from the dominant world view, large organizations might actually accelerate innovation. Emergent communities that span the boundaries of an organization are likely conduits of external and innovative views into the organization – John Seely Brown, VP and Chief Scientist, Xerox Corp.

Knowledge management is a very complex phenomenon that can be tackled from several perspectives: socio-organizational, economical, technical, human and legal. There have been various KM definitions, perspectives, frameworks, paradigms and measurements proposed to explain (a) what knowledge management is; (b) what its main techniques and methods are; (c) what its value is; and (d) what its functions for supporting individual and organizations are (Liao, 2003, p. 156).

Knowledge management tools are technologies, methodologies and practices which enable knowledge generation, codification and transfer (Ruggles 1997, p. 3). Their design should intend to ease the burden of work as well as better resource allocation. It is important to realize that not all knowledge tools are computer-based. Simple pen and paper can be utilized to do the activities mentioned above (i.e. knowledge generation, codification and transfer). Knowledge management tools can only be fully understood in the context in which they are used and the methodologies that support them. They have to take into account that knowledge is a "fluid mix of framed experience, values, contextual information, and expert insight that provides a framework for evaluating and incorporating new experiences and information" (Tyndale 2002, p. 184).

Different tools are applied to help the various goals of modern knowledge management. In the case of the knowledge generation, these tools stimulate creativity (e.g. brainstorming and morphological analysis). Knowledge codification (i.e. putting knowledge in a form that can be transmitted to others) can be supported among others by artificial intelligence tools (e.g. expert systems), databases, data warehouses and organizational knowledge maps. Knowledge sharing has attracted a remarkable amount of attention due to advances in groupware and networking tools, which are designed to enable the flow of knowledge among groups and individuals. The goal of such tools is ultimately shared memory and understanding (Ruggles 1997, p. 6). These tools strive to achieve something that is very difficult due to the "stickiness" of knowledge. Knowledge is usually placed in the context which gives it meaning. The term stickiness (Szulanski, 2003) in the case of knowledge refers to inability or unwillingness to transfer knowledge. Such situations may occur in big multinational companies where different branches or departments may be geographically separated or may have diverse organizational cultures (Chia-Ying & Chang-Tseh, 2009). Moreover knowledge is constantly changing and growing. It may also go out of date and become irrelevant. ICT enables "KM activities for collaborative decision support, organizational learning, organizational memory and information sharing" (Liao 2003, p. 158). Dieng et al (1999) examined corporate KM tools. The authors investigated the concept of "corporate memory" and its various flavours: non-computational corporate memory, document-based corporate memory, knowledge-based corporate memory, case-based corporate memory and distributed corporate memory. The last kind is the most interesting given the objectives of this thesis as it supports "collaboration and knowledge sharing between several groups of people in an organization or in several collaborating organizations, such groups being possibly dispersed geographically" (ibid, p. 581).

Communities of practice (CoPs) are one of the most recognised knowledge sharing tools, making it a very highly valued tool of knowledge management. One of the characteristics of CoPs, which appeals to knowledge managers, is their ability to traverse geographical, organisational and culture barriers. They are also known to be informal unlike most of the corporate practices and tools and therefore it is easier to share both explicit and implicit knowledge after locating the right subject expert(s) (Brown and Grey, 1995; Lesser and Everest 2001). Lave and Wenger (1991) described it as an activity system that brings together individuals with common values, interests, and varied experiences to share among them. CoPs are not part of the formal structures but rather informal entities that "exist" in the mind of each member (Loyarte and Rivera, 2007). CoPs are also defined as informal groups of people that are held together by a "common sense of purpose and a real need to know what each other knows" (Brown and Grey 1995, p. 2).

Becoming a member of a CoP is usually performed in an informal way and may be described as a self-selecting process. In some cases, however, some organizations, for example, BP in the oil exploration business, are beginning to formalize this process (Newell et. al., 2002, p. 119). It is however necessary to note that a CoP is not just an informal network based on friendship or shared affiliations. A CoP, unlike other types of social networks, directly supports work processes by allowing individuals to share experiences about their work and thus understand them better. Also CoPs may easily cross traditional organizational boundaries as they may often emerge from existing networks of individuals that are present in different organisations. Because of that they are also very useful in quickly identifying experts - individuals with the right subject expertise necessary to provide the best answer to a given problem. This is especially important in multinational organizations where expertise may be separated by distance, time zones, different economic and political systems or organizational boundaries (Lesser and Everest 2001, p. 3-4).

Participants of traditional CoPs meet face to face to discuss and share knowledge. However, modern ICT technologies enable participants to enjoy the benefits of being part of a community irrespective of residing at different geographical locations and time zones. They use ICT tools ranging from email to virtual conferences to "extend the boundaries of traditional face-to-face communities by creating virtual communities that enable global asynchronous and real-time collaboration" (Usoro et al., 2007, p. 200). It is their reliance on computer mediation that adds "virtual" dimension to the name of CoPs; hence "virtual communities of practice" (VCoPs).

Technology is an enabler of the VCoPs' main activity, i.e. "an active participation of a substantial part (ideally, all) of its members" (Ardichvili et. al., 2003, pp. 65-66). Participants can play two distinguishable roles - either a provider or a receiver of knowledge.

3. RESEARCH MODEL

A variety of factors influence knowledge management processes. This is reflected in Becerra-Fernandez et. al.'s (2004) statement that "various KM solutions may have different impacts on performance, depending on the circumstances" (ibid, p. 66). Research has revealed key factors that affect people's online behaviour (Ardichvili 2003). The most prominent is trust (Chowdhury 2005). Furthermore there are different components that constitute trust: integrity, competence and benevolence (Chiu et al. 2006, Usoro et al. 2007, Holste & Fields, 2010, McNichols, 2010). In most cases the high value of these components is highly correlated with the level, density and quality of knowledge sharing (Usoro et al. 2007). Andrews & Delahaye (2000) point out that "perceived trustworthiness – based on perceptions of what colleagues were likely to do with sensitive information – was the factor that influenced knowledge sharing decisions" (p. 797). Chowdhury (2005) demonstrated that trust facilitates complex knowledge sharing. Lambiotte et. al. (2009) indicated how important trust is in the way online communities function and that it influences knowledge sharing among their members. In real life factors combine to influence knowledge sharing.

Other important factors are risk and perceived benefits (rewards, incentives, reputation, appreciation) (Bock et al., 2006), reciprocity (norm of reciprocity, perceived reciprocity) (Bock et al., 2006; Chiu et al. 2006; Lin et al., 2009), community (social ties, social network, social relationships) (Chiu et al. 2006, Holste & Fields, 2010), organization-related supervision and the provision of incentives such as promotion, time, knowledge sharing self-efficacy (Bock et. al., 2006, Lin et al., 2009), perceived relative advantage of knowledge sharing (Lin et al., 2009) and perceived compatibility of knowledge sharing (Lin et al., 2009).

The perception of community drives virtual communities as reflected by Chiu et al. (2006) that "people who come to a virtual community are not just seeking information or knowledge to solve problems but they also treat it as a place to meet other people, to seek support, friendship and a sense of belonging" (p. 1874). Although they were focusing on the knowledge provision perspective, they recognized that the sense of community has to be shared, even if at a less extent, by receivers as well. Knowledge receivers are often expected to and/or they often feel obliged to reciprocate by also giving their knowledge, skills, values or something else of value more so with the consequent development of trust in such relationships.

Thus Chiu et al (2006) appreciated not only a sense of community but also reciprocity as antecedents of knowledge sharing. The role of reciprocity in this way was also deduced by Kankanhalli et al. (2005a). Both knowledge sharing and sense of community may be enhanced by the notion of reciprocity. Thus, reciprocity can be viewed as an antecedent of perception of community which in turn should influence knowledge sharing. This research uses "perception" rather than "sense" of community because it is anticipated to capture the member's perception of the existence of a community whether or not he/she feels a belonging to the community. To illustrate this point, a member on the fringe or even an outsider may recognize the existence of a strong community even though he does not belong or is accepted there. Perception of community does not only affect the giver but also the receiver of knowledge. Members are more likely to value knowledge that comes from a community with an established reputation than from a new one with little or no track record.

Another important group of factors is one embracing benefits, gains and various incentives. Kankanhalli et al (2005b) argued out that "the exchange of intellectual capital can be facilitated by norms of collaboration and sharing" (p. 1158). In this context the norms of collaboration and sharing reflect the existence or perception of community while exchange of intellectual capital includes knowledge reception. Kankanhalli et al. (2005b) also indicate that the potential incentives or benefits are positively associated with knowledge sharing. The expected benefits may differ between the seeker and the giver of knowledge. To the seeker the benefit can be the received knowledge itself (Kankanhalli et al., 2005b). Nebus (2004) therefore concludes that there is a positive relationship between the perceived expectation of obtaining knowledge and knowledge seeking behaviour. The benefit expected by the receiver can also be increased performance (Li, 2010) or some "social reward" e.g. friendship (Chiu et al., 2006).

To the knowledge provider the benefit may not be so obvious. They may be economic such as "increased salary, larger bonuses, greater job security, and career advancement prospects" (Kankanhalli et al, 2005b, p. 1159), appraisal, respect, being seen as skilled, and of higher status in the community (Butler et al., 2002), or networking opportunity (Zhang & Hiltz, 2003). Mayfield (2010) notes that "targeted rewards are the most powerful means to increase worker tacit knowledge sharing" (p. 25). As rewards influence behaviour, tacit knowledge sharing will respond accordingly. Rewards also signal that management is committed to tacit knowledge sharing, and thus help shape an organization's cultural lens.

Another set of factors that may influence knowledge sharing are those related to medium or means of communication. Participants of CoPs communicate face-to-face while VCoP participants use ICT to communicate. Technologies utilised may range from email and simple discussion boards to sophisticated knowledge management systems and dedicated virtual world environments as it was described previously. The importance of technological considerations is also noted by Ensign & Hébert (2009).

(V)CoPs are considered as a KM environment where barriers to knowledge-sharing are lowered (Newell et. al., 2002, p. 120). Members of such communities also develop a set of shared meanings deriving from their common experience. They can also employ more specialized forms of language such as technical jargon. Although this may enhance knowledge sharing for the more experienced members of the CoP it may pose a difficulty for the new-comers. Another potential barrier to knowledge sharing in (V)CoPs is the potential loss of objectivity. It may occur where large groups of people come to share a similar world-view or perspective (Newell et. al., 2002, p. 122). Negative influences to knowledge sharing also exist and these can be fears, risks or costs of on-line knowledge sharing. Ardichvili et al. (2003) identified fear of losing face as an impediment to online knowledge sharing. The fear of being laughed at by more experienced members may hinder knowledge provision or even asking questions (knowledge seeking). For a knowledge provider, it may also be the fear of taking additional responsibility and, even more hindering, losing competitive advantage over others. These fears could be regarded as costs; the fear of losing face can be termed as the cost of losing face, for instance. Kankanhalli et al. (2005b) make the point that "incentives may be needed to encourage knowledge reuse to counteract the inertia to seek knowledge and the propensity of employees to "reinvent the wheel," i.e., come up with their own solutions to tasks" (p. 1159). Perceived costs as a hindrance of knowledge sharing can be in terms of money and time which often has to be significantly spent to make meaningful contributions to VCoP (Bock et al., 2006, p 358).

Based on the literature this research tries to develop a comprehensive model of knowledge sharing in (Virtual) Communities of Practice that would take into account both technological as well as social factors across two dimensions of knowledge sharing: knowledge provision and knowledge reception.

It is necessary to acknowledge in existing research (e.g. Kankanhalli et al. 2005a and 2005b), that VCoP members may act as knowledge givers and knowledge receivers. Therefore, it is necessary to perceive these two roles or perspectives as antecedents to on-line knowledge sharing in VCoPs thus:

H₁: Knowledge *provision* is positively associated with online knowledge sharing.

H₂: Knowledge *reception* is positively associated with online knowledge sharing.

Perception of community may be influenced by such factors as trust and norm of reciprocity. Kankanhalli et al. (2005a) noted that reciprocity is positively related to knowledge sharing. The hypotheses that can be derived are that:

H₃: The norm of reciprocity is positively associated with the perception of community while providing knowledge.

H₄: The norm of reciprocity is positively associated with the perception of community while seeking knowledge.

Trust is another factor that affects knowledge reception. It is trust in the credibility, expertise and reputation of the contributor (knowledge source) that matters. "Perceived value from knowledge seeking depends on the contributor's (source's) expertise and credibility, while perceived expectation of value is determined by trust, obligation, and the contributor's willingness to help" (Bock et al., 2006). It is possible to say that trust in on-line community affects the perception of the community on the knowledge receiver side. If the community is perceived as competent in answering queries it is expected that a knowledge seeker will keep posting his or her questions. Other trust components count as well, because a knowledge receiver needs to be able to rely on the knowledge provided by the community. Thus benevolence and integrity are also important. It is possible to formulate the following hypotheses based on these facts:

H₅: Trust is positively associated with the perception of community while providing knowledge.

H₆: Trust is positively associated with the perception of community while receiving knowledge.

H₇: The norm of reciprocity is positively associated with trust while providing knowledge.

H₈: The norm of reciprocity is positively associated with trust while receiving knowledge.

At this point it is possible to propose a conceptual model consisting of the proposed hypotheses and embracing both roles that can be played by the participants of VCoP. This conceptual model is presented in Figure 1.

This conceptual model was operationalized into a questionnaire and interview questions (Appendix I and II). The next section focuses on the research methodology utilized.

4. RESEARCH METHODOLOGY

This research follows the deductive approach to research starting with literature review and theory, through hypotheses formulation, and participant observation, finishing with confirmation and in some cases rejection of formulated hypotheses. Hypotheses are presented as relationships between theoretical constructs. Testing of hypotheses is performed using statistical methods. Therefore this type of research can be classified as correlation research. Additionally its subtype may be specified as one that deals with relationships.

The hypotheses were tested by way of qualitative and quantitative research with the Lucky Tribe group in Second Life, which was carefully selected to reflect the Second Life environment. This immersive virtual world embraces profit-oriented organisations as well as people that seek different sorts of entertainment. This group was used to promote various vendors across the grid as well as generate traffic on their lands. Enter-

Figure 1. Conceptual model of factors influencing knowledge sharing in VCoP in immersive virtual environment

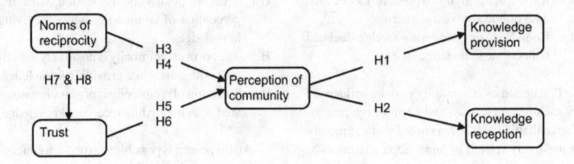

taining activities were used to attract potential customers. The comprehensive economic analysis of the whole venture is beyond the scope of this chapter; however it is possible to say that in this case knowledge sharing between participants has some economic aspect in the background.

Lucky Tribe group at the time of the research had more than 1,480 members. Members of this group performed a variety of functions in Second Life for which they were awarded the group own "currency"–kudos points. Furthermore, tools and practices were used to enhance the strength of the social ties: dedicated Heads Up Display (HUD) showing achievements of a given member and also ability to check status (by showing number of kudos points a given person has). The practices that enhance the social ties were special events or quests where members needed to gather together to collaboratively do a given task. For successfully accomplishing a given activity members are rewarded kudos points and a special badge that is visible in their HUD. Additionally a special set of interviews were developed to further validate the model. Interview data is available in Appendix III. Group owners were contacted and asked for permission to do the research. This is an alternative approach to the Second Life social research conducted by Messinger et al. (2009). After acquir-

ing permission, a few members of the community were asked to evaluate the questionnaire. Their feedback was the basis for the improvement of the questionnaire items.

A link to an online version of the questionnaire was designed and distributed by way of group notices (special group mechanism available in Second Life), so that all of the members had the opportunity to access it. The questionnaire required 15 to 20 minutes to complete. The members of the group were truly global and came from a variety of countries and backgrounds. The interviews were performed with the group owner, top members (number of kudos points) and random members of the community.

5. DATA ANALYSIS

Descriptive analysis was used to provide demographic data regarding participants of VCoPs. In general descriptive statistics are used to summarize the elementary characteristics of the studied data. These summaries are straightforward for and easy to understand by the reader. Therefore they are considered as rudimentary techniques utilized in almost every quantitative analysis.

Figure 2. Participants' country of origin

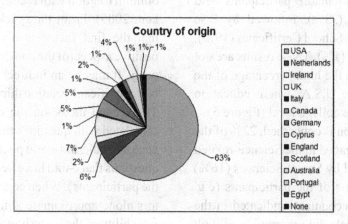

Figure 3. Participants' gender

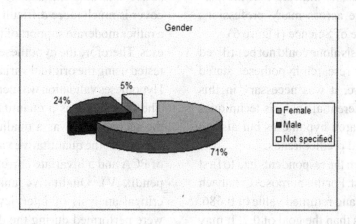

Data was collected for the time period between 13 September 2009 and 23 November 2009. There were a total of 161 responses. Incomplete surveys were removed and after data cleaning 152 responses were available for analysis. In terms of demographic data the participants of the survey were mainly from the U.S.A. (63%), followed by the U.K. (10%; some of them selected England - 2% and Scotland - 1%), the Netherlands (6%), Germany (6%), Canada (6%), Australia (4%) and some other countries (Figure 2).

Participants were mainly female (71%) with some fraction of males (24%) and 5% did not specify their gender (Figure 3). These results provide insight that IVW are quite popular with

women as compared with the game-based industry where males dominate the statistics. It may also be that the social part of IVW fits female inclination more and constitutes their main attraction to IVW.

As far as age of participants is concerned the leading group are people below 20 and 29 (more than 50 participants), followed by those in their thirties (almost 40 participants) (Figure 4). The number of participants decreases with age; older participants are significantly few. It is also surprising that the people below 20 were not that well represented. A possible explanation is that a separate grid (Teen Grid) exists for people below 18 years of age.

Most of the questionnaire participants held College Certificates (33%), followed by BSc (21%) and Secondary School Certificates (19%), MSc (10%) and PhD (1%). These results are not very surprising given the high percentage of the participants from the U.S.A. where education usually finishes at the college level (Figure 5).

As far as profession is concerned, 22% of the participants were engaged in the Science-related professions, followed by Social Sciences (16%) and Arts (15%). Some of the participants (e.g. one working as an accountant) indicated in the comments that the scale did not provide enough choices. It may be necessary to adjust the scale in future studies. Results indicate that the participants were active across many professions with little dominance of Science (Figure 6)

Descriptive analysis alone could not be utilized to confirm or falsify research hypotheses stated previously. Therefore, it was necessary in this research to apply inferential analysis techniques to not only test research hypotheses but also to draw conclusions and predict trends.

Data gathered from the respondents had to first undergo reliability test. For this purposes Cronbach alpha was evaluated and returned value of 0.686, which is slightly less than the goal of 0.7. It may still be considered as a good reliability and thus it is possible to say that the questionnaire items measure the same variable or concept – in this case this concept could be knowledge sharing. Figure 7 presents the results.

Apart from measuring the reliability of the scales it was also necessary to examine their validity. Validity is a term which describes how well a questionnaire or survey measures what it is purposed to measure. Factorial validity with the most common technique, such as principal components analysis (PCA) or confirmatory factor analysis, has been identified as one of the most appropriate in IS research (Straub *et al*, 2004, p 10). The results of the principal components analysis are provided in Appendix IV in supplementary files. Five factors were extracted using

oblimin rotation with Kaiser Normalization (Pallant, 2005). From the quick analysis it appears that the first factor is highly correlated with positive aspects of the constructs discussed previously. It may be an indirect indication that there is a significant relationship between the items. The second factor on the other hand is highly correlated with questions that were added to balance the scale and avoid positive slant (except the questions that could have been misunderstood by the participants). When combined, these two factors alone approximate almost 50% of the total variability of the underlying variables. The other three factors are scattered among different constructs and thus explanation of what they could cover is much more difficult. The PCA provides a rather moderate support of the research hypotheses. Therefore the hypotheses for this study were tested using the original variables and constructs. Hypotheses validation was performed in two steps. The first step was a quantitative validation and the second step was a qualitative validation. In the case of the quantitative validation it consisted of PCA and a bivariate correlation analysis (Appendix V). Qualitative analysis consisted of critical analysis of interviews data. Interviews were performed during the distribution of questionnaire in order to capture a specific time in the lifecycle of the community.

Respondents belonged to the list of 20 participants who had the most kudos points (achievement points awarded for a variety of tasks). This may indicate a higher involvement in the group and a tendency to share their knowledge with others. Apart from that, questionnaires were also distributed to mid-level and low-level kudos members of immersive VCoP. From the responses of the high achievers it was apparent that they kept to themselves by carving out a common subgroup: one of them actually confirmed that they were closer to each other than to other members.

Two of them described their strategy of figuring out how to perform a given task before the rest of the group; thus in most cases they were playing

Figure 4. Participants' age

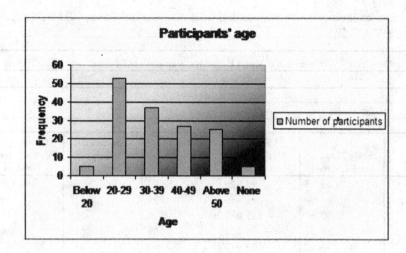

Figure 5. Participants' educational level

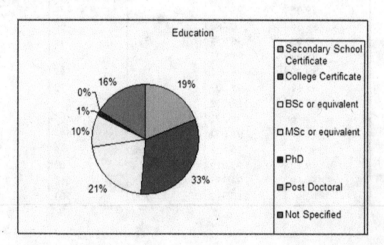

Figure 6. Participants' profession

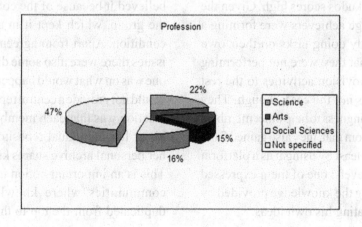

Figure 7. Reliability of the questionnaire items

(a) Reliability statistics

Cronbach's Alpha	Cronbach's Alpha Based on Standardized Items	N of Items
.686	.708	21

(b) Item-total statistics

	Scale Mean if Item Deleted	Scale Variance if Item Deleted	Corrected Item-Total Correlation	Squared Multiple Correlation	Cronbach's Alpha if Item Deleted
NR1	88.53	98.529	.500	.504	.657
NR2	88.68	95.436	.534	.571	.649
NR3	93.34	111.681	-.130	.610	.704
TRP1	89.12	96.251	.559	.516	.650
TRP2	93.11	109.941	-.068	.574	.706
TRP3	88.96	93.429	.620	.662	.641
PCP1	88.78	96.109	.511	.597	.652
PCP2	92.78	110.052	-.089	.299	.718
PCP3	89.05	93.157	.511	.474	.647
KP1	93.36	110.482	-.079	.467	.702
KP2	90.07	96.054	.382	.446	.661
KP3	89.90	91.705	.518	.477	.644
TKR1	89.20	98.932	.232	.364	.679
TKR2	88.81	95.003	.579	.692	.646
TKR3	93.15	113.772	-.200	.554	.716
PCKR1	88.76	98.291	.362	.507	.664
PCKR2	88.87	95.964	.541	.604	.650
PCKR3	92.96	116.528	-.298	.546	.723
KR1	89.12	93.019	.550	.560	.644
KR2	88.89	94.333	.608	.661	.643
KR3	92.97	117.311	-.300	.503	.730

the knowledge provider role: "I tend to figure things out before most others in the group". This strategy keeps their kudos scores high. Given the two facts that the high achievers were forming a subgroup and usually doing tasks on their own one could deduce that they were not performing much knowledge provision activities to the rest of the group. This is not the case, though. They expressed a true willingness to help other members of the group. Apart from that, they also gained from group knowledge at least by using it as a platform to aspire to higher levels: one of them expressed his practice of testing the knowledge provided by others before generating his own ideas.

All of the respondents stated that the group was working well and acting in a friendly way. They believed it because of the contributions made to the group, which kept it in a good and healthy condition. Apart from agreement on most of the issues there were also some differences. The first one was on what would happen if the group owner would not provide a central repository. The general reaction was that each member was improvising his or her individual repository and from his or her personal archive shares knowledge to others. This is an important notion in the case of fractal communities where knowledge is somehow duplicated from the top to the bottom level of a

VCoP and thus can be easily retrieved even in the case of failure of a given repository. In the case of immersive VCoPs it is even easier to acquire such a structure as compared with other VCoPs.

There were some difficulties mentioned by the respondents as well. One of them was the difficulty of locating sources of information. This is one of the difficulties often experienced by newcomers to a VCoP. This difficulty is however tackled by the owner with the 'mentor tiki'. It can be described as a special "mechanism" in the workings of the immersive VCoP. It would be hard to achieve this sort of mechanism in plain VCoPs. It is a sort of special occasion that is used to establish mentorship. Each case is made up of a mentor and a student, which resembles real world settings in a way. These two roles are a clear representation of a knowledge provider (mentor) and a knowledge receiver (student). In reality a mentor also sometimes has the opportunity to learn from his or her student. This process therefore was designed in order to strengthen the bonds within the group and thus enhance knowledge sharing processes.

Findings

The outcomes of both quantitative and qualitative data analyses indicate that the hypotheses tested were to be accepted. It came out from the findings that Second Life was not only for pure business and entertainment as originally envisioned but also mixing knowledge sharing activities into it was possible without harm for the other two. Actually knowledge sharing was supporting the business and entertainment carried out in the environment.

The three-dimensional environment provided enhanced opportunities for interaction and socialisation unseen in contemporary environments. This interaction and socialisation through the surrogate users – avatars – resulted in high levels of knowledge sharing. The summary of findings is provided in Figure 8. Unlike in the other research, all hypotheses gained strong positive support.

Figure 8. Summary of the findings of a study with Second Life

	Quantitative Analysis	Qualitative Analysis	Outcome
Hypothesis	**First Step**	**Interview**	
H_1	Strong	Strong	Positive
H_2	Strong	Strong	Positive
H_3	Strong	Strong	Positive
H_4	Strong	Strong	Positive
H_5	Strong	Strong	Positive
H_6	Moderate	Strong	Positive
H_7	Strong	Strong	Positive
H_8	Moderate	Strong	Positive

Weak = 1	Positive if the value is 5 or above
Moderate = 2	Undecisive if the values is 3 or 4
Strong = 3	Negative if the value is below 3

6. CONCLUSION AND AREAS FOR FURTHER RESEARCH

Knowledge sharing in virtual communities of practice requires the existence of reciprocity, trust and a sense of community. The research shows that the existence of a sense of community and active participation of community members are essential to the working of a VCoP. The research study with a group from Second Life investigated whether the knowledge sharing motivations in immersive VCoPs are different from those in "flat" static web environments. From earlier studies and findings in the latter environments, a research model was developed, operationalized and tested in Second Life. It was found that although immersive VCoP undoubtedly provide a richer and more exciting experience to knowledge sharers the same factors that influence KS in "flat" static web environments operate in them.

Meanwhile, it is necessary to note that perception of community, trust and reciprocity are very important for keeping and growing virtual communities in immersive environments. At the same time care has to be exercised to ensure that the amount of social part introduced is in line with the goals of the community. This study acknowledged but not examined the economic aspect of knowledge sharing in immersive virtual worlds. This is a possible area for future research. It would be interesting to know how and which economic incentive has greater positive impact on knowledge sharing.

REFERENCES

Allee, V. (2003). *The future of knowledge: Increasing prosperity through value networks*. USA: Elsevier Science.

Anderson, J. C., & Gerbing, D. W. (1988). Structural equation modeling in practice: A review and recommended two-step approach. *Psychological Bulletin, 103*(3), 411–423. doi:10.1037/0033-2909.103.3.411

Andrews, K. M., & Delahaye, B. L. (2000). Influences on knowledge processes in organizational learning: the psychological filter. *Journal of Management Studies, 37*(6), 797–810. doi:10.1111/1467-6486.00204

Ardichvili, A., Page, V., & Wentling, T. (2003). Motivation and barriers to participation in virtual knowledge-sharing communities of practice. *Journal of Knowledge Management, 7*(1), 64–77. doi:10.1108/13673270310463626

Barquin, R. C. (2001). What is knowledge management? In Barquin, R. C., & Bennet, A. (Eds.), *Knowledge management: The catalyst for electronic government*. Vienna, VA: Management Concepts Publications.

Becerra-Fernandez, I., Gonzalez, A., & Sabherwal, R. (2004). *Knowledge management, challenges, solutions and technologies*. Pearson Education.

Beckman, T. (2001). Creating business value from knowledge management: The fusion of knowledge and technology. In Barquin, R. C., & Bennet, A. (Eds.), *Knowledge management: The catalyst for electronic government*. Vienna, VA: Management Concepts Publications.

Bock, G.-W., Kankanhalli, S. S., & Sharma, S. (2006). Are norms enough? The role of collaborative norms in promoting organizational knowledge seeking. *European Journal of Information Systems, 15*, 357–367. doi:10.1057/palgrave.ejis.3000630

Boland, R. (1985). Phenomenology: A preferred approach to research in information systems. In Mumford, E., Hirschheim, R. A., Fitzgerald, G., & Wood Harper, T. (Eds.), *Research methods in information systems* (pp. 193–201). Amsterdam, The Netherlands: North Holland Publishers.

Braa, K., & Vidgen, R. (1999). Interpretation, intervention, and reduction in the organizational laboratory: A framework for in-context information system research. *Accounting, Management, and Information Technology, 9*, 25–47. doi:10.1016/S0959-8022(98)00018-6

Brown, J. S., & Gray, E. S. (1995). The people are the company. *Fast Company, 1,* 78. Retrieved from http://www.fastcompany.com/magazine/01/people.html

Butler, B., Sproull, L., Kiesler, S., & Kraut, R. (2002). Community effort in online groups: Who does the work and why? In S. Weisband & L. Atwater (Eds.), *Leadership at a distance*, (pp. 2–32). Mahwah, NJ: Lawrence Erlbaum Publishers. Retrieved from http://opensource.mit.edu/papers/butler.pdf

Castelfranchi, C., & Falcone, R. (1999). The dynamics of trust: From beliefs to action. *Proceedings of the Autonomous Agents Workshops on Deception, Fraud and Trust in Agent Societies*.

Chia-Ying, L., & Chang-Tseh, H. (2009). The impact of knowledge stickiness on knowledge transfer implementation, internalization, and satisfaction for multinational corporations. *International Journal of Information Management, 29*(6), 425–435. doi:10.1016/j.ijinfomgt.2009.06.004

Chiu, C.-M., Hsu, M.-H., & Wang, E. T. G. (2006). Understanding knowledge sharing in virtual communities: An integration of social capital and social cognitive theories. *Decision Support Systems, 42*, 1872–1888. doi:10.1016/j.dss.2006.04.001

Choudrie, J., & Dwivedi, Y. K. (2005). Investigating the research approaches for examining technology adoption issues. *Journal of Research Practice, 1*(1). Retrieved from http://jrp.icaap.org/index.php/jrp/article/view/4/7

Chow, W. S., & Chan, L. S. (2008). Social network, social trust and shared goals in organizational knowledge sharing. *Information & Management, 45*, 458–465. doi:10.1016/j.im.2008.06.007

Chowdhury, S. (2005). The role of affect and cognition based trust in complex knowledge sharing. *Journal of Managerial Issues, 17*(3), 310–326.

Davenport, T., & Probst, G. (2000). *Knowledge management case book*. Siemens Best Practices.

Davenport, T. H., & Prusak, L. (1998). *Working knowledge*. Boston, MA: Harvard Business School Press.

Davenport, T. H., & Prusak, L. (1998). *Working knowledge*. Boston, MA: Harvard Business School Press.

Denzin, N. K. (1970). *The research act in sociology*. Chicago, IL: Aldine.

Dieng, R., Corby, O., Giboin, A., & Ribiere, M. (1999). Methods and tools for corporate knowledge management. *International Journal of Human-Computer Studies, 51*, 567–598. doi:10.1006/ijhc.1999.0281

Dube, L., Bourhis, A., & Jacob, R. (2005). The impact of structuring characteristics on the launching of virtual communities of practice. *Journal of Organizational Change Management, 18*(2), 145–166. doi:10.1108/09534810510589570

Gambetta, D. (2000). Can we trust trust? In *Trust: Making and breaking cooperative relations* (*Vol. 13*, pp. 213–237). Oxford, UK: Blackwell.

Garavelli, C., Gorgoglione, M., & Scozzi, B. (2002). Managing knowledge transfer by knowledge technologies. *Technovation*, *22*, 269–279. doi:10.1016/S0166-4972(01)00009-8

Golafshani, N. (2003). Understanding reliability and validity in questionnaire research. *Qualitative Report*, *8*(4), 597–607.

Groff, T. R., & Jones, T. P. (2003). *Introduction to knowledge management: KM in business*. Woburn, MA: Butterworth-Heinemann.

Groves, R., Fowler, F. J., Couper, M. P., Lepkowski, J. M., Singer, E., & Tourangeau, R. (2010). *Survey methodology* (2nd ed.).

Gupta, A. K., & Govindarajan, V. (2000). Knowledge management's social dimension: Lessons from Nucor steel. *Sloan Management Review*, *42*(1), 71–80.

Halal, W. E. (1998). *The infinite resource*. San Francisco, CA: Jossey-Bass Inc.

Holste, J. S., & Fields, D. (2010). Trust and tacit knowledge sharing and use. *Journal of Knowledge Management*, *14*(1), 128–140. doi:10.1108/13673271011015615

Hooff van den, B., & Huysman, M. (2009). Managing knowledge sharing: Emergent and engineering approaches. *Information & Management, 46*, 1-8.

Jiacheng, W., Lu, L., & Calabrese, A. F. (2010). A cognitive model of intra-organizational knowledge-sharing motivations in the view of cross-culture. *International Journal of Information Management*, *30*, 220–230. doi:10.1016/j.ijinfomgt.2009.08.007

Kankanhalli, A., Tan, B. C. Y., & Wei, K.-K. (2005a). Contributing knowledge to electronic knowledge repositories: An empirical investigation. *Management Information Systems Quarterly*, *29*(1), 113–143.

Kankanhalli, A., Tan, B. C. Y., & Wei, K.-K. (2005b). Understanding seeking from electronic knowledge repositories an empirical study. *Journal of the American Society for Information Science and Technology*, *56*(11), 1156–1166. doi:10.1002/asi.20219

KMEdge. (2010). *How do communities work in leading organizations?* Retrieved April 10, 2010, from http://kmedge.org/wp/howdocop.html

Lai, L. F. (2007). A knowledge engineering approach to knowledge management. *Information Sciences*, *177*, 4072–4094. doi:10.1016/j.ins.2007.02.028

Lambiotte, R., & Panzarasa, P. (2009). Communities, knowledge creation, and information diffusion. *Journal of Informatrics*, *3*, 180–190. doi:10.1016/j.joi.2009.03.007

Lave, J., & Wenger, E. (1991). *Situated learning: Legitimate peripheral participation*. New York, NY: Cambridge University Press.

Lesser, E., & Everest, K. (2001). Communities of practice: Making the most of intellectual capital. *Ivey Business Journal*, *65*(4), 37–41.

Li, W. (2010). Virtual knowledge sharing in a cross-cultural context. *Journal of Knowledge Management*, *14*(1), 38–50. doi:10.1108/13673271011015552

Liao, S.-H. (2003). Knowledge management technologies and applications – Literature review from 1995 to 2002. *Expert Systems with Applications*, *25*, 155–164. doi:10.1016/S0957-4174(03)00043-5

Lin, M.-J. J., Hung, S.-W., & Chen, C.-J. (2009). Fostering the determinants of knowledge sharing in professional virtual communities. *Computers in Human Behavior*, *25*, 929–939. doi:10.1016/j.chb.2009.03.008

Litwin, M. S. (1995). *How to measure survey reliability and validity*. London, UK: Sage Publications.

Loyarte, E., & Rivera, O. (2007). Communities of practice: A model for their cultivation. *Journal of Knowledge Management, 11*(3), 67–77. doi:10.1108/13673270710752117

Lukkarinen, H. (2005). Methodological triangulation showed the poorest quality of life in the youngest people following the treatment of coronary artery disease: A longitudinal study. *International Journal of Nursing Studies, 42*, 619–627. doi:10.1016/j.ijnurstu.2004.09.016

Marsh, S. (1994). Formalising trust as a computational concept. Ph. D. Thesis, Department of Computing, Science and Mathematics, University of Stirling, Stirling, Scotland.

Matsuo, M., & Easterby-Smith, M. (2008). Beyond the knowledge sharing dilemma: The role of customization. *Journal of Knowledge Management, 12*(4), 30–43. doi:10.1108/13673270810884237

Mayer, R. C., Davis, J. H., & Schoorman, F. D. (1995). An integrative model of organisational trust. *Academy of Management Review, 20*(3), 709–734.

Mayfield, M. (2010). Tacit knowledge sharing: techniques for putting a powerful tool in practice. *Development and Learning in Organizations, 24*(1), 24–26. doi:10.1108/14777281011010497

McNichols, D. (2010). Optimal knowledge transfer methods: A generation X perspective. *Journal of Knowledge Management, 14*(1), 24–37. doi:10.1108/13673271011015543

Mingers, J. (2001). Combining IS research methods: Towards a pluralist methodology. *Information Systems Research, 12*, 240–259. doi:10.1287/isre.12.3.240.9709

Mingers, J. (2003). The paucity of multimethod research: A review of the information systems literature. *Information Systems Journal, 13*(3), 233–249. doi:10.1046/j.1365-2575.2003.00143.x

Monclar, R., Tecla, A., Oliveira, J., & de Souza, J. M. (2009). MEK: Using spatial–temporal information to improve social networks and knowledge dissemination. *Information Sciences, 179*, 2524–2537. doi:10.1016/j.ins.2009.01.032

Nebus, J. (2004). Learning by networking: Knowledge search and sharing in multinational organizations. In *Proceedings of the 46th Academy of International Business, Bridging with the Other: The Importance of Dialogue in International Business*, Stockholm, Sweden.

Newell, S., Robertson, M., Scarbrough, H., & Swan, J. (2002). *Managing knowledge work*. New York, NY: Palgrave.

O'Donnell, E., & David, J. S. (2000). How information systems influence user decisions: A research framework and literature review. *International Journal of Accounting Information Systems, 1*, 178–203. doi:10.1016/S1467-0895(00)00009-9

Orlikowski, W., & Baroudi, J. (1991). Studying information technology in organizations: Research approaches and assumptions. *Information Systems Research, 2*, 1–28. doi:10.1287/isre.2.1.1

Pallant, J. (2005). *SPSS survival manual*. Maidenhead, UK: Open University Press.

Robertson, J. (2004). *Developing a knowledge management strategy*. Step Two Designs Pty Ltd. Retrieved September 16, 2010, from http://www.steptwo.com.au/papers/kmc_kmstrategy/index.html

Ruggles, R. L. III, (Ed.). (1997). *Knowledge management tools*. Newton, MA: Butterworth-Heinemann.

Saliola, F., & Zanfei, A. (2009). Mulitnational firms, global value chains and the organization of knowledge transfer. *Research Policy, 38*, 369–381. doi:10.1016/j.respol.2008.11.003

Schutz, A. (1967). *The phenomenology of the social world*. Chicago, IL: University of Chicago Press.

Shaw, G., & Williams, A. (2009). Knowledge transfer and management in tourism organisations: An emerging research agenda. *Tourism Management, 30*, 325–335. doi:10.1016/j.tourman.2008.02.023

Sittig, D. F., Wright, A., Simonaitisc, L., Carpenter, J. D., Allene, G. O., & Doebbeling, B. N. (2010). The state of the art in clinical knowledge management: An inventory of tools and techniques. *International Journal of Medical Informatics, 79*, 44–57. doi:10.1016/j.ijmedinf.2009.09.003

Smith, M. L. (2006). Overcoming theory-practice inconsistencies: Critical realism and information systems research. *Information and Organization, 16*, 191–211. doi:10.1016/j.infoandorg.2005.10.003

Snyder, W. M., Wenger, E., & de Sousa Briggs, X. (2004). Communities of practice in government, leveraging knowledge for performance. *Public Management, 32*(4), 17–21.

Sowe, S. K., Stamelos, I., & Angelis, L. (2008). Understanding knowledge sharing activities in free/open source software projects: An empirical study. *Journal of Systems and Software, 81*, 431–446. doi:10.1016/j.jss.2007.03.086

Spender, I.-C. (2005). An overview: What's new and important about knowledge management? Building new bridges between managers and academics. In S. Little & T. Ray (Eds.), *Managing knowledge: An essential reader 2005*, 2nd ed., pp. 126-128. London, UK: Sage. Retrieved September 2, 2010, from http://www.jcspender.com/uploads/Spender_B823_Little___Ray_reader_Ch06.pdf

Stankosky, M. (2005). Advances in knowledge management: University research toward an academic disciplin. In *Creating the discipline of knowledge management*. Burlington, MA: Elsevier Inc. doi:10.1016/B978-0-7506-7878-0.50005-3

Straub, D., Boudreau, M., & Gefen, D. (2004a). Validation guidelines for IS positivist research. *Communications of the Association for Information Systems, 13*, 380–427.

Straub, D., Gefen, D., & Boudreau, M.-C. (2004b). *The ISWorld quantitative, positivist research methods website*, (D. Galletta, Ed.). Retrieved from http://www.dstraub.cis.gsu.edu:88/quant/

Szulanski, G. (2003). *Sticky knowledge: Barriers to knowing in the firm*. SAGE Strategy Series.

Tang, F., Mu, J., & MacLachlan, D. L. (2008). Implications of network size and structure on organizations' knowledge transfer. *Expert Systems with Applications, 34*, 1109–1113. doi:10.1016/j.eswa.2006.12.020

Tomek, J. (2001). Knowledge management and collaborative virtual environments. *Journal of Universal Computer Science, 7*(6), 458–471.

Trochim, W. M. (2006a). *The research methods knowledge base*, 2nd ed. Retrieved September 19, 2011, from http://www.socialresearchmethods.net/kb/statdesc.php

Trochim, W. M. (2006b). The research methods knowledge base, 2nd ed. Retrieved September 9, 2011, from http://www.socialresearchmethods.net/kb/statinf.php

Tyndale, P. (2002). A taxonomy of knowledge management software tools: Origins and applications. *Evaluation and Program Planning, 25*, 183–190. doi:10.1016/S0149-7189(02)00012-5

Usoro, A., Sharratt, M. W., Tsui, E., & Shekhar, S. (2007). Trust as an antecedent to knowledge sharing in virtual communities of practice. *Knowledge Management Research & Practice, 5*, 199–212. doi:10.1057/palgrave.kmrp.8500143

Vaccaro, A., Parente, R., & Veloso, F. M. (2010). Knowledge management tools, inter-organizational relationships, innovation and firms performance. *Technological Forecasting and Social Change, 77*, 1076–1089. doi:10.1016/j.techfore.2010.02.006

Van den Hooff, B., & Huysman, M. (2009). Managing knowledge sharing: Emergent and engineering perspectives. *Information & Management, 46*(1), 1–8. doi:10.1016/j.im.2008.09.002

Walsham, G. (1995). Interpretive case studies in IS research: Nature and method. *European Journal of Information Systems, 4*, 74–81. doi:10.1057/ejis.1995.9

Wenger, E., McDermott, R., & Snyder, W. M. (2002). *Cultivating communities of practice: A guide to managing knowledge*. Boston, MA: Harvard Business School Press.

Wiig, K. M., De Hoog, R., & Van Der Spek, R. (1997). Supporting knowledge management: A selection of methods and techniques. *Expert Systems with Applications, 13*(1), 15–27. doi:10.1016/S0957-4174(97)00019-5

Willem, A., & Buelens, M. (2009). Knowledge sharing in inter-unit cooperative episodes: The impact of organizational structure dimensions. *International Journal of Information Management, 29*, 151–160. doi:10.1016/j.ijinfomgt.2008.06.004

Wolf, P. (2003). Interview with Etienne Wenger on communities of practice. Retrieved October 27, 2010, from http://www.knowledgeboard.com/cgi-bin/item.cgi?id=458

Yang, S.-C., & Farn, C.-K. (2009). Social capital, behavioural control, and tacit knowledge sharing – A multi-informant design. *International Journal of Information Management, 29*, 210–218. doi:10.1016/j.ijinfomgt.2008.09.002

Zhang, P., & Li, N. (2004). An assessment of human-computer interaction research in management information systems: Topics and methods. *Computers in Human Behavior, 20*, 125–147. doi:10.1016/j.chb.2003.10.011

Zhang, Y., & Hiltz, S. R. (2003). Factors that influence online relationship development in a knowledge sharing community. In *Proceedings of the Ninth American Conference on Information Systems*, (pp. 410 – 417).

APPENDIX I (OPERATIONALISATION)

No.	Construct	Operationalisation	Source	Questionaire item
1	Norms of reciprocity (NR)	Reciprocity (KP)	Chiu et al. (2006) p. 1874, Kankanhalli et al. (2005a), Lin et al. (2009), p. 932, Kankanhalli et al., 2005b, p. 1158, Usoro et al., 2007, p. 203, Gannon-Leary & Fontainha E, 2007, p. 6, Bock et al., 2006, p. 359, Chow & Chan, 2008, p. 459-460	Questions 1 and 2
		Negative Aspect		Question 3
2	Trust (KP)		Kankanhalli et al. (2005a), Chiu et al. (2006) p. 1874, Usoro et al., 2007; Willem & Buelens, 2009, Chow & Chan, 2008, Van den Hooff & Huysman, 2009, Lin et al. (2009), p. 932, Bock et al., 2006, Gannon-Leary & Fontainha E, 2007, p. 6,	Question 1 and 3
		Negative Aspect		Question 2
3	Trust (KR)		Bock et al., 2006, p. 358, Chow & Chan, 2008, Van den Hooff & Huysman, 2009, Lin et al. (2009), p. 932, Gannon-Leary & Fontainha E, 2007, p. 6,	Question 2 and 3
		Negative Aspect		Question 1
4	Perception of community (PCKP)		Kankanhalli et al. (2005a), Chiu et al. (2006) p. 1874, Chiu et al 2009, p. 1874, Zhang & Hiltz, 2003, Usoro et al., 2007, p. 203, Butler et al., 2002 p. 5, Gannon-Leary & Fontainha E, 2007, p. 6,	Question 1 and 3
		Negative Aspect		Question 2
5	Perception of community (PCKR)		Bock et al., 2006, 2005b p. 359, Butler et al., 2002 p. 5, Gannon-Leary & Fontainha E, 2007, p. 6, Kankanhalli et al., 2005b, p. 1158, Usoro et al., 2007,	Question 1 and 2
		Negative Aspect		Question 3
6	Knowledge provision (KR)	KP Frequency	(based on) Usoro et al., 2007	Question 2 and 3
		Negative Aspect	Chiu et al. (2006) p. 1874	Question 1
7	Knowledge reception (KR)	KR Evaluation	(based on) Usoro et al., 2007	Question 1 and 2
		Negative Aspect		Question 3

APPENDIX II (QUESTIONNAIRE DISTRIBUTION)

Questionnaire

Knowledge in SL may be shared by exchanging notecard, objects, and tutoring on how to do given task (e.g. Maze, elemental quest). Questionnaire items were based on Lin et al. (2009) and Usoro et al. (2007).

    Scale 1 – strongly disagree, 7 – strongly agree

    Norm of reciprocity (NR) (Knowledge provider and seeker perspective)

1. I know that other (lucky tribe group) members will help me so it's fair to help other members in this virtual community.
2. When I share knowledge with other (lucky tribe group) members, I believe that others would help me if I need it.
3. In general I don't answer questions of others as it is waste of my precious time and there will be someone to help me if I need it anyway.

Trust (TR) (Knowledge provider perspective)

Definition: The degree of belief in good intentions, behaviours, competence and integrity of members with respect to sharing knowledge in VCs (Usoro et al., 2007)

4. I can trust members of this lucky tribe group while sharing my experience and knowledge.
5. Members of the lucky tribe group may criticise me heavily that's why I prefer not to share my knowledge.
6. I am eager to trust (lucky tribe group) members and share my knowledge on how to accomplish specific tasks (e.g. Maze, Elements ritual).

Perception of Community (PC) (Knowledge provider perspective)

7. This group encourages knowledge and experience sharing.
8. In general members that share their knowledge and help others are not much recognized.
9. Group rituals (e.g. mentor ritual, initiation ceremony) strengthen sharing of information and experience among group members.

Knowledge Provision (KP)

10. Sharing my knowledge and helping others is unfair because it interferes with the competition.
11. I spend time in activities that contribute knowledge to the lucky tribe group.
12. I frequently share knowledge with community members on a one-to-one basis (e.g. IM, public chat).

Trust (TR) (Knowledge seeker perspective)

13. I am afraid to ask questions in this community, because I may be laughed at or criticised.
14. I can trust other members when they answer my questions.
15. I am not afraid that my questions would be termed as stupid questions.

Perception of Community (PC) (Knowledge seeker perspective)

16. This group is welcoming to new members and their questions.
17. Members of this group usually answer if they are asked a question.
18. It is hard to have your questions answered or getting help as everyone seems to be busy with hunting their kudos.

Knowledge Reception (KR)

19. Lucky tribe group is a good source of information and knowledge.
20. Members of the community are providing accurate information on most of the queries.
21. Lucky tribe group lacks important information that could be useful for new members.

APPENDIX III (INTERVIEW). QUALITATIVE DATA (INTERVIEW WITH VCOP MANAGERS AND MEMBERS)

Interview with group members

1. What do you think of the lucky tribe community as compared with other SL groups?
2. Do you prefer to help or share your knowledge with members that you already know or that have helped you in the past (e.g. with initiation ceremony, elements rituals)?
3. Do you rely more on information or knowledge provided by members you are affiliated or there is no difference between them and ordinary members?
4. Does the way community functions as a whole affects your eagerness to contribute to it?
5. Does the way community functions as a whole affects your eagerness to rely on the information stored in the community?
6. Does trust and former behaviour of community members affects your sense of the community?
7. Do you have any additional information to add with regards to knowledge sharing in Lucky Tribe group?

First Participant

1. What do you think of the lucky tribe community as compared with other SL groups? Most groups in sl are not communitys .. just there to make group anouncements. Lucky tribe is one of the few that i know where there is a real community of people helping each other and communicating with each other.

2. Do you prefer to help or share your knowledge with members that you already know or that have helped you in the past (e.g. with initiation ceremony, elements rituals)?
    I'm willing to help or share knowledge with anyone and do so, but it is natural that you tend to offer help with those that you already know. I think the various ceremonies and rituals within the Lucky tribe group act to break down these barriers and make people more likely to help strangers.

3. Do you rely more on information or knowledge provided by members you are affiliated or there is no difference between them and ordinary members?
    I take all the help i can get from whoever is offering it:). The only thing that effects this is past evidence of how helpful, or not, that person has been.

4. Does the way community functions as a whole affects your eagerness to contribute to it?
    Yes. The community functions well and so that has increased my eagernes to contribute.

5. Does the way community functions as a whole affects your eagerness to rely on the information stored in the community?
    The way lucky tribe functions you have to rely on information stored in the community. There is no central place where you can get information on all the activities available. Fortunately members of the community are documenting and sharing this information.

6. Does trust and former behavior of community members affects your sense of the community?
    Absolutely. If someone helps you then you feel obligated to help them back, or pay it on and help others.

7. Do you have any additional information to add with regards to knowledge sharing in Lucky Tribe group?
    I think there is a barrier to some of the newcomers. the group is very large and while the community does help the newcomers they do not always know who to ask for help, or like asking for help from strangers. As the group continues to grow there may be a need to put a more formal support structure in place - possibly asking some of the group to take on a more formal responsibility to helping others.

Second Participant

1. What do you think of the lucky tribe community as compared with other SL groups?
    I'm in 2 other groups besides Lucky Tribe that are willing to help each other and are friendly and polite. It is a pleasure to be among people with whom you are instantly accepted.

2. Do you prefer to help or share your knowledge with members that you already know or that have helped you in the past (e.g. with initiation ceremony, elements rituals)?
    No, I'll help anyone who asks.

3. Do you rely more on information or knowledge provided by members you are affiliated or there is no difference between them and ordinary members?
    No difference.

4. Does the way community functions as a whole affects your eagerness to contribute to it?
    Yes, it's comraderie and friendly competition. We want the points but we cheer each other on.

5. Does the way community functions as a whole affects your eagerness to rely on the information stored in the community?
    Yes

6. Does trust and former behavior of community members affects your sense of the community?
   Yes, as stated above.
7. Do you have any additional information to add with regards to knowledge sharing in Lucky Tribe group?
   Not that I can think of.

Third Participant

1. What do you think of the lucky tribe community as compared with other SL groups?
   About the same as other groups.. maybe a bit more friendly since there are no advertisers in the group.
2. Do you prefer to help or share your knowledge with members that you already know or that have helped you in the past (e.g. with initiation ceremony, elements rituals)?
   Prefer over what? Over not helping? Sure.. that's one of the reasons I update a notecard with all the Tribe spots (see attached)
3. Do you rely more on information or knowledge provided by members you are affiliated or there is no difference between them and ordinary members?
   I'm a little confused on the wording... "members you are affiliated"? Are you refering to friends? By definition those in the group are automatically affiliated with other members of the group. Overall however I treat all members the same.. friends list or not. I get most of my information from the blog or through trial and error.. I tend to figure things out before most others in the group.
4. Does the way community functions as a whole affects your eagerness to contribute to it?
   Not really, only that I'm more likely to partiicpate to a group if it's not spammed with advertisers etc..
5. Does the way community functions as a whole affects your eagerness to rely on the information stored in the community?
   Not particularlly... I'm not sure really what you mean by "the way the community functions".
6. Does trust and former behavior of community members affects your sense of the community?
   Of course... if people started to become idiots and ranting they become muted.. too many mutes and I'd abandon the Tribe. Luckily that has not happened at all. This is no different from ANY SL group or online community.
7. Do you have any additional information to add with regards to knowledge sharing in Lucky Tribe group?
   Well... I think shep (author note: group owner) did a great job with the "mentor tiki' which encourages one member to help and mentor another... however it has a flaw in that you cannot 'reset' your mentee. In my case for example, the person no longer visits Second life.. thus I do not have any incentive to mentor another person since I can no longer receive the Kudo badge. That's not to say I dont' help people... but I don't go out of my way nearly as much.

APPENDIX IV (PRINCIPAL COMPONENT ANALYSIS)

	Component				
	1	**2**	**3**	**4**	**5**
NR1	.525				
NR2	.729				
NR3		.775			
TRP1	.789				.302
TRP2		.436		-.661	
TRP3	.727				
PCP1	.570				
PCP2		.665			
PCP3	.545			-.363	
KP1		.810			
KP2			-.867		
KP3	.332		-.675		
TKR1	.483				
TKR2	.760				
TKR3				-.682	.431
PCKR1	.424	-.364			
PCKR2	.800				
PCKR3		.377			.405
KR1	.646				
KR2	.833				
KR3					.847

Extraction Method: Principal Component Analysis.
Rotation Method: Oblimin with Kaiser Normalization.
a Rotation converged in 19 iterations.

APPENDIX V (CORRELATION ANALYSIS)

Correlation (Knowledge provision items)

		NR1	NR2	NR3	TRP1	TRP2	TRP3	PCP1	PCP2	PCP3	KP1	KP2	KP3
NR1	Pearson Correlation	1	.547(**)	-.275(**)	.457(**)	-.155	.541(**)	.482(**)	-.170(*)	.366(**)	-.200(*)	.337(**)	.339(**)
	Sig. (2-tailed)		.000	.001	.000	.056	.000	.000	.036	.000	.014	.000	.000
	N	152	152	152	152	152	152	152	152	152	152	152	152
NR2	Pearson Correlation	.547(**)	1	-.302(**)	.546(**)	-.220(**)	.625(**)	.501(**)	-.332(**)	.448(**)	-.205(*)	.322(**)	.336(**)
	Sig. (2-tailed)	.000		.000	.000	.006	.000	.000	.000	.000	.011	.000	.000
	N	152	152	152	152	152	152	152	152	152	152	152	152
NR3	Pearson Correlation	-.275(**)	-.302(**)	1	-.279(**)	.564(**)	-.396(**)	-.269(**)	.410(**)	-.207(*)	.598(**)	-.130	-.247(**)
	Sig. (2-tailed)	.001	.000		.000	.000	.000	.001	.000	.011	.000	.111	.002
	N	152	152	152	152	152	152	152	152	152	152	152	152
TRP1	Pearson Correlation	.457(**)	.546(**)	-.279(**)	1	-.299(**)	.622(**)	.471(**)	-.185(*)	.359(**)	-.182(*)	.254(**)	.441(**)
	Sig. (2-tailed)	.000	.000	.000		.000	.000	.000	.022	.000	.025	.002	.000
	N	152	152	152	152	152	152	152	152	152	152	152	152
TRP2	Pearson Correlation	-.155	-.220(**)	.564(**)	-.299(**)	1	-.322(**)	-.205(*)	.269(**)	-.028	.368(**)	.092	-.104
	Sig. (2-tailed)	.056	.006	.000	.000		.000	.011	.001	.733	.000	.260	.203
	N	152	152	152	152	152	152	152	152	152	152	152	152
TRP3	Pearson Correlation	.541(**)	.625(**)	-.396(**)	.622(**)	-.322(**)	1	.581(**)	-.196(*)	.506(**)	-.280(**)	.358(**)	.479(**)
	Sig. (2-tailed)	.000	.000	.000	.000	.000		.000	.016	.000	.000	.000	.000
	N	152	152	152	152	152	152	152	152	152	152	152	152
PCP1	Pearson Correlation	.482(**)	.501(**)	-.269(**)	.471(**)	-.205(*)	.581(**)	1	-.204(*)	.424(**)	-.317(**)	.304(**)	.361(**)
	Sig. (2-tailed)	.000	.000	.001	.000	.011	.000		.012	.000	.000	.000	.000
	N	152	152	152	152	152	152	152	152	152	152	152	152
PCP2	Pearson Correlation	-.170(*)	-.332(**)	.410(**)	-.185(*)	.269(**)	-.196(*)	-.204(*)	1	-.176(*)	.364(**)	-.031	-.025
	Sig. (2-tailed)	.036	.000	.000	.022	.001	.016	.012		.030	.000	.702	.763
	N	152	152	152	152	152	152	152	152	152	152	152	152

continued on following page

Continued

		NR1	NR2	NR3	TRP1	TRP2	TRP3	PCP1	PCP2	PCP3	KP1	KP2	KP3
PCP3	Pearson Correlation	.366(**)	.448(**)	-.207(*)	.359(**)	-.028	.506(**)	.424(**)	-.176(*)	1	-.231(**)	.313(**)	.376(**)
	Sig. (2-tailed)	.000	.000	.011	.000	.733	.000	.000	.030		.004	.000	.000
	N	152	152	152	152	152	152	152	152	152	152	152	152
KP1	Pearson Correlation	-.200(*)	-.205(*)	.598(**)	-.182(*)	.368(**)	-.280(**)	-.317(**)	.364(**)	-.231(**)	1	-.111	-.154
	Sig. (2-tailed)	.014	.011	.000	.025	.000	.000	.000	.000	.004		.175	.057
	N	152	152	152	152	152	152	152	152	152	152	152	152
KP2	Pearson Correlation	.337(**)	.322(**)	-.130	.254(**)	.092	.358(**)	.304(**)	-.031	.313(**)	-.111	1	.518(**)
	Sig. (2-tailed)	.000	.000	.111	.002	.260	.000	.000	.702	.000	.175		.000
	N	152	152	152	152	152	152	152	152	152	152	152	152
KP3	Pearson Correlation	.339(**)	.336(**)	-.247(**)	.441(**)	-.104	.479(**)	.361(**)	-.025	.376(**)	-.154	.518(**)	1
	Sig. (2-tailed)	.000	.000	.002	.000	.203	.000	.000	.763	.000	.057	.000	
	N	152	152	152	152	152	152	152	152	152	152	152	152

** Correlation is significant at the 0.01 level (2-tailed).
* Correlation is significant at the 0.05 level (2-tailed).
Correlation (Knowledge reception items)

		NR1	NR2	NR3	TKR1	TKR2	TKR3	PCKR1	PCKR2	PCKR3	KR1	KR2	KR3
NR1	Pearson Correlation	1	.547(**)	-.275(**)	.321(**)	.479(**)	-.250(**)	.392(**)	.483(**)	-.315(**)	.385(**)	.473(**)	-.437(**)
	Sig. (2-tailed)		.000	.001	.000	.000	.002	.000	.000	.000	.000	.000	.000
	N	152	152	152	152	152	152	152	152	152	152	152	152
NR2	Pearson Correlation	.547(**)	1	-.302(**)	.366(**)	.470(**)	-.267(**)	.429(**)	.495(**)	-.355(**)	.438(**)	.524(**)	-.261(**)
	Sig. (2-tailed)	.000		.000	.000	.000	.001	.000	.000	.000	.000	.000	.001
	N	152	152	152	152	152	152	152	152	152	152	152	152
NR3	Pearson Correlation	-.275(**)	-.302(**)	1	-.300(**)	-.312(**)	.342(**)	-.417(**)	-.322(**)	.500(**)	-.207(*)	-.217(**)	.289(**)
	Sig. (2-tailed)	.001	.000		.000	.000	.000	.000	.000	.000	.011	.007	.000
	N	152	152	152	152	152	152	152	152	152	152	152	152
TKR1	Pearson Correlation	.321(**)	.366(**)	-.300(**)	1	.433(**)	-.414(**)	.254(**)	.425(**)	-.308(**)	.293(**)	.395(**)	-.356(**)

continued on following page

Continued

		NR1	NR2	NR3	TKR1	TKR2	TKR3	PCKR1	PCKR2	PCKR3	KR1	KR2	KR3
	Sig. (2-tailed)	.000	.000	.000		.000	.000	.002	.000	.000	.000	.000	.000
	N	152	152	152	152	152	152	152	152	152	152	152	152
TKR2	Pearson Correlation	.479(**)	.470(**)	-.312(**)	.433(**)	1	-.460(**)	.507(**)	.607(**)	-.427(**)	.586(**)	.713(**)	-.327(**)
	Sig. (2-tailed)	.000	.000	.000	.000		.000	.000	.000	.000	.000	.000	.000
	N	152	152	152	152	152	152	152	152	152	152	152	152
TKR3	Pearson Correlation	-.250(**)	-.267(**)	.342(**)	-.414(**)	-.460(**)	1	-.238(**)	-.300(**)	.435(**)	-.351(**)	-.312(**)	.423(**)
	Sig. (2-tailed)	.002	.001	.000	.000	.000		.003	.000	.000	.000	.000	.000
	N	152	152	152	152	152	152	152	152	152	152	152	152
PCKR1	Pearson Correlation	.392(**)	.429(**)	-.417(**)	.254(**)	.507(**)	-.238(**)	1	.560(**)	-.457(**)	.406(**)	.482(**)	-.378(**)
	Sig. (2-tailed)	.000	.000	.000	.002	.000	.003		.000	.000	.000	.000	.000
	N	152	152	152	152	152	152	152	152	152	152	152	152
PCKR2	Pearson Correlation	.483(**)	.495(**)	-.322(**)	.425(**)	.607(**)	-.300(**)	.560(**)	1	-.472(**)	.516(**)	.604(**)	-.314(**)
	Sig. (2-tailed)	.000	.000	.000	.000	.000	.000	.000		.000	.000	.000	.000
	N	152	152	152	152	152	152	152	152	152	152	152	152
PCKR3	Pearson Correlation	-.315(**)	-.355(**)	.500(**)	-.308(**)	-.427(**)	.435(**)	-.457(**)	-.472(**)	1	-.322(**)	-.368(**)	.468(**)
	Sig. (2-tailed)	.000	.000	.000	.000	.000	.000	.000	.000		.000	.000	.000
	N	152	152	152	152	152	152	152	152	152	152	152	152
KR1	Pearson Correlation	.385(**)	.438(**)	-.207(*)	.293(**)	.586(**)	-.351(**)	.406(**)	.516(**)	-.322(**)	1	.575(**)	-.382(**)
	Sig. (2-tailed)	.000	.000	.011	.000	.000	.000	.000	.000	.000		.000	.000
	N	152	152	152	152	152	152	152	152	152	152	152	152
KR2	Pearson Correlation	.473(**)	.524(**)	-.217(**)	.395(**)	.713(**)	-.312(**)	.482(**)	.604(**)	-.368(**)	.575(**)	1	-.389(**)
	Sig. (2-tailed)	.000	.000	.007	.000	.000	.000	.000	.000	.000	.000		.000
	N	152	152	152	152	152	152	152	152	152	152	152	152
KR3	Pearson Correlation	-.437(**)	-.261(**)	.289(**)	-.356(**)	-.327(**)	.423(**)	-.378(**)	-.314(**)	.468(**)	-.382(**)	-.389(**)	1
	Sig. (2-tailed)	.000	.001	.000	.000	.000	.000	.000	.000	.000	.000	.000	
	N	152	152	152	152	152	152	152	152	152	152	152	152

** Correlation is significant at the 0.01 level (2-tailed).

* Correlation is significant at the 0.05 level (2-tailed).

Compilation of References

Abrams, L. C., Cross, R., Lesser, E., & Levin, D. Z. (2003). Nurturing interpersonal trust in knowledge-sharing networks. *The Academy of Management Executive*, *17*(4), 64–77. doi:10.5465/AME.2003.11851845

Adams, D. A., Nelson, R. R., & Todd, P. A. (1992). Perceived usefulness, ease of use, and usage of information: A replication. *Management Information Systems Quarterly*, *16*, 227–247. doi:10.2307/249577

Adams, W. (2000). Getting real: Santa Cruz and the crisis of liberal education. In DeZure, D. (Ed.), *Learning from change: Landmarks in teaching and learning in higher education from Change Magazine, 1969-1999* (pp. 131–134). Sterling, VA: Stylus.

Adler, P. S., & Kwon, S.-W. (2002). Social capital: Prospects for a new concept. *Academy of Management Review*, *27*(1), 17–40.

Adloff, F. (2006). Beyond interests and norms: Toward a theory of gift-giving and reciprocity in modern societies. *Constellations (Oxford, England)*, *13*(3), 407–427. doi:10.1111/j.1467-8675.2006.00399.x

Adloff, F., & Mau, S. (2006). Giving social ties, reciprocity in modern society. *European Journal of Sociology*, *47*(1), 93–123. doi:10.1017/S000397560600004X

Agarwal, R., Sambamurthy, V., & Stair, R. M. (2000). Research report: The evolving relationship between general and specific computer self-efficacy--An empirical assessment. *Information Systems Research*, *11*(4), 418. doi:10.1287/isre.11.4.418.11876

Agrawal, R., & Srikant, R. (1994). Fast algorithms for mining association rules in large databases. In *20th International Conference on Very Large Data Bases*, (pp. 478-499).

Agre, P. (2002). Real-time politics: The Internet and the political process. *The Information Society*, *18*(5), 311–331. doi:10.1080/01972240290075174

Ahlbrant, R., & Cunningham, J. (1979). *A new public policy for neighborhood preservation*. New York, NY: Praeger.

Akyol, Z., & Garrison, D. R. (2011). Understanding cognitive presence in an online and blended community of inquiry: Assessing outcomes and processes for deep approaches to learning. *British Journal of Educational Technology*, *42*(2), 233–250. doi:10.1111/j.1467-8535.2009.01029.x

Albright, M. D., & Levy, P. E. (1995). The effects of source credibility and performance rating discrepancy on reactions to multiple raters. *Journal of Applied Social Psychology*, *25*, 577–600. doi:10.1111/j.1559-1816.1995.tb01600.x

Al-Khalifa, H., & Davis, H. (2006). The evolution of metadata from standards to semantics in E-learning applications. *Proceedings of the Seventeenth Conference on Hypertext and Hypermedia*, (pp. 69-72).

Allee, V. (2003). *The future of knowledge: Increasing prosperity through value networks*. USA: Elsevier Science.

Ally, M. (2004). Foundations of educational theory for online learning. In Anderson, T., & Elloumi, F. (Eds.), *Theory and practice of online learning* (pp. 3–31). Athabasca, Canada: Athabasca University.

Alvesson, M., Ashcraft, K. L., & Thomas, R. (2008). Identity matters: Reflections on the construction of identity scholarship in organization studies. *Organization*, *15*(1), 5–28. doi:10.1177/1350508407084426

Anderson, B. (1991). *Imagined communities: Reflections on the origin and spread of nationalism*. London, UK: Verso.

Anderson, J. C., & Gerbing, D. W. (1988). Structural equation modeling in practice: A review and recommended two-step approach. *Psychological Bulletin*, *103*(3), 411–423. doi:10.1037/0033-2909.103.3.411

Anderson, T. (2004). Teaching in an online learning context. In Anderson, T., & Elloumi, F. (Eds.), *Theory and practice of online learning* (pp. 273–294). Athabasca, Canada: Athabasca University.

Andrejevic, M. (2007). *iSpy: Surveillance and power in the interactive era*. Lawrence, KS: University Press of Kansas.

Andreoni, J. (1990). Impure altruism and donations to public goods: A theory of warm-glow giving. *The Economic Journal*, *100*(401), 464–477. doi:10.2307/2234133

Andrews, K. M., & Delahaye, B. L. (2000). Influences on knowledge processes in organizational learning: the psychological filter. *Journal of Management Studies*, *37*(6), 797–810. doi:10.1111/1467-6486.00204

Anonymous. (2007). Amazon.com acquires DPReview.com. *Business Wire Press Release*. Retrieved March 21, 2008, from http://www.dpreview.com/news/0705/07051402amazonacquiresdpreview.asp

Anzaldua, G. (1987). *Borderlands/La Frontera*. San Francisco, CA: Spinsters/Aunt Lute.

Arbaugh, J. B. (2004). Learning to learn online: A study of perceptual changes between multiple online course experiences. *The Internet and Higher Education*, *7*, 169–182. doi:10.1016/j.iheduc.2004.06.001

Ardichvili, A. (2008). Learning and knowledge sharing in virtual communities of practice: Motivators, barriers, and enablers. *Advances in Developing Human Resources*, *10*(4), 541. doi:10.1177/1523422308319536

Ardichvili, A., Maurer, M., Li, W., Wentling, T., & Stuedemann, R. (2006). Cultural influences on knowledge sharing through online communities of practice. *Journal of Knowledge Management*, *10*(1), 94–107. doi:10.1108/13673270610650139

Ardichvili, A., Page, V., & Wentling, T. (2002). Virtual knowledge-sharing communities of practice at Caterpillar: Success factors and barriers. *Performance Improvement Quarterly*, *15*(3), 94–113. doi:10.1111/j.1937-8327.2002.tb00258.x

Ardichvili, A., Page, V., & Wentling, T. (2003). Motivation and barriers to participation in virtual knowledge-sharing communities of practice. *Journal of Knowledge Management*, *7*(1), 64–77. doi:10.1108/13673270310463626

Argote, L., Beckman, S., & Epple, D. (1990). The persistence and transfer of learning in industrial settings. *Management Science*, *36*(2), 140–154. doi:10.1287/mnsc.36.2.140

Argyle, K. (1996). Life after death. In Shields, R. (Ed.), *Cultures of the internet: Virtual spaces, real histories, living bodies*. London, UK: Sage.

Armstrong, A., & Hagel, J. III. (1996). The real value of on-line communities. *Harvard Business Review*, (May-June): 131–141.

Aronova, E., Baker, K., & Oreskes, N. (2010). Big science and big data in biology: From the international geophysical year through the international biological program to the long term ecological research (LTER) network, 1957–present. *Historical Studies in the Natural Sciences*, *40*(2), 183–224. doi:10.1525/hsns.2010.40.2.183

Arvidsson, A. (2006). Quality singles: Internet dating and the work of fantasy. *New Media & Society*, *8*(4), 671–690. doi:10.1177/1461444806065663

Ashby, W. R. (1958). Requisite variety and its implications for the control of complex systems. *Cybernetica*, *1*(2), 83–99.

Atton, C. (2006). Far-right media on the Internet: Culture, discourse and power. *New Media & Society*, *8*(4), 573–587. doi:10.1177/1461444806065653

Augé, M. (1994). *Pour une anthropologie des mondes contemporains*. Paris, France: Flammarion.

Australia, E. (2004). *Accreditation management system. December 2004, Engineers Australia*. Melbourne: Aust.

Bachrach, K.M, & Zautra, A. (1985). Coping with a community stressor: The threat of a hazardous waste facility. *Journal of Health and Social Behavior, 26*(2), 127–141. doi:10.2307/2136602

Bagozzi, R. P., & Dholakia, U. M. (2002). Intentional social action in virtual communities. *Journal of Interactive Marketing, 16*(2), 2–21. doi:10.1002/dir.10006

Bakardjieva, M., & Feenberg, A. (2002). Community technology and democratic rationalization. *The Information Society, 18*(3), 181–192. doi:10.1080/01972240290074940

Baker, R., & Yacef, K. (2009). The state of educational data mining in 2009: A review and future visions. *Journal of Educational Data Mining, 1*, 3–17.

Bandura, A. (1989). Social cognitive theory. In Vasta, R. (Ed.), *Annals of child development* (pp. 1–60). Greenwich, CT: Jai Press LTD.

Banks, D., & Daus, K. (2002). *Customer community: Unleashing the power of your customer base*. San Francisco, CA: Jossey-Bass.

Banks, J., & Humphrey, S. (2008). The labour of user co-creators: Emergent social network markets? *Convergence, 14*(4), 401–418. doi:10.1177/1354856508094660

Barber, B. R., Mattson, K., & Peterson, J. (1997). *The state of the electronically enhanced democracy*. Rutgers, NJ: Walt Whitman Center.

Barkley, E. F. (2010). *Student engagement techniques: A handbook for college faculty*. San Francisco, CA: Jossey-Bass.

Barney, D. (2004). Communication versus obligation: The moral status of virtual community. In Tabachnick, D., & Koivukoski, T. (Eds.), *Globalization, technology, and philosophy* (pp. 21–41). New York, NY: SUNY Press.

Barquin, R. C. (2001). What is knowledge management? In Barquin, R. C., & Bennet, A. (Eds.), *Knowledge management: The catalyst for electronic government*. Vienna, VA: Management Concepts Publications.

Barros, B., & Verdejo, M. F. (2000). Analyzing student interaction processes in order to improve collaboration: The degree approach. *International Journal of Artificial Intelligence in Education, 11*, 221–241.

Barr, R. B., & Tagg, J. (1995). From teaching to learning: A new paradigm for undergraduate education. *Change, 27*(6), 154–166.

Barth, F. (1989). The analysis of culture in complex societies. *Ethnos, 34*, 120–142. doi:10.1080/00141844.1989.9981389

Barth, F. (1990). *Cosmologies in the making*. Cambridge, UK: Cambridge UP.

Barton, J., Currier, S., & Hey, J. (2003). Building quality assurance into metadata creation: an analysis based on the learning objects and e-prints communities of practice. *Proceedings of the 2003 International Conference on Dublin Core and Metadata Applications: Supporting Communities of Discourse and Practice—Metadata Research & Applications,* Dublin Core Metadata Initiative, (p. 5).

Bataille, G. (1967). *La part maudite: Precede de La notion de depense*. Paris, France: Minuit.

Bateman, P. J. (2008). *Online community referrals and commitment: How two aspects of community life impact member participation*. PhD Dissertation, University of Pittsburgh.

Bateman, P. J., Gray, P. H., & Butler, B. S. (2006). Community commitment: How affect, obligation, and necessity drive online behaviours. *Twenty-Seventh International Conference on Information Systems*, 2006, Milwaukee (pp. 983-1000). Milwaukee.

Bates, B. R., Romina, S., Ahmed, R., & Hopson, D. (2006). The effect of source credibility on consumers' perceptions of the quality of health information on the Internet. *Medical Informatics and the Internet in Medicine, 31*, 45–52. doi:10.1080/14639230600552601

Batini, C., Cappiello, C., Francalanci, C., & Maurino, A. (2009). Methodologies for data quality assessment and improvement. *ACM Computing Surveys, 41*(3), 1–52. doi:10.1145/1541880.1541883

Baudrillard, J. (1981). *Simulacres et simulations*. Paris, France: Galilee. boyd, d., & Ellison, N. B. (2007). Social network sites: Definition, history, and scholarship. *Journal of Computer-Mediated Communication, 13*(1). Retrieved from http://jcmc.indiana.edu/vol13/issue1/boyd.ellison.html

Baudrillard, J. (1993). *Symbolic exchange and death*. London, UK: Sage.

Bauer, L. (2010). *Measuring student behavior and learning in an online environment*. Distance Learning Symposium, Learning Enhancement Center, Metropolitan College of New York. Retrieved from http://vimeo.com/12856497

Baumeister, R. F. (1998). The self. In Gilbert, D. T., Fiske, S. R., & Lindzey, G. (Eds.), *The handbook of social psychology* (pp. 680–740). New York, NY: McGraw-Hill.

Baym, N. (1995). The emergence of community in computer-mediated communication. In Jones, S. (Ed.), *Cybersociety: Computer-mediated communication and community* (pp. 138–163). Thousand Oaks, CA: Sage Publications.

Baym, N. (1997). Interpreting soap operas and creating community: Inside an electronic fan culture. In Keisler, S. (Ed.), *Culture of the Internet* (pp. 103–120). Mahweh, NJ: Lawrence Erlbaum Associates.

Baym, N. (2000). *Tune in, log on: Soaps, fandom, and online community*. Thousand Oaks, CA: Sage.

Baym, N. K. (1998). The emergence of online community. In Jones, S. (Ed.), *Cybersociety 2.0 revisiting computer-mediated communication and community* (pp. 35–68). Newbury Park, CA: Sage Publications.

Baym, N. K. (2000). *Tune in, log on: Soaps, fandom, and online community*. Thousand Oaks, CA: Sage Publications.

Baym, N. K. (2005). Introduction: Internet research as it isn't, is, could be, and should be. *The Information Society*, *21*(4), 229–232. doi:10.1080/01972240591007535

Bayus, B. L. (2010). Crowdsourcing and individual creativity over time: The detrimental effects of past success. Retrieved February 3, 2012, from http://ssrn.com/abstract=1667101

Becerra-Fernandez, I., Gonzalez, A., & Sabherwal, R. (2004). *Knowledge management, challenges, solutions and technologies*. Pearson Education.

Becker, E. (1973). *The denial of death*. New York, NY: Simon & Schuster.

Beckman, T. (2001). Creating business value from knowledge management: The fusion of knowledge and technology. In Barquin, R. C., & Bennet, A. (Eds.), *Knowledge management: The catalyst for electronic government*. Vienna, VA: Management Concepts Publications.

Beenen, G., Ling, K., Wang, X., Chang, K., Frankowski, D., Resnick, P., & Kraut, R. E. (2004). Using social psychology to motivate contributions to online communities. *Proceedings of the 2004 ACM Conference on Computer Supported Cooperative Work*, (p. 221).

Behar, R. (1991). Death and memory: From Santa Maria del Monte to Miami Beach. *Cultural Anthropology*, *6*(3), 346–384. doi:10.1525/can.1991.6.3.02a00050

Beike, D., & Wirth-Beaumont, E. (2005). Psychological closure as a memory phenomenon. *Memory (Hove, England)*, *13*(6), 574–593. doi:10.1080/09658210444000241

Bell, C., & Newby, H. (1976). Community, communion, class and community action: The social sources of the new urban politics. In D. T. Herbert & R. J. Johnston (Eds.), *Social areas in cities: Vol. II. Spatial perspectives on problems and policies* (pp. 189–207). Hoboken, NJ: Wiley.

Bell, D. (1973). *The coming of post-industrial society: A venture in social forecasting*. New York, NY: Basic Books.

Bell, D. (2001). *An introduction to cybercultures*. London, UK: Routledge.

Benjamin, W. (1968). Unpacking my library: A talk about book collecting. In Arendt, H. (Ed.), *Illuminations* (pp. 59–68). New York, NY: Schocken Books.

Benkler, Y. (2006). *The wealth of networks*. New Haven, CT: Yale University Press.

Benkler, Y., & Nissenbaum, H. (2006). Commons-based peer production and virtue. *Journal of Political Philosophy*, *4*(14), 394–419. doi:10.1111/j.1467-9760.2006.00235.x

Benlian, A., & Hess, T. (2011). The signaling role of IT features in influencing trust and participation in online communities. *International Journal of Electronic Commerce*, *15*(4), 7–56. doi:10.2753/JEC1086-4415150401

Berking, H. (1999). *Sociology of giving*. London, UK: SAGE.

Berkman, L. F., & Glass, T. (2000). Social integration, social networks, social support, and health. In Berkman, L. F., & Kawachi, I. (Eds.), *Social epidemiology* (pp. 137–173). New York, NY: Oxford University Press.

Berlin, J. (1987). *Rhetoric and reality: Writing instruction in American colleges, 1900-1985*. Carbondale, IL: Southern Illinois UP.

Bermudez, L., & Piasecki, M. (2006). Metadata community profiles for the Semantic Web. *GeoInformatica*, *10*(2), 159–176. doi:10.1007/s10707-006-7577-2

Bernard, J. (1973). *The sociology of community*. Glenview, IL: Scott, Foresman.

Bhattacherjee, A. (2001). Understanding information systems continuance: An expectation-confirmation model. *Management Information Systems Quarterly*, *25*(3), 351–370. doi:10.2307/3250921

Bianchi, M., Boyle, M., & Hollingsworth, D. (1999). A comparison of methods for trend estimation. *Applied Economics Letters*, *6*(2), 103–109. doi:10.1080/135048599353726

Bijker, W. (1993). Do not despair: There is life after constructivism. *Science, Technology & Human Values*, *18*(1), 113–138. doi:10.1177/016224399301800107

Birch, A., & Irvine, V. (2009). Preservice teachers' acceptance of ICT integration in the classroom: Applying the UTAUT model. *Educational Media International*, *46*(4), 295–315. doi:10.1080/09523980903387506

Bishop, J. (2005). The role of mediating artifacts in the design of persuasive e-learning systems. *Proceedings of the First International Conferences on Internet Technologies and Applications*, University of Wales, NEWI, Wrexham, (pp. 548-558).

Bishop, J. (2009c). Increasing membership in online communities: The five principles of managing virtual club economies. *Proceedings of the 3rd International Conference on Internet Technologies and Applications - ITA09*, Glyndwr University, Wrexham.

Bishop, J. (2010). *Multiculturalism in intergenerational contexts: Implications for the design of virtual worlds*. Paper Presented to the Reconstructing Multiculturalism Conference, Cardiff, UK.

Bishop, J. (2011b). Transforming lurkers into posters: The role of the participation continuum. *Proceedings of the Fourth International Conference on Internet Technologies and Applications (ITA11)*, Glyndwr University.

Bishop, J. (2007a). Ecological cognition: A new dynamic for human-computer interaction. In Wallace, B., Ross, A., Davies, J., & Anderson, T. (Eds.), *The mind, the body and the world: Psychology after cognitivism* (pp. 327–345). Exeter, UK: Imprint Academic.

Bishop, J. (2007b). Increasing participation in online communities: A framework for human–computer interaction. *Computers in Human Behavior*, *23*(4), 1881–1893. doi:10.1016/j.chb.2005.11.004

Bishop, J. (2007c). Increasing participation in online communities: A framework for human–computer interaction. *Computers in Human Behavior*, *23*(4), 1881–1893. doi:10.1016/j.chb.2005.11.004

Bishop, J. (2009a). Enhancing the understanding of genres of web-based communities: The role of the ecological cognition framework. *International Journal of Web Based Communities*, *5*(1), 4–17. doi:10.1504/IJWBC.2009.021558

Bishop, J. (2009b). Increasing capital revenue in social networking communities: Building social and economic relationships through avatars and characters. In Dasgupta, S. (Ed.), *Social computing: Concepts, methodologies, tools, and applications* (pp. 1987–2004). Hershey, PA: IGI Global. doi:10.4018/978-1-60566-984-7.ch131

Bishop, J. (2009d). Increasing the economic sustainability of online communities: An empirical investigation. In Hindsworth, M. F., & Lang, T. B. (Eds.), *Community participation: Empowerment, diversity and sustainability*. New York, NY: Nova Science Publishers.

Bishop, J. (2011a). *The equatrics of intergenerational knowledge transformation in techno-cultures: Towards a model for enhancing information management in virtual worlds*. *Unpublished MScEcon*. Aberystwyth, UK: Aberystwyth University.

Bjorkeng, K., Clegg, S., & Pitsis, T. (2009). Becoming (a) practice. *Management Learning*, *40*(2), 145–159. doi:10.1177/1350507608101226

Blair, K. L., & Monske, E. A. (2003). Cui bono? Revisiting the promises and perils of online learning. *Computers and Composition, 20*, 441–453. doi:10.1016/j.compcom.2003.08.016

Blanchard, A. (2004). The effects of dispersed virtual communities on face-to-face social capital. In Huysman, M., & Wulf, V. (Eds.), *Social capital and information technology* (pp. 53–73). Cambridge, MA: The MIT Press.

Blumer, T. (2010). Face-to-face or Facebook: Are shy people more outgoing on social networking sites? In N. Carpentier, I. Trivundza, P. Pruulmann-Vengerfeldt, E. Sundin, T. Olsson, R. Kilborn … B. Cammaerts (Eds.), *Media and communication studies interventions and intersections* (pp. 201-212). Estonia: Tartu University Press.

Boccia Artieri, G. (2009). SuperNetwork: Quando le vite sono connesse. In Mazzoli, L. (Ed.), *Network effect. Quando la rete diventa pop*. Torino, Italy: Codice Edizioni.

Bock, G.-W., Kankanhalli, S. S., & Sharma, S. (2006). Are norms enough? The role of collaborative norms in promoting organizational knowledge seeking. *European Journal of Information Systems, 15*, 357–367. doi:10.1057/palgrave.ejis.3000630

Bodea, V. (2003). Standards for data mining languages. *The Proceedings of the Sixth International Conference on Economic Informatics - Digital Economy*, (pp. 502-506). ISBN 973-8360-02-1

Bodea, V. (2007). Application and benefits *of knowledge management in universities – A case study on student performance enhancement. Informatics in Knowledge Society, The Proceedings of the Eight International Conference on Informatics in Economy*, May 17-18, (pp. 1033-1038).

Bodea, V. (2008). *Knowledge management systems*. Ph.D thesis, supervised by Prof. Ion Gh. Roşca, The Academy of Economic Studies, Bucharest.

Bodea, V., & Roşca, I. (2007). Analiza performanţelor studenţilor cu tehnici de data mining: Studiu de caz în Academia de Studii Economice din Bucureşti. In Bodea, C., & Andone, I. (Eds.), *Managementul cunoaşterii în universitatea modernă. Editura Academiei de Studii Economice din Bucureşti*.

Bogenrieder, I., & Baalen, P. (2007). Contested practice: Multiple inclusion in double-knit organizations. *Journal of Organizational Change Management, 20*(4), 579–595. doi:10.1108/09534810710760090

Boghossian, P. (2006). Behaviorism, constructivism, and Socratic pedagogy. *Educational Philosophy and Theory, 38*(12), 713-722. Retrieved on June 18th, 2010 from http://www3.interscience.wiley.com/journal/118600926/abstract?CRETRY=1&SRETRY=0, DOI: 10.1111/j.1469-5812.2006.00226.x

Boisot, M., & Canals, A. (2004). Data, information and knowledge: Have we got it right? *Journal of Evolutionary Economics, 14*(1), 43–67. doi:10.1007/s00191-003-0181-9

Boland, R. (1985). Phenomenology: A preferred approach to research in information systems. In Mumford, E., Hirschheim, R. A., Fitzgerald, G., & Wood Harper, T. (Eds.), *Research methods in information systems* (pp. 193–201). Amsterdam, The Netherlands: North Holland Publishers.

Bolter, J. D., & Grusin, R. (1999). *Remediation: Understanding new media*. Cambridge, MA: MIT Press.

Bolter, J. D., & Grusin, R. (2000). *Remediation: Understanding new media*. Cambridge, MA: MIT Press.

Bonsu, S. K. (2007). The presentation of dead selves in everyday life: Obituaries and impression management. *Symbolic Interaction, 30*(2), 199–219. doi:10.1525/si.2007.30.2.199

Bonsu, S. K., & DeBerry-Spence, B. (2008). Consuming the dead: Identity and community practices in death rituals. *Journal of Contemporary Ethnography, 37*(6), 694–719. doi:10.1177/0891241607310631

Bos, N., Zimmerman, A., Olson, J., Yew, J., Yerkie, J., & Dahl, E. (2007). From shared databases to communities of practice: A taxonomy of collaboratories. *Journal of Computer-Mediated Communication Education, 12*(2).

Bouckaert, R., Frank, E., Hall, M., Kirkby, R., Reutemann, P., Seewald, A., & Scuse, D. (2010). *WEKA manual for version 3-6-2*. Hamilton, New Zealand: University of Waikato.

Bourdieu, P. (1988). *Homo Academicus*. Stanford, CA: Stanford University Press.

Bowker, G. C., Baker, K., Millerand, F., & Ribes, D. (2010). Toward information infrastructure studies: Ways of knowing in a networked environment. In Hunsinger, J., Klastrup, L., & Allen, M. (Eds.), *International handbook of internet research* (pp. 97–117). doi:10.1007/978-1-4020-9789-8_5

boyd, d. (2008). Facebook's privacy train wreck: Exposure, invasion, and social convergence. *Convergence, 14*(1), 13-20.

boyd, d. (2008). *Teen socialization practices in networked publics.* http://www.danah.org/papers/talks/MacArthur2008.html

boyd, d. m., & Ellison, N. B. (2007). Social network sites: Definition, history, and scholarship. *Journal of Computer-Mediated Communication, 13*(1), article 11.

Boyer, E. L. Sr. (1987). *College: The undergraduate experience in America.* New York, NY: HarperCollins.

Boyer, E. L. Sr. (1990). *Campus life: In search of community – A special report for the Carnegie Foundation for the Advancement of Teaching.* Lawrenceville, NJ: Princeton University Press.

Boyer, K. K., Olson, J. R., Calantone, R. J., & Jackson, E. C. (2002). Print versus electronic surveys: A comparison of two data collection methodologies. *Journal of Operations Management, 20*, 357–373. doi:10.1016/S0272-6963(02)00004-9

Braa, K., & Vidgen, R. (1999). Interpretation, intervention, and reduction in the organizational laboratory: A framework for in-context information system research. *Accounting, Management, and Information Technology, 9*, 25–47. doi:10.1016/S0959-8022(98)00018-6

Braga, D. B., & Busnardo, J. (2004). Digital literacy for autonomous learning: Designer problems and learner choices. In Snyder, I., & Beavis, C. (Eds.), *Doing literacy online* (pp. 45–68). Cresskill, NJ: Hampton Press.

Brandt, A. (2000). Agentes inteligentes: O próximo passo da Internet. *Inteligência Empresarial, 3.*

Braskamp, L. A., Trautvetter, L. C., & Ward, K. (2006). *Putting students first: How colleges develop students purposefully.* San Francisco, CA: Jossey-Bass.

Brent, J. (2004). The desire for community: Illusion, confusion and paradox. *Community Development Journal, 39*(3), 213–223. doi:10.1093/cdj/bsh017

Brew, L. S. (2008). The role of student feedback in evaluating and revising a blended learning course. *The Internet and Higher Education, 11*, 98–105. doi:10.1016/j.iheduc.2008.06.002

Brodie, L. (2006). Problem based learning in the online environment – Successfully using student diversity and e-education. *Internet Research 7.0: Internet Convergences*, Hilton Hotel, Brisbane, Qld, Australia. Retrieved from http://conferences.aoir.org/viewabstract.php?id=586&cf=5

Brodie, L. M., & Gibbings, P. D. (2007). *Developing problem based learning communities in virtual space.* Connected International Conference on Design Education, University of New South Wales, Sydney, Australia.

Brodie, L. (2009). E-problem based learning – Problem based learning using virtual teams. *European of Engineering Education, 34*(6), 497–509. doi:10.1080/03043790902943868

Brodie, L., & Porter, M. (2008). Engaging distance and on-campus students in problem based learning. *European Journal of Engineering Education, 33*(4), 433–443. doi:10.1080/03043790802253574

Bronfenbrenner, U. (1979). *The ecology of human development: Experiments by nature and design.* Cambridge, MA: Harvard University Press.

Brook, C., & Oliver, R. (2003). Designing for online learning communities. *World Conference on Educational Multimedia, Hypermedia and Telecommunications 2003*, AACE, Honolulu, Hawaii, USA, (pp. 1494-1500). Retrieved January 13, 2007, from http://www.editlib.org/index.cfm/files/paper_14026.pdf?fuseaction=Reader.DownloadFullText&paper_id=14026

Brouwer, D. C. (2001). ACT-ing up in congressional hearings. In Asen, R., & Brouwer, D. C. (Eds.), *Counterpublics and the state* (pp. 87–110). Albany, NY: State University of New York Press.

Brown, J. S., & Gray, E. S. (1995). The people are the company. *Fast Company, 1*, 78. Retrieved from http://www.fastcompany.com/magazine/01/people.html

Brown, J., Duguid, P., & Haviland, S. (1994). Toward informed participation: Six scenarios in search of democracy in the information age. *Aspen Institute Quarterly*, *6*(4), 49–73.

Bruce, B. C., Parliament, F., Kimmo, E. M., Studies, I., Reijo, E. M., & Sanna, E. M. (2005). Information literacy as a sociotechnical practice 1 Kimmo Tuominen, 2 Reijo Savolainen, 3 and Sanna Talja 4. *Most*, *75*(3), 329–345.

Bruhn, J. (2004). *The sociology of community connections*. New York, NY: Kluwer Academics.

Bulu, S. T., & Yildirim, Z. (2008). Communication behaviors and trust in collaborative online teams. *Journal of Educational Technology & Society*, *11*(1), 132–147.

Burbules, N. C. (1993). *Dialogue in teaching theory and practice*. New York, NY: Teachers College Press.

Burke, K. (1969). *A grammar of motives*. Berkeley, CA: University of California Press.

Burton, L., Westen, D., & Kowalski, R. (2009). *Psychology*, 2nd ed. John Wiley & Sons Australia Ltd.

Butler, B., Sproull, L., Kiesler, S., & Kraut, R. (2002). Community effort in online groups: Who does the work and why? In S. Weisband & L. Atwater (Eds.), *Leadership at a distance*, (pp. 2–32). Mahwah, NJ: Lawrence Erlbaum Publishers. Retrieved from http://opensource.mit.edu/papers/butler.pdf

Butler, B. (2001). Membership size, communication activity, and sustainability: A resource-based model of online social structures. *Information Systems Research*, *12*, 346–362. doi:10.1287/isre.12.4.346.9703

Butler, B., Sproull, L., Kiesler, S., & Kraut, R. (2007). Community effort in online groups: Who does the work and why? In Weisband, S. P. (Ed.), *Leadership at a distance: Research in technologically-supported work*.

Byoungho, J., Park, J. Y., & Kim, H.-S. (2010). What makes online community members commit? A social exchange perspective. *Behaviour & Information Technology*, *29*(6), 587–599. doi:10.1080/0144929X.2010.497563

Byrne, J. A., Brandt, R., & Port, O. (1993, February 8). The virtual corporation. *BusinessWeek*, 36-41.

Cairncross, F. (1997). *The death of distance*. Harvard Business School Press.

Calhoun, C. (1992). Introduction: Habermas and the public sphere. In Calhoun, C. (Ed.), *Habermas and the public sphere* (pp. 1–48). Cambridge, MA: MIT Press.

Campbell, J. A. (2001). Internet finance forums: Investor empowerment through CMC or market manipulation on a global scale? *Proceedings of AMCIS*, *2001*, 2161–2163.

Carey, J. (1988). *Communication as culture*. New York, NY: Routledge.

Castelfranchi, C., & Falcone, R. (1999). The dynamics of trust: From beliefs to action. *Proceedings of the Autonomous Agents Workshops on Deception, Fraud and Trust in Agent Societies*.

Castells, M. (1989). *The information city: Information technology, economic restructuring and the urban-regional process*. Oxford, UK: Blackwell.

Castells, M. (1996). *The rise of the network society*. Oxford, UK: Blackwell.

Centola, D. (2010). The spread of behavior in an online social network experiment. *Science*, *329*(5996), 1194. doi:10.1126/science.1185231

Chandler, D. (1995). *Technological or media determinism*. Retrieved March 10, 2008, from: http://www.aber.ac.uk/media/Documents/tecdet/tecdet.html

Chapman, C., Clinton, J., & Kerber, R (2005). *CRISP-DM 1.0, Step-by-step data mining guide*.

Charpentier, M., Lafrance, C., & Paquette, G. (2006). *International e-learning strategies: Key findings relevant to the Canadian context*. Retrieved from http://www.ccl-cca.ca/pdfs/CommissionedReports/JohnBissInternationalELearningEN.pdf

Chavan, V., & Penev, L. (2011). The data paper: A mechanism to incentivize data publishing in biodiversity science. *BMC Bioinformatics*, *12*(Suppl 15), S2. doi:10.1186/1471-2105-12-S15-S2

Chen, C. J. (2004). The effects of knowledge attribute, alliance characteristics, and absorptive capacity on knowledge transfer performance. *R & D Management*, *34*(3), 311–321. doi:10.1111/j.1467-9310.2004.00341.x

Cheng, W. (1996). The virtual enterprise: Beyond time, place and form. *Economic Bulletin*. Singapore International Chamber of Commerce, 5-7 February.

Chen, I. Y. L. (2007). The factors influencing members' continuance intentions in professional virtual communities—A longitudinal study. *Journal of Information Science*, *33*(4), 451–467. doi:10.1177/0165551506075323

Chen, Y., Harper, F. M., Konstan, J., & Li, S. X. (2009). Group identity and social preferences. *The American Economic Review*, *99*(1). doi:10.1257/aer.99.1.431

Chia-Ying, L., & Chang-Tseh, H. (2009). The impact of knowledge stickiness on knowledge transfer implementation, internalization, and satisfaction for multinational corporations. *International Journal of Information Management*, *29*(6), 425–435. doi:10.1016/j.ijinfomgt.2009.06.004

China Internet Network Information Center (CNNIC). (2001). *The 8th Statistical Survey Report on the Internet Development in China*. July 2001. Retrieved from http://j2j.cn/download/2003/10/10/171539.pdf

China Internet Network Information Center (CNNIC). (2006). The 17th Statistical Survey Report on the Internet Development in China, January 2006. Retrieved from http://www.cnnic.org.cn/images/2006/download/2006011701.pdf

China Internet Network Information Center (CNNIC). (2009). *Research report on social events and the influence of online media*. Retrieved July 19, 2010, from http://research.cnnic.cn/img/h000/h11/attach200912231659420.pdf

China Internet Network Information Center (CNNIC). (2011). *Statistical survey report on Internet development in China*. Retrieved December 14, 2011, from http://www1.cnnic.cn/uploadfiles/pdf/2011/2/28/153752.pdf

Chin, W. W. (1998). The partial least squares approach to structural equation modeling. In Marcoulides, G. (Ed.), *Modern methods for business research* (pp. 295–336). Mahwah, NJ: Lawrence Erlbaum Associates.

Chipuer, H., & Pretty, G. (1999). A review of the sense of community index: Current uses, factor structure, reliability and further development. *Journal of Community Psychology*, *27*(6), 643–658. doi:10.1002/(SICI)1520-6629(199911)27:6<643::AID-JCOP2>3.0.CO;2-B

Chiu, C. M., Hsu, M. H., Sun, S. Y., Lin, T. C., & Sun, P. C. (2005). Usability, quality, value and e-learning continuance decisions. *Computers & Education*, *45*(4), 399–416. doi:10.1016/j.compedu.2004.06.001

Chiu, C.-M., Hsu, M.-H., & Wang, E. T. G. (2006). Understanding knowledge sharing in virtual communities: An integration of social capital and social cognitive theories. *Decision Support Systems*, *42*(3), 1872–1888. doi:10.1016/j.dss.2006.04.001

Choudrie, J., & Dwivedi, Y. K. (2005). Investigating the research approaches for examining technology adoption issues. *Journal of Research Practice*, *1*(1). Retrieved from http://jrp.icaap.org/index.php/jrp/article/view/4/7

Chowdhury, S. (2005). The role of affect and cognition based trust in complex knowledge sharing. *Journal of Managerial Issues*, *17*(3), 310–326.

Chow, W. S., & Chan, L. S. (2008). Social network, social trust and shared goals in organizational knowledge sharing. *Information & Management*, *45*, 458–465. doi:10.1016/j.im.2008.06.007

Chumney, E. C., & Simpson, K. N. (2006). *Methods and designs for outcome research*. American Society for Health Systems Pharmacists.

Clark, D. (Ed.). (1993). *The sociology of death*. Oxford, UK: Blackwell.

Clifford, J., & Marcus, G. E. (Eds.). (1986). *Writing culture: The poetics and politics of ethnography*. Berkeley, CA: University of California Press.

Cocea, M., Hershkovitz, A., & Baker, R. S. J. D. (2009). The impact of off-task and gaming behaviors on learning: immediate or aggregate? *Proceedings of the 14th International Conference on Artificial Intelligence in Education*, (pp. 507-514).

Cohen, J. (1992). A power primer. *Psychological Bulletin*, *112*(1), 155–159. doi:10.1037/0033-2909.112.1.155

Cohen, N. (2008). The valorization of surveillance: Towards a political economy of Facebook. *Democratic Communiqué, 22*(1), 5–22.

Consalvo, M. (1997). Cash cows hit the web: Gender and communications technology. *The Journal of Communication Inquiry, 21*(1), 98–115. doi:10.1177/019685999702100105

Constant, D., Sproull, L., & Kiesler, S. (1996). The kindness of strangers: The usefulness of electronic weak ties for technical advice. *Organization Science, 7*, 119–135. doi:10.1287/orsc.7.2.119

Contractor, N., & Eisenberg, E. (1990). Communication networks and new media in organizations. In Fulk, J., & Steinfield, C. W. (Eds.), *Organizations and communication technology* (pp. 143–172). Newbury Park, CA: Sage Publications.

Cooperrider, D. (1986). *Appreciative inquiry: Toward a methodology for understanding and enhancing organizational innovation.* Unpublished Doctoral dissertation. Case Western Reserve University, Cleveland, Ohio.

Cooperrider, D. L., & Whitney, D. (2005). *Appreciative inquiry: A positive revolution in change.* San Francisco, CA: Berrett-Koehler.

Coppock, P. J., & Violi, P. (1999). Conversazioni telematiche. In Garatolo, R., & Pallotti, G. (Eds.), *La conversazione: Un'introduzione allo studio dell'interazione verbale.* Milano, Italy: Raffaello Cortina.

Corradi, G., Gherardi, S., & Verzelloni, L. (2010). Through the practice lens: Where is the bandwagon of practice-based studies heading? *Management Learning, 41*(3), 265–283. doi:10.1177/1350507609356938

Cortes, C., Pregibon, D., & Volinsky, C. (2002). Communities of interest. *Intelligent Data Analysis, 6*(3), 211–219.

Cote, M., & Pybus, J. (2007). Learning to immaterial labour 2.0: MySpace and social networks. *Ephemera, 7*(1), 88–106.

Counts, D. A., & Counts, D. (2004). The good, the bad, and the unresolved death in Kaliai. *Social Science & Medicine, 58*(5), 887–897. doi:10.1016/j.socscimed.2003.10.040

Cowart, M. (2006). Embodied cognition. *The internet encyclopedia of philosophy.* Retrieved January 24, 2012, from http://www.iep.utm.edu/e/embodcog.htm

Cox, A. M. (2007). Beyond information–factors in participation in networks of practice. *The Journal of Documentation, 63*(5), 765–787. doi:10.1108/00220410710827790

Cox, A. M. (2008). An exploration of concepts of community through a case study of UK university web production. *Journal of Information Science, 34*(3), 327–345. doi:10.1177/0165551507084354

Craig, J. (2010). Introduction: E-learning in politics. *European Political Science, 9*(1), 1–4. doi:10.1057/eps.2009.36

CRoss Industry Standard Process for Data Mining. (n.d.). Retrieved from http://www.crisp-dm.org/

Cross, K. P. (1998). Why learning communities? Why now? *About Campus, 3*(3), 4–11.

Csikszentmihalyi, M. (1990). *Flow: The psychology of optimal experience.* New York, NY: Harper & Row.

Culnan, M. J., & Markus, M. L. (1987). Information technologies. In Jablin, F. M., Putnam, L. L., Roberts, K. H., & Porter, L. W. (Eds.), *Handbook of organizational communication: An interdisciplinary perspective* (pp. 420–443). Newbury Park, CA: Sage.

Cummings, J. N., Sproull, L., & Kiesler, S. B. (2002). Beyond hearing: Where real world and online support meet. *Group Dynamics, 6*(1), 78–88. doi:10.1037/1089-2699.6.1.78

Curran, C. (2004). *Strategies for e-learning in universities.* Research & Occasional Paper Series: CSHE.7.04. Center for Studies in Higher Education, University of California, Berkeley

Currier, S., Barton, J., O'Beirne, R., & Ryan, B. (2004). Quality assurance for digital learning object repositories: Issues for the metadata creation process. *ALT-J, 12*(1), 5–20. doi:10.1080/0968776042000211494

Czarniawska, B. (1998). *A narrative approach to organization studies (Vol. 43).* Thousand Oaks, CA: Sage Publications.

Czarniawska, B. (2004). On time, space, and action nets. *Organization, 11*(4), 773–791. doi:10.1177/1350508404047251

Daft, R. L., & Lengel, R. H. (1986). Organizational information requirements, media richness and structural design. *Management Science, 32*(5), 554–571. doi:10.1287/mnsc.32.5.554

Daft, R. L., Lengel, R. H., & Trevino, L. K. (1987). Message equivocality, media selection, and manager performance: Implications for information systems. *Management Information Systems Quarterly, 11*(3), 355–366. doi:10.2307/248682

Dahlander, L., & Frederiksen, L. (2011). The core and cosmopolitans: A relational view of innovation in user communities. *Organization Science, 2011*, 1–20.

Dahlberg, L. (2001). The Internet and democratic discourse: Exploring the prospects of online deliberative forums extending the public sphere. *Information Communication and Society, 4*(4), 615–633. doi:10.1080/13691180110097030

Dahl, D., & Vossen, G. (2008). Learning object metadata generation in the Web 2. 0 era. *International Journal of Information and Communication Technology Education, 4*(3), 1–10. doi:10.4018/jicte.2008070101

Dahlgren, P. (2005). The Internet, public spheres, and political communication: Dispersion and deliberation. *Political Communication, 22*, 147–162. doi:10.1080/10584600590933160

Dal Lago, A., & De Biasi, R. (Eds.). (2002). *Un certo sguardo. Introduzione all'etnografia sociale.* Roma-Bari, Italy: Laterza.

Dantas, J., Silveira, R. M., & Ruggiero, W. V. (2010). *Metadata in digital video repositories: An analysis on author-generated metadata.* International Conference on Information Society (i-Society 2010), June 28-30, 2010, London, UK.

DataOne. (n.d.) *About DataONE.* Retrieved February 2, 2012, from http://www.dataone.org/about

Davenport, T. (2001). Successful knowledge management projects. *Sloan Management Review, 39*(2).

Davenport, T. H., & Prusak, L. (1998). *Working knowledge.* Boston, MA: Harvard Business School Press.

Davenport, T., & Probst, G. (2000). *Knowledge management case book.* Siemens Best Practices.

Davidow, W. H., & Malone, M. S. (1992). *The virtual corporation – Structuring and revitalizing the corporation for the 21st century.* New York, NY: HarperCollins.

Davis, S. (2008). With a little help from my online friends: The health benefits of internet community participation. *The Journal of Education, Community and Values, 8*(3).

Davis, F. D., Bagozzi, R. P., & Warshaw, P. R. (1989). User acceptance of computer technology: A comparison of two theoretical models. *Management Science, 35*, 982–1003. doi:10.1287/mnsc.35.8.982

Davis, K., Seider, S., & Gardner, H. (2008). When false representations ring true (and when they don't). *Social Research, 75*, 1085–1108.

Davy, C. (2006). Recipients: The key to information transfer. *Knowledge Management Research & Practice, 4*, 17–25. doi:10.1057/palgrave.kmrp.8500081

Day, M. (2001). Metadata in a nutshell. *Information Europe, 6*(2), 11.

Day, P., & Schuler, D. (2004). *Community practice in the network society: Local action/global interaction.* London, UK: Routledge.

de Certeau, M. (1990). *L'invention du quotidien. I Arts de faire.* Paris, France: Gallimard.

de Moora, A., & Weigandb, H. (2007). Formalizing the evolution of virtual communities. *Information Systems, 32*(2), 223–247. doi:10.1016/j.is.2005.09.002

Delavari, N., Beikzadeh, M. R., & Amnuaisuk, S. K. (2005). Application of enhanced analysis model for data mining processes in higher educational system. *Proceedings of ITHET 6th Annual International Conference,* Juan Dolio, Dominican Republic.

Delavari, N., Beikzadeh, M. R., & Shirazi, M. R. A. (2004). A new model for using data mining in higher educational system. *Proceedings of 5th International Conference on Information Technology based Higher Education and Training: ITEHT '04,* Istanbul, Turkey.

DeLone, W. H., & McLean, E. R. (1992). Information systems success: The quest for the dependent variable. *Information Systems Research*, *3*, 60–95. doi:10.1287/isre.3.1.60

DeLone, W. H., & McLean, E. R. (2003). The DeLone and McLean model of information systems success: A ten-year update. *Journal of Management Information Systems*, *19*, 9–30.

Denzin, N. K. (1970). *The research act in sociology*. Chicago, IL: Aldine.

DeSanctis, G., & Gallupe, R. B. (1987). A foundation for the study of group decision support systems. *Management Science*, *33*, 589–609. doi:10.1287/mnsc.33.5.589

Dewey, J. (1927). *The public and its problems*. Athens, OH: Swallow Press.

Dewey, J. (1933). *How we think*. Lexington, MA: Heath.

Dholakia, R., & Sternthal, B. (1977). Highly credible sources: Persuasive facilitators or persuasive liabilities? *The Journal of Consumer Research*, *3*, 223–232. doi:10.1086/208671

Dholakia, U. M., Bagozzi, R. P., & Pearo, L. K. (2004). A social influence model of consumer participation in network- and small-group-based virtual communities. *International Journal of Research in Marketing*, *21*(3), 241–263. doi:10.1016/j.ijresmar.2003.12.004

Dieng, R., Corby, O., Giboin, A., & Ribiere, M. (1999). Methods and tools for corporate knowledge management. *International Journal of Human-Computer Studies*, *51*, 567–598. doi:10.1006/ijhc.1999.0281

DiMaggio, P., Hargittai, E., Neuman, W., & Robinson, J. (2001). Social implications of the Internet. *Annual Review of Sociology*, *27*, 307–336. doi:10.1146/annurev.soc.27.1.307

Donath, J. S. (1999). Identity and deception in the virtual community. In Smith, M. A., & Kollock, P. (Eds.), *Communities in cyberspace* (pp. 29–59). New York, NY: Routledge.

Donath, J., & Boyd, D. (2004). Public displays of connection. *BT Technology Journal*, *22*(4), 71–82. doi:10.1023/B:BTTJ.0000047585.06264.cc

Drucker, P. (1994). The age of social transformation. *Atlantic Monthly*, (November): 53–80.

Dube, L., Bourhis, A., & Jacob, R. (2005). The impact of structuring characteristics on the launching of virtual communities of practice. *Journal of Organizational Change Management*, *18*(2), 145–166. doi:10.1108/09534810510589570

Duncan-Howell, J. (2010). Teachers making connections: Online communities as a source of professional learning. *British Journal of Educational Technology*, *41*(2), 324–340. doi:10.1111/j.1467-8535.2009.00953.x

Duranti, A. (1997). *Linguistic anthropology*. Cambridge, UK: Cambridge University Press.

Dutton, W. (1996). Network rules of order: Regulating speech in public electronic fora. *Media Culture & Society*, *18*(2), 269–290. doi:10.1177/016344396018002006

Duval, E., Hodgins, W., Sutton, S., & Weibel, S. (2002). Metadata principles and practicalities. *D-Lib Magazine*, *8*(4), 1082–9873. doi:10.1045/april2002-weibel

Dyer, J. H., & Nobeoka, K. (2000). Creating and managing a high-performance knowledge-sharing network: The Toyota case. *Strategic Management Journal*, *21*(3), 345–367. doi:10.1002/(SICI)1097-0266(200003)21:3<345::AID-SMJ96>3.0.CO;2-N

Dyson, M. C., & Campello, S. B. (2004). Evaluating virtual learning environments: What are we measuring? *Electronic Journal of e-Learning*, *2*(2). Retrieved June 15th, 2010, from http://www.ejel.org/volume-1-issue-1/issue1-art2.htm

Eckstein, S. (2001). Community as gift-giving: Collectivistic roots of volunteerism. *American Sociological Review*, *66*(6), 829–851. doi:10.2307/3088875

Ecological Research. (2011). *Ecological research: Guidelines for data papers*. Retrieved February 26 from http://www.springer.com/cda/content/document/cda_downloaddocument/EcolRes11284_DataPaper-Guidelines20110426.pdf?SGWID=0-0-45-1081937-0

Eco, U. (1976). *A theory of semiotics*. Bloomington, IN: Indiana University Press.

Eco, U. (1979). *The role of the reader*. Bloomington, IN: Indiana University Press.

Eco, U. (1984). *Semiotics and the philosophy of language.* Bloomington, IN: Indiana University Press.

Eco, U. (1994). *The limits of interpretation.* Bloomington, IN: Indiana University Press.

Edwards, S. L., Watson, J. A., Nash, R. E., & Farrell, A. (2005). Supporting explorative learning by providing collaborative online problem solving (COPS) environments. *OLT 2005 Conference: Beyond Delivery*, QUT, Brisbane, (pp. 81-89). Retrieved February 8, 2008, from http://eprints.qut.edu.au/archive/00002146/02/2146.pdf

Efimova, L. (2009). Weblog as a personal thinking space. *Proceedings of the 20th ACM Conference on Hypertext and Hypermedia,* (pp. 289-298).

Einsenhardt, K. M. (1989). Building theories from case study research. *Academy of Management Review, 14*(4), 532–550.

Eklund, J., Kay, M., & Lynch, H. (2003). *E-learning: Emerging issues and key trends.* Australian Flexible Learning Framework discussion paper. Retrieved from http://www.flexiblelearning.net.au

Elias, N. (1985). *The loneliness of the dying.* Oxford, UK: Blackwell.

Ellis, D., Oldridge, R., & Vasconcelos, A. (2004). Community and virtual community. *Annual Review of Information Science & Technology, 38*(1), 145–186. doi:10.1002/aris.1440380104

Ellison, N. B., Steinfield, C., & Lampe, C. (2007). The benefits of Facebook 'friends': Social capital and college students' use of online social network sites. *Journal of Computer-Mediated Communication, 12*(4), 1143–1168. doi:10.1111/j.1083-6101.2007.00367.x

Ellul, J. (1964). *The technological society.* New York, NY: Alfred A. Knopf.

Emerson, R. M. (1976). Social exchange theory. *Annual Review of Sociology, 2,* 335–362. doi:10.1146/annurev.so.02.080176.002003

Esarey, A., & Xiao, Q. (2008). Below the radar: Political expression in the Chinese blogosphere. *Asian Survey, 48,* 752–772. doi:10.1525/AS.2008.48.5.752

Esposito, J. J. (2010). Creating a consolidated online catalogue for the university press community. *Journal of Scholarly Publishing, 41*(4), 385–427. doi:10.3138/jsp.41.4.385

Etzioni, A. (1993). *The spirit of community: The reinvention of American society.* New York, NY: Touchstone.

European Commission. (2005). *Mobilizing the brainpower of Europe: Enabling universities to make their full contribution to the Lisbon Strategy.* Brussels, Communicate no. 152.

Eurostat. (2009). *The Bologna Process in higher education in Europe, key indicators on the social dimension and mobility, European Communities and IS, Hochschul-Informations-System GmbH, 2009.* Retrieved from http://epp.eurostat.ec.europa.eu/portal/page/portal/education/bologna_process

Facebook. (2011). *Company information.* Retrieved from http://newsroom.fb.com/content/default.aspx?NewsAreaId=22

Fairfield, H. (2007, April 15). Baby on board, and a photography business, too. *The New York Times.* Retrieved July 1, 2010, from http://www.nytimes.com/2007/04/15/business/yourmoney/15cameras.html?_r=1&oref=slogin

Faraj, S., Jarvenpaa, S. L., & Majchrzak, A. (2011). Knowledge collaboration in online communities. *Organization Science, 22*(5), 1224–1239. doi:10.1287/orsc.1100.0614

Faraj, S., Kwon, D., & Watts, S. (2004). Contested artifact: Technology sensemaking, actor networks, and the shaping of the Web. *Information Technology & People, 17*(2), 186–209. doi:10.1108/09593840410542501

Farquharson, K. (2011). Doing 'race' on the internet: A study of online parenting communities. *Journal of Intercultural Studies (Melbourne, Vic.), 32*(5), 479–493. doi:10.1080/07256868.2011.593115

Feenberg, A. (1999). *Questioning technology.* London, UK: Routledge.

Feenberg, A., & Bakardijeva, M. (2004). Virtual community: No killer implication. *New Media & Society, 6,* 37–43. doi:10.1177/1461444804039904

Feigenbaum, L., Herman, I., Hongsermeier, T., Neumann, E., & Stephens, S. (2007). The semantic web in action. *Scientific American Magazine, 297*(6), 90–97. doi:10.1038/scientificamerican1207-90

Feldman, M. S., & Orlikowski, W. J. (2011). Theorizing practice and practicing theory. *Organization Science, 22*(5), 1240–1253. doi:10.1287/orsc.1100.0612

Feldman, M. S., & Pentland, B. T. (2003). Reconceptualizing organizational routines as a source of flexibility and change. *Administrative Science Quarterly, 48*(1), 94–118. doi:10.2307/3556620

Felski, R. (1989). *Beyond feminist aesthetics: Feminist literature and social change*. Cambridge, MA: Harvard University Press.

Fernback, J. (2007). Beyond the diluted community concept: A symbolic interactionist perspective on on-line social relations. *New Media & Society, 9*, 49–69. doi:10.1177/1461444807072417

Ferraro, G. (2001). *Il linguaggio del mito*. Roma, Italy: Meltemi.

Festinger, L. (1957). *A theory of cognitive dissonance*. Evanston, IL: Row, Peterson.

Fischer, G., Scharff, E., & Ye, Y. (2004). Fostering social creativity by increasing social capital. In Huysman, M., & Wulf, V. (Eds.), *Social capital and information technology* (pp. 355–399). Cambridge, MA: MIT Press.

Fiske, A. P. (1991). *Structures of social life: The four elementary forms of human relations*. New York, NY: The Free Press.

Flanagin, A. J., & Metzger, M. J. (2001). Internet use in the contemporary media environment. *Human Communication Research, 27*(1), 153–181. doi:10.1093/hcr/27.1.153

Fontanille, J. (2006). *The semiotics of discourse*. New York, NY: P. Lang.

Fornell, C., & Larcker, D. F. (1981). Evaluating structural equation models with unobservable variables and measurement error. *JMR, Journal of Marketing Research, 18*, 39–50. doi:10.2307/3151312

Foucault, M. (1980). *Power/knowledge: Selected interviews and other writings, 1972-1977* (Gordon, C. (Trans. Ed.)). New York, NY: Pantheon Books.

Foucault, M. (2008). *The birth of biopolitics: Lectures at the College de France*. New York, NY: Picador.

Fraser, N. (1992). Rethinking the public sphere: A contribution to the critique of actually existing democracy. In Calhoun, C. (Ed.), *Habermas and the public sphere* (pp. 109–142). Cambridge, MA: MIT Press. doi:10.2307/466240

Freeman, C. (1991). Networks of innovators: A synthesis of research issues. *Research Policy, 20*, 499–514. doi:10.1016/0048-7333(91)90072-X

Freud, S. (1933). *New introductory lectures on psychoanalysis*. New York, NY: W.W. Norton & Company, Inc.

Friedland, L. A. (2001). Communication, community, and democracy: Toward a theory of the communicatively integrated community. *Communication Research, 28*(4), 358–391. doi:10.1177/009365001028004002

Fuch, C. (2006). The self-organization of virtual communities. *Journal of New Communications Research, 1*(1), 29–68. Retrieved from http://fuchs.icts.sbg.ac.at/VC.pdf

Fulk, J., Schmitz, J., & Steinfield, C. (1990). A social influence model of technology use. In Fulk, J., & Steinfield, C. (Eds.), *Organizations and communication technology* (pp. 117–142). Newbury Park, CA: Sage.

Furman, E., & Peltola, T. (2012). Developing socio-ecological research in Finland: Challenges and progress towards a thriving LTSER network. In Singh, S. J., Haberl, H., Chertow, M., Mirtl, M., & Schmid, M. (Eds.), *Long term socio-ecological research: Studies in society: Nature interactions across spatial and temporal scales*. Springer.

Gabelnick, F., MacGregor, J., Matthews, R. S., & Smith, B. L. (1990). *New directions for teaching and learning: No. 41. Learning communities: Creating connections among students, faculty, and disciplines*. San Francisco, CA: Jossey-Bass.

Gächter, S., & Fehr, E. (1999). Collective action as a social exchange. *Journal of Economic Behavior & Organization, 39*(4), 341–369. doi:10.1016/S0167-2681(99)00045-1

Gambetta, D. (2000). Can we trust trust? In *Trust: Making and breaking cooperative relations* (*Vol. 13*, pp. 213–237). Oxford, UK: Blackwell.

Gamson, Z. F. (2000). The origins of contemporary learning communities: Residential colleges, experimental colleges, and living and learning communities. In DeZure, D. (Ed.), *Learning from change: Landmarks in teaching and learning in higher education from Change Magazine, 1969-1999* (pp. 113–116). Sterling, VA: Stylus.

Gannon-Leary, P., & Fontainha, E. (2007). Communities of practice and virtual learning communities: Benefits, barriers and success factors. *eLearning Papers, 5,* 13. Retrieved January 3, 2010, from http://www.elearningeuropa.info/files/media/media13563.pdf

Garavelli, C., Gorgoglione, M., & Scozzi, B. (2002). Managing knowledge transfer by knowledge technologies. *Technovation, 22,* 269–279. doi:10.1016/S0166-4972(01)00009-8

Garcia, A. C., Standlee, A. I., Bechkoff, J., & Cui, Y. (2009). Ethnographic approaches to the internet and computer-mediated communication. *Journal of Contemporary Ethnography, 38*(1), 52–84. doi:10.1177/0891241607310839

Gardner, J. (1990). *On leadership.* New York, NY: Free Press.

GBIF. (2011). *First database-derived 'data paper' published in journal.* Retrieved February 2, 2012, from http://www.gbif.org/communications/news-and-events/showsingle/article/first-database-derived-data-paper-published-in-journal/

GBIF. (n.d.). *About GBIF.* Retrieved February 2, 2012, from http://www.gbif.org/index.php?id=269

Geels, F. W. (2004). From sectoral systems of innovation to socio-technical systems Insights about dynamics and change from sociology and institutional theory. *Research Policy, 33*(6-7), 897–920. doi:10.1016/j.respol.2004.01.015

Geertz, C. (1973). *The interpretation of cultures.* New York, NY: Basic Books.

Geertz, C. (1975). *The interpretation of cultures.* New York, NY: Basic Books.

Geiger, R. S., & Ribes, D. (2011). Trace ethnography: Following coordination through documentary practices. In *Proceedings of the 44th Annual Hawaii International Conference on Systems Sciences.*

Genette, G. (1987). *Seuils.* Paris, France: Seuil.

Gerbner, G., Gross, L., Morgan, M., & Signorielli, N. (1986). Living with television: The dynamics of the cultivation process. In Bryant, J., & Zillman, D. (Eds.), *Perspectives on media effects* (pp. 17–40). Hilldale, NJ: Lawrence Erlbaum Associates.

Gherardi, S. (2009). Practice? It's a matter of taste! *Management Learning, 40*(5), 535–550. doi:10.1177/1350507609340812

Gibbings, P. D., Lidstone, J., & Bruce, C. (2008). *Using student experience of problem-based learning in virtual space to drive engineering educational pedagogy.* Paper presented to the 19th Annual Conference for the Australasian Association for Engineering Education - To Industry and Beyond, Yeppoon, Queensland, Australia, 7th - 10th December

Gibbings, P. D., & Brodie, L. M. (2008b). Team-based learning communities in virtual space. *International Journal of Engineering Education, 24*(6), 1119–1129.

Gibbings, P. D., Bruce, C., & Lidstone, J. (2009). *Problem-based learning (PBL) in virtual space: Developing experiences for professional development.* VDM Verlag Dr Muller Aktiengesellschaft & Co KG.

Gibbings, P., & Brodie, L. (2008a). Assessment strategy for an engineering problem solving course. *International Journal of Engineering Education, 24*(1), 153–161.

Gibson, J. J. (1986). *The ecological approach to visual perception.* Lawrence Erlbaum Associates.

Gibson, M. (2007). Death and mourning in technologically mediated culture. *Health Sociology Review, 16,* 415–424. doi:10.5172/hesr.2007.16.5.415

Giddens, A. (1984). *The constitution of society.* Cambridge, MA: Polity.

Giddens, A. (1991). *Modernity and self identity: Self and society in the late modern age.* Stanford University Press.

Gil, I. S., Baker, K., Campbell, J., Denny, E. G., Vanderbilt, K., & Riordan, B. (2009). The long-term ecological research community metadata standardisation project: A progress report. *International Journal of Metadata. Semantics and Ontologies, 4*(3), 141–153. doi:10.1504/IJMSO.2009.027750

Glaser, B. G., & Strauss, A. L. (1967). *The discovery of grounded theory: Strategies for qualitative research.* New York, NY: Aldine de Gruyter.

Glassmeyer, D. M., Dibbs, R. A., & Jensen, R. T. (2011). Determining utility of formative assessment through virtual community: Perspectives of online graduate students. *Quarterly Review of Distance Education, 12*(1), 23–35.

Godbout, J., & Caillé, A. (1998). *The world of the gift* (Winkler, D., Trans.). Montreal, Canada: McGill-Queen's University Press.

Golafshani, N. (2003). Understanding reliability and validity in questionnaire research. *Qualitative Report, 8*(4), 597–607.

Golder, S., & Huberman, B. (2006). Usage patterns of collaborative tagging systems'. *Journal of Information Science, 32*(2), 198–208. doi:10.1177/0165551506062337

Goldman, S., Nagel, R., & Preiss, K. (1995). *Agile competitors and virtual organizations: Strategies for enriching the customer.* New York, NY: van Nostrand Reinhold.

Gongla, P., & Rizzuto, C. R. (2001). Evolving communities of practice: IBM Global. *IBM Systems Journal, 40*(4), 842–862. doi:10.1147/sj.404.0842

Goodman, P. (1964). *Compulsory mis-education and the community of scholars.* New York, NY: Random House.

Granovetter, M. (1973). The strength of weak ties. *American Journal of Sociology, 78*(6), 1360–1380. doi:10.1086/225469

Greenberg, J., & Robertson, W. (2002). Semantic Web construction: An inquiry of authors' views on collaborative metadata generation' *Proceedings of the 2002 International Conference on Dublin Core and Metadata Applications: Metadata for E-Communities: Supporting Diversity and Convergence,* Dublin Core Metadata Initiative, (pp. 45-52).

Greenberg, J., Pattuelli, M., Parsia, B., & Robertson, W. (2001). Author-generated Dublin Core metadata for web resources: A baseline study in an organization. *Journal of Digital Information, 2*(2), 38–46.

Greenberg, J., White, H. C., Carrier, S., & Scherle, R. (2009). A metadata best practice for a scientific data repository. *Journal of Library Metadata, 9*(3-4), 194–212. doi:10.1080/19386380903405090

Greimas, A. J., & Courtés, J. (1979). *Sémiotique: Dictionnaire raisonné de la théorie du langage.* Paris, France: Hachette.

Grewal, D., Goflieb, J., & Marmorstein, H. (1994). The moderating effects of message framing and source credibility on the price-perceived risk relationship. *The Journal of Consumer Research, 21,* 145–153. doi:10.1086/209388

Grigoriadis, V. (2009, 13 April). Do you own Facebook? Or does Facebook own you? *New York Magazine.* Retrieved from http://nymag.com

Groff, T. R., & Jones, T. P. (2003). *Introduction to knowledge management: KM in business.* Woburn, MA: Butterworth-Heinemann.

Grossman, L. (2006, December). You – yes, you – are *Time's* person of the year. *Time, 168*(26). Retrieved from http://time.com

Groves, R., Fowler, F. J., Couper, M. P., Lepkowski, J. M., Singer, E., & Tourangeau, R. (2010). *Survey methodology* (2nd ed.).

Guarasci, R., & Cornwell, G. (1997). *Democratic education in an age of difference.* San Francisco, CA: Jossey-Bass.

Guardado, M., & Shi, L. (2007). ESL students' experiences of online peer feedback. *Computers and Composition, 24,* 443–461. doi:10.1016/j.compcom.2007.03.002

Gu, B., Konana, P., Rajagopalan, B., & Chen, H. W. M. (2007). Competition among virtual communities and user valuation: The case of investing-related communities. *Information Systems Research, 18*(1), 68. doi:10.1287/isre.1070.0114

Gulati, R., & Garino, J. (2000). Get the right mix of bricks and clicks. *Harvard Business Review,* (July-August): 107–114.

Guo, C., Shim, J., & Otondo, R. (2010). Social network services in China: An integrated model of centrality, trust, and technology acceptance. *Journal of Global Information Technology Management, 13*(2), 76–99.

Gupta, A. K., & Govindarajan, V. (2000). Knowledge management's social dimension: Lessons from Nucor steel. *Sloan Management Review, 42*(1), 71–80.

Gusfield, J. (1975). *Community: A critical response.* New York, NY: Harper & Row.

Habermas, J. (1989). *The structural transformation of the public sphere: An inquiry into a category of bourgeois society.* Cambridge, MA: MIT Press.

Habermas, J. (1992). Further reflections on the public sphere. In Calhoun, C. (Ed.), *Habermas and the public sphere* (pp. 421–461). Cambridge, MA: MIT Press.

Haddawy, P., & Hien, N. (2006). *A decision support system for evaluating international student applications. Computer Science and Information management program.* Asian Institute of Technology.

Haeckel, S., & Nolan, R. (1993). Managing by wire. *Harvard Business Review,* (September-October): 122–132.

Hagel, J., & Armstrong, A. G. (1997). *Net gain: Expanding markets through virtual communities.* Boston, MA: Harvard Business School Press.

Halal, W. E. (1998). *The infinite resource.* San Francisco, CA: Jossey-Bass Inc.

Hammond, T., Hannay, T., Lund, B., & Scott, J. (2005). Social bookmarking tools (I). *D-Lib Magazine, 11*(4), 1082–9873. doi:10.1045/april2005-hammond

Hansen, D. L. (2007). *Knowledge sharing, maintenance, and use in online support communities.* PhD Dissertation, University of Michigan.

Hansen, M. (1993). Foreword. In Negt, O., & Kluge, A. (Eds.), *Public sphere and experience: Toward an analysis of the bourgeois and proletarian public sphere* (pp. ix–xli). Minneapolis, MN: University of Minnesota Press.

Haraway, D. J. (1991). *Simians, cyborgs, and women: The reinvention of nature.* New York, NY: Routledge.

Hardin, G. (1982). Discriminating altruisms. *Zygon, 17*(2), 163–186. doi:10.1111/j.1467-9744.1982.tb00477.x

Harding, S. (2004). Rethinking standpoint epistemology: What is "strong objectivity"? In Harding, S. (Ed.), *The feminist standpoint theory reader: Intellectual and political conversations* (pp. 127–140). New York, NY: Routledge.

Hardt, M. (1999). Affective labor. *Boundary 2, 26*(2), 89–100.

Harris, A. (2003). *Notions of embodied knowledge.* Retrieved September 5, 2011 from http://www.thegreenfuse. org/harris/notions-of-ek.htm

Harvard (2007). *Report of the Task Force on General Education.* Last retrieved on 2012FEB22 at: http://www. sp07.umd.edu/HarvardGeneralEducationReport.pdf.

Hassanein, K., & Head, M. (2006). The impact of infusing social presence in the Web interface: An investigation across product types. *International Journal of Electronic Commerce, 10*(2), 31–55. doi:10.2753/ JEC1086-4415100202

Hauser, G. A. (2001). Prisoners of conscience and the counterpublic sphere of prison writing: The stones that start the avalanche. In Asen, R., & Brouwer, D. C. (Eds.), *Counterpublics and the state* (pp. 35–58). Albany, NY: State University of New York Press.

Hawisher, G. E., & Selfe, C. L. (1992). The rhetoric of technology and the electronic writing class. *College Composition and Communication, 42*, 55–65. doi:10.2307/357539

Haythornthtwaite, C. (2002). Building social networks via computer networks. creating and sustaining learning communities. In Renninger, K. A., & Shumar, W. (Eds.), *Building virtual communities. Learning and change in cyberspace* (pp. 159–190). Cambridge, UK: Cambridge University Press. doi:10.1017/CBO9780511606373.011

Haythornthwaite, C. (2002). Strong, weak, and latent ties and the impact of new media. *The Information Society, 18*(5), 385–401. doi:10.1080/01972240290108195

Haythornthwaite, C. (2005). Social networks and Internet connectivity effects. *Information Communication and Society, 8*(2), 125–147. doi:10.1080/13691180500146185

Haythornthwaite, C., & Wellman, B. (1998). Work, friendship and media use for information exchange in a networked organization. *Journal of the American Society for Information Science American Society for Information Science, 49*(12), 1101–1114. doi:10.1002/(SICI)1097-4571(1998)49:12<1101::AID-ASI6>3.0.CO;2-Z

Heartel, E. (1990). Performance tests, simulations and other methods. In Millman, J., & Darling Hammond, L. (Eds.), *The new handbook of teacher evaluation* (pp. 278–294). Newbury Park, CA: Sage.

Hedberg, B., Dahlgren, G., Hansson, J., & Olve, N. (1997). *Virtual organizations and beyond: Discover imaginary systems.* New York, NY: John Wiley & Sons Ltd.

HEFCE. (2005). *HEFCE strategy for e-learning. Higher Education Funding Council for England (HEFCE), Joint Information Systems Committee (JISC), and Higher Education Academy.* HEA.

HEFCE. (2009). *Enhancing learning and teaching through the use of technology: A revised approach to HEFCE's strategy for e-learning. Higher Education Funding Council for England.* HEFCE.

Helble, Y., & Chong, L. C. (2004). The importance of internal and external R&D network linkages for R&D organisations: Evidence from Singapore. *R&D Management, 34*(5), 605 – 612. Retrieved June 15th, 2010, from http://www3.interscience.wiley.com/journal/118761805/abstract

Heron, S. (2009). Online privacy and browser security. *Network Security,* (6): 4–7. doi:10.1016/S1353-4858(09)70061-3

Hess, C., & Ostrom, E. (2007). *Understanding knowledge as a commons - From theory to practice.* Cambridge, MA: MIT Press.

Hildreth, P., & Kimble, C. (2000). Communities of practice in the distributed international environment. *Journal of Knowledge Management, 4*(1), 27–38. doi:10.1108/13673270010315920

Hill, P. J. (1985). *The rationale for learning communities.* Paper presented at the Inaugural Conference of the Washington Center for Improving the Quality of Undergraduate Education, Olympia, WA.

Hinds, D., & Lee, R. M. (2008). Social network structure as a critical success condition for virtual communities. In R. H. Sprague, Jr. (Ed.), *Proceedings of the 41st Hawaii International Conference on System Sciences – 2008,* (pp. 323-333).

Hine, C. (2000). *Virtual ethnography.* Thousand Oaks, CA: Sage Publications.

Hoadley, C. M., & Pea, R. D. (2002). Finding the ties that bind: Tools in support of a knowledge-building community. In Renninger, K. A., & Shumar, W. (Eds.), *Building virtual communities: Learning and change in cyberspace* (pp. 321–354). New York, NY: Cambridge University Press. doi:10.1017/CBO9780511606373.017

Hockey, J. (1993). The acceptable face of human grieving? The clergy's role in managing emotional expression during funerals. In Clark, D. (Ed.), *The sociology of death: Theory, culture, practice* (pp. 129–148).

Holste, J. S., & Fields, D. (2010). Trust and tacit knowledge sharing and use. *Journal of Knowledge Management, 14*(1), 128–140. doi:10.1108/13673271011015615

Holt, R. (2004). *Dialogue on the internet: Language, civic identity, and computer-mediated communication.* Westport, CT: Praeger.

Hong, S. J., Thong, J. Y. L., & Tam, K. Y. (2006). Understanding continued information technology usage behavior: A comparison of three models in the context of mobile internet. *Decision Support Systems, 42*(3), 1819–1834. doi:10.1016/j.dss.2006.03.009

Hong, T. (2006). The influence of structural and message features on Web Site credibility. *Journal of the American Society for Information Science and Technology, 57,* 114–127. doi:10.1002/asi.20258

Hooff van den, B., & Huysman, M. (2009). Managing knowledge sharing: Emergent and engineering approaches. *Information & Management, 46,* 1-8.

Horrigan, J. B., Rainie, L., & Fox, S. (2001). *Online communities: Networks that nurture long-distance relationships and local ties.* Retrieved October 11, 2007, from http://www.pewinternet.org/pdfs/PIP_Communities_Report.pdf

Howard, P. N. (2002). Network ethnography and the hypermedia organization: New media, new organization, new methods. *New Media & Society*, *4*(4), 550–574. doi:10.1177/146144402321466813

Howard, P., & Jones, S. (2004). *Society online: The Internet in context*. Thousand Oaks, CA: Sage Publications.

Howard, T. W. (2010). *Design to thrive: Creating social networks and online communities that last*. Morgan Kaufmann.

Hrastinski, S. (2008). What is online learner participation? A literature review. *Computers & Education*, *51*(4), 1755–1765. doi:10.1016/j.compedu.2008.05.005

Hrastinski, S. (2009). A theory of online learning as online participation. *Computers & Education*, *52*(1), 78–82. doi:10.1016/j.compedu.2008.06.009

Hsu, M. H., Chiu, C. M., & Ju, T. L. (2004). Determinants of continued use of the WWW: An integration of two theoretical models. *Industrial Management & Data Systems*, *104*, 766–775. doi:10.1108/02635570410567757

Hsu, M. H., Ju, T. L., Yen, C. H., & Chang, C. M. (2007). Knowledge sharing behavior in virtual communities: The relationship between trust, self-efficacy, and outcome expectations. *International Journal of Human-Computer Studies*, *65*(2), 153–169. doi:10.1016/j.ijhcs.2006.09.003

Hsu, M., Ju, T. L., Yen, C., & Chang, C. (2004). Knowledge sharing behavior in virtual communities: The relationship between trust, self-efficacy, and outcome expectations. *International Journal of Human-Computer Studies*, *65*(2), 153–169. doi:10.1016/j.ijhcs.2006.09.003

Hung, K., Yiyan Li, S., & Tse, D. K. (2011). Interpersonal trust and platform credibility in a chinese multibrand online community. *Journal of Advertising*, *40*(3), 99–112. doi:10.2753/JOA0091-3367400308

Hunter, J., Khan, I., & Gerber, A. (2008). Harvana: Harvesting community tags to enrich collection metadata. *Proceedings of the 8th ACM/IEEE-CS Joint Conference on Digital Libraries*, (pp. 147-156).

Hurd, S. N., & Stein, R. F. (Eds.). (2004). *Building and sustaining learning communities: The Syracuse University experience*. New York, NY: John Wiley & sons, Inc.

Hurley, P. J. (2000). *A concise introduction to logic*. Belmont, CA: Wadsworth.

Huwe, T. (2008). Where the sidewalk ends and the community begins. *Computers in Libraries*, *28*(4), 33–35.

Huysman, M., & Wulf, V. (2006). IT to support knowledge sharing in communities, towards a social capital analysis. *Journal of Information Technology*, *21*(1), 40–51. doi:10.1057/palgrave.jit.2000053

Ihde, D. (2008). *Ironic technics*. LaVergne, TN: Automatic Press/VIP.

Iivari, J. (2005). An empirical test of the DeLone-McLean model of information system success. *The Data Base for Advances in Information Systems*, *36*, 8–27. doi:10.1145/1066149.1066152

In der Smitten, S. (2008). Political potential and capabilities of online communities. *German Policy Studies/Politikfeldanalyse*, *4*(4), 32-62.

Innes, R. B. (2007). Dialogic communication in collaborative problem solving groups. *International Journal for the Scholarship of Teaching and Learning*, *1*(1), 1-19. Retrieved October 16, 2007, from http://www.georgiasouthern.edu/ijsotl/v1n1/innes/IJ_Innes.pdf

International Working Group on Educational Data Mining. (2010). *Educational data mining*. Retrieved from http://www.educationaldatamining.org/

iResearch. (2006). *China internet community user development report 2006*. Retrieved from http://www.iresearch.com.cn

Iriberri, A., & Leroy, G. (2009). A life-cycle perspective on online community success. *ACM Computing Surveys*, *41*, 11:1-11-29.

Iriberri, A., & Leroy, G. (2009). A life cycle perspective on online community success. *ACM Computing Surveys*, *41*(2), 11. doi:10.1145/1459352.1459356

Jagers, H., Jansen, W., & Steenbakkers, W. (1998). Characteristics of virtual organizations. In P. Sieber & J. Griese (Eds.), *Organizational Virtualness, Proceedings of the VoNet-Workshop*, April 27-28. Bern, Switzerland: Simowa Verlag.

Jaggar, A. M. (2004). Feminist politics and epistemology. In Harding, S. (Ed.), *The feminist standpoint theory reader. Intellectual and political conversations* (pp. 55–66). New York, NY: Routledge.

Jain, R. (2005). I want my IPTV. *IEEE MultiMedia, 12*(3), 96. doi:10.1109/MMUL.2005.47

James, M. C., Wotring, E., & Forrest, E. J. (1995). An exploratory study of the perceived benefits of electronic bulletin board use and their impact on other communication activities. *Journal of Broadcasting & Electronic Media, 39*, 30–50. doi:10.1080/08838159509364287

Jamieson, L. (2007). *Engineering education in the changing world*. Paper presented to the EPICS Conference, University of California, San Diego.

Japan, L. T. E. R. (n.d.). *About JaLTER*. Retrieved February 25, 2012 from http://www.jalter.org/modules/about/

Jarvenpaa, S. L., & Staples, D. S. (2000). The use of collaborative electronic media for information sharing: An exploratory study of determinants. *The Journal of Strategic Information Systems, 9*, 129–154. doi:10.1016/S0963-8687(00)00042-1

Jarvenpaa, S. L., & Tanriverdi, H. (2003). Leading virtual knowledge networks. *Organizational Dynamics, 31*(4), 403–412. doi:10.1016/S0090-2616(02)00127-4

Jasperson, J. S., Carter, P. E., & Zmud, R. W. (2005). A comprehensive conceptualization of post-adoptive behaviors associated with information technology enabled work systems. *Management Information Systems Quarterly, 29*(3), 525–557.

Jasperson, J., Carter, P., & Zmud, R. (2005). A comprehensive conceptualization of post-adoptive behaviors associated with IT enabled work systems. *Management Information Systems Quarterly, 29*, 525–557.

Jayanti, R. K., & Singh, J. (2010). Pragmatic learning theory: An inquiry-action framework for distripbuted consumer learning in online communities. *The Journal of Consumer Research, 36*(6), 1058–1081. doi:10.1086/648689

Jenkins, H. (2002). *Textual poachers: Television, fans and participatory culture*. London, UK: Routledge.

Jenkins, H. (2006a). *Fans, gamers, and bloggers: Exploring participatory culture*. New York, NY: New York University Press.

Jenkins, H. (2006b). *Convergence culture*. New York, NY: New York University Press.

Jennings, S., & Gersie, A. (1987). *Drama therapy with disturbed adolescents* (pp. 162–182).

Jeong, H., & Biswas, G. (2008). Mining student behavior models in learning-by-teaching environments, *Proceedings of the 1st International Conference on Educational Data Mining*, (pp. 127-136).

Jeppesen, L. B., & Frederiksen, L. (2006). Why do users contribute to firm-hosted user communities? The case of computer-controlled music instruments. *Organization Science, 17*(1), 45–63. doi:10.1287/orsc.1050.0156

Jeppesen, L. B., & Laursen, K. (2009). The role of lead users in knowledge sharing. *Research Policy, 38*(10), 1582–1589. doi:10.1016/j.respol.2009.09.002

Jhally, S., & Livant, B. (2006). Watching as working: The valorization of audience consciousness. In *S. Jhally (Author), The spectacle of accumulation: Essays in culture, media, & politics* (pp. 25–43). New York, NY: Peter Lang. doi:10.1111/j.1460-2466.1986.tb01442.x

Jiacheng, W., Lu, L., & Calabrese, A. F. (2010). A cognitive model of intra-organizational knowledge-sharing motivations in the view of cross-culture. *International Journal of Information Management, 30*, 220–230. doi:10.1016/j.ijinfomgt.2009.08.007

Jiang, M., & Xu, H. (2009). Exploring online structures on Chinese government portals: Citizen political participation and government legitimation. *Social Science Computer Review, 27*(20), 174–195. doi:10.1177/0894439308327313

JISC. (2007). *Transforming institutions through e-Learning*. Retrieved December 19, 2011, from http://www.elearning.ac.uk/features/Transformation

JISC. (2010). *New study urges colleges to develop e-learning strategies for higher education*. Retrieved December 19, 2011, from http://www.jisc.ac.uk/news/stories/2010/12/vle.aspx

Johnson, S. L. (2010). Should I stay or should I go? Continued participation intentions in online communities. *Proceedings of Academy of Management Annual Conference*, 2010, (pp. 1-6).

Johnson, J. (1988). Mixing humans and non-humans: The sociology of a door closer. *Social Problems, 35*(3), 298–310. doi:10.1525/sp.1988.35.3.03a00070

Joia, L. A. (2000b). Tecnologia da informação para gestão do conhecimento em organização virtual. *Produção, 9*(2).

Joia, L. A. (1999). A new model for workers' retraining in Brazil. *Journal of Workplace Learning, 11*(4), 140–145. doi:10.1108/13665629910276070

Joia, L. A. (2000a). W3E - A web-based instruction system for leveraging corporate intelligence. *Journal of Workplace Learning, 12*(1), 5–11. doi:10.1108/13665620010309747

Joia, L. A., & Costa, M. F. C. (2008). Some key success factors in web-based corporate training in Brazil: A multiple case study. *International Journal of Web-Based Learning and Teaching Technologies, 3*(4), 1–28. doi:10.4018/jwbltt.2009092201

Jones, Q., Ravid, G., & Rafaeli, S. (2004). Information overload and the message dynamics of online interaction spaces: A theoretical model and empirical exploration. *Information Systems Research, 15*(2), 194–210. doi:10.1287/isre.1040.0023

Jones, S. (1997). *Virtual culture: Identity and communication in cybersociety*. London, UK: Sage Publications.

Jones, S. (Ed.). (1995). *Cybersociety*. Thousand Oaks, CA: Sage.

Jones, S. (Ed.). (1998). *Cybersociety 2.0*. Thousand Oaks, CA: Sage.

Jones, S. G. (1997). The Internet and its social landscape. In Jones, S. G. (Ed.), *Virtual culture: Identity and communication in cybersociety* (pp. 7–35). London, UK: Sage Publications.

Jones, S. G. (2002). Building, buying, or being there: Imagining online community. In Renninger, K. A., & Shumar, W. (Eds.), *Building virtual communities: Learning and change in cyberspace* (pp. 368–376). Cambridge, UK: Cambridge University Press. doi:10.1017/CBO9780511606373.019

Jung, I. (2001). Building a theoretical framework of web-based instruction in the context of distance education. *British Journal of Educational Technology, 32*(5), 525–534. doi:10.1111/1467-8535.00222

Kahn, B., Strong, D., & Wang, R. (2002). Information quality benchmarks: Product and service performance. *Communications of the ACM, 45*(4), 192. doi:10.1145/505999.506007

Kalathil, S., & Boas, T. (2003). *Open networks, closed regimes: The impact of the Internet on authoritarian rule*. Washington, DC: Carnegie Endowment for International Peace.

Kankanhalli, A., Tan, B. C. Y., & Wei, K.-K. (2005a). Contributing knowledge to electronic knowledge repositories: An empirical investigation. *Management Information Systems Quarterly, 29*(1), 113–143.

Kankanhalli, A., Tan, B. C. Y., & Wei, K.-K. (2005b). Understanding seeking from electronic knowledge repositories an empirical study. *Journal of the American Society for Information Science and Technology, 56*(11), 1156–1166. doi:10.1002/asi.20219

Karagiorgi, Y., & Lymbouridou, C. (2009). The story of an online teacher community in Cyprus. *Professional Development in Education, 35*(1), 119–138. doi:10.1080/13674580802269059

Karahanna, E., Straub, D. W., & Chervany, N. L. (1999). Information technology adoption across time: A cross-sectional comparison of pre-adoption and post-adoption beliefs. *Management Information Systems Quarterly, 23*, 183–213. doi:10.2307/249751

Karim, K. (2003). *The media of diaspora*. London, UK: Routledge.

Kates, S. (2002). *Elocution and African American culture: The pedagogy of Hallie Quinn Brown. Activist rhetorics and American higher education, 1885-1937* (pp. 53–74). Carbondale, IL: Southern Illinois University Press.

Katz, E. (1996). And deliver us from segmentation. *The Annals of the American Academy of Political and Social Science, 546*, 22–33. doi:10.1177/0002716296546001003

Kazmer, M. M. (2005). How technology affects students' departures from online learning communities. *ACM SIGGROUP Bulletin, 25*, 25–40.

Kearl, M. C. (1989). *Endings*. New York, NY: Oxford University Press.

Keen, P. (1991). *Shaping the future*. Harvard Business School Press.

Kehrwald, B. (2010). Being online: Social presence as subjectivity in online learning. *London Review of Education, 8*(1), 39–50. doi:10.1080/14748460903557688

Kelly, H. F., Ponton, M. K., & Rovai, A. P. (2007). A comparison of student evaluations of teaching between online and face-to-face courses. *The Internet and Higher Education, 10*, 89–101. doi:10.1016/j.iheduc.2007.02.001

Kendall, L. (2002). *Hanging out in the virtual pub: Masculinities and relationships online*. Berkley, CA: University of California Press.

Kennedy, H. (2006). Beyond anonymity, or future directions for identity research. *New Media & Society, 8*(6), 859–876. doi:10.1177/1461444806069641

Kil, S. H. (2010). Telling stories: The use of personal narratives in the social sciences and history. *Journal of Ethnic and Migration Studies, 36*(3), 539–540. doi:10.1080/13691831003651754

Kim, J. S. (2005). The effects of a constructivist teaching approach on student academic achievement, self-concept, and learning strategies. *Asia Pacific Education Review, 6*(1), 7-19. Retrieved January 24, 2012, from http://www.eric.ed.gov/ERICWebPortal/search/detailmini.jsp?_nfpb=true&_&ERICExtSearch_SearchValue_0=EJ728823&ERICExtSearch_SearchType_0=no&accno=EJ728823

Kim, A. J. (2000). *Community building on the web: Secret strategies for successful online communities*. Berkeley, CA: Peachpit Press.

Kimble, C., Barlow, A., & Li, F. (2000). *Effective virtual teams through communities of practice*. Retrieved June 6, 2008, from http://ssrn.com/abstract=634645

Kim, H.-s., Park, J. Y., & Jin, B. (2008). Dimensions of online community attributes: Examination of online communities hosted by companies in Korea. *International Journal of Retail & Distribution Management, 36*(10), 812–830. doi:10.1108/09590550810901008

Kim, J. W., Choi, J., Qualls, W., & Han, K. (2008). It takes a marketplace community to raise brand commitment: The role of online communities. *Journal of Marketing Management, 24*(3-4), 409–431. doi:10.1362/026725708X306167

Kim, S. S., & Malhotra, N. K. (2005). A longitudinal model of continued is use: an integrative view of four mechanisms underlying post-adoption phenomena. *Management Science, 51*, 741–755. doi:10.1287/mnsc.1040.0326

Kirkby, J. (2006). Remembrance of the future: Derrida on mourning. *Social Semiotics, 16*(3), 461–472. doi:10.1080/10350330600824383

Kirschner, P. A., Sweller, J., & Clark, R. E. (2006). Why minimal guidance during instruction does not work: An analysis of the failure of constructivist, discovery, problem-based, experiential, and inquiry-based teaching. *Educational Psychologist, 41*(2), 75–86. doi:10.1207/s15326985ep4102_1

KMEdge. (2010). *How do communities work in leading organizations?* Retrieved April 10, 2010, from http://kmedge.org/wp/howdocop.html

Knowledge Network for Biocomplexity. (n.d.). *Ecological metadata language (EML) specification*. Retrieved February 3, 2012, from http://knb.ecoinformatics.org/software/eml/eml-2.0.1/index.html

Ko, D. G., Kirsch, L. J., & King, W. R. (2005). Antecedents of knowledge transfer from consultants to clients in enterprise system implementations. *Management Information Systems Quarterly, 29*, 59–85.

Koh, J., Kim, Y.-G., Butler, B., & Bock, G.-W. (2007). Encouraging participation in virtual communities. *Communications of the ACM, 50*(2), 69–73. doi:10.1145/1216016.1216023

Koka, B. R., & Prescott, J. E. (2002). Strategic alliances as social capital: A multidimensional view. *Strategic Management Journal, 23*(9), 795–816. doi:10.1002/smj.252

Koku, E., Nazer, N., & Wellman, B. (2001). Netting scholars: Online and offline. *The American Behavioral Scientist, 44*, 1752–1772. doi:10.1177/00027640121958023

Komito, L. (1998). The Net as a foraging society: Flexible communities. *The Information Society, 14*(2), 97–106. doi:10.1080/019722498128908

Komter, A. (2007). Gifts and social relations: The mechanisms of reciprocity. *International Sociology, 22*(1), 93–107. doi:10.1177/0268580907070127

Kosonen, M. (2009). Knowledge sharing in virtual communities - A review of the empirical research. *Journal of Web-based Communities, 5*(2), 144–163. doi:10.1504/IJWBC.2009.023962

Kozinets, R. V. (2002). The field behind the screen: Using netnography for marketing research in online communities. *JMR, Journal of Marketing Research, 39*(1), 61–72. doi:10.1509/jmkr.39.1.61.18935

Kozinets, R. V. (2006). Click to connect: Netnography and tribal advertising. *Journal of Advertising Research, 46*(3), 279–288. doi:10.2501/S0021849906060338

Kraut, R., Kiesler, S., Boneva, B., Cummings, J., Helgeson, V., & Crawford, A. (2002). Internet paradox revisited. *The Journal of Social Issues, 58*(1), 49–74. doi:10.1111/1540-4560.00248

Kraut, R., Maher, M., Olson, J., Malone, T. W., Pirolli, P. L., & Thomas, J. C. (2010). Scientific foundations: A case for technology-mediated social-participation theory. *Computer Magazine, 43*(11), 22–28.

Kraut, R., Patterson, M., Lundmark, V., Kiesler, S., Mukophadhyay, T., & Scherlis, W. (1998). Internet paradox: A social technology that reduces social involvement and psychological well-being? *The American Psychologist, 53*(9), 1017–1031. doi:10.1037/0003-066X.53.9.1017

Krumm, J., Davies, N., & Narayanaswami, C. (2008). User-generated content. *IEEE Pervasive Computing / IEEE Computer Society and IEEE Communications Society, 7*(4), 10–11. doi:10.1109/MPRV.2008.85

Kuh, G. D. (1996). Guiding principles for creating seamless learning environments for undergraduates. *Journal of College Student Development, 37*(2), 135–148.

Kumar, T. (2001). An introduction to data mining in institutional research. Retrieved from www.ir.uni.edu/dbweb/pdf/present/dm_intro.pdf

Lai, L. F. (2007). A knowledge engineering approach to knowledge management. *Information Sciences, 177*, 4072–4094. doi:10.1016/j.ins.2007.02.028

Lakhani, K. R., & von Hippel, E. (2003). How open source software works: Free user-to-user assistance. *Research Policy, 32*(6), 923–943. doi:10.1016/S0048-7333(02)00095-1

Lambiotte, R., & Panzarasa, P. (2009). Communities, knowledge creation, and information diffusion. *Journal of Informatrics, 3*, 180–190. doi:10.1016/j.joi.2009.03.007

Lampe, C., & Resnick, P. (2004). Slash (dot) and burn: Distributed moderation in a large online conversation space. *Proceedings of the SIGCHI Conference on Human Factors in Computing Systems,* (pp. 543-550).

Lampe, C., Ellison, N., & Steinfield, C. (2006). *A Face (book) in the crowd: Social searching vs. social browsing.* Paper presented at the CSCW-2006, New York.

Landowski, E. (1985). Eux, nous et moi: régimes de visibilité. *Mots, 10*, 9–16. doi:10.3406/mots.1985.1182

Landowski, E. (1989). *La société réfléchie.* Paris, France: Seuil.

Langerak, F., Verhoef, P. C., Verlegh, P. W. J., & de Valck, K, (2003). *The effect of members' satisfaction with a virtual community on member participation.* ERIM Report Series Research in Management, Reference No. ERS-2003-004-MKT, Erasmus Research Institute of Management, Erasmus University Rotterdam.

Latour, B. (2005). *Reassembling the social: An introduction to actor-network theory.* Oxford, UK: Oxford University Press.

Laurillard, D. (2002). *Rethinking teaching for the knowledge society.* Retrieved June 8, 2005, from http://www.educause.edu/ir/library/pdf/erm0201.pdf

Lave, J., & Wenger, E. (1991). *Situated learning: Legitimate peripheral participation.* New York, NY: Cambridge University Press.

Law, J., & Hassard, J. (1999). *Actor network theory and after.* Oxford, UK: Blackwell.

Lazar, J., & Preece, J. (1998). Classification schema for online communities. *Proceedings of the Americas Conference on Information Systems 1998* (pp. 84-86). Association for Information Systems.

Lazzarato, M. (2006). Immaterial labor. In Virno, P., Buckley, S., & Hardt, M. (Eds.), *Radical thought in Italy* (pp. 133–150). Minneapolis, MN: University of Minnesota Press.

Lécuyer, C., Brock, D. C., & Last, J. (2010). *Makers of the microchip: A documentary history of fairchild semiconductor*. Cambridge, MA: The MIT Press.

Lee, F. S. L., Vogel, D., & Limayem, M. (2002). Virtual community informatics: What we know and what we need to know. *35th Hawaii International Conference on System Sciences* (pp. 2863–2872).

Lee, F. S. L., Vogel, D., & Limayem, M. (2003). Virtual community informatics: A review and research agenda. *Journal of Information Technology Theory and Application, 5*, 47–61.

Lee, G. K., & Cole, R. (2003). From a firm-based to a community-based model of knowledge creation: The case of the Linux kernel development. *Organization Science, 14*(6), 633–649. doi:10.1287/orsc.14.6.633.24866

Lee, H. L., & Whang, S. (2001). Winning the last mile of e-commerce. *Sloan Management Review, 42*(4), 54–62.

Lee, J., & Lee, H. (2010). The computer-mediated communication network: exploring the linkage between the online community and social capital. *New Media & Society, 12*(5), 711–727. doi:10.1177/1461444809343568

Lee, M. J. W., & McLoughlin, C. (2009). Social software as tools for pedagogical transformation: Enabling personalization, creative production, and participatory learning. In Lambropoulos, N., & Romero, M. (Eds.), *Educational social software for context-aware learning: Collaborative methods and human interaction* (pp. 1–22). Hershey, PA: Information Science Reference. doi:10.4018/978-1-60566-826-0.ch001

Lee, T., Hendler, J., & Lassila, O. (2001). The Semantic Web. *Scientific American, 284*(5), 34–43. doi:10.1038/scientificamerican0501-34

Lee, Y., Strong, D., Kahn, B., & Wang, R. (2002). AIMQ: A methodology for information quality assessment. *Information & Management, 40*, 133–146. doi:10.1016/S0378-7206(02)00043-5

Lerner, J., & Tirole, J. (2002). Some simple economics of open source. *The Journal of Industrial Economics, 50*(2), 197–234. doi:10.1111/1467-6451.00174

Lesser, E., & Everest, K. (2001). Communities of practice: Making the most of intellectual capital. *Ivey Business Journal, 65*(4), 37–41.

Lessig, L. (2001). *The future of ideas: The fate of the commons in a connected world*. New York, NY: Random House.

Lessig, L. (2004). *Free culture: How big media uses technology and the law to lock down culture and control creativity*. New York, NY: Penguin Press.

Leung, C. H. (2010). Critical factors of implementing knowledge management in school environment: A qualitative study in Hong Kong. *Research Journal of Information Technology, 2*(2), 66–80. doi:10.3923/rjit.2010.66.80

Lévy, P. (1994). *L'intelligence collective. Pour une anthropologie du cyberspace*. Paris, France: La Découverte.

Li, H. L., & Lee, K. C. (2010). Behavior participation in virtual worlds: A Triandis model perspective. *Proceedings of the 2010 Pacific Conference in Information Systems (PACIS2010)*, Paper 94. Retrieved January 24, 2012, from http://aisel.aisnet.org/pacis2010/94/

Liao, P., & Hsieh, J. Y. (2011). What influences internet-based learning? *Social Behavior & Personality: An International Journal, 39*(7), 887–896. doi:10.2224/sbp.2011.39.7.887

Liao, S.-H. (2003). Knowledge management technologies and applications – Literature review from 1995 to 2002. *Expert Systems with Applications, 25*, 155–164. doi:10.1016/S0957-4174(03)00043-5

Lima, N. C., & Joia, L. A. (2009). Empirical evidence of key success factors in web-based corporate training. *Proceedings of the 15th Americas Conference on Information Systems*. Association for Information Systems - AIS.

Limayem, M., Cheung, C. M. K., & Chan, G. W. W. (2003). Explaining information systems adoption and post-adoption: Toward an integrative model. *Twenty-Fourth International Conference on Information Systems* (pp. 720-731).

Limayem, M., & Cheung, C. M. K. (2008). Understanding information systems continuance: The case of Internet-based learning technologies. *Information & Management, 45*(4), 227–232. doi:10.1016/j.im.2008.02.005

Limayem, M., Hirt, S. G., & Cheung, C. M. K. (2007). How habit limits the predictive power of intention: The case of information systems continuance. *Management Information Systems Quarterly, 31*(4), 705–737.

Lin, C. F. (2008). The cyber-aspects of virtual communities: Free downloader ethics, cognition, and perceived service quality. *Cyberpsychology & Behavior, 11*(1), 69–73. doi:10.1089/cpb.2007.9932

Lin, C.-C., Porter, J. H., Hsiao, C.-W., Lu, S.-S., & Jeng, M.-R. (2008). Establishing an EML-based data management system for automating analysis of field sensor data. *Taiwan Journal for Science, 23*(3), 279–285.

Lin, M.-J. J., Hung, S.-W., & Chen, C.-J. (2009). Fostering the determinants of knowledge sharing in professional virtual communities. *Computers in Human Behavior, 25*, 929–939. doi:10.1016/j.chb.2009.03.008

Litwin, M. S. (1995). *How to measure survey reliability and validity*. London, UK: Sage Publications.

Liu, B., Hsu, W., & Ma, Y. (1998). Integrating classification and association rule mining. In *Fourth International Conference on Knowledge Discovery and Data Mining*, (pp. 80-86).

Li, W. (2010). Virtual knowledge sharing in a cross-cultural context. *Journal of Knowledge Management, 14*(1), 38–50. doi:10.1108/13673271011015552

Locke, J. (1988). *Two treatises of government*. New York, NY: Cambridge University Press. (Original work published 1689)

Lounsbury, J., Loveland, J., & Gibson, L. (2003). An investigation of psychological sense of community in relation to big five personality traits. *Journal of Community Psychology, 31*(5), 531–541. doi:10.1002/jcop.10065

Lowry, P. B., Zhang, D., Zhou, L., & Fu, X. (2010). Effects of culture, social presence, and group composition on trust in technology-supported decision-making groups. *Information Systems Journal, 20*(3), 297–315. doi:10.1111/j.1365-2575.2009.00334.x

Loyarte, E., & Rivera, O. (2007). Communities of practice: A model for their cultivation. *Journal of Knowledge Management, 11*(3), 67–77. doi:10.1108/13673270710752117

Luan, J., Zhai, M., Chen, J., Chow, T., Chang, L., & Zhao, C.-M. (2004). *Concepts, myths, and case studies of data mining in higher education*. AIR 44th Forum, Boston.

Luan, J. (2001). *Data mining applications in higher education. New directions for institutional research* (1st ed.). San Francisco, CA: Jossey-Bass.

Luan, J. (2002). Data mining and its applications in higher education. In Serban, A., & Luan, J. (Eds.), *Knowledge management: Building a competitive advantage for higher education. New directions for institutional research, No. 113*. San Francisco, CA: Jossey Bass. doi:10.1002/ir.35

Lukkarinen, H. (2005). Methodological triangulation showed the poorest quality of life in the youngest people following the treatment of coronary artery disease: A longitudinal study. *International Journal of Nursing Studies, 42*, 619–627. doi:10.1016/j.ijnurstu.2004.09.016

Lyotard, J. F. (1984). *The postmodern condition: A report on knowledge*. Minneapolis, MN: University of Minnesota Press.

Ma, M. (2005). *IT design for sustaining virtual communities: An identity-based approach*. Dissertation, Decision of Information Technologies Department, University of Maryland, Maryland.

Ma, Y., Liu, B., Wong, C. K., Yu, P. S., & Lee, S. M. (2000). Targeting the right students using data mining. *Proceedings of the Sixth ACM SIGKDD International Conference on Knowledge Discovery and Data Mining*, Boston, (pp. 457-464).

Machlup, F. (1962). *The production and distribution of knowledge in the United States*. Princeton, NJ: Princeton University Press.

Maffesoli, M. (1996). *The time of the tribes: The decline of individualism in mass society* (Smith, D., Trans.). London, UK: Sage Publications.

Mahar, G. (2007). *Factors affecting participation in online communities of practice*. PhD Dissertation, Nardi, B. A., & Whittaker, S. (2002). The place of face-to-face communication in distributed work. In P. Hinds & Kiesler, S. (Eds.), *Distributed work: New research on working across distance using technology*, (pp. 83-110). Cambridge, MA: MIT Press.

Mallapragada, M. (2006). Home, homeland, homepage: Belonging and the Indian-American web. *New Media & Society, 8*(2), 207–227. doi:10.1177/1461444806061943

Ma, M., & Agarwal, R. (2007). Through a glass darkly: Information technology design, identity verification, and knowledge contribution in online communities. *Information Systems Research, 18*(1), 42–67. doi:10.1287/isre.1070.0113

Manetti, G. (1998). *La teoria dell'enunciazione*. Siena, Italy: Protagon.

Margolin, V. (2009). Design history and design studies. In Clark, H., & Brody, D. (Eds.), *Design studies - A reader*. Oxford, UK: Berg.

Margolis, M., & Resnick, D. (2000). *Politics as usual: The cyberspace "revolution."*. Thousand Oaks, CA: Sage Publications.

Markus, M. L. (1994). Electronic mail as the medium of managerial choice. *Organization Science, 5*(4), 502–527. doi:10.1287/orsc.5.4.502

Marlow, C., Naaman, M., Boyd, D., & Davis, M. (2006). HT06, tagging paper, taxonomy, Flickr, academic article, to read. *Proceedings of the Seventeenth Conference on Hypertext and Hypermedia*, ACM, (pp. 31-40).

Marrone, G. (1999). *C'era una volta il telefonino. Un'indagine socio semiotica*. Roma, Italy: Meltemi.

Marsh, S. (1994). Formalising trust as a computational concept. Ph. D. Thesis, Department of Computing, Science and Mathematics, University of Stirling, Stirling, Scotland.

Marshall, J. P. (2010). Ambiguity, oscillation and disorder: Online ethnography and the making of culture. *Cosmopolitan Civil Societies Journal, 2*(3), 1-22. Retrieved from http://epress.lib.uts.edu.au/ojs/index.php/mcs/article/view/1598

Marshall, J. P. (2007). *Living on cybermind: Categories, communication and control*. New York, NY: Peter Lang.

Marton, F., & Booth, S. (1997). *Learning and awareness*. Lawrence Erlbaum Associates.

Marx, K., & Engles, F. (1848). Manifesto of the communist party. In Tucker, R. C. (Ed.), *The Marx-Engel reader* (pp. 331–362). New York, NY: Norton.

Mascio, A. (2004). Virtual communities and the socio-semiotical approach. *Internet-Journal of INST, i.e. TRANS Internet-Zeitschrift fuer Kulturwissenschaften 15/2004, 1.2. Signs, Texts, Cultures. Conviviality from a Semiotic Point of View / Zeichen, Texte, Kulturen. Konvivialität aus semiotischer Perspektive*. Retrieved from http://www.inst.at/trans/15Nr/01_2/01_2inhalt_part1_15.htm

Mascio, A. (2008). *Virtuali comunità*. Milano, Italy: Guerini & Associati.

Maslow, A. H. (1943). A theory of motivation. *Psychological Review, 50*(4), 370–396. doi:10.1037/h0054346

Mathes, A. (2004). *Folksonomies-Cooperative classification and communication through shared metadata*. Technical Report, Graduate School of Library and Information Science, University of Illinois Urbana-Champaign.

Mathwick, C., Wiertz, C., & De Ruyter, K. (2007). Social capital production in a virtual P3 community. *The Journal of Consumer Research, 34*, 832–849. doi:10.1086/523291

Matsuo, M., & Easterby-Smith, M. (2008). Beyond the knowledge sharing dilemma: The role of customization. *Journal of Knowledge Management, 12*(4), 30–43. doi:10.1108/13673270810884237

Mauss, M. (1950). *Sociologie et anthropologie*. Paris, France: Universitaires de France.

Maxwell, J. A., & Miller, B. A. (2008). Categorizing and connecting strategies in qualitative data analysis. In Leavy, P., & Hesse-Biber, S. (Eds.), *Handbook of emergent methods* (pp. 461–477).

Mayer, R. C., Davis, J. H., & Schoorman, F. D. (1995). An integrative model of organisational trust. *Academy of Management Review, 20*(3), 709–734.

Mayfield, M. (2010). Tacit knowledge sharing: techniques for putting a powerful tool in practice. *Development and Learning in Organizations*, 24(1), 24–26. doi:10.1108/14777281011010497

McCarthy, C. (2007). Amazon snaps up digital photography review. *CNet News*. Retrieved March 21, 2008, from http://www.news.com/2102-1038_3-6183488.html

McDonald, M., Dorn, B., & McDonald, G. (2004). A statistical analysis of student performance in online computer science courses. *Proceedings of the 35th SIGCSE Technical Symposium on Computer Science Education*, Norfolk, Virginia, (pp. 71-74).

McEvily, S. K., & Chakravarthy, B. (2002). The persistence of knowledge-based advantage: An empirical test for product performance and technological knowledge. *Strategic Management Journal*, 23(4), 285–305. doi:10.1002/smj.223

McFarland, D., & Hamilton, D. (2006). Factors affecting student performance and satisfaction: Online versus traditional course delivery. *Journal of Computer Information Systems*, 46(2), 25–32.

McKenna, K. Y. A., & Bargh, J. A. (1999). Causes and consequences of social interaction on the internet: A conceptual framework. *Media Psychology*, 1(3), 249–269. doi:10.1207/s1532785xmep0103_4

McKinney, V., Yoon, K., & Zahedi, F. M. (2002). The measurement of web-customer satisfaction: An expectation and disconfirmation approach. *Information Systems Research*, 13, 296–315. doi:10.1287/isre.13.3.296.76

McLaughlin, L. (1993). Feminism, the public sphere, media and democracy. *Media Culture & Society*, 15, 599–620. doi:10.1177/016344393015004005

McLuhan, M. (1967). *Understanding media: The extensions of man*. New York, NY: McGraw Hill.

McMillan, D. W., & Chavis, D. M. (1986). Sense of community: A definition and theory. *Journal of Community Psychology*, 14, 6–23. doi:10.1002/1520-6629(198601)14:1<6::AID-JCOP2290140103>3.0.CO;2-I

McNichols, D. (2010). Optimal knowledge transfer methods: A generation X perspective. *Journal of Knowledge Management*, 14(1), 24–37. doi:10.1108/13673271011015543

Meiklejohn, A. (1932). *The experimental college*. New York, NY: HarperCollins.

Mendelson, A., & Papacharissi, Z. (2011). Look at us: Collective narcissism in college student Facebook photo galleries. In Papachariss, Z. (Ed.), *A networked self: Identity, community, and culture on social network sites* (pp. 252–273). New York, NY: Routledge.

Mergel, B. (1998). *Instructional design and learning theory*. Retrieved November 28, 2005, from http://www.usask.ca/education/coursework/802papers/mergel/brenda.htm

Merleau-Ponty, M. (1962). *Phenomenology of perception*. London, UK: Routledge.

Messinger, P. R., Stroulia, E., Lyons, K., Bone, M., Niu, R. H., Smirnov, K., & Perelgut, S. (2009). Virtual worlds - Past, present, and future: New directions in social computing. *Decision Support Systems*, 47(3), 204–228. doi:10.1016/j.dss.2009.02.014

Metcalf, P., & Huntington, R. (1991). *Celebrations of death: The anthropology of mortuary ritual* (2nd ed.). Cambridge University Press.

Meyers, E. M. (2009). Tip of the iceberg: Meaning, identity, and literacy in preteen virtual worlds. *Journal of Education for Library and Information Science*, 50(4), 226–236.

Meyrowitz, J. (1985). *No sense of place: The impact of electronic media on social behavior*. New York, NY: Oxford University Press.

Mezirow, J. (1991). *Transformative dimensions in adult learning*. San Francisco, CA: Jossey-Bass.

Miles, M. B., & Huberman, A. M. (1994). *Qualitative data analysis: An expanded sourcebook* (2nd ed.). Thousand Oaks, CA: Sage.

Mingers, J. (2001). Combining IS research methods: Towards a pluralist methodology. *Information Systems Research*, 12, 240–259. doi:10.1287/isre.12.3.240.9709

Mingers, J. (2003). The paucity of multimethod research: A review of the information systems literature. *Information Systems Journal*, *13*(3), 233–249. doi:10.1046/j.1365-2575.2003.00143.x

Miranda, S. M., & Saunders, C. S. (2003). The social construction of meaning: An alternative perspective on information sharing. *Information Systems Research*, *14*, 87–106. doi:10.1287/isre.14.1.87.14765

Misanchuk, M., & Anderson, T. (2001). Building community in an online learning environment: Communication, cooperation and collaboration, (pp. 1-14). Retrieved January 13, 2007, from http://www.mtsu.edu/~itconf/proceed01/19.html

Mislove, A. (2009). *Online social networks: Measurement, analysis, and applications to distributed information systems.* Doctor of Philosophy PhD Thesis, Rice University, Houston, Texas.

Mitchell, T. R., & Daniels, D. (2003). Motivation. In Borman, W. C., Ilgen, D. R., & Klimoski, R. J. (Eds.), *Handbook of psychology, volume twelve: Industrial and organizational psychology* (Vol. 12, pp. 225–254). New York, NY: John Wiley.

Monclar, R., Tecla, A., Oliveira, J., & de Souza, J. M. (2009). MEK: Using spatial–temporal information to improve social networks and knowledge dissemination. *Information Sciences*, *179*, 2524–2537. doi:10.1016/j.ins.2009.01.032

Monolescu, D., & Schifter, C. (2000). Online focus group: A tool to evaluate online students' course experience. *The Internet and Higher Education*, *2*, 171–176. doi:10.1016/S1096-7516(00)00018-X

Mook, D. G. (1987). *Motivation: The organization of action.* London, UK: W.W. Norton & Company Ltd.

Moore, J. (1996). *The death of competition.* HarperCollins Publishers.

Moore, M. G. (1972). Learner autonomy: The second dimension of independent learning. *Convergence*, *5*(2), 76–88.

Moore, M. G., & Kearsley, G. (1996). *Distance education: A systems view.* New York, NY: Wadsworth.

Moran, J. (2007). Generating more heat than light? Debates on civil liberties in the UK. *Policing*, *1*(1), 80. doi:10.1093/police/pam009

Morra, L., & Friedlander, A. C. (1999). *Case study evaluations.* OED (Operations Evaluation Department) Working Paper Series, No. 2, May, World Bank.

Moule, P. (2007). Challenging the five-stage model for e-learning: A new approach. *ALT-J*, *15*(1), 37–50. doi:10.1080/09687760601129588

Mu, J., Peng, G., & Love, E. (2008). Interfirm networks, social capital, and knowledge flow. *Journal of Knowledge Management*, *12*(4), 86–100. doi:10.1108/13673270810884273

Mulkay, M. (1993). Social death in Britain. In Clark, D. (Ed.), *The sociology of death: Theory, culture, practice.*

Murugesan, S. (2007). Understanding Web 2.0. *IT Professional*, *9*(4), 34–41. doi:10.1109/MITP.2007.78

Nack, F., van Ossenbruggen, J., & Hardman, L. (2005). That obscure object of desire: Multimedia metadata on the Web, part 2. *IEEE MultiMedia*, *12*(1), 54–63. doi:10.1109/MMUL.2005.12

Nagel, L., Blignaut, A. S., & Cronje, J. C. (2009). Read-only participants: A case for student communication in online classes. *Interactive Learning Environments*, *17*, 37–51. doi:10.1080/10494820701501028

Nahapiet, J., & Ghoshal, S. (1998). Social capital, intellectual capital, and the organizational advantage. *Academy of Management Review*, *23*(2), 242–266.

Nardi, B. A., Whittaker, S., & Schwartz, H. (2000). It's not what you know, it's who you know: Work in the information age. *First Monday*, *5*(5).

National Center for Ecological Analysis and Synthesis (NCEAS). (n.d.). *Overview.* Retrieved February 26, 2012, from http://www.nceas.ucsb.edu/overview

NBC News. (2011, August 13). Flash mobs turning violent across the country. *NBC Nightly News with Brian Williams.*

Nebus, J. (2004). Learning by networking: Knowledge search and sharing in multinational organizations. In *Proceedings of the 46th Academy of International Business, Bridging with the Other: The Importance of Dialogue in International Business*, Stockholm, Sweden.

Negt, O., & Kluge, A. (1993). *Public sphere and experience: Toward an analysis of the bourgeois and proletarian public sphere*. Minneapolis, MN: University of Minnesota Press.

Neus, A. (2001). Managing information quality in virtual communities of practice. In E. Pierce & R. Katz-Haas (Eds.), *6th International Conference on Information Quality at MIT*. Boston, MA: Sloan School of Management.

Newell, S., Robertson, M., Scarbrough, H., & Swan, J. (2002). *Managing knowledge work*. New York, NY: Palgrave.

Newmann, F., & Oliver, D. (1967). Education and community. *Harvard Educational Review, 37*(1), 61–106.

Ngwenyama, O. K., & Lee, A. S. (1997). Communication richness in electronic mail: Critical social theory and the contextuality of meaning. *Management Information Systems Quarterly, 21*(2), 145–167. doi:10.2307/249417

Nielsen, B. B. (2005). The role of knowledge embeddedness in the creation of synergies in strategic alliances. *Journal of Business Research, 58*(9), 1194–1204. doi:10.1016/j.jbusres.2004.05.001

Nilsson, M., Palmér, M., & Naeve, A. (2002). Semantic Web meta-data for e-learning–some architectural guidelines. *Proceedings of the 11th World Wide Web Conference*, (pp. 7-11).

Nisbet, R. (1969). *The quest for community*. New York, NY: Oxford University Press.

Noblit, G. W., & Hare, R. D. (1988). *Meta-ethnography: Synthesizing qualitative studies (Vol. 11)*. Newbury Park, CA: Sage Publications.

Nonaka, I., & Konno, N. (1998). The concept of 'Ba': Building a foundation for knowledge creation. *California Management Review, 40*(3), 40–54.

Nonaka, I., & Takeuchi, H. (1997). *Criação de conhecimento na empresa: Como as empresas Japonesas geram a a dinâmica da inovação* (pp. 65–71). Editora Campus.

Nonnecke, B., & Preece, J. (1999). *Shedding light on lurkers in online communities* (pp. 123-128). Nonnecke, B., & Preece, J. (2000). *Lurker demographics: Counting the silent*. ACM SIGCHI CHI 2000 Conference on Human Factors in Computing Systems, The Hague.

Nonnecke, B., & Preece, J. (2000). Lurker demographics: Counting the silent. *Proceedings of CHI 2000*. The Hague, The Netherlands: ACM

Nonnecke, B., & Preece, J. (2001). *Why lurkers lurk*. Americas Confenrence on Information Systems 2001 Boston.

Nonnecke, B., & Preece, J. (2003). Silent participants: Getting to know lurkers better. *From Usenet to CoWebs: Interacting with Social Information Spaces*, (pp. 110-132).

Nonnecke, B., Preece, J., & Andrews, D. (2004b). What lurkers and posters think of each other. *Proceedings of the 37th Hawaii International Conference on System Sciences - 2004*, (pp. 1-9).

Nonnecke, B., Andrews, D., Preece, J., & Voutour, R. (2004a). *Online lurkers tell why* (pp. 2688–2694).

Norman, D. A. (1991). Cognitive artifacts. In Carroll, J. M. (Ed.), *Designing interaction: Psychology at the human-computer interface* (pp. 17–38). New York, NY: Cambridge University Press.

Normore, L. F., & Tebo, M. E. (2011). *Assessing user requirements for a small scientific data repository*. ASIST 2011, October 9-13, 2011, New Orleans, LA, USA.

Norris, P. (2004). The bridging and bonding role of online communities. In Howards, P. N., & Jones, S. (Eds.), *Society online the interned in context* (pp. 31–41). Thousand Oaks, CA: Sage Publications. doi:10.1177/108118002129172601

Noy, N., Griffith, N., & Musen, M. (2010). Collecting community-based mappings in an ontology repository. *The Semantic Web-ISWC, 2008*, 371–386.

O'Donnell, E., & David, J. S. (2000). How information systems influence user decisions: A research framework and literature review. *International Journal of Accounting Information Systems, 1*, 178–203. doi:10.1016/S1467-0895(00)00009-9

O'Neill, J., & Conzemius, A. (2006). *The power of SMART goals: Using goals to improve student learning.* Bloomington, IN: Solution Tree.

O'Reilly, T., & Battelle, J. (2009). *Web squared: Web 2.0 five years on.* Retrieved December 20, 2009.

O'Rourke, D. (2007). Mourning becomes eclectic. *American Ethnologist, 34*(2), 387–402.

O'Brien, J. (1999). Writing in the body: Gender (re) production in online interaction. In Smith, M. A., & Kollock, P. (Eds.), *Communities in cyberspace* (pp. 76–104). London, UK: Routledge.

Obst, P., & White, K. (2004). Revisiting the sense of community index: A confirmatory factor analysis. *Journal of Community Psychology, 32*(6), 691–705. doi:10.1002/jcop.20027

OECD. (2005). *E-Learning in tertiary education: Where do we stand?* OECD Publishing. Retrieved January 24, 2012, from http://www.oecd.org/dataoecd/55/25/35961132.pdf

Olaniran, B. A., & Williams, I. M. (2009). Web 2.0 and learning: A closer look at transactional control model in e-learning. In Lambropoulos, N., & Romero, M. (Eds.), *Educational social software for context-aware learning: Collaborative methods and human interaction* (pp. 23–37). Hershey, PA: Information Science Reference. doi:10.4018/978-1-60566-826-0.ch002

Oldenburg, R. (1991). *The great good place: Cafés, coffee shops, bookstores, bars, hair salons, and other hangouts at the heart of a community.* New York, NY: Marlowe and Company.

Oldenburg, R. (1999). *The great good place.* New York, NY: Paragon House.

Oliver, R. L. (1980). A cognitive model for the antecedents and consequences of satisfaction. *JMR, Journal of Marketing Research, 17,* 460–469. doi:10.2307/3150499

Or-Bach, R. (2005). Educational benefits of metadata creation by students. *ACM SIGCSE Bulletin, 37*(4), 93–97. doi:10.1145/1113847.1113885

Orem, S. L., Binkert, J., & Clancy, A. L. (2007). *Appreciative coaching: A positive process for change.* San Francisco, CA: Jossey-Bass.

Orland-Barak, L. (2004). Portfolios as evidence of reflective practice: What remains untold. *Educational Research, 47*(1), 25–44. doi:10.1080/0013188042000337541

Orlikowski, W. J. (2002). Knowing in practice: Enacting a collective capability in distributed organizing. *Organization, 13*(3), 249–273. doi:10.1287/orsc.13.3.249.2776

Orlikowski, W. J. (2007). Sociomaterial practices: Exploring technology at work. *Organization Studies, 28*(9), 1435–1448. doi:10.1177/0170840607081138

Orlikowski, W., & Baroudi, J. (1991). Studying information technology in organizations: Research approaches and assumptions. *Information Systems Research, 2,* 1–28. doi:10.1287/isre.2.1.1

Orr, E., Sisic, M., Ross, C., Simmering, M., Arseneault, J., & Orr, R. (2009). The influence of shyness on the use of Facebook in an undergraduate sample. *CyberPscyhology & Behavior, 12*(3), 337–340. doi:10.1089/cpb.2008.0214

Ozuem, W., Howell, K. E., & Lancaster, G. (2008). Communicating in the new interactive marketspace. *European Journal of Marketing, 42*(9-10), 1059–1083. doi:10.1108/03090560810891145

Page, S. E. (1999). Computational models from A to Z. *Complexity, 5*(1), 35–41. doi:10.1002/(SICI)1099-0526(199909/10)5:1<35::AID-CPLX5>3.0.CO;2-B

Pallant, J. (2005). *SPSS survival manual.* Maidenhead, UK: Open University Press.

Palloff, R., & Pratt, K. (2005). Online learning communities revisited. *Proceedings of the 21st Annual Conference on Distance Teaching and Learning.* Retrieved from http://www.uwex.edu/disted/conference/Resource_library/proceedings/05_1801.pdf

Palloff, R., & Pratt, K. (2007). *Building online learning communities.* San Francisco, CA: John Wiley & Sons.

Papacharissi, Z. (2002). The virtual sphere: The Internet as a public sphere. *New Media & Society, 4*(1), 9–27. doi:10.1177/14614440222226244

Papakyriazis, N. V., & Boudoudrides, M. A. (2001, May 17-18). *Electronic weak ties in network organizations.* Paper presented at the The 4th GOR Conference, Goettingen, Germany.

Parasuraman, A., & Zinkhan, G. M. (2002). Marketing to and serving customers through the Internet: An overview and research agenda. *Journal of the Academy of Marketing Science*, *30*, 286–295. doi:10.1177/009207002236906

Park, C.-H., & Kim, Y.-G. (2006). The effect of information satisfaction and relational benefit on consumers' online shopping site commitments. *Journal of Electronic Commerce in Organizations*, *4*, 70–90. doi:10.4018/jeco.2006010105

Parks, M. R., & Floyd, K. (1996). Making friends in cyberspace. *Journal of Computer-Mediated Communication*, *1*(4). Retrieved from http://www.ascusc.org/jcmc/vol1/issue4/parks.html

Pauleen, D. J., & Yoong, P. (2001). Facilitating virtual team relationships via Internet and conventional communication channels. *Internet Research: Electronic Networking Applications and Policy*, *11*(2), 190–202.

Pena-Shaff, J. B., & Nicholls, C. (2004). Analyzing student interactions and meaning construction in computer bulletin board discussions. *Computers & Education*, *42*, 243–265. doi:10.1016/j.compedu.2003.08.003

Pentland, B. T., & Feldman, M. S. (2005). Organizational routines as a unit of analysis. *Industrial and Corporate Change*, *14*(5), 793–815. doi:10.1093/icc/dth070

Pentland, B. T., & Feldman, M. S. (2007). Narrative networks: Patterns of technology and organization. *Organization Science*, *18*(5), 781–795. doi:10.1287/orsc.1070.0283

Peowski, L. (2010). Where are all the teens? Engaging and empowering them online. *Young Adult Library Services*, *8*(2), 26–28.

Peters, J. D. (1993). Distrust of representation: Habermas on the public sphere. *Media Culture & Society*, *15*, 541–571. doi:10.1177/016344393015004003

Peterson, M. (2008). Loser generated content: From participation to exploitation. *First Monday*, *13*(3). Retrieved from http://frodo.lib.uic.edu/ojsjournals/index.php/fm/article/view/2141/1948

Petty, R. E., & Cacioppo, J. T. (1986). *Communication and persuasion: Central and peripheral routes to attitude change*. New York, NY: Springer-Verlag.

Phang, C. W., Kankanhalli, A., & Sabherwal, R. (2009). Usability and sociability in online communities: A comparative study of knowledge seeking and contribution. *Journal of the Association for Information Systems*, *10*(10), 721–747.

Piaget, J. (1974). *Biology and knowledge*. Chicago, IL: University of Chicago Press.

Piccoli, G., Ahmad, R., & Ives, B. (2001). Web-based virtual learning environments: A research framework and a preliminary assessment of effectiveness in basic IT skills training. *Management Information Systems Quarterly*, *25*(4), 401–426. doi:10.2307/3250989

Pino-Silva, J., & Mayora, C. A. (2010). English teachers' moderating and participating in OCPs. *System*, *38*(2). doi:10.1016/j.system.2010.01.002

Pipino, L., Lee, Y., & Wang, R. (2002). Data quality assessment. *Communications of the ACM*, *45*(4), 211–218. doi:10.1145/505248.506010

Pitta, D. A., & Fowler, D. (2005). Internet community forums: An untapped resource for consumer marketers. *Journal of Consumer Marketing*, *22*, 265–274. doi:10.1108/07363760510611699

Poor, N. (2005). Mechanisms of an online public sphere: The website slashdot. *Journal of Computer-Mediated Communication*, *10*(2).

Porter, C. E. (2004). A typology of virtual communities: A multi-disciplinary foundation for future research. *Journal of Computer-Mediated Communication*, *10*(1), 00–00.

Porter, E. (2004). A typology of virtual communities: A multi-disciplinary foundation for future research. *Journal of Computer Mediated Communication*, *10*(1). Retrieved April 10, 2007, from http://jcmc.indiana.edu/vol10/issue1/porter.html

Porter, C. E., & Donthu, N. (2008). Cultivating trust and harvesting value in virtual communities. *Management Science*, *54*(1), 113–128. doi:10.1287/mnsc.1070.0765

Porter, M. (1985). *Competitive advantage*. New York, NY: The Free Press.

Porter, M. (2001). Strategy and the Internet. *Harvard Business Review*, (3): 62–78.

Postareff, L., & Lindblom-Ylänne, S. (2008). Variation in teachers' descriptions of teaching: Broadening the understanding of teaching in higher education. *Learning and Instruction, 18*(2), 109–120. doi:10.1016/j.learninstruc.2007.01.008

Postelnicu, M., Martin, J., & Landreville, K. (2004). The role of campaign web sites in promoting candidates and attracting campaign resources. In Williams, A., & Tedesco, J. (Eds.), *The Internet election: Perspectives on the web in campaigning in 2004*. Lanham, MD: Rowman & Littlefield.

Poster, M. (1995). *CyberDemocracy: Internet and the public sphere*. Retrieved July 20, 2010, from http://www.hnet.uci.edu/mposter/writings/democ.html

Poster, M. (2001). *What's the matter with the internet?*Minneapolis, MN: University of Minnesota Press.

Postman, N. (1985). *Amusing ourselves to death: Public discourse in the age of show business*. New York, NY: Penguin.

Powazek, D. M. (2002). *Design for community: The art of connecting real people in virtual places*. New Riders.

Pozzato, M. P. (2001). *Semiotica del testo*. Roma, Italy: Carocci.

Preece, J. (2000). *Online communities: Designing usability, supporting sociability*. Chichester, UK: John Wiley & Sons.

Preece, J. (2001). Sociability and usability in online communities: Determining and measuring success. *Behaviour & Information Technology, 20*, 347–356. doi:10.1080/01449290110084683

Preece, J., Nonnecke, B., & Andrews, D. (2004). The top 5 reasons for lurking: Improving community experiences for everyone. *Computers in Human Behavior, 2*(1), 42.

Preece, J., & Shneiderman, B. (2009). The reader-to-leader framework: Motivating technology-mediated social participation. *Transactions on Human-Computer Interaction, 1*(1), 13–32.

Priluck, R. (2004). Web-assisted courses for business education: An examination of two sections of principles of marketing. *Journal of Marketing Education, 26*(2), 161–173. doi:10.1177/0273475304265635

Prosser, M., & Trigwell, K. (1999). *Understanding learning and teaching: The experience in higher education*. Buckingham, UK: Open University Press.

Prykop, C., & Heitman, M. (2006). Designing mobile brand communities: Concept and empirical illustration. *Journal of Organizational Computing and Electronic Commerce, 16*(3/4), 301–323.

Putnam, R. (1995). Bowling alone: America's declining social capital. *Journal of Democracy, 6*(1), 65–78. doi:10.1353/jod.1995.0002

Putnam, R. D. (1995). Bowling alone: America's declining social capital. *Journal of Democracy, 6*(1), 65–78. doi:10.1353/jod.1995.0002

Pybus, J. (2007). Affect and subjectivity: A case study of Neopets.com. *Politics and Culture, 2*. Retrieved March 27, 2008, from http://aspen.conncoll.edu/politicsandculture/page.cfm?key=557

Qiu, J. L. (2000). Virtual censorship in China: Keeping the gate between the cyberspaces. *International Journal of Communications Laws and Policy, 4*, 1–25.

Qiu, J. L. (2006). The changing web of Chinese nationalism. *Global Media and Communication, 2*(1), 125–128. doi:10.1177/1742766506061846

Rafaeli, S., & Ariel, Y. (2008). Online motivational factors: Incentives for participation and contribution in Wikipedia. In Barak, A. (Ed.), *Psychological aspects of cyberspace: Theory, research, applications*. Cambridge, UK: Cambridge University Press.

Rainie, L. (2007). *28% of online Americans have used the internet to tag content*. Pew Internet & American Life Project.

Rambusch, J., & Ziemke, T. (2005). The role of embodiment in situated learning. *Proceedings of COGSCI 2005: XXVII Conference of the Cognitive Science Society*. Retrieved January 24, 2012, from http://www.cogsci.rpi.edu/CSJarchive/Proceedings/2005/docs/p1803.pdf

Ramsden, P. (2003). *Learning to teach in higher education* (2nd ed.). London, UK: Routledge Falmer.

Ranjan, J. (2008). Impact of Information Technology in academia. *International Journal of Educational Management, 22*(5), 442–455. doi:10.1108/09513540810883177

Ranjan, J., & Malik, K. (2007). Effective educational process: A data mining approach. *Vine, 37*(4), 502–515. doi:10.1108/03055720710838551

Rao, A. S., & Georgeff, M. P. (1998). Decision procedures for BDI logics. *Journal of Logic and Computation, 8*(3), 293. doi:10.1093/logcom/8.3.293

Rashid, A. M., Ling, K., Tassone, R. D., Resnick, P., Kraut, R., & Riedl, J. (2006). Motivating participation by displaying the value of contribution. *Proceedings of the SIGCHI Conference on Human Factors in Computing Systems,* (p. 958).

Reckwitz, a. (2002). Toward a theory of social practices: A development in culturalist theorizing. *European Journal of Social Theory, 5*(2), 243-263.

Reeves, T. C., & Reeves, P. M. (1997). Effective dimensions of effective learning on the World Wide Web. In Kahn, B. H. (Ed.), *Web-based instruction* (pp. 59–66). Educational Technology Publications.

Reice, S. R. (1994). Nonequilibrium determinants of biological community structure. *American Scientist, 82*(5), 424–435.

Reid, L. (1996). Informed consent in the study of on-line communities: A reflection on the effects of computer-mediated social research. *The Information Society, 12*(2), 169–174. doi:10.1080/713856138

Reiss, S. (2004). Multifaceted nature of intrinsic motivation: The theory of 16 basic desires. *Review of General Psychology, 8*(3), 179–193. doi:10.1037/1089-2680.8.3.179

Renninger, A. K., & Schumar, W. (Eds.). (2002). *Building virtual communities*. Cambridge, UK: Cambridge University Press. doi:10.1017/CBO9780511606373

Ren, Y., Kraut, R., & Kiesler, S. (2007). Applying common identity and bond theory to design of online communities. *Organization Studies, 28*(3), 377–408. doi:10.1177/0170840607076007

Reushle, S. E. (2005). *Inquiry into a transformative approach to professional development for online educators*. Doctoral thesis, University Southern Queensland, Toowoomba, Toowoomba.

Reushle, S. E. (2006). A framework for designing higher education e-learning environments. In T. C. Reeves & S. F. Yamashita (Eds.), *World Conference on E-Learning in Corporate, Government, Healthcare, & Higher Education*. Association for the Advancement of Computing in Education (AACE), Honolulu, Hawaii.

Rheingold, H. (1994). *The virtual community homesteading on the electronic frontier*. New York, NY: Harper Perennial.

Rheingold, H. (2000). *The virtual community: Homesteading on the electronic frontier* (2nd ed.). London, UK: MIT Press.

Ribes, D., & Polk, J. B. (2012). Historical ontology and infrastructure. *Proceedings of the 2012 iConference*, Toronto, CA, (pp. 252-264).

Rice, R. E. (1992). Task analyzability, use of new media, and effectiveness: A multi-site exploration of media richness. *Organization Science, 3*(4), 475–500. doi:10.1287/orsc.3.4.475

Rice, R., & Love, G. (1987). Electronic emotion: Socioemotional content in a computer-mediated communication. *Communication Research, 14*(1), 85–108. doi:10.1177/009365087014001005

Ridings, C. M., Gefen, D., & Arinze, B. (2002). Some antecedents and effects of trust in virtual communities. *The Journal of Strategic Information Systems, 11*(3-4), 271–295. doi:10.1016/S0963-8687(02)00021-5

Ridings, C., Gefen, D., & Arinze, B. (2002). Some antecedents and effects of trust in virtual communities. *The Journal of Strategic Information Systems, 11*(3-4), 271–295. doi:10.1016/S0963-8687(02)00021-5

Ridings, C., Gefen, D., & Arinze, B. (2006). Psychological barriers: Lurker and poster motivation and behavior in online communities. *Communications of the Association for Information Systems, 18*(16). Retrieved from http://aisel.aisnet.org/cais/vol18/iss1/16

Rieh, S. Y., & Belkin, N. J. (1998). Understanding judgment of information quality and cognitive authority in the WWW. *Proceedings of the 61st Annual Meeting of the American Society for Information Science* Vol. 35 (pp. 279-289). Retrieved from http://www.si.umich.edu/rieh/papers/asis98.pdf

Rieh, S. Y. (2002). Judgment of information quality and cognitive authority in the Web. *Journal of the American Society for Information Science and Technology, 53,* 145–161. doi:10.1002/asi.10017

Riger, S., & Lavrakas, P. (1981). Community ties: Patterns of attachment and social interaction in urban neighborhoods. *American Journal of Community Psychology, 9,* 55–66. doi:10.1007/BF00896360

Riger, S., LeBailly, R., & Gordon, M. (1981). Community ties and urbanites fear of crime: An ecological investigation. *American Journal of Community Psychology, 9,* 653–665. doi:10.1007/BF00896247

Robertson, J. (2004). *Developing a knowledge management strategy*. Step Two Designs Pty Ltd. Retrieved September 16, 2010, from http://www.steptwo.com.au/papers/kmc_kmstrategy/index.html

Roberts, P., & Lourdes, A. V. (1999-2000). Perpetual care in cyberspace: A portrait of memorials on the web. *Omega, 40*(4), 521–545.

Roberts, T. L., Lowry, P. B., & Sweeney, P. D. (2006). An evaluation of the impact of social presence through group size and the use of collaborative software on group member voice in face-to-face and computer-mediated task groups. *IEEE Transactions on Professional Communication, 49*(1), 28–43. doi:10.1109/TPC.2006.870460

Robey, D., Koo, H., & Powers, C. (2000). Situated learning in cross-functional virtual teams. *IEE Transactions of Professional Communication, 43*(1), 51–66. doi:10.1109/47.826416

Romano, S. (1993). The egalitarianism narrative: Whose story? Which yardstick? *Computers and Composition, 10,* 5–28.

Romero, C., & Ventura, S. (2007). Educational data mining: A survey from 1995 to 2005. *Expert Systems with Applications, 33,* 135–146. doi:10.1016/j.eswa.2006.04.005

Romm, C. T., & Setzekom, K. (2008). *Social network communities and E-dating services: Concepts and implications*. London, UK: Information Science Reference. doi:10.4018/978-1-60566-104-9

Roos, J., Roos, G., Dragonetti, N., & Edvinsson, L. (1997). *Intellectual capital*. MacMillan Press Ltd.

Rosewood, B. (2008). *Cybermind novel*. Sydney, Australia: Alchemical Elephant. Retrieved from http://uts.academia.edu/jonmarshall/Books/130911/Cybermind_Novel

Rountree, J. C. (1998). Coming to terms with Kenneth Burke's Pentad. *American Communication Journal, 1*(3).

Rousseau, J. J. (1998). *The social contract*. Hertfordshire, UK: Wordsworth Editions. (Original work published 1762)

Rovai, A. (2002). Building sense of community at a distance. *International Review of Research in Open and Distance Learning, 3*(1), 1-16. Retrieved January 13, 2007, from http://www.irrodl.org/index.php/irrodl/article/view/79/153

Roversi, A. (2001). *Chat line*. Bologna, Italy: Il Mulino.

Roversi, A. (2006). *L'odio in Rete*. Bologna, Italy: Il Mulino.

Ruggiero, T. E. (2001). Uses and gratifications theory in the 21st century. *Mass Communication & Society, 3*(1), 3–37. doi:10.1207/S15327825MCS0301_02

Ruggles, R. L. III, (Ed.). (1997). *Knowledge management tools*. Newton, MA: Butterworth-Heinemann.

Ryan, M. (2001). *A collegiate way of living: Residential colleges and a Yale education*. New Haven, CT: John Edwards College, Yale University.

Saarinen, L. (2002). Imagined community and death. *Digital Creativity, 13*(1), 53–61. doi:10.1076/digc.13.1.53.3212

Saeed, K. A., Grover, V., & Hwang, Y. (2003). Creating synergy with a clicks and mortar approach. *Communications of the ACM, 46*(12), 206–212. doi:10.1145/953460.953501

Saffo, P. (1989). Information surfing. Retrieved on June 24th, 2010, from http://www.saffo.org/infosurfing.html

Saliola, F., & Zanfei, A. (2009). Mulitnational firms, global value chains and the organization of knowledge transfer. *Research Policy*, *38*, 369–381. doi:10.1016/j.respol.2008.11.003

Salmon, G. (2005). Flying not flapping: A strategic framework for e-learning and pedagogical innovation in higher education institutions. *ALT-J. Research in Learning Technology*, *13*(3), 201–218. doi:10.3402/rlt.v13i3.11218

Saltmarsh, S., & Sutherland-Smith, W. (2010). S(t)imulating learning: Pedagogy, subjectivity and teacher education in online environments. *London Review of Education*, *8*(1), 15–24. doi:10.1080/14748460903557613

Sangwan, S. (2005) Virtual community success: A uses and gratifications perspective. *Proceedings of the 38th Hawaii International Conference on System Sciences*. Los Alamitos, CA: IEEE Press.

Sarason, S. (1974). *The psychological sense of community: Prospects for a community psychology*. San Francisco, CA: Jossey Bass.

Sargeant, A., & Woodliffe, L. (2007). Gift giving: an interdisciplinary review. *International Journal of Nonprofit and Voluntary Sector Marketing*, *12*(4), 275–307. doi:10.1002/nvsm.308

Sargenti, P., Lightfoot, W., & Kehal, M. (2006). Diffusion of knowledge in and through higher education organizations. *Issues in Information Systems*, *3*(2), 3–8.

Scardamalia, M., & Bereiter, C. (2006). Knowledge building: Theory, pedagogy, and technology. In Sawyer, R. K. (Ed.), *The Cambridge handbook of the learning sciences* (pp. 97–115). New York, NY: Cambridge University Press.

Schatzki, T. R. (2005). Peripheral vision: The sites of organizations. *Organization Studies*, *26*(3), 465–484. doi:10.1177/0170840605050876

Schatzki, T. R. (2006). On organizations as they happen. *Organization Studies*, *27*(12), 1863–1873. doi:10.1177/0170840606071942

Schoem, D. (2004). Sustaining living-learning programs. In Laufgraben, J. L., & Shapiro, N. S. (Eds.), *Sustaining and improving learning communities* (pp. 130–156). San Francisco, CA: Jossey-Bass.

Scholing, A., & Emmelkamp, P. M. G. (1993). Exposure with and without cognitive therapy for generalized social phobia: Effects of individual and group treatment. *Behaviour Research and Therapy*, *31*(7), 667–681. doi:10.1016/0005-7967(93)90120-J

Scholz, T. (2007). What the MySpace generation should know about working for free. *Re-Public*. Retrieved from http://www.re-public.gr/en/?p=138

Schon, D. (1987). *Educating the reflective practitioner*. San Francisco, CA: Jossey-Bass.

Schroeder, R. (Ed.). (2002). *The social life of avatars*. London, UK: Springer.

Schudson, M. (1996, March-April). What if civic life didn't die? *The American Prospect*, *25*, 17–20.

Schultze, U., & Boland, R. J. (2000). Knowledge management technology and the reproduction of knowledge work practices. *The Journal of Strategic Information Systems*, *9*, 193–212. doi:10.1016/S0963-8687(00)00043-3

Schultze, U., & Orlikowski, W. J. (2004). A practice perspective on technology-mediated network relations: The use of internet-based self-serve technologies. *Information Systems Research*, *15*(1), 87–106. doi:10.1287/isre.1030.0016

Schumpeter, J. (1947). *Capitalism, socialism, and democracy*. New York, NY: Harper.

Schutz, A. (1967). *The phenomenology of the social world*. Chicago, IL: University of Chicago Press.

Schwier, R., & Balbar, S. (2002). The interplay of content and community in synchronous and asynchronous communication: Virtual communication in a graduate Seminar. *Canadian Journal of Learning and Technology*, *28*(2), 21–30.

Seliger, E., & Engstrom, T. (2007). On naturally embodied cyborgs: Identities, metaphors, and models. *Janus Head*, *9*(2), 553–584.

Senge, P. M. (1990). *The fifth discipline: The art and practice of the learning organization*. London, UK: Currency Doubleday.

Shaw, G., & Williams, A. (2009). Knowledge transfer and management in tourism organisations: An emerging research agenda. *Tourism Management, 30*, 325–335. doi:10.1016/j.tourman.2008.02.023

Shepherd, M. M., Martz, J., & Benjamin, W. M. (2001). Media richness theory and the distance education environment. *Journal of Computer Information Systems, 47*(1), 114–122.

Sherry, L. (1996). Issues in distance learning. *International Journal of Distance Education, 1*(4), 337–365.

Sherwin, A. (2006, April 3). A family of Welsh sheep - The new stars of Al-Jazeera. *Times (London, England)*, (n.d), 7.

Shimizu, H. (1995). *Ba*-principle: New logic for the real-time emergence of information. *Holonics, 5*(1), 67–79.

Short, J., Williams, E., & Christie, B. (1976). *The social psychology of telecommunications*. Toronto, Canada: Wiley.

Shumar, W., & Renninger, K. A. (2002). On conceptualizing community. In Renninger, K. A., & Shumar, W. (Eds.), *Building virtual communities: Learning and change in cyberspace* (pp. 1–20). Cambridge, UK: Cambridge University Press. doi:10.1017/CBO9780511606373.005

Shyamala, K., & Rajagopalan, S. P. (2006). Data mining model for a better higher educational system. *Information Technology Journal, 5*(3), 560–564. doi:10.3923/itj.2006.560.564

Silver, D. (2000). Looking backwards, looking forward: Cyberculture studies 1990-2000. In Gauntlett, D. (Ed.), *Web.Studies: Rewiring media studies for the digital age*. New York, NY: Oxford University Press.

Silverstone, R. (1990). From audiences to consumers: The household and the consumption of communication and information technologies. In Hay, J., Grossberg, L., & Wartella, E. (Eds.), *The audience and its landscapes* (pp. 281–296). Boulder, CO: Westview. doi:10.1177/026732319100600202

Simmons, L. L., & Clayton, R. W. (2010). The impact of small business B2B virtual community commitment on brand loyalty. *International Journal of Business and Systems Research, 4*(4), 451–468. doi:10.1504/IJBSR.2010.033423

Sittig, D. F., Wright, A., Simonaitisc, L., Carpenter, J. D., Allene, G. O., & Doebbeling, B. N. (2010). The state of the art in clinical knowledge management: An inventory of tools and techniques. *International Journal of Medical Informatics, 79*, 44–57. doi:10.1016/j.ijmedinf.2009.09.003

Skågeby, J. (2009b). Online friction: Studying sociotechnical conflicts to elicit user experience. *International Journal of Sociotechnology and Knowledge Development - Special Issue on New Sociotechnical Insights in Interaction Design, 1*(2), 62-74.

Skågeby, J., & Pargman, D. (2005). File-sharing relationships - Conflicts of interest in online gift-giving. *Proceedings of the Second International Conference on Communities and Technologies* (pp. 111-128). Milano, Italy: Springer.

Skågeby, J. (2004). Gifting technologies. *First Monday, 9*(12).

Skågeby, J. (2007). Analytical dimensions of online gift-giving: 'Other-oriented' contributions in virtual communities. *International Journal of Web-based Communities, 3*(1), 55–68. doi:10.1504/IJWBC.2007.013774

Skågeby, J. (2008). Semi-public end-user content contributions: A case study of concerns and intentions in online photo-sharing. *International Journal of Human-Computer Studies, 66*(4), 287–300. doi:10.1016/j.ijhcs.2007.10.010

Skågeby, J. (2009a). Exploring qualitative sharing practices of social metadata: Expanding the attention economy. *The Information Society, 25*(1), 60–72. doi:10.1080/01972240802587588

Smedlund, A. (2008). The knowledge system of a firm: Social capital for explicit, tacit and potential knowledge. *Journal of Knowledge Management, 12*(1), 63–77. doi:10.1108/13673270810852395

Smith, G. J. H. (1996). Building the lawyer-proof web site. Paper presented at the *Aslib Proceedings, 48,* (pp. 161-168).

Smith, M. A., & Kollock, P. (1999). *Communities in cyberspace*. London, UK: Routledge. doi:10.5117/9789056290818

Smith, M. L. (2006). Overcoming theory-practice inconsistencies: Critical realism and information systems research. *Information and Organization, 16*, 191–211. doi:10.1016/j.infoandorg.2005.10.003

Snyder, W. M., Wenger, E., & de Sousa Briggs, X. (2004). Communities of practice in government, leveraging knowledge for performance. *Public Management, 32*(4), 17–21.

Sohn, D., & Leckenby, J. D. (2007). A structural solution to communication dilemmas in a virtual community. *The Journal of Communication, 57*(3), 435–449. doi:10.1111/j.1460-2466.2007.00351.x

Soo, C. W., Midgley, D. F., & Devinney, T. (2000). *The process of knowledge creation in organizations*. INSEAD Working Paper, 2000/71/MKT.

Sousa, D. A. (2001). *How the brain learns: A classroom teacher's guide* (2nd ed.). Thousand Oaks, CA: Corwin Press, Inc., A Sage Publications Company.

Sowe, S. K., Stamelos, I., & Angelis, L. (2008). Understanding knowledge sharing activities in free/open source software projects: An empirical study. *Journal of Systems and Software, 81*, 431–446. doi:10.1016/j.jss.2007.03.086

Spears, R., & Lea, M. (1992). Social influence and the influence of the 'social' in computer-mediated communication. In Lea, M. (Ed.), *Contexts of computer-mediated communication* (pp. 30–65). New York, NY: Harvester Wheatsheaf.

Spender, I.-C. (2005). An overview: What's new and important about knowledge management? Building new bridges between managers and academics. In S. Little & T. Ray (Eds.), *Managing knowledge: An essential reader 2005*, 2nd ed., pp. 126-128. London, UK: Sage. Retrieved September 2, 2010, from http://www.jcspender.com/uploads/Spender_B823_Little___Ray_reader_Ch06.pdf

Splichal, S. (1999). *Public opinion*. Lanham, MD: Rowman & Littlefield.

Sproull, L., & Faraj, S. (1997). Atheism, sex, and databases: The net as a social technology. In Kiesler, S. (Ed.), *Culture of the Internet* (pp. 35–51).

Sproull, L., & Kiesler, S. (1986). Reducing social context cues: Electronic mail in organizational communication. *Management Science, 32*(11), 1492–1513. doi:10.1287/mnsc.32.11.1492

Sproull, L., & Kiesler, S. (1992). *Connections: New ways of working in the networked organization*. The MIT Press.

Squires, C. R. (2001). The black press and the state: Attracting unwanted(?) attention. In Asen, R., & Brouwer, D. C. (Eds.), *Counterpublics and the state* (pp. 111–136). Albany, NY: State University of New York Press.

Squires, C. R. (2002). Rethinking the black public sphere: An alternative vocabulary for multiple public spheres. *Communication Theory, 12*(4), 446–468. doi:10.1111/j.1468-2885.2002.tb00278.x

Stafford, T. F., Stafford, M. R., & Schkade, L. L. (2004). Determining uses and gratifications for the Internet. *Decision Sciences, 35*(2), 259–288. doi:10.1111/j.00117315.2004.02524.x

Stankosky, M. (2005). Advances in knowledge management: University research toward an academic disciplin. In *Creating the discipline of knowledge management*. Burlington, MA: Elsevier Inc.doi:10.1016/B978-0-7506-7878-0.50005-3

Steinfield, C., & Salvaggio, J. L. (1989). Toward a definition of the information society. In Salvaggio, J. L. (Ed.), *The information society: Economic, social and structural issues* (pp. 1–14). Hillsdale, NJ: Lawrence Erlbaum Associates.

Stein, R. F. (2004). Learning communities: An overview. In Hurd, S. N., & Stein, F. S. (Eds.), *Building and sustaining learning communities: The Syracuse University experience* (pp. 1–18). Boston, MA: Anker.

Stein, R. F., & Hurd, S. N. (2000). *Using student teams in the classroom: A faculty guide*. Boston, MA: Anker.

Sterne, J. (2006). The mp3 as cultural artifact. *New Media & Society, 8*(5), 825–842. doi:10.1177/1461444806067737

Stewart, T. A (1997). *Intellectual capital*. Doubleday/Currency.

Stewart, A. (1998). *The ethnographer's method*. Thousand Oaks, CA: Sage Publications.

Stoddart, L. (2007). Organizational culture and knowledge sharing at the United Nations: Using an intranet to create a sense of community. *Knowledge and Process Management, 14*(3), 182–189. doi:10.1002/kpm.283

Stone, A. R. (1995). *The war of desire and technology, at the close of the mechanical age.* Cambridge, MA: M.I.T. Press.

Straub, D., Gefen, D., & Boudreau, M.-C. (2004b). *The ISWorld quantitative, positivist research methods website,* (D. Galletta, Ed.). Retrieved from http://www.dstraub.cis.gsu.edu:88/quant/

Straub, D., Boudreau, M., & Gefen, D. (2004a). Validation guidelines for IS positivist research. *Communications of the Association for Information Systems, 13,* 380–427.

Studdert, D. (2005). *Conceptualizing community beyond the state and individual.* New York, NY: Palgrave/Macmillan.

Sum, S., Mathews, M., Pourghasem, M., & Hughes, I. (2009). Rapid communication: Internet use as a predictor of sense of community in older people. *Cyberpsychology & Behavior, 12*(2), 235–239. doi:10.1089/cpb.2008.0150

Sundar, S. S., Knobloch-Westerwick, S., & Hastall, M. R. (2007). News cues: Information scent and cognitive heuristics. *Journal of the American Society for Information Technology, 58,* 366–378. doi:10.1002/asi.20511

Sussman, S. W., & Siegal, W. S. (2003). Informational influence in organizations: An integrated approach to knowledge adoption. *Information Systems Research, 14,* 47–65. doi:10.1287/isre.14.1.47.14767

Sveiby, K. E. (1997). *The new organisational wealth.* Berret-Koehler Publishers, Inc.

Szulanski, G. (2003). *Sticky knowledge: Barriers to knowing in the firm.* SAGE Strategy Series.

Talamo, A., & Ligorio, B. (2001). Strategic identities in cyberspace. *Cyberpsychology & Behavior, 4*(1), 109–122. doi:10.1089/10949310151088479

Talavera, L., & Gaudioso, E. (2004). Mining student data to characterize similar behavior groups in unstructured collaboration spaces. *Workshop on Artificial Intelligence in Computer Supported Collaborative Learning at European Conference on Artificial Intelligence,* Valencia, Spain, (pp. 17-23).

Tallent-Runnels, M.-K. (2005). The relationship between problems with technology and graduate students' evaluations of online teaching. *The Internet and Higher Education, 8,* 167–174. doi:10.1016/j.iheduc.2005.03.005

Tang, F., Mu, J., & MacLachlan, D. L. (2008). Implications of network size and structure on organizations' knowledge transfer. *Expert Systems with Applications, 34,* 1109–1113. doi:10.1016/j.eswa.2006.12.020

Tapscott, D., & Williams, A. D. (2010). *Macrowikinomics: Rebooting business and the world.* Canada: Penguin Group.

Taxonomic Databases Working Group (TDWG). (2009). *Darwin Core.* Retrieved February 2, 2012, from http://rs.tdwg.org/dwc/

Taylor, S., & Todd, P. A. (1995). Understanding information technology usage: A test of competing models. *Information Systems Research, 6,* 144–176. doi:10.1287/isre.6.2.144

Tedjamulia, S., Olsen, D. R., Dean, D. L., & Albrecht, C. C. (2005). Motivating content contributions to online communities: Toward a more comprehensive theory. In J. F. Nunamaker, Jr. & R. O. Briggs (Eds.), *Proceedings of the 38th Hawaii International Conference on System Sciences – 2005,* 03-06 Jan. 2005.

Thelwall, M. (2008). Social networks, gender, and friending: An analysis of MySpace member profiles. *Journal of the American Society for Information Science and Technology, 59*(8), 1321–1330. doi:10.1002/asi.20835

Thoben, K., & Schwesig, M. (2002). *Meeting globally changing industry needs in engineering education.* ASEE/SEFI/TUB Colloquium, American Society for Engineering Education, Berlin, Germany. Retrieved from http://www.asee.org/conferences/international/papers/upload/Global-Education-in-Manufacturing.pdf

Tian, W., & Tan, F. B. (2009). *Guanxi, social capital and knowledge exchange: A cross-dimensional view*. Paper presented at the the 6th International Conference on Knowledge Management, Hong Kong, China.

Tillema, H. H. (2001). Portfolios as developmental assessment tools. *International Journal of Training and Development*, *5*(2), 126–135. doi:10.1111/1468-2419.00127

Timmerman, P., & Harrison, W. (2005). The discretionary use of electronic media. *Journal of Business Communication*, *42*(4), 379–389. doi:10.1177/0021943605279059

Timm, P. (1976). The bulletin board: Economy and effectiveness in organizational communication. *Journal of Business Communication*, *13*(2), 37–44. doi:10.1177/002194367601300205

Tinto, V. (1997, November/December). Classrooms as communities: Exploring the educational character of student persistence. *The Journal of Higher Education*, *68*(6), 599–623. doi:10.2307/2959965

Tiwana, A., & Bush, A. A. (2005). Continuance in expertise-sharing networks: A social perspective. *IEEE Transactions on Engineering Management*, *52*(1), 85–101. doi:10.1109/TEM.2004.839956

Toffler, A. (1980). *The third wave*. New York, NY: Bantam.

Tomek, J. (2001). Knowledge management and collaborative virtual environments. *Journal of Universal Computer Science*, *7*(6), 458–471.

Tönnies, F. (1957). *Community and society (Gemeinschaft und Gesellschaft)* (Loomis, C. P. (Trans. Ed.)). East Lansing, MI: Michigan State University Press. (Original work published 1887)

Torrey, C., Burke, M., Lee, M., Dey, A., Fussell, S., & Kiesler, S. (2007). *Connected giving: Ordinary people coordinating disaster relief on the Internet. HICSS 07* (*Vol. 40*, p. 2956). IEEE.

Trochim, W. M. (2006a). *The research methods knowledge base*, 2nd ed. Retrieved September 19, 2011, from http://www.socialresearchmethods.net/kb/statdesc.php

Trochim, W. M. (2006b). The research methods knowledge base, 2nd ed. Retrieved September 9, 2011, from http://www.socialresearchmethods.net/kb/statinf.php

Tseng, F.-C., & Kuo, F.-Y. (2010). The way we share and learn: An exploratory study of the self-regulatory mechanisms in the professional online learning community. *Computers in Human Behavior*, *26*(5), 1043–1053. doi:10.1016/j.chb.2010.03.005

Turban, E., Lee, J., King, D., & Chung, H. M. (2004). *E-commerce – A managerial perspective* (3rd ed.). Prentice-Hall, Inc.

Turkle, S. (1995). *Life on screen: Identity in the age of the internet*. New York, NY: Simon and Schuster.

Turner, J. W., Grube, J. A., & Meyers, J. (2001). Developing an optimal match within online communities: An exploration of CMC support communities and traditional support. *The Journal of Communication*, *51*(2), 231–251. doi:10.1111/j.1460-2466.2001.tb02879.x

Tussman, J. (1969). *Experiment at Berkeley*. London, UK: Oxford University Press.

Tyndale, P. (2002). A taxonomy of knowledge management software tools: Origins and applications. *Evaluation and Program Planning*, *25*, 183–190. doi:10.1016/S0149-7189(02)00012-5

US LTER. (n.d.). *About LTER*. Retrieved February 2, 2012, from http://www.lternet.edu/overview/

Usoro, A., Sharratt, M. W., Tsui, E., & Shekhar, S. (2007). Trust as an antecedent to knowledge sharing in virtual communities of practice. *Knowledge Management Research & Practice*, *5*, 199–212. doi:10.1057/palgrave.kmrp.8500143

Vaast, E. (2007). What goes online comes offline: Knowledge management system use in a soft bureaucracy. *Organization Studies*, *28*(3), 283–306. doi:10.1177/0170840607075997

Vaast, E., & Walsham, G. (2005). Representations and actions: The transformation of work practices with IT use. *Information and Organization*, *15*(1), 65–89. doi:10.1016/j.infoandorg.2004.10.001

Vaccaro, A., Parente, R., & Veloso, F. M. (2010). Knowledge management tools, inter-organizational relationships, innovation and firms performance. *Technological Forecasting and Social Change*, *77*, 1076–1089. doi:10.1016/j.techfore.2010.02.006

Van den Hooff, B., & Huysman, M. (2009). Managing knowledge sharing: Emergent and engineering perspectives. *Information & Management, 46*(1), 1–8. doi:10.1016/j.im.2008.09.002

Van Dijk, J. (1999). *The network society: Social aspects of new media.* Thousand Oaks, CA: Sage Publications.

Van Dijk, J. (2009). Users like you? Theorizing agency in user-generated content. *Media Culture & Society, 31*(1), 41–58. doi:10.1177/0163443708098245

Van Velsen, L., & Melenhorst, M. (2009). Incorporating user motivations to design for video tagging. *Interacting with Computers, 21*(3), 221–232. doi:10.1016/j.intcom.2009.05.002

Varman, R., & Costa, J. A. (2008). Embedded markets, communities, and the invisible hands of social norms. *Journal of Macromarketing, 28*(2), 141–156. doi:10.1177/0276146708314594

Vat, K. H. (2000). Training E-commerce support personnel for enterprises through action learning. In *Proceedings of the 2000 ACM SIGCPR Conference* (pp. 39-43). April 6-8, Chicago, Illinois, USA.

Vat, K. H. (2009a). Developing REALSpace: Discourse on a student-centered creative knowledge environment for virtual communities of learning. *International Journal of Virtual Communities and Social Networking, 1*(1), 43–74. doi:10.4018/jvcsn.2009010105

Vat, K. H. (2009b). The generative potential of appreciative inquiry for CoP: The virtual enterprise's emergent knowledge model. In Akoumianakis, D. (Ed.), *Virtual community practices and social interactive media: Technology lifecycle and workflow analysis* (pp. 60–85). Hershey, PA: Information Science Reference. doi:10.4018/978-1-60566-340-1.ch004

Vat, K. H. (2010). Virtual organizing professional learning communities through a servant-leader model of appreciative coaching. In Inoue, Y. (Ed.), *Cases on online and blended learning technologies in higher education: Concepts and practices* (pp. 183–206). Hershey, PA: Information Science Reference.

Venkatesh, V., & Davis, F. D. (2000). A theoretical extension of the technology acceptance model: Four longitudinal field studies. *Management Science, 46*, 186–204. doi:10.1287/mnsc.46.2.186.11926

Venkatesh, V., Morris, M. G., Davis, G. B., & Davis, F. D. (2003). User acceptance of information technology: Toward a unified view. *Management Information Systems Quarterly, 27*(3), 425–478.

Venkatraman, N., & Henderson, J. C. (1998). Real strategies for virtual organizing. *Sloan Management Review, 40*(1), 33–48.

Virilio, P. (2007). *The original accident.* Malden, MA: Polity.

von Bertalanffy, L. (1968). *General system theory: Foundations, development, applications.* New York, NY: G. Braziller.

Vovides, Y., Sanchez-Alonso, S., Mitropoulou, V., & Nickmans, G. (2007). The use of e-learning course management systems to support learning strategies and to improve self-regulated learning. *Educational Research Review, 2*(1), 64–74. doi:10.1016/j.edurev.2007.02.004

Vygostsky, L.S. (1978). *Mind in society: The development of higher psychological processes.* Cambridge, MA: Harvard University Press.

Vygotsky, L. S. (1930). *Mind in society.* Cambridge, MA: Waiton, S. (2009). Policing after the crisis: Crime, safety and the vulnerable public. *Punishment and Society, 11*(3), 359.

Vygotsky, L. S. (1978). *Mind in society.* Cambridge, MA: Harvard University Press.

Wade, R. C., & Yarbrough, D. B. (1996). Portfolios: A tool for reflective thinking in teacher education. *Teaching and Teacher Education, 12*, 63–79. doi:10.1016/0742-051X(95)00022-C

Waiyamai, K. (2004). *Improving quality of graduate students by data mining.* Faculty of Engineering, Kasetsart University, Frontiers of ICT Research International Symposium.

Wakao, A. (2007). *Nikon eyes double-digit growth in compact digicams*. Retrieved March 24, 2008, from http://www.reuters.com/articlePrint?articleId=UST KU00283620070220

Wallace, P. (1999). *The psychology of Internet*. Cambridge, UK: Cambridge University Press.

Wallace, R. M. (2003). Online learning in higher education: A review of research on interactions among teachers and students. *Education Communication and Information*, *3*(2), 241. doi:10.1080/14636310303143

Walsham, G. (1995). Interpretive case studies in IS research: Nature and method. *European Journal of Information Systems*, *4*, 74–81. doi:10.1057/ejis.1995.9

Walther, J. B. (1992). Interpersonal effects in computer-mediated interaction: A relational perspective. *Communication Research*, *19*(1), 52–90. doi:10.1177/009365092019001003

Walther, J. B. (1997). Group and interpersonal effects in international computer-mediated collaboration. *Human Communication Research*, *23*(3), 342–369. doi:10.1111/j.1468-2958.1997.tb00400.x

Walther, J. B., & Burgoon, J. K. (1990). Relational communication in computer-mediated interaction. *Human Communication Research*, *19*, 50–80. doi:10.1111/j.1468-2958.1992.tb00295.x

Walther, J.; & Borgoon, J. (1992). Relational communication in computer-mediated interaction. *Human Communication Research*, *19*(1), 50–88. doi:10.1111/j.1468-2958.1992. tb00295.x

Waltzer, K. (1992, Fall). Mad about Madison. *MSU Alumni Magazine*.

Wang, X. (2007). *An ecological perspective on online communities*. Ph.D. Dissertation, University of Pittsburgh.

Wang, X., Butler, B., & Ren, Y. (2011). *The impact of membership overlap on growth: An ecological competition view of online groups* (pp. 1-36).

Wang, J. C., & Chiang, M. J. (2009). Social interaction and continuance intention in online auctions: A social capital perspective. *Decision Support Systems*, *47*(4), 466–476. doi:10.1016/j.dss.2009.04.013

Ward, J. (2006). *The student's guide to cognitive neuroscience*. Psychology Press - Taylor & Francis Group.

Warren, J. T. (2006). Introduction: Performance ethnography: A TPQ symposium. *Text and Performance Quarterly*, *26*(4), 317–319. doi:10.1080/10462930600828667

Wasko, M. M., & Faraj, S. (2000). "It is what one does": Why people participate and help others in electronic communities of practice. *The Journal of Strategic Information Systems*, *9*(2-3), 155–173. doi:10.1016/S0963-8687(00)00045-7

Wasko, M. M., & Faraj, S. (2005). Why should I share? Examining social capital and knowledge contribution in electronic networks of practice. *Management Information Systems Quarterly*, *29*, 35–57.

Wasko, M. M., Faraj, S., & Teigland, R. (2004). Collective action and knowledge contribution in electronic networks of practice. *Journal of the Association for Information Systems*, *5*(11-12), 493–513.

Wasko, M., & Faraj, S. (2000). It is what one does: why people participate and help others in electronic communities of practice. *The Journal of Strategic Information Systems*, *9*(2-3), 155–173. doi:10.1016/S0963-8687(00)00045-7

Wasko, M., & Faraj, S. (2005). Why should I share? Examining social capital and knowledge contribution in electronic networks of practice. *Management Information Systems Quarterly*, *29*(1), 35–57.

Waterman, A. S. (2004). Finding someone to be: Studies on the role of intrinsic motivation in identity formation. *Identity: An International Journal of Theory and Research*, *4*(3), 209–228. doi:10.1207/s1532706xid0403_1

Waterson, P. (2006). Motivation in online communities. In Dasgupta, S. (Ed.), *Encyclopedia of virtual communties* (pp. 334–337). Hershey, PA: Idea Group. doi:10.4018/978-1-59140-563-4.ch062

Watson-Manheim, M. B., & Bélanger, F. (2007). Communication media repertoires: Dealing with the multiplicity of media choices. *Management Information Systems Quarterly*, *31*(2), 267–293.

Watson, N. (1997). Why we argue about virtual community: A case study of the phish.net fan community. In Jones, S. G. (Ed.), *Virtual culture: Identity and communication in cybersociety* (pp. 102–132). Thousand Oaks, CA: Sage.

Watt, S. E., Lea, M., & Spears, R. (2002). How social is internet communication? A reappraisal of bandwidth and anonymity effects. In Woolgar, S. (Ed.), *Virtual society? Technology cyberbole, reality* (pp. 61–77). Oxford, UK: Oxford University Press.

Weaver, M. (2007). Contextual metadata: faceted schemas in virtual library communities. *Library Hi Tech, 25*(4), 579–594. doi:10.1108/07378830710840527

Webster, F. (1995). *Theories of the information society.* London, UK: Routledge.

Weiler, J. H. H. (2002). A constitution for Europe? Some hard choices. *Journal of Common Market Studies, 40*(4), 563–580. doi:10.1111/1468-5965.00388

Wellman, B., Quan-Haase, A., Boase, J., Chen, W., Hampton, K., de-Diaz, I., & Miyata, K. (2003). The social affordances of the Internet for networked individualism. *Journal of Computer-Mediated Communication, 8*(3). Retrieved March 15, 2007, from http://jcmc.indiana.edu/vol8/issue3/wellman.html

Wellman, B. (1979). The community question: The intimate networks of East Yorkers. *American Journal of Sociology, 84*(5), 1201–1231. doi:10.1086/226906

Wellman, B. (1997). An electronic group is virtually a social network. In Kiesler, S. (Ed.), *Culture of the Internet* (pp. 179–205). Mahwah, NJ: Lawrence Erlbaum Associates.

Wellman, B. (1999). The network community: An introduction. In Wellman, B. (Ed.), *Networks in the global village: Life in contemporary communities* (pp. 1–48). Boulder, CO: Westview Press.

Wellman, B. (2002). Little boxes, glocalization, and networked individualism. In Tanabe, M., van den Besselaar, P., & Ishida, T. (Eds.), *Digital cities II: Computational and sociological approaches* (pp. 10–25). Berlin, Germany: Springer. doi:10.1007/3-540-45636-8_2

Wellman, B., & Gulia, M. (1999). *Net*-surfers don't ride alone: Virtual communities as communities. In Wellman, B. (Ed.), *Networks in the global village* (pp. 331–366). Boulder, CO: Westview Press.

Wellman, B., & Gulia, M. (1999). Virtual communities as communities. Net surfers don't ride alone. In Smith, M. A., & Kollock, P. (Eds.), *Communities in cyberspace.* London, UK: Routledge.

Wellman, B., & Haythornthwaite, C. (2002). *The Internet in everyday life.* Oxford, UK: Blackwell. doi:10.1002/9780470774298

Wenger, E. (1998). *Communities of practice.* New York, NY: Cambridge University Press.

Wenger, E., McDermott, R. A., & Snyder, W. (2002). *Cultivating communities of practice: A guide to managing knowledge.* Boston, MA: Harvard Business Press.

Wiggins, G. (1993). *Assessing student performance: Exploring the purposes and limits of testing.* San Francisco, CA: Jossey-Bass.

Wiig, K. M., De Hoog, R., & Van Der Spek, R. (1997). Supporting knowledge management: A selection of methods and techniques. *Expert Systems with Applications, 13*(1), 15–27. doi:10.1016/S0957-4174(97)00019-5

Wilbur, S. P. (2000). An archaeology of cyberspaces. Virtuality, community, identity. In Bell, D., & Kennedy, B. M. (Eds.), *The cybercultures reader* (pp. 45–55). London, UK: Routledge.

Wilczynski, V., & Jennings, J. (2003). Creating virtual teams for engineering design. *International Journal of Engineering Education, 19*(2), 316–327.

Wilkinson, G. (2006). Commercial breaks: An overview of corporate opportunities for commercializing education in US and English schools. *London Review of Education, 4*(3), 253–269. doi:10.1080/14748460601043932

Willem, A., & Buelens, M. (2009). Knowledge sharing in inter-unit cooperative episodes: The impact of organizational structure dimensions. *International Journal of Information Management, 29*, 151–160. doi:10.1016/j.ijinfomgt.2008.06.004

Williams, R., & Pollock, N. (2009). Beyond the ERP implementation study: A new approach to the study of packaged information systems: The biography of artifacts framework. In *Proceedings of the Thirtieth International Conference on Information Systems* 2009.

Williams, B. T. (2008). "Tomorrow will not be like today": Literacy and identity in a world of multiliteracies. *Journal of Adolescent & Adult Literacy, 51*(8), 682–686. doi:10.1598/JAAL.51.8.7

Williams, P. W. (2009). *Assessing mobile learning effectiveness and acceptance*. US: ProQuest Information & Learning.

Williams, R. (1975). *Television: Technology and cultural form*. New York, NY: Schocken. doi:10.4324/9780203450277

Wilson, A. (2007). Toward releasing the metadata bottleneck: A baseline evaluation of contributor-supplied metadata. *Library Resources & Technical Services, 51*(1), 16–28.

Winarnita, M. S. (2008). Motherhood as cultural citizenship: Indonesian women in transnational families. *The Asia Pacific Journal of Anthropology, 9*(4), 304–318. doi:10.1080/14442210802506412

Winner, L. (1977). *Autonomous technology: Technics-out-of-control as a theme in political thought*. Cambridge, MA: MIT Press.

Wirth, L. (1938). Urbanism as a way of life. *American Journal of Sociology, 44*, 1–24. doi:10.1086/217913

Witten, I., & Frank, E. (2005). *Data mining: Practical machine learning tools and techniques*. Elsevier.

Woerner, S. L., Orlikowski, W. J., & Yates, J. (2004). The media toolbox: Combining media in organizational communication. *Proceedings of the Academy of Management*, Orlando FL.

Wolf, D., Bixby, J., Glenn, J., & Gardner, H. (1991). To use their minds well. In G. Grant (Ed.), *Review of Research in Education, 17*, 31-74. Washington, DC: AERA.

Wolf, P. (2003). Interview with Etienne Wenger on communities of practice. Retrieved October 27, 2010, from http://www.knowledgeboard.com/cgi-bin/item.cgi?id=458

Woodfill, W. (2009, October 1). The transporters: Discover the world of emotions. *School Library Journal Reviews, 59*.

Woodsworth, J. S. (1911). *My neighbor*. Toronto, Canada: University of Toronto Press.

Wu, J.-H., & Wang, Y.-M. (2006). Measuring KMS success: A respecification of the DeLone and McLean's model. *Information & Management, 43*, 728–739. doi:10.1016/j.im.2006.05.002

Xenos, M., & Foot, K. (2005). Politics as usual, or politics unusual: Position-taking and dialogue on campaign web sites in the 2002 U.S. elections. *The Journal of Communication, 55*(1), 169–185. doi:10.1111/j.1460-2466.2005.tb02665.x

Xiao, B., & Benbasat, I. (2007). E-commerce product recommendation agents: Use, characteristics, and impact. *Management Information Systems Quarterly, 31*(1), 137–209.

Xiao, Y., Du, X., Zhang, J., Hu, F., & Guizani, S. (2007). Internet protocol television (IPTV): The killer application for the next-generation Internet. *IEEE Communications Magazine, 45*(11), 126–134. doi:10.1109/MCOM.2007.4378332

Xu, Y., Tan, C. Y., & Yang, L. (2006). Who will you ask? An empirical study of interpersonal task information seeking. *Journal of the American Society for Information Science and Technology, 57*, 1666–1677. doi:10.1002/asi.20339

Yang, G. (2009). *The power of the Internet in China: Citizen activism online*. New York, NY: Columbia University Press.

Yang, S.-C., & Farn, C.-K. (2009). Social capital, behavioural control, and tacit knowledge sharing – A multi-informant design. *International Journal of Information Management, 29*, 210–218. doi:10.1016/j.ijinfomgt.2008.09.002

Yeh, C. (2010). Analyzing online behaviors, roles, and learning communities via online discussions. *Journal of Educational Technology & Society, 13*(1), 140–151.

Yen, H. R., Hsu, S. H.-Y., & Chun-Yao, H. (2011). Good soldiers on the Web: Understanding the drivers of participation in online communities of consumption. *International Journal of Electronic Commerce, 15*(4), 89–120. doi:10.2753/JEC1086-4415150403

Yeow, A., & Faraj, S. (2011). Using narrative networks to study enterprise systems and organizational change. *International Journal of Accounting Information Systems, 12*(2), 116–125. doi:10.1016/j.accinf.2010.12.005

Yimam-Seid, D., & Kobsa, A. (2003). Expert-finding systems for organizations: Problem and domain analysis and the DEMOIR approach. *Journal of Organizational Computing and Electronic Commerce, 13*(1), 1–24. doi:10.1207/S15327744JOCE1301_1

Yin, R. (1994). *Case study research: Design and methods* (2nd ed.). Thousand Oaks, CA: Sage Publications.

Young, A., & Norgard, C. (2006). Assessing the quality of online courses from the students' perspective. *The Internet and Higher Education, 9*, 107–115. doi:10.1016/j.iheduc.2006.03.001

Yountz, B. (1984). The Evergreen State College: An experiment maturing. In Jones, R. M., & Smith, B. L. (Eds.), *Against the current: Reform and experimentation in higher education* (pp. 93–118). Cambridge, MA: Schenkman.

Yu, G. (2010). *Annual report on public opinion in China (2010)*. Beijing, China: People Daily Press.

Yukawa, J. (2005). Story-lines: A case study of online learning using narrative analysis. *Proceedings of the 2005 Conference on Computer Support for Collaborative Learning: Learning 2005: The Next 10 Years!* (p. 736).

Zack, M. H. (1993). Interactivity and communication mode choice in ongoing management groups. *Information Systems Research, 4*(3), 207–238. doi:10.1287/isre.4.3.207

Zapalska, A., Shao, D., & Shao, L. (2003). *Student learning via WebCT course instruction in undergraduate-based business education. Teaching Online in Higher Education (Online)*. Conference.

Zhang, W., & Watts, S. (2003). Knowledge adoption in online communities of practice. *2003 Twenty-Fourth International Conference on Information Systems* (pp. 96-109).

Zhang, Y., & Hiltz, S. R. (2003). Factors that influence online relationship development in a knowledge sharing community. In *Proceedings of the Ninth American Conference on Information Systems*, (pp. 410 – 417).

Zhang, P., & Li, N. (2004). An assessment of human-computer interaction research in management information systems: Topics and methods. *Computers in Human Behavior, 20*, 125–147. doi:10.1016/j.chb.2003.10.011

Zhang, P., Ma, X., Pan, Z., Li, X., & Xie, K. (2010). Multi-agent cooperative reinforcement learning in 3D virtual world. In *Advances in swarm intelligence* (pp. 731–739). London, UK: Springer. doi:10.1007/978-3-642-13495-1_90

Zhang, W. (2006). Constructing and disseminating subaltern public discourses in China. *Javnost-The Public, 13*(2), 41–64.

Zhang, W., & Watts, S. (2008). Online communities as communities of practice: A case study. *Journal of Knowledge Management, 12*(4), 55–71. doi:10.1108/13673270810884255

Zhao, Y. (2008). *Communication in China: Political economy, power, and conflict*. Lanham, MD: Rowman & Littlefield.

Zhou, T. (2011). Understanding online community user participation: A social influence perspective. *Internet Research, 21*(1), 67–81. doi:10.1108/10662241111104884

Zimmerman, A. (2007). Not by metadata alone: The use of diverse forms of knowledge to locate data for reuse. *International Journal on Digital Libraries, 7*(2), 5–16. doi:10.1007/s00799-007-0015-8

Zollers, A. (2007). *Emerging motivations for tagging: Expression, performance, and activism*. WWW 2007.

Zwick, D., Bonsu, S., & Darmody, A. (2008). Putting consumers to work: Co-creation and new marketing governmentality. *Journal of Consumer Culture, 8*(2), 163–196. doi:10.1177/1469540508090089

About the Contributors

Honglei Li is currently a senior lecturer in Enterprise Information Systems at School of Computing, Engineering, and Information Sciences, Northumbria University. Before joining Northumbria University, she worked as a lecturer in Information Systems at School of Business & Economics, Swansea University, United Kingdom. She received her BS and M.Phil. in Computational Mathematics and Management Information Systems, respectively, from Nanjing University in China. Later she received her PhD in Management Information Systems from The Chinese University of Hong Kong. Her current research interests include virtual communities, virtual worlds, electronic business, business process management, and information systems project management. Being in the field of information systems for many years, she is especially enthusiastic about virtual communities and virtual worlds but keeps a very keen interest in enterprise systems analysis and development. Her research papers have been published in academic journals such as *Information & Management, Journal of the American Society for Information Science and Technology,* and *International Journal of Electronic Business.* She has also presented her research papers in many international conferences including the American Conference on Information Systems and the International Conference on Information Systems.

* * *

Jonathan Bishop is a leading researcher in increasing participation in online communities. Regarded as one of 'Britain's foremost exporters of online community and e-learning research to the USA and Mainland Europe', he has over 20 publications in the field and a number of innovative technologies that have reached national finals in innovation competitions. Jonathan is the Principal Chair of the Centre for Research into Online Communities and E-Learning Systems, heading up its Information Technology, Arts, Law and Science Group. Since 2008 he has developed a range of expertise on Internet trolling specifically, founding the Trolling Academy in 2011. By mid-2012 he had written over 12 letters and Op-Eds, and quoted in 8 different news media outlets on the subject. His seminal research paper on 'Increasing participation in online communities' has received huge accolades. Being cited over 100 times, it is one of the most cited papers in its journal, being rated as one of the Top 8 posts about online communities and ranked as one of the Top 25 articles in computer science in 2007 when it was first published.

Constanţa-Nicoleta Bodea is a professor at the Academy of Economic Study Bucharest (ASE), Faculty of Cybernetics, Statistics and Economic Informatics, Economic Informatics Department. Currently, she teaches Artificial Intelligence, Data Mining, and Project Management. She coordinates numerous research projects at the national level and achieved a high expertise in managing projects with multiple consortia.

She is author of 11 books and more than 50 papers on Project Management, Information Systems, and Artificial Intelligence, being honored by IPMA with the Outstanding Research Contributions in 2007.

Vasile Bodea holds a PhD Diploma, obtained at the Academy of Economic Study Bucharest (ASE), in 2008. He is the author of several books and papers in the field of project management and knowledge management, a member in numerous research projects and also a member of International Project Management Association and PM Forum, a research center in ASE.

Lyn Brodie is an Associate Professor in the Faculty of Engineering and Surveying. Her research interests include engineering education, Problem Based Learning, assessment and the first year experience. She is a board and founding member of the USQ Teaching Academy and Director of the Faculty Engineering Education Research Group. Lyn was the academic team leader for the teaching team which successfully designed a strand of PBL courses for the faculty. Her work has been recognised through several awards including a University Award for Design and Delivery of Teaching Materials, Carrick Institute Citation and Australian University Teaching Award for Innovation in Curricula Learning and Teaching, USQ Associate Learning and Teaching Fellowships for curriculum and assessment development and recognition from the Australian Association of Engineering Educators for innovation in curricula. On several occasions Lyn has been a visiting Associate Professor to the University of Hong Kong consulting in both PBL and online curriculum development and assessment.

Christy M. K. Cheung is Associate Professor at Hong Kong Baptist University. She received her Ph.D. from City University of Hong Kong. Her research interests include virtual community, knowledge management, social computing technology, and IT adoption and usage. Her research articles have been published in MIS Quarterly, Decision Support Systems, Information & Management, Journal of the American Society for Information Science and Technology, and Information Systems Frontiers. Christy received the Best Paper Award at the 2003 International Conference on Information Systems and was the PhD fellow of 2004 ICIS Doctoral Consortium. She also serves on the editorial board of several research journals in the field.

Andrew Cox is a Lecturer at the Information School of The University of Sheffield, and holds the Direction of Learning and Teaching of this department. His main interests are in online community and use of social media, be that on the open web, in organisations (including communities of practice) and in learning contexts. He is interested in the intersection of information and media/cultural studies paradigms. Most of his research uses qualitative methods.

Joana Sócrates Dantas received the degree in Business Mangement from the University of São Paulo, Brazil in 1996, and her MA in Digital Media from London Metroplitan University, England in 2003. From 1998 to 2003 she has worked as head of Visual Communication Department at Rede Globo Broadcasting Co., Paraná, Brazil and as Web Designer at BBC World Service in England. She has also partipated and worked as producer and designer for Interactive TV and IPTV projects at different production companies in London between 2003 and 2005. Currently she is pursuing her PhD diploma in Computer Engineering at the University of São Paulo and the University of Catalunya.

Maria-Iuliana Dascălu has a Master's Degree in Project Management from the Academy of Economic Studies, Bucharest, Romania (2008) and a Bachelor's Degree in Computer Science from the Alexandru-Ioan Cuza University, Iasi, Romania (2006). She obtained a PhD diploma in Economic Informatics at the Academy of Economic Studies (July 2011), after combining her work experience as a programmer with numerous research activities. Her research relates to computer-assisted testing with applications in e-learning environments for project management, competences development systems and their benefits to adult education. Maria Dascălu is a Certified Project Management Associate (2008). She also conducted a research stage at the University of Gothenburg, Sweden, from October 2009 to May 2010. Currently, she works as a teaching assistant at the Politehnica University of Bucharest, Department of Engineering Taught in Foreign Languages.

Peter Gibbings is an Associate Professor and the Associate Dean (Learning and Teaching) in the Faculty of Engineering and Surveying at the University of Southern Queensland. His professional background is in land surveying and his key research interests include problem-based learning, remote access laboratories, and engineering education. His academic achievements have been recognised by receiving a University Medal in 2003 for excellence in design and delivery of problem-based learning. In 2005, he received a national award from the Australasian Association for Engineering Education for excellence in engineering education. In the same year, he was a finalist in the Australian Awards for University Teaching. In 2006, he won a Citation for Outstanding Contributions to Student Learning Carrick Australian Awards for University Teaching and was runner up in the Pearson Education UniServe Science Teaching Award. In 2007, he won the Carrick Australian University Teaching Award for Programs that Enhance Learning. In 2008, he won the individual Queensland Spatial Excellence Award for Education and Professional Development, and in the same year, he went on to win the individual Asia Pacific Spatial Excellence Award for Education and Professional Development.

Gibran Rivera Gonzalez is a PhD student at the Information School of The University of Sheffield. His research focuses on online communities within organizational settings. He is particularly interested in looking at how Information Technologies are adopted in organizations to support their working practices. He is finishing his PhD studies by mid 2012 in which he is currently using Practice Theories and Actor-Network Theory to understand participation in a HR professional online community.

Xiao-Ling Jin is currently an Assistant Professor in the Management School of Shanghai University. She obtained her PhD degree in information systems and electronic commerce from a joint program of City University of Hong Kong and University of Science and Technology of China in August 2009. Her research interests mainly focus on consumer behavior including online shopping and information exchange in new digital social media, virtual community, and IT adoption and usage. She has published several papers in international journals and conferences, such as Journal of Management Information Systems, Computer in Human Behavior, Behaviour and Information Technology, International Journal of Information Management, ECIS, and HICSS, etc.

Luiz Antonio Joia is an Associate Professor and Principal of the *e:lab* – Research Laboratory on e-Government and e-Business at the Brazilian School of Public and Business Administration at Getulio Vargas Foundation. He is also an Adjunct Professor at Rio de Janeiro State University. He holds a B.Sc.

in Civil Engineering from the Military Institute of Engineering, Brazil, and a M.Sc. in Civil Engineering and a D.Sc. in Production Engineering from the Federal University of Rio de Janeiro. He also holds an M.Sc. in Management Studies from the Oxford University, U.K. He was a World Bank consultant in Educational Technology and is an invited member of the Technical Board of the Working Group WG 8.5 (Informatics in the Public Administration) of the IFIP (International Federation for Information Processing). His research interests lie on IT for Development, Information Systems Resistance, e-Government, e-Business, e-Learning, Strategic Use of IT, Intellectual Capital, and Actor-Network Theory.

Matthew K. O. Lee is a Chair Professor of Information Systems & E-Commerce at the College of Business, City University of Hong Kong. He holds a PhD degree from the University of Manchester in the UK and he is a qualified Barrister-at-Law, a Chartered Engineer (UK Engineering Council), and a professional member of the British Computer Society. Professor Lee has a research and professional interest in IT based innovation adoption and diffusion (focusing on systems implementation management issues), knowledge management, social computing, electronic commerce, and legal informatics. Professor Lee's publications in the information systems and electronic commerce areas include a book as well as over one hundred refereed articles in international journals, conference proceedings, and research textbooks. His work has appeared in leading journals such as MIS Quarterly, Journal of Management Information Systems, Communications of the ACM, and the Journal of International Business Studies.

Ben Li studies information infrastructures as a doctoral student at the University of Oulu, Finland. Ben has previously examined innovation in city regions as a Research Associate at the University of Calgary, Canada. He has also developed and implemented ways to engage online and offline stakeholders on international issues as a Policy and Communication Analyst at the Legislative Assembly of Alberta. Ben holds degrees in biology, political science and open source innovation.

Jonathan Paul Marshall is an anthropologist who is an Australian Research Council supported QEII fellow at the University of Technology Sydney. He is working on a project about the disorder created by computer software in the workplace and the information society generally. A co-authored book called *Disorder and the Disinformation Society: The social dynamics of networks and software,* summarising some of this research, is forthcoming from Routledge. He has previously carried out ethnographic fieldwork on the internet Mailing List Cybermind and his PhD thesis was published as *Living on Cybermind: categories, communication and control* (Peter Lang 2007). He also has edited a special issue of the Transforming Cultures Ejournal about the uses of gender on Cybermind – *the Cybermind Gender Project.* Current work also engages with the psychology of climate change, and he edited *Depth Psychology, Disorder and Climate Change* (JungDownunder books 2009).

Radu-Ioan Mogo□ obtained his PhD diploma at the Academy of Economic Studies, the Faculty of Cybernetics, Statistics and Economic IT, in July 2011. He is working as an IT analyst at the IT Department. He is a member of the Romania Project Management Association. His research domains include artificial intelligence and project management. He is the author of one book and he is project member in several research projects.

Ion Gh. Ro□ca is a university professor within the Bucharest Academy of Economic Studies. He holds a PhD in sciences, specialization Economic Calculation and Economic Cybernetics from the same institution. He has a long experience in books, manuals, articles, essays, studies' writing in the area of economics, informational societies, electronic business, new educations forms, systems' security, projects management, GRID systems, qualitative and quantitative research methods. He is also author of many articles, essays and published papers. He has occupied prestigious positions both academic and administrative. He received numerous scientific rewards and distinctions, such as the prize for "Best manual in the field of applicative economic sciences" for "Electronic Trade, Concepts, Technologies and Applications", from Economica Publishing House. In 2004, he was given by General association of Economists in Romania the Georgescu Roegen Diploma, Academy of Economic Studies of Bucharest, for the scientific research activity in years 1999, 2000, 2001, 2002, 2003, 2004. He was also a nominee in the Experts Catalogue, published by Academic Society in Romania, First Edition, 1997, pg. 130. He also wan a Romanian Academy Prize, for book the book *Informatics (Informatica)*.

Sergey Rybas teaches rhetoric and professional writing at Capital University in Columbus, Ohio. His research areas include power, subjectivity, and identity issues in computer-mediated communication; performances of online community; multimodal teaching and learning; and epistemologies of the information age. He has also been involved in projects exploring politics, practices, and performances of nationality and nationalism and has specifically focused on issues of national identification and difference in Eastern Europe and the former USSR. Seeing the application of his research to a broad spectrum of disciplines in humanities and social sciences, he advocates critical cultural literacy as a primary goal of an interdisciplinary and intercultural dialogue on problems related to production, dissemination, and interpretation of knowledge.

Regina Melo Silveira is an Assistant Professor at Escola Politecnica of University of Sao Paulo. Her research and teaching interests include computer networks, Internet information systems, multimedia applications for high speed networks, transmission, management, Quality of Service (QoS), Quality of Experience and metadata of digital medias. She participated on Poli-Virtual Projects, Multimedia System under Demand, RMAV-SP (Internet 2 of São Paulo), GTGV, Tidia-Ae, KyaTera and Brazilian System of Digital TV (SBTVD) in partnership with researchers from other research institutions. Prof. Silveira received her B.S. in Physics from the Pontificia Universidade Catolica de São Paulo (1988) and M.S. in Experimental Physics from the Institute of Physics of University of São Paulo (1994). She received her Doctorate degree in Computer Engineering from Escola Politecnica of University of Sao Paulo (2000).

Jörgen Skågeby is a Research Fellow at the Department of Media Studies, Stockholm University. He researches the social practices that emerge with increasing everyday use of interactive media platforms. The dissertation 'Gifting Technologies – ethnographic studies of end-users and social media sharing' examines the applicability of gifting concepts to digital sharing milieus. His research has been published in several renowned international journals including Journal of Information Technology, The Information Society and The International Journal of Human-Computer Studies.

Robert N. Spicer is a doctoral candidate in Media Studies in the School of Communication and Information at Rutgers University. He is also an Assistant Professor of Communication at DeSales University. Spicer's research focuses on political discourse drawing on theories of affect, immaterial labor and audience studies. His work looks at political discourse in popular culture, campaigns, new media and media law. As of this printing Spicer is working on his dissertation tentatively entitled *Discourses of deceit: An analysis of lying in politics*. His most recent publications include an analysis of *The Daily Show* and photographs from news coverage of the 2008 U.S. Presidential Election. His work can be found at www.robertnspicer.com.

Felix B. Tan is Professor of Information Systems, Head of the Department of Business Information Systems and Director of the Centre for Research on Information Systems Management (CRISM) at Auckland University of Technology, New Zealand. He served as the Editor-in-Chief of the Journal of Global Information Management from 1997 to 2012 and was on the Council of the Association for Information Systems from 2003-2005. . His research interests include user behaviour in e-commerce, m-commerce and Web 2.0 and IS strategy, management and governance.

Stella W. Tian received a joint Ph.D. in Information Systems from the University of Science and Technology of China (USTC) and City University of Hong Kong (CityU). She received her Bachelor's degree from School of Management, University of Science and Technology of China in 2006. Her research interests include knowledge management, Web 2.0 for learning, and business intelligent applications.

Abel Usoro lectures in the School of Computing, University of the West of Scotland, UK. His current research interests are information systems which include knowledge management, e-learning and tourism. He has published book chapters, in refereed international conferences and journals (such as International Journal of Global Information Management and International Journal of Knowledge Management). His academic work and research have taken him to countries in Africa, Europe, Asia, North and South America. He is Editor-in-Chief of Computing and Information Systems Journal, Associate Editor of JEDMIFM, and member of editorial boards of other international journals. He is a member of scientific committees of many international conferences and chairs one of them (Conference on Information Technology and Economic Development). He is also a member of the British Computing Society and the lead editor of Leveraging Developing Economies with the Use of Information Technology published by IGI Global.

Kam Hou Vat is currently a senior instructor in the Department of Computer and Information Science, under the Faculty of Science and Technology, at the University of Macau, Macau SAR, China. His research interests include learner-centered design with constructivism in Software Engineering, architected applications developments for Internet software, information systems for learning organizations, information technology for knowledge synthesis, and collaborative technologies in electronic organizations. He can be reached at fstkhv@umac.mo.

Doug Vogel is Professor of Information Systems at the City University of Hong Kong and an AIS (Association of Information Systems) Fellow as well as AIS President-elect. He has been involved with computers and computer systems in various capacities for over 40 years. He received his MS in Computer Science from UCLA in 1972 and PhD in Information Systems from the University of Minnesota in 1986. His research interests bridge the business and academic communities in addressing questions of the impact of information systems on aspects of interpersonal communication, group problem solving, cooperative learning, and multi-cultural team productivity and knowledge sharing. He is especially engaged in introducing communication technology into educational systems and virtual teams. Additional details can be found at http://www.is.cityu.edu.hk/staff/isdoug/cv/.

Kevin Y. Wang is an Assistant Professor at Butler University's College of Communication in Indianapolis, USA. He holds a PhD in Mass Communication from the University of Minnesota-Twin Cities and a M.C. in Digital Media from the University of Washington. Before joining the Butler faculty in 2011, he was a Consortium for Faculty Diversity Fellow at DePauw University. Kevin teaches public relations and advertising in the strategic communication program at Butler and conducts research on the social and political implications of new communication technologies. He has authored scholarly articles on e-government, online consultation, online public diplomacy, political campaigns on the Web, and virtual communities.

Michael Weeks is an Associate Professor of Management at the University of Tampa. His research interests include technology management, innovation, and organizational theory. He has BEE and MBA degrees from Auburn University as well as MSc and DPhil degrees from the University of Oxford. He served for 21 years in the U.S. Air Force as a pilot and educator before retiring in 2007.

Weiyu Zhang is an Assistant Professor at the Department of Communications and New Media, National University of Singapore. She received her PhD from Annenberg School for Communication, University of Pennsylvania. Her research focuses on ICTs and civic engagement, with an emphasis on the Asian region. She has published works on electronic deliberation, Chinese online communities and social networking sites, political participation and media usage in Singapore and Taiwan, as well as media multitasking and its explanations and influences. Her current project is a cross-nation study on youth, new media and civic engagement in six Asian countries.

Zhongyun (Phil) Zhou is currently an Assistant Professor in the Department of Management Science and Engineering, School of Economics and Management, Tongji University. He holds a Ph.D. in Management Science from University of Science and Technology of China, and a joint Ph.D. degree in Information Systems from City University of Hong Kong. His current research focuses on IT/IS usage and cross-cultural issues. His work has appeared or is forthcoming in such journals as *Journal of Management Information Systems, International Journal of Information Management, Computers in Human Behavior, Behaviour and Information Technology,* and others.

Index